SIXTH EDITION

Therapeutic Counseling and Psychotherapy

LAWRENCE M. BRAMMER

University of Washington

PHILIP J. ABREGO

University of Washington

EVERETT L. SHOSTROM

Newport Beach, California

PRENTICE HALL, Englewood Cliffs, New Jersey 07632

Library of Congress Cataloging-in-Publication Data

Brammer, Lawrence M.
   Therapeutic counseling and psychotherapy / Lawrence M. Brammer,
Philip J. Abrego, Everett L. Shostrom.—6th ed.
     p. cm.
   Previous ed. published under the title: Therapeutic psychology.
   Includes bibliographical references and index.
   ISBN 0-13-912817-4
   1. Psychotherapy. 2. Counseling. I. Abrego, Philip J.
II. Shostrom, Everett L. III. Brammer, Lawrence M. Therapeutic
psychology. IV. Title.
   RC480.5.B7 1993
   616.89′14—dc20   92-26700
                               CIP

Acquisitions editor: Susan F. Brennan
Production editor: Cecile Joyner
Editorial/production supervision
  and interior design: Joan Stone
Copy editor: Rene D. Lynch
Cover designer: Bruce Kenselaar
Prepress buyer: Kelly Behr
Manufacturing buyer: Mary Ann Gloriande
Editorial assistant: Jennie Katsaros

Previously published under the title *Therapeutic Psychology:
Fundamentals of Counseling and Psychotherapy*

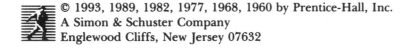 © 1993, 1989, 1982, 1977, 1968, 1960 by Prentice-Hall, Inc.
A Simon & Schuster Company
Englewood Cliffs, New Jersey 07632

Printed in the United States of America

10 9 8 7 6 5 4 3 2

ISBN 0-13-912817-4

PRENTICE-HALL INTERNATIONAL (UK) LIMITED, *London*
PRENTICE-HALL OF AUSTRALIA PTY. LIMITED, *Sydney*
PRENTICE-HALL CANADA INC., *Toronto*
PRENTICE-HALL HISPANOAMERICANA, S.A., *Mexico*
PRENTICE-HALL OF INDIA PRIVATE LIMITED, *New Delhi*
PRENTICE-HALL OF JAPAN, INC., *Tokyo*
SIMON & SCHUSTER ASIA PTE. LTD., *Singapore*
EDITORA PRENTICE-HALL DO BRASIL, LTDA., *Rio de Janeiro*

Contents

iii

8   Barriers to Actualizing Relationships, *200*

PART III

SPECIAL AREAS OF APPLICATION

9   Group Principles and Methods, *228*

PART IV

VALUES AND PROFESSIONAL ISSUES

Preface

The specialties of counseling and clinical psychology have been growing closer together. The authors of this text—one from university teaching of counseling psychology and the other two from medical center work and private clinical practice—have worked together to produce this sixth edition. We have each contributed from our unique experience to this common approach to counseling and psychotherapy. This sixth edition attempts to reassess the current status, trends, and problems in research and practice of general counseling and psychotherapy with mildly dysfunctional people experiencing normal developmental problems.

The authors wish to thank their students and colleagues who have contributed criticisms and suggestions for this revision. We are grateful for the criticism provided by Professors Roberta Driscoll of the University of Central Florida, Harold E. Engen of the University of Iowa, Warren F. Shaffer of the University of Minnesota, Minneapolis, and Fred Borgen of Iowa State University. We are also grateful to the large number of dedicated people in research and practice of counseling and psychotherapy who put their findings and thoughts on the pages of technical journals and papers. We wish to acknowledge the generous permission of Robert Knapp, President of Educational and Industrial Testing Service, to quote extensively from *Actualizing Therapy*. We also wish to acknowledge the special support of Marian Brammer, Sharon Shostrom, and Martha, Poppy, Taylor, and Kipp Abrego, and we acknowledge with thanks the careful editorial work of Susan F. Brennan, Joan Stone, Rene D. Lynch, and Cecile Joyner.

Lawrence M. Brammer
Philip J. Abrego
Everett L. Shostrom

CHAPTER 1

Theoretical Foundations of Therapeutic Psychology

The helping professions of counseling and psychotherapy offer great challenges, rewards, and opportunities to persons intrerested in helping their fellow human beings. Help is defined as providing conditions for people to fulfill their needs for life meaning, security, love and respect, self-esteem, decisive action, and self-actualizing growth; help also means providing resources and skills that enable people to help themselves. This helping process involves listening to the deeply personal life stories of people, their hopes as well as their defeats, passions, and tragedies, and the problems they encounter in their lives. The purpose of this text is to help counselors become more understanding, intentional, and effective in their counseling roles.

In being helpful, professionals strive to become aware of their limitations. They examine their feelings, attitudes, and behavior to learn about their own ethnocentrism, needs for control, and requirement that clients fulfill their own needs for love, power, or prestige. Counselors need rewards for their efforts, however; seeing clients realize their hidden potentials and function at higher levels of effective living provides such rewards.

In addition to describing the fundamental techniques of counseling and psychotherapy, this volume presents historical and sociocultural foundations, personality theory, professional issues, and applications of therapeutic psychology to special population groups and work settings.

To facilitate growth in others, professional psychologists must have a clear conception of what they are doing. For example, what goals do they have for the helping process? What assumptions do they make about the nature of personality and behavior change? What are the conditions for change and how are they established? What are reasonable outcomes? This book presents principles for developing and evaluating theories of psychotherapy and learning how to tailor helping strategies to the needs of clients.

Counseling approaches in the 1990s must address the needs of a pluralistic, multicultural society. The practice of formal counseling and psychotherapy has been primarily a North American and European cultural development, based on shared values, for example, of rugged individualism manifested as autonomy, control, and personal responsibility for choice and action. These values are part of a distinctive world view that is basically linear, analytical, and empirical. Large countries with pluralistic cultures and many nations of Africa, the Middle East, and Asia, however, have world views and personal myths different from countries with European roots. These differences affect the importance of counseling for individuals and their societies. Differences in how normality and adjustment are defined and conflicts over individual/family/community values contribute to differing views of the importance of formal counseling.

As a result of the differences cited above, counselors, psychologists, and case workers must meet the changes imposed by increasing ethnic diversity and shifting demographics. In North America, for example, the demand for change is mounting to meet the most rapid shift in racial mix in its history. The 1990 U.S. Census, compared to past surveys, revealed that nonwhite ethnic and racial minorities will soon become the majority. White Americans in twenty years will constitute about 48 percent of the U.S. population (Sue, 1992). Census projections also predict that by the year 2000 one-third of the U.S. population will consist of Spanish-speaking cultural groups. These groups have not had counseling and psychotherapy as part of their traditions until recently because the family has traditionally been the primary source of informal counseling.

Some implications of the data cited above are that traditional counseling is not suited to many cultural groups. Language alone is a barrier for many. Therefore, counselor training and counseling theory must take into account the different cultural views about the whole enterprise of counseling and psychotherapy. Adaptations must be made, hence multicultural considerations must be a special dimension of counseling theory. Theory in therapeutic psychology must consider the individual client's particular world view as well as his or her interpersonal and cultural context. We encourage students to begin the complex process of developing a personal theory of counseling that includes these dimensions of human experience.

This text is divided into four parts. Part I includes chapters covering an overview of the counseling process, psychotherapeutic theories, and principles for synthesizing a personal counseling theory. The principal purpose of Part I is to prepare the reader with theory and concepts of human change processes as background for the discussion of counseling process and applications in Parts II and III. Part I contains four unique key terms. The first, *therapeutic psychology*, encompasses much of the accumulated wisdom of the helping professions. *Creative synthesis* is our term for efforts to develop a comprehensive integrative outlook on personality structure and change as a basis for counseling practice. *Multidimensional* refers to the varied modalities of theory underlying the helping process—philosophical, structural, functional, developmental, and research. *Actualizing counseling and psychotherapy* is our illustrative understanding and action approach described in Chapter 3.

Part II describes the process dimensions of counseling and psychotherapy. Beginning with Chapter 4 and continuing through Chapter 7, important points are described related to relationship building, assessment, and intervention strategies. Chapter 8 describes barriers that impede the therapeutic relationship. A basic assumption underlying Part II is that psychotherapeutic attitudes and skills are learned, not endowed. Hence, effective counseling methods can be acquired with conscientious study, practice, and evaluation. It is intended that readers, whatever their professional setting, will be able to choose those interventions that have particular applications to their specialties and institutional roles.

Part III includes applications of skills to particular populations and settings. Chapters 9, 10, and 11 describe applications of therapeutic psychology to group counseling, marriage and family therapy, and career counseling. Chapter 12 discusses special issues related to gender roles, gay and lesbian clients, and ethnically diverse groups. Applications in cross-cultural settings, aging, business, education, health care, and independent practice settings are also discussed.

Part IV discusses both value issues in counseling and present status and trends in professional psychology. The purpose of Part IV is to sensitize professional psychologists to the moral and values issues inherent in the counseling process and to provide a current description of professional disciplines, issues, and trends affecting the counseling profession.

The overview of this volume will help the reader to understand the nature of *Therapeutic Psychology.* Much material has been included that is not technique but rather knowledge and values considered necessary to the professional background of professional counselors and psychotherapists. Although we do not assume that this material represents *all* that should be known for competence in this field, we hope that the student in training and the practitioner already at work will find this volume a useful description of how counseling skill is developed and applied.

THERAPEUTIC PSYCHOLOGY

Therapeutic psychology represents a body of knowledge that gathers its data from various related professions. All embody the helping function. In psychology, applied specialties have emerged as research and clinical practice expand into new areas. The clinical specialty, with its traditional emphasis on diagnostic evaluation, concentrates more on psychotherapy and counseling with severely distressed and dysfunctional people. Counseling psychology incorporates traditional decision making and assessment in education, mental health, industry, and rehabilitation with new emphases on life-long personal development and performance effectiveness.

School psychology is a specialization that has broadened its identity to include counseling, assessment, and prevention emphases within educational and health care settings. With its growing emphasis on assessment of neurological functioning of children with learning problems, it has become a specialization in child clinical psychology.

The American Psychological Association recognizes four specializations in professional psychology: clinical, counseling, school, and industrial. Clinical and counseling, especially, have moved so close to one another in functions, settings, and training that they are hardly distinguishable as separate specializations. This accelerating trend toward a generic professional psychologist fits closely our concept of the therapeutic psychologist. In Chapter 14, we expand on the concept of therapeutic psychology. We also comment on the similarities and differences among the professional specializations and deal with the issues and trends surrounding professional practice in detail.

New specialties within psychology are emerging in diverse domains such as neuropsychology, forensic psychology, health psychology, sport psychology, family psychology, and gerontology. Other professionals contributing to therapeutic psychology include mental health counselors, marriage and family therapists, social workers, psychosocial nurses, pastoral counselors, and psychiatrists. Each professional group adds a unique contribution to the overall body of knowledge and practice in applied psychology.

The establishment of a formal area of therapeutic psychology that incorporates contributions from many helping professions is a natural phenomenon. For many years psychology has collaborated with other professions in contributing its unique approaches to understanding human behavior. In order to succeed in counseling and psychotherapeutic efforts, it is necessary that professionals in applied psychology recognize and utilize the understandings of all the established helping professions in addition to capitalizing on the unique findings of their own science.

The study of therapeutic psychology, then, has four broad purposes: (1) to create an appreciation of the scope and depth of learning necessary for competency as a skilled counselor and psychotherapist; (2) to develop an understanding of relevant knowledge from behavioral sciences; (3) to develop competencies for the various specialties in counseling and psychotherapy; and (4) to understand research results and needs.

Counseling and Psychotherapy

Because therapeutic psychology embraces both counseling and psychotherapy, it is useful to comment on the similarities and differences. Figure 1-1 illustrates the scope of therapeutic psychology. *Counseling* and *psychotherapy* are viewed as overlapping areas of professional competence. Historically, counseling has been characterized by the following words: educational, preventive, voca-

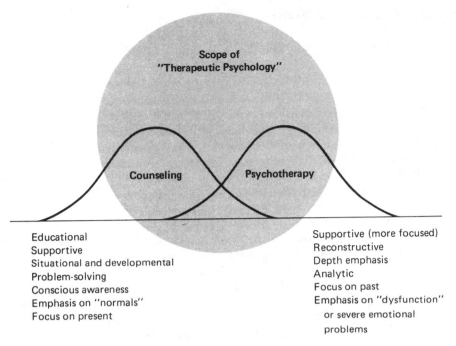

FIGURE 1-1   The Scope of Counseling and Psychotherapy within the Framework of Therapeutic Psychology.

tional, supportive, situational, problem solving, conscious awareness, normal, developmental, present-time, and short term. *Counseling* has been viewed as a process concerned with assisting people functioning normally to achieve their goals or function more effectively. *Psychotherapy* has been described with terms such as supportive (as in a crisis setting), reconstructive, depth, analytical, and focus on the past. The emphasis was on more dysfunctional or severe emotional problems. *Psychotherapy* also has been considered a longer term and more intense process concerned with alleviating severe problems in living.

To many clinicians, distinctions between psychotherapy and counseling appear to be primarily quantitative rather than qualitative in nature, meaning that the functions performed look similar. Professionals in most settings find that they provide both counseling and psychotherapy in accordance with their education and training and the needs of their clients. In current usage, the terms counseling and psychotherapy tend to be used interchangeably depending on the service setting. Therefore, in the remainder of this volume we will use either term to encompass the other, unless otherwise stated. For purposes of this text, we will also use interchangeably terms such as psychotherapist, clinician, mental health counselor, and psychologist in describing providers of mental health counseling and psychotherapy. We recognize that there are some differences in usage of terms in educational and health care settings.

THE SIGNIFICANCE OF THEORY

Scientist/Practitioner Model

The premise of the scientist/practitioner model is that the counselor can be both subject and object, that is, he or she can be an objective observer, critical of what goes on, yet a participant in the counseling process at the same time. The essences of scientific method used by this model counselor are observation, inference, and verification. Counseling practice involves the application of principles deduced from generalizations or theories as well as from specific experiences. One foundation of the scientific practice of psychotherapy and counseling, therefore, is theory. By *counseling theory* we mean a structure of hypotheses and generalizations based on counseling experience and experimental studies. Generally, theory includes four elements: goals and values, assumptions, intervention strategies, and expected outcomes. Since these elements change with experience, a person's theories are in a constant state of development.

When speaking of the counselor as a scientist, two related meanings should be distinguished. First, the counselor acts as a careful observer of the process. The counselor describes accurately what behavior is seen and may go to the second stage of making inferences about the meaning of the observations. In this descriptive sense everyone can be a scientist. The second is the scientific attitude that the counselor assumes so that he or she can verify the rough hypotheses and improve services. This second view of a counselor as scientist applies the scientific process. It requires control of extraneous variables and manipulation of experimental variables according to established rules of scientific research. This control is rarely possible in a counseling situation, unless a deliberate study is designed to test certain hypotheses about counseling. Therefore, the scientific approach to counseling in the latter sense remains primarily an ideal.

Although counselors are interested in the applications of scientific attitudes and methods to improve practice, they are also interested in behavioral science as a science. That is, they are interested broadly in the greater understanding of human behavior, whether or not it leads to any practical results in counseling.

Theory helps to explain what happens in a counseling relationship and assists the counselor in predicting, evaluating, and improving results. Theory provides a framework for making systematic observations about counseling. Theorizing encourages the coherence of ideas about counseling and the production of new ideas. Hence, counseling theory can be very practical by helping to make sense out of the counselor's observations. What behaviors exemplify the scientific attitude? A counselor or psychotherapist who proceeds through daily tasks without asking the following questions is not likely to progress in therapeutic effectiveness, nor is he or she likely to contribute new ideas to the profession. The scientific attitude leads to questions such as: What is happening here? What is my model? What are my assumptions? What accounts for this event? What will happen if I try this? Unscientific counselors who do not ask themselves these vital questions are likely to feel smug about their counseling methods, a dangerous attitude to take.

A counseling interview may be regarded as an N of 1 experiment (Tracey, 1983). The counselor begins with some observations and hunches about client needs and some preferred interventions that will fill those needs. This thinking serves as a hypothesis about what goals, intervention strategies, and outcomes are likely to meet the client's needs the best. Thus, the hypothesis is supported or rejected by the experience of working with this client. The counselor must be careful, however, about generalizing from this N of 1 to other clients without instituting the usual controlled procedures of scientific method.

The next step in theorizing is to observe additional experiences with clients, noting patterns and exceptions. Counselors start with a question or problem; then they observe what happens in the interaction between themselves and their clients. They examine the data and formulate hypotheses about what is happening. These hypotheses are the inferences based on the observations and require further testing. Sets of refined hypotheses are generally referred to as theories. From these theories, counselors attempt to explain or predict further events in counseling. They must check the validity of their new theories against the reality of their observations to bring the two closer together. The refined theories then are used to make more precise explanations and predictions of counseling events. For example, counselors observe that when they "push" clients too hard with questions or interpretations, the clients get angry or stop talking. Counselors observe the various conditions under which clients behave in this negative fashion and speculate why this might be so. Clinicians observe similar cases and note a pattern and a consistency. They hypothesize that clients become negativistic or "defensive" when they are threatened, or perceive counselors as a source of frustration and even psychological danger. The counselors may postulate some personality structures that function inconsistently. The therapists may be "pushing" their clients too fast, so they check their hypothesis about threat and generalizations to the point where the theories are useful in predicting what will happen to clients under threat. Counselors are then in a better position to evaluate both their hypotheses and techniques.

As a final step in theory building, the counselors' "miniature" theories, or confirmed hypotheses, are combined with additional data and confirmed hypotheses into more consistent and larger theories about personality structure and function. This broader theory is then used in a deductive fashion to produce more hypotheses to be tested experimentally or through counseling experience.

Although the preceding section expresses the ideal of the scientist/practitioner approach, the novelty of the scientific attitude for many practicing counselors makes it difficult to use in practice. Some counselors see this kind of theorizing as interfering with their attempts to relate to their clients. In addition, there is no compelling evidence that counseling effectiveness in producing client-specified outcomes definitely depends upon the extent and explicitness of one's espoused theoretical foundations, nor that one theory of personality or psychotherapy is superior to another. The important question is: Which theories work best with which clients, in which settings, and with which expected outcomes?

THE ROOTS OF PSYCHOTHERAPY

Practitioners must develop their own theories and styles of counseling and psychotherapy. To give precision, coherence, and promise to their counseling and psychotherapy techniques, they must become familiar with certain aspects of human-change processes as well as with highlights of specific theories about helping. One of our basic assumptions is that counseling or therapy becomes an impulsive application of "cookbook" recipes to human problems unless the clinician has a firm foundation in the current thinking and research of other practitioners and a consistent set of assumptions about personality growth and development. These principles must be tested and understood within a broad sociocultural context lest they reflect limited ethnocentric ideas that may be unhelpful or even damaging to their clients.

We therefore begin this chapter with an overview of cross-cultural models of healing to place psychotherapy within a structural context. By examining culture-specific and universal aspects of formal helping processes across cultures, we can begin to identify some core elements of helping relationships. What we learn from this broader cross-cultural view of helping can help us better understand psychotherapy as a particular form of healing. In this chapter, we trace the evolution of psychotherapy approaches and consider challenges to our current scientific paradigms of counseling theory. This overview of the evolution of counseling can provide the basis for developing new integrative theories of counseling and psychotherapy. Finally, at the end of this chapter, we discuss principles for building and testing a personal approach to therapy, which integrates multiple theories.

Cross-Cultural Perspectives on Healing

Many practitioners from non-Western and pluralistic societies are uncomfortable with solely utilizing the Western paradigm of psychotherapy as an understanding of how healing occurs. They consider Western psychotherapy as merely one indigenous form among a wide assortment of symbolic healing systems, that is, a therapy based on words, myth, and ritual uses of symbols (Kleinman, 1988). Examples of other systems include forms of religious healing, shamanism, and Asian systems of traditional medicine. Each particular healing approach is unique and yet shares common features with other approaches in terms of its structure and process.

All forms of healing deal with different manifestations of distress and demoralization. Ethnographic studies demonstrate that concepts of emotions, self and body, and general illness categories differ significantly across cultures. Distress may be attributed to divergent culturally meaningful explanations ranging from religious beliefs, diet, biology, and life stress to ancestral ghosts, depending upon individual and cultural world views.

The experience of distress, as well as the course and outcome of symptom patterns, is always strongly shaped by culture. It is clear that major mental disorders such as schizophrenia, depression, and anxiety occur universally across cultures (Kleinman, 1988). However, the expression of symptom patterns tends to differ widely across cultures. Distress may be expressed in many forms of culture-specific syndromes. For example, within non-Western societies, anxiety may be expressed in culture-bound syndromes related to witchcraft, soul loss, and fear of strangers. Depression and anxiety are manifested through a marked predominance of somatic symptoms among depressed and anxious persons in non-Western societies. In contrast, depressed Westerners more commonly experience feelings of guilt and self-reproach than do non-Westerners. It has been hypothesized that the more somatized depression may have an easier course and better outcome than psychologized depression, owing to less preoccupation with and negative expectation in the experience of one's distress (Kleinman, 1988). Course and outcome of symptom patterns may also be related to social expectations and interpersonal reactions to the client that impede the person's expectation for improvement. Other important social factors include the economics of disability and the level of effective support programs for distressed persons.

Cross-cultural research shows that levels of distress and demoralization may universally be related to such social factors as political upheaval, social change, crowding, information overload, poor housing, violence, social isolation, social disintegration, unemployment, and stressful work conditions. For example, uprooting and forced acculturation among refugees, immigrants, and migrants have repeatedly been shown to create increased rates of mental distress. Southeast Asian "boat people" who have resettled in North America experience high rates of depression, anxiety, and somatic disturbance. Some social problems are so common among particular minority or oppressed populations in many areas of the world (for example, frequency of diagnosis of antisocial personality among ethnic minority youth in the United States) that these forms of demoralization are thought to represent long-term responses to historical forces that create an underclass in society. Worldwide, women in most studies bear higher rates of mental illness than men and research points to the importance of their relative powerlessness (McGrath, Keita, Strickland, & Russo, 1990). Brown and Harris (1978) found that working-class women in England who experienced relative powerlessness, absence of emotional support, the social pressures of childrearing, and no job outside the home significantly increased their vulnerability to life event stressors. Those women with marginal self-esteem were more likely to experience generalized hopelessness and clinical depression. However, these types of social factors are not the sole determinants of mental distress. Mental distress involves a complex interaction among biological, psychological, and social sources of vulnerability.

An important implication for counselors is the need for us to learn about the cultural context of our own client's experience of distress. We need to look beyond the individual to cultural, social, and political factors that may affect each client's experience of distress. Although much of psychotherapy in North America operates from a disease model, it is apparent from cross-cultural research that psychological and biological vulnerability reciprocally interact with social norms and cultural pressures to evoke a spectrum of affective, anxiety, and somatic complaints.

Patterns of help seeking and coping also differ in different societies and ethnic groups. Healing approaches have both culture-specific features and universal characteristics, and it is important for counselors to be aware of both of these aspects. Depending on the acculturation experience and ethnicity of our clients, we may need to tailor approaches in more culture-specific ways. In our own theory construction, we need to be aware of core elements of helping behavior across cultures. As we progress through this text, more will be said about adapting theory and techniques toward specific client groups.

The major similarities of healing approaches cross-culturally may present some important understanding about how psychotherapy produces its effects. Several authors (Kleinman, 1988; Frank & Frank, 1991) have described important similarities in non-Western healer-client relationships. There is evidence that the more successful indigenous healers in the non-Western world may possess personalities that inspire confidence and respect for their personal power and demonstrate empathy for the client's experience. In North America, research on psychotherapists has identified the tendency of effective therapists to have warm, supportive personalities (Truax & Carkhuff, 1962; Luborsky, Singer, & Luborsky, 1985).

The structure and process of indigenous healing also share common elements. Initially, indigenous healers share a mode of clinical communication with their clients, which may be somatic, psychological, moral, religious, or cultural, to describe the client's distress. The healing practitioner must provide a causal attribution of the client's distress within a particular taxonomy. For example, in a traditional Buddhist healing in Thailand, the explanation for distress may be that "a ghost is clinging to the back of bereaved family members." The healer must persuade the client that his or her redefinition of the problem is valid. The healer often creates a set of positive expectations about the course and outcome of the distress. Most indigenous healers then guide therapeutic change through mediating symbols that are related to the problem taxonomy. The healer affects the client's emotional and physical reactions by manipulating the source of distress through therapeutic rituals that may be sacred or secular. Healing processes often create emotional arousal in clients and provide opportunities for catharsis. Many evoke an altered state of consciousness such as trance or possession. Finally, the cause of distress is removed (that is, the ghost is exorcised) and the client is ceremonially cured. Although the client's life problems may or may not have been directly affected by this process, the client's perception and experience of the problems has been changed. The client feels better and the client and healer believe in the efficacy of the treatment.

In Western societies, psychotherapy has become a primary means of healing distress. Some parallels between the above description of indigenous healing and Western schools of psychotherapy are apparent. Western approaches to psychotherapy must articulate an explanation of the client's suffering that both the client and counselor agree upon. Interventions related to the model are used by the counselor to guide the client through change, interventions that often arouse the client's emotions, redefine the problem in some way, and provide a pathway to change or recovery. For example, the presenting depression of an adult client abused or neglected as a child becomes transformed as client and therapist agree to work together through the grief of childhood in a way that alters the client's present experience. The client works within a shared therapeutic model, which attributes current pain to unresolved childhood grief. Through the therapeutic techniques of "grief work," the therapist guides the client's recovery even though the individual's circumstances may not necessarily have changed.

The study of cross-cultural healing suggests that there is an important structure to the healing process that transcends any one particular "school" of therapy. This is not to say that psychotherapeutic healing is related solely to nonspecific structural factors such as a shared framework of therapeutic meaning. We are suggesting that each separate school of therapy, although perhaps distinct in its underlying assumptions about human change processes, shares a similar counselor-client helping structure. In Chapter 2, we will explore more of these distinctions among traditional Western approaches to therapy.

Students must learn skills that transcend particular schools of therapy so that they can develop a personal framework for making sense of the major symbolic tasks of healing and for maximizing the symbolic effects of psychotherapy. More will be said of this in Chapter 3 as we discuss the complex task of developing an integrative therapy. This task of modifying existing theory in light of what is known about healing across cultures has become particularly important in the current decade. We are realizing that many of our predominant schools of therapy are based in traditional European values and need to be modified or replaced in order to work with clients of other beliefs and values.

Psychotherapy and counseling have been concerned with the healing process for people who have been suffering or have become dysfunctional due to their personal problems. Counseling especially has focused also on developmental issues, such as making decisions at critical transition points regarding education, career, marriage, and life style. The development of personality and vocational tests became a key part of this counseling endeavor because prediction of success in education or career was the primary focus of the decision making and planning. A wide range of cognitive and personality trait theories developed out of this counseling activity. Educational and career counseling involved a heavy emotional component also because key life decisions are encrusted with anxiety and uncertainty. Decision making and commitment processes, along with achievement motivation, became the objects of research and practice by counselors and therapists. At the present time counselors and psychotherapists in educational institutions have a broad orientation to healing and developmental decision making. In mental health and family counseling centers, the focus is more on the healing process.

Most of the thrust for career counseling arose in private agencies, but it quickly moved into schools in the early 1900s when secondary education flourished. Colleges and universities were slower to incorporate services for student emotional problems and life planning. Student counseling services did not develop much until mid century, when counseling services for World War II veterans proved their value.

Before we examine particular schools of therapy in Chapter 2, we want to provide a meta-view of the development of therapeutic approaches over historical periods. It is hoped that students can avoid the pitfalls of overly identifying with a particular counseling approach but can instead learn to synthesize important contributions from the various theories.

THE EVOLUTION OF PSYCHOTHERAPY

Science historian Thomas Kuhn (1977) traced the evolution of scientific disciplines. He found that most disciplines begin in what he called a "preparadigmatic period," during which the practitioners of a science are split into many competing schools, each of which approaches the same subject differently. In this period, each competing school claims that its way is the best. This stage lasts until a major scientific breakthrough makes most of the schools obsolete, after which, in the "postparadigmatic period," the discipline is dominated by one school. Kuhn proposes that this pattern of evolution of science, from a period during which there are many competing schools to the dominance of one school that is subsequently overthrown by a new one, is characteristic of all fields.

Richard Schwartz (1985) has described a similar framework for understanding the evolution of psychotherapy. His equivalent of the preparadigmatic stage is what he calls an *essentialist* stage. In this stage there are many models, which provide great variation. There have been a number of competing schools, each claiming validity. The development of many schools of counseling can be accounted for, in part, by the relative youth of psychological sciences and by the complexity of the phenomena that theories of psychotherapy are trying to explain or predict.

The essentialistic stage of ideas is often characterized by a period of professional zeal, high productivity, and creativity. Developers of a model are both excited by and committed to the belief that they have found the essence to understanding a complex phenomenon. This stage can have a down side, however, because essentialism breeds either/or thinking and polarization: One model is right and all others are wrong. As the developers of the model become overinvested in the model, they have greater trouble examining their results critically. It then takes them longer to discover that their model is limited or flawed. Essentialists often behave like enlightened crusaders who must defend their model. The more invested they become in the model the more they pursue confirmatory data and explain away contrary evidence. The essentialistic stage is likely to continue until the point when a model's limitations begin to emerge or when the established orthodoxy accepts or accommodates to the new model.

According to Schwartz, a *transitional* stage begins when some essentialists start to recognize that their model is limited or flawed. For example, as theorists raised concerns about radical behaviorism's lack of attention to the role of thinking, early experience, and unconscious processes in mediating behavior, behaviorism began to change. Many theorists began to acknowledge the interactive influence of thoughts on the environment (Bandura, 1977) and some even incorporated a view that included the role of unconscious experience under the term "schema" (Beck et al., 1979). This transitional stage can be a tumultuous period, depending upon how extreme the essentialistic period was. The transitional period is often marked by increased polarization within a model and between models. Some adherents defend the existing model while others become interested in new directions. The zealousness and naive optimism of an essentialistic stage generates a pendulum-swinging process. Disillusioned former adherents of the model and outsiders, polarized by the essentialists' narrowness, spin off new, opposite, but equally extreme models.

The paradigm shift is often related to significant new research findings. For example, psychotherapy research revealed that there was great variation in both therapeutic behaviors and outcomes among therapists who were of the same theoretical orientation (Luborsky et al., 1975). Additionally, it was observed that therapists of similar experience but different theoretical allegiances behaved quite similarly to each other (Fiedler, 1950; Sloane, Staples, Cristol, Yorkston, & Whipple, 1975). Building upon these results, researchers began to compare therapists of different theoretical orientations on common nonspecific relationship factors and process variables that appeared important to effective therapy. These new research directions formed the foundation for a growing movement toward theoretical eclecticism.

As the pendulum swings in a new direction, an essentialistic stage in the model's development begins again, which is often characterized by tunnel vision, zeal, and chauvinism. Tunnel vision seems necessary temporarily in order to fully explore the complex possibilities of the new approach without the distraction of old or alternative points of view.

This pendulum-swinging process seems to be useful in that the extremes are quickly explored, allowing for a gradually increasing drift toward a middle ground. For example, Freud's extreme focus on the power of the unconscious was countered by the behaviorist movement that discounted the intrapsychic and emphasized environmental reinforcers. Next, the reductionistic focus on the individual of the Freudian and behaviorist schools was countered by family therapy's extreme emphasis on the power of the family system. The emphasis on behavior to the exclusion of thoughts and meaning as mediating variables has been replaced by a renewed interest in cognitive psychology.

Some of those who remain loyal to the original model through this transitional stage will be inclined to retrench in the face of the chaos and polarization and become even more rigidly dogmatic about the model's assumptions and methods. Others, however, gradually accept the model's limitations and begin to see it in context. They are able to drop the tunnel vision that was necessary earlier and see the commonalities as well as the differences with other models. Their zeal is replaced with a new opennness and modesty as they become comfortable with a shift in goal from finding the quintessential discovery to contributing a piece to a larger puzzle.

The questioning of the model is often accompanied by the fear that its unique qualities will be lost. Ideally, the tension of this process forces theorists to a "meta" position—a perspective from which they can look down upon the larger field and see their model as one among an ecology of models. They become better able to see the pattern that connects their model with other models that they once believed to be contradictory or incompatible. This *ecological* period is characterized by increased communication and cooperation among models. In this way the ecological period may produce a new meta-theory that is able to account for and deal with a much wider range of phenomena than any of the individual models.

Counselors and psychotherapists will likely experience the essentialist, transitional, and ecological stages described above as they develop their own increasingly complex, personalized theory of counseling. They may begin with an identification with a particular school of therapy. As new experiences as a counselor emerge, they may develop an eclectic integration within or across schools.

Psychotherapy has gone through several periods when a given theory was in ascendancy and a large number of practitioners were aligning themselves with that theory. At the present time proportionately fewer individuals report strict theoretical allegiance, the preponderance of therapists identifying with some form of eclecticism (Garfield & Kurz, 1977; Smith, 1982; Norcross & Prochaska, 1982; Watkins, Lopez, Campbell, & Himmell, 1986; Mahoney, 1991).

There has been a proliferation of writings (Goldfried, 1980, 1982; Ivey, 1980; Beutler & Clarkin, 1990; Mahoney, 1991) in the past decade advocating the development of eclectic and integrative therapies. Mahoney (1991) found in a recent survey of psychotherapists that there is much agreement across theoretical orientations about what constitute optimal practices in successful psychotherapy. His findings include the importance of active exploration of novel experiences by the client, encouragement of self-examination, necessary changes in the client self-system, and the fact that such changes are facilitated by a safe and caring human relationship.

The search for common ground is taking place at the strategy level as well as the levels of basic assumptions of counseling theory. The psychotherapy research of Strupp (1986) has described the imprecision involved in comparing labels or "schools" of therapy. He points out the difficulties in separating the two major components of psychotherapeutic influence-interpersonal factors and procedures (techniques). Describing the therapeutic process, Strupp (1986) says,

> The therapist's skill is significantly manifested by an ability to create a particular interpersonal context and, within that context, to foster certain kinds of learning. In other words, the therapist may be said to develop, maintain, and manage a specialized human relationship with therapeutic intent. The goal is to promote learning within a benign and constructive interpersonal context. The therapist's contribution, therefore, appears to be partly attitudinal and partly technical. (p. 126)

Rather than compare schools of therapy, Strupp prefers to research detailed accounts of the treatment "system" to be evaluated. It is then possible to research the extent to which the therapist is adhering to a particular set of technical operations and the level of competence or skill manifested by the therapist. However, Strupp believes that because the variables involved in human functioning are highly complex and intertwined, attempts to attribute segments of the outcome variance to single technique variables may result in spuriously weak effects. Consequently, the outcome literature results in a blurred image of the phenomena the researcher is studying and can provide only crude markers of therapeutic effectiveness. By analogy, Strupp suggests "it is largely meaningless to examine the surgeon's scalpel to discover why a particular operation is successful, but one may learn a great deal by focusing on the manner in which the surgeon (compared to, say, a layperson) employs it. Similarly, it appears pointless to account for surgical skills by referring to 'common factors' in 'cutting,' an activity that is also performed by butchers, tailors, and many others." To develop an understanding of the organizing principles that underly successful psychotherapy, it is essential to examine both technical factors and relationship factors.

Gelso and Carter (1985) have edited a special journal issue focusing on the counseling relationship and its impact on therapeutic outcome. They suggest that the therapeutic relationship is complex and should be conceptualized in specific components (for example, agreement over goals and tasks, transference, and an accurately perceived "real relationship") rather than in global terms such as "nonspecific factors" or "placebo effects." It is important for counselors to examine what aspect of the relationship is emphasized by their therapeutic approach. The essential question regarding the influence of the therapeutic relationship becomes, "which component is most important when practiced within which theoretical system by what kind of counselor, with what client, and in which of a number of counseling settings?" (p. 235). Thus, while agreeing with others that it is difficult to determine differential effects from differing therapeutic approaches, Gelso and Carter have proposed that we reconceptualize the therapeutic relationship in order to understand how relationship factors influence the process and outcome of psychotherapy.

ADOPTING AN APPROACH TO THEORY

Much work has been done in the last few years in the area of systematic theory construction. A satisfactory general counseling and psychotherapeutic theory, however, is not yet available. Because counselors attempt to explain what they see with their unique and limited perception, there are over 250 "schools" of counseling or therapy (Herink, 1980). This multiplicity of theories is a healthy state of affairs in a young profession, but, ultimately, it is expected that a unified theory of behavior and of counseling practice will evolve. After tracing the history of theory building in counseling and psychotherapy in his Address to the Society for the Advancement of Psychotherapy Integration, London (1987) asserted that we have identified the common elements and are much closer to a unified theory. In the meantime, counselors must examine the thinking of others as well as work on formulating their own hypotheses about the structure and function of the human personality and the counseling process, as in the creative synthesis described below. Even though most counselors cannot be creative theoreticians, they can develop an attitude of careful critical observation of everyday practice and an understanding of formal experimental approaches to counseling problems. They can also strive to be open to new ideas for expanding their own theory.

Counselors and psychotherapists can take one of three positions: identify with one of the theories already published and tested in practice, develop an eclectic position, or strive for a personalized creative synthesis of theory and practice.

The Single Theory

The case for a single theoretical approach is argued in terms of having a ready-made set of assumptions, concepts, and related strategies, which have been proven useful over a long period. Research productivity flowing from a single theory is offered as another advantage. While numerous practitioners state their allegiance to a single approach such as analytic, behavioral, or person-centered, their actual practice, as indicated later in this chapter, is not so parochial. They tend to move beyond their favorite theory quickly. Having an allegiance to a single-theory group has the personal advantage of a solid professional identity and often substantial status.

The single-theory approach tends to promote the "great creator" myth—a view that the original formulator was a genius of some kind with special gifts. While some persons, such as Freud, had special conceptualizing abilities, they were seeing events in terms of their unique life experiences and times. A highly elaborated system, such as analytic, tends over the years to become a closed system, and adherents tend to act more like disciples or hero worshipers than creative clinicians.

Eclectic Views

In one sense all theories are eclectic in that they incorporate previous viewpoints and philosophies. We define eclectic, however, as the process of selecting concepts, methods, and strategies from a variety of theories that work. Eclecticism has taken several forms; *theoretical eclecticism* integrates at the theoretical level rather than the intervention level. Theoretical eclecticists combine concepts from different theories or translate the terms used by one theory into those employed by other theories. A second type of eclecticism, *technical eclecticism,* integrates various treatment approaches at the level of specific procedures, rather than at the level of theory. The technically eclectic clinician endeavors to select the best and most useful procedures for a given client from the many procedures available, regardless of the theories from which these procedures derive. *Common factors eclecticism* is a third eclectic approach, which tries to identify the common qualities that exist among effective practitioners regardless of their theoretical models.

Theoretical eclecticism has advanced both within specific therapy schools and across schools. For example, within psychoanalysis, there have been theoretical variations from Freud's theories based on different concepts of motivation (for example, Adler) symbols (for example, Jung) and goals (for example, Horney). Among different theoretical schools, Dollard and Miller (1950) and Wachtel (1977) have integrated behavioral and psychoanalytic theory. Wachtel and Wachtel (1986) proposed an integration of psychoanalytic and family systems theories.

Technical eclecticism has incorporated a broad application of methods in an equally wide theoretical framework. One widely recognized technically eclectic approach is Lazarus's Multimodal Therapy (1976, 1981). While Lazarus's basic approach is behavioral in the traditional sense, he employs numerous cognitive and affective processes and explores systematically modalities of behavior, affect, sensation, imagery, cognition, interpersonal relationships, and biochemical factors.

Common factors eclecticism highlights the role of nonspecific factors in facilitating treatment outcome. The cross-cultural approaches we described earlier in this chapter (Kleinman, 1988; Frank & Frank, 1991) are examples of the common factors approach to eclecticism. These approaches examine specific structures or processes in psychotherapy, such as the therapist's ability to show empathy, credibility, and support, which seem to contribute toward effectiveness and train therapists to develop these qualities. Shostrom (1987), in work he produced on psychotherapists demonstrating their styles, has extracted six emphases, or general factors he calls FACETS. This acronym represents commonalities of feeling, acting, corporal, empathic, thinking, and self-actualizing that exist in varying degrees among all styles of psychotherapy. This work is a continuation of earlier studies (Shostrom & Riley, 1968) that extracted six parameters common to the three diverse therapies in their study. Shostrom's observations support further the growing trend toward commonality among therapist styles in practice. Currently, a number of clinicians are creatively combining these types of integration. Many of the advances in the convergence of models are reported in the *Journal of Psychotherapy Integration*.

An important direction is to develop a theoretical model that can match specific treatment interventions to particular problems at specific phases of treatment. Two complementary models of treatment stages have been proposed by Prochaska (1984) and Beitman (1987). Prochaska proposed four sequential phases of personal problem solving: precontemplation, contemplation, action, and maintenance. Thus, there is a stage prior to making any plans to change, followed by a planning period and an action stage, and finally a stage in which the desired change is maintained. Beitman has identified common phases of

psychotherapy regardless of theoretical allegiance. These include phases of relationship building, a search for patterns in the client's responses, the instigation of
personal change, and preparing for termination. These conceptions of the
change process over time can be useful in helping eclectic theorists suggest more
systematic ways in which different interventions may be targeted toward clients
at different phases of the change process.

Beutler (1983) and Beutler and Clarkin (1990) developed an approach
known as Systematic Eclectic Psychotherapy, which proposes three client dimensions matched with three complementary aspects of technique. These client dimensions include symptom complexity or severity, defensive style, and interpersonal reactance level. Assessment of symptom severity is used to determine if
treatment should be symptom or conflict focused. The client's defensive style
determines whether cognitively, behaviorally, or affectively oriented procedures
will be selected. The interpersonal reactance level determines the degree of
therapist directiveness to be used. Treatment plans change across time as the
client's experience of his or her problem changes.

Howard and his colleagues (1986) have proposed a promising eclectic system known as adaptive counseling and therapy (ACT). ACT, adapted from Hersey and Blanchard's Situational Leadership Theory (1977), attempts to systematically match therapist style with characteristics of the client and the issues brought
to therapy. Therapist style is described as operating along two independent
continuums: support and direction. Therapists high on the support behavior
dimension would devote considerable time, thought, and energy to showing
concern for the client, demonstrating support, being empathic, and building
rapport. Such techniques are designed to help clients feel understood, approved
of, cared for, and supported by the therapist. Techniques that do not include
facilitating the therapeutic relationship would be classified as low on the support
behavior continuum. Behaviors directed toward the accomplishment of an identified goal are on the direction continuum of therapist behavior. What varies is
how much structure or directive behavior is provided by the therapist and how
much by the client. Therapist levels of directiveness and support are matched to
client "task readiness," described in terms of competence, confidence, and motivation. In the ACT model, therapy is conceptualized as a series of affective,
cognitive, and/or behavioral tasks to be accomplished. The style of therapeutic
intervention will vary systematically depending on the specific task and the client's competence, confidence, and motivation related to the task. Central to ACT
theory is the belief that the therapist should behave differently along the dimensions of direction and support with (1) different clients, (2) the same client, at
different points in time, or (3) the same client for different tasks. The therapist's
behavior varies systematically with the diagnosis and treatment goals. Howard's
model seems to have heuristic value and will undoubtedly add to a better understanding of the therapeutic process.

Many eclectic counselors have difficulty articulating their own approach.
They often limit themselves by having only an intuitive sense of what works for
them. Some eclectic counselors choose this position out of inertia or feelings of

defeatism or to avoid the rigorous thinking necessary in developing a unique position. Their practice is based on an additive process of picking and choosing among many theories, often relying on a superficial knowledge to suit their needs of the moment. Thus, a kind of faddism tends to develop, which changes tomorrow when a more attractive method comes along. Howard (1986) notes that "a recurring problem with eclecticism has been the lack of an organizing framework. Although the need has existed for systematizing the current body of therapeutic knowledge, there have been few organizing principles to guide the eclectic in deciding under what circumstances a given therapeutic approach should be used." The principal limitations of the eclectic position are that it often attempts to equate opposite views, gloss over irreconcilable differences, or ignore larger philosophical issues.

To be fair to many persons who label themselves systematic eclectics, it must be stated that such persons struggle to integrate, to be consistent, to validate, and to create a unique personalized theoretical position. This approaches a different stage, however, which we have described in the next section as creative synthesizing. We feel this effort goes beyond what is currently regarded as eclecticism.

The Creative Synthesis Approach

It is our view that each counselor and psychotherapist ultimately must develop a point of view that is uniquely his or her own. Freud was not a Freudian, Jung not a Jungian, and Rogers not a Rogerian. Each of them was himself most fully and completely, while building upon the wisdom of the past. Each practitioner must feel that his or her counseling practice reflects such individuality. This is the reason why no one text or school is fully adequate, and why we try to exemplify an approach which we have termed "creative synthesizing." This approach is not an arrogant attempt to put down predecessors. Ideas are rarely developed in solitary efforts. Usually, they are the results of many years of cumulative cross-fertilization of numerous minds. Isaac Newton is alleged to have said on this point, "If I have seen further, it is because I have stood on the shoulders of giants."

The "creative" element comes in when the counselor not only puts together concepts and practices from other theories in new ways but also transforms them into ideas and methods that have continuing relevance for himself or herself. As each new Gestalt emerges, it becomes more than the sum of its parts. Each new Gestalt goes a step beyond: It expands, modifies, and amplifies. Synergy is involved in that summated systems create a new whole that exceeds the power of the individual systems.

The "synthesis" element comes into the theory-building process as counselors strive to integrate in incremental fashion what appear to be separate ideas and uncoordinated methods. They synthesize dynamic and structural elements to form a basic personality model; they describe strategies and methods that follow from their assumptions and values. This could include culling relevant methods from psychoanalytic practices, cognitive strategies, existential viewpoints, and behavioral methods, which are supported by the basic assumptions of the theorizer. In this process one must be careful about excessive conceptualizing beyond known empirical data. It is easy to get caught up in attractive metaphors that can go well beyond explanatory functions and inject a note of mysticism. Therefore, the criteria that must be applied to such synthesizing processes are that they must be simple, based on data, consistent, open to criticism and change, and useful to explain and predict behavior.

A number of people have attempted this difficult type of synthesis. Assagioli (1965) with his psychosynthesis, Gendlin (1978) with his synthesis views, Perls (1969) with his Gestalt synthesis, Schutz's work (1971) with group processes, Ivey's (1986) and Mahoney's (1991) developmental counseling approaches are some examples of efforts to integrate a wide range of psychological ideas, research findings, and methods into a broad and consistent point of view.

Our actualizing counseling and psychotherapy model is another effort at creative synthesizing. It will be described in the next chapter and will be used as an illustrative model in the remainder of the book.

Steps in Personal Theory Building

Developing one's own view is a very demanding life-long task. In addition to knowing current theories of personality structure and behavior change, counselors must know their own assumptions about the nature of man and the process of knowing, their own values and views of the good life, and their models of the mature well-functioning person. This goal is accomplished through self-study of client-counselor relationships and personal therapeutic experiences resulting in increased self-understanding. These understandings and assumptions are then related to one's goals for counseling, which in turn are matched with strategies and methods to reach those goals most effectively. Counselors borrow from other theorists in the sense that they stand on their shoulders to reach higher levels of understanding and effectiveness in practice. Then, they synthesize these pieces incrementally into a unifed system that is comfortable and effective in a particular setting. Finally, counselors test the theory in practice and formulate hypotheses that can be tested experimentally. The results then are incorporated into their system, or they revise the system.

Lebow (1987) has suggested several useful principles for developing a personal approach to therapy, which integrates multiple theories. First, he suggests that an integrative approach must have a clear and internally consistent theoretical underpinning. This involves asking oneself questions such as, "How does change occur?" "What aspects of experience are most important?" "What constitutes normality?" "What ultimate goals are most important in treatment and what mediating goals are sought to achieve these ends?"

Secondly, Lebow suggests that the theoretical formulation should lead to a method of practice consistent with that formulation. Interventions should be purposeful. The therapist must ask questions such as, "What interventions will be attempted, with what types of cases, in what particular situations?" "How will interventions vary across presenting problems or types of cases?" "What will the ordering of interventions be when there are multiple problems assessed across level, e.g., will a psychodynamic interpretation precede, parallel or follow a systemic intervention?" "How much will one focus on client-stated goals and how much on therapist-observed difficulties outside of client awareness?" The therapist needs to delineate the nature of the intervention model and relate it to his or her theoretical stance.

Thirdly, Lebow reminds us that no perfect theory will emerge. Nor is it likely that an integrative theory will integrate all of the competing conceptions of the human condition that underlie the major theory groups. He suggests that rather than looking for the ultimate therapy, we should emphasize each therapist's development of a clinical posture that maximizes a particular individual's unique strengths.

SUMMARY

In this chapter emphasizing the significance of counseling theory, we have provided a discussion of the origins and development of approaches to the helping process. We have placed psychotherapy in the broader sociocultural process of healing in order to highlight the important structure of the helping relationship as well as to give the student a glimpse of the diverse perspectives from which clients in multicultural, pluralistic societies enter into a helping relationship. The evolution of helping paradigms, with an emphasis on integrative approaches, was discussed. This important process of paradigm shifts occurs not only on a large-scale basis within the field but is also a description of how each student's own theorizing is likely to progress through stages as he or she develops a personalized approach to counseling.

In Chapter 2, we will describe the traditional Western theories that form the basis of most eclectic psychotherapies. Key contributions of each school of therapy will be highlighted. We will also discuss the limitations of these models, which must be incorporated into new paradigms of helping.

CHAPTER 2

Major Theory Groups

The following section contains a summary of the major theories of personality with implications for counseling theory and practice. Critiques of these theories are also presented as a basis for helping the student consider his or her own modifications of these theories in light of new perspectives on the importance of gender and sociocultural context.

PSYCHOANALYTIC APPROACHES

Psychoanalytic approaches provide an example of how an approach has been modified over time to incorporate new ideas. Psychoanalytic therapy is best associated with the works of Freud, who incorporated principles of physics and energy transfer from his day into his view of psychopathology. Freud developed a hydraulic metaphor for human emotional processing in which instinctual urges were viewed as accumulating impulses that could be either discharged or diverted but not eliminated. Freudian therapy has gone through numerous modifications in which new therapies such as Jungian, Rankian, Adlerian, Ego Psychology, Object Relations Therapy, and Self-Psychology have been conceived.

Key Concepts

The psychoanalytic approach stresses the importance of the client's life history (psychosexual development), the influence of genetic impulses (instincts), a life energy (libido), the influence of early experiences on later personality of the individual, and the irrationality and unconscious sources of much of human behavior. The psychoanalytic concepts of levels of awareness are significant contributions. The conscious level consists of those ideas of which the individual is aware at the moment. The preconscious contains those ideas of which the individual is not aware at the moment but which can be recalled. The unconscious level consists of those memories and ideas which the individual has forgotten. Freud conceived the unconscious as making up the bulk of the personality and of having a powerful influence on behavior.

A significant psychotherapeutic issue raised by the psychoanalytic approach is this: Do we need a "depth" approach that postulates that the origin and solution of human problems lie deep within the personality, or do the explanation and solution lie more within the perceptual organization of the individual? Psychoanalytic counselors emphasize the importance of having a concept of depth in personality and postulate a series of structural elements known as Freud's "iceberg" concept, which are illustrated in Figure 2-1. The largest element is the *id*, which has the characteristics of being unconscious, irrational, unorganized, pleasure oriented, primitive, the source of *libido* or life force and energy, and the source of drives and basic wishes for life and death.

Another element of structure is the *ego*, which functions as a controlling, reality-oriented, mastery mechanism. The ego functions also as a mediating element among superego, id, and reality demands. One of the principal functions of the ego is that of controlling the id and keeping impulses and feelings, such as anxiety, out of consciousness. Ego control is accomplished through the mechanism of "defense," of which the main type is "repression." The id impulse, thwarted in direct expression, penetrates the ego barrier in a disguised and usually safer derivative form known as sublimation.

Although the early psychoanalytic theorists placed great emphasis upon repression of anxiety and the consequent symptoms, more recent classical or

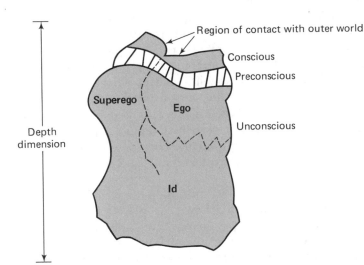

Depth dimension

Region of contact with outer world

Conscious

Preconscious

Superego

Ego

Unconscious

Id

FIGURE 2-1 Psychoanalytic Conception of Personality Structure. J.F. Brown, *Psychodynamics of Abnormal Behavior* (New York: McGraw, 1940); adapted from W. Healy, A. Bronner, and A. Bowers, *The Structure and Meaning of Psychoanalysis* (New York; Knopf, 1930).

"orthodox" psychoanalytic therapists have been giving greater attention to ego psychology, which emphasizes the adaptive mastery functions of personality.

The *superego* is another Freudian concept that functions as a controlling agent in the personality. It is conceived generally as parental moral attitudes and social mores learned in early years, which become an important structural and functional part of personality in later years. In many ways, the concept is similar to the popular term "conscience."

Later students of Freud, such as Jung and Rank, not only modified but also abandoned many of his basic postulates. Adler, a colleague of Freud, emphasized the goal-directedness or purposiveness of human beings more than did Freud, who saw clients more as blind victims of their impulses operating in a rather mechanical deterministic fashion. Adler felt that power and status motives were more significant for behavior than the broadly sexual motives of Freud. Adler saw superiority attitudes as compensations for perceived weakness or the "inferiority complex." Related to Adler's drive for mastery is his notion of the "masculine protest" of some women who envied the status and power of men.

Adler emphasized also the "social interest" or current "life style," as well as the biological determinants of behavior. One of the Adlerian therapist's devices to gain clues to his or her client's life style is to ask for "first recollections." This approach gives the therapist an idea of the experiences on which the client's style of life is based.

Adler is well known for his concept of the *ego ideal* or the person's model of the kind of person he would like to be, a prelude to the now popular concept of *self-image*. Helping the client become more aware of his unique life style, ideals, and self-images is one of the major goals of counseling. Adlerian concepts form the basis of a currently popular form of family counseling.

Jung stressed the uniqueness of human motives and the striving toward individuation. Jung postulated a broad *collective unconscious,* consisting of inherited *archetypes,* which are collections of primordial universal motives and human images. His second structural element is the *personal unconscious,* which contains forgotten and repressed material. The *conscious* is the external awareness level concerned with problems of everyday living. The *persona* is a type of mask hiding the deeper personality characteristics from others. Jung felt that the persona was an important and healthy element of personality, except where it tended to dominate the "real" personality or to blind the person to what Jung called his "shadow." The shadow part of the personal unconscious is considered to be impulsive and generally not consciously nor socially acceptable. In addition to the persona and shadow, there are other examples of archetypes—*animus* (masculine aspect of women), *anima* (feminine element in men), and *self* (the achievement of oneness and unity).

Jung emphasized that the psychotherapist must help the individual replace his neuroses and "build" an individual self. Hence, he placed high value on religion and the integration of religion and psychology. Jung's descriptions of the paradoxes in human personality, such as the mixed feminine and masculine components, are often useful concepts in the interpretation phase of psychotherapy. Both Jung and Adler stressed the value of the direct, face-to-face contact of the psychotherapist with the client, as contrasted with the less direct, couch-centered treatment of the Freudians.

Rank contributed much to psychoanalytic theory by his emphasis upon the traumatic events of birth and separation from the mother. These ideas were expanded to include the security-seeking efforts of people. Rank pointed out many implications from the growth and development as a child for development of independence and security as an adult, thus offering counseling theory a significant and meaningful developmental point of view. One implication, for example, is the importance of "limits." According to this concept, the client is helped to gain a feeling of security by setting limits to his behavior, such as making him stay within the time and place of the interview. With children, especially, this is a significant part of the therapeutic process.

Rank's central concept is the *will*, which is a guiding, integrating, and instinct-inhibiting force. He views resistance as the operation of the will in maintaining the integrity of the personality. Rank's views placed considerable emphasis upon the positive motivations of the client and his present feelings, rather than upon the therapist and his interpretations of the past.

Rank's major contributions to counseling were his insistence on viewing the client as a person, and his casting of the psychotherapist into a more personalized role. Rank believed strongly in "ethical self-determination," implying that the counselor should be careful not to force values on the client. Rank's view sharpens another significant issue in counseling: Where should the content of the process come from, primarily—the client's field of awareness or the counselor's?

Rank's theories have influenced several American psychotherapeutic writers. In addition to Carl Rogers in the adult psychotherapy field, Jesse Taft in social work and F. H. Allen in child psychotherapy have extended Rank's special adaptations of psychoanalytic theory. Rank's will is interpreted as a positive growth force. The conflict between dependence and independence needs is seen as a tendency to regress to earlier dependent relationships when the demands of life become too overpowering. Allen perceives that the basic adjustment difficulties of clients result from excessive demands being made upon them before they have the resources to cope with them. Rank's insistence upon the therapeutic power of the relationship itself has led naturally to a strong emphasis being placed on the attitudes held by the counselor and the importance of having clients assume their own psychotherapeutic responsibility.

Therapeutic Process

In describing key elements of the therapeutic process in psychoanalytic treatment, it is important to recognize that many deviations from the classical psychoanalytic model exist. It is helpful to distinguish between three levels of psychoanalytic treatment.

The most intensive level is *classical psychoanalysis*. Classical psychoanalytic treatment often involves the client visiting the therapist four or five times per week over a period of years. In classical psychoanalysis, the client-therapist relationship is highly central. Change cannot occur without the establishment of a certain kind of therapist-client relationship. Analysts disclose very little about themselves and try to maintain a sense of neutrality. They attempt to foster a transference relationship in which their client will make projections onto them. Analysts believe that if they say little about themselves and rarely share their personal reactions, then whatever the client feels toward them is largely the product of feelings associated with other significant figures from the past. These projections that have their origins in unfinished and repressed situations are considered the object of analysis. The transference (the client's inaccurate perceptions of the analyst) are of central interest. This transference component must be developed, because the client will have a propensity toward such misperceptions and toward behaving in other relationships on the basis of those incorrect perceptions. In effect, transference must develop so that the analyst can show the client, *in vivo*, what he or she does in relationships to perpetuate his or her unhappiness. The analyst's neutral analytic posture helps cultivate the transference, and then his or her interpretative activity renders the eventual insight and working through (seeing the pattern in manifold situations) that is necessary for basic personality change.

Psychoanalytic therapists use techniques such as abreaction of feelings, free association, and interpretation of resistance, dreams, and transference material. The assumptions, style, and length (usually two to five years) of psychoanalytic therapy make it of limited utility in psychotherapeutic counseling. A prominent feature of psychoanalytic technique is to encourage regression to promote exploration of early experiences. The therapist can help clients work through experiences that otherwise might have been beyond their awareness. An example is the transference event where clients see in the therapist characteristics from important persons in their past. Therapists interpret these transference relationships to enhance client awareness.

Psychoanalytically oriented psychotherapy is a less intense form of psychodynamic therapy. Clients meet with their therapist two or three times per week. The therapist adheres less to the stance of neutrality and does not rely solely on interpretation. Transference phenomena and resistance are dealt with and remain central, but transferences are not resolved on the basis of interpretive techniques alone. A greater focus is placed on outside events in the patient's life than in classical analysis (Blanck & Blanck, 1968).

In the third level, *supportive analytic therapy* (usually occurring once a week), there is more give and take between the participants, a greater focus on events outside the therapy, less emphasis on transference phenomena, and a much wider range of therapeutic responses. Psychoanalytic understandings are used to guide the therapist's efforts in the treatment but he or she is much less neutral, more gratifying, and less bound by the rules of classical analysis. The therapist can provide suggestions and otherwise take a more flexible role with the client.

Supportive analytic therapy is not concerned with attempting *major* personality transformations through detailed interpretation of early and persistent unconscious conflicts as is psychoanalysis. Psychotherapy is concerned more with conflicts and feelings which are already in, or dimly in, present awareness and with helping the client to develop resources for handling them. In other words, the psychotherapist concentrates more on the "here and now," whereas the psychoanalyst is concerned with lifting repressions of deeply unconscious material. The analytic method of free association has applications in everyday counseling to help clients let thoughts and feelings flow freely to enhance awareness. The relevance of analytic techniques to psychotherapeutic counseling is treated in later chapters on relationship techniques.

Psychoanalysts tend to view classical psychoanalysis as the most powerful and far-reaching treatment. Modified analytic approaches are usually recommended for more disturbed clients, such as those with borderline personality organization.

Psychoanalytic therapy has made a major contribution through Freud's theory of defense mechanisms. Psychoanalytic thought has made us more aware of the unconscious bases of behavior, with the result that counselors are less concerned with the symptoms (defenses) and more concerned with the origins of the defensive behaviors. The importance placed on developmental issues has led many counselors to do more careful history taking as part of their assessments. Counselors of many theoretical orientations acknowledge the value of analytic notions about transference. A potential shortcoming of analytic therapy is its overemphasis on the past and consequent undervaluing of current interpersonal behavior in maintaining the client's difficulties.

One key implication of a deterministic system like Freud's, in which one has a blocked urge, then repression, then the neurotic symptom, is that individuals tend to deemphasize their personal responsibility for their behavior: "It is not I who is at fault; it is my frustrated id impulses which are causing me trouble." For example, "My hunger stole the fruit, not I." Psychotherapeutic counselors operate on the assumption that the client must, sooner or later, accept personal responsibility for his or her behavior. Existential therapists, for example, place great stress on the client's feeling a sense of "ownership" of himself or herself.

Jung's and Adler's amplification of psychoanalytic theory includes more of the social determinants, such as cooperativeness, and the purposive character of behavior. Rank, as well, stresses the person's integrating powers and the necessity for understanding the client's feelings and potentialities. This concept paved the way for later therapists such as Sullivan, Horney, Taft, Allen, and Rogers to develop theoretical positions of even greater value to psychological counselors.

Recent Positions.   Sullivan is known for his theory of interpersonal relationships, including the interaction between personality development and culture. According to the interpersonal theory, people appear quite different, both to themselves and to others, depending upon the particular personalities with whom they are interacting at the moment. The practical import of this view is that the individual can be understood only within the context of his or her friendships (real or imaginary), and broader social groups.

Sullivan postulates two basic goals of human behavior—physical satisfactions (food, drink, rest, sex) and security (defined as a state of pleasantness or euphoria resulting from fulfilled social expectations). Children, in the process of acculturation, frequently find themselves in conflict between need satisfaction and security. As parents use prohibitions and disapprovals in the acculturation process, children begin to feel anxiety as a result of their inability to fulfill these expectations. They develop increased muscle tension. They exclude from consciousness selected phases of experience that have proved anxiety provoking. Their attempts to resolve these tensions through activity do not result in complete relief, since anxiety reduction does not tend to follow release patterns of other physiological tensions.

If children can obtain both satisfaction and security, they gain a sense of mastery or power; hence, they begin to experience a higher evaluation of themselves. This self-regarding attitude is thus determined by the attitude of others toward them. Self-attitudes, in addition, seem to determine the attitudes that they have toward others.

It is important to realize, therefore, that much anxiety originates in an interpersonal context. If considerable anxiety has been generated during the acculturation process, then useful learning, awareness, and capacity for insight will be greatly reduced. Sullivan speaks of this process as "selective inattention." When other persons in the interpersonal situation mention words or feelings that provoke anxiety in one's self, the evaluation of others tends to change in a negative direction; hence, individuals are alienated from one another. It helps, therefore, to understand that aggressive clients respond in this manner largely because they have been rebuffed in their bids for affection and understanding. Through their inability to receive as well as to give affection, they maintain hostile attitudes even toward those who attempt to satisfy their needs.

Sullivan traces self-development through a series of stages from preverbal infancy through adult maturity. The principal implications for counselors are the necessity to provide security relationships, to accept emotional outbursts, which are indicative of tension buildups, and to organize learning situations, which result in enhancement of self-regarding attitudes of worth and confidence. Therapists and counselors must realize that affectional growth may be poorly developed owing to disturbances in interpersonal relationships and, as a result, the client needs a treatment environment where he or she can develop self-esteem and confidence adequate to any situation. He or she needs an opportunity to develop the ability to love another person whose welfare is as significant as his or her own.

The counselor must be cautious, however, in interpreting the explanations of personality dynamics to the individual. Counselors must recognize also that they too have developed through the same social processes as their clients and that the present counseling relationship is changing them further through what Sullivan describes as his "participant-observer" status. This topic will be treated in Chapter 8 under *countertransference*.

In summary, the principal implication of Sullivan's theory for therapists and counselors is that the individual can be understood mainly in light of his or her interpersonal history. The quality of the client's interpersonal relationships must be examined, in particular, as a key to the client's understanding of his or her attitudes. The counselor must realize that the client's responses to the counselor are affected by these past relationships and that feelings expressed are displacements of feelings from previous personal relationships. Sullivan's ideas are related to the current emphasis in counseling known as the "communications approach."

Karen Horney (1937), who may be classified among the so-called neo-Freudians, differs from the earlier psychoanalysts in that she too stresses the cultural determinants of behavior and emphasizes that maladaptive behaviors arise largely from disturbances in human relationships. Horney, while remaining in the general framework of psychoanalytic theory, shifted the stress from early childhood experiences and repression of biological drives to presently existing character structure and conflicts. She does this, however, without negating the significance of early experience in personality formation. Horney feels that the totality of early childhood experiences and conflict forms a unique character structure which predisposes the person to later neurotic difficulties. This view differs somewhat from the earlier Freudian idea that adult conflicts and neuroses are essentially repetitions of isolated childhood experiences.

An example of the cultural origin of personal problems is the American emphasis on competition, which appears to produce considerable frustration and hostility. Our hostilities are projected to others who are then viewed as competitors. This creates anxiety about the potential danger from others and fear of retaliation for having hostilities of our own. This situation results in a need for security, which is satisfied partially through love relationships. Since deeply satisfying affectional relationships are infrequent for many persons in our society, we are subjected to further frustration.

Horney stresses the competing and contradictory demands of our culture upon the person as one source of tensions. Examples are the conflicts between stimulation of demand for material goods and the limited means for satisfying them, independence and free choice as opposed to the limitations imposed by birth and social circumstances, brotherhood and love for your neighbor against competition and "an eye for an eye and a tooth for a tooth."

The conflicts in the culture are often internalized and express themselves in various forms of aggressiveness and yielding, personal power and helplessness, self-aggrandizement and self-sacrifice, trust of people and fear of them. An implication here for psychological counseling is that these conflicts, faced by all people in our society, become accentuated or reappear as unintegrated childhood conflicts, causing feelings of distress. Individuals may then develop defense mechanisms annoying to themselves or others. The awareness of these conflicts, or the associated anxiety, drives people to seek psychological counseling. An example is the person with a self-effacement defense, so common in our middle-class culture. He feels it is important to "be nice to everyone, so they will be nice to me and will love me." He finds, however, that other people often dislike him anyway, so he is baffled, concludes that he is fighting a losing battle, and becomes even less assertive.

Another useful distinction that Horney makes is between "normal" anxiety, which is fear of concrete events such as accident and death, and "neurotic" or "basic" anxiety, which is fear that arises in early relationships when the person faces a potentially hostile world and which leads to neurotic defenses. One of the psychological counselor's tasks is to help individuals to recognize their basic anxieties and to help them build more satisfying ways of handling them.

Closely related to Horney's concept of basic anxiety is "basic hostility." Horney postulates that much neurotic anxiety stems from the presence of repressed hostility which has been projected to others. The perception of the world as a hostile place generates anxiety and further repression of hostility, and so begins the "vicious circle."

Of further interest to counselors is Horney's concept of the *basic conflict*, which exists largely at an unconscious level. This conflict concerns the feelings of dependence and affection which one has for parents versus feelings of hostility toward them for having to be dependent. The conflict may not be recognized at the conscious level because one cannot easily alienate one's self from those on whom one depends. The more normal individual moves freely between the opposing tendencies of independence and dependence, whereas the more neurotic people are more compulsive about their behavior and experience their independence-dependence feelings as being in direct conflict with one another. This condition has the effect of limiting spontaneity and of giving the victim a feeling of helplessness, indecision, and fatigue. One of the therapist's tasks, according to Horney, is to make the client aware of his or her basic conflicts and his or her attempts to solve the conflict by moving toward, against, or away from people.

One of Horney's (1950) formulations of interest to therapists is her description of the basic types of personalities that come for psychotherapy: (1) *Expansive types* give an impression of glorified self-regard, exhibit an arrogant and contemptuous demeanor, and seem to feel that they can impress and fool others into believing they are someone they are not. This type of client is difficult to involve in a therapeutic relationship initially, but later, when their defenses are reduced, they become involved quite easily; (2) *self-effacing types* tend to subordinate themselves to others, to be dependent upon others, and to seek protection and affection. They are characterized by a strong feeling of failure, inferiority, and self-hate. They exhibit a demeanor of passivity and obsequiousness. They generally become involved easily in a counseling relationship. (3) *Resigned types* put on an air of disinterest, reflecting retreat from inner feelings and from the rigors of life. They take on more of a detached observer's role in life's activities. They lack a strong achievement drive and avoid serious effort. This type of client maintains an emotional distance from others and avoids pressures to get involved in any kind of close human relationship. This avoidance behavior makes involvement in a counseling relationship very difficult.

Additional utilitarian concepts for counselors are Horney's "alienation from self" and the "tyranny of the shoulds" (1950). The former term refers to common client conditions involving fear of losing identity, hazy thoughts and feelings, and feelings of remoteness from one's thoughts and feelings. Horney's "tyranny of the shoulds" refers to the strong tendency in many clients to strive compulsively to be their ideal selves without due regard for reality conditions in their lives. Such clients, for example, operate on the assumption that nothing is or should be impossible for them.

Erich Fromm (1941, 1947), like Sullivan and Horney, is concerned with the social influences on behavior. He, too, stresses the client's individuality, goal-directedness, and productive possibilities.

Fromm was one of the first to use the term *self-realization* in a therapeutic context, viewing growth as an unfolding process of psychological powers. He places the responsibility for many personal conflicts on the economic structure and guilt formation. More broadly, Fromm conceives that the main problems of the modern person center around ethical conflicts and relatedness, particularly in regard to loving and being loved. An example would be the social emphasis upon unselfishness versus social competitiveness and self-interest, both of which involve problems of relatedness and ethics. The relatedness of people to their world, particularly to other people, is an unending human problem. The counselor helps clients on these matters through improving their ability to lead creative lives and to relate to their worlds. The unifying "glue" in Fromm's discussion of human relationships is mature love, which will be elaborated upon in later chapters of this book.

Alexander and French (1946), though adhering closely to more classical Freudian assumptions and techniques, have modified the practice of psychoanalytic therapy so as to reduce the time required to achieve results. The amount of time that should be spent on a client is one of the key issues of professional counseling. Alexander and French have reduced the time required for therapy by selecting carefully therapists to match clients' particular needs, by keeping techniques flexible in order to suit individual styles, and by varying the time between interviews. They emphasize that psychotherapy is a "corrective emotional experience" achieved through forced insight and liberal use of supportive techniques. This latter approach highlights another counseling issue concerning the effectiveness of very direct therapist activity and liberal use of support.

Eric Berne developed a position called *transactional analysis* (1961). He postulates that each of us carries with him three basic ego states—parent, adult, and child—which we use to test reality. The main subject matters for the helping process are the defensive and gratification interactions of these states within and between individuals. For example, one person may react with his archaic "child ego" to the "parent ego" of another person in such a way that the communication is marked by manipulation or distortion. Berne calls these defensive interactions "games." He tries to help clients see more clearly the use of their various ego states and how they can strengthen their more adaptive adult ego. They do this through a progressive structural analysis of their own ego states, a transactional analysis of their communications with others, and analysis of the games they play with others. A key activity in transactional work is reconstruction and analysis of "life scripts," which are basically life-style histories. The stroke is a rewarding condition, such as love and attention. Transactional analysis devotes much time to the client's history of gaining and losing strokes in his or her life script. Transactional analysis incorporates methods from several theoretical positions, such as contracting and Gestalt awareness. For many counselors TA has become a viable and flexible theoretical framework.

In the past decade, Heinz Kohut's self-theory (1971, 1977, 1984) has gained prominence in the analytic community. Kohut has emphasized the key role of empathy in fostering a mature self. Kohut has a similarity to Carl Rogers in postulating that humans have a tendency toward growth, health, and fulfillment. Kohut's concept of the self involves three "constituents," the maturation of which constitutes healthy development. One sector consists of the child's exhibitionistic and grandiose needs. A second constituent is referred to as idealizing needs—the normal child needs to admire, idealize, and seek strength and nurturance from an all-powerful other. The third constituent need is an alterego need to be close and yet separate from a significant other. Healthy development is facilitated when empathic others provide for these early developmental needs. Over time, children gradually acquire the capacity to take over the functions of the empathic other. Thus, needs for a significant other's approval become less important as the child can provide more internal nurturance. These needs gradually become transformed into healthy self-esteem, ambitions, talents, values, and principles. If the childhood environment is not sufficiently empathic, the self becomes fragmented. The person is not able to regulate his or her self-esteem, nurturance, or other needs and seeks external sources, such as people or drugs to meet these needs. Like other psychoanalytic therapists, Kohut takes a "reconstructive-interpretive" approach to work through childhood transference. Kohut's contribution to current analytic therapy is his emphasis on establishing a face-to-face empathic understanding with his clients. He seeks to provide this empathic understanding as well as to interpret transference.

Currently, many psychoanalytic therapists practice a form of Object Relations Theory that builds on many of the theories described previously. Object relations therapists are a theoretically diverse group who believe that the establishment of meaningful relationships or "objects" is the ultimate goal of human behavior. A common thread among object relations therapists is an emphasis on how the client's internal representations of significant early relationships lead to dysfunction in present-day interpersonal relations. Object relations theorists focus on the development of attachment and separation from significant others (Klein, 1975; Bowlby, 1988; Mahler, Pine, & Bergman, 1975) and on development of identity coherence and identity diffusion (Kernberg, 1980).

In object relations therapy, the therapist becomes personally drawn into the client's pathology through the process of "projective identification." According to Cashdan (1988), "projective identifications are patterns of interpersonal behavior in which a person induces others to behave or respond in a circumscribed fashion." In the projection of dependency, for example, persons who project assume that dire consequences are likely to occur unless people provide help for them. Through the projection of helplessness, they induce caretaking from others. Projection involves the behavioral and emotional manipulation of others, usually around themes of dependency, power, sexuality, or ingratiation (Cashdan, 1988). The role of the therapist is to use the therapist-client relationship itself as the focus of change. Through a process of identifying and interpreting these projections within a secure emotional relationship, the therapist guides the client in the resolution of dysfunctional identity splits and into the formation of healthy emotional attachment.

Summary of Recent Psychoanalytic Positions. In summary, the current directions and implications of neo-psychoanalytic theory are as follows: (1) greater recognition of the cultural determinants of behavior; (2) more concern with clients' present circumstances, especially people close to them, and less preoccupation with infantile development and traumata; (3) more emphasis upon the quality of the therapeutic relationship and how the client perceives it; (4) a deemphasis of sexual needs and aberrations, and increasing stress on other needs and feelings such as love, hostility, and ambivalence; and (5) a greater emphasis on rational ego functions in solving life problems.

Research

There are few adequately controlled studies on the outcome of psychoanalytic therapy. Quantitative research on psychoanalysis is rare. The complexity of the theory, difficulty in defining terms, and a past suspicion of quantitative research among analysts have contributed to the lack of adequate research. A promising development for research has been the development of written manuals for short-term psychodynamic therapy (Horowitz, Marmar, Krupnick, Wilner, Kaltreider & Wallerstein, 1984; Luborsky, 1984; Strupp & Binder, 1984). These programs emphasize formulations about the nature of internal and interpersonal conflicts.

A review of comparative treatment studies by Luborsky, Chandler, Auerbach, Cohen, and Bachrach (1971) showed that no one counseling therapeutic treatment may be established as superior to another. Research on the transference concept, thought to be the core of change in effective psychoanalytic treatment, is practically nonexistent. Current research suggests that the quality of the relationship (working alliance) between client and therapist accounts for a large proportion (as much as 30 percent) of the outcome variance in analytic treatment. These findings suggest that much further research is needed to explore various factors related to how a positive working alliance is established, maintained, and contributes to therapeutic outcome. For a comprehensive review of the research on psychoanalytic therapy, read Luborsky and Spence (1978).

PHENOMENOLOGICAL APPROACHES

Phenomenological approaches to psychotherapy have their historical roots in psychodynamic and existential writings. In contrast to psychodynamic approaches, which emphasize therapist interpretations, phenomenological approaches stress that how individuals feel and behave in the present is far more crucial to self-understanding than focusing on why they behave as they do. Phenomenological approaches focus on the expression of the client's and therapist's underlying experience in the counseling relationship. Phenomenological approaches share a respect for the client's subjective experience and a trust in the capacity of the client to make positive and constructive conscious choices. They have in common an emphasis on concepts such as self-actualization, choice, personal responsibility, values, and meaning.

Therapeutic processes of phenomenological therapies emphasize basic therapist attitudes rather than attention to technique. Phenomenological approaches emphasize expanding self-awareness, accepting personal responsibility for who one is and what one does, and unifying or integrating the person. As people become more aware of themselves, they are able to make better choices and live more meaningful existences. A basic assumption of phenomenological approaches is that people themselves can deal effectively with their life problems if they make full use of their awareness of what is happening in and around them.

The primary therapeutic approaches we will describe as phenomenological are person-centered and Gestalt therapy. Other approaches that would be considered as phenomenological include those of Maslow, Carkhuff, Glasser, and May.

Carl Rogers's Person-Centered Therapy

Carl Rogers has been the leading figure in the development of phenomenological therapy. Rogers's controversial volume, *Counseling and Psychotherapy,* appeared in 1942. Rogers's position became known as "nondirective." It was considered radical because it was counter to the psychoanalytic and directive methods of therapy that dominated American psychotherapy during the 1930s. Rogers emphasized the clients' creative responsibility in enhancing themselves toward self-actualization.

Rogers himself is a good example of a creative person at work. Rogers has continued to expand and revise his theory. He has applied his work to diverse clinical groups and settings including school systems, hospitals, management, family therapy, group therapy, and foreign relations (Rogers, 1970, 1977, 1980, 1984).

Key Concepts. Rogers's person-centered approach to counseling emphasizes the important dimension of "self." The self-concept is the person's picture of the self and the self-evaluation of this picture. The self is a construct typically defined as "the individual's dynamic organization of concepts, values, goals, and ideals which determine the ways in which he should behave" (Shostrom & Brammer, 1952, p. 8). It is the individual's consistent picture of self and is best represented by what he or she calls "I" or "me." Various terms such as "concept of self," "self-images," and "self-structure" are used to describe this personality construct. The main sources of these personal evaluations are direct experience and the values and concepts of parents, which are incorporated as if directly experienced.

The concept of self is a learned attribute, a progressive concept starting from birth and differentiating steadily through childhood and adolescence like an unfolding spiral. For example, one of the earliest manifestations of the self is the negativistic attitude of the two-year-old child when he or she begins to realize that he or she has an individuality of his or her own with pressing and distinctive needs and powers. This growing awareness of himself or herself as a unique person is his or her concept of self. This self takes on various subjective attributes in the form of "I am" (his nature), "I can" (his capacities), "I should or should not" (his values), and "I want to be" (his aspirations) (Shostrom & Brammer, 1952).

The development of a self-concept is influenced by an individual's need for positive regard or approval from his or her parents or primary caregivers. Rogers believes the need for positive regard is a universal need. The developing child learns an internalized sense of worth based on his or her perception of the regard received from significant others. One's self-regard comes to depend on the conditions of worth that one has learned through interaction with significant others.

Inevitably, the child's need to retain the love of his or her parents gets in conflict with his or her own needs and desires. When this happens he or she may avoid or deny his or her organismic experiences which he or she has learned are not worthy of positive regard. Experiences perceived to be *incongruent* (inconsistent) with the self-concept will lead to feelings of being threatened, anxious, confused, and inadequate. Because incongruent experiences tend to threaten their self-images, people attempt to use "defense mechanisms" to deny or distort their perceptions of these experiences to reduce the threat to the self-concept.

An example of this phenomenon is the young man who comes for counseling in an anxious state. His first attempts at handling the feelings of anxiety have been to deny or distort them. The client describes his mixed feelings about going to college and continues, "My parents keep telling me I can make it; my aptitude test scores indicate I can do it; I would like to do it; but I am somehow convinced I can't. I feel caught between, so I freeze when I take exams. I would like to junk the whole idea." The client continues to describe his discomfort and other symptoms.

The client's *self-definitions,* capacity concepts, and aspirations run partially along these lines: "I am a young adult; I respect my parents' opinions; I do not have the ability to do college work; I want a college degree; I want to be liked and admired." Yet, the client experiences the fact that he is in college now; his parents have expressed themselves and he values their judgment; the tests indicate that he has the ability to do the work. He is very much *aware* of the anxiety which results and is aware that this anxiety expresses itself in "exam panic." He does not yet perceive, however, that he is experiencing *threat* because his self-concepts are so incongruent with the data. The *symptom* is anxiety, which is experienced when threat occurs. He is tempted to deny (defense mechanism) the conflict by running away from the situation. This evasive action may reduce his awareness of the threat, but not the threat itself. Unless counseling or other life experience breaks this defensive chain reaction and strengthens his self-concept, the defensive behavior (exam troubles, running away) will very likely increase his susceptibility to further threat and guilt, thereby creating more distortion and more mechanisms. The preceding sequence is a summary of the self-theorist's threat and defense theory.

Another common example of the threat-anxiety-defense sequence is that of the young woman who feels a conflict between career and marriage. If she falls in love she would satisfy the need for marriage, but it would threaten her career. However, if she does well in her grades in school and spends much time on training instead of social activities, it would support her career needs but would seriously threaten her marriage goal. The preceding analysis of threat-defense sequences could be applied to this situation where there are two seemingly opposing self-concepts. In this case, the counselor tries to help the client recognize and accept both desires.

When the person above is not acting in accord with her self-concept, we might say she is incongruent in the sense that her awareness of threat and anxiety, and her consequent defensiveness, are high. Her concept of self and her experience as perceived by herself are dissimilar, as indicated in Part (a) of Figure 2-2. The student in the former illustration who feels deeply that he cannot do college work, yet denies the significance of parental judgments and test data, fits this paradigm also.

Conversely, when the person's concept of self is in relative harmony with his perceived experience and he feels that he is acting in accordance with his values, ideals, and past experiences, we might say he has good adjustment. Our student illustration recast in hypothetical terms to match Part (b) of Figure 2-2 would say, "I'm convinced I can make it. My parents expect it; my grades and test scores all point to the fact that my plans are realistic."

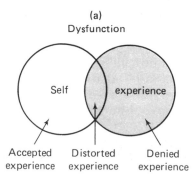

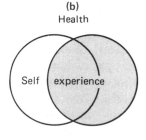

FIGURE 2-2 Dysfunction and Health from the Person-centered Viewpoint. Adapted from Rogers (1951, p. 526).

Congruence is the term used by self-theorists, particularly Rogers (1951) to imply the close matching of awareness and experience. If a client is aware of communicating a feeling that he is genuinely experiencing, his behavior is said to be congruent or integrated. If a client is *aware* of trying to *communicate* a feeling of love to another person, for example, yet he *experiences* hostility toward that person, the recipient of his feelings may experience an awareness of phony communication. The recipient is often aware, furthermore, of the unconsciously motivated defensiveness underlying the client's inaccurate communication. This illustration points up the clear incongruence between experience and awareness, because what the client is aware of and what he is genuinely experiencing are two different phenomena. This condition is also an illustration of the nature of defense from a self-theorist's viewpoint.

A further example of incongruence is the bored guest who insists he is having a wonderful time. Here the guest is aware of the incongruence between his real feeling of boredom and a desire to be polite. Rogers would say this is a type of incongruent behavior that is deceptive rather than defensive because he is aware that his communication is incongruent with his genuine experience of boredom.

The principal counseling implication of this theory of congruence, it would seem, is that the counselor's problem is how to help clients to face courageously the incongruence between awareness and experience so that communication of their real experiences is in full awareness and not defensively distorted.

Although the "self" is the key structural construct, Rogers's principal assumption or central hypothesis of the self-theory group is that the individual has a self-actualizing growth tendency or need. The organism strives not only to maintain itself but also to enhance itself in the direction of wholeness, integration, completeness, and autonomy. Hence, the client is believed to have the capacity and the motivation to solve his or her own problems. The main implication of this view is that the counselor's role is to create an interview "climate" and to use techniques that allow these natural growth forces to emerge in the direction of mentally healthy and creative behaviors. Thus, the self and growth theories are rooted in existential philosophy and humanistic psychology. Both are based on views of present existence and quality of living. Questions such as, Who am I? What does my life mean? and What is real? are in the forefront. Existentialism emphasizes responsibility for individual choice and self-actualizing goals.

Although the "self-actualizing tendency" is postulated as being biologically determined, the direction of the growth tendencies is assumed to be culturally determined by parents, peers, teachers, and other persons significant to the child. Since the individual tends to deny perceptions that conflict with his self-concept, these growth forces often become distorted in the developmental process. This condition often gives the picture of a person devoid of positive growth motives. There seems to be a strong belief on the part of the self-theorists that the positive growth forces will ultimately triumph. For example, independence will supersede dependence; integration will overcome disintegration; social behavior will replace antisocial behavior.

A third assumption, central to *phenomenological views*, is that people's "reality" is that which they perceive. External events are significant for individuals only insofar as they experience them as meaningful. The phenomenologists say that the way to understand individuals is to infer the "phenomenological field" from their behavior. In other words, to really know a person, the observer, or counselor, must know how the individual views his environment and himself. Thus, the term *internal frame of reference* has come into common use in counseling with the implication that counselors must try to perceive clients' perceptual worlds as closely as they can. This intimate understanding is a necessary prelude to "acceptance" of the client's feelings. This viewpoint explains why the client-centered counseling group focuses on deep understanding and acceptance of client attitudes. Thus, the phenomenological approach places a premium on the empathic skill of the psychotherapist. Rogers has been the model of this skill of entering the unique perceptual world of the client. A key assumption of client-centered counseling is that clients who have been heard in this understanding way are better able to become self-actualized.

Therapeutic Process. One of the basic contributions of this view for counseling and psychotherapy is that the experiencing individual becomes the center of focus in the counseling process. Since the client holds the power of growth and meaningful perception internally, the responsibility for change and the "locus of evaluation" of his or her experience must be within the client. The client's internal frame of reference is generally close enough to "objective reality" so that the counselor can follow meaningfully what the client is saying. The counselor, nevertheless, constantly must ask, "What is the client trying to say, and, what does this mean to the client?" The counselor's understanding of the perceptual world of the client is then communicated to the client in fresh language. This condition facilitates further elaboration and clarification of feelings, which leads to insight, and in turn results in positive planning and action.

In person-centered therapy, the counseling relationship is considered the central means for promoting healing and growth. The function of the counselor is to establish a therapeutic climate in which clients experience the necessary freedom to explore areas of their lives that now are either denied to awareness or distorted. According to Rogers, change occurs as a result of an interaction between the therapist and the client. There is strong emphasis on being in a relationship of unconditional positive regard toward the client and on the client's experiencing him- or herself within that relationship. In the safety of this relationship climate, individuals experience permission to experience and work through their internal conflicts. There is less concern about the *direction* in which clients will move and more concern about providing a *relationship* where they can move freely and safely in exploring their own feelings. When "delinquents," for example, are given this type of relationship, the expectancy is that they will move in a socializing direction because they see this as the most rewarding way to go. Thus, there is little emphasis upon changing basic motivations or habits. The person-centered theorist claims that these behaviors automatically change in a socially desired direction when the client's perception is more finely differentiated and when the client discovers for one's self more satisfying ways of meeting his or her own and society's needs.

This therapeutic climate is fostered by relationship conditions of *empathy, positive regard, and genuineness* offered by the therapist. Therapy focuses on the client's current experiencing rather than on interpreting past history or the transference relationship. This exclusive focus in therapy on the present personalized experience of the client is the source of the terms client-centered or person-centered therapy. The therapist focuses his or her attention on the needs and experience of the client. Rogers believes that this empathic understanding has a curative effect on the client.

The second necessary therapeutic condition, unconditional positive regard, means that the therapist genuinely cares for the client and that any therapist behavior that is overtly or covertly judgmental or evaluative is avoided. The therapist completely trusts the client's resources for self-understanding and positive change. The therapist believes and conveys to the client that he or she can effectively follow his or her own process of change.

Genuineness or congruence refers to the therapists' capacity to sense and share their own felt experience as they interact with the client. The therapists trust their own organismic responses in the situation and convey those feelings which they intuitively believe have relevance in the counseling relationship. The therapists' willingness and consistency in truthfully reporting their feelings and experience in the relationship removes some of the risk of the client's sharing him- or herself with another (Meador & Rogers, 1984).

Rogers believes that healing occurs through the client's experiencing an intensely human interaction within the context of an emotionally real relationship. In person-centered therapy, it is the therapist's openness to his or her own experiencing and willingness to share that with the client that provides the basis for therapeutic change.

Person-centered therapy has undergone an evolution since its inception. Hart and Tomlinson (1970) have described Rogers's work as occurring within three phases. The first phase (1940–1950) might be called the *nondirective therapy* phase. The functions of the therapist were to create a permissive, nondirective atmosphere. The therapist aimed at creating a safe therapeutic climate. Rogers's technical interventions consisted primarily of accepting the client and clarifying what the client was saying. During the second *reflective psychotherapy* phase (1950–1957), emphasis was placed on creating a nonthreatening relationship. The therapist's major task was to reflect the client's underlying feelings so that the client was able to experience more congruence between self-concept and the ideal self. The counselor's role was not to interpret but rather to attend to the client's felt experiencing or affect. The *experiential psychotherapy* phase (1957–1970) began with Rogers's statement of the "necessary and sufficient conditions" for personality change to occur. To a much greater extent than in earlier years, a wide range of therapist behaviors was permitted in order to express the basic relationship attitudes of empathy, positive regard, and congruence. There was a greater focus on the therapist's experiencing and expressing his or her own immediate feelings in the relationship. Rogers's emphasis shifted away from attention to technique (such as reflection of feelings) and toward an increased focus on the importance of basic therapist attitudes.

Research.   Rogers's person-centered therapy has generated numerous research contributions to the science and practice of counseling. Many researchers have studied the facilitative conditions of empathy, genuineness, and acceptance that Rogers hypothesized as necessary and sufficient conditions for effective therapy. Truax and Mitchell (1971) reviewed research on these conditions and concluded that counselors who are accurately empathic, genuine, and non-possessively warm in attitude tend to be effective with a wide variety of clients regardless of their training or theoretical orientation. They also concluded that clients receiving low levels of facilitative conditions showed deteriorated functioning. However, in a more recent review of the literature, Gelso and Carter (1985, p. 220) state that "the conditions originally specified by Rogers are neither necessary nor sufficient, although it seems clear that such conditions are facilitative." They also suggest that client deterioration is not related in a "clear, linear way" to low counselor facilitativeness but rather to a complex constellation of therapist and client relationship variables. Gelso and Carter point out that much of the research based on Rogers's theories has looked at therapist variables and has ignored the two-way interaction that a therapeutic relationship involves.

Summary of the Person-Centered Approach.   The principal mark of Rogers's person-centered theory is its postulation of a self-concept. A second distinguishing characteristic is the belief in the innate positive growth potential or self-actualizing power of the organism. The main focus in therapy is on the relationship of counselor to client. In this relationship, the counselor's attitudes of honesty, trustworthiness, and genuine concern are crucial. A main difference from other dynamic approaches appears to be the effort to build and maintain a nonthreatening, anxiety-reducing relationship in which growth can take place from the very beginning. Another difference from other approaches is the increased amount of responsibility placed upon the client compared to that ascribed to the counselor.

Gestalt Therapy

Gestalt therapy has its roots in European Gestalt psychology developed by such familiar figures as Koffka, Kohler, Wertheimer, and Lewin. The Gestalt approach shares many basic goals with person-centered therapy, including expanding one's awareness, accepting personal responsibility for who one is, and unifying or integrating the sometimes conflicting dimensions of the client. There is an emphasis on the here and now experiencing of both the client and the therapist and on the importance of openly sharing that experiencing in the therapeutic relationship. Our summary of Gestalt therapy is drawn from the writings of its founders, Fritz and Laura Perls, and key Gestalt therapists such as Perls, Hefferline, and Goodman (1951) and Perls (1969a, 1969b, 1973), Polster and Polster (1973), Zinker (1977), and Simkin and Yontef (1984).

Key Concepts.   In Gestalt therapy, the goal always is to increase growth and autonomy through an increase in awareness or insight. Perls believed that people prevent themselves from experiencing their full potential. Gestalt therapy is a process that can help people live more full lives through increasing self-awareness, assuming more responsibility for satisfying their needs, becoming more aware of their environments, and increasing their ability to give and receive from others.

Gestalt therapists attempt to help individuals more fully experience themselves and their environments. Gestalt therapists explore ways that individuals resist becoming authentic through games and roles that cut themselves off from themselves and their environments.

Gestalt therapists pay particular attention to ways people avoid living in the here and now. Perls believed that anxiety was the result of individuals escaping from the present into the past or future and either bemoaning their past shortcomings or filling their lives with resolutions and plans for the future. People avoid authenticity by hanging onto the past or future and developing "games" in order to justify their unwillingness to take responsibility for their present lives. Games include being phoney (living through roles as if they are a person who they are not), avoiding emotional pain by denying aspects of themselves, and trying to manipulate their environment to get others to do what they are afraid to do. These forms of avoiding the experience of uncomfortable emotions prevent people from taking the necessary risks that growth demands.

Therapeutic Process.   Gestalt therapy is an exploration rather than a direct modifying of behavior. Gestalt therapy facilitates problem solving through increased self-regulation and self-support by the client. Beginning clients are usually concerned with the solution of problems. As therapy goes on, the client and therapist turn more attention to general personality issues of the client.

The Gestalt therapy method involves the contacting and focusing of awareness. The therapist actively engages with the client. Rather than maintaining distance and interpreting, the Gestalt therapist meets the client and guides active awareness work. The therapist's active presence is alive and warm, honest, and direct. As appropriate, clients are told how they are experienced, what is seen, how the therapist feels, and what the therapist is like as a person. Growth occurs from real contact between real people. Clients learn how they are seen and how their awareness process is limited, not primarily from talking about their problems, but how they and the therapist engage each other around the process. The focusing runs the range from therapist empathy to exercises and experiments. The therapist attitude is to provide direct experience, not interpretation. The task in therapy is to have the person become aware of previously alienated parts and explore them and assimilate them if they want to.

Simkin and Yontef (1984) describe three descriptive therapeutic principles: *I and Thou, What and How,* and *Here and Now.* The *I and Thou* principle describes the horizontal relationship between client and therapist. Therapists as well as clients show their full presence. Both are responsible for themselves. Therapists are responsible for the quality and quantity of their presence, for knowledge about themselves and the client, for maintaining a nondefensive posture, for keeping their awareness clear and for establishing and maintaining the therapeutic climate.

The *What and How* principle refers to the emphasis on increasing awareness of what the client does and how, through direct and immediate sharing of observations and directing the client's attention. The client's attention may be directed in various ways such as therapist feedback, ready-made exercises or experimental tasks designed to *expand the client's direct experience.* For example, therapists may share their immediate feelings, ask clients to attend to incongruities between verbalizations and body language, alter their language into words that claim personal responsibility, or dialogue with various parts of themselves.

The *Here and Now* principle refers to the importance placed on present experience for both the client and the therapist. Therapy remains present oriented. Even in discussing childhood memories or dreams that occurred, the therapist will work with them in ways that involve the client describing them in the present tense.

Research. There is only a limited amount of research on Gestalt approaches to therapy in their meta-analysis of psychotherapy effectiveness. Smith, Glass, and Miller (1980) found that Gestalt therapy ranked eleventh out of eighteen different approaches to therapy. Gestalt approaches have been found to be more effective than other approaches to therapy on measures of self-esteem. Greenberg and his colleagues (1979, 1980, 1982) have researched the Gestalt two-chair technique and reported it as an effective technique for resolving decisional conflict. Gestalt therapists as a group have not been in favor of statistical research. Perls (1951, p. 7) is quoted as saying, "We present nothing that you cannot verify for yourself in terms of your own behavior." The lack of Gestalt research reflects philosophical objection, difficulties in separating technique effects from general relationship effects, and the tendency for Gestalt therapists to work in nonacademic settings.

BEHAVIORAL AND COGNITIVE-BEHAVIORAL APPROACHES

Key Concepts

Historically, this group evolved from the Pavlovian conditioned-response approach to learning and the Watsonian behaviorism of the 1920s. Their objective orientation resulted in a heavy emphasis on studying behavior in its most simple forms through the medium of animal experiments. In the 1950s and 1960s, a number of theorists began to translate learning theory concepts into counseling principles. Pioneers associated with the behavior therapy movement included Mowrer (1950), Dollard and Miller (1950), Wolpe (1958), Krasner and Ullmann (1965), Krumboltz (1966), and Bandura (1969).

Early behaviorists were concerned with changing *overt* dysfunctional behavior in their clients through principles of *classical* and *operant conditioning*. Exposure treatments, such as Stampl's implosion therapy and Wolpe's desensitization, are examples of behavioral approaches designed to reduce anxiety about specific fears. Wolpe's techniques of systematic desensitization and counterconditioning were based on the principle of reciprocal inhibition derived from classical conditioning. These techniques are still commonly used in treatment of anxiety and fear, although investigators now question Wolpe's explanation that these techniques actually work because of classical conditioning principles (Wilson & Davison, 1971; Goldfried, 1971).

Strategies such as use of reinforcements (for example, token economies) and stimulus control are based on principles of operant conditioning. Stimulus control involves reducing the number of antecedent stimuli associated with an undesirable behavior and simultaneously increasing the antecedent cues associated with a desirable response (Thoreson & Mahoney, 1974). For example, overeating has been found to be associated with many environmental cues. Stimulus control strategies would aim to reduce the number of cues (watching TV, walking by the refrigerator, driving by McDonald's, etc.) associated with the undesirable response while increasing cues that will elicit desirable behavior (exercise, eating healthful foods). Stimulus-control procedures have been used for behavior change in weight loss (Carroll & Yates, 1981), to decrease insomnia (Lacks, Bertelson, Sugerman, & Kunkel, 1983), to increase exercise (Keefe & Blumenthal, 1980), and to enhance social interaction among elderly nursing home residents (Quatrochi-Turbin & Jason, 1980), as well as many other applications.

In the evolution of behavioral therapies, the more complex the problems, the less strictly behavioral treatments have been found to be suited to the solution. Anxiety and simple phobias seemed most amenable to treatment by operant methods. However, as problems showed greater complexity, cognitive aspects of behavior began to be addressed as important mediating factors in treatment.

Bandura (1969, 1971) pioneered applications of *observational learning* or *modeling* to the modification of behavior. Perry and Furukawa (1986) have reviewed the applications of modeling to a variety of counseling concerns. These include learning social skills, assertion training, alleviating fears related to surgery, and treating phobias.

A later group of theorists have applied learning principles to influence covert behavior, that is, the *cognitions* of their clients. These *cognitive-behavioral* therapists include investigators such as Ellis, Beck, Mahoney, and Meichenbaum. These therapists believe that the internal dialogue or "self-talk" of clients plays a major role in their behavior. Behavior and emotions are viewed as resulting from cognitive processes. Maladaptive behavior and emotions are changed by correcting dysfunctional beliefs. The therapist's function is to be a diagnostician and educator in uncovering dysfunctional cognitions and helping clients develop new cognitive and behavioral patterns.

Therapeutic Process

Ellis is perhaps the most well-known therapist who has written about dysfunctional beliefs. In contrast to other cognitive-behavior therapists, Ellis's work has a pronounced philosophic emphasis. Ellis believes that people are happier and more productive when they are thinking and behaving rationally. His therapy stresses values of learning to be tolerant of oneself and others. Ellis's rational emotive therapy stresses an "ABC" model of understanding change. The "A" refers to an activating event that precedes a belief about this event, "B," which is followed by emotional and/or behavioral consequences, "C". For example, a client may complain that he was turned down for a date with a woman he wanted to get to know better. He believes he is a failure with women and that he will never find a woman that he likes who will also want to get to know him (Belief "B"). His emotional reaction is that he feels depressed and distances himself from any woman he is attracted to date.

A rational emotive therapist targets the irrational beliefs, "B," for change because the therapist believes it is faulty beliefs that cause the client's dysfunctional reaction. The therapist will be directive in disputing the client's irrational beliefs and in teaching the client to dispute his or her own irrational beliefs. The therapist may use reasoning, confrontation, role playing, humor, and homework assignments to confront irrational thinking and replace it with more rational ideas that are believed to lead to better mental health. In the counseling situation described above, the counselor would challenge the client's belief that he is "a failure with women" and that he will never meet a woman he likes who will also like him. The counselor might offer possible alternative interpretations for being turned down for a date (for example, the woman is not interested in dating anyone) and would challenge the irrational idea that any man turned down for a date is a failure with women. He might also refute the client's dismal beliefs about the future by reviewing evidence that the client had, in fact, met women in the past whom he liked and who were attracted to him. An RET therapist would teach the client to apply such rational disputing methods in situations where the old irrational beliefs arose. An RET therapist believes that, as the client substitutes rational thinking for irrational beliefs, he will feel better and will not distance himself from women toward whom he feels attracted.

Cognitive behavioral therapy has become much more developed in the past twenty years. Therapists such as Beck (1976), Mahoney (1991), and Meichenbaum (1977) have developed cognitive behavioral approaches that are widely used in the treatment of depression, anxiety, fears, pain, and many other areas. Rather than considering clients' beliefs as "irrational," they prefer to consider them as either distorted or dysfunctional thinking patterns. Much of the research from this perspective is reported in the journal *Cognitive Therapy & Research*.

Many cognitive behavioral approaches involve cognitive restructuring. These strategies often involve an initial phase when the client self-monitors his or her thoughts, feelings, and behaviors. In a manner similar to RET therapy, clients then learn to substitute more realistic (less distorted) self-talk for cognitive distortions.

Cognitive approaches have also been used to teach people skills in coping with stressful life events. Meichenbaum's stress inoculation training helps clients to rehearse self-talk in preparation for entering and managing situations likely to produce high levels of anxiety. D'Zurilla and Goldfried (1971) have applied cognitive behavioral principles to teach problem-solving skills. Brammer and Abrego (1981) utilize a wide variety of cognitive and behavioral methods in their taxonomy of skills for coping with life transitions. Their intervention strategies include changes in perception of control, cognitive message awareness and restructuring, construction of external support systems, management of stress, and various styles of problem solving.

Many traditional behavioral strategies have been enhanced by adding cognitive components. Progressive relaxation strategies include a cognitive component of relaxing self-instructions. Systematic desensitization often utilizes covert modeling and rehearsal. Self-management programs often involve covert positive and negative reinforcement.

Research

Research evidence shows that many behavior modification and cognitive behavioral strategies have been effective in both clinical and controlled analogue studies. Much of the voluminous research in behavior modification involves studies of which treatment components are related to effective outcomes with different types of clients. Ellis (1977, 1984) has reviewed research findings related to rational emotive therapy. Studies generally support the effectiveness of RET and its ABC theory of personality. A variety of authors have summarized research and utilization of behavioral and cognitive behavioral therapy with various clinical populations. For further information, it is suggested that the reader consult Mahoney (1974), Rimm and Masters (1979), Kendall and Hollon (1981). Karoly and Kanfer (1982), Meichenbaum (1985), Kanfer and Goldstein (1986), and Mathany et al. (1986).

SYSTEMS APPROACHES

In contrast to the psychoanalytic, phenomenological, and behavioral theories we have previously described, systems theories emphasize a more contextual way of understanding behavior. System theories tend to operate on less individualistic assumptions than other therapies. Traditional personality models have emphasized individual responsibility and individual causes of behavior. These assumptions about the meaning of behavior have led to the individual as being the unit of treatment and have generated individually oriented diagnostic schemes and forms of therapy. The effect of this individualistic paradigm development has been to minimize the role of interpersonal environments as influences contributing to the client's behavior. Systems theories consider the role of the individual as part of a larger interpersonal system. Therapy from this perspective pays less attention to intrapersonal dynamics and, instead, emphasizes the role of transactions between people in shaping personality and behavior.

Systems theory is primarily a way of conceptualizing therapy. Because systems theories are often associated with family therapy, there is a common misconception that systems therapy mostly concerns the number of people in the therapist's office. While it is the system that is the focus of treatment, the therapist may choose to intervene with a particular unit of the system (including an individual "subsystem"). Thus, a systems therapist may choose to see an individual in the session but will *think systematically* about that individual.

A main contribution of systemic views for therapists is that they provide a more contextual way of considering ourselves and our clients. Systems theories build on the work of neo-analytic theorists such as Sullivan and Horney, and social psychological approaches (Strong, 1979), which described therapy in interpersonal terms. Systems theorists have expanded these ideas to consider how individuals shape and are shaped by larger interpersonal and societal networks. Systems therapies have also added new interpretations and responses to the traditional concept of client "resistance." Systems therapists suggest therapeutic responses to resistance that place more responsibility on the therapist to be flexible and creative rather than blaming of the client for being uncooperative.

Key Concepts

1. The individual is embedded within a larger relational context. A central tenet of systems theory is that the individual is embedded in a larger relational system, which is the unit of therapeutic intervention. This larger relational system is a highly complex organization that includes many parts or subsystems such as the individual, the nuclear family, the extended family, and the community. Each subsystem is both a whole and a part, not more one than the other. Part and whole are connected to each other in a continuing, current, and ongoing process of communication and interrelationship. Subsystems may be individuals or groups organized according to generational or hierarchical characteristics (parents, children, employers, employees), gender, interest, or task (parenting or work role). Any part of the system (that is, the individual) is best understood by examining his or her position in the larger system structure.

2. Transactional patterns in the system are involved in shaping the behavior of individuals within the system. For the systems therapist, the meaning of behavior is derived from an appreciation and examination of relational contexts. A systems therapist assumes that the meaning of an individual's behavior is best understood through an examination of the relational context in which he or she is embedded as well as the relational outcomes that the behavior functionally elicits from others. In other words, the systems therapist must explore the meaning and function of symptomatic behavior within the client's larger relational system. That relational system may include the client's family of origin, marriage, current work or school setting, or other significant subsystem.

3. Dysfunction is related to recursive patterns within the system. Systems therapists tend to use circular rather than linear thinking to describe symptom manifestation and therapeutic process. Most Westerners automatically tend to apply reductionistic habits and "punctuate" reality by dividing interaction processes into small segments. For instance, one might note that event A precedes event B. So, one's linear paradigm then leads one to "know" that A "*caused*" B. For example, a husband's criticism caused his wife's sadness. Preoccupation with causes often leads to the conclusion that A intended the occurrence of B (i.e., the husband intended to hurt the wife's feelings). These presumed intentions then become subject to moral judgments by the client or therapist (i.e., "What a malicious or crazy person that husband is!").

In order to understand beliefs and behavior as a circular process, a deliberate attempt must be made to suspend linear punctuation of events and look for recursive sequences of behavior. When employing a circular orientation, the therapist might note that when the wife becomes sad, the couple's child misbehaves, and when the child misbehaves the husband is critical, and when the husband is critical the wife becomes sad, etc. The systems therapist might conclude that the wife shows sadness as part of a recursive pattern of interaction between the husband, wife, and child. Judgment is against the pattern rather than the individual. The therapist becomes more neutral than in therapies that emphasize identifying cause and effect. Systems therapists focus on exploring how each part of the system "shapes" and is "shaped by" its position in the larger system. There is a shift away from evaluating the intentions of a person to evaluating the *effects* of behavior in terms of circular patterns. The therapist is always considered part of the pattern that he or she is observing.

In contrast to individually oriented therapies, systems therapies assume that mental phenomena reflect social phenomena. Thus, mental problems may be regarded as problems in patterns of social interaction. This assumption channels therapeutic interventions toward patterns of interaction between persons rather than toward a particular individual or specific symptom he or she may be manifesting. Attention is given to circular processes that show the function of symptoms rather than to the specific content of the symptom. The person within a system who shows symptoms is usually designated as the "identified patient" or "I.P." This term indicates that the symptom bearer is the person who has been *labeled* as the problem person by himself or herself and/or others in the system.

This contextual view of behavior is reflected in the careful use of systemic language. Systems therapists are wary of linguistic conditioning that is oriented toward linear thinking. For instance, systems therapist Karl Tomm suggests substituting the verb "to show" for the verb "to be." Tomm (1984a, p. 119) illustrates the differences in meaning by stating, "one could make the statement that the 'father is depressed' or that the 'father shows depression.' If one employs the former, one implicitly separates the father from his context and becomes oriented towards looking inside him for the basis of the depression. One might look for psychodynamic factors in superego functioning or for some biochemical abnormality in his nervous system. On the other hand, if one describes him by saying the 'father shows depression,' one tends to wonder to whom is he showing this depressive behavior and what effect this might be having. Thus one becomes inclined to examine what is happening in the father's context (in his relationships) to explain why he shows this difference in his behavior."

Therapeutic Process

Systemic therapists use a variety of techniques to intervene in a system. They tend to look at the system's ability to define roles, solve problems, adjust to developmental or situational change, balance separateness and togetherness, manage power, and maintain boundaries. The therapist works to substitute new behavior patterns for dysfunctional feedback patterns. Choice of therapeutic strategies will depend on the particular systemic approach adopted by the therapist. The major adherents of systemic therapy can be grouped into several approaches: intergenerational, structural, and strategic therapies.

Intergenerational Therapies. Intergenerational therapies emphasize a multigenerational process of symptom development. Theorists associated with this group include Bowen, Boszormenyi-Nagy, and Framo. In describing this approach, we will primarily describe the work of Bowen as being representative of the intergenerational group.

In explaining the emergence of emotional symptoms in a family member, Bowen (1978) suggests that its origin lies in difficulties family members of the previous generation have had in separating from their families of origin. This difficulty is mitigated, if not solved, by unconsciously involving or triangulating a person from the next generation as an identified patient. As this process unfolds from generation to generation, family members' inability to individuate intensifies until one or more children exhibit symptoms that keep them stuck forever in the family, and the family stuck forever around them. It is a kind of repetition compulsion applied to the generations. The identified patient finds him- or herself either over- or underfunctioning with little freedom within the family system to function differently. The "I.P." can be stuck in "positive" roles such as an overfunctioning "strikingly high achiever" or may assume a role as an underfunctioning "bum." Either kind of role reflects *triangulation* into one's family of origin.

For Bowen, symptoms develop when a family system is unable to balance the counterbalancing life forces of individuality and togetherness. The degree to which individuals can balance these forces is described as the person's *level of differentiation* or sense of solid self. A well-differentiated person is able to achieve an optimum balance of individuality and togetherness forces. The person can define his or her own life's goals and values apart from the surrounding togetherness pressures. He or she can say "I" when others are demanding "you" and "we." Differentiation includes the capacity to maintain a (relatively) nonanxious presence in the midst of anxious systems, and to assume maximum responsibility for one's own destiny and emotional well-being. It is somewhat reflected by the breadth of a person's repertoire of responses when confronted with a crisis. Differentiation is not to be confused with autonomy but is rather an interdependent capacity to be an "I" while remaining connected to others. Such differentiated persons can think about their feelings and be intentional about their behavior in a relationship system. They are not at the mercy of emotional pressures from others to think and act in certain ways and can clearly define the boundaries between self and other.

Less differentiated persons are said to experience *relationship fusion*. The greater the fusion or lack of differentiation, the greater the influence of the togetherness life forces on a person's functioning. This fusion is manifested by a strong need to be approved by others in order to feel emotionally secure. Such persons may become overly dependent or withdraw from the risk of closeness. They may also become emotionally reactive and find themselves courting disapproval and rebelling against the perceived wishes of others as a way of fighting the togetherness forces. Fusion is manifested by poorly defined boundaries between self and others and a fusion of intellectual and emotional functioning that leads to unrealistic assessments (overvaluing or undervaluing) of oneself and others.

Fused individuals are also vulnerable to stress. Anxiety is extremely uncomfortable for them to experience. When such people become anxious, they either distance and emotionally cut themselves off from others or become more fused through triangulation. For example, an undifferentiated person experiencing conflict will "resolve" his or her discomfort by becoming fused or overinvested in a third person, thing, or activity (i.e., job, hobby) and avoiding conflict with the original person. Distancing and triangulation are common means of avoiding conflict or internal discomfort. Triangulation of children into adult conflicts often occurs. This pattern of handling conflict tends to replicate patterns in one's family of origin.

Therapy from an intergenerational systems perspective involves efforts to increase the identified patient's level of differentiation. The therapist's role is usually to coach clients to gain enough knowledge about themselves and their systems to be able to change themselves in relationship to others. The therapist educates clients about typical emotional processes and helps clients become aware of their own defenses or "reactivity" within their surrounding emotional systems. The therapist will coach the client about ways to recognize and manage anxiety without defensive distancing or triangulation. Clients are asked to make visits to their own families of origin when appropriate to gather information about family roles as well as to practice maintaining a strong sense of self within an emotional system that might normally elicit fusion from the client. A key role of the therapist in intergenerational therapy is to maintain his or her sense of self and not become triangulated or pulled into the client's conflicts.

Structural Therapies. Structural therapies have their roots in innovative community mental health programs of the 1960s when there was a great deal of experimentation in methods of treating poor families. Because of these roots, structural approaches have particularly focused on family problems. A structural approach, however, can be useful in assessing and intervening with a variety of issues people face by transferring the basic concepts to other significant relationship or work contexts. Structural therapy is primarily associated with pioneers such as Minuchin, Fishman, Montalvo, and Aponte.

Structural therapists have been concerned with assisting families to develop an internal structure or organization that will provide family members with a sense of belonging while, at the same time, allowing for separation and individuation. Optimal family organizations must have flexibility to adapt to the situational and developmental stresses that every family encounters as well as to maintain enough cohesion to provide for a sense of belonging. Symptoms appear in the system when the system lacks a sufficient range of patterns, available alternative transactional patterns, and the flexibility to mobilize these patterns when necessary.

Structural therapists believe that an appropriately organized family will have clearly marked boundaries or rules defining who participates, and how, in each subsystem. Structural family therapists believe that the optimal marital subsystem will have closed boundaries to protect the privacy of the spouses. The parental subsystem will have clear boundaries between it and the children, but not so impenetrable as to limit the access necessary for good parenting. The sibling subsystem will have its own boundaries and will be organized hierarchically so that children are given tasks and privileges consonant with sex and age as determined by the family's culture. Finally, the boundary around the nuclear family will also be respected, although this is dependent on cultural, social, and economic factors.

The therapist's role is to assess the family's organization and redesign it as necessary so that it will approximate the normative model more closely. It is assumed that symptoms will disappear as family organization becomes more normal. The therapist joins the family system and "maps" family organization indicating important factors such as membership in coalitions, the nature of boundaries, and how the subsystems are structured. The therapist maps family organization by attending to family process. The family's established transactional patterns underpin and are indicators of family organization.

There are three main strategies of structural therapy, each of which is served by a group of techniques. The three strategies are *challenging the symptom, challenging the family structure,* and *challenging the family reality*. Challenging the symptom involves reframing the family's view of the problem so that members can establish more functional transactional patterns. A structural therapist will search for the function of a problem within the system. Minuchin and Fishman (1981, p. 68), for example, describe treatment of a boy who urinated on the floor whenever he was angry at his mother. The therapist explored alternative ways of expressing resentment and disagreement in the family. The therapist examined the different intensities of each parent's involvement with the symptom, the meaning the symptom held for each family member, and the function of the symptom in the marital and sibling subsystems. The symptom was redefined as a way for the system to reengage the mother, who had recently changed her relationship with the child and her husband. This redefinition opened up new perspectives on the conflictual relationship between the spouses, the distancing between father and son, and the privileged position of the son in the sibling subsystem. As the family members found themselves exploring new territory, their mood changed, becoming more intense and at the same time more hopeful.

Challenging the family structure involves building "walls" and "bridges" between people to set boundaries, unbalance the system, and help members to see themselves in complementary roles (i.e., as a system). Because many relational conflicts involve over- or underaffiliation, therapy is seen as a process for monitoring and regulating proximity and distance among family members.

Structural therapy postulates that transactional patterns depend on and contain the way people experience reality. Therefore, to change the way family members look at reality requires the development of new ways of interacting in the family. The therapist takes the family data and, reorganizing it, presents it to the family with a new interpretation. "Reframing" behavior in this way helps family members experience themselves and one another differently so that new transactional possibilities appear.

Strategic Therapy.   Strategic therapy is mostly associated with therapists such as Haley, Madanes, Milton Erikson, Watzlawick, Weakland, and Fisch. The strategic school focuses on the problem as the unit to be treated. The strategic therapist tries to identify how a system becomes organized around a problem in a manner that maintains the problem. These therapists believe that most problems consist of self-reinforcing cycles of patterned behavior. These problem sequences may involve various members of a client's system.

Strategic therapists see symptoms as the results of misguided attempts at changing an existing difficulty. For example, the depressed person whose family frantically tries to cheer him up may only become more and more depressed. In such cases Watzlawick et al. (1974) note that "the family is unable to see (and the patient to say) that what their help amounts to is a demand that the patient have certain feelings (joy, optimism, etc.) and not others (sadness, pessimism, etc.). As a result, what for the patient might originally have been a temporary sadness becomes infused with feelings of failure, sadness, and ingratitude toward those who love him so much and are trying so hard to help him" (p. 34). Thus the family's attempt to alleviate the problem only exacerbates it.

According to Watzlawick et al. (1974), problems are created or maintained when a normal difficulty is encountered and either (1) action is necessary but is not taken (pretending a problem doesn't exist); (2) action is taken when it should not be (often based on the premise that things should be different than they are); or (3) action is taken at the wrong level (as in the "mishandling" of the depressed person in our previous illustration). Such actions are often based on common sense but are not appropriate to the situation.

Strategic therapists attempt to change the recurrent sequence or pattern of behavior that creates or maintains the client's problems. In strategic therapy, the therapist assumes responsibility for determining the structure of the therapeutic process. Treatment is usually brief (ten sessions or so) and time limited. The therapist is usually directive, giving the client directive tasks and homework assignments. Therapy is pragmatic. The therapist uses whatever technique he or she believes will be effective in changing the dysfunctional pattern of behavior.

Watzlawick et al. (1974) describe their therapeutic procedures as a four-step process. The first step is to get a clear definition of the problem in concrete terms. The purpose of this step is to explore the client's personalized and specific meaning of the problem. This is followed by an investigation of the solutions attempted so far (i.e., looking for how problems are created and maintained by poor problem-solving attempts). Exploration of these attempted solutions not only shows what kind of change must not be attempted but also reveals what maintains the situation that is to be changed and where change has to be applied. The third step involves clearly defining the concrete change to be achieved. This step ensures that the client's goals for success are attainable and not utopian. For example, it may be impossible to cure chronic pain but it may be possible to learn how to better manage the pain. The fourth step is the formulation and implementation of a plan to produce change. The target of change is the sequence of behaviors that represents the client's attempted solution to his or her problems.

Because most clients have already tried to solve their problems in ways that make sense to them, many strategic interventions may appear strange or illogical to the client. Tactics must be presented to clients in forms that utilize their own ways of conceptualizing reality. Otherwise, clients may resist the therapist's directives. When client motivation is high and resistance is low, therapist pattern-prescribing directives are straightforward. However, strategic therapists are particularly well known for interventions with clients who resist change. Typical strategic interventions for these clients include communicating through story or metaphor and paradoxical interventions such as symptom prescriptions (i.e., bringing on an anxiety attack), restraining strategies (i.e., discouraging change), positively connoting symptoms, and accepting and exaggerating a client's position (i.e., "outdoing" a client's pessimism by defining the situation as even more dismal than the client had originally held it to be). Paradoxical interventions must be carefully reframed in order to fit the data and provide a new view of "reality" for the client.

Recently, a new movement, known as *constructivism* (Mahoney, 1991; Efran, Lukens, & Lukens, 1990) has shifted the focus of strategic therapy from the client's problem-solving efforts to a focus on the underlying premises a client has assigned to his or her problems. Constructivism is a complex and abstract theory that has incorporated elements of biology (Maturana & Varela, 1987), cognitive psychology (particularly Kelly's personal construct theory), and systems theory. Constructivism takes a relativistic point of view that emphasizes the client and therapist's subjective construction of reality. The client and therapist's realities are both believed to be arbitrarily created. There is no normal model of individual development or "valid" way to live one's life. Thus, each "story" of reality is discussed with mutual respect and without judgment.

In constructivist therapy, subjective meaning that the client has attributed to his or her problems becomes the target of therapy. This therapy is sometimes termed "meaning-focused therapy." In this form of therapy, the therapist has conversations with the client in order to understand the client's "problem-saturated" stories. These client narratives typically involve narrow, pessimistic underlying premises that shape their lives in ways that generate rigid, ineffective, attempted solutions. The goal of therapy is to come up with a new story or explanation of reality that leads clients to redescribe themselves in a new, empowered story.

Externalizing Therapy (White & Epston, 1990) and Solution-Focused Therapy (de Shazer, 1988; O'Hanlon & Weiner-Davis, 1989) are examples of meaning-focused therapies. In each of these therapies, clients are asked to focus on exceptions, that is, times when their problems either did not occur or did not defeat them. The therapist then looks for ways to expand or build on those times of success. For example, if a client has difficulty with overeating but remembers that several times in the previous weeks her eating was acceptable and those times occurred when she was having fun with other people, she may decide to direct her energy by building relationships with people rather than focusing on her eating. Solution-oriented therapists claim that if both client and therapist can reorient themselves in the direction of strengths, and can initiate small changes that can lead to larger changes, then therapy can be quite brief.

Constructionist approaches have held appeal because of their orientation to client strengths and brief treatment. One difficulty with the constructivist viewpoint is that the belief in subjective relativism may inadvertently collude with certain types of clients who overly deny problems such as chemical dependency or abuse. Such individuals may not believe that their problems are as bad as they think and the constructivist therapist must decide whether to confront those realities.

Research

Although there has been an increase in research on systems theories in recent years, there is generally a lack of solid empirical research on the concepts and applications of the theories. Of the three approaches described above, the intergenerational approaches have had the least empirical study. A significant relationship between family triangulation and personal adjustment levels of adolescents has been found by numerous researchers (Flemming & Anderson, 1986; Bell & Bell, 1982; Kleiman, 1981; Teyber, 1983a, 1983b). These studies add support to intergenerational theory as well as to structural theory by supporting the positive relationship between clear parental coalitions and family adjustment. Development of a family of origin scale (Hovestadt, Anderson, Piercy, Cochran, & Fine, 1985; Mazer, Mangrum, Hovestadt, & Brashear, 1990) may advance research on intergenerational therapy.

Structural family therapy research has been reported by Minuchin, Rosman, and Baker (1978), Stanton and Todd (1979), and others. Because structural therapy employs a wide choice of techniques, it is difficult to validate central aspects of the theory and identify components of the treatment that uniquely contribute to its efficacy. Most of the research conducted has been with families presenting child problems. The issue of its applicability with adults needs further research. Structural approaches need testing in other clinical settings with a broad range of problems.

Existing research shows that strategic therapy has been effective with particular kinds of problems. However, research is needed regarding its application to a broader range of problems. Watzlawick, Weakland, and Fisch (1974) have described research on strategic therapy. Also, Weeks and L'Abate (1982) have reviewed extensively research on the paradoxical therapeutic techniques that are frequently used by strategic therapists.

One of systems therapy's greatest contributions to the mental health field is to stress the importance of understanding people's behavior in their social context. Prior to this recognition, the symptoms of a client were examined in isolation, apart from his or her network of significant relationships. When the development or presence of behavior patterns are viewed within a social or family context, they often seem less strange and can be understood as a necessary aspect of living within a particular family or social group.

CHALLENGES TO THE CURRENT PSYCHOTHERAPEUTIC PARADIGMS

In Chapter 1 we described the nature of paradigm shifts in psychotherapeutic systems. In this chapter we have seen how each of the theories we have discussed has evolved around a central focus of change. Psychoanalytic theory has focused on development of a coherent self and effective regulation of unconscious motivations. The phenomenological or humanistic theories have asserted the primacy of current emotional experience in effecting changes in behavior and attitudes. Behaviorists have favored behavior as the primary force of human experience and suggested that behavioral changes produce changes in attitude and emotions. In contrast, the cognitive-behaviorists have emphasized the important role of thinking and rationality in producing changes in behavior and feeling. Systemic therapists have asserted that changes in the individual's social context lead to changes in thoughts, behavior, feeling and definition of the self.

As we discussed in Chapter 1, there are movements to integrate these theories. Along with a desire to incorporate clients' needs for meaning, there has been a movement among some cognitive therapists toward embracing emotional experience. In cognitive behaviorism, intense and seemingly irrational affect has been seen as a problem rooted in irrational and unrealistic cognitions. A major aim of cognitive therapy has been to enhance self-control over such emotions through rational supremacy (Mahoney, 1991). In systems therapy, there has been a movement toward acknowledging the important role of the individual within the family system.

In spite of these new evolutions, important biases and blind spots in these theories have become apparent in the last decade. In this last section of Chapter 2, we try to highlight several important developments that therapists may need to consider as they develop a creative theoretical synthesis for the coming decades.

Gender-Role Concerns

Feminist critiques of psychotherapy in the 1980s (Gilbert, 1987; Hare-Mustin & Maracek, 1990) made us painfully aware that all of the theories we have discussed previously in this chapter inadvertently applied sexist notions to counseling and therapy. Psychotherapy has often focused on restoring troubled women to their traditional gender-role model of mental health, which has included characteristics of submissiveness, inhibition of activity, and suppression of anger that may predispose women to depression. Counseling has fostered the status quo without attending to relational differences in women or elements of their societal context that put women at increased risk for emotional distress. Specific life experiences of women, such as increased care-giver roles, family violence (for example, abuse, sexual harassment), physiological changes (for example, menstrual cycle, childbirth, infertility, menopause), and medical procedures undergone only by women (for example, abortion, hysterectomy), have not been incorporated into mental health theory or treatment.

The power of male therapists over female clients has been seen by feminist therapists as paralleling an oppressive social order in which men have defined women's needs and passed judgments about women's optimal functioning. Counseling theories predominantly developed by men have emphasized autonomy, achievement, and the use of intrapersonal and cognitive problem-solving methods rather than a reliance on interpersonal problem solving. These criticisms have given rise to a feminist-informed therapy, which promotes an understanding of women's experiences within their social context and advocates social and relational changes to empower women for freer, less stereotyped roles.

In the current decade, there has been a rise in the awareness of how traditional conceptions of male gender roles can also be detrimental to emotional health (Scher, Stevens, Good, & Eichenfield, 1987; Levant, 1992). Men's restricted emotional expression and their drive to achieve power and control are examples of some of the traditional gender-role stereotypes that may make men prone to health and relational distress. While the attention to men has not led to revisions in counseling theory to the extent of feminist critiques, the attention to the issues of men will likely increase in the coming years.

A significant challenge to any new paradigm of counseling will be that it must be a "gender aware" therapy (Good, Gilbert, & Scher, 1990). The research on the effect of sex and gender-role attitudes on the therapy process is still in the early stages (Mintz & O'Neil, 1990); it is clear, however, that the influence of gender on the counseling process is quite complex. Future research will need to explore variables such as gender-role orientation, attitudes, conflict, multi-cultural gender issues, and counselor sex/gender-role pairings with clients.

Multiculturalism

As we discussed in Chapter 1, multiculturalism challenges our current paradigms of counseling. The majority of theories we have described in this chapter have been developed from an ethnocentric point of view and lack a multicultural perspective. In our increasingly pluralistic and ethnically diverse society, any new paradigm of counseling must address both the universality of human distress and the cultural and intracultural uniqueness in how that distress is expressed.

The challenge to counselors is to develop a personal theory and practice that precludes "cultural encapsulation" (Wrenn, 1985). This encapsulation refers to the tendency of counselors to depend upon one authority, one theory, and become trapped in a blind way of thinking that resists adaptation. The essence of the cross-cultural approach we are proposing is that clinicians seek to understand how their clients think about *their* world and *their* problems. The counselor is respectful in the face of alternative knowledge and explanations, treating them as comparable but different from his or her own. The contribution of this cross-cultural perspective is not to falsely romanticize what is different but to encourage a perspective that is integrative, flexible, and sensitive to diversity and pluralism in human experience.

We agree with Kleinman (1988) that each counselor must learn to incorporate basic ethnographic methods into his or her practice. These include learning about the key cultural values, behavioral norms and practices, styles of communication, and family and other social institutions that significantly affect behavior. Clinicians can also learn about culturally specific distress syndromes as well as norms for the expression of complaints and typical help-seeking methods of their client groups. Supervision in methods, such as ethnographic interviewing skills and community participation, will help the counselor elicit information important to understanding culture-specific and within-group cultural variations to values and norms. The purpose is to come to an understanding of the client's unique world view. Clinical supervision is also important in coming to terms with the counselor's own ingrained biases about people who come from different backgrounds. These types of information are critical for developing client-specific interventions in multicultural settings.

Powerlessness and Empowerment

Any new paradigm of counseling will need to address needed changes in a societal context in which certain populations are at greater risk for mental health problems because of cultural, linguistic, gender, and socioeconomic influences (Brody, 1990; McWhirter, 1991). This became apparent as we discussed the challenges of gender-role concerns and multiculturalism. It is impossible to talk of personal change without implicating social change for groups that are blocked from access to sources of societal power. Across cultures, persons are relegated to minority status because of such socially visible characteristics as race, class, religion, ethnicity, nationality, or caste.

To ignore the socioeconomic context within which the client lives is to miss many external variables that contribute to client problems. According to Brody (1990), individuals who lack access to power also lack (1) freedom of opportunity to become self-determining and to attain higher socioeconomic status; (2) justice in the sense of equal access to social goods and equal freedom from restraint; and (3) beneficent treatment aimed at their best interest. For instance, high-socioeconomic-status patients receive more voluntary explanations from doctors about illness and treatment, regardless of diagnosis, than do low-socioeconomic patients (Benson, 1984). The minority person who is distant from sources of societal power is at a greater risk to enter the mental health system through the legal judicial system.

The challenge for counselors is to develop a new paradigm of counseling that includes recognition of social power differences and emphasizes a process of client empowerment. According to McWhirter (1991), the counseling process may be disempowering when the counselor holds a negative or deterministic view of human nature, when there are wide discrepancies between counselor and client power, when the client's subjective experience of reality or cultural values is ignored or downplayed, and when the client's problem is defined without acknowledgment of the social context within which the client operates. In contrast, empowerment is a process in which the client grows in life skills, develops an awareness of how power dynamics are played out in his or her life context, shows a sense of identity with similar others, participates in his or her community, and supports the empowerment of others.

SUMMARY

This chapter maintains the view that counselors and psychotherapists should have a consistent and explicit theory of personality to guide their practice as scientist-practitioners in therapeutic psychology. Although there is no one theory of personality that is suitable to frame the practice of counseling and psychotherapy, each position has unique implications for practice. The various psychodynamic, phenomenological, behavioral, and systemic models of personality can be drawn upon to help understand this unique client in this particular setting. Gender concerns, multiculturalism, and issues of empowerment are discussed as major challenges to the current theoretical paradigms. Each counselor is encouraged to assume responsibility for developing a personalized approach to counseling.

CHAPTER 3

Actualizing Counseling and Psychotherapy

A MULTIDIMENSIONAL VIEW

The title of this chapter expresses our views on a creative synthesis approach to counseling theory and human growth. The whole point to growth is to become one's true person and to realize all the potentials within one's self, that is, to continue actualizing into a responsible, fulfilled human being. In the preceding chapter we surveyed a variety of theories intended to achieve the goals of counseling and psychotherapy and described our creative synthesis approach. We emphasized that any one theory is not yet sufficiently comprehensive or systematic to guide the counselor through the multitudinous problems in everyday practice. Therefore, our multidimensional view is described to cope with the complexities of the counseling endeavor.

As counselors grow, their theories progress. Psychodynamic and phenomenological approaches become integrated with behaviorally oriented action approaches. Systemic approaches also become reconciled with models that emphasize internal beliefs and dynamics. Historical approaches become mixed with theories that emphasize the individual's present perceptual matrix and conditioned behavior.

We have struggled with the problem of devising a parsimonious, yet multidimensional, approach to counseling, which involved selection of concepts that would hold up with growth, crisis, and prevention models, or which were at least workable for the majority of our clients. The selection of a personality model that had consistency for the universe in which we worked, and the selection of techniques that fitted our personalities, gave us a vocabulary and a frame of reference within which to verbalize, communicate, and test our observations about counseling relationships.

This chapter is our effort to make the events of counseling and psychotherapy more understandable to us, and we hope more understandable to the reader. We have discovered that it is much easier to develop a point of view for a restricted clientele in a special setting than a theory for counseling in general. Yet we know from our teaching and conferring with colleagues that most counselors work in settings with wide varieties of human problems requiring a multidimensional dynamic theory and a flexible approach to methods.

It is important for each of us to remember that the theories we use to describe persons within the counseling process are only metaphors or "maps" to guide our work. Just as a map is not the same as the terrain it describes, our theories about the person are psychological constructs and not the actual person. We must be careful that we not lose sight of theory as a fallible guide. Our clients often serve as examples of persons who get stuck because of the dysfunctional or distorted theories they hold (about themselves). Counselors, too, become ineffective when they try to fit their clients into their theories rather than finding theories that are useful in helping their clients.

Other theories have made their unique and rich contributions to our thinking, for which we are grateful. We have added reflections, however, from our combined experiences in counseling and psychotherapy over a broad spectrum of clients and settings. Figure 3-1 represents perceptions of the current state of our thinking in reference to other wide and overlapping categories of theory. Major conceptual contributions to actualizing counseling flow from phenomenological psychology. Perl's Gestalt therapy ideas about perception, awareness, and encounter in the present moment are examples. The contributions of Maslow on self-actualization, May on human encounter, Rogers on sensitivity to feelings, and Jourard on transparency and self-disclosures are central also. Cognitive-behavioral views such as those of Krumboltz, Lazarus, Bandura, Meichenbaum, and Mahoney emphasize behavior reinforcement, cognitive restructuring, and specific client goals. These views are important for actualizing because they focus on problem solving and actualizing goals desired by clients. The cognitive approaches of Ellis (1962), Beck (1976), and others have been influential in their emphasis on conscious and preconscious determinants of behavior, on the use of present cognitive processes rather than past traumatic events, and on the significant way in which humans intervene between stimulus and response by means of cognitive processes. Analytic views have made their impact in the form of levels of functioning, in focus on the ego, and with the phenomenon of defense. Transpersonal psychology has contributed many holistic principles of mind-body relationships and numerous techniques to explore our fantasy and dream worlds. Systemic therapy has shifted our attention to important current and transgenerational interpersonal behavior patterns that shape and maintain personal identity and behavior.

The principal tenets of actualizing counseling are progressive awareness

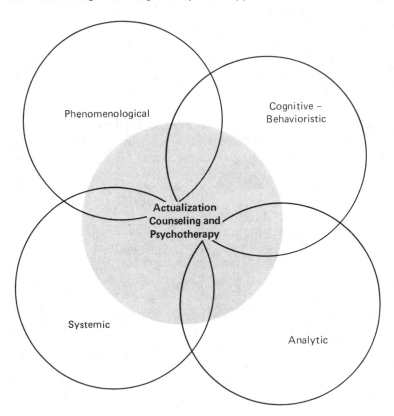

FIGURE 3-1 Relationship of Actualizing Counseling and Therapy to Four Overlapping Historical Approaches.

and growth toward the actualized person. This growth process stresses responsible social action within a self-fulfilling framework. The term *actualization* was used originally by Goldstein (1940) to describe the becoming process of the organism. We use Maslow's and Goldstein's concept as a departure point, emphasizing the process term *actualizing*.

MULTIDIMENSIONAL SCOPE OF THE ACTUALIZING MODEL

Because of the broad context in which most counselors and psychotherapists perform their helping functions, we feel strongly that a multidimensional approach must be utilized in maximizing their helpfulness. Frequently counselors must approach clients on a wide front, utilizing many interacting modalities of feeling, cognition, sensation, imagery, and action. For maximum effectiveness, however, it appears that counselors must focus on one or two modalities at one time, drawing on numerous techniques to reach client goals. For example, a counselor may focus on expression of feeling during the early stages, use fantasy to facilitate expression, move to a desensitization method to assist with management of specific fears, model new behaviors through role playing, interpret growth goals according to the polarity hypothesis, and set up a schedule of reinforcement to perpetuate new adaptive behaviors over the next few months. We are fully aware of the difficulties in attempting integration of the broad spectrum of theoretical views of personality and behavior change, but we are convinced that this task needs continuous effort by every counselor.

We see six dimensions comprising the actualizing point of view. A *philosophical dimension* is an essential consideration because of the emphasis on goals of actualization. We have assumptions about the nature of personal development as well as an "ideal image" of well-functioning persons. This model incorporates a series of value judgments about the human condition and the nature of reality.

We also incorporate a schematic conceptualization of *personality organization*. This cognitive map provides a view of the actualizing process in a given moment of time. Closely related is the *dynamic dimension*, which emphasizes basic processes of growth and motivation. A *developmental dimension* includes much of what we know about human development.

Since counseling is performed in extremely varied cultural contexts around the world, a *multicultural dimension* for counseling is essential. The focus of multicultural counseling is on adaptations of basically North European models, concepts, and language to fit the needs of clients from diverse cultural backgrounds. Actualization counselors strive to get within the cultural framework of the client to understand the differences and to adapt to the client.

Finally, a *research dimension* is essential to an enterprise as new and dynamic as actualizing counseling and psychotherapy. The actualizing counselor is a true scientist, as described in Chapter 1. Counselors are curious, critical, truthful, logical, objective, and precise in this role, as opposed to their more subjective emotional functioning as participants in the client's actualizing process. The actualizing counselor must strive to reconcile these frequently contradictory roles through employing them in a kind of synergic alternating of awareness, or as a check and balance system. We feel strongly that an overemphasis in either direction is not appropriate at this stage of development in actualizing counseling. Maslow has approached this problem in depth through his extended essay *The Psychology of Science: A Reconnaissance* (1966), recommended to the reader for more ideas on reconciling these conflicts.

THE PHILOSOPHICAL DIMENSION

Counseling and psychotherapy, being such profound growth processes, constantly face questions of what values and goals to promote, how free the individual is or should be, and how much influence the actualizing counselor should have on client values. These questions will be discussed more extensively in Chapter 13 on the actualizing counselor as a valuing person. The purposes of this section, however, are to emphasize the importance of the counselor's philosophy and to present some philosophical assumptions underlying actualizing counseling. The vastness of this subject requires restating that this discussion is illustrative and does not do justice to the importance and complexity of this topic.

Assumptions of Actualizing Counseling

Actualizing counseling is based in part upon assumptions drawn from the four major theoretical approaches described in Chapter 2. We have drawn from each school of therapy in our own creative synthesis of the major theories.

First of all, actualization counseling represents a developmental therapy derived from *historical and psychodynamic approaches* to counseling. The person is viewed from a perspective of development over time: past, present, and future.

1. Development is cumulative in the sense that early experiences influence the kinds of later experiences a person will have. The meaning and impact of events is influenced by past history, which shapes our expectations and desires.
2. Unresolved conflicts and grief from previous generations can become transmitted in an intergenerational process, which may constrict current personal growth and contribute toward symptom development.
3. Personal development becomes actualized as individuals develop clear internal boundaries. Clear boundaries within oneself involve an awareness of one's own moment-to-moment thoughts and feelings, inner polarities and conflicts, and defensive style.
4. Personality development is dynamic, changing its focus and pattern over time.
5. Development is enhanced by a consistent core identity, which can orchestrate changing life structures or "seasons," and a broad repertoire of skills to anticipate and manage situational and developmental stress.
6. Insight into one's development over time can be an invaluable assistance in self-actualization. However, insight is of limited usefulness unless it is accompanied by the experience of changed behavior patterns.

Actualization therapy derives important assumptions from *phenomenological approaches* to counseling.

7. We affirm the uniqueness of each individual. We believe that personal development involves learning to become aware of one's own unique strengths, limitations, and purpose.
8. One's representation of events determines behavior more than events themselves. These internal beliefs guide one's behavior with others. Concurrently, circular recursive interactional patterns with others shape one's expectations and interpretations of events. This ongoing feedback from others intentionally or unintentionally confirms or disconfirms existing internal psychological beliefs and structures.
9. One has freedom to choose much of one's future. While much of human behavior is shaped by personal history and systemic forces, the actualizing process assumes that one's future is largely undetermined and a person has wide ranges of freedom to choose.
10. The assumption of freedom places corresponding responsibility on the person for his or her own actualizing. Even though growth takes place in a social context, each person is responsible for initiating and maintaining changes for his or her own life, based on an examined and considered choice of values and principles. The thera-

pist maintains an active neutrality, emphasizing accurate empathic understanding while valuing the person's responsibility to choose his or her own goals.

Behavior therapy contributes an action focus to actualizing therapy as well as an understanding of how change occurs.

11. While some primitive behaviors are reflexive, hence largely genetically determined, and some are the result of chemical or neurological changes, a fundamental assumption of actualization counseling is that social behavior is learned and changes in behavior follow an active learning process. Important life skill deficits, such as competencies in social and work roles, may be mastered through new learning.

12. Most human learning is not automatic but is mediated by cognitive processes. A reciprocal interaction takes place between thoughts, emotions, actions, and feedback from others. Change can begin at any of these processes.

Systems approaches remind us that each individual is embedded within a larger relational context.

13. Actualization is achieved primarily in social interaction with a counselor, teacher, minister, group, friend, or family, but it can also be achieved through self-help methods, such as meditation and imagery. Social interaction becomes the main vehicle for conditions of actualization such as honesty with feelings, awareness of self, freedom of expression, and trust in oneself and others. Therapist support is an important component in helping others to achieve their potential.

14. Transactional patterns play an important role in shaping behavior. Therapeutic change is facilitated by disrupting dysfunctional interactional patterns and providing new feedback. This usually involves altering either the client's interpretation of other people's behavior or the behavior itself.

15. Actualization involves learning to set clear external boundaries with others. These boundaries are evidenced by the ability to maintain a clear sense of self in the midst of an anxious emotional field. Additionally, an actualized person has a capacity for intimacy and a readiness for closeness based on a firm sense of identity to risk the self with others.

16. Actualization is reflected in an attitude of interdependency. An actualizing person has a systematic ethic of responsibility. Personal decisions are made in terms of their impact on the total web of relationships that the person is involved in, both in the present and in the future. An interdependent person attempts to balance his or her own rights over against the claims of others and learns to deal with the inevitable tensions that this will involve.

17. Actualization is in part a byproduct of an interdependent attitude in which one transcends self-interest to cooperate with others working for the common good of justice and love. Actualization involves widening the inclusiveness of the circle of those we consider as our "neighbor" from the narrowness of our familial beginnings toward real solidarity with a commonwealth of people. Pursuit of self-actualization apart from an attitude of interdependency produces alienation from others.

Goals of Actualizing Counseling and Psychotherapy

A philosophy of counseling must contain some indications of outcomes expected from the growth process. The following statements of personality growth are just that—ideals of the ongoing actualizing process and not fixed quantitative end points. While some of these goals are preludes to more remote growth stages and could be organized in a hierarchy such as Allport's and Maslow's schemas, we prefer at this point merely to list and describe some of our objectives of actualizing counseling and therapy.

There are three kinds of goals. The first is a category of *process goals,* which are means toward broader actualization. Examples are free spontaneous verbalization and continued working through of problems. *Client goals* are the manifest purposes of the client's initial search for help. Examples are reduction of anxiety, desire for information, removal of annoying symptoms, making a crucial decision, or easing a situational pressure. Clients do not come initially asking to be "actualized." *Actualizing goals,* however, are broader, more generalized growth outcomes than solutions to immediate problems. It should be emphasized that these actualizing goals are tied closely to social values and the kinds of behaviors required to live effectively in Western culture. In another sense, these goals are characteristics of a theoretical model personality which would seem to "fit" Western cultural settings. This statement does not imply that psychological counseling leads to passive adjustment or conformity to a heavily bureaucratized world. The principal emphasis is upon developing the individuality of clients, at the same time helping them to see their social responsibilities for contributing to, and possibly changing, the culture about them. This discussion and the values to follow flow mainly from the humanistic tradition, since this approach to counseling emphasizes the potentiality of people for psychological growth. This view pushes the person beyond adjusting and coping with life. The discussion of actualizing goals follows from our philosophical assumptions.

Much of actualization counseling is concerned with helping clients to become more differentiated and set better boundaries between themselves and others. Some examples of ideal actualizing growth goals are listed below.

1. Differentiation involves having a clearer *sense of personal identity* as well as greater *awareness of one's own emotional processes.* A differentiated person can distinguish between his or her thoughts and feelings and draw on both. Various phrases are used as synonyms for this goal, such as spontaneity freedom to be, flexibility in meeting change, openness to one's own and others' experience, and reduction of rigidity. Spontaneity may be construed as the polar opposite of defensiveness. Rogers (1954) describes this characteristic as "increasing openness to experience." The world of experience for the client is no longer threatening. Clients picture themselves in a way more congruent with the way they are seen by others; therefore, they need not defend themselves as strenuously as they did before counseling.

There are objective indices of such a characteristic as spontaneity on psychological instruments. Rorschach protocols, for example, show how spontaneity follows as the constrictive control indices decline. Flexibility takes its place. Shostrom's *Personal Orientation Inventory* (1963) also has a spontaneity scale which measures this quality.

Tolerance of intellectual ambiguity and their own emotional ambivalence is also characteristic of these people. One can live comfortably with value and factual conflicts or unclear situations. One can hold beliefs in a tentative fashion while sifting conflicting evidence. One is not compulsively bound to seek definiteness in all things.

2. An important outcome of actualization therapy is that the client can *affirm his or her own unique strengths, limitations, and purpose.* Persons who experience their uniqueness are freed from competing with others to achieve something great that will justify their lives. They believe that there is no shortage of significant ways to contribute to life. They feel a broad *sense of purpose* and yet experience the freedom and *ability to determine their unique pathway* through life.

Such persons are not anxious about meeting an inflated ideal of seeking to become "super competent" nor are they deflated when they encounter their limitations or failures. Other people's strengths are valued as a complementary division of labor and they do not feel diminished or threatened by them. When individuals are not caught in frantic efforts to prove themselves, they seek a responsible *balance* in their investment of time and energy.

3. As a result of actualization therapy, individuals should be *able to set goals* for themselves and *initiate new learning.* They learn to *face their anxieties and fears* and seek help when needed. *Decisiveness* based on examined values and principles is also an outcome of counseling.

4. As individuals become more differentiated, they attempt to *balance their self-interest with the interests of others*, both in present and future generations. They are involved in responsible action, which enhances their own welfare and that of others. Such people show the courage to resist social demands and trends that run counter to their own values. They *take responsibility* for their own choices and utilize their own style of problem solving. They *extend themselves into the lives of others* beyond those who share similar values, interests, and life styles. They learn to see life as an *adventure* and to balance security needs with risking. Such persons try to maintain a creative tension between their security needs and leaving their "comfort zones."

Thus, while much actualizing behavior is concerned with inner development of pleasure and fulfillment, active outgoing interpersonal contact is equally significant. This focus includes an activist stance that concentrates on enhancing others' welfare and serving as an advocate for the weak, helpless, alienated, and deprived. This role also means functioning as a force for community change by attempting to transform community norms, attitudes, and behaviors to those more in line with the actualizing goals cited above.

5. An important goal of counseling is to help clients to form a *developmental view of life.* Clients who accept this view can reflect and learn from their past, live in the here and now, and anticipate that their lives will proceed through periods of flux and stability. They understand that they will encounter both anticipated and unexpected personal transitions. Where possible, such people plan for transitions by developing broad flexible coping skills. These individuals show *flexibility* in meeting change, *openness* to their own and others' experiences, and lack of emotional rigidity.

Rogers's summary of his philosophical paper entitled *A Therapist's View of the Good Life* emphasizes the significance of a philosophy based on awareness and acceptance of one's own nature:

> I believe it will have become evident why, for me, adjectives such as happy, contented, blissful, enjoyable, do not seem quite appropriate to any general description of this process I have called the good life, even though the person in this process would experience each one of these feelings at appropriate times. But the adjectives which seem more generally fitting are adjectives such as enriching, exciting, rewarding, challenging, meaningful. This process of the good life is not, I am convinced, a life for the faint hearted. (It involves stretching and growing, becoming more and more of one's potentialities. It involves the courage to be. It means launching oneself fully into the stream of life. Yet the deeply exciting thing about human beings is that when the individual is inwardly free, he chooses as the good life this process of becoming.) (1954, p. 13)

6. Differentiated people show a *capacity for closeness.* They can balance needs for independence and dependence. They have a capacity for intimacy based on a firm sense of identity. They can risk themselves in closeness to others, without a paralyzing fear of the loss or compromise of the self. This capacity for closeness includes a readiness to engage in conflict without withdrawal or the need to destroy the opponent. A repertoire of conflict management skills are available within the person.

7. While overlapping and summarizing many of the actualized characteristics above, the goal of increased human *effectiveness* is central to actualizing counseling. Effectiveness in living is related to life stages, since effectiveness is defined in terms of the expectancies and skills the person possesses at his or her particular stage in life and particular cultural setting. The actualizing person meets life's demands effectively and flexibly at each of his or her developmental stages. Ivey and Simek-Downing (1986) use the term *intentionality* to describe an overall goal for counseling. A person possessing this quality can approach problems flexibly from a variety of viewpoints and can act with a sense of capability to develop new thoughts and behaviors appropriate to the present time and place.

The list above is not exhaustive of actualizing goals. Empirical studies of ideal growth have been made by investigators such as Maslow (1970), with his "self-actualized young persons," Rogers (1961) on personal growth, and Shostrom (1963) with dimensions of self-actualizing. Much of the counseling, mental hygiene, and existential literature is replete with statements of ideal maturation for our culture. Mental health is a term to describe this ideal mature state. Jahoda (1958) developed six key criteria after reviewing the extensive literature on mental health. These are:

1. Attitude toward self.
2. Degree of realizing self-actualization potential through action.
3. Integration of personality function.

4. Autonomy or independence of social influence.
5. Perception of reality.
6. Taking life as it comes and environmental mastery.

Key problems for counselors are to find observable indicators of the above criteria and then to specify the conditions for achieving them.

PERSONALITY AND INTERPERSONAL STYLE

The following outline of structural and functional dimensions of personality is presented as an example of a way of conceptualizing the *individual* "subsystem" within the client's social system. Several basic concepts characterizing this model will be described followed by a detailed listing of functions and actualizing goals for each of the levels.

Five levels—facade, actualizing, manipulative, character, and core—are shown in Figure 3-2. They are hypothesized as interlocking "subsystems" of the individual with unique functions to perform for the person. Together, they form dynamic interactive functional levels of personality.

A Dynamic System.   This is a key concept because it denotes the unstable changing character of the personality system. Permeable boundaries exist among levels of personality so that there is constant movement along the polarities in an interweaving fashion.

Another dynamic aspect is the view of personality expression as varying within its social context. It appears from Mischel's extensive review (1973) of the personality literature and his own research that personality traits are not stable but rather vary from situation to situation.

The term *dynamic* implies the action element so central to the actualizing model. We assume that awareness is moving continuously from vague experiencing into active behavior change in the direction of the client's specific goals and the general actualizing goals cited earlier.

Energy.   It is assumed that energy is a characteristic of all personality levels and provides the motivational force impelling the person to action. It is predicted upon a biologically based need system. It is postulated that energy flows freely among the levels in the system. All levels are "grounded" in the body where feelings are expressed in the musculature and organs.

Polarities.   The actualizing model attempts to come to grips with one of the baffling issues in counseling, namely, the paradoxes inherent in the idea of feeling polarities. The idea of polarities in existence is an old one—for example, the idea that if dependence is a pronounced characteristic, a dormant independence opposite is present also. Leary (1957) brought the concept of polarities and continua of polar characteristics to the center of personality theory. This concept of polarities is central to actualizing counseling and therapy because we think that helping the client to become more aware of these polar traits and to accept their seemingly contradictory functions in our lives is a key actualizing goal. One of the additional goals, furthermore, is to develop both poles in the service of the person. In Maslow's research on self-actualizing people (1970), he found that they could express anger or tender love with ease. They were competent and strong, yet were aware of their weaknesses. In Figure 3-2 only four polar points, with illustrative feelings, are included, for the sake of simplicity and because we regard these four points of anger-love and strength-weakness as key polarities. Others, such as dominance-submission, masculinity-femininity, dependence-independence, are significant also. The descriptive terms along the polar continua express the polar characteristics for that level of personality; for example, actualizing on the weakness pole has unsure and helpless feeling qualities.

FIGURE 3-2   An Actualizing Model. Adapted from E.L. Shostrom, L. Knapp, and R. Knapp, *Actualizing Therapy* (1976, p. 137).

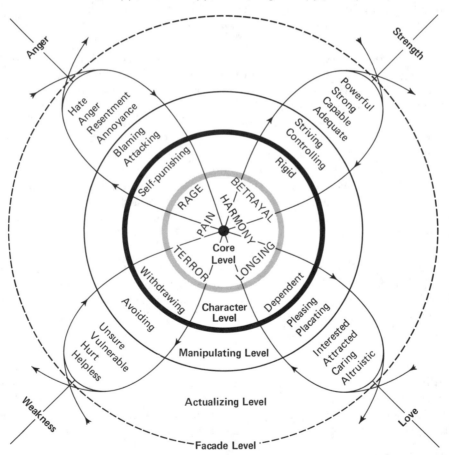

Functional Levels within Individual Personality

Facade Level.   This level is defined as a permeable boundary between the actualizing level and contact with the interpersonal world. This permeability, indicated by a dotted line in Figure 3-2, varies with the person's needs for defense or freedom of contact. Openness to others, for example, can be thought of in terms of permeability of the facade.

The principal functions of the facade level are to manage the balance of emotional closeness and distance with others. The facade level functions to defend the person from psychological threats from without; to "hide" feelings at the other personal functioning levels from others; and to present a "public image" or impression. The facade functions are controlled largely by the manipulating or managing level. Here, the defensive functions, such as projection, deception, denial, and manipulation, are initiated. These defensive functions are learned in the process of development and become quite automatic, even though partially under the control of the manipulating level. They are part of our "programming" for survival.

Additionally, defensive functions can become embedded in dysfunctional interpersonal patterns. Bowen's (1978) concept of "triangulation" and Minuchin's (1974) concept of "detouring" describe how a two-person system resolves stress by bringing in a third party. Framo (1981, p. 138) describes how individual conflict can also be resolved through projective identification with a partner. He states, "a main source of marital disharmony is that spouses project disowned aspects of themselves onto the mate and then fight them in the mate." Individuals may become incorporated into group (i.e., family) defensive patterns such as "scapegoating," which involve projective identification to preserve the desired functioning of the group.

An objective of the actualizing process is to make the person more aware of facade-level functions, to make defensive maneuvering functions more serviceable to the person, and to place them more under the control of the actualizing level. For example, "game" behavior, as Berne (1961) defined it, has a deceptive or manipulative effect on others and has many "payoffs" for the person, such as social advantage and satisfaction of aggressive needs at the expense of others. Actualizing processes attempt to put these functions in juxtaposition with actualizing behaviors so the person can make some basic adaptive and rational choices and achieve some balance in expression of his or her polarities. Another goal is to achieve some measure of congruence between the public image put forth at the facade level and the private images one has of one's self at other levels. An example of such a discrepancy would be the person's behavior at a cocktail party. Here, the manipulative type of person responds in terms of what others expect rather than in terms of his or her private feelings. In other words, open, flexible, and congruent facade functions are the basic goals.

Actualizing Level.   This is the first level of awareness in the system. First, it serves an *objectifying function* such that people can look at themselves as both subjects and objects. That is, they can get outside of themselves to observe themselves as objects. Thus, it has many functions of an ego system in the analytic models. It is the equivalent of the "I" or "me" of everyday language. In the objectifying function, the actualizing level also is the locus of rationality and ordering of experience.

Through its rational functions, the actualizing level performs a type of filter effect for selecting stimuli to which the person will attend. This actualizing function includes symbolizing and externalizing much of the feeling that comes from the other levels within the system. As a symbolizing agent, the actualizing level helps the person to rationalize conflict by attempts to reduce apparent inconsistencies. Hence, the actualizing level contains the major integrating force.

Thus, one of the important related functions of the actualizing level is construing the world in a manner so as to make perceptions "fit." Following the above-mentioned symbolizing and filtering functions, this system organizes and attaches meanings to current sensations in light of past experiences. The actualizing system also compares perceptions with past experiences and data from the other levels.

When the actualizing level is functioning in the ways described above, which are effective and satisfying for the person, it is said that one has a "strong" actualizing system. The person is perceiving events as accurately as possible with his or her unique experience background. The person is aware of a feeling of competence to master both internal and external pressures and to reconcile polarities. The person is also aware of a feeling of value and individuality, which is a goal in the actualizing process.

A second important function of the actualizing level is *action*. Many of the problem-solving, decision-making, and energy-mobilizing functions of the person have their locus here, as well as in the manipulating level, to be described next. The actualizing level is the locus of activity in the person, where actualizing behaviors are focused and find expression in interpersonal contacts.

A third function is serving as a vehicle for *expression of feeling*, usually in contact with others. In Figure 3-2, it may be noted that these feelings follow the axis of the polarities and are characteristic in both kind and intensity of the actualizing level. The aim in the actualizing process is to facilitate the active expression of basic polar feelings freely and appropriately. A function of the actualizing level is to translate the feelings in nonfunctional or dysfunctional forms from other levels such that the actualizing goals of the person are achieved. This is accomplished in the rhythmic style described earlier and illustrated with arrows in Figure 3-2.

Manipulating Level.   The chief function of this level in the system is to manage or control for purposes of protecting the person, manipulating others, gaining support from the environment, or coping with environmental demands. A key synonym for manipulating would be *managerial*, since one consequence of this level of functioning in interpersonal events is that the other person feels controlled. The manipulator functions without much feeling. This nonsensitivity to others is understandable, since the main function of the managing level is to protect the person. The manipulator is driven by the fear of experiencing one's own confusing and sometimes frightening emotional polarities. An overemphasis on this function leads to a "thick-skinned" protective reaction, which is perceived by others as insensitive and rigid. A counselor may say, for example, "What sort of feelings might you be afraid of experiencing if you were to let someone get close to you?" (From here the counselor works on specific actions clients can take to loosen their behaviors and increase their contact skills.)

Character Level.   This level functions as an identity base for the person. The basic personal styles, or character patterns, are stylized ways of responding to the world. For example, in terms of the basic polarities of the actualizing model, a character style would be the typical personal patterns of handling hostility, dependency, and rejection or acceptance of others. Much of the reaction is experienced by the musculature in the form of tenseness or by organ dysfunction, such as colitis. Holding back on feelings, for example, is associated with muscular rigidity.

Another function of the character level is to provide a definition of self, that vague, undifferentiated part of the person which one defines as the "real me" or the "self." It is a learned pattern of responses to characteristic life situations, which are expressed in the form of stereotyped responses along the polarity dimensions. As in the manipulating level, the character level performs essentially negative protective functions. The challenge of actualizing is how can one's basic character structure be made over sufficiently to act in the service of actualizing the whole person, instead of maintaining essentially stereotyped responses? The level of awareness of the person in regard to the character level is usually low. One of the goals of the actualizing process is to loosen the boundaries between the core and actualizing levels so that the basic character of the person can be modified sufficiently to serve the actualizing goals of that person. This process means taking risks so that the manipulating level can release sufficient controls to allow change to take place. This loosening process can be monitored to a limited degree by keeping in touch with body developments. For example, as the control and caution needs lessen, the body can loosen. Muscular rigidity is the body's way of communicating that the person does not consider that release of feelings or revelation of core polarities is safe.

Core Level.   This center of the person is the locus of basic feelings and what is popularly called "human nature." Paradoxically, the core has the common elements of feeling polarities that characterize all human beings; at the same time, it defines the uniqueness of a person. It is the center of one's existence and has the function of providing a harmonious and satisfying home in a world of loneliness and isolation from others; or it can be a living "hell on earth" of accumulated painful feeling experiences of which one is only vaguely aware.

We have been impressed over the years with people's basic need for privacy—a place in their existence that is uniquely their own. We view the main function of the core, then, as providing this center of one's existence where the vectors of many polar feelings cross. It is here that much of the painful hurt of the past is experienced. It is often expressed in deep longing for contact as, "Why wasn't I loved?" or in a form of rage as, "Why wasn't I given the freedom to be?" Sometimes, an awareness of being rejected is experienced as betrayal. Core pain is thus a basic reaction to the denial of the person's fundamental right to exist as a person. The actualizing process consists, in part, then, of aiding the person to be aware of those feelings of hurt and denial, to own them, and to take responsibility for actualizing himself or herself to the point of effective and satisfying living.

The core level is the locus of experiencing positive and strong qualities also. These qualities are expressed frequently as awareness of well-being, harmony, peace, confidence, worth, beauty, oneness with nature or with the universe. One goal of the actualizing process is to bring these feelings to awareness and to reinforce them with actualizing level behaviors that validate the positive core feelings.

We view the core level, therefore, as being neither positive nor negative from an external judging point of view. It is much like Fromm's description of the unconscious, which he describes as follows:

> In Freud's thinking the unconscious is essentially that in us which is bad, the re-pressed, that which is incompatible with the demands of our culture and of our higher self. In Jung's system the unconscious becomes a source of revelation, a symbol for that which in religious language is God Himself. In his view the fact that we are subject to the dictates of our unconscious is in itself a religious phenomenon. I believe that both of these concepts of the unconscious are one-sided distortions of the truth. Our unconscious—that is, that part of our self which is excluded from the organized ego—*contains both the lowest and the highest, the worst and the best [emphasis ours]*. We must approach the unconscious not as if it were a god whom we must worship or a dragon we must slay but in humility, with a profound sense of humor, in which we see that other part of ourselves as it is, neither with horror nor with awe. We discover in ourselves desires, fears, ideas, insights which have been excluded from our conscious organization and which we have seen in others but not in ourselves. (1950, p. 97)

The core level is a powerful motivating agent in the person, since it is from here that much of the energy for action stems. If our hypotheses are correct—that is, that basic drives for security, sexuality, and aggression originate here through learned life experiences—then it is understandable what a dominating force the core could be in the personality. This is the case particularly in times of threat or crisis. The biological and anthropological evidence on the inferred nature of the core level is fragmentary and conflicting. Generally, people seem to come into this world with basically outreaching, cooperating, security-seeking need systems. In the normal processes of family life, many frustrations and learnings are experienced that affect the person's basic outlook on life and himself or herself. It is assumed, therefore, that the feeling propensities and characteristics of the core level are learned rather than inherited.

Since core feelings are learned, and work in such individualistic ways to influence the behavior of persons, it is difficult to generalize about "human nature." While some people seem motivated by "blind" pleasure and seek to minimize pain and effort, others appear to be motivated by challenge and search. One goal of the actualizing process is that persons seek meaningful activity and meaningful relationships to fulfill complex longings for worth and dignity. This goal and the value premise underlying it have profound political implications as we visualize a society which makes possible the full actualization of its members.

A basic principle of the actualizing process is to open communication between the core and the actualizing levels of the person. One of the main methods is release of affect through talk, body sensory work, fantasy, or other projective method. The safety of a counseling relationship offers the person an opportunity to face the frightening feelings of rage, deep longing for contact, terror, or rejection and betrayal by trusted persons. This relationship offers opportunities for release of these feelings to awareness and the companion approach of taking responsibility for constructive action to change one's behavior. This awareness serves to prevent use of these past experiences and feelings as excuses for not realizing one's potential for growth. Often the labored expression of these painful core feelings with a caring helper results in feelings experienced as harmony, peace, and well-being. In terms of our postulate of system energy, this energy that was so bound to the core feelings is now released for constructive use at the actualizing behavior level. A basic principle of many therapy models, the actualizing model included, is that release from emotional conflict equals available emotional energy for actualizing pursuits. This release of energy coupled with action methods for behavior change offers clients a wide spectrum of actualizing possibilities.

DEVELOPMENTAL DIMENSION

Counseling is frequently construed as a process of facilitating optimum life-long development. In addition, each stage in life has its unique physical and psychological tasks to accomplish. Some of these tasks must be finished before moving to the next stage, such as achieving a sense of personal identity by late adolescence. Unless a clear answer to the question, "Who am I?" is achieved by young adulthood, later years of life are preoccupied with answering it. If certain tasks are not accomplished by the expected age for that culture, a life crisis could erupt. Counseling is concerned with these developmental crisis points also. So, the value of a developmental perspective for a counselor is that it provides a kind of lifeline map to identify tasks and crisis points for each roughly defined stage.

The idea of life stages with definable boundaries is very controversial. Levinson and associates (1978), for example, identify a number of fairly stable stages in adult development separated by usually unstable transitional periods of one to three years. Brim (1977), on the other hand, says his data do not support the concepts of stages and predictable crises during life transitions. In the following section we present a few developmental counseling issues; but we refer the reader to specialized texts on life-long development.

Recent developmental research and text writing have focused on cognitive developmental work (Collins, 1977; Fowler, 1981; Kegan, 1982; Gilligan, 1982). It appears from the developmental research of Kohlberg (1981), Fowler, Kegan, and Gilligan that cognitive developmental maturity is reflected in the context of how individuals view their own needs with respect to others. Gilligan's study of female moral development and Kohlberg's research suggest that males and females progress through different paths of moral development but may end up converging in a mature balance of autonomy and interdependency. These studies of cognitive competencies from infancy to old age help counselors decide what interventions are likely to succeed or fail at a given age. Examples are the findings on moral judgments and social role-taking ability. Designing psychological education programs on the basis of cognitive-developmental theory is another example.

General Periods of Growth

Life-long development can be divided into two general periods: from birth to about thirty-five years, and from age thirty-five to death. The first mastery stage is one in which people have broad capacities for learning and building their lives. Unfolding intelligence and physical and emotional maturation are in their service to pursue countless goals, which are both created and limited by their physical and cultural environments. In this period people develop habits to cope with parental demands; then they meet pressures to develop rational skills, acquire an education, enter and progress on a career.

At the end of this first period, the individual's intellectual, physical, and emotional potentials have taken direction; habits have been formed; choices have been made; mastery skills have been developed; and a life style has been chosen. Following this first broad period, people begin to think of ways to consolidate their gains. They have in some fashion mastered their economic and social environment. Efficiency and physical strength begin to diminish, and the maintenance period begins. The goals of youth begin to be replaced by the goals of maturity and old age. They find themselves beginning to scrutinize their values and to look for a way of life that will support and reward them and those they love until the end of life.

The idea of precise stages of adult development is not supported by sufficient data. What is impressive to us, though, is the increasing diversity with age. While it makes some sense to talk about the typical seven-year-old, it makes no sense whatever to describe the typical fifty- or seventy-year-old. Even retirement planning, for example, is no longer following the conventional counseling approaches because of the great variability in ages of retirement and perceptions of what that event means.

Counselors must study developmental psychology to understand the changing demography and the impact of social change on different age groups in a given culture. For example, counselors need to know what is happening to the older American adult group in numbers and use of psychological services. From census projections, for example, adults over age 65 by the year 2020 will comprise over 16 percent of the population, whereas only 11 percent are currently over 65 (Jarvik, 1978). Where only 2 percent of mental health services clients now are from the elderly, it is estimated that demand for counseling will skyrocket when the current middle-age generation arrives in the older-age brackets. Myths about older adults are crumbling also. Their potential for growth is great and their mental declines are not as severe as once was believed (Butler, 1975; Heath, 1991). Their special problems of facing multiple losses and the imminent prospects of death or disability, for example, are unlike those of younger age groups. Suicides among older adult white men are more frequent per unit of population than any other age group. Above all, counselors need to face their own biases about aging, their own fears of becoming "useless," and, finally, their own deaths (Schlossberg, Troll, & Leibowitz, 1978).

Basic Principles of Growth. Psychological growth has several general underlying principles that affect the counselor's perceptions. Growth is *progressive* and *cumulative;* that is, it moves by steps and through rough stages. Growth is *integrative* and *disintegrative;* that is, growth is a building- and fitting-together process as well as a tearing-down process. For example, childhood patterns are fairly stable and when undergoing transformation force the person into an unstable transition period. These transitions may vary from a month to two years and are characterized by discontinuity with patterns of the past. Such transitions usually call forth coping abilities the person did not know he or she had and often are a means to growth. If a transition is "off time," such as a young person losing a spouse through death, the transition usually has crisis proportions and heads the person into an intensive mourning process. Even chosen transitions, such as job change or early retirement, involve a loss of some kind and may thrust a person into a mourning process also. Counselors need to be wary of changes in people's lives, and how these changes affect their coping capacities.

Psychological growth depends upon the twin principles of *maturation* and *learning.* Maturation implies a potential for development which unfolds under the proper stimulating conditions when the organism is ready to respond. Restrictive environments and restrictive adaptations of the individual, such as intense psychological threat, inhibit psychological growth. Finally, psychological growth is dependent upon contact with people. It is believed that one reason why the helping relationship provides a powerful growth medium is that special optimum human relationship qualities prevail.

The principle that growth takes place through intimate human contact is highly significant for the helping professions. The relationship techniques discussed in Chapter 5 have the purpose of establishing an environment between the therapist and the troubled client to provide a maximum climate for growth. The capacity to love is perhaps the most important growth ingredient. Fromm, who has written extensively on the topic of love, asserts: "Analytic therapy is essentially an attempt to help the patient gain or regain his capacity for love" (1950, p. 87). He defines love as "the active concern for the life and growth of that which we love" (1956, p. 26). In a similar vein, Sullivan says, "Love begins when a person feels another person's needs to be as important as one's own" (1953, p. 246).

A principal quality of mature love is deep concern about the other person's welfare. We postulate that the experiencing of this kind of love from parents or their surrogates is necessary for normal growth. Experiencing and expressing love have special meaning for psychological growth and health of the individual at every stage from infancy through old age.

Some therapists say that people become "ill" when the conditions for growth are not fulfilled. But the problems with which the counselor and client struggle are not so much "mental illness" as they are inhibition of normal growth processes. In an individual client, these growth problems may take one or both of two general forms. On the one hand, the person may be experiencing difficulties that are endemic to his or her particular age level. On the other hand, problems inhibiting growth may be those which, considering age and capacity, he or she should have mastered earlier.

We further postulate that individuals are the product of all those experiences that they have had until the time they receive counseling or therapy. Moreover, the experiences to which they have been subjected in their early formative years determine, in large part, the type of adjustment that they will make at any later level of development. All individuals have "problems" in growing up. When these are solved successfully and successively, people are well equipped to progress in their psychological development. When the problems have been too threatening or too difficult to resolve, they falter in growth or develop a shield of defensive mechanisms that inhibits or distorts their creative potentials.

THE MULTICULTURAL DIMENSION

In Chapter 1 the importance of multicultural considerations was stressed, and in Chapter 2 we discussed multiculturalism as one of the imperatives for changes in counseling theory. It is a key dimension in actualization theory since different cultural groups often need different counseling approaches. As early as 1962 Wrenn wrote of the "culturally encapsulated counselor" (Wrenn, 1962). A decade later Cheek (1976) advocated counseling varied cultural groups differently because of the perception that counselors and psychotherapists use "white techniques." Cheatham (1990) argues that individual counseling of minority racial clients must include family networks and community contexts. He cautions that counseling should not become another oppressive force in the client's life by emphasizing protection of the cultural status quo. For these clients, counseling must be experienced as a liberating force to be effective in behavior change.

With all this diversity, is it even possible to develop a universal theory? Fukuyama (1990) contends that some human factors transcend a particular culture and have universal applications, but she cautions that some preconditions must be met: Counselors must thoroughly understand their own world view and the views and cultures of their clients.

Some additional implications of the viewpoints cited above are that traditional counseling is not suited to many cultural groups. Language alone, and the cultural differences it represents, is a barrier for many. Therefore, counselor education and counseling theory must take into account the different cultural views about the whole enterprise of counseling and psychotherapy. Counselors must be thoroughly conversant with many cultural backgrounds, and adaptations must be made in counseling practice to accommodate these differences.

Counseling theory must take into account adaptations for the large social group identified as the "disadvantaged" or "underclass." If we are going to extend the basic idea of counseling as a helping service, we must reexamine our primary assumption that initiating counseling must be a voluntary act by the client. Because of the large number of people enmeshed in the criminal justice system, substance abuse, ill health, unwanted pregnancies, suicidal impulses, and interpersonal violence, an intervention strategy is necessary to make an entry into their personal lives on the assumption that they usually want counseling but do not know how to access or use such helping services in their crisis condition. Wood and Long (1991) propose a strategy called life space intervention for reaching people who do not fit the usual definition of readiness for counseling. They emphasize a proactive way of reaching children and youth in crisis— especially those involved as perpetrators or victims of violence. It is a mediational effort to build bridges of communication and trust.

Ivey, Ivey, and Simek-Morgan (1991) and Pedersen (1991) see multicultural counseling as the fourth force in counseling. Multiculturalism is a generic term that covers more than race and ethnicity. It includes diversity and complexity within cultural groups and cuts across ethnic boundaries, covering such issues as social status, gender, age, and sexual life styles.

The Association for Multicultural Counseling and Development has developed a set of standards that detail criteria, definitions, and necessary skills for counselors working in multicultural settings. Even though these standards have broad applications to many groups, they refer primarily to four ethnic groups: African-Americans, American Indians, Asian-Americans, and Hispanics or Latinos (Sue, Arredondo, & McDavis, 1992).

RESEARCH DIMENSIONS

Any approach to counseling must have an emphasis on validation of concepts and methods. Otherwise, at best it is an anecdotal accumulation of therapeutic wisdom, and at its worst reverts to the occult and mystical. There are pressing ethical and scientific obligations to validate, with the best experimental means available, the procedures advocated. Unfortunately, experimental methods are not completely adaptable to counseling settings. We depend on a rough empirical kind of validation called a tryout or pilot study, but we strive for more precise study of concepts and methods through a variety of disciplines. This research orientation to actualizing counseling and psychotherapy was described in Chapter 2 and is emphasized throughout this book. It is mentioned here only to emphasize the open-ended tentative quality of all systems. One of our current obligations is to state our assumptions, strategies, and expected outcomes in such a way that they can be tested, not only in the rough arena of comparative case experiences but also in the step-by-step detailed study of process and technique for achieving operationally definable goals of actualization.

We endorse Sanford's (1966) and Kleinman's (1988) ideas that human problems must be studied from the point of view of culture or social context as well as individual psychology, and that we need a general personality-social theory to guide us. Study of isolated part-function behaviors does not necessarily add to a deeper understanding of complex social behavior, such as clients interacting with counselors or their families. In counseling research we are stymied by methods designed primarily to study segmental rather than holistic behaviors.

OVERVIEW OF THE THERAPEUTIC PROCESS

Therapeutic process in actualization therapy places an emphasis on both establishing a therapeutic relationship with a client and on developing effective action strategies and interventions to facilitate change. In this chapter we will provide an overview of the counseling process. The steps we describe will be further elaborated in Chapters 4 through 7.

Counseling is basically a problem-solving process involving many decisions and actions. Both in and out of counseling we are making choices constantly about what to do next. Heppner and Krauskopf (1987) reviewed the counseling literature related to problem solving and found that few studies exist that detail the process steps and how to lead clients into this process. They make a convincing case for the position that counselors can teach problem-solving procedures to clients with data that already exist and that we need not wait for all the necessary studies to be completed. This is the view we take as we present this chapter. Our model of the counseling process is described in four roughly sequential steps: (1) establishing a therapeutic relationship, (2) problem identification and assessment, (3) facilitating therapeutic change, and (4) evaluation and termination.

Step 1: Establishing the Relationship.   The main process goal in the counseling process involves establishing a therapeutic alliance with one's client. The goal of this stage is to enable clients to state and clarify their concerns, problems, distress, or reasons for coming. Additionally, it is essential to build a positive relationship with the client, which has characteristics of trust based upon openness and honesty of expression. It is important for the counselor to convey professional credibility as a trustworthy and competent person at this point. A growing body of research (Barak & La Crosse, 1975; Schmidt & Strong, 1971; Strong & Schmidt, 1970) supports the idea that how the counselor is perceived in terms of expertise, attractiveness, and trustworthiness determines the effectiveness of counseling.

Many clients have a clear purpose, but some do not. Their presenting statement may or may not imply a recognition of need for help, since clients at this early stage often do not have a strong sense of "ownership" of their problem. Clients may blame others or think they are victims of fate. Seldom have they made a firm commitment to work on their problems in an intentional, responsible manner. So, a second process goal is to determine the clients' recognition of need for help and readiness to commit themselves to the process. Much of the first interview is usually devoted to these issues of need and commitment. In terms of our actualizing model, the main process goal in this step is to work through the facade-level resistance.

The process strategy during this first step is to attend to client statements and observe nonverbal behaviors for messages. Clients often come in with vague complaints and goals and very guarded reasons for coming. Their facade level is often functioning effectively to protect them. A second strategy, then, is to help clients clarify the nature of their concerns or problems. Further clarification usually is needed regarding client expectations and perceptions of the nature of counseling help and commitment to work under the counselor's counseling or therapy model.

It is important to realize that clients initially are hesitant to make a firm commitment to counseling, since this commits them to change. The prospect of change is frightening for most clients. Change means giving up something dear—a comfortable habit, a long-standing relationship, a prized thing, a cherished value, or even a painful feeling. This long-standing experience of letting go usually is painful and often sets off a mourning process. Counselors need to be sensitive to signs of distress and to be aware of this strong resistance to change in clients. Evidence suggests that there may be an optimal set for problem solving (D'Zurilla & Goldfried, 1971). This set includes an awareness that problematic situations constitute a normal part of living, behaving as if effective coping with one's problems were possible, and believing that one has control over much of one's environment. A second group of problem-solving behaviors consists of identifying bothersome situations and labeling them as such (Heppner & Krauskopf, 1987). A third class of good client problem-solving behaviors is not to act impulsively or avoid the problem situation. These attitudes set the stage for steps to be described next.

Step 2: Problem Identification and Assessment.   This step in the counseling process is concerned with identifying and assessing client problems. The principal process goal at this step is to discuss with clients what they would like to get out of the counseling process, especially if their presenting concerns and reasons were vague. This discussion averts the possibility that unrealistic goals and expectations emerge by default, such as viewing counselors as having an extraordinary power to change client behavior or make people happy. Specific goals are usually discussed along with the kinds of behaviors that would be regarded as successful outcomes. Another process goal is to obtain a clear understanding of who the client is. It is important to explore both individual problems and interpersonal or social context difficulties. Often in referrals, especially of children, the teacher or the parents may play an essential role in the problem behavior and should, therefore, be involved in the counseling process. A further process goal at this stage is the determination of the *structure* of how the process is going to proceed, of the nature of the goals, and of the "contract" regarding rules and responsibilities. It is essential for the counselor to pay close attention to his or her own immediate interpersonal process experience with the client. Manifestations of current problems often become apparent through defensiveness or nonverbal behavior of clients. Further coverage of this topic is given in later chapters.

The strategy at this point involves discussing procedures for reaching the expected outcomes and negotiating any working agreements.

Step 3: Facilitating Therapeutic Change. Step three of the counseling process involves initiating strategies and interventions to facilitate change. The process goals and strategies at this point are determined largely by the nature of the problem, the style and theory of the counselor, and the client's desires and style of communicating. During this phase, the therapist constructs alternative action plans, evaluates the possible consequences of the various alternatives, and decides how to proceed at the particular moment. Strategies may involve techniques from various therapeutic approaches aimed toward altering affective blocks, restructuring attitudes, stress management, enhancing problem solving, or altering maladaptive interaction patterns.

Although strategizing is a separate activity from establishing a therapeutic alliance and identifying the client's problem, it is very interconnected during a therapeutic interview. The counseling process is a recursive sequence of behaviors oriented toward facilitating client actualization and problem resolution. Typically the therapist begins with hypothesizing, using whatever information he or she may have about the client. Having developed a hypothesis, the counselor makes some strategic choices about how to intervene with the client. Following each intervention the therapist pays close attention to the "circular" feedback (content and process) from the client by observing the effects of the interventions. Subsequently, these observations are used in the ongoing process of modifying one's hypotheses. On the basis of a modified hypothesis, the therapist once again strategizes about how to intervene with the client. Thus, while the counseling interview is taking place the therapist is continually moving around a circuit of hypothesizing, strategizing, intervening, observing feedback, hypothesizing, and so on, as in Figure 3-3.

Step 4: Evaluation and Termination. The fourth step of counseling involves evaluating the outcomes of counseling and then termination. The principal criterion for successful counseling and the key indicator for termination is the degree to which the client has achieved the goals of counseling. Significant progress evaluation questions for the therapist include: Did the relationship help

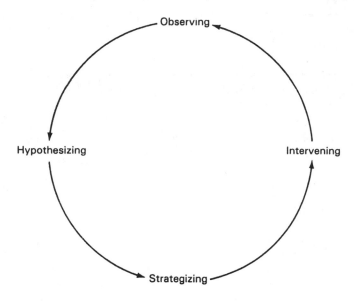

FIGURE 3-3 Therapeutic Interviewing Process.

the client? In what respects did it help? If it did not help, why not? If goals were not achieved entirely, what progress was made toward them? The decision to terminate is a joint effort on the part of the counselor and client, although it is the client who is the principal determiner of when the goals have been met. The process goal of termination is not taken seriously enough, in our opinion, since so much of counseling and psychotherapy is structured as open-ended with vaguely defined outcome criteria.

SUMMARY

A multidimensional point of view termed actualizing counseling and psychotherapy is described as a process of helping people to develop their life potentials. It includes philosophical, developmental, structural, dynamic, and research dimensions. Actualizing counseling and psychotherapy are based upon a model of the actualizing person as a developmental goal, rather than a cured state of illness or the mere solution of immediate life problems.

Counseling is basically a problem-solving process calling for continuous decisions. In this chapter we presented a brief overview of the process of actualization counseling and psychotherapy.

CHAPTER 4

The Therapeutic Relationship

In Part II of our text, we will focus on the counseling process and techniques of therapeutic psychology. We begin with an overview of the therapeutic alliance and a discussion of skills for establishing a therapeutic relationship. As a relationship is established, the therapist's next tasks involve problem identification, assessment and formulating strategies for facilitating and evaluating behavior change. The final chapter in Part II explores barriers that impede the therapeutic alliance and counseling progress.

The heart of the therapeutic process is the relationship established between the counselor and the client. In this chapter we will describe some of the various aspects of therapeutic relationships that make them distinct from other kinds of relationships. We will also examine qualities of both counselors and clients as influences in establishing an effective therapeutic alliance. Readiness as a factor in the therapeutic relationship will also be discussed. We shall describe relationship-building skills in Chapter 5, after the discussion of counselor qualities, since we regard skills as *implementations* of the therapist's basic attitudes. Using helping techniques without appropriate supporting attitudes usually is counterproductive.

The relationship is important in counseling and psychotherapy because it constitutes the principal medium for eliciting and handling significant feelings and ideas that are aimed at changing client behavior. Thus, the quality of the relationship determines not only the nature of the personal exchanges but also whether counseling will continue at all.

We are becoming increasingly convinced that the relationship in psychotherapy and counseling is a helpful agent in its own right. In special ways the counselor models how to establish and maintain a relationship. This is a positive picture of the therapist's instructional role, as opposed to a more remedial or problem-solving role. This developmental modeling role is also what makes the therapist's own relative freedom from cognitive-emotional distortion of central importance.

Relationship refers to the *affective* elements of the interaction, which can only be inferred from observation of client behavior. The therapeutic relationship or "alliance" represents the emotional alignment and mutual involvement between therapist and client. Bordin (1975) distinguished three critical aspects of this therapeutic alliance: (a) the emotional bond between client and therapist, (b) the equality of client and therapist involvement in the tasks of therapy, and (c) the degree of agreement between client and therapist on the goals of therapy.

In actualizing theory terms, a relationship provides the principal bridge for the actualizing personality levels of two people to make contact. Thus, defenses, interpersonal problem-solving skills, and polar feelings find expression in the relationship. As we discussed in Chapter 2, each basic counseling theory has a position on the significance and function of the relationship. Research on relationship variables indicates the effectiveness of relating in terms of empathy, warmth, and genuineness did not show significant differences among three divergent theorists' interviews (Fischer & Paveza, 1975). The therapeutic relationship's importance is recognized even in cognitive and behavior therapies (Beck et al., 1979; Goldfried & Davison, 1976; Wilson & Evans, 1977).

The definition of the therapist's role is an important philosophical and practical issue. The metaphor we select to identify our role will guide the way we provide psychotherapy. We can choose from a variety of metaphors, such as friend, consultant, resource collaborator, coach, teacher, expert, advice giver, empowerer, shaman, priest, and more. We believe each therapist must be flexible to assume a variety of roles. In the same way, we may hold various images of our clients such as victim, abuser, neurotic, person in transition, helpee, and others. It is important to have accurate images of therapist and client roles because these images will affect our work. More will be said about these influences in our discussion of countertransference and transference in Chapter 8.

CHARACTERISTICS AND DIMENSIONS OF THE RELATIONSHIP

Uniqueness/Commonality

Though certain general statements can be made about the therapeutic relationship, it is important to remember first that each client-counselor relationship is unique. The factors creating this uniqueness are as diverse as human differences. The unique factors include *counselor* attitudes, behaviors, and physical characteristics, in addition to *client* attitudes, backgrounds, and behaviors.

This uniqueness makes generalizing about counseling difficult. Each new counseling relationship is a fresh challenge to the counselor.

A therapeutic relationship also is distinct from other human relationships. While friends, relatives, and teachers have profound influences on behavior, one unique element of a counseling relationship is its structure. It is a carefully planned and described process framework. Because of its intimate nature, structure, and attitudes, the counseling relationship also has similarities to other human situations, for example, family, friendships, teacher-pupil, doctor-patient, and pastor-parishioner.

Objectivity/Subjectivity

Objectivity refers to the more cognitive, scientific, generic aspects of the relationship, wherein the client is regarded as an object of study or as an abstract part of suffering humanity. In extreme objectivity, therefore, a counselor would remain psychologically distant and would regard client views and values without personal judgment.

The meaning of objective counselor behavior for clients is that they feel the counselor respects their views, does not force his or her ideas on them, and looks at their problems rationally and analytically. Clients tend to reject such an objective attitude. They want the counselor to get emotionally involved, to exhibit warmth and caring, and to be personally concerned about them. This subjective feeling of involvement is one basis for feeling "understood," and seems to offer the reassurance that the counselor knows how the client feels. Conversely, some clients perceive this counselor involvement as threatening, since they are "submitting" to the control of or "revealing" themselves to another person. They experience anxiety, therefore, over feeling vulnerable and feared loss of emotional control. This anxiety is especially strong when clients see the counselor allied with their externalized or rejected feelings. A client seeing the counselor, for example, as a loving mother becomes fearful of his or her own uncontrolled dependency needs.

The nature of the emotional interaction appears to be a key variable determining the quality of the relationship, or encounter. Counselors must be *aware of the various levels of their impact* on clients, and the clients' impact on them. First, the counselor reacts at a friendship level, as one liking certain qualities in the other and experiencing pleasure at the meeting. Secondly, he or she reacts at a genuine personal encounter level, honestly and directly communicating. Then the counselor reacts at a more intense level of loving concern for the other person's welfare. The counselor must be aware also of possible erotic components of interaction, which if unrecognized may interfere with the counselor's effectiveness at other levels. Rollo May (1969) suggests that a real encounter involves all four levels.

The risk of subjective involvement for counselors is that they might respond to clients' problems as if they were their own. Yet, counselors must use their own generalized experiences and feelings as guides to experiencing the clients' feelings. For example, how can counselors really know how it feels to be loving and hostile to a parent simultaneously unless they have experienced this feeling themselves and have been aware of the implications? This does not mean that counselors must have experienced all feeling situations. They must have recognized in themselves, however, those universal human experiences such as anxiety, depression, disillusionment, and anger. They must have worked through these feelings enough to be able to tolerate, recognize, and empathize with clients. One of the key issues in counseling is the extent to which counselors should reveal themselves as distinct persons and how much emotional involvement they should allow themselves.

The most reasonable goal seems to be that the counselor get emotionally involved to the extent necessary to keep the client emotionally involved; but the counselor's keen interest in helping should be tempered with some reserve and distance so that the counselor can accept attitudes and feelings expressed by the client or confront them objectively with as little counselor projection as possible. If counselors get too emotionally involved with clients, it is difficult to be objective about such attitudinal areas as religion, for example, or moral life styles different from their own which may even disgust them personally. Counselors are objective, or "detached," in the sense that they regard these attitudes and behaviors as important manifestations of the client's personality. The term *participant-observer* is used in psychological circles to describe this dual relationship problem. Counselors participate fully in the intricate human interaction; yet, simultaneously, they maintain a detached observer role.

Cognitiveness/Affectiveness

Cognitive relationship elements refer to intellectualizing, such as exchanging information, advising on courses of action, or interpreting data, whereas the affective elements refer to feeling expressions and exchanges. In managing the relationship, the counselor must know when to encourage rational examination and interpretation of the client's problem and when to encourage more exploration of feelings and their ideational connections. Communication is going on at both levels all the time, so it behooves the counselor to be aware of the relative weight of these factors at any given moment.

Ambiguity/Clarity

The notion of relationship ambiguity, as developed by Bordin (1955), is a characteristic of a stimulus situation to which people respond differently and to which no clear-cut response is indicated. The counseling relationship is vague and ambiguous to the client. Counselors generally define themselves and the situation early by a process known as *structuring,* an effort to introduce some clarity to the relationship.

Ambiguity serves the function of allowing clients to project feelings into the ambiguous counseling situation. This projection aids clients to become more aware and concerned about their feelings. Too much ambiguity for some clients precipitates anxiety in their attempts to make something secure and structured out of the relationship. Moderate personal ambiguity is necessary so that the client can project any desired role on the counselor. The issue is *social distance* rather than *emotional distance*. If counselors are too friendly with clients in the sense that they let themselves be known too early as well-delineated personalities, counselors will find that they feel compelled to "act themselves" too strongly in an interview situation. Thus, an interview might drift in the direction of social conversation or intimate friendship. This is a difficult matter to handle in the school situation, for instance, in which counselors frequently meet student clients on social and instructional as well as therapeutic levels.

In a clinical setting the problem of socializing with clients could create relationship problems. Most clinicians, therefore, still consider it unwise to socialize with clients. The expectancies of social relationships tend to be quite different from therapeutic relationships and tend to interfere with an effective counseling relationship. This issue is controversial, however, since a growing body of therapeutic literature and practice is stressing the importance of the counselor being a natural friendly human being with clients.

Responsibility/Accountability

Accepting a client in a counseling relationship implies a willingness on the part of the counselor to assume some responsibility for the outcomes of counseling. Counseling is very serious business and must be matched by a seriousness of purpose and ethical commitment. Clients have responsibility as well, which they must assume in great part since it is their problem and behaviors which are at stake.

Counselor opinions differ on the proportion of responsibility which each participant must assume. We feel that the counselor does not take responsibility for running the client's life or selecting the counseling goals. The acceptance of the relationship, nevertheless, places counselors in a responsible leadership position where they must protect the client and assume certain liabilities for the outcomes because of the influence of their own personalities on the relationship. The latter situation holds especially in psychotherapeutic relationships where clients make such crucial decisions as whether or not to get a divorce, leave home, commit suicide, change jobs, or drop out of school. Counselors must adhere to strict ethical standards in regard to these client decisions.

It is difficult to reduce the client's responsibility to a formula. The amount of proportional responsibility depends upon such factors as the age of the client, type of problem, type of agency setting, legally designated responsibilities, and professional expectations. There is no question but that the client is responsible for setting the goals of counseling since he or she owns the problem. Usually, if the goals are ethical and feasible, a counselor agrees to facilitate the process of achieving these goals. How accountable the counselor can be for the outcomes is a debatable professional issue. The trend, however, is to hold the counselor increasingly more accountable for outcomes in line with client and agency goals. In other words, counselors increasingly must be able to produce measurable results to demonstrate responsible professional behavior and justify their salaries.

Some counselors control the responsibility factors by discouraging clients from making crucial decisions over such matters as divorce while in the counseling relationship. Such counselors claim that the relationship offers them a vehicle for exploring the ramifications of divorce which puts the client in a better position to make a sound decision and to live with it. The writers believe that responsibility cannot be handled so neatly in most cases. Counselors have more influence than they realize, because of their power and status as healers. They partake of some of the shaman's influence in more simple cultures. Some counselors have an added charisma which gives them even more influence. As a result clients tend to feel powerless, and this feeling is likely to be destructive to client decisiveness, self-esteem, and growth (Stensrud & Stensrud, 1981). Handling this power and influence humanely is a key counselor responsibility. The techniques of structuring and contracting described later can help both counselor and client to face frankly the problems of allocating exclusive and mutual responsibilities.

Counselors working in an agency setting have a further responsibility to be loyal to the institution for which they work. The preceding discussion emphasized the client's and counselor's responsibilities to each other. Mutual responsibilities of agencies and counselors are controlled somewhat by ethical and policy considerations, but they involve the hard realities of agency responsibility to provide adequate facilities and legal protection, for example. Counselors have responsibilities to their agencies to carry out agency policy. Although this aspect of accountability is not a dimension of the relationship, it has a direct bearing upon it and is occasionally in conflict with client interests.

Ethical Dimensions

A distinctive mark of the professional counselor is ethical handling of client relationships so that both the client and society are protected. The counselor's value system is an important determinant of ethical behavior. Codes that summarize ethical principles are based on dominant social values. To cover questions commonly arising in counseling, the Committee on Ethical Standards of the American Psychological Association has published a code of ethical standards (1990, 1992); this code is continuously revised to reflect changes in cultural values. The American Counseling Association (formerly The American Association for Counseling and Development) (1988) also published a revised statement of ethical standards that were originally designed for school and college counseling settings. Other professional associations have also published ethical standards to guide group leaders, marriage and family therapists, social workers, and other helping professionals. The APA code includes the following principles, stated here in greatly abbreviated form in order to indicate the general idea of the nine principles. It is important for all counselors to have personal copies of the entire code and apply the principles, subprinciples, and standards to specific cases.

1. *Responsibility*. Psychologists take responsibility for providing the highest possible standards of service.
2. *Competence*. Psychologists maintain their high standards of competence in the interest of the public and the profession as a whole.
3. *Moral and Legal Standards*. Psychologists' moral, ethical, and legal standards of behavior are a personal matter; yet they are aware of the impact that their public behavior could have on quality of service.
4. *Public Statements*. Public statements and advertising of psychologists serve the purpose of providing information to help consumers make informed choices. Therefore, they must be accurate and objective statements of qualifications.
5. *Confidentiality*. Safeguarding personal information obtained in the course of teaching, practice, or research is a primary obligation of the psychologist.
6. *Welfare of the Consumer*. Psychologists respect and protect the people with whom they work. Conflicts of interest and loyalties as well as evaluative or training procedures must be made clear to the consumer in order for participants to have freedom of choice regarding participation.
7. *Professional Relationships*. Psychologists give due regard to needs, competencies, and obligations of colleagues, other professionals, and organizations with whom or with which they associate.
8. *Utilization of Assessment Techniques*. Psychologists observe relevant APA standards when developing, publishing, and using assessment methods.
9. *Pursuit of Research Activities*. The psychologist carries out investigations with safeguards for the welfare and respect for the dignity of participants.
10. *Care and Use of Animals*. Psychologists investigating animal behavior ensure the welfare of animals and treat them humanely.

There are occasions when the codes do not apply specifically. They were intended to be guidelines only and reflections of a consensus of professionals. There are times when counselors must rely on their own experience and intuitive judgments flowing from their own personal ethics. When in doubt, it is common practice for the counselor to consult with colleagues about the specific issues and what is planned as a resolution. Many situations arise, however, when consultation is not readily available. For example, a counselor judges the client's problem to be beyond his or her competence, and a referral is considered. The American Counseling Association code says in Section B:

> The member shall decline to initiate or shall terminate a counseling relationship when he cannot be of professional assistance to the counselee or client either because of lack of competence or personal limitation. In such instances the member shall refer his counselee or client to an appropriate specialist. In the event the counselee or client declines the suggested referral, the member is not obligated to continue the relationship.

The preceding questions cover only a small sample of the many that face the counselor in everyday practice. Since they involve elements of judgment as well as fact, it would be well if the counselor consulted with colleagues concerning questions of ethics in difficult cases. Counselors should look also into their own ethics and areas of bias to find possible sources of doubt and value conflict about the ethical implications of their behaviors. Finally, one of the most important safeguards against unethical behavior is knowledge and experience. When in doubt about an ethical problem, it is usual practice to discuss the issues with a group of professional colleagues, using their consensus as a guide.

There are other significant questions to be answered, such as, what causes unethical practice? Is damage or discomfort to the client as a result of ignorance or inadequate training unethical? Schwebel (1955) asserts that unsound judgment and ignorance, though dangerous and having important selection and training implications, are not, strictly speaking, unethical. He hypothesizes further that generally it is self-interest that causes unethical practice. By *self-interest* Schwebel means seeking personal profit, self-enhancement, security, and status at the expense of others. Conflicts often arise, therefore, over the infusion of the counselor's values into the process. Recent emphasis on the methods of self-disclosure of counselors in the relationship poses a related ethical problem. While the client's trust may be enhanced by the counselor revealing his or her true feelings and values, it could have a compelling impact on client values bordering on the unethical. Wrenn (1958) stressed the personal values of the counselor as a basis for counseling ethics. He states, in addition, that ethical behavior on the part of a counselor involves more than subscribing to a code of ethics; a feeling of responsibilty to relate behavior to ethics is necessary as well.

Professional discretion involving sexual relationships with clients has become a central ethical issue. Keen judgment must be exercised around that fine line of demonstrating personal warmth and caring, on the one hand, and exploitation or harassment on the other. Informed consent is another current issue that emphasizes full disclosure of the counselor's style of counseling and then getting the client's consent to enter the relationship under these conditions. Some licensing laws require counselors to provide such disclosures in writing.

COUNSELOR INFLUENCES ON THE THERAPEUTIC ALLIANCE

The counselor's personality qualities and attitudes provide an important influence on the quality of the therapeutic relationship. Early research by Fiedler (1950) found that therapists and clients of different schools rated the ideal therapy similarly with respect to such global aspects as warmth and overall quality of the therapeutic relationship. While there have been numerous literature reviews and factor analytic studies about general therapist influences in the psychotherapy process (Goldfried & Padawer, 1982; Gomes-Schwartz, 1978; Orlinsky & Howard, 1978), research is not sufficiently definitive to select counselors according to characteristics thought to enhance therapeutic effectiveness.

The available research has pointed to a variety of characteristics associated with therapeutic effectiveness. Many of the qualities and attitudes to be discussed may seem idealistic; nevertheless, they provide yardsticks against which counselors can measure themselves. What are the characteristics of the effective counselor or therapist? While it was popular for years to compile lists of counselors' characteristics thought to be significant, we are well along in research on traits of effective and ineffective counselors and therapists. An early APA Committee on Training in Clinical Psychology, for example, compiled a list of traits which were difficult to specify behaviorally. Combs (1969) and Combs and Avila (1985) described how counselors differ from other defined helpers, such as teachers. The methods were largely standardized tests of traits correlated with specific counselor behaviors. This line of investigation did not produce very useful data about effective counselors. The following discussion of counselor characteristics is derived largely from more recent experimental studies on effective counselor characteristics, as well as from our own experience.

Person-Technician Balance

There are numerous studies that suggest that counseling effectiveness is maximal when counselors and psychotherapists have two strong and balanced components: personal relationship skills and technical qualifications. Clinicians such as Strupp (1963) support this view. The actualizing counseling approach is replete with suggested techniques for developing effective technicians for behavior change. In addition, counselors must always be in a conscious process of personal growth so their personal actualizing efforts will serve them as well as their methodolgies. There are abundant data now to validate the view that counseling effectiveness is maximal when a counselor can relate to clients in warm, understanding, and self-revealing ways. In this manner he or she serves as a personality model for the client.

Several references will be made to the data of Rogers (1953, 1957), Truax and Mitchell (1971), and Patterson (1984) on facilitative relationships characteristic of counselors. They found that counselor warmth, understanding, positive regard or caring, concreteness of counselor expression, and transparency or realness create conditions for greater client self-exploration. These characteristics in turn result in greater behavior change in a client than if these "facilitative conditions" were not present in optimal amounts. Others (Bergin & Suinn, 1975; Lambert, DeJulio, & Stein, 1978), however, have challenged this research as inconclusive because of measurement difficulties and confounded variables (i.e., therapist intensity, participation). Additional research is needed to determine the extent to which these characteristics are important with different kinds of client populations.

Before describing counselor characteristics further, we wish to reemphasize what we feel to be some focal points of this book:

1. Counselors and therapists are engaged in helping others in a professional capacity. But, more important, they are human beings with personal weaknesses and actualizing problems of their own. The therapist has the capacity to grow; as teachers learn from students, likewise therapists learn daily from clients. Counselors must take continuing responsibility for their own personal growth through counseling for

themselves, group experience, and other self-renewal experiences, such as those described by Gardner (1965) and Brammer and Abrego (1981).

2. Professional counselors are experts in helping others, but they have no mystical solutions. Their technical training can be helpful, but only the continuous attempt to increase their own self-understanding and awareness makes them believe in what they attempt to do with clients. Counseling and therapy are only partly technique; the rest is subtle human effectiveness through personal relationships.

3. Each client with whom one deals is a unique expression of human nature; hence, the textbook generalization never applies completely. Also, counselors must respect themselves as unique persons.

4. Thus, counseling and therapy can be viewed as a laboratory for the actualizing of both participants. Each client can help a counselor or therapist shed new light on his or her own personal integration.

5. A central emphasis for enlightened counselors or therapists must be the development of a core of valid technique that fits their theory, along with flexibility to ask themselves how different therapeutic interventions will work best for a particular client with a particular problem.

Intellectual Competence

To comprehend the enormous complexity of the human personality and to handle the involved abstractions of counseling theory, the counselor must be considerably above average in general intelligence. Related to intellectual competence is the requirement of vast knowledge of the culture acquired through general education and varied living. Intellectual and cultural breadth is significant also, since one basis for understanding varied clients is to have familiarity with the cultural environments those clients have experienced. Additionally, intellectual competence and flexibility help the therapist to provide the client with a new "assumptive world." Therapists help clients edit and enlarge their cognitive "maps" of the world through interpretation, information giving, questioning, modeling, and selective reinforcement.

Counselors believed for a long time that didactically presented knowledge about counseling improves effectiveness. Evidence from studies such as Joslin's (1965) indicates that, in training situations with school counselors, rated counseling competence has a low relationship to measurable knowledge about the process.

Spontaneity

What was said about spontaneity and flexibility as characteristics of the actualizing personality in Chapter 3 applies especially to the counselor. It has been mentioned several times that counseling is not a rigid mechanical application of formulas for producing behavior changes. The counselor's responses to client statements and feelings must be immediate reactions of the counselor's total being at that moment. Counselors must be free to move naturally, quickly, and easily in their thinking and feeling in order to adapt to the sublte nuances of client behavior.

While no concrete suggestions can be offered concerning how this characteristic is acquired, it seems to be a by-product of thorough preparation in counseling theory, attitudes, and methodology plus a nonrigid mature personality relatively free from threat.

Acceptance and Caring

It is questionable how much attitudes can be changed by advice, persuasion, or threats. Client attitudes appear to change most effectively in the presence of other growth-producing attitudes. The client experiences acceptance, for example, as a feeling of being unconditionally understood, loved, and respected. This attitude of positive acceptance is the counseling equivalent of a basic form of altruistic love (Sorokin, 1950). The evidence and logic presented by writers such as Fromm (1956), Montague (1950), May (1953), and Sorokin (1950) attest to the therapeutic power of altruistic love. For the past few years counselors looked to philosophy, theology, and anthropology for their concepts of therapeutic love. Psychologists have studied the components of love through ingenious experiments with primates. Harlow's (1958) studies of mothering are examples. In the context of long-range developmental studies, Harlow found that primates fed and raised under varying conditions of maternal deprivation developed maladaptive behaviors, which in human terms would be described as neurotic and sociopathic. Examples are infantile sexual behaviors, excessive and inappropriate aggression, and reduced affectional interaction. It was apparent that the deficient quality and quantity of early affectional relationships with the mother or mother surrogates had a profoundly negative effect on their later behavior. Spitz's (1949) earlier studies with children in foundling homes further support common sense observations about the powerful qualities of love relationships. Infants not fondled by home personnel had an unusually high mortality rate compared to those who obtained some human attention. Until more evidence is accumulated, however, one should be cautious about overgeneralizing in regard to the curative effect of love.

The counselor is in a position to provoke love relationships in the interview which can have constructive or destructive effects on the client's security system and capacity to give and accept love. As long as clients have unfulfilled affectional needs, the counselor's management of love in counseling will be a crucial therapeutic variable. Observations seem to indicate that people who have received sufficient love, particularly in early development, learn to be happy with themselves and to love adults around them, which, in turn, enables them to direct considerable altruistic concern to all human beings later on.

Caring is often communicated through touch. While counseling research findings support the effectiveness of nonverbal communication generally, touch has its special issues and risks. Sometimes clients feel anxious when touched; others feel the warmth and caring intended; some attach sexual overtones; and some feel patronized if in a lower status. Certainly, counselors need to exercise their best judgment about this issue since research offers little help. A few guidelines, such as making the gesture appropriate to the situation, not imposing more intimacy than the client desires, and not communicating a negative or power message, might help. Alagna and associates (1979) studied the effects of touching with mixed sex pairs. They concluded that counselors can use touch effectively in counseling, but that this complex behavior had a number of limiting boundaries that made both counselor and client potentially vulnerable.

Some counselors and psychotherapists may have reservations about using the ambiguous term *love* in a counseling context. *Caring* is a term meaning much the same as love and including the component of unconditional regard for the client's welfare. This care can be expressed in an aggressive critical fashion as well as in situations where correction or discipline are involved.

Unconditional positive regard is another euphemistic term used by counselors to describe this deep concern for the client's welfare and personhood. Truax (1963), for example, found unconditional positive regard as an effective treatment variable in his study of treatment in psychosis.

Nygren (1953) contrasts the eros and agape types of love—eros referring to the ancient Greek term for a self-centered, erotic love which satisfies the organisms's desires. Agape refers to a type of love in which a person seeks to assist other people to grow, contributes unequivocally to the welfare of the love object, and allows the loving person to be used for self-enhancement of the loved. Acceptance, as defined in therapeutic terms, has many of the attributes of agape.

Another characteristic of acceptance is *spontaneous motivation*. The presence of concern for the other person is a natural outgrowth of the basic attitudinal structure of the counselor's personality. Acceptance is *altruistic* in the sense that the other person's welfare is sought, not exploited.

Acceptance attitudes are *nonjudgmental* in that the counselor holds a "neutral interest" in values held by the client. This appears paradoxical when we assume that the counselor wants to promote the welfare of the client as the counselor views that welfare. The counselor tries to say in effect, however, "I neither approve nor disapprove of your behavior and attitudes, but I deeply respect your right to feel as you please and your right to act or feel differently from me." The counselor makes clients feel that no matter how they feel toward the counselor it doesn't matter, and that the counselor won't judge them for seeking help.

Basic Assumptions Underlying Acceptance.   Holding an attitude of acceptance presupposes several basic assumptions. First, acceptance is based on the idea that the individual has *infinite worth and dignity*. In other words, human values are extremely high in the value hierarchy of the counselor. A second basic assumption is that it is the person's *right to make his or her own decisions* and lead his or her own life. This assumption is based upon a third even more basic assumption that the client has the capacity or *potential to choose wisely* and *to live a full, self-actualizing, socially useful life*. A fourth related assumption is that each person is *responsible for his or her own life*. The counselor's value system must be such that he or she will enhance this sense of self-respect and self-responsibility in clients and in herself or himself. As a result, the counselor's credibility and trustworthiness will rise.

The basic assumption of many counselors, particularly of those leaning toward the person-centered group, is that there exist within the individual creative growth forces which, when released by the counselor's acceptance, will allow the individual to grow toward the model of the self-actualizing personality. Rogers (1951) cites evidence from several fields, which appear to support this assumption of growth needs. Allport's concept of "propriate striving" as a positive, goal-directed, motivating force deep within the personality supports this basic assumption also (1955).

The assumptions and attributes of acceptance are rooted deeply in American democratic philosophy, which in turn is based strongly in the Hebraic-Christian cultural traditions. The Leibnitzian philosophical position of viewing the human as an active, growth-motivated organism has contributed much also. The blend of eighteenth-century emphases on universal human rights and values with nineteenth-century views on human uniqueness and individuality has created a rich background for twentieth-century counseling philosophy. Thus, the present cultural and educational climate in the Western world appears to favor these assumptions and attitudes. This climate is making it easier for counselors to learn and apply basic attitudes leading to client self-actualization.

A summary definition of acceptance has been stated by Rogers (1951) as being a positive attitude toward people, which views them as persons of worth and dignity with the right to make their own decisions. We have postulated that the major element of this positive attitude is a form of love. Being loved in this accepting sense makes clients more capable of loving themselves and others. Perhaps the following is the dynamic of acceptance: when clients have experienced attitudes of acceptance, they are able to take this attitude and experience it in the same way toward themselves. Once they have accepted certain characteristics about themselves, they are able to accept those ideas, experiences, and drives which are a part of their basic selves, but which, up to now, they have been denying or distorting. Evidence from studies by Truax and Carkhuff (1964) support this idea of greater self-confrontation in the presence of warmth and understanding.

Self-Acceptance.   There is some evidence for the circular idea that acceptance of others is based on acceptance of one's self, and that self-acceptance is based largely on being accepted by others. Several early studies (Phillips, 1951; Sherman, 1945; Zelen, 1954) point to the significance of self-acceptance and other positive self-regarding attitudes as basic for acceptance of others. The significance of these findings for counselors is that they must accept themselves before they can accept clients sufficiently well to help them. The significance for clients is that acquisition of self-acceptance and understanding puts them in a position to accept and to receive social rewards from others. Fromm (1956) points out that one great difficulty with this principle is that our culture frowns on self-love yet extols loving others. This difficulty seems to stem from our cultural inability to differentiate *selfishness* from *self-respect*.

Values of Acceptance.   A point of great significance for the acceptance attitude is that clients get involved in the counseling process when clients sense that the counselor really cares about what they think and feel, that the counselor can and wants to help them, and that they will not be judged. Counseling then begins in earnest and becomes meaningful.

A second value of the acceptance attitude is its effect on the *psychological climate* of the interview. By psychological climate is meant the emotional tone resulting from the personal interaction of the client and counselor. The climate may be described, for example, as warm, cold, serious, or frivolous. Conspicuous examples of emotional climates are those surrounding funerals or football games. Porter (1950) defines psychological climate more narrowly as those elements of a situation that have implications regarding valuing one's self as a person. In other words, the counselor's attitudes affect the interview climate which, in turn, influences clients' attitudes toward themselves—attitudes of confidence, worth, and competence, for example.

The counselor, in addition, tries to keep a fairly consistent or stable attitudinal climate so that clients can express themselves freely without expecting disapproval, criticism, argument, or other traditional responses they expect on the basis of their past experiences. This accepting climate, and the fact that the counselor does not react toward them as others have reacted, makes a favorable situation, we believe, for learning new responses and extinguishing old nonadaptive behaviors.

A third value of acceptance is its salutary effect on *defensive* attitudes. Why does acceptance have such power to counteract defensiveness? A partial answer may be found in the description of personality presented in Chapter 3, which viewed the individual as being protected by a facade of protective mechanisms—mechanisms employed to reduce psychological vulnerability. Rationalization, denial, justification, projection, and development of symptoms were a few examples.

What happens when clients feel threatened? Their previously learned defenses are mobilized. They are like the old man in the fable who, when the wind began to blow, wrapped his coat around himself even tighter. You will remember that in the story it was the sun, with its warm rays, that created the atmosphere or climate that made the man want to take off his coat. Acceptance, similarly, is that attitudinal set of the counselor that seems to create in the client a feeling of being so comfortable in the counselor's presence that the client need no longer keep his or her guard or defenses up.

Acceptance—What It Is Not.   The following are some mistaken notions about acceptance. *Approval* or agreement is not acceptance. Accepting a person means neither approving nor disapproving of what he or she says or feels. It means simply taking him or her as a person with the right to feel and think differently from the way we think and feel, no matter how unfair, absurd, negativistic, wholesome, social, or pleasant the person's expressions may be. That clients, early in the counseling process, may misinterpret the counselor's acceptance attitudes as agreement with what they say and feel is a real counseling hazard.

A second misconception may occur over an attitude of *neutrality*. Acceptance is a *positive, active* attitude toward the client. It says in effect, "I *like* you even if I may not necessarily agree personally with all you think or feel." Another way of stating this idea might be, "I see, appreciate, and value these ideas and feelings along with you. You, the essential you, matter more to me than what you say or do."

A third distorted notion of acceptance is to equate it with *sympathy*. Sympathy goes much farther than acceptance, in that the counselor actually begins to feel in the way the client does—with a strong empathic response. The counselor actually feels sorry too as he or she becomes more emotionally involved. Acceptance, however, is more detached. The counselor says in effect, "I understand how badly you feel, although I do not personally feel that way." Sympathy, while intended as a supportive device, has the added disadvantage of tending to *minimize* the feeling of the client. A sympathy attitude says in effect, "You poor person, I feel so sorry for you since you cannot help yourself; let me give you encouragement and help." Clients feel incapable of handling feelings by themselves and feel that they must look to outside support. The net effect is the creation of a psychological climate in which dependent and evasive behavior is learned. When the need in the counselor to offer sympathy is strong, it is suspected that this is an expression of his or her own dependency needs.

A fourth misinterpretation of acceptance is equating it with *tolerance*. Although tolerance may be a desirable social trait, in a counseling relationship it connotes "putting up with." It implies a negative acceptance rather than a positive one, as well as a more superficial kind of respect for personality. The tolerance attitude implies that there is a characteristic, such as race difference, of which the counselor is aware, and about which the client senses he or she is trying to be tolerant.

Understanding and Empathy

Counseling and therapeutic writings are replete with suggestions to *understand* clients as a special way of being with them, yet the term is seldom defined in behavioral terms. Effective counselors seem to be able to understand their clients more than ineffective counselors can, according to several studies (Fiedler, 1950; Heine, 1950). Porter (1949) made a useful distinction between understanding diagnostically and understanding therapeutically. *Understanding diagnostically* refers to the intellectualized descriptions of the client's behavior. Examples are the information obtained through testing or observation for making diagnostic judgments to use in career planning. As one would expect, this aspect of understanding enables the counselor to make predictions about clients' overt behavior and their self-descriptions. The test, then, of the counselors' diagnostic understanding would be the extent of their ability to describe, interpret, and predict client behavior.

Understanding therapeutically refers to feeling reactions on the part of a counselor that enable the client to feel understood, accepted, and empathized with.

An attitude of therapeutic understanding emphasizes seeing clients as they see their experiences. As Gendlin (1962) so aptly described it, understanding empathically is sensing the meaning that the client is experiencing so as to help the client focus on that meaning. Raskin (1974) studied 83 counselors from eight different therapeutic orientations to arrive at a description of the ideal therapist. They agreed highly on the ideal qualities, and most put empathy in the first rank. Yet, when examining the recordings of six expert therapists, Raskin found many short of their ideal. Empathy, even though not a very operational concept, has been studied extensively and has proven to be a key ingredient for obtaining constructive outcomes in classrooms as well as in counseling (Aspy, 1975).

The evidence for empathic understanding is not all positive, however. Lesser's study (1961), although limited in scope to a few counselors and clients, found that the generally accepted idea of empathic understanding being related to client progress did not pertain. Even though all clients in his study made progress as measured by Q-sorts on ideal-self perceptions, this progress was unrelated to measures on an empathic understanding scale.

In a series of studies on the conditions that promoted constructive personality change in college and hospital clients, Truax and Carkhuff (1963, 1964) found that a sensitive and accurate attempt at therapeutic understanding of the client was very facilitative. This is an empathic response to the client's being, which clients perceive as meaning they have been understood. Truax and Carkhuff found that nonpossessive warmth and counselor genuineness were variables which, in addition to understanding, promoted client growth. The rationale for the effectiveness of these ingredients is stated by the investigators as follows:

> The greater the degree of the therapist's accurate empathic understanding of the client, the greater the degree to which the therapist shows unconditional or nonpossessive warmth or integration of the therapist within the relationship, and the more intense and intimate the therapist in the relationship, the greater will be the degree of the client's interpersonal exploration and the greater will be the consequent extent of positive behavior change. (1964, p. 861)

In other words, if the counselor conditions described above are present in the relationship, clients feel more free to be themselves and face their problems. Empathy has been stressed as a key variable in counseling success. Research data support this view. Retrospective accounts by former clients typically describe relationship qualities such as support and understanding as being the most helpful factors in successful therapy (Cross, Sheehan, & Khan, 1982).

Effective counselors apparently need both diagnostic and therapeutic types of understanding. Yet they may find that attempting to use both types of understanding is difficult indeed. There is a strong tendency to be preoccupied with the cognitive aspects of clients' difficulties and to overlook the emotional implications of their confusion and indecision. For example, while attempting to see the clients' reasons for seeking financial aid, for finding social work more suitable than teaching, or deciding which marital prospect appears most promising, the counselor might tend to ignore the threat to the clients' independence involved in the financial aid, or the need to dominate children in the career choice, or the extreme dependency interfering with a marital or occupational choice. In some cases, perhaps, more emphasis needs to be placed on the reality level of the clients' occupational choice rather than on the intricate feelings regarding their parents' wishes for success through them. This point in especially pertinent for many school counselors and advisers whose positions are structured around career planning. We assume that the really effective therapeutic psychologist has the capacity to keep the understanding emphases in balance and to know when to stress one aspect of understanding over the other.

The Internal Frame of Reference. Another useful concept in understanding the client and in assisting the counselor or psychotherapist to understand the meaning of empathy is that of the internal frame of reference (Porter, 1950; Rogers, 1942). This concept is defined as the attempt by the counselor to perceive the client's phenomenological world as seen by the client. It means the attempt to think *with*, rather than *for* or *about* the client. By frame of reference is meant simply point of view or the observational vantage point. Rogers cites an example of the counselor's thoughts as he or she assumes this role:

> To be of assistance to you I will put aside myself—the self of ordinary interaction— and enter into your world of perception as completely as I am able. I will become, in a sense, another self for you—an alter ego of your own attitudes and feelings—a safe opportunity for you to discern yourself more clearly, to experience yourself more truly and deeply, to choose more significantly. (1951, p. 35)

An example of a counselor's thinking from the *external* frame of reference would be, "What is causing this difficulty, and why is he or she so preoccupied with marital problems?" The counselor thinks, "This fellow is in bad shape; I've got to find out what is wrong and try to help him save his marriage." An example of the *internal* frame of reference thinking would be, "You see this as a very disturbing experience, and you want to do something about it." The counselor thinks, "I must try to understand how he looks at this problem and to help him clarify his own thinking about it so that he can make a decision in line with the best interests of all concerned."

As an aid in conceptualizing the problem of getting within the client's frame of reference, see Figure 4-1 (Shostrom & Brammer, 1952). In stage (1) the client and counselor are in an ordinary social interaction situation where *S* listens and *C* talks. The perceptions are formed largely on the basis of the unique past experience of each participant. Each moves down his or her respective experience lane as in stage (3). Often the counselor, who characteristically assumes the external frame of reference, tries to get the client to come into his or her lane— to see things his or her way. Under certain circumstances this may be a legitimate objective, but it does not necessarily help in understanding the client.

When counselors assume the internal frame of reference, however, they try to make their perceptual framework match that of the client as in stage (2) of Figure 4-1. Stage (4) illustrates what happens when counselors try to get into the client's lane. At least temporarily, they attempt to think and feel the way the client does.

Learning to assume the internal frame of reference and to stay within it seems to be particularly difficult. As one contemplates the reasons for this difficulty, the following examples can be considered.

Language differences constitute a major obstacle. As the adult tries to understand the adolescent or the child, or as the Easterner tries to fathom the particular lingo of the Westerner, it seems that the symbols used have different meanings to different people. This is a problem of semantics that has received much attention in the psycholinguistics literature of recent years. Researchers associated with "neurolinguistic programming" approaches to therapy have taught us to recognize important client-therapist differences in the representational systems they use to process their experiences (Bandler & Grinder, 1975). For example, a visually oriented client may process experience in a way that she cannot "see" what a feeling oriented counselor is trying to have her "feel." Language differences may be particularly important with clients of different sociocultural backgrounds from the counselor. Differences in language or dialect between counselor and client affect perceptions of counselor credibility and perceived therapist-client similarity (Russell, 1988).

Biological differences are obviously another barrier. The difficulties experienced as a man tries to assume the feminine frame of reference, and vice versa, can be easily understood. A current issue in counseling is whether white or black counselors working with clients of a different race can really empathize with

FIGURE 4-1   The Internal and External Frames of Reference.

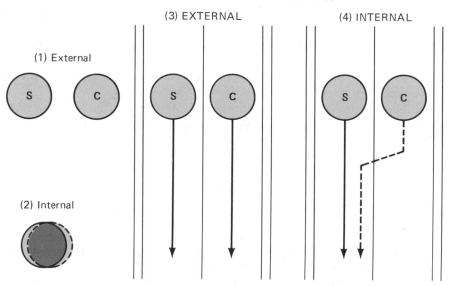

their clients since they share so little common experience. It takes unusual empathic ability to transcend these differences.

Socioeconomic differences often cause client and counselor to be in different semantic worlds. Counselors, for example, having from five to eight years of college training have difficulty assuming the frame of reference of those with little formal education. A thorough understanding of social class differences and their significance, therefore, should be part of every counselor's training. There is abundant evidence of the need for this type of understanding in studies by Havighurst (1953), Warner, Meeker, and Ells (1949), Postman, Bruner, and McGinnies (1948), Schwebel (1965), Ivey (1979), and Sue (1977).

Related to cultural differences are *experience differentials*. Counselors, having life experiences different from their clients, can only see the clients' world imperfectly in the light of their own frames of reference. Finally, *age differences* influence understanding, in that one who has lived longer often finds it difficult to "see" the significance of the conflicts and frustrations of a much younger person. Teachers, for instance, often forget "how it feels" to be a student.

It was felt that a brief analysis of some of the obstacles to assuming the internal frame of reference would help to punctuate the necessity for striving very hard for broad life experiences, as well as for asking ourselves the questions: "How does he look at this problem?" "How is she thinking and feeling about this matter?" "What is he trying to say?" This attempt at understanding the client by means of assuming the internal frame of reference pays heavy dividends in a better relationship and more appropriate counselor responses to the client's feeling and thinking.

Empathic response is another way of viewing understanding. Empathy is related to the German *einfühlung*, which means *feeling into*. An illustration is the response of the crowd as the highjumper clears the bar. All vocalize *umm-mm* and lean forward as the jumper goes up. Bowlers often experience similiar feelings when they "empathize" the ball. Similarly, counselors tend to "feel into" the attitudes of the client as they are being expressed. Although this capacity to empathize aids the counselor in maintaining the internal frame of reference, there is a tendency to get overinvolved emotionally, the dangers of which have been described previously.

The question of how a counselor manifests empathic qualities is answered by the quality of verbal responses that capture the essential feeling messages of the client. Reflecting these messages with caring concern leaves the client with a feeling of being warmly understood.

Warmth and Human Encounter

Closely related to therapeutic understanding, caring, and acceptance attitudes is *warmth*, a term used to describe an aspect of the relationship. Warmth appears to encompass the sensitive, friendly, considerate, and responsive elements of the counselor personality. *Relating easily to people* is a phrase often used to describe an aspect of warmth. Manifested warmth seems basic for an effective relationship. Truax and Carkhuff (1964) found with their warmth research scale that nonpossessive warmth was an effective therapeutic ingredient, and that the higher the level of this variable the more evidence of constructive personality change was noted.

The friendly conversation, preceding and interspersed in the process, however, adds little to the progress of counseling. It has been called "sawdust" by Rogers (1942), meaning that it helps to maintain a friendly climate but doesn't result in much therapeutic progress.

Consideration for clients is rooted in respect for them as persons and is another way of manifesting warmth. This counselor attitude conveys a feeling to clients that they are worthy of respect (a feeling that many clients do not have for themselves). Consideration is shown also in the ordinary courtesies of social communication, such as offering a chair and showing concern for the client's comfort. Consideration is shown through the intense interest exhibited in clients so that they feel they are important and worthwhile persons to the counselor, not just research subjects or practice "guinea pigs."

Bugental (1987), in describing the mature therapist, uses the term *encounter* to describe the therapist's willingness to "be there with" the client and yet take responsibility only for his or her own (the therapist's) authentic personhood. The counselor serves as a model for authenticity.

Another external manifestation of warmth in a relationship is the honest smile. This behavior is the test of the genuineness of the counselor's attitudes. Clients can sense when counselors are "just trying to be nice" and when they experience genuine pleasure in knowing their clients as distinct people.

Freedom

This corollary attitude of acceptance characterizes a freedom and lack of authoritarian and judgmental attitudes in the counselor's personality. *Permissiveness* was a term used in the past to describe therapeutic freedom, but accrued negative connotations reduced its descriptive accuracy. The counselor says in effect, "You may discuss anything you wish here without fear of judgment"; hence, he or she is neither offended nor shocked. Counselors allow clients freedom to be themselves and to grow.

A completely laissez faire attitude, however, would operate to the disadvantage of the client, since the relationship would be too ambiguous. If allowed too much free expression, the client may fear loss of emotional control and suffer anxiety. As indicated in the discussion of catharsis, too free an expression of feelings may serve to erode client defensive structures to the point where they are at the mercy of their feelings and may move toward a psychosis.

A counselor who is too permissive could be extremely cruel to the client who is vulnerable to anxiety. Such a client might flounder without direction. The counselor would abuse his or her own freedom if he or she were facetious. An extreme sample would be the client who came into the office and announced, "I just killed my mother," to which the counselor replied, "Did you use an axe or a knife?" The client assumes that counselors take their professional responsibilities seriously, and responses of this type tend to destroy respect for them.

The counselor's authority role often belies attempts to acquire a permissive attitude. The counselor's personal prestige, specialized knowledge, and professional "halo" make an atmosphere of free expression difficult to achieve. Counselors are tempted at most to use their authoritarian status to urge clients toward definite goals or, at least, to select the content of the interviews. The desirable amount of authority or direction to be given is the least amount consonant with the goals of the particular counseling case and the least amount which is comfortable for both. Techniques for implementing these attitudes will be clarified later under the subject of structuring. When used appropriately, therapeutic freedom allows clients more spontaneous expression of their feelings, thus allowing them to understand and accept the feelings.

Congruence and Transparency

There is growing evidence that, in order to elicit open, honest self-confrontation by the client, the counselor must manifest these qualities. There is little evidence, however, concerning what kind of self-congruent behavior is therapeutic. Does this mean telling the client one's own problems? In a group therapy situation, Branan (1967) found that use of the counselor's self-experience did not increase perceived counselor genuineness significantly; yet Schutz (1971) places leader self-revelation in a central place in group work.

Various terms are used to describe the condition of genuineness-realness, congruence, transparency, and authenticity. There is more than just self-awareness and nondenial of feeling in counselors. They must present themselves as real persons in the interview encounter. A common behavior running counter to this idea in counselors is the facade of professionalism—a kind of protective personal distance. In the Truax and Carkhuff studies (1964), there was a significant tendency for counselors rated high on the genuineness and self-congruence scales to have clients who were rated most improved or having the most constructive personality change.

The counselor must, above all, be honest and sincere in his attitudes. Counseling cannot be a masquerade. Honesty, as used here, is not perceived in moralistic terms but as a characteristic of *straightforwardness*. Beginning counselors, for example, learn quickly that if they try to be accepting without truly feeling this way inside, clients find this out quickly. It is this quality of honesty which again distinguishes communication in the interview from ordinary social conversation. In much of social communication both parties keep up a "front," hence conversation is often a game of mild deceit. It seems that when clients experience a relationship in which this deceit is not present and when they feel that the counselor is serious and "on the level" with them, they realize that they can drop their own facades and can accomplish little by being deceitful themselves.

In order to be completely honest, it is necessary that counselors recognize frankly their own errors—that they make errors of judgment and technique. Therapists can more easily recognize and correct errors when they can admit their possibility. Their perceptions and humble acceptance of error, however, must be balanced by a mature tolerance for the inevitable mistakes, especially the more trivial ones. Clients seem to have a remarkable tolerance for counselor error providing other aspects of the relationship are adequate. This attitude of alertness to error serves as a useful antidote to counselor complacency, or what is known as the "pedestal syndrome," or the "Jehovah complex." Bugental (1981), in describing characteristics of the mature therapist, mentions humility as a consequence of counselors' awareness of their limited knowledge and the awe they experience in the presence of potential growth. Bugental mentions further the need to accept normal guilt for being a therapist. This condition results when sensitive therapists realize that they are not doing all that can be done for persons who trust their lives to them. These are further illustrations of the need for counselors to face up to the real business of being human in the very sensitive relationship of counseling.

The studies of Truax and Carkhuff on therapeutic variables have been cited often in this chapter. Not only are they models of research procedure, but they also give valuable leads for process conceptions and counselor selection. They found that effective counselors are people who can sensitively and accurately understand clients, allow themselves to express warmth, be genuine, and still retain their integrity in the relationship. These conditions encourage clients to manifest the same characteristics, resulting in deepening self-exploration and self-awareness, which then make possible more constructive personality change. They also found that low therapeutic conditions resulted in ratings of client behavior indicating deterioration (Carkhuff & Truax, 1966). Thus, counseling can have negative effects; this may help to explain why so many studies of counseling outcomes come out negative, and why so much credence is placed in Eysenck's findings (1952), which question the efficacy of therapy. Positive growth indices are canceled out by the deteriorative effects of some counseling relationships.

We feel that, at this point in the discussion of counselor characteristics, it must be mentioned that the counselor is not some sort of inert, bland agent to be manipulated at will by the client. In attempts to accept the client wholeheartedly and to enter into a close relationship, the counselor or therapist *risks* as much as the client. Counselors, too, must open their facades to make the relationship effective. The risk element involves the possibility of failure or rejection by the client and, if this happens, the counselor may lose part of herself or himself. The counselor accepts this risk as the price of being human.

To help counteract tendencies to be incongruent, studies of matching client and counselor on compatibility variables have been performed. Fry and Charron (1980), for example, found that in their study of cognitive style and compatibility clients improved in their self-exploration skills and ease of relating to their counselors. These general findings have been confirmed in similar studies (Packer & Bain, 1978).

Flexibility

Carnes's study (1949) of counselor flexibility points up the necessity for this vital trait in the counselor's character. Therapists must be flexible in the use of their counseling techniques and attitudes as they move along all the dimensions defined at the outset of this chapter. Sometimes they must be objective and at other times subjective. Often they utilize techniques that are primarily affective; at other places they are primarily cognitive. For example, they may explain a point about client responsibility to create clarity; at other points they may deliberately promote ambiguity, as will be explained in Chapter 7. Sometimes counselors focus on aspects of client problems that are common to men and women in general. Then again, they may dwell upon the unique problems of particular clients. The essence of the creative synthesis view is flexibility in utilizing all approaches and methods as they seem appropriate and effective in achieving the anticipated client outcomes.

The counseling relationship is very complex and it is difficult to generalize about relationship conditions that are facilitative under all circumstances. Gelso and Carter (1985) conclude:

> It seems clear that there is not a simple linear relationship, at least of any magnitude, between therapist-offered conditions and outcome. The relationship is probably best viewed as highly complex, one in which therapist-offered conditions can at times impede client movement. While it seems clear that at least some minimal degree of empathy, positive regard and the like must be displayed, however subtly, evidence suggests that certain doses of these qualities with certain kinds of clients under certain conditions . . . can affect process and outcome negatively, for example, high degrees of genuineness early with delinquent boys or high degrees of empathy within the context of directive therapy. (p. 221)

It is essential for therapists to evaluate, to the best of their abilities, the effects of their behavior on the therapeutic process with each client and not assume their behavior will affect all clients in the same manner.

CLIENT INFLUENCES ON THE THERAPEUTIC ALLIANCE

Although research focused for many years on characteristics of counselors that enhanced effective therapy, the client's involvement in therapy is obviously a major ingredient in all psychotherapies. Recent research has focused on client characteristics and behavior as key determinants of therapeutic outcome. Some researchers believe that there was an overemphasis on the role of the therapist and not enough attention to either the role of the client or to more general relationship factors. For example, client reports of therapists' warmth, empathy, and genuineness can be construed as a global measure of the therapeutic alliance rather than reflecting the central importance of the counselor as a person. Those who consider the client's behavior to be critical to therapy outcome view the therapist's diverse techniques as alternative approaches to facilitating the client's involvement in therapy and the verbal exploration of the client's internal frame of reference. Client influences upon the therapeutic alliance include variables such as client disclosure, participation, and expectancies.

In their review of client disclosure research, Stiles, Shapiro, and Elliott (1986) found that client disclosure (first person utterances revealing subjective information) shows strong positive correlations with other measures of effective psychotherapy. Factor analytic studies of therapy have also found a general client participation/resistance factor to be central in effective psychotherapy.

It has been difficult to demonstrate a convincing relationship between specific client behaviors and therapy outcome. There is some evidence that the client's overall participation, positive contributions, and the total number of client disclosures in therapy are associated with beneficial therapy outcomes.

Expectancies influence profoundly the motivation for and the outcomes from counseling (Garfield, 1986; Beutler & Clarkin, 1990). Client expectancies included initial expectations as well as those developed in treatment. Initial client expectations of success can be bolstered by early outcomes; once a success of any sort has been achieved, clients in any therapy may be pulled along by their own expectations of further change. Bandura (1984) suggests that client self-efficacy (cognitive estimate of future competence on the basis of past performance) functions to forecast psychotherapy success and also enhance performance by the individual. It may be that all therapeutic techniques function to enhance clients' hopes and self-efficacy beliefs.

In addition to the expectancies growing out of the process itself, the clients bring varied backgrounds of age, gender, family, and learning experiences that influence expectations. Personal factors, such as intelligence, prior success or failure in counseling, current levels of distress, coping skills, and defensive style affect the expectancies from counseling. Older adults, for example, tend not to seek counseling for personal problems from a professional counselor largely because their expectancies for help are so low and their perceptions of the process are so threatening.

The results of research on the therapeutic relationship suggest that the client's contribution to and perception of the therapeutic alliance, rather than the therapist's, best predicts successful outcome (Luborsky et al., 1983; Horowitz et al., 1984; Marziali, 1984; Garfield, 1986).

READINESS AND THE THERAPEUTIC ALLIANCE

Readiness for learning is a well-known educational concept. Children, for instance, are not "ready" to read until they have achieved a certain level of motivation, maturation, and basic skill development. Readiness for counseling and psychotherapy is simliar in that certain conditions must be satisfied before counseling can take place. For instance, a study by Lipkin (1954) led to the conclusion that clients who view the counseling experience favorably and anticipate success undergo more change than those who are more skeptical.

A client may recognize that something is wrong in his or her life, but typically the client has to have this observation pointed out to him or her by someone else or wait for a crisis to emerge. A suggestion that the client needs help often provokes resistance—a type of protective defense against change discussed in Chapter 8. It is significant for this discussion because the typical client comes to counseling with some strong reservations.

Counseling cannot begin until people recognize a need for change and until they are ready to commit themselves to the change process. Our culture interferes with both of these steps. First of all, when people seek help for emotional difficulties, others often perceive them as weak or defective rather than viewing them as humans with limitations or special problems. Consequently, admitting to a need for help brings feelings of shame and embarrassment, which too frequently lead people to block such needs from their awareness. Assuming this first obstacle of need for change is faced, common misconceptions about the change process interfere with the second step of actively seeking competent help and using it effectively. For instance, a professional helper may be viewed as having the power to effect changes in people they don't really want or as able to solve others' problems single-handedly rather than as a collaborator in a project requiring mutually cooperative efforts. A concern of this chapter, therefore, will be methods for assisting clients in facing difficulties, seeking help, and utilizing the helping relationship effectively.

Even though clients may need assistance in pursuing help, overzealousness in these efforts should be resisted. Some groups, such as extremist religious cults and a number of the mass psychotherapies, resort to a variety of deceptions to prepare recruits or clients for changes the group leaders have decided are in the clients' best interest. We believe this ends-justifies-the-means approach is both unnecessary and destructive. We support, instead, a facilitative process based on fully voluntary and informed choice, whereby a potential client is made aware of the strengths as well as the limitations of the particular counseling approach.

Factors Determining Readiness

Several factors determine "readiness" of the client for a counseling experience. They may be a function of the client, the therapist, or the context within which counseling takes place. Factors within the client may involve expectations of the counselor and/or counseling process, intellectual or conceptualizing abilities, and openness to information about one's self.

Clients may view the change process as being similar to that of fixing an automobile. They expect the therapist to fix them with minimal involvement on their part. Elements of readiness such as this are covered under the terms *structuring* to be discussed in Chapter 5. Alternatively, a client may take a dim view of a particular therapist on the basis of his or her reputation, or lack thereof (Rippee, Harvey, & Parker, 1965), or on a cultural and socioeconomic gap which leaves the client skeptical of the therapist's ability to fully understand the client. Crider's study on conceptualizing ability (1946) found that the more intellectually able and psychologically sophisticated individuals have the best chances of therapeutic success. Individuals' openness to information about themselves usually is described in terms of the rigidity or flexibility of defense systems and levels of insight. A number of investigations have found a relationship between readiness and this flexibility and openness factor. For instance, Mendelsohn (1966) concluded that persons inclined to seek help were more open to exploring themselves, more willing to consider change, and more intuitive and perceptive (as defined by the Myers-Briggs scale) than those not so inclined. Similarly, Raskin (1961) found that increased motivation for treatment went with an increased awareness of one's psychological difficulties.

Most of the research on client readiness for counseling has studied isolated dimensions of expectancy. In a factorial study to identify the most relevant dimensions, Tinsley, Workman, and Kass (1980) found four component factors—personal commitment, facilitative conditions, counselor expertise, and nurturance. This was the first systematic study of the client commitment factor, although the importance of client commitment to change has been part of counseling lore for decades. High client commitment scores are a good prognostic sign, insofar as clients are expected to devote much time and energy to the process. The importance of preparing clients for their counseling experience with realistic information is underscored in a study by Wollersheim and associates (1958).

Raskin's study highlighted another important variable determining a client's readiness for treatment, that is, the therapist's readiness to treat that particular client. Clients who were liked by their therapists rated high on motivation. Results of Raskin's study along with findings of a national survey of psychotherapists conducted by Goldman and Mendelsohn (1969) showed that such clients tended to be imaginative, sensitive, curious, of high educational and occupational levels, and anxious. It seems that most therapists like to work with clients who are verbal, exhibit little pathology, and who are much like themselves. Critics of counseling have called this preference the "YAVIS Syndrome" (young, assertive, verbal, intelligent, socialized).

The context within which counseling takes place can also affect readiness significantly. For instance, if the physical setting is uncomfortable and lacking in privacy, clients may become ill at ease and distrustful. Similarly, some hospitals, schools, and colleges have an administrative policy or an unfortunate history of rumors which mitigate against an atmosphere of trust and acceptance. An example is having the counseling function closely tied to disciplinary activities rather than having disciplinary officers serve simply as a possible referral source. Lack of accessibility is another aspect of the counseling context which can seriously interfere with readiness. A disturbed client, for example, may arrive motivated to work. He is told he will need to make an appointment for a later date because the counselor is booked up. Often he loses interest to the point where he does not return. It would seem desirable to have an "intake" system to see clients, even if briefly, when they come the first time. This procedure would let them feel something is being done and would ascertain the degree of urgency for psychotherapy, counseling, or referral to specialists. Some counseling services maintain fixed open hours to avoid intake delays for urgent problems.

A significant contextual factor is the cultural, economic, and ethnic match of the counselor and client. While there is no compelling evidence to our knowledge that counselor and client must come from the same race or ethnic background to be effective, many clients have feelings about the issue. Sue (1977), for example, found that half of the minority clients he studied did not show for their second appointments, and a large number of these, when followed up, did not finish counseling later. Two implications emerge from cross-cultural counseling research. One is the necessity for counselors to have training in cross-cultural facts so that they can understand and deal effectively with clients different from themselves. The second is to acquire a broad kind of cultural awareness that Ivey, Ivey, and Simek-Morgan (1991) stress is necessary for the majority of counselors, so that these counselors can escape their white, middle-class orientation and respond empathically to the needs of culturally diverse clients.

Methods for Readying Clients

One way of reaching people with problems in through *talks*. Heads of agencies and counseling service directors report that every time they give a talk to a public group on mental health, family problems, study methods, or child behavior, for example, there are numerous requests for services.

A second method of motivating clients is through creating an *institutional climate conducive to seeking help*. In schools, for example, this is particulary important, since very few student clients seek counseling voluntarily.

A third method for stimulating weakly motivated clients and for building better readiness in those already seeking such services is that of *instructing referral sources*. Counselors constantly must work on sharpening the awareness of referral agents through conferences with physicians, teachers, advisers, ministers, lawyers, personnel directors, and others likely to make the first contact.

A fourth device for promoting readiness is to give the prospective clients *information about themselves*. This is quite easy in a school or college setting compared to private or clinic practice. Generally, test batteries have been given, and personal records are completed routinely and cumulatively. The students are notified that they can come in to discuss the test results. In a clinical setting inventories such as the classic Mooney Problem Checklist (1950), Shostrom's Personal Orientation Inventory (1963), the Multimodal Life History Questionnaire (Lazarus, 1980), Behavior Analysis History Questionnaire (Cautela & Upper, 1976) can be used. Computer interaction programs such as DISCOVER or SIGI may also be used to provide self-help data to clients to supplement counseling interviews.

A fifth significant source of finding motivated clients is through the *educational process* itself, such as courses in study methods, English skills, reading techniques, college orientation, psychology, and marriage preparation. Work-shops in assertiveness training, human relations, or sex role awareness often generate interest in individual counseling.

Special *precounseling orientation* meetings are a sixth means of giving clients information about counseling and related functions such as testing, helping them formulate realistic expectations about counseling and the counselor's role, acquainting them with the philosophy of the particular counseling service, and reducing anxieties about the anticipated counseling experience.

Readiness during the Interview

Most of the preceding methods of establishing readiness are concerned with locating and motivating clients. Once the client is in the office, a counselor has a special problem in readiness. Attitude, setting, and technique are impor-tant factors. Counselors must be able to size up the situation to know if they should apply support techniques to ease clients' suffering, or whether they should increase client discomfort to get them more emotionally involved and willing to work on their problems.

Counselors can be misled easily by the "facade" phenomenon. The client's resistance may result in opening the relationship on issues such as "no vocational goal," "poor name remembering," "stage fright," or "poor study habits," as the basic problem. We feel that the counselor should start at this level with the client and not jump to the conclusion immediately that this is a "facade" problem. Generally speaking, however, if the counselor's attitudes are appropriate, clients will come forth with a redefinition of their problems shortly.

Criteria the counselor can apply to ascertain the client's readiness to move forward are positive attitudes toward the therapeutic process and a lowered defensiveness, which gives an impression of spontaneity and eagerness to talk about problems. Impressions that clients are ready to deal with the emotional implications of their problems, articulateness that enables them to express ideas and feelings directly, and a general acceptance of the therapist's or counselor's role, structure, and style of counseling are further indications of client readiness. The counselor should be alert also to the client who may not be able to articulate problems or feelings directly but by attitude indicates a desire to go ahead. Similarly the counselor should be wary of the client who is too glib about going ahead, and who uses interview talk as a device to avoid taking responsible action.

SUMMARY

Psychotherapeutic and counseling relationships have several basic dimensions, such as uniqueness-commonality, objectivity-subjectivity, cognitive-affective, ambiguity-clarity, and responsibility-accountability. The counselor has the diffi-cult task of recognizing and dealing appropriately with these seemingly paradoxi-cal elements of the relationship.

Since therapeutic effectiveness hinges so much on the quality of the relationship between counselor and client, basic attitudes of the counselor are highly significant. The attitudes of acceptance and understanding have considerable consequences upon the psychological climate of the interview. The climate of the therapeutic relationship is based on qualities and behaviors brought into the relationship by both the counselor and the client. A key to an effective attitudinal climate is the counselor's assuming the internal frame of reference, which is an attempt to understand the client by taking the client's view of his situation. The counselor must have additional characteristics of warmth, intelligence, flexibility, humility, and a willingness to share the responsibility. Additionally, it is important for clients to enter counseling with a willingness to share their thoughts and feelings, an expectation to become active participants in the counseling process, and a sense of hope or self-efficacy. Various strategies to improve counselor and client readiness to begin counseling were discussed.

CHAPTER 5

Relationship Building Strategies and Methods

The purpose of this chapter is to present methods for relating easily and effectively to clients, promoting client comfort and feelings of being understood, and encouraging client exploration of feelings. In previous chapters we have stated our assumption that techniques are limited unless there is full understanding of therapeutic goals, fundamental counselor attitudes, and theoretical assumptions from which the techniques emerge. In other words, there is a danger of becoming too "technique conscious." One characteristic of a charlatan is blind adherence to pat techniques applied indiscriminately to all clients.

We emphasize a variety of relationship building methods and flexibility in their application. This emphasis on flexibility fits our actualizing model. These relationship methods are useful in dealing with problems at the facade level in handling resistance. They also have a modulating effect on feeling awareness and expression at other levels, particularly with feeling polarities. Relationship strategies are especially useful in encouraging expression of feelings along the basic polarities of loving and directing anger, for example. Thus, modulating in this context means the process of expressing a full spectrum of feelings along any polarity in a manner that achieves the growth goals of the client.

It is important to remember that the therapist's use of himself or herself in the therapeutic system is the most powerful tool in the process of helping clients change. In order to build a common ground with the client, the therapist will deliberately activate aspects of himself or herself that are congruent with the client's needs and expectations. However, the therapist will bond in a way that leaves him or her free to maintain separateness from the client. The therapist will accommodate the client, but also requires the client to accommodate to him or her. Minuchin and Fishman (1981) have stressed the value of therapist role flexibility in building a therapeutic alliance. They describe the importance of being able to join with clients from different positions of proximity—the close proximity of a supportive and nurturant counselor, the median position of an objective "coach," or a more distant "expert" role. Different clients will have different needs and each position of joining with a client will have its own strengths and weaknesses.

There has been abundant research on counseling skills over the past twenty years. Almost any verbal response method will have its supporting data; but the research methodological and classification issues are so great that consistent results and firm conclusions are rare. We know, however, that methods have differential effects. To determine these differential effects, for example, one study by Ehrlich, D'Augelli, and Danish (1979) found that feeling-type counselor responses encouraged two and a half times as many client affect responses as advice types and twice as many as open questions. So counselors need to give close attention to the kinds of responses they make to achieve the results they want.

OPENING TECHNIQUES

The first task upon meeting a client is to establish a feeling of trust. Earlier books on counseling and psychotherapy speak of building rapport, a condition of mutual understanding and comfort. Counselors establish this condition by living their accepting, warm attitudes and manifesting deep interest in clients, rather than by applying a kind of technique. Some of the accumulated experience of counselors in beginning the relationship is summarized in the following topics.

The Greeting

If counseling takes place in an office, the counselor's initial interest in a client is manifested by meeting the client in the reception room with a firm hand clasp (if socially appropriate to age level and subculture), greeting the client by name, and escorting him or her courteously into the office. If not in an office, the usual informal greeting customs appropriate to the subculture of the client would prevail. Ordinary human courtesy, therefore, goes far in opening a relationship satisfactorily.

The Topics

Counselors vary in their opinions on how to open an interview. Starting with an urbane or trite conversational topic might result in a more strained relationship than if clients were allowed to state their business frankly and immediately. This problem illustrates an area of artful judgment required of a counselor and reflects his or her personal style.

Counseling generally deals with problems that are personal and loaded with anxiety. It is often difficult to face these problems squarely and immediately, particularly in the presence of a strange person of uncertain trustworthiness. The counselor must resolve the client's fear and restraint, which is natural in a new setting, by making the client moderately comfortable. Sometimes it helps a client to mention a "conversation piece" in the office such as a picture on the desk. Clients often feel comfortable with this conventional way of starting a human relationship. It should be emphasized, however, that such openers are merely "ice breakers" to enable the client to start perceiving the therapeutic attitudes of the counselor. There is just as much danger that the relationship will get off on a conversational bent as on a "cold," resistive start.

As an additional note of caution, an effective relationship can be established just as easily on a nonverbal basis by a warm and friendly "waiting-for-you, my-time-is-yours" appearance on the counselor's part, and secondly, by competently meeting whatever lead the client gives for a starter. If a client is motivated to seek help, counselor-initiated "small talk" may tend to show a kind of disrespect for this need. Furthermore, too much "small talk" might imply that the counselor needs to protect the client from the reality of the situation. Generally, a lead something like "would you like to tell me what brings you here?" is most realistic and honest. In summary, the first remarks are largely matters of counselor preference or style.

The Physical Arrangements

One of the determinants of a good working relationship is the physical condition of the room. Research is lacking on this problem, so we depend upon opinions of counselors. While some counselors work across a desk, we feel this sets up communication barriers. Yet sitting face to face at close range is too threatening for some clients. Counselors need to experiment with the most effective arrangment and attend to cultural differences on this issue of proximity.

Other physical arrangements would seem to be taken for granted, but our experience is that they often are overlooked by counselors. It is axiomatic, for example, that clients never be placed in a position where they must face the light. This means that, if it is necessary to face the client toward the window, the blinds or drapes must be closed.

Another consideration is the nature of the client's chair. The possibilities for a good counseling relationship seem to be improved through installation of comfortable chairs for both counselor and client. This represents quite a change from traditional arrangements whereby the counselor is afforded a comfortable swivel chair and the client is given any available straight chair.

The Attitudes

A degree of mysticism seems to surround the client-therapist relationship. Counselors sometimes give the client the impression that therapy is a form of magic and that the therapist is endowed with special powers that make him or her able to help people. In our experience the relationship bridge is built best on a feeling of the natural human relationship. It is assumed here that counseling is a unique, human interaction that differs only slightly from other human relationships. The counselor may explain that there is nothing mysterious about counseling or psychotherapy, for they are largely processes of planning, relearning, and confronting one's self.

As with all other techniques, building a relationship is rather fruitless unless the counselor possesses the characteristics detailed earlier in Chapter 4. Ethical behavior must prevail. Above all, the confidential nature of the interview must be maintained. Counselors working in colleges and universities often are tempted to use illustrations from their own counseling experiences in classes in counseling, mental hygiene, and psychology. Such a procedure is doubtful, yet counselors are apt to follow this practice unless they are aware of the damaging effects this may have on relationships with future clients.

REFLECTIVE RELATIONSHIP TECHNIQUES

Reflection of Feeling

In the actualizing approach to personality described in Chapter 3, it was emphasized that much of personality is beyond awareness. Reflection technique helps the individual to go beyond the actualizing system to become more aware of obscure feelings at the core and to deal with them more effectively. What seems to happen is that clients talk of their feelings as "it" or "them"—something apart from themselves. This tendency of the client to deny ownership of his or her feelings at first serves a useful defensive function. The reflection technique, however, focuses on the subjective element of what the client says. Reflection emphasizes the pronoun "you" in the phrases, "you feel . . ." and "you think . . ." Reflection serves a useful purpose in that it leads the client to think of the feelings and ideas being expressed as part of one's own personality and not outside one's self. Thus, reflection is a useful intermediate technique to be used after the initial relationship has been built and before the information-giving and interpretation stages in the process are begun.

Reflecting feelings is a skill and, as such, can be learned by understanding and practice. Phillips and Agnew (1953) found from their data that reflection is definitely a learned helping skill, and that it is not commonly used in general interpersonal relationships by nonclinically trained, or even able and mature, people. With the prevalence of communications skills training, however, and the emphasis on listening for feelings, reflection of feelings is becoming more of an everyday occurrence (Allmon, 1981).

It is apparent from the chapters so far that to get clients to express their feelings is an important process goal. While all the basic helping skills of attending, reflecting, and nonverbal encouragement facilitate expression of feelings, Hill and Gormally (1977) found, in a careful study, that probing methods produced more discussion of feelings than either reflection or restatement. Modeling examples by the counselor is another effective method to get client self-disclosure of feeling (Zarle & Boyd, 1977). Thus, many counseling skills are needed to elicit feelings.

The Nature of Reflection

Reflection of feeling is defined as the attempt by the counselor to paraphrase in *fresh* words the essential *attitudes* (not so much the content) expressed by the client. The counselor attempts to mirror the client's attitudes for his or her better self-understanding and to show the client that he or she is being understood by the counselor. The word *fresh* is emphasized because perhaps the most glaring reflection error of the novice counselor is to express the reflection in words already used by the client. In a humorous anecdote, in which the counselor repeated almost verbatim the client's statement, the client's reply was, "What's wrong with the way I said it?" It is preferable to use sufficiently different words with an air of intense interest and effort to understand, such as "You seem to want to make a decision, yet you find it so hard to do so."

The word *attitudes* is emphasized in the definition of reflection in order to make the counselor aware that he or she must be able to grasp the underlying feeling about what is being said, not just the content. Therapy is often likened to a river, with the ripples on the surface corresponding to the content. But more important are the undercurrents—the feelings underlying the content. It takes considerable skill to develop the sensitivity necessary to identify these feelings immediately and to mirror them back as soon as the client has completed his or her statements.

A word of caution about client feelings is worth expressing. A common misconception arising from an emphasis on feeling is that the expression and identification of feelings have in themselves some great intrinsic merit. The conclusion often drawn is that feelings are more important then intellectualizations. Expression of feelings is encouraged by the reflection technique. Its effectiveness, however, seems to reside in the idea that the expression of feeling is a means to self-confrontation, and not an end in counseling.

Feelings are thought by the client to be subjective and not to be trusted. They tell the client of danger when there is no danger, of presence of symptoms when he or she is tired and discouraged. The expression of feeling, therefore, is to make possible the discovery of the idea that underlies or is attached to the feelings. The client should be taught to *trust* the expression of feelings. A person in a panic state, for example, is helped if allowed to express his or her feelings. The air is cleared of smog and, as a result of the clarification, the client can examine and deal with the underlying basis of his or her insecurity.

Individuals, through the aid of their actualizing capacities, are the evaluators of their experience. Feelings do not possess evaluational quality; they are not "right" or "wrong." Ideas, however, possess truth or falsity. But evaluation of thought is only possible after feelings have been clarified. This is why reflection of *content* is unwise in the early stages of therapy, but appears to have real value in later stages. Thus, clarifying feelings leads to clarification of the *ideas* and *experience* underlying these feelings.

Reflection of Nonverbal Experience

Nonverbal behavior of the therapist plays an important role in establishing and maintaining an effective therapeutic relationship. Some kinds of counselor nonverbal behavior facilitate the experience of trust and empathy, while other nonverbal behaviors detract from the relationship. Claiborn (1979) found that counselor nonverbal behaviors were associated with client perceptions of the therapist as expert and attractive. Certain nonverbal behaviors have been found to increase the client's experience of empathy even in the presence of a detracting verbal message (Fretz, Corn, Tuemmler, & Bellet, 1979). It is difficult to specify precisely which therapist nonverbal behaviors are related to counseling effectiveness because the effects of various counselor nonverbal behaviors are related to contextual variables in counseling, such as type of client, verbal content, timing in a session, and client's perceptual style (Hill, Siegelman, Gronsky, Sturniolo, & Fretz, 1981). We suggest that counselors attend to *matching* their nonverbal behavior to that of the client and *maintain consistency* between their verbal and nonverbal messages.

Matching or "pacing" counselor nonverbal behavior to client nonverbal behavior has been found to contribute to establishing rapport and empathy (Maurer & Tindall, 1983). For example, rapport is built as the counselor matches his or her overall body posture and position with the client's position. The counselor may also match the client's breathing, voice volume, rate of speech, speech emphasis, or other nonverbal behaviors to mirror the client's demeanor.

Sharing of Experiences

Actualizing therapy holds that the relationship between client and counselor is a key dimension of the therapeutic process. This relationship may be thought of as a *continuum of personal responsiveness* with *reflection of feeling* at the one end, with *reflection of experience* in the center, and with *sharing of experience* at the opposite end. *Sharing of experience* means the honest effort of the counselor to share her or his own experience with the client in the moment. Thus, sharing of experience is *modeling* for the client and encourages clients to share their experience. The therapist is modeling how to be a person and is not simply a technician mirroring the client's verbalizations. This stance requires risking and a willingness to share with the client the therapist's personal feelings at the moment. The following are examples:

TH: It makes me angry when you let her get to you like that.
TH: I get uncomfortable when you *always* hurt and never let yourself feel any other feelings.
TH: Your intellectualizing is boring me and I am getting sleepy.

Identifying Feelings

In teaching the technique of reflection to new counselors, we found it helpful to list and categorize the nature of human feelings so as to assist the novice in the immediate recognition of the feeling expressed. Reid and Snyder (1947) found considerable variation among counselors in their ability to name feelings expressed by clients. There was high agreement among counselors rated as good, however. This implies that ability to reflect is partly a matter of general counseling skill and experience.

In general, it may be said that feelings fall into three broad categories: positive, negative, and ambivalent. Positive feelings are ego-constructive and self-actualizing, while negative feelings are generally ego-destroying. Ambivalence refers to the presence of two or more contrasting or conflicting feelings expressed or implied at the same time toward the same object. In clinical counseling, it is found that such feelings underlie a great many interpersonal relationships; therefore, it is particularly important for the counselor to spot these apparent contradictions and to reflect them to the client. It is important for the client to see and to accept seemingly contradictory attitudes toward the same person, for this can be a source of great tension. One of the goals of psychotherapeutic counseling is to realize that one can both love and hate the same person at the same time.

The following list gives some examples of labels that fall into the two arbitrary categories of positive and negative feelings.

POSITIVE		NEGATIVE	
Happiness	Self-worth	Guilt	Disgust
Security	Love	Resentment	Antagonism
Gratitude	Optimism	Fear	Rebellion
Self-confidence	Contentment	Depression	Rejection
	Warmth		Hostility

A beginning counselor who can observe and identify common feelings will find it easier to reflect these feelings more quickly and confidently. The ability to sense fine shades of client feeling depends largely on the empathic capacities of the counselor.

Difficulties in Reflecting

Stereotypes.   A common error is made in reflection when the counselor uses a stereotyped introductory phrase, such as, "You feel . . ." This procedure, if it is not varied, will tend to arouse client feelings of resentment and attempts to analyze the process hypercritically. The following variations are suggested:

Use of the word that expresses the feeling; for example: "You were mad (sorry, confused, etc.) when that happened."
"You think . . ."
"You believe . . ."

"It seems to you . . ."
"As I get it, you felt that . . ."
"In other words . . ."
". . . is that it?"
"I gather that . . ."
Inflection—intonation of various words to express the reflection; for example:

CL: It really hurt me to hit her.
 C: It *really* hurt. (Note: This is an exception to the general rule of not reflecting content.)

Timing. Another error that counselors seem prone to make is that of waiting for clients to stop their comments before reflecting. When much content and little feeling are expressed by the client, this is not serious. As counseling develops, however, a great many feelings may come rapidly. This condition often necessitates interrupting the client so as to focus on and emphasize significant feelings. It is also easy to make the opposite error of interrupting clients too soon and completing their sentences for them.

Selection of Feeling. When Rogers introduced this reflection technique, it became associated with the Rogerian label, *nondirective.* A cursory examination of the technique suggested that since the counselor was only repeating feelings that already had been expressed by the client, the counselor, therefore, was not *directive.* A closer scrutiny of this technique reveals, however, that any reflection requires that the counselor *choose* from the verbalization of the client those elements that he or she feels have greatest quality of feeling and are in greatest need of clarification. This means that the counselor, in a sense, is highly direct and confrontative in using this technique.

Porter (1950) made a significant contribution to the use of reflection technique when he suggested that the counselor must learn to avoid the "four common errors of reflection." A paraphrased and illustrated summary is presented below.

Content. "Reflecting content" is an error in counseling that consists of reflecting back client statements in essentially the same words that the client used. When counselors do this, they do not convey understanding but merely repeat blindly what has already been said. Their reflections, moreover, are generally met with denial rather than acceptance.

CL: I've always just considered medicine because my father always dictated to all of us boys what we should be.
 C: You've always sort of considered medicine because your father dictated to you and your brothers what you should be.

A counselor who uses these techniques is fortunate if the first interview lasts over five minutes. The counselor who has a "knowledge-of-acquaintance" in reflecting techniques might reflect in the following manner:

C: You just went along with him since you never thought of disagreeing with him?

This is an attempt by the counselor to get below the surface and to touch on the undercurrent of feeling expressed by the student. The counselor disregards the words of the student in favor of the feelings being expressed.

Depth.   The counselor who fails to respond to the same degree of depth in feeling as expressed by the client is also not reflecting accurately. Some counselors are consistently too shallow in their reflections. Others are consistently too deep, and the reflection becomes an interpretation. An illustration follows:

CL: I want to be an engineer, but I just can't drive myself for four long years without her. . . . I just can't do it. . . .
C: You'd like to be an engineer, but you'd also like to get married.

The reflection obviously is too shallow. A more accurate reflection might have been:

C: It's just too long a grind without her.

Or, the counselor might have reflected:

C: You just wouldn't be able to live without her for four years.

This reflection perhaps is "too deep" and might be met with denial or by a change of subject on the part of the client.

Meaning.   It is also important that the counselor not *add to* or *take away from* the meaning of the client's statement. An illustration of such procedure is as follows:

CL: I just can't see myself as an accountant sitting at a desk all day.
C: You don't think you'd like the idea of having to balance budgets, and making profit-and-loss statements, day in and day out.

It is obvious that the client did not say all that the counselor did. The counselor has read much more meaning into the statement. The counselor might have taken away meaning by a reflection of the following nature:

C: You just don't like indoor work.

To be accurate in reflecting the proper meaning on the surface appears easy, but too often the counselor responds from his or her own frame of reference rather than from the client's frame of reference.

Language.   Experience by many trained counselors indicates that the counselor should always use the language most appropriate to the situation. Here is an example of a poor use of language:

CL: I just seem to be shy with girls. I just can't be friendly.
 C: This inferiority complex seems to be extremely active in these heterosexual relations.

The errors the counselor made in the reflection are mainly overinterpretation and pedantry as well as absence of feeling.

It should be emphasized that although reflections should be accurate, an inaccurate remark may still promote interview progress if clients perceive that the counselor is trying to understand them. For example, the counselor may say, "So you resent your father for doing this?" The client responds, "Oh no, I actually admire him for it." While inaccurate from the client's viewpoint, the remark may still be effective since the client feels compelled to clarify his or her feelings and correct the counselor. The net effect is often further self-exploration.

Types of Reflection

Immediate Reflection.   This type consists of reiterating a feeling immediately after it has been stated by the client.

Summary Reflection.   This involves "tying together" several feelings. This summary method is diagrammed in Figure 5-1. The summary reflection is a method of bringing together in one statement several feelings expressed previously. An illustration is, "From your descriptions of your family relationships, school experiences, and now your new job, you seem to have strong feelings of personal failure in all of them."

Terminal Reflection.   This is a technique of summarizing the important aspects of the entire counseling hour. Terminal reflection may also include certain content material that summarizes the proceedings of the hour.

Reasons for Effective Reflection

It seems appropriate in the discussion of this technique to examine some of the possible reasons for its effectiveness in achieving the goals of counseling. Reflection helps the individual to feel *deeply understood*. Most disturbed clients are defensive and feel misunderstood. When confronted with this technique their fear of feeling misunderstood diminishes. The clarity with which the counselor

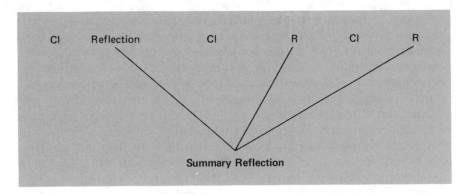

FIGURE 5-1 The Summary Reflection.

reflects their deepest unverbalized feelings can cause disturbed clients to feel deeply understood. Thus, reflection serves a supportive function and is used most effectively in the early and middle phases of counseling.

The reflection technique helps to break the so-called neurotic cycle, often manifested in marital counseling and expressed by such phrases as, "She won't understand me and therefore I won't understand her." The counselor, relying on the reflection technique, helps break this tenaciously held line of reasoning.

Reflection impresses clients with the inference that *feelings are causes of behavior.* Perhaps the most significant contribution that reflection of feeling makes to the counseling process is that it affords a vehicle for conveying understanding of causes. Feelings are elusive and often difficult to control. Frequently we feel that we do not understand ourselves because of the emergence of strange or unwanted feelings. When another human being tries so genuinely to understand us and appears so capable of clarifying for us the elements of our own experience that are cloudy and fearful, we start to value this human being. Reflection serves, therefore, as a clarifying and simplifying function.

Reflection keeps the *locus of evaluation* in the client. Another reason that reflection is so effective is that it challenges individuals to take responsibility for themselves. It subtly suggests that a value system is not something inherent in any experience or object, but that value is placed on it by the individual. Bombardment of the individual with such phrases as "you feel" and "you think" and "you believe" teaches people that they are the evaluators of their own experience and that values are alterable. Clients see that values are judgments made by individuals based upon their experiences. Values are also alterable if and when new experience gives new evidence. The term *locus of evaluation* is helpful here. In the early phases of therapy, clients tend to put the locus of evaluation of their behavior *outside* of themselves in parents, friends, or social groups. Toward the end of counseling, the individual finds that one can place and must place this evaluation of behavior in one's self. Clients learn that they own their feelings.

Proper reflection gives clients the feeling that they have the *power of choice.* A current tendency in our culture has been to shy away from assuming personal responsibility and to trust the "expert." The specialist is expected to tell us how to rear our children, to advise us on marriage or divorce, to choose our career, to advise in matters of love making, budgeting, ad infinitum. In matters of personal concern, the result is a continuous cycle of helplessness. The more the expert is consulted, the greater the feeling of helplessness, the greater the need for further advising. In counseling, the aim should be to create self-direction in the client. The reflection technique along with the lack of advice on these matters encourages the individual to achieve this end of self-help.

Reflection *clarifies client thinking* so that he or she can see the situation more objectively. Reflection technique by its very nature involves an attempt by the counselor to draw out essential elements of the client's conversation for reconsideration. The natural result of such a procedure is to mirror to clients the high points of their thinking, and to enable them to clarify their present situation and to see it in a more objective and focused fashion. Clarification, a technique that summarizes the substance of the client's verbalization, is designed to accelerate client awareness through simplification of their wandering and scattered responses without feeling they are being "pushed."

Reflection helps clients to *examine their deep motives.* When counselors concentrate on the individual's feelings rather than the ideational content of his or her remarks, they are reaching the individual at a deep motivational level. This observation is illustrated by the common question with which all of us have been faced: "Why did you do that?" The answer may have been, "Because I felt like it." People often do things just because they "feel like it." Feelings are manifestations of the needs and drives that compel us to act. Careful scrutiny of our feelings leads us to examine the motivating forces underlying these feelings. This process is illustrated by the comment, "Well, I felt like it because . . ." The word *because* often leads us right to the core motive or experience.

ACCEPTANCE TECHNIQUES

Nature and Value of Acceptance Techniques

This is a simple technique of responding mainly with short phrases, such as "mm-hm," "Yes, go on," which imply attitudes of attention and acceptance. It is employed usefully in the early stages of counseling when much content or narrative material is produced, often without much associated feeling. Acceptance techniques are employed also in the later stages when clients are delving deeply into themselves and bringing out painful material. It is simply a verbalization of the attitudes of acceptance of the counselor that says in effect: "Go on, it's safe, you needn't be ashamed of expressing how you really feel." The values of expressions like, "I see" or "Uh huh" are that they reinforce discussion and provide a bridge between ideas, which gives a smooth flow to the process.

Elements of Acceptance Technique

Simple acceptance technique has at least four major observable elements. The first is simple *attending behavior,* largely maintaining eye contact. Eyes are very expressive for most people and are a key vehicle for counselors to express acceptance and caring. Second is the *facial expression* and nodding of the counselor. The counselor must convey genuine interest in her or his face. The counselor who puts on a feigned expression of interest will be discovered by the sensitive client.

Third, *tone of voice* and inflection tell the client whether the counselor is accepting, even if he or she uses conceptually meaningless vocalizations such as "mm" instead of words. Of course, counselors who speak so quietly that clients must strain to hear them hamper the process by conveying an impression of disinterest. But the counselor who speaks with an overbearing voice conveys an impression of dulled sensitivity to the expressions of the client or is exhibiting his or her own needs for controlling the interview.

Distance and posture are a fourth consideration in acceptance. If the counselor leans over and sits comfortably close to the client, the client will infer a friendly attitude. This conveying of "towardness" as opposed to "away-from-ness" by posture is important, since the former attitude conveys the qualities of openness and sincerity of the counselor. Since many clients are hypersensitive to cues like these, they may interpret the slightest negative gesture of the counselor as rejection or disinterest. Yawning, crossing and recrossing of legs, and grasping the arms of the chair tightly are examples of such negative cues that are easily discerned by the client.

Ellis (1955), in surveying the literature on couch and face-to-face therapy positions of clients, concluded that face-to-face therapy was preferable, partly because acceptance techniques could operate more effectively. In terms of a microcounseling approach, the above acceptance methods have come to be known as attending behaviors (Ivey & Authier, 1978).

STRUCTURING TECHNIQUES

Nature and Value of Structuring

Structuring technique is the counselor's definition of the nature, conditions, limits, and goals of the process. In other words, structuring provides clients with a framework or orientation for therapy. They then feel that the relationship has a rational plan. Structure provides them with a counseling road map and with a dossier of their responsibilities for using the road map, thus reducing the ambiguity of the relationship. Clients should know *where* they are, *who* the interviewer is, and *why* they are there. Thus, the structure of counseling has three elements; the first is implicit in that the very setting and known role of the counselor automatically set limits that are generally understood by the client. The second element, formal structuring, consists of the counselor's purposeful statements to explain and limit the counseling process. The third, or contractual element, is described later in this chapter.

The use of May's analogy (1939) to illustrate the nature of implicit structuring may be helpful: Each person is traveling through life as though he or she were in a boat going down a river. Without the structure of the riverbank, the water would flow in all directions. The banks of the river provide the limiting factors that guide the boat and give it added power to go downstream. Individuals, likewise, are free to make their own choices, but always there seems to be a frame of reference that limits and gives direction to those choices.

Another illustration of the directional value of structuring is provided by a former client: "It was kind of like going down the highway on a foggy night. I drove my own car but the counselor provided the illuminated white line in the middle of the road for me."

The therapeutic value of setting limits can be distilled to the following general principles: (1) limits should be *minimal*, consonant with the security of the client and therapist; (2) limits should be applied in a *nonpunitive* manner; (3) limits should be *well defined* in regard to such things as action, time, and number of appointments; and (4) limits should be structured *at the proper time*. Too early or too rigid structuring may destroy a relationship. Sue and Sue (1977) make the case for structuring when counseling with minority clients, because counselors' unfamiliarity with the client role in counseling may hinder their success.

Dangers of Inadequate Structuring

The counselor who fails to provide structure would be unfair to many of the clients who have no notion of what counseling is all about. In this age of consumer rights and regulations, it is a legal as well as an ethical obligation to present accurately what the client is buying. Curran stresses this point:

> A confused person is likely to approach the first interview feeling a minimum of responsibility for himself and a maximum of fear, insecurity and defensiveness. Continued miscues on the part of the counselor in structuring the relationship seem to cause the client to depend on the counselor and to feel rejected and hostile if the counselor refuses to solve his problems, and finally in defensiveness and fear to flee the interviews and not keep subsequent appointments. (1944, p. 189)

Structuring, therefore, has value in preventing such early misconceptions about counseling as magical cures, fast help, single causes, advice giving, smooth sailing, inevitability of cure, and counselor responsibility. By focusing on the positive learnings and roles of client and counselor and the reasonable expectations of the process, many misconceptions can be offset. This aspect of structuring, by the way, must be a continuous process.

Rogers stated that the structure of therapy can be provided for the individual at the nonverbal level; that is, the client will "get the idea" as he or she participates in the process. This may be true with highly sophisticated clients but does not seem to be adequate for average clients. Ingham and Love, on the other hand, suggest that undesirable insecurity develops when structuring is not provided:

> The patient may at first feel that his task is unorganized and formless and that there are no rules. Then he experiences a strange feeling of helplessness and dissatisfaction. It is as though the therapist did not care what he talked about or how he spoke of it. (1954, p. 81)

Lack of structuring arouses anxiety in clients and perhaps accounts for some counseling failures. It is important, therefore, that the structure be made a *means* to enhance the security of the relationship and not an *end* in itself. Otherwise, permissiveness and acceptance values are lost. Structuring in the beginning phases of counseling must be approached with caution, since there is a danger of conveying a feeling that the counselor has a definite preconceived way of doing things that the client had better follow as an ultimatum. Another danger is that the counselor might convey an impression of how clients ought to feel rather than encouraging them to feel the way they really feel.

Sherman (1945) found that failure to structure, thus leaving the client too much on his or her own resources early in the process, results in strong resistance. A feeling for the right amount of structure for each individual client is a paramount counseling skill. If structuring is done badly, it can be a relationship barrier. Similarly, if it is ignored in institutional settings, the results may be equally undesirable, since the client may build unreal expectations about the outcomes. Structuring has a positive value if it reduces the anxiety of clients who are not cognizant of the dual roles of their counselors or are not aware of situational limits that exist. An example is the counselor who has instructional or administrative relationships with a student. The counselor must point out that these relationships are different from his or her relationship as a counselor, and that authoritarianism will not spill into the relationship.

The counselor's compulsion to structure frequently, to set the client straight, may be a symptom of his or her lack of assurance. Another caution in structuring is the tendency to imply that the relationship will continue with this particular client. It may turn out that the counselor will decide not to work with this client or that the client may not be suitable for this counselor. Hence, the client or the counselor may feel too committed to the relationship if it has been overstructured. Overstructuring can be avoided by matching degree of structure to the conceptual level (need for structure) of the client. Clients vary considerably on need for structure, and the importance of matching intervention method with the person is supported increasingly with data (Stein & Stone, 1978).

Types of Structure and Contracts

Earlier, we described structuring as a technique that defines the limits and potentialities of the process. Paradoxical as it may seem, the provision of clear-cut limits provides the client with permission and power to change. Structuring methods extend to contracting, which is an agreement on how and when counseling goals are to be achieved.

Contracts.   Several theories of counseling use the term *contract* to describe structuring agreements. Some contracts, especially with young clients, take on a formal character. They list privileges extended, responsibilities incurred, bonuses or sanctions, and how and by whom the contract is to be monitored. Contracts have characteristics of *specificity,* that is, clients know exactly what is expected of them, and *feasibility,* meaning it is within the capabilities of clients to carry out the contract. Contracting works most effectively when the client is acquiring or getting rid of a specific behavior, such as smoking or excess eating. The key value of a contractual form of structure is that a counselor knows when he or she has been successful—that is, when clients reach the goals they agreed to work on, and in the way both agreed. Contracts tend to focus on expected *outcomes.*

Time Limits.   Perhaps the time limit is paramount in school and other public agency counseling, in which only a limited amount of time can be given for each interview. The counselor, therefore, must explain at the onset of the interview just how much time is available. We suggest that when time limits are presented, clients very often hasten the therapeutic processes in an effort to accomplish as much as possible in the time available. This suggestion applies to short five- or ten-minute interviews as well as those lasting longer. An example is, "We have forty-five minutes; let's see what we can accomplish."

A second aspect of time limits concerns the time required for the process as a whole. It appears that one of the contributing factors to the success of psychoanalytic therapy, for example, is that the analyst emphasizes very carefully to the patient that the process might take two to three years and will be costly. It is admitted that many clients cannot accept this, but at the same time, for the clients who can, the process seems to be facilitated. The counselor, in similar fashion, indicates that to reach the agreed goals, several sessions will be required. The counselor is careful to point out, however, that no commitments can be made as to specific outcome. For example, a counselor might say, "Ordinarily we get together a couple of times to go over the test data and other material collected, then we spend a session or two helping you plan a specific course of action. In all, it should take four or five hours to get where we want."

In more emotional problems counselors may feel that they do not want to become committed to a long-term therapeutic relationship. Structuring may help them prevent misunderstandings with clients, as the following example shows:

C: We have been talking about "first-aid" methods for a while. Perhaps we had better talk a bit about where we go from here. As you realize, we cannot become committed to a major personality overhaul (pause).

CL: I see, more of a tune-up job then.

In structuring time limits the counselor must guard against being over-anxious for the client by making promises or raising false hope or even by stating that counseling "is a good investment." Promising success violates the ethics of psychotherapy. An optimistic counselor attitude, however, creates client confidence in the process as well as assists an insecure and anxious client to begin working confidently.

Although it is difficult for counselors to make definite long-range time commitments to clients, they should discuss fees frankly and early in the first interview. Phone calls and missed appointments, generally, are billed, since this fact is part of the contract. The counselor who does not charge for long phone calls and uncanceled missed appointments plays into the manipulative client's hands. Also, it is not sound therapeutically because it does not take cognizance of the *reality* of the relationship. A clear contract should help on these issues.

Time-limited or short-term therapy is a popular topic at professional meetings. Most counselors are interested in making the most of their time with clients, but economic pressures are forcing this topic to the front. Health maintenance organizations, for example, which contract with individual therapists or group practices for specific services at fixed amounts with caps on total hours find this short-term model attractive. Garfield (1989) asserts that it is only recently that even discussion of short-term therapy was respectable. This is an active, cognitively based problem-solving activity, an approach that has an integrative quality for counseling theories. Brief time is difficult to define, but it means from four to eight hours contact time. Currently, much effort is going into one-session models of psychotherapy. The research indicates moderate levels of efficacy for limited psychotherapy compared to longer forms, which have not demonstrated any superiority of outcome (Garfield, 1989).

Action Limits.   There are also what might be termed action limits. The counselor does not limit verbal expression, no matter how absurd, unfair, or foolish it sounds; but there are certain feelings that cannot be permitted direct expression in action. Younger clients, for example, cannot break windows or destroy furniture and equipment. They can say they don't like the therapist, but they cannot physically attack the therapist. As Rogers (1942) points out, hurting the therapist may arouse the child's deep guilt and anxiety in relation to the only person who can help him or her. Fear of retaliation and threat of withdrawal of this unique kind of supporting relationship may destroy the possibility of therapy.

Role Limits.   In educational, industrial, religious, or medical settings, we find that the counselor often has dual roles: teacher-counselor, supervisor-counselor, administrator-counselor, minister-counselor, and physician-counselor. This means that these people also have a role of authority in the life of the client, as well as the role of nonjudgmental listener. These roles must be so structured. The teacher, after a hearing, points out to John that he must take certain prescribed courses whether he wants to or not. Thus, one role of the adviser is to maintain the school structure. A foreman, counseling one of his men, cannot permit him to come and go on the job whenever he wishes. A teacher cannot permit a student client to avoid handing in class work. These are limits defined by the role of authority that these people also have.

In situations that make it necessary for the counselor to take dual roles, the use of the "coat analogy" is often helpful. The following is an example of how it may be used:

C: Well, Jack, before we start I want to clarify my role with you. You might say I wear two coats around here—my teacher's coat and my counselor's coat. When I wear my teacher's coat, I have to be evaluating and judging to a certain degree in order to state your progress as a student. When I see you personally, however, in a relationship such as this, I am wearing my counselor's coat. This means that you can feel free to talk about anything you like and I won't hold it against you or make judgments about you. Okay?

Procedural or Process Limits.   If counseling is to be successful, clients must accept the nature of the process. In the first place, clients must accept their *responsibility* for carrying on the major share of the interview. There are certain things they must know to utilize the process most effectively. Ingham and Love (1954, pp. 79–81) suggest six basic process values that must be conveyed to clients in the early structuring remarks and through basic attitudes.

1. "... that it is appropriate and good to investigate ourselves." *This means facing his disturbing problems as much and as fast as he is comfortably able. This value suggests that there are causes of his difficulties that can be known and understood.*
2. "... that it is better to investigate than to blame." *This approach conveys the idea that there is a difference between a "bad" person and the "bad" act. The counselor stresses that he is trying to understand, not blame him. Thus, he will be better able to accept what he discovers within himself.*
3. "... to regard emotion as a real and important thing." *This value stresses the idea that emotions and their free expression are important realities and not signs of weakness.*
4. "... that there must be relatively complete freedom of expression." *The idea emphasized here is that the emotional importance of a topic, not its social acceptability, is the criterion of topic choice. This means that swearing, sex topics, and unconventional ideas are acceptable.*
5. "... the use of investigation of the past in developing an understanding of the present." *This focus on the past is a controversial value among counselors and therapists.*
6. A *series of process* values centering about the client's present view of his world *are often mentioned in structuring. These are his capacity for human relationships, his own individual importance, and his own life values and morals as a basis for further changes through counseling. A keen interest in the client's basic style of life is indicated.*

Structuring Process Values.   It should be emphasized that all of the aforementioned process values need not be made explicit. Clients have differing needs for explanations about how counseling proceeds. Generally, the counselor lets clients bring up their own topics, and as it becomes apparent that they have misconceptions, or feel bewildered, helpless, or dissatisfied with this new experience, the counselor aids them through structuring. The counselor should start counseling on grounds familiar to clients and get them involved in the main job of counseling as quickly and comfortably as possible.

A second important use of structuring as a means of describing the process comes in the *handling of direct requests for advice*. In general, we recommend reflecting the feeling underlying this request first. This often allows the client to continue and to see his or her dependency as a problem. It is often necessary, however, to define this limit, as given by the following example:

CL: Can't we do something about this? The tension is really getting me. Can you tell me what to do? It might help both of us.

C: I can understand how desperate you feel; but we have found that there are certain answers that only the individual can give himself. By working together I think that we can arrive at some answers for you.

Unfortunately, it is easy to give the client a feeling of getting the "brushoff" with a response like this. The anxious, dependent client tends to miss the structuring and reassuring intent of the counselor's response and may interpret it as, "So, you also don't want to help me."

A third use of process structuring is to present to the client the philosophy underlying the method of counseling. Porter (1950, p. 60) gives an example of this method:

> Counselor: "I don't believe I know much about why you are here. The Dean mentioned you some time ago, but I know very little about it."
>
> Frank: "Well, the Dean and Professor R. wanted me to see you. They said you were a good psychologist, and that if you studied me you might be able to diagnose my adjustment. They think I'm not getting along very well and if you diagnosed what was the matter, you would be able to help me."
>
> Counselor: "They think you need some help, and you are trying to do what they wish?"
>
> Frank: "Well, they say I'm not doing as well as I should, and if you studied me, you could say why."
>
> Counselor: "Well, now I'll tell you, Frank, I really haven't had much luck helping students with problems that the Dean thinks they have. I don't know whether I can be of help to you along that line or not. When a student is concerned about some problem that *he* thinks he has, then frequently we can work out something together, but otherwise, I don't believe I get very far. I wonder, quite aside from what the Dean thinks about you, whether you feel there is anything about your situation that is causing you concern?"
>
> Frank: "Well, I don't know—I suppose I don't live up to my ability."
>
> Counselor: "That is something you feel a little concerned about?"
>
> Frank: "Yes, I don't know, I guess I procrastinate; I just don't get things done on time. I don't see why. I've thought about that a lot and tried to analyze it but I don't seem to have helped it."
>
> Counselor: "So you feel you really do procrastinate, and that you've been unable to do anything about it?"

Timing of Structuring

Cardinal principles of structuring are that it is a continuous and individualized process. With some clients who demand more structure or seem to be confused, formal structuring of the process must come early. With others, the formal structuring can come later when attempts to shift responsibility to the counselor are made. With other clients who seem to take to the process easily, a very minimum of formal structuring is necessary in the beginning. In fact, if too many structuring remarks preface counseling, the client may experience them as constricting and annoying. Sophisticated clients expect that the structure will grow out of the relationship rather than be dictated to them in a formal, instructional manner. Day and Sparacio (1980) summarized the basic themes of structures from their survey of the literature. One theme dealt with practical issues such as length and time of counseling, appointments, and other procedural matters. The second theme covered consumer issues such as outcomes, records, costs, risks, rights, and methods. Process issues involved definitions of counseling, how to begin a session, statement of client goals, and role descriptions for counselor and client.

From this presentation the reader may rightly infer that structuring is a controversial issue in counseling practice. Some writers emphasize its value, while others stress its limitations. We have attempted to present various sides of the issue so that counselors can develop a style most effective for themselves.

LISTENING TECHNIQUES

Listening is an active attending process with little or no verbalization. It may seem strange, at first, to give prominence to listening as a technique of counseling. Yet, all the systems of helping skills give listening a prominent place. We believe that therapeutic listening is a technique that must be learned. Perhaps this is so because the ethics of social conversation in our culture discourage silence. Hence, we have learned to become uncomfortable with silences and to regard long pauses as synonymous with a social vacuum. Beginning counselors often feel that when pauses are long they are not doing enough for the client. The appropriate mix of counselor response and listening is one of the most difficult counselor behaviors to learn.

The Meaning and Handling of Client Silence

In evaluating the significance of a pause, the time of its occurrence and whether it was initiated by client or counselor are significant. A long pause initiated by the client early in the initial interview conveys a different meaning to the counselor from one occurring later in the process. Pauses made by the client early in the interview may reflect embarrassment or resistance. As the counseling progresses, silence gradually comes to be a vibrant communicative medium for support, emotional expression, and thought.

In addition, it should be emphasized that counseling interviews are characterized by pauses of varying lengths from a few seconds to several minutes. It is difficult to assess the meaning of all pauses and no attempt is made here to catalog these possibilities. The following are offered merely as suggestions for interpreting and handling interview silences initiated by either counselor or client.

Any discussion of silence requires that recognition be given to two types: negative or rejecting, and positive or accepting. Socially, we often use the "silent treatment" as a form of rejection, defiance, or condemnation. In social situations, when we argue with people we are saying in effect that we respect them enough to want to change them. The negative silent treatment, however, says coldly in effect that the other person is not even worth talking to. Unfortunately, before a proper counseling relationship is established, it is possible for a client to interpret early silence in the interview as being this negative or rejecting type. This is true particularly when clients are still afraid of what the counselor is thinking about them. Appropriate acceptance techniques frequently have a reassuring effect, so that clients feel they do not have to impress the counselor.

A second meaning of silence is that the client or counselor has reached the end of an idea and is merely wondering what to say next. An extended pause may mean, also, that both have lost their way temporarily and that the interview has become confusing to both. The client may realize also that he or she has come to the end of the conversational period and must get down to work. Characteristically, there is an extended silence before getting down to serious work. The counselor can help the client over this hump by saying something like, "It is sort of hard to get down to serious business." The counselor's silence points up dramatically the transparency of small talk in later interviews. If the pause is of this "thought-collecting" type, it is considered wise not to interrupt. Tindall and Robinson (1947) found in study-improvement interviews that this type of contemplative silence accounted for half the pauses.

A third meaning of silence is that of hostility-motivated resistance or anxiety-motivated embarrassment. This is true particularly when the client has been called for or sent in. At first, the client may be waiting cautiously for the counselor to make all the first moves and may answer or comment in short words or phrases followed by a long expectant pause. This kind of silence is an effective client manipulative device.

The pause with a fourth meaning may be the signal that the client is experiencing some particularly painful feeling that he or she is not ready to verbalize, whereas consciously he or she may want to express the feeling desperately. The counselor may say something like, "It is all right if you want to wait until words come along," or, "It seems hard to say what you want at times, doesn't it?" Without pushing the client, the counselor might say, "Perhaps if you gave me some hint where your thoughts are moving, maybe I can help you put them into words." We have facilitated expression in this type of client by handing the client a pencil and paper without comment so that he or she can write what the client wants to say as a starter.

In the resistive type of silence the participants may appear to be engaging in a contest to see who can outwait the other, like children trying to stare one another down. This may be due to a preconceived notion of counseling in which the client expects the counselor to ask questions or has a cautious "wait and see" attitude. This silent response may indicate to the counselor that there is a need for structuring or for a brief exploration of some personal items to get the client talking. The counselor may provoke the hostility-motivated client to talk by making a disarming reflection, "You don't feel like talking just now, do you?" Another way is to ask her or him to interpret the silence, "What do you think has brought this about?" However, the client may infer that the counselor who takes the attitude of, "Well, I'll wait until you decide to talk," or who pauses too long, is rejecting the client.

If shyness seems to be the difficulty, it might be overcome if the counselor starts with some items from the client's life history, for example, "Here we've spent quite a bit of time together and you haven't mentioned your mother (pause)."

A fifth meaning of silence might be labeled as "anticipatory," wherein the client pauses expecting something from the counselor—some reassurance, information, or interpretation. Tindall and Robinson (1947) found that counselors were quite sensitive in assessing and responding appropriately to this type of pause.

A sixth meaning of client pausing is that they may be thinking over what they have just said. In this case interruption of the pause may be inappropriate, since it might destroy the client's train of thought and may throw the interview off the client's main theme.

Finally, a pause may mean that the client is merely recovering from the fatigue of a previous emotional expression. Here again, quiet acceptance of the silence is probably the best approach.

The problem for the counselor in the preceding illustrations might be simply stated as follows: Shall I interrupt the pause or shall I wait and let the client go on? In general, our view is to let the client assume responsibility for going on when he or she was responsible for pausing originally. This avoids interfering with a forward-moving activity. Yet, the counselor must be alert to those situations in which it seems best to support clients over rough places rather than to force them to face their problems, feelings, and responsibilities before they are ready. Problems of handling the negative silence are treated in the following chapter under *resistance*, which will be defined and illustrated. In any case, the counselor is asking himself or herself continually during the silences, "What is going on?"

Values of Counselor Listening

One of our basic assumptions is that listening of the positive and accepting type is a most promising counseling technique. The counselor's silence forces the client to talk. Similarly, being in the presence of another silent person often moves the client's attention to the task at hand—the client's problems. Silence on the part of the counselor then can have the value of focusing responsibility on the client.

A second value, emphasized from research with the Rorschach technique, indicates that introversive persons may be deeply creative individuals, with rich inner lives. They should not necessarily be seen as people inferior to the more socially valued extroverted individual. In counseling, clients discover that they can be silent and still be liked. Perhaps this acceptance of silence in the client gives the less articulate person a feeling of worth and thereby helps people to accept themselves for what they are. By feeling accepted as a shy and quiet person, a client is able then to experience this same attitude toward herself or himself. The following case comments by Rogers suggest the therapeutic value of silence.

> I have just completed the strangest counseling case I've ever had. I think you might be interested in it.
> Joan was one of my very first clients when I started counseling one half-day each week at the local high school. She told the girls' adviser, "I feel so shy I couldn't even tell her what my problem is. Will you tell her for me?" So the adviser told me before I saw Joan that she worried about having no friends. The adviser added that she had noticed that Joan seemed always to be so alone.
> The first time I saw Joan she talked a little about her problem and quite a bit about her parents of whom she seemed to be quite fond. There were, however, long pauses. The next four interviews could be recorded verbatim on this small piece of paper. By the middle of November Joan remarked that "things are going pretty good." No elaboration on that. Meanwhile the adviser commented that the teachers had noticed that Joan was now smiling a friendly greeting when they met her in the halls. This was unheard of before. However, the adviser had seen little of Joan and could say nothing of her contacts with other students. In December there was one interview during which Joan talked freely; the others were characterized by silence while she sat, apparently in deep thought, occasionally looking up with a grin. More silence through the next two and one-half months. Then I received word that she had been elected "woman of the month" by the girls of the high school! The basis for that election is always sportsmanship and popularity with other girls. At the same time I got a message from Joan, "I don't think I need to see you any more." No, apparently she doesn't, but why? What happened in those hours of silence? My faith in the capacity of the client was sorely tested. I'm glad it did not waver. (1951, pp. 158–159)

Apparently the therapeutic value of spending time with someone who understood her and who had faith in her ability to solve her problem was helpful even though little was said.

A third value of counselor listening is that, after a significant expression of feeling, the client is allowed to think and to come up with profound awareness. Had the counselor forced continued exploration or verbalized too much, the awareness might not have followed. The client often uses silence to delve deeply into feelings, to struggle with alternative courses of action, or to weigh a decision. Clients want to feel that the counselor approves of this behavior, and that they are not letting the counselor down by this behavior. In fact, one extreme style of therapy, called the silent interview method, consists almost entirely of this nonverbal type of communication wherein the therapist conveys to the client the therapist's understanding that the client is struggling with deep, difficult feelings. Hence, one value of silence is that it forces depth of client penetration into feelings.

A fourth value of counselor listening is that it reduces the pace of the interview. Often the counselor senses that the client is rushing or that the counselor feels compelled to push too hard. A counselor can reduce the intensity and pace to a more tolerable level for both participants by making the pauses longer. The counselor suggests in effect, "We are not in a hurry; take it easy." Thus, counselor silence in later interviews tends to have a beneficially calming effect on the client.

Pauses can be classified into three types: deliberate (for emphasis), organizational (for transitions), and natural termination (to close counseling). Organizational pauses, in most cases, help most to clarify the subject discussed and prepare the way for information to be given by the counselor.

Difficulties in Using Listening Techniques

In the training of counseling psychologists, we have found that it has been necessary to teach toleration of client silence without embarrassment. To the untried therapist a minute of silence seems like an hour. He or she has, consequently, an overwhelming desire to interrupt the client's thought. One of the errors of reflection is that of completing sentences for the client. Many clients find it difficult to state what they mean precisely without fumbling for words. Therefore, a very common error that inexperienced counselors make is to put words into the client's mouth, or in some way to take the conversational initiative away from the client.

Using listening technique does not mean being passive or uncommunicative, however. There has been a growing conviction among counselors, arising from studies and clinical experience, that the activity level of the counselor is a significant variable in client response and indeed affects whether the client stays in counseling. It is difficult to do conclusive studies on such a variable as counselor activity-passivity; but Heller, Davis, and Myers's (1966) laboratory-type study on effects of interview style suggest that clients verbalize much more actively, rate counselors as more friendly, and continue in counseling when counselors are more active than passive and silent. While these terms need more definition to be useful as guides to counselors, such evidence contradicts long-standing views that interviews should start with low structure and a more passive stance to allow the client to do more projecting and talking.

One of the most difficult aspects of using the listening technique is keeping silent when the client wants to talk. A greater proportion of client talk, however, is not necessarily an indicator of a more effective working relationship or greater client awareness. The relationship between insight and talk ratio is inconclusive.

Carnes and Robinson (1948) found a strong relationship between client talk and amount of client responsibility assumed for the discussion unit. (The discussion unit is the verbal exchange between client and counselor on a discrete subject.) When clients felt primarily responsible for interview progress, they talked more. It is interesting to note also that Carnes and Robinson found that the stronger the counselor's lead, the less the client talked. The general conclusions of their study are that the causal relationship between desired interview outcomes and amount of client talk are not clear, and that it is not possible, therefore, to use the amount of client talk as a measure of counseling effectiveness.

LEADING TECHNIQUES

General Principles and Values of Leads

The term *lead* is used with two meanings. One usage refers to the extent to which the counselor is ahead or behind the client's thinking. Another view concerns the extent to which the counselor directs or influences the client's thinking. Counselor questions, for example, would have high influence compared to the accepting vocalization "mm." Silence would have a lower impact or lead.

Leading in counseling means working together, where the counselor's remarks seem to state the point he is ready to accept. It is analogous to passing a football down the field so that the receiver's path intersects the flight path of the ball at the same time. All techniques can be rated according to degree of lead involved, but in the present discussion the topic will be limited to general leading as a technique by itself.

Using Leads

Three general usages of leading are recommended. One principle is to lead *only as much as the client can tolerate* at the present level of ability and understanding. Enough old material must be mentioned to form a bridge of understanding to the next new idea. A lead too far ahead of the client generally arouses resistance to counseling. Similarly, too little lead may annoy clients who feel that the counselor should carry more of the responsibility for the interview talk.

The second general principle of leading is *to vary the lead*. The amount of lead changes from topic to topic or within a discussion unit so as to match the pace and lead of the client.

A third principle is *to start the counseling process with little lead*. For example, begin the counseling process with relationship techniques that have low lead, until the relationship is well established. Then increase the lead as needed with information and interpretation, which are useful in developing awareness.

The *indirect lead* may be used to help clients elaborate upon a topic of their choice. Examples are, "Would you explain that a little more?" "How do you mean that?" This type of lead is used also in the form of general questions to start an exploration, such as "What would you like to talk about today?" "Is there anything more you would like to discuss?"

The *direct lead* indicates the area of discussion desired from the client. Examples of the direct lead are: "Tell me more about your father"; "Suppose we explore more fully the idea of teaching"; "What do you think that means?" Asking the client a question, whether rhetorical or for information, is a means of shifting responsibility to the client. Conversely, if the client asks many questions of the counselor, it may indicate more than a desire for information or interpretation; it may mean the client is expressing a need to shift responsibility to the counselor.

Interpretive techniques that are described in Chapter 7 employ various degrees of lead. The concept of lead is introduced in this chapter, however, to emphasize that some degree of lead is always present in the relationship techniques that the counselor uses. Even silence is a leading technique, since lack of verbal response on the counselor's part causes the client to make a judgment about the significance of the material just presented. Thus counselors, through their manipulation of the pauses, often are responsible for the direction of the interview.

REASSURANCE AND SUGGESTION METHODS

Nature and Value of Reassurance

One relationship technique that has wide utility for conveying support is reassurance. In Chapter 7 the concept of support is discussed as a necessary ingredient of the counseling relationship. Reassurance is essentially a type of reward that has a reinforcing effect on behavior and builds expectations for future rewards. The counselor suggests directly, or in effect, "You are a capable person; you can be consistent; you can be reasonable; you can be organized; you can feel better; you can solve this problem."

Reassurance also is a process of fitting counseling to the client's present belief system. Reassurance encourages exploration of new ideas or tryout of different behaviors. In this capacity reassurance is a temporary expedient to keep the client in the relationship, like string and baling wire used to hold structures together until more solid or productive work can be done. Reassurance also prevents fragmentation of the client's ideas, even though eventually the client may want to change his or her maladaptive responses.

A second value of reassurance is the means it provides to reduce anxiety and insecurity directly. Although anxiety in the proper amount is a positive motivating force to keep the person in counseling, excess amounts interfere with the therapeutic process. Reassurance tends to keep the anxiety generated by the counseling process itself under control by assuring clients that they don't have to explore feelings too quickly. This use of reassurance is particularly valuable in controlling anxiety outside the relationship, for example, over weekends and vacations. An example is offering simple suggestions to a mother who is having problems with her child so that weekend crises are lessened.

A third value of reassurance is the reinforcing effect it has on new patterns of behavior. It is often difficult to launch a new course of action, even after significant insights have been achieved. The client often feels discouragement, leading to loss of confidence. An example is the student who is attempting to improve her failing grades. Reassurance in the form of praise for her attempts, assurances that she will pull through the temporary setbacks, and the encouragement of confident attitudes generally help her to retain or regain her new behaviors.

Using Reassurance

The *approval* or *acquiescence remark* is one means of reassurance. Its purpose is to give the client some feeling of security about the ideas or feelings he or she is expressing. Expressing approval of the client's remarks tends to have a reinforcing effect also. An example is:

CL: It seems that people resent being criticized or told they are wrong.
 C: That's right; a very interesting observation and a good rule about personality.

This technique goes beyond acceptance; it is actual agreement with the client. Though generally reassuring, it may be hazardous, because clients may feel they cannot change position without admitting error. Thus, the approval technique tends to have the unfortunate effect of rigidifying the client's thinking. The client may be communicating feeling on a different meaning level also, so a reassuring counselor response may be disruptive.

The counselor who suggests that there are other ways of thinking and acting builds expectations of success in clients. For example, the counselor assures clients that they can change themselves and that counseling can be an effective means to help them change.

Prediction of outcomes describes the consequences of counseling or psychotherapy over the following few days. Avoiding sweeping predictions, the counselor makes a limited forecast about how the client is likely to feel between conferences. An example is: "We've been talking about your problems in a more intensive fashion. You will probably find that you will be more uncomfortable and moody the next few days. Don't be alarmed, because this is part of the process. You will be able to handle it all right."

Postdiction of outcomes is a related reassuring technique. An example is, "It is my guess that during the last few days things have been tougher for you to handle. We opened up many sensitive areas last time that have upset you during the week. Is this correct?" Another example is, "Perhaps you were disturbed by our session last time, but this is a normal part of the process." The reassuring value of such comments comes from the client's impression that his or her behavior makes sense to the counselor and is predictable.

The *interview conditions* tend to be reassuring. As we pointed out in our earlier discussion of support, it is the acceptance, structured limits, attention, affectional warmth, and outward signs of friendship in the counselor that have a powerful reassuring effect. This is true particularly with children, whose behaviors can often be drastically changed through the reassuring effect of emotional support. Thus, meeting specific emotional needs of the client is one of the key uses of reassurance.

Factual reassurance can be given to the client who feels his or her problem is unique. When the client knows that many other people suffer from the same feelings, the fearful bewilderment may subside. Related to this point is the reassurance that the problem has a solution and that the cause of the difficulty is known. Thus, people can tolerate anxiety and annoying symptoms when they know that they are, very likely, temporary reactions to their basic problems. Clients also feel reassured that they can reach specific objectives, such as achieving an educational goal, formulating a vocational plan, getting better grades, or saving their marriages.

Often, the counselor's reassurance of his or her clients that they do not have to feel ashamed, guilty, or alarmed about their problem helps. The client can feel that the problem does not have to be viewed moralistically, but as a personal problem to be solved in an objective way.

Reassurance that the best of help available to science will be given to a client is an often successful means that the counselor can employ to reduce the client's anxiety about the efficacy of treatment. Sharing diagnostic and prognostic formulations with the client when they are favorable is a very convincing type of reassurance.

Reinstating defenses is another psychotherapeutic "first-aid" method. Clients may be using a defense, such as vigorous sarcasm, to handle their hostilities. In the course of counseling, such a client sees the inappropriateness of the extrapunitive tendencies. But the client has not worked them through sufficiently, so he or she develops incapacitating migraine headaches that appear to be manifestations of intrapunitive hostility. Clients are better off if they are "given back" their former defensive mechanisms through being encouraged to express their hostilities more outwardly—the social consequences of which are less severe than the personal consequences of repressed hostility.

A *support system* is an important outcome from a supporting relationship. While this is partly a goal to replace the supportive counseling relationship, it is also an important coping skill to have for future problems. Counselors can help their clients to identify and use their support network. Who are the significant people in a client's life? What differential functions do they perform—nurturance, information, motivation, pleasure, constructive feedback? How is the client using the network? What alterations and additions does the client need? A network is especially useful in crisis situations, so we do our clients a great service through helping them to identify, assess, use, and develop a personal support network.

Using Suggestion

Suggestion is a powerful supportive tool when used in the context of a helping relationship. We need to recognize that we are giving suggestions in subtle ways all the time. While the counselor gives direct suggestions under conditions of high client receptivity, the goal is to teach clients more creative imagery so that they can perform self-suggestion, or autosuggestion, on their own initiative. Several conditions make the use of suggestion possible to improve client functioning. The prestige and attributed power of the counselor is an influential beginning. A relationship of trust and confidence is a second positive variable for suggestion. Having the client at ease, relaxed, calm, and receptive is an essential condition. The counselor's soft, calm voice aids this state of receptivity. Under these conditions, telling clients that they are calm and relaxed, yet alert and energetic, makes them even more receptive to natural and sincere suggestions that they are, for example, competent to pass an impending examination, confident in social situations, able to remember names, or able to curb their appetite for sweets. They imagine themselves able to do these things in the future also, and with the same confident, competent, self-regarding attitude. The emphasis is on having positive qualities, not on the removal of negative images. Then it is suggested that clients can do this imaging on their own initiative. They can develop this state of relaxed alertness or "flow" by themselves.

The reader might ask whether the methods just described are applications of hypnosis. There are similarities between suggestion and hypnosis, since the latter is primarily a hypersuggestive state induced by more direct and formal methods than those described above. Being ready for positive suggestions is a kind of trance state, but it is much lighter and more limited than traditional hypnosis. Because of their manner, language, and status, counselors have the power of suggestion, and they need to become more aware of it and to develop more explicit methods to use that power constructively for client development.

This suggestion method has great potential for helping clients to function at higher levels of effectiveness and pleasure (Barber, Spanos, & Chaves, 1976).

Limitations and Cautions

Limitations of reassurance methods are mentioned in the following paragraphs to acquaint the student with the fact that reassurance is a two-edged sword in many ways. It can be most helpful when utilized properly as a reinforcer in the situations described and most detrimental when used indiscriminately.

Reassurance is a technique that is particularly vulnerable to misfiring. Reassurance is so easy to use that there is a temptation to be overliberal. Direct verbal reassurance is a vehicle so common in everyday human relationships that it may be stated fairly that reassurance is much overused in counseling. A frequent misuse of reassurance, for example, is in false concealment of the true nature of a serious situation. This is an ethical problem as well as a procedural concern.

Reassurance is used crudely in the approach that "everything will come out in the wash." The "just relax, everything will come out all right" attitude and the old aphorisms, such as "every cloud has a silver lining," serve only to create resentment in clients.

Reassurance might be interpreted by a very disturbed person as artificial and insincere sympathy. Reassurance, at best, is a temporary expedient and the counselor must be reconciled to the possible slowing of progress if he or she uses it. There is the obvious limitation that the whole relationship can be put in jeopardy because subsequent events do not bear out the optimistic predictions of the counselor.

Reassurance has the additional liability of promoting a dependency relationship between client and counselor. The periodic need for reassurance is a type of substitute satisfaction for real accomplishment. The responses reinforced by reassurance tend to become fixed learnings, and the client feels a strong need to get reassurance from this particular person. Some clients use reassurance as an excuse not to change their behavior.

If clients interpret reassurance as agreement, they may limit themselves in the sense that they will feel guilty about changing their behavior or experimenting with new methods of viewing their problems. In other words, they may feel trapped in their present efforts and may think that they can't find any solutions to their problems.

It has been stated earlier that reassurance is most valuable in supporting the anxious, distressed client. It can be grossly misused if given to the client who is already overly aggressive or self-confident. Thist type of client needs discouragement of her or his often insensitive, rigid, egocentric behavior, rather than support for it.

Use of suggestion has some liabilities for the client. In a suggestible state the client can be influenced easily; so he or she would be vulnerable to an unethical practitioner. Even ethical counselors need to be fully aware of their power when the client is in a suggestible state. Counselors must see that this power is not abused; there must be no unwarranted influence on client values or behaviors.

TERMINATING SKILLS

The effective termination of counseling is as important for successful outcomes as the establishment of the relationship. How neatly the counselor "settles the dust" or "ties up the package" determines the ease with which clients can assume complete responsibility for themselves and the extent to which their progress toward their goals can be determined.

Since the problems and procedures for closing interviews and changing discussion units during the counseling process are related to techniques for terminating, these are considered together in the following discussion.

Terminating a Discussion Unit

A discussion unit can be closed by the summary reflection described earlier, wherein the counselor ties together the loose ends of several related ideas. The net effect of this summary is to give a feeling of closure and progress to the client, whereupon the client generally proceeds to another topic.

A second device for ending the discussion unit is a *capping technique*. This consists of shutting off the flow of talk or feeling in such a way that the client does not stop talking or feel rejected. Frequently the counselor senses that the more the person delves into feelings, the more uncomfortable he or she becomes or the more dissociated he or she seems to get. When the counselor feels that clients' defenses are not sufficiently functional to protect themselves, he or she helps clients regain their defensive armor through capping techniques. The counselor does this with the hope that it is a temporary expedient and that the client will be more ready to attack the conflict at a later time.

Capping techniques consist of *changing the subject* to something less intense. The subject can be changed back to a topic previously discussed, the original symptoms, or a new and less loaded topic. Reducing the *length of counselor lead* and the general *pace* of the interview often reduces the client's discomfort, resistance, or undesired feelings toward the counselor. The counselor can help to decelerate the pace by *pausing* longer and more frequently. In order to cap exploration that has become too intense, he or she can *reduce the frequency of interviews*. It is well known in counseling and psychotherapeutic practice that the intensity of the relationship varies directly with the frequency of interviews per week. The counselor, for example, may suggest meeting every two weeks instead of once a week. Sometimes reassurance that there is plenty of time to work through the problems helps to take feelings of pressure off the client. Increasing the amount of *counselor talk* has a "shutting off" effect on client communication, thus preventing deeper exploration of problems.

There may be times, also, when the quality of the relationship is such that the counselor can use *direct interpretation* to terminate a topic. An example is, "You are getting quite disturbed about this. Suppose we drop it for a while and go on about your plans after graduation." Clients may need further explanation for changing the subject and reassurance that they can come back to this topic at a later time.

Terminating an Interview

The counseling literature contains very little information about the nature of skills for terminating an interview. Yet, most counselors would agree that it is important that the interview be drawn to a definite close and not left with the client feeling that nothing has been accomplished. Beginning counselors report that ending an interview is one of the most difficult tasks they face. The following are some "tricks of the trade." The reader should note that detailing of such methods can be carried to the point of misleading absurdity. Ordinary honesty and natural courtesies common to our culture are the best guides.

Reference to time limits is one natural way to remind the client that the hour is up. No matter what the length of the interview, it is important that the counselor inform clients at the beginning of the interview that they have a fixed length of time. In a clinical setting, a forty-five- or fifty-minute period is usually standard. In other settings, such as public schools, a much shorter time may be more appropriate. Interview time is a matter of agency policy, case load, and the purpose of the interview.

Generally, it is felt that a minimum of forty-five minutes is needed to deal with clients' most pressing problems. This allows clients a few minutes for "warmup," wherein they move slowly into the main content of the interview and pick up the loose threads from the preceding session, and gives them a few minutes at the end of the hour to "pull themselves together." This is especially necessary after a therapeutic counseling session that delved deeply into feelings.

In school counseling, however, time and case load pressures often force the problem to be stated and analyzed in interviews of ten or fifteen minutes. In any case, as long as the time limit is set, the successful conclusion of the interview can be more assured. At the end of the interview, for example, the time limit can again be brought up by such a statement as, "Our time is nearly up; when would you like to come back again?" or "Well, that does it for today," or "It seems we've reached the end of the hour." This provides an easy transition to the calendar, the door, or the receptionist.

Summarizing is a second means of terminating the interview. This can be done by the counselor, the client, or as a collaborative act. When the counselor sees that the interview is drawing short, he or she can summarize the essential factors of the interview. Again, the terminal reflection technique can be used if the counselor is disposed to summarizing the essential feelings that have been expressed by the client during the interview. A topical summary to reflect the major content of the interview also would be in order.

From the counseling literature, it appears that client summaries are used widely. The counselor asks the client for a summarization of key feelings and ideas as follows: "Tell me how you think the situation looks now," or "Now suppose you tell me what you think you have accomplished in this interview."

The counselor usually precedes the collaborative summary with such a phrase as, "Suppose now we take a look at what we have done today. As I see it, we have said . . . Perhaps you could state how you have seen it."

Reference to the future is a third and graceful way for the counselor to terminate an interview; at the same time, an indication of his or her desire to maintain the relationship is made by the use of a statement that would refer to subsequent meetings with the client. Such a statement would be as follows: "I see our time is about up today. When would you like to come in again?" or "Would you like to make it at the same time next week?" or "I have Thursday at three and Friday at two open. Which would you prefer?" It is important to end in a warm positive tone, following the setting of the exact date and time, with a parting phrase such as, "Fine, I'll be expecting you then at two next Friday," rather than a doubtful "Then you'll come next week at two?"

Fourth, *standing up* is frequently a persuasive technique for ending the interview. With particularly difficult clients, such as obsessive-compulsive people who do not wish to terminate the contact, it may be necessary for the counselor to stand up as a more blunt means of indicating that the interview is finished. This can be done gracefully at a "low point" before the client has a chance to delve into another topic of conversation. In more formal situations, especially with adults and at the end of first interviews, the offering of the hand as a parting gesture is helpful, too.

Subtle gestures are a fifth category of cues to close the interview. While most counseling contacts close naturally at the fixed time, some clients continue to chat on. Most counselors develop certain gestures to indicate that the interview is to be terminated and that it is time for the client to depart. Examples of counselor cues that even the most obtuse client can perceive are to glance at his or her watch or desk clock and lean forward. It should be mentioned that the counselor should be alert to and evaluate the wisdom of common devices such as fidgeting, distractibility, irritability, and shuffling desk papers to cue clients that the hour is up.

Ushering clients to the door and opening it for them could aid a graceful and prompt departure. Ordinary courtesy demands that the counselor rise with clients and walk to the door with them. This makes it much easier for the client to leave than it would be if the counselor left the whole burden for terminating the interview upon the client.

Summary notes are a sixth useful aid to terminating interviews. In certain types of counseling where decisions are being made, some counselors find it useful to jot down notes while the interview is in process. They may have another sheet with carbon between so that at the end of the interview the client is handed the carbon of the counselor's notes. This is especially important in career planning, where data are profuse and significant. Many counselors feel that the client will remember the interview if they make a concrete summary of the salient features of the interview. Other counselors encourage clients to make their own notes, thus encouraging independent action.

The *"homework"* or *"prescription" method* can be utilized as a terminating device. An example would be: "Before you leave I'd like to suggest a little 'homework' . . ." or "I wonder if you could give some thought to these questions that have arisen in our conversation today (mention items)." Specific tasks such as taking dance lessons, baking a cake, seeking out a friend, or trying a new behavior are assigned also. Counselors from most theoretical positions rationalize homework of some kind to encourage generalization of interview learnings to real life.

Related to the activity approach is the *arrangement for tests or occupational reading* if the problem is primarily educational or vocational. This is another natural way to end the interview. It should be stressed that endings are arrived at cooperatively and by counselor suggestion; they are not coerced.

It is important that the interview end on a note of positive planning so that clients know exactly what they are going to do. If the counselor is ambiguous about plans or expectations concerning the client, he or she may arouse insecurity and confusion.

One of the rules in terminating an interview is to start *tapering off* in intensity a few minutes before the scheduled end. A counselor should never let a client leave without allowing the client to pull himself or herself together again and to reduce the feelings stirred up by the interview. Yet this very condition makes it difficult for the client to leave. Clients tend to relax when they feel the pressure is off and often become very spontaneous. They will try to detain the counselor with new and interesting material. Counselors can hold to their structure, or they can use the "five-minutes-more" technique. This technique is ushered in as follows: "I have a few minutes between the interviews. I'll share them with you. You may have five minutes more if you wish. Then we will have to close for today."

The counselor may decide that the material coming out is so significant that it warrants using the "extra hour" device if by chance he or she has the next hour free. One might say, "I have this next hour free; I gather this is a significant area for you. Suppose we take more time, then, while the matter is still hot." This hour may be extremely productive since the usual defenses may not be prepared for it. The client is likely, therefore, to be exceedingly spontaneous. It is our experience that material often comes out in this hour that very likely would not arise in interviews for which the client is more "set."

One danger of the "extra hour" technique should be mentioned. Once an extra hour has been given to a manipulative client, he or she may try to get extra hours again and again. The approach would be "You helped me then—why don't you again?" It may also result in the client remaining superficial in the first hours as his or her defenses get reset. In any case, this technique is useful if used with discretion.

Regardless of the device used to end the interview and to get clients out the door, the interview should end on a positive and friendly note. The counselor should not adopt a cold, neutral attitude, in an effort, perhaps, to avoid deciding for clients whether they will continue and when they will return.

Techniques for terminating interviews should be planned in advance and should be friendly, definite, and collaborative. These characteristics are necessary to help the client feel wanted, focus on accomplishment, know what to do next, and realize that he or she collaborated in solving the problems.

SUMMARY

The techniques for implementing the basic principles of relationship in the preceding chapter have been classified into eight categories—opening, reflecting, accepting, structuring, listening, leading, reassuring, and terminating. Each method has its unique values as well as limitations for creating the optimal kind of relationship necessary for the development of insight and self-actualization. In the next chapter, we will discuss the assessment phase of counseling, in which the nature of the client's difficulties is explored and a treatment plan is developed.

CHAPTER 6

Assessment and Diagnosis in Counseling and Psychotherapy

ISSUES OF DIAGNOSIS

Diagnosis in the medical sense means a process of examining symptoms, inferring causes, integrating observations and fitting them into general categories, and, finally, pinning specific labels on disease entities. Psychiatric or psychological diagnosis is a similar process of ferreting out causation and of naming symptom clusters—for example, schizophrenia, reading disorder, or anxiety state—but there is no clear-cut psychological analogue to a medical concept like diptheria or thrombosis, which have definite etiology. In these diseases it is mandatory that diagnoses precede treatments.

In the psychological arena, however, the diagnostic process takes on several meanings and is not as clear as it is in medicine. Psychological diagnosis generally means an assessment of the problems or present status of the client, probable cause of the difficulty, possible counseling techniques to solve the problems, and a prediction of counseling outcomes or future client behavior. A diagnostic formulation may also include a survey of the strengths of the client.

Psychodiagnosis has meant historically a descriptive *classification*, or taxonomy of problems. This process is often called *differential diagnosis*, wherein the clinician attempts to differentiate one category of problems from another. Various differential classification schemes have been devised for different types of dysfunctional behavior. The American Psychiatric Association's *Diagnostic and Statistical Manual of Mental Disorders* (called DSM-III and DSM-III-Revised) is the most widely used diagnostic classfication system.

DSM-III-R

DSM-III-R (1987) consists largely of descriptions of more than 200 distinguishable mental and psychological disorders classified into 18 major diagnostic categories (Table 6.1). Specific diagnostic criteria are provided for each category. These criteria are intended to provide the counselor with a way to evaluate and classify each client's problems.

The DSM-III-R (1987) diagnostic system is "multiaxial" in that it consists of an assessment on five axes. *Axes I and II* comprise the clinical syndromes (i.e., schizophrenia, affective disorders, mental retardation) and conditions not attributable to a mental disorder (i.e., uncomplicated bereavement, parent-child problems) that are a focus of treatment. The counselor documents any current physical disorders or conditions of the client that are potentially relevant to the understanding or treatment of the client on *Axis III*. *Axis IV* provides a seven-point rating scale for identifying and evaluating the frequency and severity of psychosocial stressors relevant to the assessment and treatment of the client. Such information is important because the person's prognosis may differ when a disorder develops as a consequence of marked stress than when it develops after minimal stress. *Axis V* permits the counselor to gauge the highest level of adaptive functioning that the client has been able to maintain for a period of time during the previous year. Adaptive functioning is defined as a composite of three major areas: social relations, occupational functioning, and use of leisure time.

Field studies with the DSM-III and DSM-III-R yielded reliabilities for diagnostic descriptions higher than those formerly obtained with the DSM-II system. This apparently resulted from the increased comprehensiveness and specificity of the DSM-III's diagnostic criteria. It should be noted, however, that the reliabilities for specific classes of personality disorders were comparatively low. Since personality disorders are characterized by maladaptive and enduring responses and since they are less acute than other classes of disorder, it is harder to distinguish normal from abnormal in unambiguous terms. Nevertheless, the DSM-III-R is proving to be a more useful counseling tool to classify atypical behaviors.

The DSM-IV is scheduled for publication early in 1993. The principal changes are increased compatibility of diagnostic categories with the ISD-10 (International Classification of Disorders), incorporation of recent research findings, and inclusion of new categories, such as mixed anxiety/depression. Some controversial categories, such as self-defeating personality disorder, are eliminated. New categories, such as cognitive impairment disorders, are included and distinctions between organic and inorganic bases for cognitive disorders are eliminated. Opinions of those working with the revision indicate that the categories have moved farther in the biological direction.

Counselors working in private practice, community mental health agencies, or health service settings are increasingly being required to classify client problems according to the DSM-III-R taxonomy for all cases on which they may collect health insurance. The DSM-III-R is the best tool for accomplishing this

TABLE 6-1. DSM-R CLASSIFICATIONS.

The DSM-III-R Axes I and II Diagnostic Categories

Disorders Usually First Evident in Infancy, Childhood or Adolescence: disorders usually evident in infancy, childhood, or adolescence (i.e. developmental disorders, disruptive behavior disorders, anxiety disorders, eating disorders, gender identity disorders, tics, elimination disorders, speech disorders).

Organic Mental Syndrome and Disorders: include conditions such as deliriums, dementias (i.e. Alzheimers), intoxication and withdrawal symptoms related to intake or cessation of alcohol and other drugs, and organic disorders associated with physical conditions (i.e. dementia associated with a brain tumor).

Psychoactive Substance Use Disorders: includes symptoms and maladaptive behavioral changes associated with dependence or abuse of alcohol and other drugs.

Schizophrenia: involves the presence of characteristic psychotic symptoms such as delusions, hallucinations, or characteristic disturbances in affect and in the form of thought.

Delusional (Paranoid) Disorder: features the presence of a persistent, nonbizarre delusion that is not due to any other mental disorder.

Psychotic Disorders Not Elsewhere Classified: includes psychotic disorders (i.e. brief reactive psychosis) that cannot be classified as any of the above categories.

Mood Disorders: includes mood disturbances accompanied by a full or partial manic or depressive syndrome that is not due to any other physical or mental disorder (i.e. manic episode, major depression, bipolar disorders).

Anxiety Disorders: involve symptoms of anxiety and avoidance behavior. Includes panic disorders, phobias, obsessive compulsive disorder, post-traumatic stress disorder, and generalized anxiety disorder.

Somatoform Disorders: features disorders with physical symptoms suggesting physical disorder for which there are no demonstrable organic findings or known physiologic mechanisms, and for which it is presumed that the symptoms are linked to psychological factors or conflicts.

Dissociative Disorders: involves disturbance in the normally integrative functions of identity, memory, or consciousness. Examples are multiple personality disorder, fugue, amnesia, and depersonalization disorder.

Sexual Disorders: includes paraphilia disorders characterized by arousal in response to sexual objects or situations that are not part of normative arousal-activity patterns and that may interfere with the capacity of the reciprocal, affectionate sexual activity, and sexual dysfunctions characterized by inhibitions related to sexual desire, excitement, orgasm or resolution.

Sleep Disorders: features chronic sleep disturbances related to the amount, quality or timing of sleep (i.e. insomnia, hypersomnia, sleep-wake disorders) or an abnormal event occurring during sleep (i.e. nightmares, sleep terrors, sleep walking).

Factitious Disorders: characterized by physical or psychological symptoms that are intentionally produced or feigned.

Impulse Control Disorders Not Elsewhere Classified: includes disorders related to loss of impulse control (i.e. dysfunctional anger, kleptomania, pyromania, pathological gambling).

Adjustment Disorder: involves a maladaptive reaction to an identifiable psychosocial stressor (i.e. business, health, or marital difficulties) which leads to impairment in occupational (or school) functioning, social activities or relationships, or symptoms that are in excess of a normal and expectable reaction to the stressor.

Psychological Factors Affecting Physical Condition: applies to any physical condition to which psychological factors are judged to be contributory (i.e. obesity, tension headaches, pain, nausea and vomiting, ulcerative colitus).

Personality Disorders: refers to behaviors or traits that are characteristic of the person's recent and long-term functioning since early adulthood and which cause either significant impairment in social or occupational functioning or subjective distress (i.e. dependent, paranoid, antisocial borderline, avoidant, schizoid).

V Codes for Conditions Not Attributable to a Mental Disorder That Are a Focus of Attention or Treatment: includes conditions such as academic problems, malingering, marital problems, noncompliance with medical treatment, uncomplicated bereavement, phase of life problems, occupational problems, parent-child problems.

task. We have found also that the Millon Clinical Multiaxial Inventory (MCMI) is a useful aid in this diagnosis, for it gives scores for both Axis I (clinical syndrome) and Axis II (personality disorders).

Millon (1981) suggests that there is a parallel between the immune system of the body and the immune system that exists between the personality disorders and the clinical syndromes. The body's immune system determines whether or not physical viruses and bacteria can be counteracted with ease. Likewise, the same interactive pattern exists between the personality disorders and the clinical syndromes at the psychiatric level. Here it is the client's personality pattern of coping skills and adaptive flexibilities of Axis II that determine whether or not the individual will master or succumb to the symptoms of Axis I. Axis II thus becomes the foundation for the individual's capacity to function in healthy or predominantly enduring ways. Thus, the personality disorders have come to have a more enhanced role in the development of DSM-III-R.

ADVANTAGES AND DISADVANTAGES OF DIAGNOSIS

The main purpose of diagnostic thinking in counseling and psychotherapy is to plan differential treatments for clients. Shaffer (1976, 1986) and Beutler and Clarkin (1990) have been principal exponents of this view. The rationale for this kind of thinking is that the counselor must help clients and therapists decide on an appropriate treatment approach based on the nature, breadth, and severity of a client's problems. No one counseling approach is equally efficacious for all behavior changes.

Diagnosis has been a controversial concept among many mental health professionals. Those who favor diagnosis point to its advantages. Taylor (1983) observes that, in spite of the apparent conceptual and practical limitations of diagnosis, the process can aid therapists in assessing problem behaviors and in selecting appropriate interventions for treatment. Nelson and Barlow (1981) note that selected features of DSM-III are useful for suggesting additional information about the problem behaviors, the controlling variables, and the course of particular disorders. Additionally, diagnosis may be useful in suggesting treatment strategies that have been effective with similar problems. A standard diagnostic system also provides a framework for research into various treatment approaches.

Others caution therapists to consider some of the possible pitfalls involved in diagnosis. Meehl (1973) has described the limitations of diagnosis when it does not lead to differential treatment for clients with different types of problems. Also, reliability can become a problem if therapists are not adequately trained to use the diagnostic classification system or if the system itself poorly defines its diagnostic classifications. Critics also note that counselors can become overly preoccupied with the client's history and neglect current attitudes and behavior. The diagnostic process must be rooted in the individual's current psychological milieu to be effective.

Losing sight of the client's individuality is another difficulty in the diagnostic process (Herbert, Nelson, & Herbert, 1988). For example, the therapeutic psychologist may possess much comparative data from test and case history data but may lose sight of the subtle distinctions that make the client a unique person responding in his or her own individual style to common social stimuli.

Since diagnosis has been associated historically with pathology, there is a further danger that the clinician will be preoccupied with the client's pathology to the exclusion of client strengths. Stiver (1986) suggests that the very descriptions of diagnostic categories such as "Histrionic" and "Dependent Personality," found more frequently in women than in men, may reflect assumptions and misunderstandings about what behaviors are considered healthy and unhealthy in women. She believes that women in American society are socialized and encouraged to be emotionally expressive and to put others' needs ahead of their own. However, women who closely adhere to their gender-role socialization are vulnerable to becoming diagnosed as unhealthy for their patterns of behavior.

Other links exist between diagnostic classification systems and gender-role assumptions. Stiver (1986) suggests that the DSM-III Axis II categories associated more often with women than with men (e.g., histrionic personality, dependent personality, borderline personality) all have characteristics that involve interactions with others and intense expressions of affect. In contrast, the types of pathology more typical of men (paranoid personality and antisocial personality) involve symptomatology that distances rather than engages with others. Thus, diagnostic categories reflect a potential for pathologizing certain aspects of behavior that are normative for women and men who have been well socialized. Women are apt to express their conflicts and concerns more in emotional relational terms and men need to defend against the intensity of their own feelings and yearnings for connection. The client's interpersonal context is largely ignored by the current diagnostic system. It is important to consider systemic aspects of a diagnosis such as histrionic personality because the intense emotional expression "in reaction to minor crises" suggests that it is relatively unprovoked or unexplained by the social context. This behavior may represent an exaggerated expression of affect in order to be heard. Additionally, it reflects a woman's compliance with the expectation of how she needs to behave in order to engage another person to respond to her in some fashion, even if it is in an angry or uncaring fashion. Gender-role and sociocultural influences underlying diagnostic and treatment approaches are an important issue that will be discussed further in Chapter 12.

Rogers (1951) was particularly adamant on the question of diagnosis. He claimed that diagnosis was a detriment to counseling. Rogers did not ignore the significance of behavior causation, but he claimed that the meaning of behavior lies within the particular way clients perceive their reality. Clients, according to Rogers, are really the only ones who can know fully the dynamics of their own perceptions and behavior. In order to change client behavior, therefore, a perceptual change must be experienced. Just getting more intellectual data about the problem is not likely to help change that client's behavior very much. In fact, the

DSM-III-R diagnostic system excludes many problems for which people seek help.

Rogers also felt that a diagnostic point of view tends to pull the counselor away from a client frame of reference and to cause him or her to become too preoccupied with intellectualizations about the client. Certain counselors would be prone to this overdiagnosing because of their particular judgmental attitudes. Rogers claimed, further, that therapy is diagnosis in the sense that it is the client who is experiencing the process and really does the diagnosing in terms of formulating his or her own experience in meaningful terms.

Another more subtle social danger that Rogers observed (1951) was that too much emphasis on diagnosis sets up the consequent temptation to make evaluative prescriptions. If clients rely on the expertness of the counselor, there is the potential danger of social control and influence where the counselor specifies the goals and makes the value judgments on whether a behavior is appropriate or inappropriate, mature or immature.

RESOLUTION OF THE DIAGNOSIS ISSUE

We find it difficult to escape the fact that the therapeutic psychologist must make some decisions, do some therapeutic planning, be alert for pathology to avoid serious mistakes, and be in the position to make some prognosis or predictions. It seems that the therapeutic psychologist is forced to play a delicate role between the Rogerian position of withholding judgment and attempting to stay within the client's frame of reference as much as possible and at the same time trying to understand the client diagnostically.

It is proposed that we simultaneously understand diagnostically and understand therapeutically. This is done through a process of hypothesis or hunch making. Although counselors may decide to avoid some of the formal diagnostic steps, they nevertheless develop a series of hypotheses about such questions as: "How serious is this behavior?" "What would be the most appropriate intervention approach at this time?" "How far should I attempt to go?" "What seem to be the basic dynamics (defenses, needs, symptoms, environmental pressures) that are operating?" "What will the likely outcomes be?"

We consider diagnosis and assessment to be *an ongoing orientation* of the therapist, occurring on both content and process levels. Assessment is not simply an activity occurring in the initial interview. Rather, we continuously gather information and hypothesize about the client's current difficulties and needs throughout the initial and subsequent interviews. Information is gathered about the client in circular feedback both from the content of what is said and from the process feedback received by the therapist from each therapeutic intervention. The counseling interview itself becomes a process of "hypothesis formulation and testing, a process of approximation and correction" (Pepinsky, 1954, p. 198).

How clinicians conceptualize this hypothesizing process depends, in part, on their underlying theoretical assumptions about the interaction between the individual and the context in which he or she lives. Therapists will tend to use assessment "templates" that indicate the client behaviors they consider most important. For example, a behaviorist may use a functional analysis to determine why particular behaviors occur. The behavioral therapist attempts to discover the stimulus conditions that evoke, reinforce, and maintain behavior with the environment. The therapist then determines whether a response needs to be added, weakened, or strengthened. Cognitive therapists may pay particular attention to irrational beliefs and cognitive distortions. Analytically oriented therapists will explore drives, conflicts, and defenses. Phenomenological counselors may attend to the unique world view of the client and the congruence of their inner feelings and expression and differences between the ideal self and actual self. In contrast, systems therapists focus attention on interactional patterns and sequences between client and therapist and pay less attention to the client's internal conflicts.

Therapeutic assessment methodologies will differ depending on the therapist's assumptions about what constitutes health and beliefs about how people change. Cognitive therapists may be more inclined toward client self-monitoring of antecedents and consequences surrounding a particular behavior. Analytic therapists may utilize projective methods, such as the TAT, to help assess client motivations and defenses. Phenomenologically oriented therapists may pay close attention to their internal feelings in relation to the client. A systems therapist with an intergenerational approach may draw a family genogram in the assessment.

We believe a key purpose of assessment is to provide information to both the client and therapist about the nature of the client's difficulties and to guide the selection of appropriate interventions. In actualization therapy, assessment should increase client awareness of different aspects of himself or herself. The actualization therapist generates hypotheses and predictions by engaging the actualizing level of the client and exploring the functioning of the facade level, manipulating level, character level, and core level with a neutral, accepting attitude. The process of testing boundaries among the various awareness levels within the client and with the therapist provides assessment feedback about the nature of the client's internal and external boundaries. The assessment process itself provides an opportunity for the client to begin the process of change by creating more permeable boundaries.

GUIDELINES FOR ASSESSMENT

We would like to suggest that integrative assessment attempts to answer several important questions. What are the client's presenting problems? How do these problems fit into a comprehensive picture of client functioning? How does the client's unique history influence his or her experience of and manner of dealing with the problem? Does the client's problem have a function in the client's larger systemic context? What is the therapist's experience of the client and his or her interpersonal style? How the therapist uses this information to select appropriate intervention strategies will be discussed in Chapter 7.

The Client's Presenting Problems

Generally, the therapist wants to gather a description of the client's difficulties. There may be a variety of presenting problems that the counselor and client must sort through, clarify, and prioritize in importance to the client. In gathering information about the nature of client difficulties, it is important to ask for specific information from the client. Such information usually includes a detailed description of the situations in which the problems occur. The therapist notes antecedents, consequences, intensity, severity, frequency, and duration of the problem behavior. The therapist also examines the client's thoughts, feelings, and behaviors when confronted with difficulties. The effect on others of the client's behavior may be important information for determining how one's social context may reinforce or contribute to the individual's difficulties. For example, a client who reports feeling uncomfortable loneliness may be asked to discuss situations when the loneliness is most likely to be felt. The therapist can explore how these situations seem to be related to the development, experience, or expression of loneliness. The therapist may ask how the client experiences loneliness—the particular cognitions, feelings, physiological indicators, and the behavioral manner in which loneliness is manifested. The therapist will note what happens as a consequence of the person's loneliness and its effect on others. For instance, a lonely individual may not make eye contact with others. Consequently, others do not initiate conversation and the client may label himself or herself as unlovable or uninteresting. It is often helpful to identify exceptions to the typical patterns that emerge. The therapist can use this information to identify for himself or herself and the client exceptional times in which the client shows the ability to control the problem behavior. Such information both identifies client strengths and defines the problem in situation-specific rather than global terms.

The therapist also wants to identify the personalized meaning of the problem. In what particular way is this a problem for the client? To follow our example of loneliness, some clients may fear their loneliness will hold them back in their jobs, whereas others may define themselves as being dull, ugly, and, consequently, fear they will never be able to establish close ties with others. Although it may be useful for the therapist to imagine all the concomitant difficulties typically associated with loneliness or other problems, it is essential to discover the unique way in which the individual defines the problem. The intervention strategies developed by the therapist are likely to differ depending on the client's unique framework for understanding his or her difficulties.

As the therapist attempts to understand the client's presenting difficulties, it is important to assess the client's previous attempts to remedy the problem. As the strategic therapists note, there are a variety of instances in which the client's attempts to deal with his or her problems paradoxically make them worse. In other words, the solution becomes the problem. For example, the person who is lonely may feel depressed because he derives little comfort or pleasure from the people in his life. When asked what he does when he feels down, he indicates that he wants to tell some of his acquaintances from work how he is feeling but believes he should always try to be cheerful. He tells his acquaintances in a casual manner, "I've been feeling down, but I'm better now," when in fact he is still feeling quite miserable and alone. He does this both because he feels that if he works at being cheerful he will feel better and because he does not believe that revealing how he feels will be acceptable. However, if his acquaintances do not pick up on his depression, he becomes more discouraged. He may seek another solution such as giving off an air of being socially active so that people will think he would be a desirable friend. Ironically, just as his acquaintances misunderstood his statements about depression, they may interpret the statements about his social life as indicating he doesn't need or want any more friends. Information about ineffective solutions is useful in revealing how the client may contribute to the problem and may also prevent the therapist from suggesting strategies that have already proven ineffective with the client.

It is important to assess client expectations of themselves and the therapist. During initial sessions, in particular, the therapist and client need to discuss the role each will take in the counseling. The therapist, for example, may indicate she will act as a coach and will assign homework, but it will be the client's responsibility to follow through with the assignments. Client expectations about their ability to change and their faith that the therapist can help them are also important to clarify. As we mentioned in the previous chapter, research indicates that such client expectations are strongly associated with the effectiveness of therapy.

Assessment of presenting problems also provides a baseline of data about the client's problems that can be used to evaluate therapeutic progress. Assessment data from sources such as self-monitored problem frequency, severity, and duration or from psychological test results can be compared with subsequent data to assess and evaluate client progress and the effects of various treatment strategies. This evaluation helps the practitioner decide whether to continue or modify the treatment plan or intervention strategy.

Comprehensive Picture of the Client's Current Functioning

An integrative assessment attempts to view the client's symptoms within a comprehensive understanding of the client. It is important to assess the client's current functioning beyond the feelings and behaviors immediately presented by the client as a problem. Lazarus's Multimodal Assessment (1980), termed BASIC ID, provides a useful way to remember seven important assessment areas: the client's (1) behavior, (2) affect, (3) sensations, (4) imagery, (5) cognitions, (6) interpersonal relationships, and (7) drug use. The counselor's understanding of the client's difficulties might change through assessing further aspects of the client's current functioning. If we apply Lazarus's BASIC ID model to our client who is presenting loneliness as a difficulty, the counselor would assess the client's behavior when lonely, feelings of isolation and depression, body sensations of tiredness or anxiety, images of himself as ugly, self-defeating thoughts, lack of friendships, and ways he might be avoiding painful feelings through mood-altering drugs. The revelation of drug use in this assessment would probably make an important difference in treatment approach. The client might not mention heavy drinking because he or she does not believe that the drinking is a problem or that it relates to interpersonal problems and depression. However, the counselor might decide that the alcohol abuse needs to be treated before the loneliness can be effectively resolved. Such information about drug abuse might not be offered unless the client included it in his or her presenting problem description.

Developmental assessment is another aspect of assessing the client's current functioning. Various developmental models exist for understanding client growth. Authors such as Erikson, Gould, Levinson, Perry, Fowler, Gilligan, and Ivey have described frameworks for understanding individual developmental growth patterns and issues. It is important to consider differences in qualities of male and female developmental experiences. Gilligan (1982) and others have discussed how the developmental processes of males and females differ. Male developmental processes stress separation, individuation, and the achievement of independence and autonomy as the hallmarks of maturity, whereas the female experience of maturity is organized around issues of responsibility for other people. Other researchers have described specific tasks related to development in career roles (Campbell & Heffernan, 1983; Super, 1957, 1990; Shein, 1978) or couples and family relationships (Carter & McGoldrick, 1988).

Generally, we find it useful to assess the client developmentally within the individual life cycle and the family life cycle. This information often provides a perspective on why the client's symptoms are appearing *at the current time* rather than six months ago or a year ago. Symptom onset may be associated with family developmental crises of addition and loss of family members or family role status. For example, it might be important information for understanding our lonely client if we know that his children have recently left home to enter college. Such information might help us to hypothesize that he is experiencing a major normative change in the family life cycle that typically brings about the kinds of feelings he experiences and requires reorganization for both the individual and the family system. Or, if our lonely client were a 19-year-old college student, we might hypothesize his loneliness might be related to some of the separation and differentiation the student was experiencing as he became more independent from his family and old high school friends. If our client were a woman returning to college after being a homemaker for 15 years, a developmental perspective might help us understand her sense of being different and "off time" compared to the students that surround her. Although developmental perspectives do not tell us about the unique experience of each client, they can become frameworks for adding hypotheses that may prove valuable to understanding our clients.

Client functioning must also be understood in terms of its cultural context. The normative experiences of individuals as well as the unique ways they experience difficulties are nested in their cultural frameworks. Depending on the situation, the experience of self-efficacy is likely to be different for a majority group individual than for a member of a minority group. Typical developmental experiences are also likely to differ for individuals of different ethnic or cultural groups. Family life-cycle variations of multiproblem poor families and Mexican-American families have been described by Colon (1980) and Falicov and Karrer (1980).

Again, it is important to assess the unique meaning of the client's difficulties based on cultural context. This context may vary widely within a particular ethnic group. One working-class black family will differ from another working-class black family. And white clients are as ethnically variable as ethnic minority clients; the working-class Italian woman whose parents were immigrants will be culturally very different from the upper-middle-class Italian woman whose great-grandparents were immigrants. Cultural influences may play an important role in understanding the client's difficulties. Certainly, an individual from a sexual or ethnic minority group who is fired from a job by a majority employer may have a different understanding of her experience than a fired person who shares her employer's ethnic and cultural background.

An effective clinician should know something of the society and culture from which clients come, including characteristic ways of expressing anxiety and conflict and expectations and fears of helpers. Background studies in the social sciences, personal exposure to minority communities, and clinical supervision by minority mental health providers will help the counselor learn about culturally conventional ways of complaining and seeking help and a group's concepts of normal and abnormal behavior. Such knowledge will help the counselor to know whether to expect the members of a cultural group to be relatively expressive or inhibited, to perceive typical communicative codes, and to understand types of complaints that carry special cultural significance. For example, AIDS in North America, mental illness among Chinese, and afflictions owing to witchcraft in African peoples hold special culturally salient meanings. These types of complaints may demoralize or change the client's life course because of social stigmas attached.

Counselors can adopt an ethnographic approach to cross-cultural encounters, which begins with techniques to develop trust and rapport and then moves on to discovering the complaints and explanatory models of the client. It is important to elicit the client's explanatory model of his or her problems so that the counselor may understand the problem's idiosyncratic meaning to the client. To understand the client's model of distress, it is important to seek the client's perspective about its etiology, reason for onset at a particular time, experience of distress, and expected and desired treatment. If it is culturally appropriate, the counselor may ask family members or interpreters to serve as key informants to understand the communication in light of its cultural significance. The counselor thus draws on insiders' knowledge to reformulate questions that clarify the presenting complaints and draw out the client's narrative. This mini-ethnography can assist the counselor to pinpoint culturally salient roles and client expectations about the counseling process.

Brown (1986) has provided several guidelines for cultural assessment. She suggests gathering information regarding age cohorts, religions raised in and currently practicing, degree and meaning of religious orthodoxy, family history in regard to ethnicity and participation in ethnic culture, generations from immigration (where appropriate), languages spoken in the parental home, family history for client's name and any symbolic meanings of name, family roles of women and men, class backgrounds and education of parents, class and cultural differences between parents, and information about the consequences of gender membership in one's family of origin. For individuals who come from any kind of stigmatized or oppressed cultural background, it is important to determine the meaning given to deviance by the family of origin. The woman or man whose culturally oppressed family copes with oppression by emphasizing compliance and assimilation is likely to respond very differently to her or his own deviation than is the person from a family where difference was given positive connotation by means of cultural identification or separation from mainstream culture. Issues of ethnicity will be further discussed in Chapter 12.

An assessment of current functioning should also include an assessment of client strengths. It may be helpful to know that although the client is experiencing loneliness, he feels that he is learning to become successful at his work or avocation. Assessing strengths is helpful to the client because it helps pinpoint specific problem areas and situations and disrupts global self-deprecating labeling such as "I'm a complete failure." Assessment of client strengths gives the counselor valuable information about personal resources that the client may be able to draw upon during the counseling process.

The Client's Unique Developmental History

History taking by the counselor can add an important perspective in understanding how clients experience and manage their problems. We suggest that counselors in most settings will need to solicit general information about the client's background. Information about the client's educational, work, health, social/developmental, marital and family, and sexual history as well as previous counseling experiences are considered important. Among ethnic minority clients, it may be helpful to explore their acculturation experience if they are a first- or second-generation minority, as well as the evolution of their sense of their own ethnic identity.

The therapeutic psychologist is interested in learning about the client's development over time. Information about how developmental issues have been managed, including tasks such as emotionally separating from one's family of origin, establishing a sense of identity, a career direction, close friendships, and making decisions regarding one's purpose in life, provide a more complete picture of the client. Brown (1986) suggests guidelines for identifying gender-role expectations as well as the consequences of gender-role compliance or deviance.

We are often interested in information about the client's family of origin. Information about the client's parents, siblings, and extended family reveals family themes and patterns that are being continued by the client. Family "scripts" or themes can be identified by exploring the larger family context and development.

For example, family themes often are apparent when the use of alcohol is traced through the family tree or the incidence of cancer is followed. More subtle patterns also emerge such as patterns of emotional cutoffs, family attitudes, and roles. Current client attitudes about work, marriage, money, independence, conflict, or other important issues may reflect family patterns. More will be said about this in our description of the use of genograms later in this chapter.

We believe that clients' unique views of themselves and the world can often be traced to their developmental histories. Wachtel and Wachtel (1986, p. 19) write that "early experiences are seen as crucial not because they are somehow stamped into the psyche in an almost indelible way, but because they *influence the kinds of later experiences the person will have. . . .* Later behavior and experience show the effects of such traumas indirectly, in the particular way the person encounters, interprets, and (partially) masters a lifelong series of developmental tasks." Information about the client's history can help clients to understand the "reasonable" manner in which they came to acquire what has now become dysfunctional thinking and behavior. For example, a college student who reported difficulties with dating found that he held self-doubts based on experiences he had in junior high when he was teased for his prepubescent appearance.

Client developmental histories can also provide information about client strengths and skills that have proven helpful in managing previous difficulties. Clients can be helped to recall resources from within and outside themselves that were helpful in the past and might prove helpful in their current difficulties. An individual might remember a helpful self-affirmation or a strategy for building a support system that could be utilized in the current situation. In the same respect, clients are sometimes able to remember and describe skills that they lack and now need to learn in order to overcome adversity.

The Client's Systemic Context

We believe it is important for therapists to hypothesize about the possible function of the client's symptoms for the client's larger systemic context. There are times in which a family system as a whole might be needing the client to be symptomatic. For example, a middle-school student caught shoplifting may appear to be a young juvenile delinquent. Closer examination of the student's family system may reveal that the student's parents are in constant conflict and only get along well together when they are focusing on how to "straighten out" their problem child. In such a system, a child who cares about his parents is likely to continue to steal until the parents find another way to get along without their child acting out. The therapist's view of the child as well as his or her therapeutic formulations are likely to differ if the therapist understands the function of the child's symptom for the larger family system. In this situation, as in many others, the larger social system's operation unintentionally makes the patient's symptom necessary. The therapist needs to look beyond the family to examine how other systems, such as schools, extended family, government programs, or other interlocking systems, might be either maintaining the problem or of assistance in resolving the problem. Child abuse, for example, is a situation in which treatment strategies will need to be systemic, involving a network of school, agency, and counseling personnel.

Dysfunctional interpersonal patterns such as triangulation, family projection, and persistent dysfunctional communication often reveal the manner in which the client's symptomatology is connected with the larger family patterns.

The Therapist's Experience of the Client

The therapist's experience of the client provides an important source of process feedback in assessment. The therapeutic relationship in many ways can become an "enactment" of how the client behaves with significant others. The manner in which the client uses "I language" with the therapist, sets boundaries, manages difficulties, takes interpersonal risks, and shows awareness of thoughts and feelings reveals important information that can be used to hypothesize about the nature of the client's difficulties and resources. The counselor's experience of transference and countertransference, which we discuss in Chapter 8, can lead to important information. For example, a counselor's own countertransference response to an ethnic or sexual minority client may reveal unconscious feelings and attitudes about members of different groups. Examples of feelings might influence the counseling process include prejudice toward such clients, guilt about being "privileged," or unusual interest in the client's background. Counselors sometimes get confused about how much of client behavior is a response to counselor behaviors. However, counselors under training with supervisors who view interviews through video or live observation can learn to identify important elements of the client's self-presentation and interpersonal style.

In the actualizing model, the assessment process reveals information about the client's various subsystems or levels as well as the permeability of the client's boundaries in interpersonal relationships. By engaging with the actualizing level of the client, the counselor is able to discuss and experience the facade level or defensive functioning of the individual. Information about the character and manipulating levels of the person is often provided through the client's developmental history report as well as behavior with the therapist. The empathic process of seeking to understand the "unique person behind the symptoms" often leads clients to reveal something of their core-level experiences to a therapist whom they trust.

An assessment formulation must be made before the therapy proceeds to the next stage of treatment, since treatment goals and intervention plans must be based on the formulation. The integration of assessment information requires a process of developing a description and explanation of the client's problems that will be used as the basis for developing a therapeutic plan. The therapist is interested in linking the client's presenting problems to the client's own personalized meaning of the problem, unique developmental history, family system interactions and in formulating explanations that hypothesize about why the client has become symptomatic at this particular time.

ASSESSMENT METHODS

A variety of assessment tools are available to the therapeutic psychologist. The choice of tools will depend on factors such as the theoretical orientation of the therapist, his or her training and experience, the nature of the client's difficulties, and factors related to the agency or service delivery setting. In this section, we wish to highlight some of the tools utilized in assessment. We have selected examples of methods that represent a spectrum of clinical practice. We have not included many other tools, such as role playing, that are both effective interventions and assessment tools.

Intake and Client Histories

A client history is a systematic collection of facts about the client's current and past life. This history may take many forms, depending on the style and preference of the counselor or therapist and the type of problem situation. In some settings, client histories are taken as "intake interviews." An intake interview is often an initial interview that is viewed as primarily informational and is conducted by someone other than the therapist assigned to see the client. The information is summarized by the intake worker in writing and passed along to the therapist. In other settings, counselors conduct their own intake interviews.

The authors have found that it serves the best interests of the client to collect some information on a systematic self-report form and to supplement this with data offered by the client in the course of a statement and elaboration of the problem. It is important not to let concern for collecting systematic data interfere with establishing an effective helping relationship.

Counselors may supplement interview data with other methods of data collection. While some counselors use brief, structured questionnaires, others ask clients to write autobiographies, keep journals, write poetry, and draw time graphs marking key life points along a time continuum. It is often most helpful to use such methods when clients describe themselves as good journal writers, or poets, so that the method does not become an arduous task for the client.

Circular Questioning

Circular questioning is a method of interviewing based on principles of circularity underlying systems theories. Circular interviewing was first elaborated by a group of Italian therapists known as the "Milan team" (Selvini Palazzoli, Boscolo, Cecchin, & Prata, 1980) and has subsequently been described by various writers (Hoffman, 1981; Penn, 1982; Tomm, 1984a, 1984b, 1987a, 1987b; Fleuridas, Nelson, & Rosenthal, 1986). An underlying assumption of this questioning method is that the manner in which a specific event is reported by a client is influenced by the wording and tone of the therapist's questions. A circular interview is oriented toward identifying the "patterns that connect" persons, actions, contexts, events, ideas, beliefs, and so on in recursive or cybernetic sequences. When the questions of the therapist are formulated to reveal these recursive connections, both the client and the therapist are able to develop a more systemic understanding of the problematic situation. As the context in which the client's problem is embedded becomes clearer, constructive alternatives for managing or eliminating the difficulties emerge.

Patterns of Therapeutic Questions.   Tomm (1987a, b) has identified four patterns of therapeutic questioning that can be utilized in client assessments and interventions. Tomm's circumplex model categorizes types of therapeutic questions based upon their underlying *intent and assumptions.* (See Figure 6.1.) An intersection of these two basic dimensions (therapist intentionality and therapist assumptions) yields four quadrants, which may be used to distinguish four basic types of questions.

According to Tomm, one basic dimension for *differentiating* questions, represented by the horizontal axis, is a continuum regarding the intended locus of change that lies behind the question. At one extreme of this continuum is a predominantly *orienting intent* (left quadrants of Figure 6-1), for change in the therapist, and at the other end is a predominantly *influencing intent* (right quadrants of Figure 6-1), for change in clients.

The second major dimension for differentiating questions, represented by the vertical axis, has to do with varying assumptions about the nature of mental phenomena and the therapeutic process. At one extreme of this continuum are

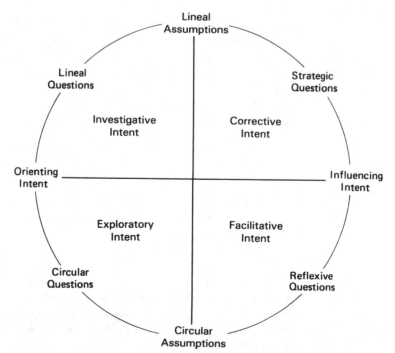

FIGURE 6-1   A Typology of Therapeutic Questions. Adapted from Tomm (1985).

predominantly *lineal* or cause-and-effect assumptions (top quadrants of Figure 6-1), and at the other, predominantly *circular* or cybernetic assumptions (bottom quadrants of Figure 6-1).

Questions of Orienting Intent. According to Tomm, the most common intention behind the questions asked by a therapist is to increase therapeutic understanding by eliciting client responses that will enable the therapist to understand the client's unique experiences and generate clinically useful explanations regarding his or her problems. Thus, the purpose for many questions in the early parts of an interview is to orient the therapist to the client's unique understanding of the problem rather than to expect client change. *Orienting questions* guide the therapist in developing an understanding of the client's unique situation and help to establish client rapport.

The first quadrant of *orienting* questions Tomm refers to as *lineal questions* because they are based on lineal or "cause-and-effect" logic and they have an investigative intent. Lineal orienting questions ask clients to describe and explain their problems. These questions are concerned with "who, what, when, where, how, how much?" and elaboration from the client (why, how come, in what way?). For instance, these questions may ask about sequences of behavior "After you felt rejected, what did you do?" or may connect thoughts, feelings, and actions such as, "When you feel depressed, what are you thinking about? What do you do?" A therapist often begins a session with a sequence of lineal questions. The focus of these questions is to determine the precise nature of the problem and to focus on the meaning or function of the problem in the context of the client's system. Tomm hypothesizes that the type of question asked is likely to have an effect on both the client and the therapist. Although lineal questions provide some useful information for the therapist, Tomm believes that these questions can set a judgmental tone to an interview as people may think there is a right and wrong response and may blame themselves or others when asked to attribute causes to their behavior. The therapist may also be drawn from a neutral stance into a judgmental role.

The second quadrant of *orienting questions* are referred to as *circular questions*. These questions have an explanatory intent and seek information about recursive interpersonal connections. They focus on behavioral effects or on differences between people. A behavioral effect question might, for example, ask, "When you are feeling depressed, how do your co-workers treat you?" An example of a difference question would be, "When you are depressed, do your co-workers treat you differently from how your wife treats you?" Difference questions may also explore differences over time (i.e., between past and present, past and future). For example, "Are you feeling more isolated since you've returned to school?" "How do you think your feelings of isolation might change after you graduate next year?" It is important to ask these questions concretely. The potential hazard with these questions is that the enquiry may drift into areas that seem irrelevant to the immediate needs of the client.

The effects of circular questioning are often very beneficial. As the therapist seeks to identify and understand recursive interactional patterns, clients become more aware of the circularity of their interaction. This increased awareness may free them to approach their difficulties from a fresh perspective. For instance, through a series of behavioral effect questions, the client begins to see how his depressive behavior triggers the withdrawal of his family and friends. The client realizes that it is not simply the family and friends' distancing that further activates his depression but also his depression that activates their withdrawal. He may then learn to interpret others' actions differently and act differently himself when his friends withdraw from his depression. Descriptive circular questions also reveal important information about situations when people act differently from their usual style—when a typically calm person becomes anxious, or when a typically optimistic person expresses worry as well as the context that elicits such behavior. The effect of circular questions on the therapist is to increase his neutrality and his capacity to accept clients. This acceptance itself has healing potential in the therapeutic system by countering the immobilizing effects of blame on self or others.

A specific version of circular questions, known as gender questions, has been developed by Sheinberg and Penn (1991) to help individuals and couples explore gender norms and gender ideals. These questions move clients from examining their current norms of what it means to be masculine or feminine toward the relational consequences of changing these norms. For example, after specifying the current norms, a couple might be asked hypothetical questions such as, If a man is frightened or dependent, can he show it to his partner without risking her loss of esteem? If you show the feelings you keep silent, will your partner think less of you? If you change your ideas about being a man or woman, do you think it will affect your sexual performance? Additional questions examine the modeling influence of their parents' gender norms and the potential for establishing new norms in the future.

Circular questions are also useful in orienting the client from an individualistic perspective to a systemic perspective. For example, notice the change of perspective as the counselor elicits descriptions about monadic, dyadic, and triadic processes, as described by Terry (1989).

PROBLEM DEFINITION QUESTIONS

Monadic: What is the problem?

Dyadic: Who else thinks this is a problem? What would he or she say is the problem? Who was the first (second, third . . . last) to notice there is a problem?

Triadic: If your (partner, mother, father, child, other) were here today, what would he or she say your (partner's, mother's, father's, child's, other's) view of the problems would be?

SYSTEM RESPONSIVENESS TO CHANGE QUESTIONS

Monadic: If this problem were to disappear, what would you hope to do that you are not able to do now?

Dyadic: If this problem were to get better (or worse), who would be the first to notice? Who would be the happiest (saddest, most relieved, most surprised) if the problem improved? How would this relationship change?

Triadic: If your (a significant other) were here today, what would he or she say your (a different significant other) would hope you would be able to do, if this problem disappeared?

These circular questions elicit information about the interpersonal consequences of change, explore the client's ambivalence about change, and suggest which system members would be allies in change and who might be adversely affected by a change in the client's situation. This kind of information provides a broader perspective from which the counselor may select treatment interventions.

Questions of Influencing Intent.   In the course of assessing the client's situation, occasions arise when the therapist may wish to *influence* the client's beliefs or behaviors. Rather than making statements, the therapist may choose to formulate questions that are liable to trigger therapeutic change. *Strategic questions,* the first quadrant of influencing questions, are stimulated by corrective intent. The therapist tries through his or her questions to get clients to change and begin to think or behave in ways the therapist believes are more constructive. Strategic questions tend to have a constraining effect on clients. The constraint may be of two forms: (1) to not do something that the therapist thinks is contributing to the problem and (2) to be limited to do what the therapist thinks the client ought to do. Categories of strategic questions include confrontational questions, leading questions, attributional change questions, and others. For example, an attributional change question might be, "If you thought that he were confused rather than 'out to get you,' how would you respond differently toward him?" The effect of strategic questions on the therapist is to orient him or her toward an oppositional stance with the client.

The second category of influencing questions are *reflexive questions.* Reflexive questions arise from a facilitative intent and are based on circular assumptions about the nature of the therapeutic process. Whereas lineal and circular questions are primarily descriptive and designed to better the therapist's understanding of the client, reflexive questions are interventive in that they both gather assessment information and are designed to influence clients to change their understanding of their difficulties. The therapist designs questions that he or she hopes will trigger clients into finding new solutions on their own. Tomm describes various categories of reflexive questions including questions that introduce clarification, expectations for the future, embedded suggestions, and others. For example, the therapist might ask a question which clarifies by drawing distinctions or suggesting metaphors, i.e., "Is he getting more like a porcupine: the closer you get the more prickly he becomes?" "When you are crying, is it because you are frustrated at not being understood or do you cry because you feel sad?" A future-oriented question might explore the anticipated consequence of behavior, i.e., "If you continue in this pattern for the next five years, what do you expect will be the result?" An embedded suggestion question might include a subtle reframing of the client's perspective such as asking an anorectic client, "When did you *decide* to stop eating?" The effect on the client is generative. Clients may first become confused but then begin to reframe their self-understanding. The effect on therapists is to lead them toward becoming more creative in the questions they ask.

The intent of therapists never guarantees the effect of their questions. Strategic questions could have an orienting effect on the therapist. An orienting question could have an influencing effect on the client. Selecting appropriate questions involves the therapists' estimating an *anticipated effect* of a question based on their past clinical experience as well as information derived from hypothesizing, strategizing, intervening, and then observing the circular interaction with the client. However, Tomm's circumplex model is useful in helping therapists to become more mindful of their intentions as well as the potential effects of their interviewing styles on themselves, the client, and the nature of the client's explanation of his or her difficulties.

Genograms

The genogram (Pendagast & Sherman, 1977; Wachtel & Wachtel, 1986; McGoldrick & Gerson, 1985) is essentially an emotional family tree. Family relationships going back three generations or more are charted and explored via a structured technique. Genograms are intended to provide a larger social context within which to understand the individual. The emphasis in contructing genograms is on the elucidation of three basic categories of information: (1) significant facts or events, (2) multigenerational patterns and family influences, and (3) the idiosyncratic world view of the client.

The process of constructing a genogram with the client is as important as the content that emerges. The genogram is usually constructed during the initial counseling sessions. It is drawn as a family tree. Exploring one generation at a time, the client is asked to describe all of the family members and to talk about their lives, interrelationships, values, and beliefs. Clients are asked for one or two "stories" that the individual has heard about his grandparents and the members of his own family. The counselor draws inferences based on the content of what is said as well as from the accompanying affect. The client is continuously given feedback regarding counselor inferences so that the process becomes a dialogue between therapist and client.

Factual information about the client can provide an important perspective on the client's difficulties. Sometimes material that may go unmentioned by the client because of its seeming irrelevance proves particularly valuable to the counselor. For example, a history of early death and incapacitating illness among males in the family could provide useful insight into some of the dynamics of a male client's mid-life crisis, even though the client might not make a conscious connection between himself and other men of his family. Excellent checklists of factual information to obtain through genograms are provided by Pendagast and Sherman (1977) and McGoldrick and Gerson (1985).

Information is also obtained about multigenerational patterns and systems. This information can increase understanding of how the client may have learned current problematic patterns and how these patterns have functioned within the client's family system. The therapist explores patterns of conflict and triangulation, overfunctioning and underfunctioning, management of closeness and distance, and stresses at various stages of the family's developmental history. These previous patterns are often transformed and manifested in the client's current behavior. Information about family patterns can serve to increase awareness of the clients' own dynamics and can offer guidance about how clients can begin to change their roles and patterns. The genogram can also alter clients' individualistic frames of reference to understand themselves in a more developmental, contextual context.

The genogram also serves as a projective tool to understand the clients idiosyncratic world view (Wachtel & Wachtel, 1986). Client stories, descriptions of family members, and affect provide clues to the individual's concerns. By focusing on the dimensions along which family members are evaluated, the therapist learns more about the client's values and concerns.

The usefulness of the genogram depends on the sensitivity of the clinician and on the quality of the therapeutic relationship. The genogram provides data that we might not ordinarily have or that might not ordinarily be highlighted in the same way.

Client Self-Monitoring

Client self-monitoring provides another source of information about the nature of the client's problems. Self-monitoring involves observing one's own behavior in a variety of real-life settings. Generally, the client maintains a daily log that charts information about problem behaviors, their time and place, their situational antecedents and consequences, as well as information about client cognitions and feelings in those situations.

The client's log becomes a baseline record that is useful in establishing the direction and level of change desired by the client. As counseling progresses, these baseline data may help clients evaluate their progress. Also, this information helps to identify a pattern among the problem behaviors, including factors that cue or elicit the problem behaviors and activities that maintain, strengthen, or weaken those behaviors. Client self-monitoring of problem situations and behaviors outside the interview can add more accuracy and specificity to the information discussed in the first interview.

Self-monitoring is often the initial step in beginning the change process. It is important to begin with a simple log that does not require a great deal of recording and then increase the amount of information the client observes and records. Research summarized by Kendall and Hollon (1981) suggests that clients with certain types of problems experience predictable difficulties in implementing self-monitoring. For example, depressed clients often initially feel overwhelmed by the task of self-monitoring or report feeling pessimistic about it.

Anxious or angry clients sometimes fear that self-monitoring will become a cue for feeling anxious or angry.

Self-monitoring can also be used to promote client change. Self-monitoring can have a positive reactive effect. As clients begin to pay close attention to a particular aspect of their behavior, that behavior is likely to change, even though no change may be intended. Cormier and Cormier (1985) have summarized research in which self-monitoring has been the major treatment strategy. Self-monitoring is often combined with other strategies such as self-reward and stimulus control to become a combined self-management treatment program.

Use of Psychological Tests

Psychological tests are often used as assessment tools to generate hypotheses about clients and select appropriate psychological treatment procedures. Through the use of tests and inventories, the counselor attempts to appraise the personality characteristics, typical behaviors, and potential problems of the client. A key purpose of psychological testing is to obtain samples of behavior in a standardized situation. In counseling relationships, psychological tests and inventories can sometimes facilitate and accelerate a client's self-understanding. Tests may be used to enhance short-term therapy, measure progress in therapy, provide a source of feedback discussion about client strengths and weaknesses, and aid in decision making (Duckworth, 1990).

A variety of testing instruments are available to the trained therapeutic psychologist. Instruments include personality inventories, projective instruments, career inventories, behavior schedules, and tests such as aptitude, reading, or neurological batteries that are designed for specific assessment purposes.

Psychological tests are sometimes based on a particular assessment framework. For example, the Millon Clinical Multiaxial Inventory provides results based on the DSM-III diagnostic system. Other instruments, such as the MMPI-2, are not bound to a particular theory. Inventories such as the Family Adaptability and Cohesion Evaluation Scales (FACES) and PREPARE are based on a systemic model of therapy.

Test selection should be based on the specific assessment purposes and needs of the client. The client should understand clearly how the results will be useful to both the client and counselor. Responsibilities of test users are summarized in guidelines published by the Association for Counseling and Development and a joint committee of the American Psychological Association and other measurement associations (1985). They discuss issues such as defining purposes for testing, qualifications of test users, test selection, test administration and scoring, test interpretation, and communication of test results. Users of psychological tests should become familiar with these documents.

While test results can provide much useful information about clients, counselors should not neglect the shortcomings of test information. Trait-oriented measures tend to cause the counselor to assume that traits may be interpreted in a relatively constant manner across situations. Test results are often assumed to reflect stable and consistent personality traits. However, tests do not pay sufficient attention to situational aspects of behavior. Nor do they recognize the possible wide intraindividual variations in behaviors. For example, traits of introversion-extroversion may vary widely in expression depending upon whether the client is with friends or strangers, in a one-on-one conversation, or within a large group of people. The counselor can often explore the situational patterns in the feedback discussions with the client. Other counselors tend to rely on behaviorally oriented checklists that focus on situational determinants of difficulties such as excessive anger or anxiety.

Tests often do not address gender-role issues, unless the test interpreter deliberately takes such issues into account. For example, Scale 5 on the Minnesota Multiphasic Personality Inventory (MMPI-2); although purportedly a measure of masculinity and femininity, in fact tends to reveal the client's interests and activity/passivity. Projective instruments reflect biases inherent in psychoanalytic theories regarding masculinity and femininity (Brown, 1986). Rosewater (1985) reported research regarding assessment of battered women with the MMPI. She comments that when gender-role analysis and an awareness on the part of an assessor regarding the meaning of battering were not integrated into the interpretation of test results, such women were often inaccurately diagnosed paranoid schizophrenic when standard MMPI code types were utilized. Brown has found similar results using the MMPI with women who have been sexually harassed at work, sexually exploited by psychotherapists, and sexually abused as children. These findings suggest the importance of interpreting test data within a broader framework that includes the importance of gender-role analysis. Gender-role identification information can be gathered through instruments such as the Bem Sex-Role Inventory that typically have been used more in research than in clinical practice.

Testing with recent immigrants and with other minority populations must be conducted with sensitivity to the complexities of cross-cultural mental health encounters. Testing may be adversely influenced by cultural differences in personality, disparate expectations about the testing situation, language difficulties, and different conceptions of what is normal or what causes difficulties. Many objective personality tests are inappropriate because they lack appropriate norms, utilize a verbal or written format that is inappropriate for a cultural group, or are based upon personality constructs that lack cultural relevance. Checklists such as the Symptom Check List 90 are not dependent on norms and thus may be less culture bound, so that they can be used with clients from different ethnic backgrounds.

Computer Utilization in Assessment

The advent of sophisticated minicomputers has brought new applications of computer technology to therapeutic assessment. Therapists in institutional settings as well as small independent practices are able to utilize computers in interviewing, diagnosis, targeting behaviors for change, psychological testing, maintaining a client database, and implementing psychotherapy evaluation programs (Butcher, Keller, & Bacon, 1985; Butcher, 1987).

Programs for computer-assisted diagnoses have been developed by a number of researchers (Fowler, 1985; Erdman & Foster, 1986). Some programs have been oriented toward assessment in focused areas such as prediction of suicidal risk (Greist, Gustafson, et al., 1973) and drug abuse (Greist, Klein, et al., 1975). Other programs have been developed that are oriented toward identifying a range of problems and diagnoses (McCullough, Stout, Longabaugh, & Stevenson, 1982). Researchers are currently developing more sophisticated programs that lead to both a diagnostic formulation and a recommendation for a particular type of counseling.

The Computerized Assessment System for Psychotherapy Evaluation and Research (CASPER; McCullough & Farrell, 1983; McCullough, Farrell, & Longabaugh, 1986) represents one of the most ambitious attempts to develop a computerized assessment system. During the initial therapy session, clients are given information about how to enter data into a microcomputer. They are then seated in front of the computer, and they respond to computerized intake interview questions. This comprehensive, 40-minute interview assesses psychological functioning across a broad range of content areas and generates a list of target complaints relevant to each client. The therapist and client then review a report based on these interview data and decide on treatment goals. During each subsequent therapy session, the therapist enters progress and process data. At termination of treatment the client is asked to retake the full intake interview, and the therapist rates the degree of improvement on each targeted problem.

Although computerized assessment programs such as CASPER currently lack adequate research evaluation, it appears that these programs will be advantageous to counselors in various respects. They help maintain a therapy focus by targeting and following specific problem areas over the course of treatment. Such systems can also tailor assessment to the individual, collect data on therapy outcome, incorporate a standardized format for collecting data on target complaints, and gather data from both the client's and therapist's perspectives. Computerized systems also gather a wide array of data on the relationship among client and therapeutic treatment variables that can be used in clinical research.

PLANNING A COURSE OF PSYCHOLOGICAL COUNSELING

In addition to psychological assessment, the therapist must develop a tentative plan for the course of counseling. Client problems identified through the assessment may fall along a continuum from trauma and crisis-related counseling to treatment for clients who are anticipating change. The type and extent of help offered will depend in part on client, counselor, and agency factors.

Client needs and variables are important considerations in determining the course of counseling. The client has a problem to solve, such as choice of a partner, selection of an occupation, dealing with distress related to family-of-origin experiences, recovering from depression, or managing anxiety. These expressions of client need may be construed by the counselor as unidimensional problems to be solved by symptom-focused treatment or, as more complex difficulties evolve, a treatment that deals with underlying personality conflicts. The client may be an individual or may be a group such as a couple, family, or roommates who present a common difficulty. The counselor will need to decide who the client will be, the nature of the treatment, and whether the counselor can be a good match for the client in terms of personality, skills, and setting. If the counselor and client decide to work together, a treatment plan will need to be formulated that includes goals and outcomes to be evaluated within an estimated time period.

Treatment Format

Treatability is an important element of treatment planning. A basic initial question to answer is whether counseling is likely to have a positive or a negative effect on the client. The answer depends on the appropriateness of the setting, the training of the counselor, the nature of the problem, and the motivation of the client for seeking treatment. For example, if the client is likely to need frequent or crisis services and the setting cannot provide such services, then it is best to refer the client to a more appropriate setting. Or if the client is likely to need medical follow up that is not available at the counselor's setting, referral is appropriate.

The decision about the appropriateness of counseling involves determining the best treatment format for the client. This decision depends upon the nature of the client's symptoms or problems. Beutler and Clarkin (1990) suggest that if the symptom or conflict reflects a transient or uncomplicated pattern that primarily concerns the individual client, with little confounding from the current family environment, then it can be dealt with in either individual or group therapy. Other problems that are amenable to individual treatment are those involving internal conflicts and coping styles that are manifested in repetitive life patterns. An example is the difficulties of an adolescent or young adult who is striving for autonomy from his or her family of origin.

If the client's conflicts are confounded by the marital and family environment, then marital and family treatment formats are often most appropriate. Problems typically treated through this format include those for which a child or adolescent is the identified patient, sexual problems, marital conflict, and family transitions. We will discuss these formats in more detail in Chapter 10.

Interpersonal conflicts that would be apparent in group interactions may be treated in group format. As we discuss further in Chapter 9, a group format may be helpful in treating specific issues such as eating disorders, fears, and recovery from abuse or chemical dependency.

The choice of which treatment may be most appropriate also may depend on the phases of problem resolution (for example, precontemplation, contemplation, action, and maintenance) and the preference of the client. Sometimes a client may benefit from simultaneously participating in several treatment formats (for example, individual and group) or select one format in the early stages of therapy and then change formats at later stages of problem resolution.

Duration

Duration of the counseling is another factor to consider in treatment planning. Duration of counseling involves a number of considerations, such as efficiency, treatment setting, problem severity, and counselor and client influences. Individual treatment is often more costly to provide than group therapy and the nature of the setting may dictate that the client receives the most efficient form of therapy. Many school and university counseling centers as well as Health Maintenance Organizations (HMOs) are only willing to provide short-term counseling and may want to refer longer-term clients initially to an outside agency or counselor.

The duration of counseling and therapy is determined by the nature of the goals. The extent to which the client wants to get deeply involved and to stay involved is also a significant determinant of length. Some client variables important to treatment duration include motivation, cooperation with treatment, social support, and problem complexity.

In general, short-term counseling is most appropriate for situational reactions and unidimensional problems. The less complex the problems, the more the focus and goals of counseling can be restricted to symptom reduction or growth issues. The more complex the problems, the longer counseling will be needed and the more it will focus on underlying conflicts. Treatment frequency is also increased with more intense symptoms, complex problems, and limited coping abilities and may be decreased with low-intensity, less complex problems.

Crisis counseling is sometimes needed to cope with unexpected situational demands such as death, disasters, sudden unemployment, or severe illness. The goal of crisis counseling is to stabilize the client and return him or her to the level of functioning experienced prior to the crisis. Currently, helping agencies are experimenting with a multiple-impact strategy with families, where several specialists offer immediate and comprehensive help to a family undergoing a crisis. Here a team of specialists meets the family right at the hospital, in case of severe accident, for example, and provides intensive help to get the family functioning as normally as possible. Crisis centers run largely by volunteers trained in basic crisis-helping skills are part of almost every large community. Much of the supportive contact work is done by telephone. Skills for managing crisis are presented in detail in *The Helping Relationship: Process and Skills* (Brammer, 1993).

Crisis intervention methodology and strategy has become a specialized helping field. The Rusk model (1971) emphasizes a process of providing support and mutual problem solving. Rusk's steps are (1) counselor presents self as concerned helper; (2) client is encouraged to express and discuss affect; (3) counselor empathizes with expressed affect; (4) counselor gains information about the crisis situation; (5) counselor helps client formulate a statement about the problem; (6) counselor and client agree on strategies to resolve crisis-induced stress; and (7) counselor and client review and implement a mutually established strategy for management of the stress and ways of coping with future stress.

Sometimes in the course of counseling clients will need to be referred for medication and medical follow up due to the level of symptom severity. This decision is usually made together by the counselor and client. The major areas for medical referral include psychotic confusion, anxiety, depression, and mania.

It is difficult to estimate how long counseling will last for any particular individual. Some normative data on duration have been provided from a review of carefully controlled psychotherapeutic studies of 2431 outpatients in individual nonbehavioral therapies (Howard, Kopta, Krause, & Orlinsky, 1986). These researchers arrived at estimates of the expected percentage improved for the selected number of sessions. They found that 10 to 18 percent of clients can be expected to show some improvement during the first session. By eight sessions, 48 to 58 percent can be expected to have measureable improvement. About 75 percent of the clients showed measurable improvement after 26 sessions. Fifty to 90 percent of clients diagnosed with anxiety and depression improved by 13 sessions of treatment. In contrast, in the borderline psychotic groups, 50 percent of patients did not improve by clinical ratings until the interval between 26 and 52 sessions. There has been little research that has compared the efficacy of short-term and long-term therapies, in part because of the difficulties in manualizing long-term therapies. Garfield's (1989) review of the history and research on short-term or brief psychotherapy indicated that this style had become very popular over the years. In addition, he found that when the problems were focused, brief psychotherapy was more effective than long-term therapy.

Relationship Variables

Treatment planning also involves finding a good match between counselor and client, a match that is complex and involves many factors. In general, research indicates that similarities between client and counselor in terms of ethnicity, socioeconomic status, and age may be helpful initially, but that differences may be more important as therapy progresses (Beutler & Clarkin, 1990). Variables affecting the initial compatibility may also involve trying to relate to specific therapeutic needs (for example, having a woman's perspective) or to a particular client's level of ethnic identity in which having a counselor of the same ethnic background may be important. This is not always as clear as it might seem. For example, in matching people of similar ethnic background, social status differences within that background may become barriers to forming a therapeutic alliance. As we will discuss throughout this text, it is important for counselors to remember that development of an effective therapeutic alliance involves much more than initial compatibility.

Formulating Treatment Goals

For clients with situational problems, treatment goals usually involve changing the specific problems or specific symptoms by which the client defines the problem. Goals may involve changing one's situation or simply gaining insight and acceptance about one's life. Treatment goals for more complex problems are derived from the counselor's theory and often involve changes in underlying defenses or coping styles. It is helpful for the counselor and client to specify how they will know when the counseling has reached its goals. As we discussed in Chapter 1, it is important that the client be involved in setting the goals and that the rationale for treatment be acceptable to the counselor and client.

Treatment Setting

The most desirable treatment setting is an unrestricted one. The setting must be restrictive only with the more seriously disturbed client who exhibits acute symptoms that are out of control and that pose a danger to self and others. Hospitalization for acute and serious symptoms such as suicidal behavior and psychotic symptoms may be indicated for a brief period of time, especially if crisis intervention is not adequate to the task. The purpose of hospitalization is to restore the client to preacute levels of functioning. Clients with long-standing symptomatic behavior and extremely low levels of social functioning may need a more restricted environment that focuses on the reduction of bizarre behaviors and improved social skills.

SUMMARY

In this chapter we have highlighted the key roles of assessment and treatment planning in counseling and psychotherapy. We have discussed some of the key questions that counselors need to attend to as they seek to understand their clients. Regardless of one's theoretical orientation, we have stressed the need for counselors to gather specific information about the client's difficulties as well as general information that provides a developmental and sociocultural context in which to view the client. Several tools for assessment were described as well as new developments in computer-assisted diagnosis. Important factors to consider in planning a course of counseling were identified. We mentioned specific considerations for crisis counseling. We will build on these concepts in our discussion in Chapter 7 of strategies for facilitating change.

Strategies for Facilitating and Evaluating Change

PRINCIPLES FOR SELECTING INTERVENTION STRATEGIES

Most approaches to psychotherapy involve similar process stages. The therapist begins by establishing a therapeutic alliance with the client. Once a relationship is established, the counselor enters the assessment phase described in Chapter 6. Assessment is followed by stages of formal or informal contracting, therapeutic intervention, and termination. This chapter will discuss these latter phases of counseling and psychotherapy.

Because we have emphasized a synthesis model of therapy, we will first explore some important principles for therapists who wish to create their own integrative models of theory and techniques. These principles form a context for considering different types of interventions. We will describe intervention strategies drawn from various counseling approaches. We believe methods drawn from a variety of therapy "schools" can be shown to be compatible with our integrative approach to counseling. We have conceptually grouped these strategies into generic categories of (1) strategies for restructuring client self-perceptions; (2) strategies for reducing physiological and emotional distress; and (3) strategies for behavior change.

Most clients will present a multitude of presenting difficulties. The therapist then has the task of conceptualizing these complaints within a theoretical frame of reference and selecting from among an array of potential therapeutic strategies. This is a complex and sizable task. To help counselors work through these complexities, we present some models and guidelines, beginning with models by Beutler and Clarkin and Lebow.

Beutler and Clarkin (1990) have developed a model for systematic treatment selection that matches interventions to the needs of the client. In the first stage of this model, the complexity of the presenting problem is used as an indicator for establishing either symptom- or conflict-oriented goals. Unidimensional problems are assigned symptom-alleviating goals while multidimensional problems involve goals oriented toward resolving underlying conflicts. For example, in the client with a situationally specific problem, such as test anxiety, the treatment focus can be on the symptomatic behaviors that define the problem. The treatment might be a cognitive-behavioral approach that focuses on recognizing the symptoms, precipitating environments, consequences, and dysfunctional cognitive processes associated with anxiety.

When the presenting problem is more complex, the treatment necessitates finding agreement with the client on a rationale or philosophy of treatment. In counseling involving complex problems, the therapist incorporates strategies to alleviate symptoms into the treatment and seeks to change underlying processes that are related to problem difficulties. Thus, the therapist must have a theoretical rationale that can describe how the various layers of problem difficulties are interrelated and how interventions relate to both symptom relief and greater insight into dysfunctional underlying processes.

Counseling goals may also be targeted toward one of four stages of psychotherapy that we discussed in Chapter 3: establishing the relationship, problem identification and assessment, facilitating changes, and planning for termination. Strategies in the initial stage might be oriented toward acquiring knowledge, insight, and emotional awareness of the nature of the client's problems. Interventions in the assessment stage are associated with defining the nature of the focal goals, which might include alleviating symptoms or understanding and changing underlying recurrent conflicts. In the third stage of therapy, strategies are aimed at altering dysfunctional personal and interpersonal patterns. Termination strategies involve evaluating counseling progress, anticipating future problems, and planning resolution strategies. In Beutler and Clarkin's (1990) model, the selection of strategies can also be designed to accommodate to the client's coping style.

Lebow (1987) has offered some valuable principles for considering how to integrate one's theoretical assumptions with appropriate therapeutic interventions. He states that:

1. The potential to synthesize various theories and techniques exists because many of the concepts identified as unique within schools of therapy actually overlap with concepts of other schools (Orlinsky & Howard, 1986). Similarly, there appear to be common overlapping treatment approaches from various schools of therapy (Strupp, 1986). Whatever the problem may be, the therapist aids the client in identifying, understanding, and mastering it. Psychotherapy

usually presupposes an interpersonal framework, involves learning, and utilizes a variety of means to foster behavior change. Therefore, it becomes possible to delineate both core theoretical concepts and interventions that exist across various therapeutic approaches.

2. Integrative therapists can sometimes add a new perspective onto a strategy derived from another model. For example, the therapist may use a behavior exchange strategy for treating a couple's relationship problems. In employing this strategy the therapist can limit herself or himself to the behavioral theoretical frame within which this technique originated or can expand this frame to include the individual dynamics of the client, systemic factors in the client's significant relationships, and the influence of extended family and the broader social system. Although these insights may not alter the intervention itself, the broader frame alters the view of the intervention and may lead to other interventions that encompass different levels of experience.

3. Theories, strategies, and techniques may add in synchronous ways to either give more power or lead to negative interactions that reduce overall effectiveness. In other words, simply employing more concepts and techniques does not necessarily lead to greater effectiveness. Some action-oriented interventions drawn from behavioral and Gestalt approaches may mix well because they share an action focus and because the therapist's directive position is similar. However, adding a paradoxical intervention strategy, with its consequent distant therapeutic position (Kanter & Neal, 1985), to a supportive treatment could result in the undoing of the basic support.

4. In selecting appropriate interventions, it becomes critical that the therapist consider what is the most efficient and comprehensive path to change at this moment. Rarely is there one treatment that can be pointed to as the only intervention of choice for a client's problems. Client problems are manifested simultaneously on a number of levels: biochemical or somatic, intrapsychic, and family system. For example, depression is often related to a multidetermined causal structure that includes reinforcement patterns, cognitions, ways of handling emotions, defenses, the intrapsychic structure of the individual, biological factors, interpersonal relations, and the familial and societal context within which the individual resides. The therapist's theory should guide him or her in choosing on which levels to intervene.

5. In choosing intervention strategies, the therapist must be aware of the importance of who is seen as well as what is done. The therapist should consider the indications and contradictions for different modalities (e.g., individual, couples, family therapy). The therapist must also be concerned with how treatment in one modality impacts the other contexts. For example, if a child is treated alone in therapy, how will it affect the family system?

6. In selecting intervention approaches, each of the stages of treatment must be considered. The treatment plan should address an engagement stage where the therapeutic alliance is built, an assessment stage, a contract (formal or informal), a working stage, and termination.

7. Interventions are most effective in the context of a strong therapeutic alliance. Technique is no substitute for a therapeutic relationship. The style and context in which an intervention is delivered largely determines how that intervention will be experienced. The therapist needs to be attentive to the fit between his or her personality and approach.

8. For each client, the therapist must choose among an array of available theoretical explanations and parallel interventions. The therapist must select a strategy that will maximize the accomplishment of the specific goals of that treatment. An important aspect of this strategy is when, and under what conditions, the method of intervention will be changed. Counselors need to evaluate the effectiveness of their approaches and consider both alternative conceptualizations and interventions when their current strategies do not lead clients toward the stated treatment goals.

9. In choosing a specific intervention strategy, the therapist also must consider such pragmatic factors as its acceptability to the client and the resources available to serve this particular client. A treatment can be effective only if the client agrees to participate and allows the treatment to be delivered. The resources available must also be considered. Different strategies may be preferable across school-based, inpatient, agency, and outpatient practice settings. Cost considerations and agency policies may play a role. For example, many schools, colleges, and health maintenance organizations are only able to deliver time-limited services that may not avail themselves to the strategies of longer-term therapy.

10. In treating each client, the synthesizing therapist must balance a coherence of approach and the flexibility to move to additional modes of intervention. The potential for flexibility is a principal strength of an integrative approach. However, the hazard of synthesizing approaches is that treatment can be conducted without sufficient planning and may be experienced by clients as disjointed and confusing. On the other hand, therapy based strongly on one "school" or approach can degenerate into rigidity and insensitivity. The therapist must find a balance between coherence and flexibility.

11. In selecting interventions, the counselor should remember that an integrative approach is not a static entity but an evolving method. The specific content of one's theory and technique can be expected to change over time as the counselor evaluates and revises his or her approach.

12. New techniques should be added to one's therapeutic repertoire with care. Counselors should have both a technical understanding of their interventions and a theoretical understanding of the context within which they were created.

We would add to this list the importance of selecting interventions that are likely to strengthen the client's expectations of personal effectiveness, are supported by research literature where possible, and do not repeat unsuccessful past attempts by the client to solve the problem.

STRATEGIES FOR RESTRUCTURING THE CLIENT'S SELF-PERCEPTION

Strategies for restructuring the client's self-perception are intended to clarify the client's own thoughts and feelings, provide new perspectives on the problem, and lead the client toward new avenues for dealing with his or her difficulties. We have selected a sample of techniques drawn from various schools of therapy which we believe useful to the therapeutic psychologist.

Interpretive Techniques

Definitions of Interpretation.   Interpretation has been defined as an attempt by the counselor to impart meaning to the client. Interpretation means presenting the client with a *hypothesis* about *relationships* or *meanings* among his or her behaviors. Interpretation from this viewpoint gives the client more freedom in the resolution of his or her problems. Interpretation varies with one's theoretical viewpoint because, in part, it is a process of *imposing meaning* on events. It is not a quest for some mythical true meaning of an event. Interpretation merely brings a fresh look at the behavior in the forms of different language, new frames of reference, or revised theoretical outlooks. The ultimate criterion of interpretive effectiveness is whether it facilitates behavior change in the direction desired by the client.

Interpretation, like so many psychotherapeutic terms, is construed differently by therapists. A *psychodynamic* therapist, for example, would view interpretation primarily as a means to make conscious client anxieties and conflicts. *Client-centered* therapists do not favor interpretation techniques. They feel that interpretation fosters resistance and puts too much therapeutic responsibility on the counselor. *Gestalt* therapists ask clients to do their own interpretations. For instance, the therapist's role might be to draw attention to a discrepancy between the client's words and body posture. The therapist would then help the client to interpret the meaning of this discrepancy for himself or herself. *Cognitive-behaviorists* consider interpretation as a form of attribution therapy (Haaga & Davison, 1986) or cognitive restructuring. *Systemic* therapists consider interpretation as "reframing" the situation for the client (Watzlawick, Weakland, & Fisch, 1974; Weeks & L'Abate, 1982).

The person-centered view holds that interpretation fosters resistance and puts too much therapeutic responsibility on the counselor. We believe, however, that most reflections of feelings are really mild or conservative interpretations. Whenever counselors reflect feeling, they must always *select* from the material which the client has presented. These feelings are emotionally toned ideas which the counselor judges to be the most significant of all that have been expressed. Therefore, reflection of feeling is interpretive in the sense that the counselor's judgment of significance is involved. The counselor, through additional efforts to clarify feeling, generally adds more meaning than the client did originally. On this issue, person-centered counselors would claim that they are not interpreting because they try to remain completely within the client's meaning framework. The evidence and opinions are contradictory. There is a continuum of differences between reflection of feeling and interpretation, with much blending of the two. It seems, furthermore, that the alternatives are not either interpretation or reflection but rather *what kind* and *degree* of interpretive-reflective response the counselor chooses to use.

Person-centered and Gestalt therapists, particularly, emphasize the liabilities of overintellectualization. There is a growing body of evidence, however, which supports the interpretive techniques of the cognitive restructuring psychotherapies. Most impressive to date is a study conducted by Rush et al. (1977), which showed Beck's cognitive psychotherapy to be more effective than pharmacotherapy in the treatment of depressed outpatients. Also noteworthy is an investigation by Lipsky, Kassinove, and Miller (1980) which indicated that Ellis's rational-emotive therapy produced more significant changes in an adult outpatient population than supportive therapy.

More complex clinical trials research designs were utilized to compare treatment approaches to a specified disorder. For example, the pilot NIMH Treatment of Depression Collaborative Research Program (Elkin et al., 1985) was designed to compare various approaches to the treatment of depression. In this pilot research program, subjects were assigned at random to one of four treatment conditions: cognitive-behavior therapy, interpersonal psychotherapy, imiprimine (antidepressant medication), or a pill-placebo. Further clinical trials, such as the NIMH program, are likely to provide us with a better understanding of what treatment approaches are most effective for different individuals with a specified disorder.

A Continuum of Techniques Involving Therapist Interpretations

Reflection. In the chapter on relationship techniques, great emphasis was placed upon reflection of feeling. The key idea underlying reflection of feeling is that the counselor goes no further than the client has already *explicitly* gone with verbal productions, although the counselor is selective in what he or she reflects.

Clarification. A technique that goes slightly beyond reflection is called "clarification," which means clarifying to the client what is *implicit* in what the client has just said. Clarification, therefore, reflects relationships or meanings for the client that are *suggested* or *implied* in the feelings or ideas brought out by the client's actual responses. Clarification deals with material which, in the judgment of the counselor, is just beyond the awareness of the client. Clarification requires knowledge of psychodynamics and mechanisms of which the client is usually not aware. The counselor adds strong cognitive elements to his or her reflection of feelings. It gives the client a feeling of forward movement in that it verbalizes material that the client may have felt only vaguely. It is analogous to the pacing of a young racehorse by a more mature one. The counselor goes far enough beyond the client's conscious verbalizations to stimulate further thinking, but not so far that he or she loses the client.

Confrontation.   A third point on the interpretive continuum is a technique called "confrontation." Here the counselor brings to the attention of the client ideas and feelings which are *implicit* but of which the client is unaware or which he or she refuses to acknowledge. In using this technique, the counselor confronts clients with their own words but relates past to present, pointing out similarities, differences, and discrepancies of which they are unaware at that moment.

Depth Interpretation.   Finally, in depth interpretation, the counselor introduces new concepts, relationships, and associations that are rooted in the client's experiences but that are considerably beyond their awareness. Some examples of the above levels of interpretation follow:

CL: Last night I was really bothered by a wet dream I had which involved a little seven-year-old girl who looked partly like my baby sister and partly like my little daughter.

1. Reflection:
"It was really disturbing to have such a dream."
2. Clarification:
"It bothered you to have an experience which suggested erotic impulses toward your daughter or sister."
3. Confrontation:
"You apparently have similar erotic impulses toward your daughter as you reported you had toward your little sister."
4. Interpretation:
"You are becoming more free to admit your past and present impulses toward those whom you love, even though it is disturbing to express feelings that are so strictly forbidden in our society."

Clarification Methods

Associative Type.   The counselor presents a hypothesis that draws together or makes associations between the client's explicit or implicit thoughts or feelings. Four major forms of association can be distinguished.

1. *Similarity.* The counselor may draw together two ideas with similar content as follows: "What you are saying now about your wife appears to be very closely related to the feelings that you expressed about your mother a few weeks ago. Would you say that is a fair statement?"
2. *Contrast.* The counselor may associate two dissimilar ideas. An example of this form would be: "I gather, from what you said, your feelings about your father are almost the opposite of those you have about your mother."

3. *Contiguity.* The counselor may associate ideas that are close in space and time. For example, "You seem to get these feelings of tension whenever you come into the biology laboratory?"

4. *Distance.* The counselor may associate ideas or feelings which are far apart in space and time. For instance, "You seem to have many of the feelings toward this person that you had toward your mother several years ago under similar circumstances."

The counselor may relate feelings or ideas to each other that have been evident in prior sessions and that seem to have some relevance to the client's present expressions. The counselor may thus be said to reduce the distance in time and space between the client's feelings and thoughts in order to make them more comprehensible, to stimulate finer differentiations, or to promote integration of feelings and ideas.

Suggestive Type.   In this type, the counselor suggests to the client certain ideas and feelings that are related to material already presented. Suggestive clarification verbalizes this connection. An example is, "You seem to understand that your feelings of hostility might be at the root of your social difficulties."

Suggestive clarification differs from general interpretation in that nothing new is brought out in the interview expect that which is only dimly in awareness or, by remote implication, suggested by the client's comments. In contrast, by the general interpretation method, hypotheses or meanings are imparted to the client which may or may not have been suggested by the client.

Systemic Interpretations.   Systemic interpretations may involve educating the client about the client's family structure, the function of the client's symptom in the context of his or her larger family system, or sharing feedback about how the client's behavior may be perceived by others.

Feedback about the client's family structure may involve understanding either the client's current family role or role in his or her family of origin. For example, a woman who had been triangulated into an "emotional caretaker" support role with her own mother found that she had triangulated her own daughter as her primary emotional support within her tenuous relationship with her husband. Understanding this family pattern of triangulation gave her a new perspective on her present experience and contributed to her ability to establish a different kind of relationship with her husband and daughter.

Interpreting the meaning of the client's symptom within their family context can shift attention from the intrapsychic to the interpersonal and vice versa. For instance, the therapist might say, "You help your spouse ward off depression by fighting with him" or "You fight with your spouse rather than experience your own depression." These types of interpretations educate the client about collusive defenses.

Interpretation of how their behavior may affect significant others can help clients become aware of recursive interactions that become vicious circles in which they maintain or escalate their problems. Such interpretations guide clients toward examining the potential interactional *effects* of their behavior on others' thoughts, feelings, and behaviors.

We believe that interpretation can be helpful in various ways to clients. Interpretations can reinforce a positive therapeutic alliance by reinforcing client self-disclosure. Interpretations also draw patterns and connections that may introduce a new frame of reference for the client. This new frame of reference can be a form of "second-order change" (Watzlawick, Weakland, & Fisch, 1974; Claiborn, Ward, & Strong, 1981), which opens up new alternative solutions for the client's problems.

General Guidelines for Interpretation

Although there are no universally valid rules for interpretation, there are some guidelines which, if individualized and applied judiciously by the counselor, can help the client toward awareness.

What to Interpret.   The content of interpretation is determined by the particular stage in the counseling process. In the early interviews it may be necessary for the counselor to interpret attitudes toward counseling and the meaning of resisting efforts. Counselors keep interpretations very general and tentative at first, the main purposes being to explain the process to the client and to open up new areas for consideration.

Later, interpretations take the form of explanations of how defenses function to keep us from becoming aware. Here, in the middle of the process, the counselor makes interpretations more specific in terms of his or her basic theory. Toward the end of counseling, counselors make the interpretations more general and vague to encourage clients to do their own interpreting. Counselors also have the goal of closing issues, rather than stirring up new problems. So, interpretations become fewer and more general toward the end of the process.

When to Interpret.   Perhaps the most important consideration in the use of interpretation is that of timing. In general, interpretations are made very cautiously and, in the counselor's judgment, not until the client is ready to accept them and is at the point where the client can almost formulate the interpretations by himself or herself.

It is wise for the counselor to interpret, or to elicit interpretations from the client, after that client has gained some awareness of the subject area of the proposed interpretation. In other words, interpretations should rarely be offered "blindly." There are occasions, however, when clients may be accelerated by a thoughtful "shot in the dark."

In person-centered therapies, reflection of feeling dominates the early phases of counseling, followed by the tentative formulations of clarifications. In the later stages, when awareness must be expanded and insights tested, general interpretation in terms of a specific theory, as illustrated later in this chapter, is

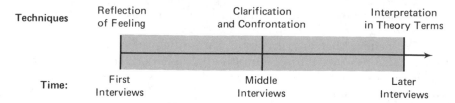

FIGURE 7-1 Timing of Interpretations.

used. Figure 7-1 illustrates the time relationships of this technique to the counseling process.

More direct approaches assume that a new conceptualization of the presenting problem and a clearly understandable rationale for treatment are established in the initial phase of counseling. This direct view holds that many clients come in feeling out of control. So, the sooner a conceptual framework can be offered that imparts hope and defines the counseling rationale, the sooner the client will become motivated and involved in counseling (Meichenbaum, Turk, & Burstein, 1975). It should be noted that these alternative conceptualizations could be foisted on the client or developed through a collaborative process in which the client became an active participant. We favor the latter approach since it promotes more sustained client motivation for counseling.

There are times when interpretation may be inappropriate because the counselor senses that the emotional dam of the client may break. On the other hand, clients can be prepared for interpretations that would otherwise be highly threatening by establishing a context of unconditional acceptance, as described in Chapter 5. For example, the counselor could discuss a "hypothetical" situation close to something the client is experiencing, explaining to the client that the situation is given to make a point. The counselor can then demonstrate that even if the client had done this hypothetical act, he or she could accept this and still feel worthwhile as a person. Frequently, this method frees clients from the fear of lowered self-esteem so they can express themselves more freely.

Often counselors make interpretations early in an interview so that there will be sufficient time to work through the client's reactions. This is true especially when potentially threatening interpretations have to be made.

There are occasions when interpretations are given more appropriately toward the end of the interview. In these situations it is necessary to prepare the client carefully and to present current documentation to support the interpretation. There are occasions also when counselors could suggest interpretations at the end of the interview to stimulate the client's thinking between sessions.

Focus on Controllable Causes. Research indicates that interpretations that focus on beliefs or behaviors the client can control are more effective than those that attribute difficulties to situations the client cannot change. This principle highlights the shaping and reinforcement role of interpretation. Interpretation should shape and guide clients toward an increased internal locus of control and awareness of where they can take responsibility for changing their behavior.

Provide Positive Interpretations.   The wording of interpretation will have an important effect on how it is received by the client. We suggest primarily offering interpretations that utilize positive connotations and are permission oriented. Permission-oriented interpretations address an aspect of the client's experience that he or she has disavowed or obscured and convey the message that it is all right to be more accepting toward that experience (Wachtel & Wachtel, 1987). Phrases such as "You're avoiding . . . ," "You're denying . . . ," often convey a rebuke to the client. An interpretation that conveys ambivalent feelings is often more gentle, such as, "You seem to feel angry toward your father but you think it's awful to feel that way." Research by Beck and Strong (1982) suggests that wording interpretations with a positive connotation promotes more enduring change than wording interpretations negatively.

Use a Tentative Approach.   Counselors frequently are critical of their more active colleagues because they feel that their interpretations are given dogmatically and without finesse. This is a gross misconception, because even the highly direct cognitive counselor generally suggests interpretations rather than stating them harshly. He does not say, "This is the way it is," but rather, "This appears to be this," or "This seems to be this way with you." Tentative phrasing also acknowledges that much of one's behavior is situationally defined rather than cemented as an unchangeable trait. This "seeds" or suggests the idea to clients that their behaviors are possible to change.

Use Repetition.   Repetition is an important interpretive principle. Since a useful and valid interpretation may be resisted, it may be necessary for the counselor to repeat the interpretation at appropriate times, in different forms, and with additional supporting evidence. Clients often achieve understanding after this kind of concerted effort (Raimy, 1975).

Although repetition is an important learning principle, it is important that counselors reexamine their interpretive hypotheses and try to understand the supporting evidence, rather than pushing them repetitively on the client. One of the best tests is whether the therapist's hypothesized model of the client's dynamics can explain the *resistance* to the interpretation as well as the interpretation itself.

Limitations of Interpretation.   Although much has been written about the value of interpretation for promoting awareness, there have been strong arguments and some data advanced against the overuse of the technique. The principal limitation cited is that interpretation is threatening; hence, resistance is aroused that blocks spontaneous new perceptions and understandings. Interpretation may have the effect of reducing client self-explorations. Bergman (1951), for example, in studying recorded interviews, found that when counselors interpreted at the client's request for evaluation, there was a significant drop in further self-exploratory responses.

Interpretation technique may tend to overintellectualize the client's problems prematurely, thus encouraging the use of interpretation as a type of defense mechanism. This happens because the client is searching for all means possible to keep feelings from awareness. The client is not ready to invest responsibility for control of feelings in the counselor.

On the other side of the above argument, it should be emphasized that there is a tendency on the part of many counselors to think that interpretation is simply intellectual. This is not so, because many counselors are most effective in utilizing interpretation to get *emotional involvement*. The following response is an example:

C: You've told me about your family as though you were a disinterested observer; what do you feel when you are with them?

Another example:

C: You've several times lost the train of thought as you got around to the topic of your mother's death; I wonder if you're hesitant to show how deeply it still affects you?

Techniques Utilizing Client Interpretations

The methods we have discussed above place responsibility on the therapist to interpret client thoughts, feelings, and behavior. Other techniques can be utilized in which the client provides an interpretation for himself or herself. Several of these techniques are described in more detail elsewhere in this text. One technique described in Chapter 6 to increase client interpretations is the use of circular questioning. Circular questions are intended to lead clients into a new framework for understanding their difficulties. Experiential awareness techniques and cognitive restructuring also represent efforts to help clients provide new interpretations about the way they perceive themselves and their situations.

Experiential Awareness Techniques

Therapeutic Metaphors.   Communication through therapeutic metaphors involves techniques that can be used either as therapist interpretation strategies or to assist clients to interpret their situations in a new way. Metaphoric communication may involve visualization, story telling, or adopting a client's metaphoric description of their circumstances or themselves and using the metaphor as a mirror of the client's life circumstances and choice conflicts. Metaphors are thought to bypass normal client defenses and to stimulate divergent thinking of alternative solutions.

Gordon (1978) has described construction of metaphoric stories, which parallel a client's circumstances. These stories subtly suggest or "seed" possible solutions to the client's difficulties. For example, a client who enjoys outdoor recreation tells of being "burned out" by taking on too many activities and projects. The counselor then constructs a detailed story about a backpacker who carries a lot of equipment on a long trip. Along the way, the backpacker unexpectedly develops difficulties (i.e., lack of adequate food) so that she is faced with the choice of possible starvation or else needing to return to the trailhead at a rapid pace. To return home safely, the backpacker must sort through all of the equipment and leave behind everything that is not necessary in order to lighten her load. She carefully sorts through each item in her pack to determine which items in her load are absolutely necessary for her to carry. She realizes that in order to survive she must carry only the most important items and leave the rest behind.

Metaphors can also be used to make therapeutic interpretations in a language that utilizes the client's life experiences. For example, a client was self-critical about his slow progress. Because the client gardened as a hobby, his counselor drew analogies between the client and plants. No plant is perfect. Every healthy plant has some imperfect leaves. There are "winter" periods in a plant's growth cycle when no growth appears to be occurring and yet the plant's roots are growing underground in preparation for spring blossoming.

Sometimes, a therapist can ask clients to create metaphors that describe their lives. A client may describe himself as a domineering "tank" that can overrun others in his interpersonal relationships. Another client described her job difficulties as stemming from her being a "kaleidoscopic person in a telescopic job." Metaphors may also be used to help clients become more aware of themselves. Counselors may, for example, ask a client to "become a toy" that incorporates characteristics the client likes and dislikes about himself. One client enacted his metaphor of being a "jack-in-the-box" toy, which incorporated his self-perception of having a pleasurable self hidden within a hard defensive shell.

Dreamwork. Therapists from Gestalt, psychoanalytic, and Jungian traditions have been known for their interest in dream interpretation. Some counseling approaches place responsibility on the therapist to interpret dreams while others ask the client to attribute meaning to the dreams. Gestalt therapists often have clients describe dreams in detail and then "become" both the animate and inanimate objects of the dream. The client "enacts" different objects, speaking their concerns and dialoguing with the other objects in the dream. These dialogues often help the client draw an interpretation to the dream. Gendlin (1986) has developed a series of 16 questions to help clients draw meaning from dreams. The questions focus on elements of the "drama" of the dream, the characters of the dream, symbols and analogies, and possible messages regarding their childhood, personal growth, sexuality and spirituality.

Body Awareness. One of the ways for people to get in touch with their bodies is to help them become aware of expressions that express body messages. The following phrases illustrate this awareness of the body: "You *rub* me the wrong way." "I feel *touched* by that." "You get under my *skin*." "Get off my *back*." "I can't *stomach* this." "You give me a pain in the *neck*." "I can't *stand* that." "I don't have the *guts* to do it." "You *depress* me." Everyone has heard or used these expressions many times, and yet most people are not usually aware of the significance and accuracy of the body as a vehicle of expression.

A here-and-now approach to living suggests continuous attention to the body and what it is expressing at every moment. This assumes that one's body can be trusted as a reliable indicator of one's feelings. The recent body therapies—in particular, the Reichian and Bioenergetic—make this important assumption. Alexander Lowen says:

> A person experiences the reality of the world only through his body. The external environment impresses him because it impinges upon his body and affects his senses. . . . If the body is relatively unalive, a person's impressions and responses are diminished. The more alive the body is, the more vividly does he perceive reality and the more actively does he respond. . . . The aliveness of the body denotes its capacity for feeling. In the absence of feeling the body goes "dead." . . . The emotionally dead person is turned inward: thoughts and fantasies replace feelings and actions. Despite this mental activity, his emotional deadness is manifested physically. We shall find that his body looks "dead" or unalive (1967, pp. 5–6).

Lowen further describes the therapeutic task and the relating of the body to feeling:

> Looking at the body and listening to it is a continous process. A patient's tone of voice tells me where he is, not his words. His words can lie. The body doesn't lie. The eyes may lack feeling, i.e., be dull or vacant, but that says something. His voice may be a monotone and that, too, is a sign. The lack of movement is as revealing as movement itself. But of even greater importance is the way a person holds himself, i.e., his psychological character structure (1972, p. 4).

As clients become more aware of their bodies, they are more open to awareness of feelings; and when they are aware of feelings, they become more aware of their actualizing potential. This positive focus of energy is a substitute for tying energy to defensive behaviors. Body therapies such as Reichian and Bioenergetic approaches assume that every body posture and movement expresses something of the individual's psychological character structure.

A variety of techniques are available to access emotional polarities through body awareness. Anger is elicited, for example, by a psychodrama technique having a "family argument" in the controlled environment of a therapist's office, or by having a fight with "bataccas" (soft, felt-covered clubs). The opposite end of the anger dimension, the caring dimension, can be elicted through touch. One way for a couple to discover their ability to care for one another is to touch each other facially as a parent might touch a child. The person giving the touch speaks kind words as though describing the beauty of each part of the face to a child. Other Gestalt therapy exercises can also access feelings through body awareness.

Gendlin (1978) has developed a procedure whereby one can understand

and integrate the relationships among thought, feeling, and bodily sensation. He calls this process "experiential focusing." His hypothesis is that words come from feelings and that feelings lead to freshly sensing one's bodily feelings. The following verbal exchange illustrates how a focus on feeling experience is achieved:

CL: I don't care about getting close to anyone. It makes me uncomfortable. (*Intellectualizing*)

TH: What is "it"?

CL: I'm afraid when I get too close to anybody. (*Feeling*)

TH: How do you mean?

CL: I get *really scared* of closeness! (*Deeper Feeling*)

TH: What makes that happen?

CL: I've been hurt too many times. (*Whole Problem*) My body becomes tight and freezes up in any intimate relationship. (*Bodily Response*)

Gendlin supports the goal of bringing together thinking, feeling, and bodily responses in therapy. He believes that sequences like the above illustrate that all therapeutic interactions are part of a *loosening process* that leads to freedom of expression and greater capacity to solve problems.

Polarities Awareness.   Shostrom, Knapp, and Knapp (1976) have described a variety of exercises for experiencing and interpreting the polarities of emotion. In "manipulation analysis," the therapist first describes interpersonal behavior patterns that would be experienced as manipulative. The therapist often sees a pattern emerging in which the individual is utilizing one or two of the basic manipulative patterns shown in Figure 7-2. Functions of these patterns, such as controlling others, avoiding situations, structuring time, and seducing others, are explored with the client.

In the second stage of the analysis, the therapist works to restore inner balance in the client by having the client experience polarities of anger-love and strength-weakness. The principle of inner balance is illustrated by the rhythmic loops seen in Chapter 3, which showed movement between the polarities of anger-love and strength-weakness. At any given time, a client might be at any one point on either of these polarities. If, for example, a client is mildly angry, the therapist will facilitate his or her expression in one of two ways: by encouraging *exaggeration* of the expression of anger, or by encouraging *reversal*—the expression of the opposite polar dimension. In the latter case, the therapist is likely to encounter some resistance from the client, since this is not where the client is at this moment. Thus, it may be more appropriate for the therapist to encourage the intensification of the feeling of anger. The therapist's purpose in asking clients to exaggerate the manipulative tendency is to allow them to experience its apparent foolishness when expressed to such an extreme. The therapist may ask the client to express the opposite pole of the manipulative pattern he or she is demonstrating. For example, a person who is playing weak may be asked to try to play a dictator. The reason for this technique is the fundamental hypothesis that

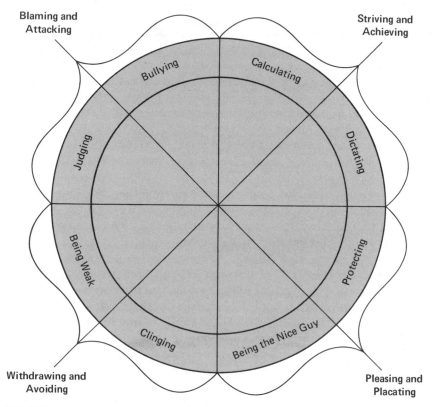

FIGURE 7-2   The Manipulative Processes. From E.L. Shostrom,
L. Knapp, and R. Knapp, *Actualizing Therapy* (1976, p. 139).

the exaggerated expression of any manipulative pattern is indicative of the underdevelopment of the opposite pattern. For example, playing weak by expressing hurt is usually indicative of covering up a strong need to express the vindictiveness that a dictator-type might feel. Expression of dependency is covering a deeper need to control others. Playing the role of a nice guy, a person may attempt to make others feel guilty for contesting him. He is often covering a need to express his hostility. The protecting person, in his need to feel responsibility for others, is often covering his need to be omnipotent. The therapist, in using this method, however, must constantly be aware of the principle of resistance and not *demand* the expression of any feeling but rather *encourage* feeling expression.

Integration, the final step in manipulation analysis, involves merging both active and passive dimensions into a unified working whole. In order to do this, the therapist continues to encourage clients to express all of their active and passive potentials, so that they might appreciate that actualizing involves the integration of all their polar styles into a unified whole. The actualizing person is like an ice skater who skates freely from one potential to another, creatively employing each in his or her movement through life.

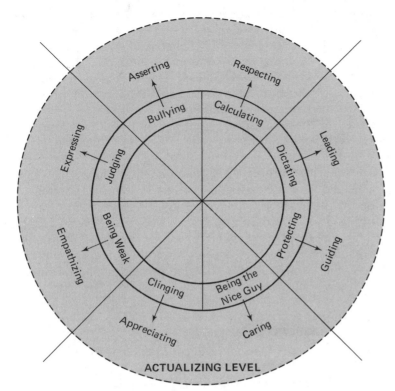

FIGURE 7-3 Manipulating Styles to Actualizing Styles. From E.L. Shostrom, L. Knapp, and R. Knapp, *Actualizing Therapy* (1976, p. 142).

In this connection, the client must realize that *self-defeating* manipulative behavior may be naturally transformed into more self-fulfilling actualizing behavior. Dictating can be transformed into leading, playing weak can be transformed into empathizing, and so on, as illustrated in Figure 7-3.

Other techniques are also available to help clients increase awareness of their emotions. Gestalt two-chair dialogues can help clients identify conflicting emotions and resolve decisional conflicts (Greenberg & Webster, 1982). Psychosynthesis approaches (Assagioli, 1965) utilize dialogues between "parts" or different aspects of oneself to interpret emotions and inner conflict.

Cognitive Techniques

Cognitive Restructuring.   Cognitive strategies focus upon adaptive thought processes that lead to constructive behavior change. Cognitive restructuring is usually associated with the names of Albert Ellis and Aaron Beck. Ellis's rational emotive therapy emphasizes disputing irrational beliefs that cause the client to feel and act in dysfunctional ways. Haaga and Davison (1986) classify these irrational beliefs as follows: (1) *awfulizing statements* describing situations (i.e., worse than merely inconvenient); (2) *shoulds, oughts, and musts,* which suggest that some unfortunate situation should or must not exist; (3) *evaluations of human worth,* which provide global evaluations of persons; (4) *need statements* involving elevating a wish into an absolute need or demand.

Ellis emphasizes attacking clients' irrational beliefs and showing clients how difficulties are sustained by holding onto irrational beliefs. He then teaches clients how to reverbalize and rethink these ideas in a more logical, self-helping way. Finally, he encourages clients to engage in activities that will prove the validity of their newly formed and valid assumptions about life.

Rather than focus on the content of cognitions as in RET, Aaron Beck (1976) emphasizes the dysfunctional form or style of a client's thinking. Typical cognitive distortions include: (1) all-or-nothing thinking, which evaluates personal qualities in black-or-white categories; (2) overgeneralization, which inappropriately applies beliefs based on particular events to dissimilar settings (a person may conclude that he or she is a failure because of a particular mistake); (3) disqualifying the positive; (4) jumping to conclusions based on an isolated detail of an event; (5) catastrophizing events or overly minimizing; (6) personalization, which relates events to oneself even when there is no connection; and (7) emotional reasoning, which assumes that one's negative emotions necessarily reflect the way things really are.

Adjunctive Techniques

Self-Help Methods. The use of literature to help people with problems is a common therapeutic practice. Audio- and videocassettes are also available as adjuncts to treatment. Bibliographic materials tend to be of two types: (1) fiction and biography, which speak to the varied expressions of human experience, and (2) popular psychology books.

Therapeutic reading can be valuable in several respects. Reading can save time in that clients can begin to think more systematically about their difficulties. Therapeutic reading can also stimulate thinking. Clients run across ideas that may increase their awareness. Parenting books, for example, may provide useful developmental information about children and ideas for handling difficult situations. Bibliotherapy sometimes can be a way for the counselor to offer support to a client. Clients find that others have similar feelings and problems.

Therapeutic reading has limitations as well. One of the foremost is the fact that people tend to rationalize their problems when they read about them. Hence, any readiness for counseling that they may have had could be reduced, and their neurotic defenses could tend to become aggravated rather than diminished. Reading could become a type of resistance to, or even substitute for, going ahead with counseling. Rosen (1987) has reviewed research suggesting that self-help treatments found in popular psychology books used without therapist assistance are less effective than when used as an adjunct to therapy and, in fact, are often detrimental to the client.

Counselors should remember several important principles for using therapeutic reading assignments. Counselors should be knowledgeable about the books they recommend. They must consider the timing of the reading and ensure that the client understands the purposes of the reading. Discussion of the reading with the client is important to ascertain the effect of the reading.

Written Communications.   Written communications have become an accepted adjunctive method for individual counseling. Pearson and his contributors (1965) have reviewed the advantages, disadvantages, and future uses of various documents such as diaries, letters, creative writing, and notebooks on fantasies and dreams. While many counselors are skeptical about the value of such materials and their use in avoiding interpersonal contact, many others are experimenting with written communications as an adjunct to counseling and have become enthusiasts for the method. Progoff's journal method (1975), for example, has been refined into an elaborate schema for recording and interpreting personal data.

STRATEGIES FOR MANAGING PHYSICAL AND EMOTIONAL DISTRESS

Selye (1974) believed that stress is a normal condition of meeting changes and threats with adaptive responses. Stress involves physiological changes (general adaptation syndrome) that may be experienced as either anxiousness (distress) or as pleasure (eustress). The task for each person is to find the optimum amount of stressful stimulation, which is exhilarating and energizing, and yet maintain a feeling state of relaxation. Each person must also seek a balance between alternating periods of stress and quietness.

Numerous strategies exist for reducing distress. Muscle relaxation exercises, meditational breathing, stress inoculation, and prioritizing are representative of these approaches. However, not all approaches to stress management necessarily involve reducing stress. Some individuals may lack sufficient stimulation to feel comfortable. The employee who is distressed because of lack of occupational promotions, for example, may need to increase his or her activity level in gathering some feedback about his or her performance in order to reduce distress.

Relaxation Methods

Progressive Relaxation Training.   Progressive relaxation training (Jacobson, 1938, 1964) involves teaching clients to relax by helping them to become aware of the sensations of tensing and relaxing major muscle groups in the body. Progressive relaxation methods have been found to be successful in the treatment of sleep difficulties, headaches, hypertension, test anxiety, speech anxiety, anger control, and various somatic difficulties (Hillenberg & Collins, 1982). The counselor usually begins by practicing the relaxation procedure with the client in order to model how the various steps are performed. After sitting or lying in a comfortable position, the client is asked to tense and then relax the major muscle groups in his or her body, one by one, and to notice the body sensations experienced. The therapist paces the client systematically through each major muscle group from head to foot drawing attention to the sensations of tension and relaxation. Detailed descriptions of these procedures can be found in Morris (1986) and Lazarus (1971). Clients are usually given an audiotape of the procedure and asked to practice the relaxation at home twice a day. The goal is to teach clients how to induce deep muscular relaxation by themselves.

Meditation.   Meditative relaxation procedures can take a variety of forms. These include Zen breathing methods, transcendental meditation, prayer and meditation, self-hypnosis, and other similar processes. Benson (1975) studied a variety of strategies and found that they elicited a physiological relaxation response. He identified four common elements to these strategies: a quiet environment, a mental device, a passive attitude, and a comfortable position. Benson found that clients could elicit the relaxation response within about five minutes by sitting comfortably in a quiet place, attending to their normal breathing pattern and inwardly repeating the words "in," "out," and "relax" as they inhaled, exhaled, and paused before their next breath. Focusing on the words appears helpful in countering the influence of anxious thoughts on the body's relaxation. Meditation strategies have been used successfully with insomnia, reducing blood pressure, and decreasing somatic stress (Cormier & Cormier, 1985).

Imagery.   Mental imagery can be used in various ways to reduce emotional and physiological distress. *Covert conditioning* (Cautela, 1976) is a term often applied to strategies that attempt to condition clients' verbal, symbolic, and imaginal representations of events. In covert sensitization, the client is asked to visualize a scene that portrays a pleasurable but undesirable behavior that the client would like to change (i.e., excessive alcohol consumption). The client is then asked to imagine a highly aversive event occurring (i.e., client sickness and vomiting). The client is then instructed to flee the event and picture herself finding relief in a safe environment (i.e., feeling healthy and self-respectful). In covert conditioning, dysfunctional behavior is paired with aversive consequences. Escape from the situation is then rewarded by the relief experience. Covert sensitization is often used in nausea imagery with alcohol problems but has been shown to be effective in a variety of situations (Elkins, 1980; Little & Curran, 1978).

Imagery is also used in modeling. *Covert modeling* involves having the client imagine a problematic situation and rehearse various ways of handling the situation successfully. Susskind (1970) utilizes imagery to help clients develop an idealized self-image. The client is first helped to formulate ideal self-characteristics. Then, clients superimpose the ideal characteristics onto a picture of themselves in their various life roles. As they imagine their ideal self-image, the clients attend to details of how they appear, think, feel, and behave as their ideal self. The clients then select specific behaviors from their ideal self-image that they would like to focus on developing in vivo prior to their next counseling appointment.

Imagery has also been applied to problems related to variety of life areas.

Imagery has been used as an adjunct to cancer recovery (Simonton, Matthews-Simonton, & Creighton, 1980) and in health promotion. DeMille (1973) has designed children's imagination games to develop divergent thinking. Bry and Bair (1978), Gawain (1982), and Lazarus (1982) have applied imagery techniques to a variety of problem areas.

Systematic Desensitization. Systematic desensitization (Wolpe, 1958) refers to a procedure used to reduce anxiety. Morris (1986) has described this process in detail. The technique involves two stages: (1) a relaxation training stage and (2) development of a fear hierarchy that is used in counterconditioning or desensitizing tenseness to anxiety-eliciting situations. The relaxation phase generally involves teaching the client progressive relaxation procedures. The second phase involves construction of an anxiety hierarchy. Clients are asked to identify specific fears and rank them in terms of how much anxiety they elicit. Once the client and therapist have constructed a hierarchal list of situations from least anxious to most anxious, the systematic desensitization begins. Each hierarchy scene is presented, beginning with a "control scene" in which the client feels very relaxed. The client is asked to picture each scene vividly and to indicate with a finger cue to the counselor if the client is still feeling calm and relaxed. The counselor continues through the hierarchy scenes until a signal is given by the client indicating anxiety is felt. At that point the counselor switches to the control scene until the client is again relaxed and can proceed through the next scene in the hierarchy. Eventually, the client learns to feel relaxed while picturing each scene of the hierarchy. The desensitization can then be followed by an *in vivo* desensitization.

Hypnotherapy. Hypnotherapy is an additional strategy that can be utilized to promote calmness and anxiety reduction. Hypnotherapy induction strategies vary along a continuum from the therapist-inducing hypnosis to self-hypnosis in which the therapist may only have given written instructions to the client or modeled induction via videotape. Hypnosis is a complex phenomenon and is described more fully by other authors (Lankton & Lankton, 1983; Zeig, 1982). Hypnotherapy shows many similarities with strategic therapies in its methods and attention toward brief problem-focused treatment.

We consider hypnotic methods as *communication strategies* to help clients shift their attention away from anxious cues toward experiences of relaxation and calmness. Gilligan (1982, p. 101) states, "The hypnotist works to secure and hold the subject's attentional processes, thereby making it possible to access unconscious processes to develop hypnotic experiences. To the extent that the subject's conscious processes interfere with this development, the hypnotist uses distraction, confusion, and boredom techniques." Once a client has entered a trance, it is possible to provide alternative ways for clients to "reframe" their difficulties or offer alternative solutions that the client might not have previously considered.

Clients can be taught self-hypnosis by a variety of means. Fife (1975) examined three different methods for inducing self-hypnosis: videotaped demonstration, videotaped demonstration plus self-hypnosis manual, and no training. No differences were found in effectiveness. Self-hypnosis has been used successfully for managing anxiety, habit control, and pain management (Crasineck & Hall, 1975).

STRATEGIES FOR PLANNING AND IMPLEMENTING BEHAVIOR CHANGE

Problem-Solving and Coping Skills Strategies

These two approaches look at behavior disorders in terms of the absence of adaptive cognitive skills rather than, as in the case of cognitive restructuring, in terms of the presence of dysfunctional cognitions. They differ, however, in that problem-solving therapies focus on deficits in cognitive processes or skills when a person is free from stress, whereas coping skill strategies analyze deficits that occur within the actual problem situation. An example of problem-solving deficit is described by D'Zurilla and his associates (D'Zurilla & Goldfried, 1971; D'Zurilla & Nezu, 1982), who interpret disorders in terms of an inability to specify a problem, generate alternative solutions, and use means-ends thinking to evaluate and choose a particular alternative. Research on the effectiveness of problem-solving training is promising in a variety of clinical applications (Haaga & Davison, 1986; Heppner, 1990).

Meichenbaum's stress inoculation training (1986) emphasizes learning coping skills, especially skill in identifying nonadaptive self-statements that emerge in stressful situations. The stress inoculation model involves three phases: cognitive preparation, skill acquisition, and application practice. During the preparation phase, the counselor educates the client about the cognitive, physiological, and behavioral concomitants of anxiety as well as external contingencies that elicit anxiety. The second phase involves developing self-statements that can be used by the client to cope with anxious arousal. The final stage involves practicing these skills both covertly and in vivo.

Self-Management

Self-management methods involve a combination of behavioral and cognitive-behavioral strategies to increase a client's self-control and ability to change his or her behavior. Self-management programs have been developed for a variety of problem areas including weight control, interpersonal skills training, anxiety reduction, insomnia, and academic performance (Cormier & Cormier, 1985).

Kanfer and Gaelick (1986) have reviewed extensively self-management strategy methods and research. They suggest the therapist's role is important in four different areas: (1) assessing the problem behavior and designing a change program; (2) enhancing client motivation; (3) teaching the client specific behavior change techniques; and (4) supporting the client's efforts and successes.

Self-management programs rely on therapist and client negotiated tasks and homework assignments to both enhance client motivation and structure the change program. Contracts between client and therapist are also used to provide a set of rules to govern the change process and to articulate the steps involved in behavior change. Self-monitoring is used to measure progress over time and as an activity that can produce change itself. Clients are taught to administer both verbal and material reinforcers for personal progress.

Sometimes modification of the environment is included in a self-management program. These techniques, known as stimulus control, set up environmental conditions that make it either impossible or unfavorable for the undesired behavior to occur. For example, these strategies may involve avoiding certain social environments where overeating or smoking is likely or studying only in locations where other activities are restricted (i.e., no music or TV). Other strategies, such as self-help groups, covert rehearsal, and bibliographic materials, may be utilized where appropriate.

Researchers have identified characteristics of successful self-management programs. Effective programs tend to utilize multiple methods and to employ them consistently over a period of time (Heffernan & Richards, 1981). Effective programs included some process for self-evaluation, utilized self-reinforcements, and environmental support.

Modeling for Skills Training

Modeling generally refers to observational learning. Early research by Bandura (1971) has led to the wide use of modeling in training clients to develop coping skills and social skills.

Bandura found that modeling or observational learning had three effects on the observer. The first effect was that of the participant's learning new behaviors or newly integrated patterns of behavior. This finding has led to a variety of applications, such as social skills training in assertion, overcoming shyness, teaching life skills to the chronically mentally ill, and in many other areas. Bellack and Hersen (1978) described three general categories that are the components of social skills: conversational skills, social perception skills, and skills necessary for special problem situations. Modeling in social skills training has focused on development of skills in these three areas.

Secondly, modeling was found to either increase or decrease the rate of performance of a behavior currently being inhibited by the observer. In other words, observation of a model provided an expectation of what might happen to the observer when he or she performed the same behavior as the model. If the client was uncertain about the effects of being assertive and then saw assertive behavior bring positive consequences to a model, the client would become more inclined to show assertive behavior. This principle has been applied in many treatments of fears and anxieties. The inhibitory effects of modeling have been used to help clients with impulse-related problems (i.e., alcohol or impulsive stealing) to strengthen their own inhibitions against their impulsive behaviors by observing models receiving unpleasant consequences for their behavior.

The third effect of modeling was to cue or remind the observer about behavior that the observer already has learned. This effect has been utilized in habit control and social skills training to strengthen appropriate behavior. When a client sees a model decline the offer of dessert after dinner, the client is reminded that it is helpful for him or her to decline desert in order to maintain his or her weight.

Perry and Furukawa (1986) have reviewed the numerous factors enhancing the effects of modeling. Factors related to the acquisition of learning include similarity to the model, the model's perceived competence, and the observer's motivation and attentional abilities. The modeling presentation itself will affect the learning impact. Live models tend to offer some advantages but lack the consistency of video models. Multiple models often enhance the learning effect. Models that emphasize coping skills rather than mastery seem helpful. Modeling cognitive processes as well as behavior helps the observer. Having the observer rehearse what she or he observes seems to aid learning retention.

Performance of modeled behavior is enhanced by building incentives into the program that will motivate clients to perform what they observe. Therapists should consider which reinforcements are most likely to reward their clients. Performance is also enhanced by rehearsal and facilitating transfer of learning from the counseling setting to the client's daily world.

TERMINATION OF CLIENTS

Practically speaking, no client's difficulties are ever "solved." Effective counseling opens possibilities of client growth, which are never finished. Yet there comes a time in the process when either the client or counselor feels that the client should be placed completely on his or her own resources. How does the counselor tell when closure has been reached? Clients often give cues that their expectations of counseling have been satisfied or that they have hopes of reaching their goals on their own efforts, such as, "Well, I guess this answers my questions" or "I feel much better about it now."

Generally, the counseling process tends to terminate spontaneously when the client's goals have been reached. A series of elaborate studies of the counseling process indicate that client responses tend to become more positive and self-directive toward the end of counseling (Seeman et al., 1949).

There are other cues that the counselor can use to effect closure. A crucial factor is fulfillment of the counseling contract. Reference should be made to the goals set in the first interviews and the contractual agreements which were negotiated. Were the expected outcomes achieved and to what degree? Counselors can watch for indices that the general goals of counseling have been accomplished. Client goals might be understanding of self and problems, an intellectual awareness of solution and direction to the problem, diminution of such symptoms as anxiety, and, most importantly, behavior improvement. The counselor must be wary, however, of the "hello-goodbye" and "flight into health" phenomena. Clients often experience feelings of euphoria and completion after an interview or two. They may feel that their problem is solved when their symptoms subside after a cathartic interview. They feel better and frequently wish to terminate counseling. Yet, the counselor realizes that no lasting behavior changes have been achieved and that such clients will be back as soon as another decision or crisis upsets them.

A distinction must be made between termination of the process by the client and by the counselor. Clients terminate counseling for many reasons. There may be completion according to the structure or contract. They might stop because of a disruption caused by resistance, ignorance about counseling, trauma, impasse, time, finances, or a feeling that the counselor is no longer needed.

The question naturally arises as to why clients leave counseling rather than become addicted to it. In addition to the cost in time, and sometimes in money also, clients may experience pain and humiliation at having to face further personality change or to achieve a higher stage of self-actualization. Or, in successful cases, the functions that were once located in the counselor are now the clients' property. Clients no longer have a "need" for counseling since what they have learned in the process has now become part of themselves and their way of life.

Counselors terminate counseling, in contrast, when they feel that the goals of counseling have been achieved, or when lack of progress on the formal or implied contract does not warrant, in their opinion, continuation of the relationship. Many counselors, once the problem is delimited, structure the time limits of the process in such a way that when this limit is reached closure proceedings are begun. For example, the counselor starts the closure by saying something like, "Well, here we are nearing the end of the term when we said we would try to finish off our counseling. Suppose we examine where we have been, where we are now, and our next steps." This method of terminating at fixed limits has great drawbacks and some danger in that the person may not be ready to terminate, or may be ready long before the structured limit. However, we think that client anxiety, which often accompanies lengthy counseling, is alleviated when they can anticipate the approximate time of closure.

Often the counselor's skill and patience are tried by the dependent client who resists assuming personal responsibility for his or her life. The counselor can only have faith in the client's capacity for and interest in personal growth. It is assumed here that lingering feelings of dependence upon, affection for, or resentment against the counselor (to be defined under "transference" in the next chapter) have been resolved. These feelings may show in relatively short informational or supportive types of counseling too, if a client, lonely or dependent, simply cannot face the deprivation of the counseling relationship, even though the most pressing problems have been resolved. A useful procedure with this type of client is to space interviews in increasingly longer intervals prior to final closure.

Steps and Methods of Closure.   The first step to close the interviews is *verbal preparation*. The client is reminded of the time limits agreed upon in the initial interview. For example, "Well, this is our fourth and last interview. . . ." Statements of client growth as a lead to termination of contacts may be expressed as follows: "You seem to have achieved some important awareness about yourself, and some realistic plans; do you think you can go it alone from here?" Other examples are, "It seems we have come to a point where you can work this out by yourself," or "You seem to think that you can carry on from here without further help from me. . . ."

The counselor should then work out a *final summary statement* with the client. This may be a general review of accomplishments, arrangements for referral or follow up, or preparation of a plan or written summary. Examples of written summaries made during counseling on careers can be found in the workbooks of Bolles (1991) and Crites (1981).

Another step the counselor may take is to leave the door open for possible *follow ups*. This is especially necessary in short-term, highly structured interviews. Abruptness is avoided when the counselor can say something like, "Drop in to see me when you are around campus," or "When you try it alone for a while you may wish to drop in to review how things are going." It is debatable how much this type of "open-door" policy should be encouraged, since it has possibilities of renewing the dependency of the client and of laying the counselor wide open for attempts to reconstitute the relationship. However, with a younger client in a school situation, the counselor may wish to establish "standby" contacts to observe their development or to give further information. An interest inventory may be used; for example, "It is a good idea to take inventory of your developing interests occasionally. . . ." This type of statement generally has a reassuring effect on clients and permits continuous observation in standby relationships.

A variation on the third step is possible *referral*. If the counselor has gone as far as he or she feels capable of going, or if another type of therapist or agency is going to take responsibility for the relationship, referral technique is used. Here it is important that the counselor structure the nature of the referral in order to pave the way for easy transition to the new relationship without revealing the nature of that new relationship in advance. Reasons for referrals should be discussed carefully with clients so they do not get the "run-around" feeling. Clients must convince themselves that the referral is necessary or helpful. If the counselor were to say, "I think you ought to see a psychiatrist about this," the client would be likely to be resistive or frightened. To avoid these possible negative responses, the counselor might say, "Our consulting psychiatrist might be able to help us on this problem. Would you care to make an appointment?" These same principles apply whether referral is to the school librarian, a social agency, the speech therapist, employment agency, or physician.

Another consideration the counselor should keep in mind in making referrals to outside persons is the desirability of mentioning two or three names, say of physicians, from which the client may choose. It is assumed, of course, that the counselor is familiar with the intake and eligibility policies and conditions of the agencies to which he or she refers clients, as well as the policies of one's own institution regarding referral channels and procedures. Schools, for example, have definite channels established for handling relationships with social agencies, courts, and professional persons in private practice.

The fourth step is the *formal leave-taking*. What was said about concluding the final phase of the individual interview applies here, with emphasis upon parting with a cordial and confident tone. It should be recognized by the counselor that the steps just cited do not always unfold smoothly. The client may make several abortive attempts to operate alone with a new discovered insight, only to be forced to return to the same or another counselor.

Before leaving this topic of termination, the authors would like to examine Thorne's concepts of overtreatment and undertreatment (1950). Thorne places the responsibility for determining the safety and appropriateness of termination squarely with the counselor. Some of the attitudes counselors have which tend, according to Thorne, to result in undertreatment are: "therapeutic nihilism," in which the counselor has a pessimistic attitude that his or her counseling will not work with this client, as a result of which he or she gives up; "diagnostic failures," wherein the counselor fails to find or deal adequately with dysfunctional processes and so terminates counseling prematurely; "passive methods," with which a counselor fails to deal actively enough with client problems; "lack of confidence" in attempting to counsel difficult cases; "lenience" in not following up clients persistently; and "overwork" of the counselor from taking too many cases, which results in rushing through appointments, or even reaching "burnout."

Though these dangers may be valid for certain cases, Thorne cautions that the counselor may err on the side of "overtreating" also. By this he means that a counselor might carry the client beyond the point of ethical treatment, or beyond the point of his or her competence. Some overtreatment may result from a conscientious attempt to be thorough, thus perhaps reinforcing the dependent client's need for constant support. However, a loose type of relationship over an extended period may have a prophylactic effect which would prevent further deterioration of the client's problem-solving ability. As in so many other areas of counseling methodology, counselors must assess the situation, weigh the advantages and disadvantages of their courses of action, and then use their best judgment.

SUMMARY

This chapter has reviewed strategies for facilitating and evaluating client change. We have attempted to provide some guidelines to assist counselors who are attempting to develop their own synthesis of theory and practice. We have described a variety of strategies and techniques that can be utilized by counselors. We have categorized therapeutic interventions into three generic categories: (1) strategies for restructuring client's self perceptions, (2) strategies for managing emotional and physiological distress, and (3) strategies for planning and implementing behavior change. Additionally, we highlighted considerations involved in termination of clients.

In our next chapters emphasizing applications of therapeutic psychology, we will describe more clinical strategies. Particular attention will be given to interventions applied to groups, marriage and family therapy, and career counseling.

CHAPTER 8

Barriers to Actualizing Relationships

Counseling and psychotherapy are interpersonal processes that have identifiable barriers. The purpose of this chapter is to discuss some of the major obstacles to building and maintaining a therapeutic relationship. *Transference, countertransference,* and *resistance* are traditional descriptions for three conditions that may help or hinder the relating process, depending on how they are expressed and handled. Although these terms typically are associated with psychoanalytic thinking, Gelso and Carter (1985) indicate that transference and countertransference reactions occur across all theoretical persuasions and occur regardless of the duration of treatment.

TRANSFERENCE

Nature of Transference Feelings

Transference refers to the repetition of past relationships with significant others such that these earlier feelings, behaviors, and attitudes are "transferred" or projected onto the therapist or others outside of the therapeutic setting. Thus, transference involves a misperception of the therapist by the client and may take many forms. The therapist may be loved, hated, sexualized, idealized, or dependent. The client-therapist relationship may recreate similar situations that the client has experienced in the past.

Various theoretical approaches understand transference phenomena differently. Thus it is important for counselors to be able to apply alternative conceptualizations of transference to their work. For example, psychoanalytically oriented therapies view transference patterns as habitual ways in which a client sets up interpersonal relationships to avoid experiencing anxiety and emotional pain. Sullivan (1954) believed that transference reactions had once been adaptive for the individual in childhood in order to tolerate emotional pain. However, these patterns have become dysfunctional for adult interaction. Analytic therapists interpret these transference feelings as a way of increasing the client's self-understanding.

Behavioral therapists acknowledge transference phenomena as "samples" of client feelings, cognition, and/or behavior (Deffenbacher, 1986). Transference phenomena are not necessarily treated differently from other emotions, thoughts, or behaviors. The behavioral therapist may construe the pattern as learned avoidance behavior or as learned dysfunctional thinking. Transference patterns will be assessed in terms of relevance to the client's problems and interference with therapeutic progress. Transference patterns that cause difficulties in situations outside of therapy will also be assessed. If the transference patterns seem important to the client's therapeutic progress, the counselor will use cognitive-behavioral techniques to alter dysfunctional thoughts, emotions, or behaviors.

Phenomenological therapists primarily attend to the here-and-now impact of transference feelings on the quality of the client-therapist relationship. Rogers (1951) states that transference feelings develop when clients perceive that counselors understand them better than clients understand themselves. The way of viewing transference, whether as hostility or dependency, depends largely on the degrees of threat involved. May and associates (1958) view transference as delayed development such that the individual views the therapist through the same restricted, distorted "spectacles" as his or her father or mother. May (1967) cautions that too much dependence on a traditional view of transference as the re-creation of personal relationships from the past leads to a diminished significance of the present encounter with the therapist. It can rob clients of personal responsibility for their feelings in this moment, and it can serve the therapist as a protective screen to avoid the threat of direct encounters with clients. Person-centered therapists tend to accept transference feelings (Rogers, 1951), whereas Gestalt therapists may interpret or actively use them to enhance client awareness (Polster & Polster, 1973).

Systems theorists emphasize both historical and current functions of transference behavior. Intergenerationally oriented therapists such as Bowen (1978) view transference as a response to anxiety about one's balance of closeness and separation within one's own family of origin. Bowen believes that anxiety regarding relationship fusion is manifested through triangulation, conflict, and family projection. Strategic therapists will explore the here-and-now interpersonal function of the transference within the client-family and client-therapist systems. Structurally oriented therapists will presume transference to be a reflection of structural or boundary problems in the therapist-client system.

We believe it is important for the actualizing therapist to integrate the views we have discussed. Transference describes how the client construes the therapist and how the client behaves toward the therapist. We view transference as having both an historical and here-and-now function for the client-therapist relationship. We believe that transference can have a strong influence on the therapeutic alliance and can elicit countertransference behavior by the therapist. Thus, assessment of the nature and function of the transference cannot be understood apart from an examination of how transference patterns are connected to countertransference from the therapist.

Intensive transference, commonly found in long-term psychotherapy, is regarded as a type of relationship that goes beyond that considered desirable or optimal for counseling. A concept of degrees of transference relationship is illustrated in Figure 8-1; the client enters the counselor's presence with the usual mixed feelings people have as they meet strangers. Since counselors and therapists generally are cordial and emotionally warm, the relationship bridge begins to widen and client feeling flows more freely toward the counselor. At this point, the transference relationship begins. Clients with strong affection or dependency needs may project these so intensely at times that the client's perception of the counselor is grossly distorted. An extreme example of this idea is the unusual client who literally hugs or throws himself or herself upon the psychotherapist. Often, clients with weak actualizing capacities must "use" the therapist's strength. In this sense, transference may be a necessary prelude to building the client's own actualizing strength. Gelso (1979) points out how all clients enter counseling with a wish (usually below awareness) to be dependent and to have needs for affection satisfied.

Parenthetically, we believe that Step 4 of Figure 8-1 illustrates a fundamental distinction between counseling and psychotherapy. The counselor develops close personal relationships with clients but does not encourage strong transference feelings as do many psychotherapists.

The resolved or broken transference relationship is conceptualized in Figure 8-1 as a complete emotional detachment, with the vectors of the client's feeling moving away from the counselor as a person and in the direction of investing feeling in other mature human relationships. Clients, in other words, take their projections back.

Transferences may be designated as positive or negative. A positive transference would be made by clients when they project their feelings of affection or dependency to the counselor, perhaps perceiving him or her as a loving, helpful father or mother. A negative transference would be made by clients when they project their feelings of hostility and aggression. These transference feelings change form, sometimes quite suddenly. For example, a client may experience warm feelings toward the counselor while describing his or her problem, yet feel fearful and resentful for having told "all" or for having exposed his or her perceived "weaknesses." Often the client's positive transference will change to negative feelings when the counselor doesn't give all the reassurance or advice expected. Sometimes clients respond to the counselor in a manner similar to that used during childhood "confessions" to their real parents.

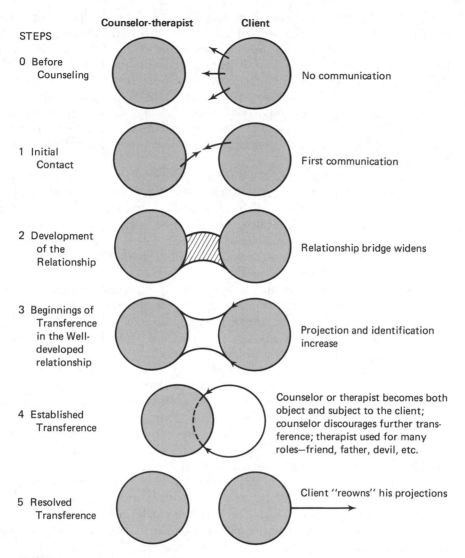

STEPS

0 Before
   Counseling — No communication

Counselor-therapist / Client

1 Initial
   Contact — First communication

2 Development
   of the
   Relationship — Relationship bridge widens

3 Beginnings of
   Transference
   in the Well-
   developed
   relationship — Projection and identification increase

4 Established
   Transference — Counselor or therapist becomes both object and subject to the client; counselor discourages further transference; therapist used for many roles—friend, father, devil, etc.

5 Resolved
   Transference — Client "reowns" his projections

FIGURE 8-1   Development and Resolution of the Transference
Relationship.

Most of us have had the experience of a first contact that was experienced as
real and meaningful. Yet, at other times, there was little, if any, meaningful contact
with the other. Freud believed that in any prolonged contact, such as a therapeutic
or employee-employer relationship, there is a transfer of many emotional responses once felt in the client's relationships with past significant others, like
parents. Our reflections about transference have led us to believe that the relationship cannot be accounted for simply by the client's relationship history. For example, we cannot view hostility once held toward parents as accounting for hostility

expressed in the here and now. So, it is not so much what the client *has been* but what the client *has not been* that is involved. It is a failure of development—a failure to move from environmental support to self-support—and this failure is a heritage from the past. Perls, in Gestalt terms, calls this "the unfinished situation" (1973). A person's hostility can be seen as a manipulation of the present situation so as to avoid contact. In other words, it is the client's fantasies of expected support, fantasies which stem from his or her *lack of being,* and not what was and has been forgotten, which is the essence of the transference. Thus, client histories are really their backgrounds of existence or being—a record of how they have become what they are.

People do not come empty-handed from their past. They bring various means of manipulating their environments. But they tend to lack self-support—an essential quality for survival: their manipulations minimize their self-support, and these manipulations are endless. For example, people break promises, play stupid, forget, lie, and continually ask questions. These manipulative behaviors annoy, embarrass, and exploit others. Thus, client styles of manipulating others are a form of transference.

Client fears of rejection and disapproval are a form of resistance. So they manipulate therapists or employers by putting on a mask of the "good child." They "bribe" with submission or pseudoacceptance of requests. So, from the Gestalt viewpoint, clients are not persons who *had* problems; they are persons with continuing here-and-now problems.

Clients need the means by which they can solve present and future problems by themselves. This self-support requires that clients become truly aware when and how they are manifesting their problems and how they can solve them in the present. This action requires that they experience their problems in the here and now rather than in the past. To achieve this focus in the present, clients must repeat the basic sentence, "Now I am aware that. . . ." The use of the word *I* develops the client's sense of responsibilty for his or her feelings and thoughts. The word *aware* provides clients with a sense of their own capacities and abilities of which they had not been aware. *Awareness, contact,* and *present* are key words to describe "being in the now." Thus, transferences can be viewed as "being deficiencies," where clients manipulate present relationships. They can learn to change these deficiencies through awareness and living authentically in the now. Bugental (1963) confirms our idea that authenticity is a central quality of being. A key counseling task is to help clients become aware that their resistance to change is their defense against being authentic. Bugental sees transference as a process of falling away from authentic communication with the counselor.

Implications for Counseling and Psychotherapy

Since a counselor of any theoretical orientation depends primarily upon a relationship of mutual trust and acceptance for success, a strong transference, especially of the negative or hostile type, tends to interfere with counseling effectiveness.

The psychotherapist, on the other hand, does not necessarily view transference as an interference. They use transference feelings to help clients recognize what they are trying to do with the relationship to the therapist—for example, how they may be trying to manipulate the therapist. The client's demands help the therapist to understand what sort of person the client is trying to be or wants to be. The transference relationship, therefore, provides valuable clues for later interpretations to the client on how his or her interpersonal relationship mechanisms are functioning.

Counselors recognize also that, though they do not depend upon a transference relationship for effective therapy, it is important to recognize that transference feelings are present in varying amounts. For example, there are the clients who fear counselors, depend on them, love them, or expect varying roles of them. These responses may be regarded with the classical view that they may be projected self-regarding attitudes related to earlier experiences with parents; nevertheless, they must be recognized and reflected effectively to maintain client involvement.

Client-centered or phenomenological counselors, in particular, do not regard a transference situation as a significant therapeutic problem. The result that persons using the client-centered style of counseling rarely confront intensive transferences, and they reflect them as they would any other feeling. Rogers's writings suggest this procedure:

> In client-centered therapy, however, this involved and persistent dependent transference relationship does not tend to develop. Thousands of clients have been dealt with by counselors with whom the writer has had personal contact. In only a small minority of cases handled in a client-centered fashion has the client developed a relationship which could in any way be matched to Freud's terms. In most instances the description of the relationship would be quite different. (1951, p. 201)

Another cause of low-intensity transference phenomena in counseling might be the counselor's approach to a transference feeling. Counselors do not usually try to analyze deeply the manifold ways in which clients manipulate life relationships. Instead, the counselor utilizes reflection and acceptance techniques, which aid clients to see that the transference feelings reside within their own inadequate perception and not within the counselor.

Counselors tend to regard expressions of negativism, hostility, and guilt as manifestations of resistance in an incomplete growing-up process. Some counselors handle transference feelings with interpretation of the unconscious impulsive nature of those feelings, whereas other counselors, dealing with the same feelings at a more superficial level, tend to use a variety of responses, including reflection of feelings. Some counselors, furthermore, look on the helping task as a continuation of the maturation process, which has been incompletely guided by the client's natural parents. The counselor generally tries to help clients understand and accept their feelings and see what they have been trying to accomplish with their attitudes. After gaining a more rational understanding, they can take their projections on the counselor back to themselves, so that, for example, they can be less dependent. The client also is helped to understand in which ways his or her former behavior was ineffective in reaching the goals of effective living.

Often, the client persistently tests the counselor's sincerity through repeated criticisms, unrealistic expectations, aggressiveness, resistance, and irritability. Gradually, however, clients feel "safe" in dropping their defensiveness and changing their perceptions of themselves and the counselor. Clients, for example, find themselves able to reconstruct satisfactory relationships with others as well as with the counselor, since they learn they may not always expect counter-aggressive acts when they are hostile to others.

Negative transferences often follow positive transferences. When clients suddenly realize they have been idealizing or have been depending upon the counselor, they begin to perceive the counselor as he or she really is rather than in the client's "God-like" image. This is the counselor's welcomed cue of client growth. The counselor must help clients work through these feelings of disillusionment, however, by "giving back" their projections. The situation is analogous to "falling out of love." The lover, in fairness to his former beloved, returns her projections of idealized images (romantic love) so that her actualizing mechanisms are restored to their former state.

Not all negative feelings expressed in the interview can be construed as transference feelings. Instead of being projected to the counselor, they may be directed inward. Intrapunitive hostility or guilt, for example, can contribute to depression. Though the counselor must be alert to clinical forms of depression, which should have more extensive treatment, he or she can interpret anxious and mildly depressed feelings as a sign that the client is struggling with important feelings. For example, the counselor says in effect, "If we stick together, we can make use of these feelings because they show us that we are very close to something important."

Therapeutic Functions of Transference Feelings for Counselors.   While strong transferences toward counselors often complicate their task, it should be recognized that this process serves significant functions for the client. The awareness of freedom to express previously repressed irrational feelings is a unique experience which often reduces anxiety.

Transference serves to build the relationship by allowing the client to express distorted feelings without the usual counterdefensive responses. For example, clients with a "chip on their shoulders" expect their irritability to arouse counterhostility from others. When the counselor does not react as expected (by getting irritated), the client can safely reduce his or her defensiveness. Hence, clients have less need to feel guilty because of hostile impulses, and less need to project hostility on others. This refusal of the counselor to respond to client projections is one of the main vehicles for accomplishing therapeutic goals. For example, if the client's former human relationships have been characterized by rejection or devaluation, the counselor is very accepting and warm. If the client has felt exploited and abused, the counselor is careful in making demands upon that client. The general principle here is that counselors should not fit themselves into the client's projections so as to satisfy the client's neurotic needs. If the counselor fulfills the client's expectations, there is the possibility the projections will be perpetuated by virtue of having been reinforced.

A second function of transference, implied above, is to promote client confidence in the counselor through wise handling of transference feelings. Such feelings also have the net effect of amplifying clients' emotional involvement with their problems, thereby enabling them to stay in counseling.

A third function of transference is to enable clients to become aware of the origin and significance of those feelings in their present life through interpretation of those feelings. The transferred feelings, along with their maladaptive behaviors, tend to disappear with insight so that they can establish more satisfying and mature relationships with people.

Working through Transference Feelings and Preventing Deep Transference Relationships.   The counselor's main task is to encourage free expression of feelings while simultaneously keeping the transference attitudes from developing into a deep transference relationship. Several general guidelines for handling and resolving transference feelings follow.

1. A primary technique for resolving transference feelings is by means of *simple acceptance,* as one would handle any type of client feeling. This procedure enables the client to "live out" his or her feelings, "take back" his or her projected feelings, or continue to express them more freely in the interview. The client recognizes, then, that transference feelings reside in herself or himself and not in the counselor.

2. The counselor may ask *clarifying questions* regarding the forms of anxiety that the client seems to be manifesting. An example would be, "You seem to be unloading on me today. Why do you suppose this is happening?" This statement is a prelude to the interpretation likely to follow, but it explores the client's attitude first and gives him or her the opportunity to do his or her own interpreting.

3. The transference feeling in the client's statement may be *reflected.* For example, the counselor might state, "You feel that we shouldn't discuss this because it may make *me* uncomfortable."

4. The counselor may *interpret* the transference feelings directly. For example, "Sometimes when people feel they have been telling too much, they get insecure about their relationship with that person. Do you suppose this is happening here?" You will note that, even with the use of interpretation, the counselor seeks the feeling response of the client, since it is his or her distortion of human relationships and feelings that very likely are at the root of the difficulties. The main goal of transference interpretation, then, is to clarify the relationship between the client's earlier interpersonal experiences and his or her present behavior. A second goal is to reassure the client that these feelings and their resolution are a normal part of the process.

The interpretations generally emphasize present problems and crises and do not dwell on earlier experiences. Interpretations also come relatively late in the process to allow the counselor to accumulate data from which to make valid interpretations. Sometimes interpretations come as "shock treatment," where the counselor says in effect, "Congratulations; you are now able to take these projections and see them as existing in yourself." (The counselor then may go on to explain the nature and function of transference feelings.)

As the client becomes comfortable with the counselor, a common question on transference would be, "Toward whom else have you had these feelings you are feeling toward me?" Such a question suggests to the client that feelings toward the therapist may be directed genuinely toward him or her, but that they should be considered in terms of the idea that feelings at the moment are often attempts to relate past expectations to the present.

5. The following suggestion by May that the counselor should focus on *what* is going on now in client feelings rather than *why* provides a most fruitful technique for handling the difficult problem of transference:

> In existential therapy "transference" gets placed in the new context of an event occurring in a real relationship between two people. . . . The only thing that will grasp the patient, and in the long run make it possible for her to change, is to experience fully and deeply that she is doing precisely this to a real person, myself, in this real moment. . . . Part of this sense of timing . . . consists of letting the patient experience what he or she is doing until the experience really grasps him. Then and only then will the explanation of *why* help.
>
> This is a point the phenomenologists make consistently, namely, that to know fully *what* we are doing, to feel it, to experience it all through our being, is much more important than to know *why*. For, they hold, if we fully know the what, the why will come along by itself. (May, Angel, & Ellenberger, 1958, pp. 83–84)

The general principle here is that not all feelings of hostility, affection, or dependency automatically need be construed as transferred from the past but may be the result of a genuine present encounter between counselor and client, or between client and client in a group.

6. In general, calling attention to the transference causes the client to react in the opposite manner. Therefore, counselors usually adhere to the principle of calling attention to negative transference feelings, but not calling attention to the positive transference unless it has reached a level where it is interfering with therapeutic movement.

7. A common method for handling transference is to regard it as a form of *projection*. The counselor can test this idea by asking the client to reverse the projection, and by encouraging repetition until the statement is felt by the client as that which he or she is really feeling. The following is an example:

CL: I have the feeling that you don't like me.
 C: Can you reverse that statement?
CL: You mean, I don't like you!
 C: Yes, can you say that again louder?
CL: I don't like you!

C: Say it again louder.
CL: I don't like you!
C: True or not true?
CL: I guess that's true!

8. The counselor may also interpret transference feelings as expression of "being deficiency," as described earlier in this chapter. An example using a role reversal method follows:

CL: You don't help me.
C: What do you want me to do?
CL: To say something helpful.
C: You be me and say something helpful.
CL: OK, Gloria, you ought to stand on your own two feet and think for yourself.
C: Now be yourself and answer.
CL: You are right!

9. The counselor may *refer* the client for more extensive psychotherapy if the relationship develops to an intensity which is beyond his or her competence and responsibility.

In the concluding phases of counseling or therapy, it is necessary that any strong residual transference feelings be discussed frankly with the client and broadly interpreted. Clients must be made aware, for example, that they must become less dependent on the counseling relationship as well as on the counselor, since the present relationship is about to terminate. The affection felt toward the counselor, in addition, must be generalized to include all human beings. Any resentments lingering toward the counselor must be completely understood by the client in light of the total psychotherapeutic discussion of parents, siblings, and so on. Thus, the client is not left struggling with unresolved feelings precipitated by the counseling process.

Transference Problems in Groups

Transference problems are compounded in group work. Every member perceives the counselor incorrectly because of transference distortions around such issues as authority, dependency, and autonomy.

According to Yalom (1975) there are two major approaches to transference resolution in group therapy: consensual validation and therapist transparency. The counselor, for example, may encourage a group member to validate his or her impressions of the counselor with those of the other group members.

A second technique is to acknowledge one's fallibility openly. The counselor shares feelings and acknowledges or refutes motives or feelings attributed to him or her. The counselor could say, "I think you touched a place where I am not entirely free myself. Maybe you could help me see what's wrong here." Another example might be, "Here we all are trying to face reality. . . . I am one of you on the same quest." The counselor might also tell the group members when their comments match his or her internal experience. An example is, "I've never heard you challenge me that way before. It's scary, but also very refreshing." So group leaders need to be models of transparency themselves, yet cope with the group's transference feelings directly.

Summary of Transference

In this section, transference was described as a largely irrational part of the counseling process wherein the client projects to the counselor self-regarding attitudes and unresolved feelings from earlier human relationships. Intensity of transference seems to be a function of the type of client involved, setting, length of counseling, extent of emotional involvement, counselor personality, and counselor technique. Although the expression and working through of transference feelings have therapeutic values, it is the intense feeling or involved relationships that create counseling problems. For intensive counseling, however, the development and working through of transferences are considered to be a significant part of long-term relationships.

The resolution or working through of transference feelings is accomplished if counselors maintain an attitude of acceptance and understanding, if they apply reflection, questioning, and interpretive techniques appropriately, and if they are willing to share some of their own feeling reactions to the client's transference. In any case, transference is a normal condition of every relationship.

COUNTERTRANSFERENCE

Nature of Countertransference Feelings

The reader may have deduced from the previous discussion that countertransference refers to the emotional reactions and projections of the counselor toward the client. In an extensive review of the writings on countertransference, Cohen (1947) concluded that, although the term transference has fairly standard meaning, countertransference has not. The counselor's resentment of the client, for example, that is based upon some objective antisocial or psychotic behavior, which would be objectionable to any human being, is on one end of the continuum. Counselor reactions to client transference feelings are at the other end. Langs (1974, p. 228) defines countertransference as "one aspect of those responses to the patient which, while prompted by some event within the therapy or the therapist's real life, are primarily based on his past significant relationships; basically they gratify his needs rather than the patient's therapeutic endeavors."

We view countertransference broadly to include any attitudes of the counselor toward real or imagined client attitudes or overt behavior. It may be simply a feeling of the moment which is a genuine response between two human beings; it also may be a form of counselor projection.

One of the counselor qualifications mentioned in Chapter 4 was that they have insight into their own immaturities, prejudices, objects of disgust, anxieties, and punitive tendencies. No counselor is free from these feelings. Unless counselors are aware of their attitudes, however, their responses to client statements will all too frequently reflect their own feelings. If negative, these attitudes tend to have a destructive effect on the relationship by arousing negative transference feelings in the client. Positive countertransferences, made by counselors, such as affection, can be even more deleterious, since they are less apt to be recognized and the client is more upset when they are withdrawn. We believe that countertransference occurs in all counseling relationships, regardless of the counselor's theoretical orientation. On the other hand, there are positive and helpful countertransference attitudes in the form of facilitating counselor traits described in Chapter 4. Attitudes of acceptance are essential in building a therapeutic relationship. The counselor, furthermore, must decide how much of a "real person" he or she must be to the client.

Since handling client feelings is reported by beginning counselors to be one of their principal difficulties, countertransference complicates the problems. These counselors are relieved to know that it is commonplace to have some mixed feelings about the client. In addition, the client often is an overvalued person in the beginning counselor's life because of his or her own strong desires to succeed in counseling.

Gelso and Carter (1985) suggest that it is important to distinguish between the counselor's internal experience and his or her behavior toward the client. The counselor's internal experience refers to countertransference feelings triggered by the client and/or therapeutic situation and rooted in the counselor's own unresolved conflicts. The counselor's behavior pertains to the counselor's enactment of countertransference feelings in the relationship. Gelso and Carter note that countertransference feelings can be of enormous aid to the counselor in understanding and dealing with the client *if* counselors are attentive to their experience and how the client's behavior stimulates such experience.

There are few studies with implications for the subject of countertransference, but an early study by Chance (1958) found that, as therapy progressed, the clients became more alike in the counselor's eyes. The results of this study suggest that as counselors anticipate client progress, clients become more like the counselors' projected "generalized clients," rather than more sharply differentiated people. Mueller's (1969) later research suggested that counselors tend to respond to client transference with countertransference behavior. Research reviewed by Singer and Luborsky (1977) indicated that such counselor behavior contributed toward unsuccessful counseling outcomes.

Research support exists for the proposition that counselor awareness of countertransference feelings and attitudes can greatly assist the counseling process. Peabody and Gelso (1982) found that counselors who reported counter-transference feelings with more of their clients also tended to be more empathic counselors. Conversely, countertransference behavior, defined as withdrawal of personal involvement, was less likely to occur among the empathic counselors.

Countertransference can lead also to negative effects on clients. Hadley and Strupp (1976) summarized their views on the negative effects of counseling around several themes. All of these factors are due to counselor misjudgments or ignorance or rigidity of style. *Misassessment of the background* of the person (culture, meaning of psychopathology, motivation, ego strength, age factors) comes from pushing the client too fast or probing too deeply. Applying the *wrong method* with a particular client out of ignorance or unrealistic confidence and allowing transferences or countertransferences to get out of hand add to the possibility of a negative effect. *Communication difficulties* and inability to recognize and confront client cognitive distortions, such as overgeneralization, add to the probability of failure as a counselor. *Lack of a focal point* or theme, where the counselor allows discussion of anything or focuses too narrowly, is a factor in failure. *Mismatch* of counselor and client or a situation where the counselor is inflexible or blind to alternative theories of causation or methodologies of treatment is a contributing factor. *Ethical misconduct,* where the counselor violates a confidence, holds the client too long in counseling, or lets the counseling process just drift, is an additional factor predicting failure of counseling.

Sources of Countertransference Feelings

Counselor anxiety is a prime source of countertransference behaviors. The counseling relationship mobilizes anxiety from former relationships in a manner similar to transference. The anxiety patterns in the counselor may be classified into three types: unresolved personal problems of the counselor, situational pressures, and communication of the client's feeling to the counselor by empathic means.

The first category, the counselor's unresolved personal problems, needs little explanation. The main solution here is counseling for the counselor. Even after personal counseling, counselors must continue to increase their self-awareness to minimize countertransference.

Situational pressures are tied to the counselor's problems but also may aggravate latent feelings. An illustration follows. A counselor had just come from a fatiguing meeting. He had to wait a few minutes for a late client who, noting the austere facial expression of the counselor, apologized profusely. The client felt that the counselor was provoked with him, when in reality it was very likely the emotional exhaustion and frustation experienced by the counselor in a previous hour that caused him to respond so severely to the client.

Situational pressures exist for counselors in the form of their feeling responsibility to see that the client improves, or feeling that their professional reputation is at stake if they fail with this client. As a result, counselors "try too hard," by pushing the client, and thereby may defeat their own purposes. Counselors must be on guard so that their anxious feelings of frustration when a client does not improve are not transmitted to the client.

Related to situational pressures are heavy case loads and long counseling hours, which result in excessive fatigue. Prolonged efforts of this kind, or just the boredom of months of counseling without breaks, lead to a condition called by many counselors the "burnout effect." This is a condition of chronic fatigue, apathy, mild depression, and loss of motivation. In severe and persistent form, it has led counselors to leave the field of counseling (Maslach, 1976; Edelwich & Brodsky, 1980). This vulnerability to burnout requires that counselors seek renewal experience regularly. These refreshment experiences go beyond the usual vacation, since they require a reexamination of basic values and thorough assessment of life-style competence. Mahoney (1991) puts counselor self-nourishment at the top of the list of priorities for maintaining counselor competence.

Some mental health professional groups have begun programs to deal with peers whose personal difficulties impede their therapeutic effectiveness. They address needs of the profession to intervene and care for the "distressed psychologist" or other professionals who may not realize the extent of their own personal difficulties (Suran & Sheridan, 1985; Kilburg, Nathan, & Thoreson, 1986). The helping professions have become acutely conscious of the "wounded healers" in their midst (Maeder, 1989). These professionals often are attracted to the healing professions to fulfill their strong personal needs at the expense of their clients.

Support networks have been a key factor stressed in recent behavioral science research findings (Maslach, 1978). A study by Casas, Furlong, and Castillo (1980) is an example of such research and it underscores the importance of a support network for helping counselors, especially minority counselors, cope with stress. The study found that those counselors who said their support group was adequate (70.4 percent) reported significantly less stress than those without an adequate support network.

A third source of countertransference is communication of client feelings to the counselor. When counselors tend to be overly sympathetic, is it because they have unwittingly responded to a strong bid for sympathy and attention? When counselors feel themselves becoming anxious or resentful, is it owing to the contagion of the client's anxious feelings? That this happens frequently is possibly due to the counselor's special training in alertness to client feelings. The counselor then responds empathically to minimal cues, such as changes in posture, voice, and manner. The counselor may not be aware that the stiff jerky walk from the reception room to the office, the grating voice, or the loud aggressive talk of the client generates tensions in him or her.

Counselor responses to client hostility were studied by Gamsky and Farwell (1966) in an experimental situation. They found that counselors reacted in a negative manner when the hostility was directed at them. Counselors so threatened reacted with significantly more reassurance, suggestions, and information than at other times. Experienced counselors handled the hostility better than the less experienced. Research by Fremont and Anderson (1986) reviews a variety of client behaviors that provoke counselor anger. Guidelines for counselor response strategies are suggested.

It should not be overlooked, perhaps, that in addition to the empathic explanation, the preceding behaviors are also related to the counselor's past personal problems. One of the ways the counselor manifests anxiety is to emit impulsively a verbalization of his or her own—a question, comment, or change of subject that may not technically be relevant to the counseling process at the moment. The net effect is often disruptive from the standpoint of stopping or diverting the flow of client feelings, throwing him or her off the loaded topic, or creating more transference feelings. An example is the counselor who has difficulty working with teen-age youth because his or her own unresolved teen-age problems are reenacted.

In addition, the counselor may reveal anxiety by uneasiness. Reusch and Prestwood, in one of the first studies of recorded therapist feelings, (1949) studied psychiatrists listening to recordings of therapeutic interviews. The investigators found that the emotional tone of the listeners varied significantly with the rate of speech, use of personal pronouns, and frequency of expression of feeling. A relaxed client resulted in a relaxed listener. Those interviews heavily laden with anxiety resulted in listener reports varying from being ill at ease to being angry.

Any discussion of the source of countertransference attitudes would not be complete without mentioning the counselor's value structure again. As indicated in earlier chapters, the very nature of the relationship puts the counselor in a position of influencing the client. This happens even though he or she claims to be objective and nonjudgmental. It is difficult for counselors to avoid conveying the feeling that they regard emotional maturity, for example, as an important goal for counseling. It is quite easy for the client to guess by emotional implication, if not verbally, the values that the counselor holds after a discussion of moral problems.

The counselor conveys two types of values to the client—those on how to live and those on how to behave in counseling. There is no question professionally that a counselor can convey counseling process values that facilitate counseling. Examples are, "It is important to express how you really feel here." "It is all right to tell me how much you resent your aunt."

There is considerable question as to how far counselors should go in promoting their own moral concepts or life styles in the interview. On the one hand, it may be desirable to help a racially prejudiced client to perceive others in a less rigid manner consonant with his or her capacity for insight; on the other hand, it might lead to unfortunate consequences to specify a particular type of religious faith.

There are two reasons for restricting value projection. One is that the counselor might succeed. We cannot safely trust even a sophisticated counselor to be a "cultural high priest," posing as the best judge about right and wrong or appropriate or inappropriate beliefs. If it is felt that the client needs more information and clarification in the area of religious values, for example, it is preferable in our opinion to refer him or her to a reliable minister from whom there is a clear understanding that he or she will receive instruction in values consonant with his or her needs and subcultural identity.

Another reason for restricting value projection is that the counselor's deliberate efforts to influence the client's values might fail. The unsuccessful attempt might interfere with a good therapeutic relationship by promoting an unwanted negative transference attitude. Yet, a counselor is an expert in decisions about life styles and applying principles of behavioral science. The counselor constantly must be aware of the client's personal standards and beliefs. He or she must try to see these values as the client sees them and help the client utilize them for the client's own benefit. Counselors must keep up with the fast-changing value contexts in society at large and with emerging subcultures so that they can help clients broaden their perspectives and make wise choices.

Ingham and Love suggest a technique for handling the instances where the client is aware of the counselor's values. The counselor explains the situation by saying, for example, "You've picked up something of my feeling about marriage. I don't mind your knowing what I think about it, but it doesn't mean that you should follow my ideas" (1954, p. 78). Here the counselor admits he or she has given his or her values and allows the client to accept or reject them, yet does not refute his or her own feelings.

The Professional Identity Defense

Gottsegan and Gottsegan (1979) described a form of countertransference they call the "professional identity defense"—an unconscious need to defend one's professional image at the expense of the client. They believe it stems from taboos set up by traditional counseling theorists regarding what must not be allowed to happen in therapy. Some examples are: (1) blindness to client data that require a response different from an orthodox theory response, (2) blaming the client when things do not go right, and (3) conducting the therapy in a rigid stylistic manner so it comes out the counselor's way.

A protection against the professional identity defense is to try new therapeutic techniques. Until counselors actually experience the new techniques, they must not summarily reject them. This approach is consonant with the theoretical position we described in Chapter 1, namely, that counselors must not rigidify their responses or acquire a thoretical identity too quickly. This means becoming a creative synthesizer and continuing to integrate new concepts and methods.

Barriers Faced by New and Early Helping Professionals

Many beginning therapists bring a variety of anxieties into their counseling sessions. These anxieties may make the beginning therapist especially vulnerable to countertransference responses. Corey (1986) has described a variety of issues for beginning therapists, including role confusion, perfectionist expectations of themselves, unrealistic expectations about how clients should change, anxiety about periods of silence, and difficulties with demanding or uncommitted clients. Close supervision focusing both on the counseling process and the counselor as a person during this period of professional growth can help counselors to understand better how their own attitudes and feelings affect the therapy process.

New professionals, especially in university training settings, face many pressures (Mintz, 1992; Watkins, 1992; Good, 1992). Among these are concerns about licensure, tenure, fears of measuring up, role conflict, promotion, and overload. In institutional settings, dealing with the local politics of the system is a source of anxiety also. Finding the right balance between role responsibilities and self-renewal is a high concern for both academic and service professionals. It is easy to get overcommitted and court professional burnout in spite of the rich personal rewards of the counseling, teaching, and research activities.

Signs of Countertransference Feelings

The following checklist of illustrative signs is offered to enable counselors to test themselves. It is hoped that it will help to distinguish positive therapeutic feelings from anxious or defensive countertransference involvement with clients.

1. Getting sleepy, not listening or paying attention, or not hearing a client's messages clearly.
2. Denying the presence of anxiety and thinking, "I feel all right about this topic and should feel upset; but I don't." (If there were no anxiety present, why would the counselor even think about it?)
3. Finding it difficult to shift positions or experiencing one's self "tighten up."
4. Becoming sympathetic rather than empathic or becoming overly emotional in the face of a client's troubles.
5. Selecting certain material to reflect or interpret and wondering afterward why this material rather than some other material was selected.
6. Consistently reflecting or interpreting too soon or incorrectly (and the result cannot be accounted for on client resistance grounds only).
7. Consistently underestimating or missing the client's depth of feeling.
8. Feeling an unreasoning dislike or attraction for the client. Getting angry at the "unappreciative" client.
9. Being unable to identify with the client. For example, when the client feels upset, the counselor feels no emotional response.
10. Overidentifying with the client, as in becoming aggressively sympathetic when the client cites maltreatment by an authority figure.
11. Discovering a tendency to argue with the client, becoming defensive, or otherwise vulnerable to client criticism.
12. Feeling that this is a "best" or "worst" client.
13. Being preoccupied with the client in fantasy between sessions, even to the extent of thinking of responses to be made.
14. Being habitually late in starting interviews or running over the hour with certain clients.
15. Attempting to elicit some strong affect from the client by making dramatic statements.
16. Being overly concerned about the confidential nature of the work with clients.

17. Feeling the compulsion to do something active; hence, making too strong an impact with "shotgun" interpretations and suggestions.
18. Dreaming about the client.
19. Being too "busy" to see the client or complaining of "administrative duties."
20. Working excessively hard with clients to the point of fatigue, then complaining of overwork.

An insidious form of countertransference expression is compulsive advice giving. This "if I were you" approach is so exceedingly common in everyday human relations that it tends to spill into counseling relationships also. The counselor may feel the need to convince the client that the course of action discussed is best for him; yet the advice, persuasion, or reassurance is motivated more by the counselor's personal needs. A possible motive for advice giving is extrapunitive hostility. It is a way of controlling others, depreciating them, and elevating one's self to a dominating role. There are conditions, however, where *information* and *opinions* can be offered.

A common form of countertransference feeling is the idea that the client must somehow like the counselor and that the counselor must please the client. Though the relationship is built upon mutual trust and cordiality, there are times when the counselor must risk this client admiration. For example, sometimes counselors must help clients see that they must give up important things, and that removal of pleasing behaviors is sometimes painful. Counselors' needs to be the "givers" may lead them to be overly accommodating in areas such as scheduling and fee setting.

Fiedler (1951) found in his studies of the factors in the counseling relationships that the poor, or nonexpert, counselors had the tendency to "not hear," "ignore," or communicate poorly with clients. The expert counselors had these tendencies significantly less often. This study suggests that such countertransference signs, as Fiedler found, are not a great problem for experienced therapists.

For counselors who feel that they are not vulnerable to countertransference tendencies, a revealing and sobering exploratory study by Fiedler is cited. He found that there was a high relationship between therapeutic competence and lack of negative countertransference attitudes. Fiedler's method consisted of comparing the similarity of the counselor's and the client's self-descriptions. The counselor's "ideal" description, then, was used to determine the nature and intensity of countertransference feelings. An implication of this study is that, as counselors grow in counseling experience and personal understanding, their harmful countertransference attitudes diminish.

Resolution of Countertransference Feelings

Although little research has been done in the area of resolving a countertransference, there is a body of clinical experience that may be useful to the counselor in handling feelings toward the client. Increasingly, encounter group experiences are helping not only beginning but experienced counselors to become more aware of their feelings toward clients. Supervision and consultation with colleagues is the accepted method for checking out countertransference concerns. Asking a colleague to review a videotape of an interview and offer feedback is accepted professional practice for professional growth (Masters, 1992).

Locating Sources of Feelings.   After awareness of the feelings, the first step consists of the counselor asking, "I wonder why this is so?" This question is precipitated by the feeling that the counselor is not communicating with clients. The following list of questions should give counselors additional reasons to ponder their countertransference attitudes.

A COUNSELOR'S GUIDE TO SELF-CRITICISM[1]

Why did I make this particular response to this client's remark? What was behind it?

What was I reacting to when making this remark?

What was I endeavoring to convey to the client?

Why did I ask that question?

Was it really asked for purposes related to helping the client?

Was I merely curious?

Was I really being judgmental by asking that question?

Why did I feel impelled at this point to give advice?

Was it because I felt that the client expected me to have all the answers?

Did I respond by being all-wise?

Why did I become so emotionally involved with the client who felt so unloved and insecure?

Could it be that basically I too still feel unloved and unlovable?

Why did I want (or did I not want) to bring the parent, husband, or wife of this client into counseling?

Can it be that I have overidentified with the client and have already rejected the spouse? (or the parent?)

Why in this first interview did I talk so much instead of letting the client tell his or her story?

Was it because I felt I had to impress the client with my own knowledge so he or she would return?

Why does it upset me when appointments are broken?

Is it because I am really insecure and uncertain concerning my skill?

Why am I so reluctant to "let go" when the counseling with a client has reached a good termination point, or when I know the client should be referred for a different kind of help?

Am I using the client for my needs or am I letting the client use me?

Counselors must accept the fact that they have varied feelings about clients and that they will be changed somewhat by the counseling experience. Counsel-

[1]Adapted from Johnson (1946).

ors must also be aware that they have anxieties coming from insecurity in the counseling role and the client's expression of anxiety.

Counselors must control their tendencies to give reassurance to the client because of their own needs for reassurance. For example:

CL: Sometimes I feel like screaming out loud in a quiet place like the library. In fact, I feel so tensed up at times I feel like wringing somebody's neck till he dies.

 C: It is all right to feel that way. After all, thinking of killing isn't the same as murder.

This counselor's response is likely to arouse more anxiety in the client, whereas the following response would recognize the main feeling, tend to tone down the reassurance, and yet not show the counselor's anxiety (even if the counselor realistically pictures himself as a possible object of the client's homicidal feelings):

C: Sometimes these feelings do seem hard to control and we feel an urge to let them go at times. Perhaps you would like to talk further about these feelings and mention some experiences with other people or situations that make you feel this way.

Counselors control their anxiety through the knowledge that nonpsychotic clients rarely assault counselors and that hostile, threatening language is often a clever device used by disturbed clients to frighten counselors.

Supervisory Assistance.   First of all, every counselor who feels uneasy about his or her responses to a client should admit to the possibility that these comments are a form of his or her own projections. All that may be necessary is to admit to this possibility frankly with a supervisor or colleague and attempt to change. There are times in the professional life of all counselors when they must admit that certain types of personalities make them defensive or are beyond their level of competence. They can handle this problem by assessing the client as "too hot to handle" and referring the client to another therapist. An additional recourse is the supervisor or a colleague with whom a counselor can discuss, with considerable candor, the feelings involved, without breaching the confidences of the relationship. For example, a counselor may recognize that he has trouble with hostile, aggressive women; hence, he might suggest that such a client change counselors. Again, discussing this problem in a counseling relationship or in a case conference with a supervisor helps counselors resolve their own feelings.

Discussion with the Client.   Although there is no objective evidence to indicate that it is expedient to discuss countertransference feelings with the client, we have found a mild reassuring and interpretive reference occasionally helpful in allaying anxiety. For example, this is a second interview with a 33-year-old married woman, after a discussion about an involved marital problem:

CL: Well, there it is—straight from the shoulder.

C: You feel you have told the story quite frankly. Perhaps you have noticed that there are times when things you say may seem to disturb me a bit. I trust though that you will not hold back any feelings for fear of disturbing me.

CL: I appreciate your telling me this. It might make it easier to talk to you.

Another example wherein a counselor rationalizes his or her unwarranted intrusion follows: The counselor has just interrupted the client and says, "I'm sorry; I didn't intend to stop you. Sometimes we are so eager to help we interrupt your train of thought."

Counselor Growth.   Counselors can use their own awareness of themselves as reflected through the therapeutic process to enhance their own growth and resolve their difficulties. Sometimes counselors doubt their own intellectual adequacy and habitually overrate or compete with their more intellectual clients. This situation makes it difficult for the counselor to help clients who use intellectualized defenses against their own anxieties. Similarly, the "burnout effect" cited earlier can be allayed or avoided by careful attention to a personal growth program of renewal, rest, and recreation.

Exemplary Encounter.   If the dialogue is seen as an *encounter,* rather than a passive helping relationship, then the counselor will not be afraid of expressing and introjecting his or her own feelings of anger and frustration. A counselor's awareness of countertransference dangers, and willingness to admit that "this may be my problem," provide the client with an open model of humanness and expression, which will help the client more than an overcautious counselor who is constricted because of countertransference fears. We see a danger in becoming too cautious for fear that countertransference may cause trouble. This caution could result in excessive "friendly, warm, and respectful" behavior. Research by Epstein (1977) warns that avoiding one's hostile or angry feelings is not always beneficial. Clients who feel worthless often tend to feel even more worthless when their counselor is always warm and accepting. By recognizing and being honest about his or her own anger, the counselor can set appropriate boundaries for himself or herself and the client. Fremont and Anderson (1986) suggest that the counselor's response of sharing anger may be inappropriate if he or she fails to recognize that the client's behavior (1) is a demonstration of the very characteristics that have alienated the client from others and (2) reflects the problem behavior that brought the client into counseling.

Analysis of Tapes and Videotapes.   An additional source of countertransference awareness is use of audio- and videotape recordings. A frank discussion with fellow staff members of the countertransference aspects of their work samples will reduce the danger of introjection of the counselor's projections into therapeutic work. Tape review allows for a more independent review of possible interactional patterns of transference and countertransference responses. Fong and Cox (1983) state that many behaviors eliciting counselor anger represent tests of the boundaries of the counseling relationship and of the counselor's trustworthiness, particularly in the early stages of therapy.

Summary of Countertransference

The purpose of this section is to emphasize the importance of counselor awareness of irrational attitudinal responses. Another purpose is to suggest ways of resolving these feelings. A counselor can resolve feelings toward the client by recognizing that he or she has countertransference feelings, by examining himself or herself concerning why the feelings exist, possibly admitting that he or she should not work with this client, and by using the recognition of countertransference feelings as information to enhance his or her own personal growth outside the interviews through counseling or encouter group work.

The next section contains a consideration of the phenomenon of resistance, which draws upon elements of the transference and countertransference discussion; yet the resistance phenomenon has unique characteristics of its own.

RESISTANCE

Nature of Resistance

One of the principal realities of building and maintaining an effective counseling relationship is the presence of resistance to change. Resistance is viewed differently by the various theoretical approaches on whether the source is in the counselor or the client.

The term *resistance* was introduced by Freud to indicate unconscious opposition toward bringing unconscious material into consciousness, as well as the mobilization of repressive and protective functions of the ego. Resistance was considered a special defensive form of transference. Psychoanalytically oriented therapists have viewed resistance as an important phenomenon for intensive analysis. They believe if they can understand the client's resistance, then they will be more able to help clients understand and change their behavior.

Phenomenological approaches also have understood resistance as serving a defensive purpose. Generally, resistance is seen as a refusal to take responsibility for one's life. May (1958, p. 79) referred to resistance as "the tendency of the client to . . . renounce the particular unique and original potentiality which is his." Rogers (1942) wrote that resistance represents the client's efforts to accelerate or to cut the process of therapy short. Perls states cogently from the Gestalt viewpoint that all resistance represents the client's refusal to be self-supportive. Therefore, he or she has to be confronted with the "gain" he or she gets from such resistance.

Behaviorists have written very little about resistance. They tend to view resistance as "noncompliance." The behavioral understanding of resistance does not blame the client for not wanting to change. Rather, responsibility for client noncompliance is placed onto the therapist for not utilizing adequate relationship enhancement or behavior-change methods (Goldstein & Myers, 1986). When resistance is encountered, the behaviorist is likely to examine specific therapist relationship offerings that are "functionally counterproductive" for the "low relatability" clients. The therapist will also assess dysfunctional client beliefs and skills that impede compliance and environmental contingencies that reinforce noncompliance.

Systems approaches to counseling often expect resistance from clients. Systems approaches view resistance differently depending on the systems theory "tradition" subscribed to by the counselor. Structural and intergenerational approaches understand resistance as a homeostatic response triggered by anxiety about possible changes in the client system. Alternatively, strategic approaches accept resistance as the client's best available response to the therapist at the given moment. Strategic therapists take a respectful attitude toward resistance by accepting such behavior as a genuine attempt by the client to respond in the best way possible. This attitude was expressed by Milton Erickson, a well-known strategic therapist, in his statement, "Sick people do want to try; usually they don't know how." Strategic therapists view resistance as client behaviors motivated by discomfort aroused by lack of congruence between the expectations of the therapist and those of the client regarding help or regarding their reciprocal roles. Systems therapists suggest that resistance is best handled by accepting and "utilizing" the client's "resistive" attitudes and behaviors. The therapist must provide interventions that are consistent with the client's world view and that offer the client a new learning experience. Inflexibility on the part of the therapist is usually considered to be the source of resistance problems.

Mahoney (1991) espouses the protective theory of resistance where reluctance to change is viewed as a natural event. When the pain or discomfort of change mounts, the resistance increases also. The counselor's task is to move with these forces rather than against them so the client feels more secure with the contemplated changes. Ivey, Ivey, and Simek-Morgan (1991) have a similar view that resistance is the client's best effort to cope with stressors and should be regarded by the counselor as a clue to the client's developmental history. Thus, the resistance to change is viewed as learned coping behavior.

Manifestations and Classifications of Resistance

Although it is futile to attempt to list the myriad forms of resistance, it may be helpful to indicate some of the subtle as well as glaring examples. We feel that a distinguishing mark of the experienced counselor is the ability to recognize resistance and deal with it appropriately.

Resistance may manifest itself in a number of negativistic ways. For example, the client criticizes the counselor, expresses dissatisfaction with the results of counseling, fails to hear or to understand the counselor, comes late or fails to keep appointments, remains silent, forgets the fee, engages in intellectual discussion using complex psychological terms, expresses negative attitudes toward psychology, desires to end counseling prematurely, is unproductive in associations or with unfamiliar material, introduces irrelevant topics, makes unreasonable demands on the counselor, is pessimistic about counseling, or expresses skepticism about interpretations.

The client's resistance may take less aggressive forms as, for example, agreeing unequivocally with everything the counselor says, refusing to get emotionally involved, being overly cooperative, prolonging a dependency transference, maintaining persistent facetiousness, forcing the process into a semantic wilderness of abstractions and philosophical notions, pressing the limits of the relationship by asking for overtime, or expressing strong interest in the counselor's personal life. Usually there is a recursive pattern of interaction and "game playing" between the client and the therapist that will elicit confusion or frustration in the therapist.

Although resistance is often considered "oppositional" by the therapist, we suggest it is important for the therapist to reframe this view for herself or himself into a more neutral stance. The strength of behavioral and systemic understandings of resistance is that these perspectives lead the therapist into more flexible and constructive behaviors than if the client is viewed only as a "resistive manipulator."

Positive Functions of Resistance

In addition to the protective or defensive functions of resistance for the client, there are valuable clues that resistance provides for the counselor. A principal value of resistance for the counselor is that it gives an indication of general interview progress and the basis for diagnostic and prognostic formulations. Noting resistance symptoms is the first step toward taking appropriate measures to ignore, reduce, or utilize them.

A second function of resistance is the glimpse it affords into the client's defensive structure. The presence of resistance tells the counselor that the client does not wish to explore these particular feelings further at this moment. Areas involving morals and deeply held beliefs are usually defended rigidly. Hence, resistance symptoms inform counselors when they are treading temporarily in taboo territory. When these areas of threat become known, therefore, they offer the counselor much valuable interpretive information.

Resistance is the counselor's cue that perhaps his usefulness has ended and that counseling should be formally terminated. Clients change their feelings of warmth and acceptance toward the counselor to resentment when they no longer feel the need of the relationship. This manifestation, therefore, may be a healthy indication for terminating the relationship.

Resistance acts as a protective mechanism for clients through keeping acute anxiety under control, and through avoiding disintegration of their defensive structures prior to establishment of new constructive behavior. In this sense, resistance often serves a useful decelerating function for the early stages in the counseling process.

Richard Lazarus (1979) has suggested that we need to reassess the idea that facing facts, or "reality testing," is one of the main ways of avoiding resistance. In fact, Lazarus suggests that denial (refusing to face the facts) and illusion (false beliefs about reality) are useful in coping with stress and may be healthy strategies for certain situations. He goes further in saying that a temporary disavowal of reality helps a person get through the devastating period of facing death, for example. The person can later face the facts and mobilize coping efforts, but, at first, denial appears to be useful.

Lazarus also distinguishes between threat and challenge to illustrate his point. Threat is a state in which a person feels blocked and coping skills are inadequate. Challenge, however, actually facilitates functioning and growth, in the long run. Another implication of threat theory is that we can teach coping skills by helping students to change maladaptive strategies to adaptive ones. An example of maladaptive self-talk would be, "This exam is too tough for me." A more effective self-statement would be, "I may be a bit anxious during the exam, but it may actually help me do better."

Techniques for Handling Resistance

In one sense, all of the readiness and relationship techniques mentioned in preceding chapters are designed to build a relationship and, consequently, to reduce or to prevent resistance. How this is accomplished is an intensely practical problem for the counselor, because the resistance variable determines to a considerable extent whether a client will leave counseling or continue. We assume at this point that the main aim for the moment is to keep clients in counseling and to prevent their loss of confidence in the counselor.

The counselor's first step in dealing with resistance is to become aware of possible external causes in himself or herself and the influence of the amount of lead in his or her techniques. The counselor then can take judicious steps according to the following suggestions.

1. Client resistance sometimes emerges because the counselor is proceeding at a pace that is too quick for the client. Slowing down the pace of therapy can reduce client resistance. Erickson (Zeig, 1982) distinguishes "pacing" versus "leading" communication. Pacing communications essentially feed back the client's experience and are intended to build trust and cooperation. Leading involves introducing interpretations or requests that are different from, but consistent with, the client's present view but are designed to lead to a new way of interpreting events. Pacing and leading can be done nonverbally as well as verbally.

2. Lessening emotional impact is a related technique that involves moving to a more intellectually loaded aspect of the topic that has aroused the resistance. This tends to reduce the pressure felt by the client. Circular questions can be used in this way. A judicious use of humor can also ease the tension felt by the

client. This must be a natural and spontaneous act, however, since a strained or awkward use of humor, or use with an implication that makes the client appear ridiculous or criticized will increase resistance.

3. Increasing emotional support and acceptance for the client are often the keys to reduction of resistance, particularly when the client can accept the counselor (Wachtel, 1980).

4. Interpretation of the resistance, a principal direct technique, involves an explanation of what the client is doing to resist. This technique helps clients develop a tolerance and acceptance of their own resistance, as well as an intellectual understanding of its uses and difficulties caused when resistance gets out of hand. The counselor expresses his or her own acceptance of the resistance along with the interpretation. This acceptance helps to decrease the likelihood that the client will take offense at the interpretation. Examples are:

CL: I just can't talk about it.
 C: You feel that sex is a topic to be avoided. Perhaps you can see that this tendency is serving some useful purpose which we cannot yet understand.
CL: Yes, that makes me feel a little better about it.

An example of interpretation of a transference problem follows:

 C: (replying after the client has made a serious of skeptical comments about the counselor after a preliminary exploration of family relationships) Do you see that your feelings toward this relationship of ours are possibly related to your feelings about your father? You felt you couldn't trust him and now you unconsciously see your father in me.
CL: I never looked at it quite that way before. I'll have to think about that.

Reflection of the feelings of resistance often is effective as a direct technique when the client appears to have an intense feeling, such as guilt, about resisting. It is an effective technique in the earlier interviews where interpretation might be premature.

Referral techniques are needed occasionally when intensive resistance is encountered. Counselors should assess their own therapeutic competence carefully before penetrating the defenses of a highly resistant client. Sometimes, if a counselor shifts the client to another counselor, he or she can remove the source of external resistance that has been inhibiting therapeutic progress.

Threats in veiled form, though a last resort, are useful occasionally in a high-risk attempt to motivate a resistive client to change his or her behavior. This situation would be apparent where the counselor's role included, in addition, that of dean, personnel manager, or other authoritarian position. For example, a student client having academic difficulties has been resisting discussion of the problem. The counselor may say, "If you don't want to work this out, I suggest we stop getting together."

5. Sometimes a personal encounter between the therapist and client can

reduce resistance. If the counselor shares how the client's specific behavior affects him or her, this personal sharing often leads the client into a degree of personal sharing that matches that of the therapist. Intellectualizing impasses are often broken in this way.

6. Providing choice to the client and employing a less authoritative structure can reduce resistance related to client needs for autonomy and power (Beutler, 1982).

7. *Body experiencing* can sometimes help, that is, to flow with the resistance and experience it in one's body. Gendlin (1978) proposed that experiencing the resistance directly in one's body is an important coping strategy. The following interview excerpt illustrates how this approach might proceed.

C: Oh, so you are afraid to experience your anger?
CL: I'm not really angry.
C: Can you let yourself experience how afraid you could be to experience your anger?
CL: I don't think so.
C: Let's suppose you are angry. How would you feel about it?
CL: I wouldn't like it.
C: Would it be scary for you if you were angry?
CL: Yes.

8. Reframing (Watzlawick et al., 1974) involves changing the meaning attributed to a situation. Weeks and L'Abate (1982) have summarized a variety of reframing methods. One method is "positive connotation" in which the therapist labels a client's behavior as "helpful" in a particular way rather than as bad or resistive. Papp (1977), for example, tells a woman that she should continue to act helpless and incompetent because that gives her husband a chance to show how strong, caring, and protective he could be. She further warned of the negative consequences that might occur should she attempt to change. Sometimes a therapist will positively relabel a client's behavior. For example, a client's anger becomes "concern," passivity becomes "the ability to accept things as they are," opposition becomes "searching for one's own way of doing things," and withdrawing becomes "taking care of oneself" (Weeks, 1977).

9. Paradoxical techniques or "paradoxical intention" (Frankl, 1967; Dowd and Milne, 1986) are also used with resistive clients. Paradoxical techniques are often appealing to the beginning therapist because of the appearance of power and the creative possibilities for the therapist. However, delivery of well-constructed paradoxical techniques is a complex process and counselors should familiarize themselves thoroughly with paradoxical methods reviewed and summarized by Dowd and Milne. The ethical and legal implications invite caution. Weeks and L'Abate (1982; Johnson, 1986) provide useful guidelines and contraindications for the use of paradoxical interventions. Paradoxical interventions fall into various categories: symptom prescriptions, paradoxical homework prescriptions related to time (i.e., symptom scheduling, predicting the negative con-

sequences of change, predicting and prescribing a relapse, declaring hopelessness, and others).

10. Resistance may sometimes be reduced by developing a better implementation plan for the client. The therapist may find it important to break down homework tasks into smaller units and take a more gradual therapeutic approach. Perhaps the client's resistance comes from being asked to do something that seems too complex or difficult. A task such as learning to juggle seems impossible if one attempts to learn it by starting with three balls. One needs to begin with one ball and gradually add more skills in order to make the goal attainable. In the same way, a task such as "learning to get close to significant others" involves many complex skills. Therapists need to remember that there is a distinction between the formation of a goal and the ability to initiate and carry out the chains of behavior and experience to fulfill it.

SUMMARY

Although transference, countertransference, and resistance are ever-present phenomena in the counseling process, the counselor must deal judiciously with these conditions to keep the process moving toward satisfactory termination. Transference patterns can adversely affect the therapeutic alliance or can provide useful psychological data. Countertransference, the transference feelings of the counselor, is a tendency which must be recognized and resolved by a counselor before counseling can progress satisfactorily. Resistance is the natural blocking of interview progress and must be resolved by a number of counseling techniques—from ignoring the resistance to direct interpretation. Resistance signs serve as useful cues concerning sensitive personality areas, general interview progress, and the nature of the client's defensive structure.

CHAPTER 9

Group Principles and Methods

INTRODUCTION TO GROUP COUNSELING AND PSYCHOTHERAPY

Group therapy continues to be a popular application of therapeutic psychology. Group experience alleviates loneliness and permits people to grow, to risk change. The encounter group encourages real relationships. Maslow said, "If ordinary [individual] therapy may be conceived of as a miniature ideal society of two, then group therapy may be seen as a miniature ideal society of ten. . . . In addition we now have empirical data that indicate group therapy . . . can do some things that individual psychotherapy cannot" (1970, p. 263). Counselors in most settings are exposed to group counseling approaches. Therapists in mental health settings usually become involved in therapy groups, life skills training, parent groups, substance abuse recovery, or groups related to managing depression or anxiety. Counselors in schools and colleges offer groups in areas such as social skills, career exploration, personal growth, and text anxiety. Psychologists in medical settings are often involved in groups oriented to pain management or living with a particular illness. Counselors in business settings may lead groups related to effective leadership, preretirement planning, or team building. In almost any setting, counselors can find applications of group work.

Advantages of Groups

Group counseling approaches offer various advantages over individual counseling. In group counseling, the presence of others provides a unique opportunity for practicing new social interactional skills with peers in a protected setting.

The group structure encourages clients to offer other clients feedback about their behavior and to offer advice about new behaviors. Individuals report valuing the feeling of being accepted, trusted, cared about, and helped by others. They also value the opportunity to learn to accept, trust, care, and help others in the group.

The group provides clients with an opportunity to recognize and change many behaviors and attitudes as they respond to the constantly changing group demands. As a group progresses through its stages, clients learn to deal with tasks related to inclusion, control, affection, and leave-taking. Clients in groups develop important leadership skills as they often play an important role in assisting others, establishing and monitoring group goals, and asking for the help and feedback they desire. As clients interact with each other, social norms are developed that enhance behavior change. Clients share a commitment to change, mutual support, and accountability.

Group approaches provide an opportunity for clients to receive help from others who share a common problem or experience. Several studies reviewing the effectiveness of group treatment components (D'Alelio & Murray, 1981; Roth, Bielski, Jones, Parker, & Osborne, 1982) showed that clients reported that "seeing that others were going through the same thing" was the most important treatment component.

DEVELOPMENTS IN GROUP WORK

Types of Groups

Cohen and Smith (1976) suggest that groups can be categorized into four types: (1) groups designed to encourage organizational development or problem solving; (2) groups for learning interpersonal and leadership skills; (3) growth groups; and (4) therapy groups. In actual practice, these four types of groups overlap. Groups differ along a number of dimensions, such as their task versus relationship orientation, leadership style, degree of structure, duration, and client population. In this chapter we will primarily describe examples of therapy, growth, skill training, and actualization groups. Additionally, we will discuss the phenomena of self-help groups.

Group Psychotherapy.   Distinctions between counseling and psychotherapy cited in Chapter 1 hold for group counseling and group psychotherapy. The focus of group counseling is on group dynamics and interpersonal skills rather than on basic personality changes. Group therapy focuses more on remediation and personality reconstruction than on managing current developmental problems. Because the client population tends to suffer from more severe emotional problems, group psychotherapy deals with past difficulties that impede current functioning. Therapy groups generally try to assist participants to reexperience painful situations and to express intensive core feelings, such as intense hatred.

As these traumatic experiences are relived in the group, participants gain insight into how their own past history or unconscious dynamics interfere with current functioning. Additionally, the group provides a supportive environment for developing new patterns of behavior. These groups tend to be of relatively long duration. Group psychotherapy can be based on various therapeutic models, including psychoanalytic, behavioral, and phenomenological frameworks.

Growth-Oriented Groups. Growth-oriented groups emphasize personal growth for people already functioning well, rather than for individuals needing to solve intense personal problems. These groups tend to focus on the "here and now" of present group interaction and communication skills, rather than on problems and feelings of the past. Growth groups, sometimes called "encounter groups" or "T-groups," explore personal blocks to intimacy and actualization.

The techniques of growth groups vary depending on their theoretical orientation. Techniques may include imagery and fantasy, encounter games, sensory-awakening experiences, body awareness, psychodrama, and dialogues with various parts of oneself.

Sometimes growth groups are focused on particular topics or issues. Zimet (1979) introduced a group concept he calls "short-term developmental task and crisis groups," which focus on life-stage issues and developmental transitions. Examples of such groups may be "managing life transitions," "women in transition," "preparing for retirement," and "divorce recovery." Examples of such groups are described by Schlossberg (1984), Brammer and Abrego (1981), and Brammer, (1991).

Marathon Groups. Marathon groups (Bach, 1966) represent a blending of growth and therapy groups. The marathon group uses intensive group work and was popular during the sixties. This was an intensive, living-in kind of therapeutic experience with a group of about 12, a therapist, and a cotherapist or two. It went on for 24 hours or more, with little time taken for vital functions. The total honesty and free expression of feelings over an intensive and extensive period of time results in greater transparency of feelings for some than would more spaced sessions. Marathon groups are not necessarily "one-shot" sessions, since follow-up sessions are conducted frequently. Sometimes a weekend is spent, with three intensive sessions interspersed with short sleep periods. Most evaluative data are in the form of personal testimonials about how one's life style has changed. Few data are available about the permanence of changes when participants return to Monday morning routines without reinforcement for new-found gains. One criticism is that current practitioners do not screen candidates for marathon groups with sufficient care; a person with weak defenses or latent emotional crises would be especially vulnerable.

Skill-Training Groups. These groups focus on teaching specific topic-related skills in areas such as assertion, parenting skills, marital communication, and stress reduction. Some groups address more general issues, however, such as "gaining control of your life," "building self-confidence," and "weight management." The tools utilized in these groups include brief lectures, specific social interactive exercises, and social skills training. Most skill-training groups rely heavily on cognitive-behavioral interventions. Groups tend to be time limited. A specific agenda at each meeting is used because of a restricted number of sessions and limited goals.

Rose (1986) describes these groups as focusing on the development of cognitive, affective, and social coping skills necessary to improve the quality of each client's relationships with others and/or to help each to cope more effectively with the numerous problematic situations with which he or she is confronted. Using cognitive-behavioral methods, clients are helped to learn a wide variety of problem-solving and coping behaviors. Strategies to reduce skill deficits include modeling, behavior rehearsal, coaching, and group feedback. Cognitive procedures such as stress inoculation and cognitive restructuring are also used, as is problem-solving training. As in other types of groups, mutual support, teaching, demonstrations, and feedback of the clients to each other are essential to group success.

Rose suggests that social skills training groups are fundamentally important since social skill deficits are related to major psychological problems and can precede a variety of clinical syndromes.

Stress Debriefing Groups.   A growing application of group processes to prevention of chronic psychological disorders is Critical Incident Stress Debriefing (CISD). This strategy offers debriefing opportunities to rescue and support personnel in community disasters such as earthquakes, plane crashes, floods, tornados, and train wrecks where large numbers of rescue personnel are on duty for sustained periods of time. Much has been done for the victims of mass disasters through the Red Cross and government agencies, but little is done for the large numbers of medical personnel, police and firefighters, rescue workers, and social agency staff who are vulnerable to Post-Traumatic Stress Disorder (PTSD). Signs of PTSD are anxiety attacks, tremors, digestive and sleep disorders, remorse, and irritability. Some rescue personnel recover their normal pretrauma state, but many caregivers who are left to their own resources develop PTSD signs (Hartsough & Myers, 1985).

The term PTSD was used originally as a descriptor for the after-effects of traumatic battle experiences, formerly called "battle fatigue." Now the term applies to any psychological disorder, similar to the description above, that is attributable to the effects of a traumatic event.

The principal application of group processes is through a debriefing event as close in time as possible, but physically removed, from the trauma scene. CISD consists of small groups gathered under an experienced group leader in a quiet setting. Participants describe their experiences, share their feelings, and discuss their plans. They assess their strengths and make arrangements for strengthening their support networks, for example. The primary goal is to help the caregivers and rescuers express and cope with their emotional needs so that they will reduce the risks of suffering permanent emotional damage. Follow-up sessions are arranged also, after they have had the experience of being reunited with their families and getting on with their regular work life. Traumatic rescue events often uncap residual emotional problems growing out of early development or current family and work environments. While the emphasis in CISD is on large-scale disasters, the group debriefing principles apply also to smaller-scale events that affect many families, such as fires, floods, accidents, illnesses, crime, and domestic violence.

Another important application of group methods to traumatic stress is community stress debriefing. The discussion above focused on caregivers, but whole communities are traumatized by events even though they may not be individual victims. They know victims and rescuers and share in some of the emotional experiences of shock, grief, and fear. These experiences need not be drastic large-scale events, such as earthquakes and plane crashes. These community crises are consequences of events such as a high school student committing suicide or a fatal auto accident. These events call for multiple group sessions on a massive scale to debrief the feelings and defuse potentially destructive proposals of the community. The required skills of the group leaders are similar to those of the counseling groups described in this chapter.

Self-Help Groups. In recent years, an increasing number of people have participated in self-help groups led by people who are not professional group leaders. Rather, they struggle with many of the same issues as group members. Lieberman (1980) suggests that there are over two hundred different types of self-help organizations. They include groups such as support groups for illnesses such as cancer, AIDS, and Alzheimer's Disease, substance-abuse-related self-help groups such as Alcoholics Anonymous, Adult Children of Alcoholics, and Narcotics Anonymous, and various other groups related to issues such as phobias, loneliness, divorce, parenting, and being widowed. These groups stress learning that comes from the sharing of experiences, mutual commitment and acceptance, and often adherence to a course of action such as the "twelve steps" of Alcoholics Anonymous.

Actualization Groups. The goals of actualizing group work cover broad outcomes to match the actualizing values cited in Chapter 3, as well as the specific outcomes expected by individual participants. These intensive actualization group experiences are conducted for periods as long as 12 weeks or as short as a two-day weekend. There is a dual emphasis—didactic (lectures, films, demonstrations) and experiential group exercises (Shostrom, Knapp, & Knapp, 1976).

Actualization groups synthesize aspects of psychotherapy groups, growth groups, and skill-training groups. Actualization groups draw upon the feeling emphasis of growth groups and utilize many encounter and interpersonal development strategies. Actualization groups are similar to skill-training groups in their combined use of didactic and experiential group exercises. Actualization groups focus on precise outcome behaviors and evaluate progress through instruments such as the Actualizing Assessment Battery and specific coping skills inventories. In their breadth and depth, actualization groups are similar to group therapy.

RESEARCH ON GROUPS

Abundant research comparing groups and individual methods with controls has appeared in the last few years (Fuhriman & Burlingame, 1990). Results are conflicting because of the difficulty controlling treatment conditions and specifying the methods of the counselors. Rose (1986) reports that in almost every study in which group cognitive-behavioral treatment is compared with individual treatment, both conditions show significant gains without either being significantly better. He concludes that group therapy is demonstrated to be at least as effective as individual treatment, and in most cases, much less costly.

Some groups are more effective and some leadership styles are more effective, depending on the peculiar characteristics of the counselor (Yalom, Lieberman, & Miles, 1971). Yalom (1975) contends that the behavior of group leaders is not predictable from their particular ideological schools. However, their behaviors and leadership styles seem to be the critical variables in determining the effectiveness of a group. Yalom cites research demonstrating that four leadership functions have a direct relationship to the outcomes of group work. First, caring is essential. Second, meaning attribution (explaining, clarifying, providing a cognitive framework for change) is directly related to positive outcome. Third, emotional stimulation (challenging, risk taking, self-disclosure, activity) is important to give vitality to a group. Fourth, the leader's executive function, which includes structuring, developing norms, and suggesting procedures, is valuable in providing the group with enough direction. Further, in researching growth groups, Yalom, Lieberman, and Miles (1971) found that leaders with either a strong, confrontative style or a pronounced laissez-faire, low-key style were least effective and had the largest number of group "casualties." A review by Fuhriman and Burlingame (1990) found that effective group counselors were characterized as having a strong and separate identity, which enables them to have a more integrative and interactive role. These therapists were seen as being more egalitarian, trustworthy, and humorous.

Gibb (1971) reviewed research addressing the question of whether group techniques yield enduring positive personality change. He concluded that intensive training experiences have therapeutic effects such as sensitivity, ability to manage feelings, positive attitudes to self and others, and interdependence. The term *interdependence* refers to interpersonal competence, teamwork in problem solving, and effectiveness as a group member. Because interdependence is also one of the chief goals of actualizing counseling and therapy, we believe Gibb's research summary is significant.

Combinations of methods appear to be most efficacious in behavior change. Research on social skills training has revealed no specific components that are universally effective across different subject populations and problems. Rose (1986) cites research indicating that different training components are effective in producing different aspects of social skills (Edelstein & Eisler, 1976; Hersen et al., 1973) and that results have different effects, depending on the subject population (Eisler, Frederiksen, & Peterson, 1978). In general it appears that a comprehensive treatment package is important when teaching complex response patterns.

Group process factors of nurturance and support play an important role in outcome. Rose (1986) indicates that when behavioral or cognitive-behavioral group packages are compared with nondirective group therapy of the same duration, the nonbehavioral group package often does as well on the behavioral measures and occasionally even better. He attributes the lack of difference to the importance of the group as a component.

Research by Yalom (1975) and Magden and Shostrom (1974) has suggested 10 curative dimensions of group effectiveness. These dimensions are:

1. *Catharsis.* Group members often ventilate feelings and/or experiences.
2. *Group as a second family.* Group members identify the therapist and/or other members in family roles.
3. *Awareness.* Group members become more aware of their thoughts, feelings, and/or bodily responses.
4. *Group cohesiveness.* Group members appear involved in the group.
5. *Receiving information.* Group members appear open to instructions, advice, and suggestions from the therapist.
6. *Imitative behavior.* Group members model their behavior after the therapist.
7. *Faith in the process.* Group members' behavior suggests that the group process will work for them.
8. *Giving and receiving help.* Group members appear to help one another through support and reassurance.

The two additional dimensions listed by Yalom (1975), but not utilized on the rating sheet, are:

9. *Universality.* Group members appear to get insight into the "universal commonness" of their ideas, feelings, and behavior.
10. *Altruism.* Group members appear to feel a sense of caring or love for one another.

More research needs to be done on comparative outcomes of different approaches and on who can use what kind of treatment best, as well as on the contribution of group process to outcome. Questions for additional research are: What personality changes are effected by group process? How do these changes affect behavior and how permanent are they? What undesired "side effects" of group processes take place? Are group experiences deleterious to the welfare of some persons? What are the best combinations of individual and group experience to maximize growth? What are the best time intervals and lengths of sessions for maximum growth? Are marathon sessions more effective than spaced sessions? What kinds of persons can profit most by group experiences? How can trust conditions be accelerated in groups? Are certain group experiences, such as T-groups, more effective in changing attitudes and traits than other types of educational experiences? What is the effect of leadership style on group outcomes?

PRINCIPLES OF GROUP DYNAMICS

Typical Leader Behaviors

Groups may function with varying degrees of leadership ranging from leaderless to a strong professional group leader. Berzon and Solomon (1966), in the first of a series of studies in leaderless group methods for encounter and therapy groups. They found that under some circumstances, self-directed groups using prepared program materials were feasible and effective in changing behavior.

Rose (1986) states that typical leader functions include organizing the group, orienting the members to the group, building group attraction, assessing client problems and the possibilities for resolving them, monitoring the behaviors determined as problematic, evaluating the progress of treatment, planning for and implementing specific change procedures, assessing group problems, modifying group attributes, and establishing transfer and maintenance programs for behavior changes occurring in the group.

The importance of leadership style for producing destructive as well as constructive outcomes was emphasized in the Yalom study cited above. This study found that leaders who were extremely active or passive had the least constructive outcomes. Implicit in the actualizing model is a leader behavior characterized by more active participation and responsibility than the more non-directive style of leadership. Yet, the leader does not dominate the group. He or she tries to "read the group" in a sensitive manner and does what appears most appropriate to achieve the actualizing goals of the group. The leader leads actively in terms of giving information, making process observations, or using confrontative or supportive interventions as indicated. He or she tries to model actualizing behavior as much as possible without setting himself or herself up as a paragon of such growth. The following list is suggestive of the various possible group maintenance functions performed by a facilitator of an actualizing group. These are general process behaviors. More specific strategies and methods are presented later in the chapter.

Problem setting. In a problem- or issue-oriented group, the leader states the issue or question to which the group is to address itself. This may occur at the outset or at various points in the discussion. The statement is made without indication of what solution should be reached or which side the leader favors.

Goal setting. Although group leaders do not set goals for their clients, they help participants set goals for themselves. Additionally, leaders help group members develop strategies for evaluating their own progress toward goals. Group leaders assist members in modifying goals if necessary.

Process moderating. The leader calls on some members or asks others to withhold comment; he or she may ask for order or attention. This category has nothing to do with content of the discussion but only with the process.

Sentiment testing. The leader seeks to learn the balance of opinion in the group. He or she may call for a show of hands or may simply state his or her impression of the trend of opinion and ask for confirmation.

Idea developing. The leader seeks to aid in the clarification and development of ideas before the group by restating, summarizing, or contrasting them. He or she does not inject new material but seeks to make issues more clear or to insure more general understanding.

Monitoring. The leader reminds the group of limits and constraints under which it is operating (for example, time limits, authority bounds, ground rules).

Energizing. The leader seeks to motivate the group to its self-assigned task. He or she may cite reasons for its work or simply enjoin the group to greater activity or chide it for inactivity.

Group serving. The leader may perform service functions for the group (for example, keeping notes, recording on a blackboard, distributing paper, adjusting lighting). There may be no verbal aspects to this function.

Content participating. The leader takes part in the discussion, as another member, without exercising leadership functions in any way.

Leaders also utilize certain *process facilitation techniques* with a view toward carrying forward the discussion of their group. The following list is a partial compilation of such techniques:

Initiating. The leader proposes new ideas, procedures, or orientation. Major content is not derived from previous work of the group but mainly from "within" the current speakers.

Amending. The leader develops ideas already before the group. He or she may add new "twists" but basically modifies more than initiates.

Supporting. The leader lends emphasis, reason, or other aid to ideas already before the group. He or she does not seek to change them but only to accelerate their acceptance.

Opposing. The leader may question, challenge, or detract from ideas before the group. He or she may seek to change them and to influence the group to reject them.

Summarizing. The leader brings out common or contrasting ideas before the group, reduces issues to essentials, and focuses or clarifies points.

Controlling. The leader may seek to control who will talk, when, or how much; he or she may intercede for less vocal members.

Informing. The leader provides information to the group (sometimes in response to a question), often simply to supply data, but he or she may have a secondary intent to influence the group. However, the main aspect of this function is to transmit facts or what are offered as facts.

Evaluating. Evaluation is an ongoing process in group counseling. The group leader evaluates the progress of the group and his or her own leadership strategies. The leader also helps the group evaluate its own movement and progress.

Leadership Strategies

Activation of the Here and Now.   Yalom suggests group leaders think "here and now." When they focus on present realities long enough, they influence the group strongly toward the here-and-now time frame. Whenever an issue is raised in the group, for example, the leader thinks, "How can I relate this issue to the group's primary task? How can I make it come to life in the here-and-now?" (Yalom, 1975, p. 134).

The leader moves the group topical focus from outside to inside, from abstract to specific. If a client described a confrontation with a spouse or room-mate, the therapist-leader may inquire, "If you were to be angry like that with anyone in the group, with whom would you be?" If a client comments that he or she lies or stereotypes people or manipulates groups, the therapist may inquire, "What is the main lie you've told in the group thus far?" or, "Can you describe the way you've stereotyped some of us?" or, "How have you manipulated the group thus far?" (Yalom, 1975, p. 134).

Focus on Process Orientation.   In making process comments, the leader initiates the process of change by escorting his or her group through the following sequence:

1. *Here is what your behavior is like.* Through feedback and, later, through self-observation, the patient learns to see himself as others see him.
2. *Here is how your behavior makes others feel.* Members learn about the impact of their behavior on the feelings of other members.
3. *Here is how your behavior influences the opinions others have of you.* Members learn that, as a result of their behavior, others value them, dislike them, find them unpleasant, respect them, or avoid them.
4. *Here is how your behavior influences your opinion of yourself.* Building on the information gathered in the first three steps, patients formulate self-evaluations; they make judgments about their self-worth and the lovability. (Yalom, 1975, pp. 155–156)

Acceptance of Basic Premises.   The therapist-leader's goal is to guide clients to a point where they can accept some important premises relative to making personal changes. These assumptions include: (1) making a personal *decision* to change, (2) believing that they are *able* to change, (3) taking personal *responsibility* for one's own change process, and (4) making a *commitment* to change even though it is likely to be a fearful process (Yalom, 1975).

Member Behaviors

Leaders must become good process observers to observe the patterns of participant behavior. Several categories of member behavior seem especially important to observe. Norms often develop in groups so that member participation is uneven. Some individuals talk more frequently and for longer duration than others. Providing the group with information about participation norms is often helpful both to individuals and in helping the group understand its own process.

Process observers also may track how group participation patterns are influenced by factors such as sex differences, age differences, and status characteristics (e.g., vocational or experience differences). For instance, do men tend to disagree more with women than with other men? Do women tend to provide more affirmation or bridge connections among group members? Nonverbal behavior may also play an important role in group communication. For example, one participant's nonverbal discomfort when discussing certain feelings or topics may be followed by another member's changing the topic. Awareness of such patterns can be helpful in identifying subtle patterns of avoidance, rescuing, and triangulation. Although the group leader constantly "tracks" process information, it is often helpful to assign the process observer role to group members on a rotating basis in order to make each participant more observant of subtle behavior patterns.

Patterns of topical development are also important to observe. In listening to a discussion, particular attention can be given to the "life history" of the topics. Though it is not possible or necessarily desirable to be highly precise about this historical analysis, nevertheless, the following scheme can help: How does the topic arise—from one individual, from the interactions of several members, from some other topic? How does the group work with the topic—by arguing contrasting aspects of it, by illustrations and examples, by emotional appeals, by responding to the influence of particular members? What changes occur in the topic as the group works on it—a part gradually displaces the topic as a whole, it is expanded and generalized, it is gradually lost sight of, it is thoroughly examined and concluded? What is the eventual fate of the topic—it is dropped, it becomes a part of the group's product, it is blended with other topics?

STAGES IN GROUP COUNSELING AND THERAPY

Although different styles of group process emerge depending on leadership style and type of group, a general pattern of group development can be described. Schutz (1975) conceptualizes stages of inclusion, control, and affection. Gazda (1978) describes five stages of groups: formation, involvement, transition, working, and ending stages. We begin our discussion of stages with an examination of some of the organizational and therapeutic issues involved in forming a group.

Pregroup Organizational Activities

Selection and Screening of Group Members.   One of the first questions that usually arises is, "Who should be in this particular group at this time?" Ethical guidelines developed by the Association for Specialists in Group Work (1980) state that the group leader needs to conduct a pregroup screening interview with prospective members. The purpose of the interview is to determine whether the client's needs and goals are compatible with the goals of the group and to ensure that the prospective participant's well-being will not be jeopardized by group participation. If selection criteria are not employed, clients may terminate the group discouraged and unhelped.

Screening should be a two-way process in which prospective group members decide whether a leader and group is suitable to them. Gazda et al. (1977) suggest that screening procedures should be designed to ensure that prospective participants understand what is expected of them and that only those members will be selected who are likely to benefit from the group experience. Prior to participation, prospective group members should be told of the limits of confidentiality, expectations regarding length of commitment to the group, and clearance required from other treatment professionals with whom they are currently involved. Yalom (1975) suggests exploring participants' misconceptions and expectations, predicting early problems, and providing a conceptual framework that includes guidelines for effective group behavior. He stresses the importance of discussing the group experience as a collaborative process between the client, therapist, and other group participants.

Group specialists differ in their screening criteria. Yalom (1975) considers the following as poor candidates for outpatient intensive group therapy: schizoid, paranoid, or sociopathic personalities, brain-damaged persons, incessant talkers, depressives, people addicted to drugs or alcohol, people who are suicidal, and extremely narcissistic people. For encounter training groups, Lakin (1972) suggests excluding (1) people who will become too defensive under stress to listen to what others say to them; (2) people who tend to project their feelings onto others and to feel victimized by them; and (3) people whose self-esteem is so low that they need constant reassurance.

Rose (1986) describes behavioral group participants as having problems with social skill deficits, depression, phobias, anxiety, stress, sexual disorders, pain management, anger or violence control, obesity or weight control, alcohol and drug abuse, and child management. Shoemaker (1977) suggests that extremely anxious clients are often not able to benefit from groups.

Bach (1954) states that the selection of an individual client is really meaningful only in relation to the factors of group dynamics in the particular group for which membership is being considered. Selection criteria will differ depending on the type of group and leader. Additional research is needed to help counselors better understand who is likely to benefit from a particular kind of group.

Regardless of group type, we believe that participants need to make the choice for themselves that they want to be in a group. We want members to have goals and an understanding of how group participation might help them reach their goals. We believe that clients need to have enough ability to trust others that they will be willing to participate in group activities.

Group Composition.   An important dimension of group composition is the homogeneity/heterogeneity of the group. This dimension refers to the extent to which the group members are alike or share some feature in common. Groups that are more time limited tend to function better with similarities among members in terms of age, sex, education, and identified problems. Yalom (1975) stresses that homogeneous groups develop an identity more quickly, are more cohesive, offer more support and less conflict, and have better attendance than heterogeneous groups.

Groups that meet for a longer time and that engage in interpersonal insight work may benefit from greater heterogeneity (Rudestam, 1982). Differences in age composition allow both cross-generational learning and more significant transference and identification opportunities for both younger and older members.

Sexual composition is an important consideration. Composition may vary in its importance as a consideration depending on the type of group. Gender is obviously a consideration in certain topic-focused groups such as "women in transition" or women's support groups. Research is lacking on the relative importance of sexual composition on other types of groups.

An empirical study (Taylor & Strassberg, 1987) of the effects of sex composition on group cohesion and interpersonal learning in personal growth groups found sexual composition to be a complex matter. Groups composed of all women were compared with all-male groups and mixed-sex groups. Significant differences were not found between the sexuall homogeneous groups, as a whole, versus the sexually heterogeneous groups.

The groups composed of all women were characterized by relatively high levels of cohesiveness, a pleasant group atmosphere, high member participation, and a sense that the group experience had been valuable for them. These groups, however, spent relatively less time involved in the interpersonal learning tasks assigned to them. In contrast, the all-male groups worked hard and relatively long on their assigned tasks but did so in a group atmosphere that was more somber than that seen in the all-female groups. These differences seem to reflect traditional sex roles.

The mixed-sex groups seemed to blend the male and female influences of the sexually homogeneous groups and combine some of the best elements of each group. These groups were characterized by high cohesion, participation, and task orientation. This initial research suggests that in order to maximize both cohesiveness and interpersonal learning, the mixed-sex format seems to be an appropriate model for personal growth groups.

Group Size and Length.   In organizing a therapy group, the question usually arises as to how many persons should be included. Optimal group size depends on various factors such as the age of the clients, the type of group, the experience of the group leaders, the number of group leaders, and the type of problems explored. A group should be large enough to allow opportunity for interaction and small enough for everyone to be involved and feel included. As groups become larger, there is a tendency for the more dominant and verbal to usurp the group's time and the likelihood that subgroups and cliques will form. When a group is too small, it ceases to operate as a group. It is generally agreed by group therapists that eight is an optimum number. Four members is the minimum for a viable group. Length is typically 90 minutes for an eight-person group. Duration varies widely and depends on the type of group.

Role of the Cotherapist in Group Therapy.   It is not uncommon for groups to employ the service of two therapists. There are a number of advantages to this arrangement. Group members can benefit from the insights of two leaders. Leaders can alternate between assuming a facilitator role and an interpreter-observer role. Coleaders can serve as important models for the members in terms of how they relate to each other.

Group leaders should pay careful attention to choosing coleaders so that they don't get into issues of control and competition with one another. They need respect, trust, cooperation, and support to be able to function as a team.

We think there are advantages to having opposite sex coleaders. We agree with Joel and Shapiro (1950) that the presence of two opposite sex therapists can re-create participants' family-of-origin dynamics. The presence of male and female leaders can also facilitate role-playing situations in which male or female participation is desirable.

Confidentiality.   There are difficult issues regarding the ethical, legal, and professional aspects of confidentiality. Is group communication protected as privileged communication? How can you enforce group members' protection of confidential information given by other group members? Group leaders should clearly contract with participants not to discuss with others what occurs in the group.

Socializing among Group Members.   We discourage group participants from socializing because of the potential for counterproductive subgroupings to emerge. Yalom (1975) emphasizes that the group teaches people how to form intimate relationships but does not provide these relationships. He suggests group members who do socialize outside the group should agree to share within the group the salient aspects of their conversations.

Closed and Continuous Groups.   There are two kinds of groups: closed and continuous. In the closed group, the same members are maintained throughout the life span of the group. This is often the case in educational settings where groups run the length of the academic semester. In the continuous group, replacements are made when a member leaves.

There is some degree of speculation among certain therapists whether closed groups offer more advantages than continuous groups. Some think that the closed group has more advantages because data can be accumulated and the group composition kept constant. If members drop out, however, because of an unavoidable circumstance, it may make the group unduly small. An advantage of an open group is that a new member, who has just come to the group, sometimes fosters a reworking of rivalries and competition in the group. Also, a new member may help therapeutic movement through a consolidation of group feeling. New members may reduce their defensiveness by identifying with other members who have already overcome theirs. The presence of less advanced group members appears to have some actualizing potential for the older members, because the older members gain therapeutically through the experience of sharing and helping new clients adjust to the group.

The Use of Videotapes

Videotape has proven to be a valuable resource for providing "focused feedback" to the group (Miller, 1970; Robinson, 1970). Berger (1968, 1970), for example, noted that client response to the first playback session differed from response to the later sessions. At first, clients attended primarily to their own self-image. Later, they responded more to their style of relating to each other and with the group's process.

Stage 1: Developing Identity and Inclusion

Inclusion is the first stage, where new members express concern about how much in or out of the process they see themselves. Inclusion needs include feelings of being prominent, significant, or worthwhile as a group member. It means searching for togetherness, belongingness, attention, and response. It is a time of decision on how much commitment one is going to make. It is a time of keen concern about how members see themselves in relationship to the total group, that is, where they fit in. This anxiety is expressed for example, in overtalking, withdrawal, exhibitionistic behaviors, or telling descriptive stories about previous group experiences.

A major task of this stage of development is building group cohesion. High group cohesion has been found to be positively associated with group effectiveness (Flowers & Booraem, 1980). Cohesion is built by providing incentives for attendance, providing guidelines of participation, modeling the facilitative dimensions of group behavior, drawing out group members' participation, using humor judiciously, and using interactive group exercises. Egan (1976) cites research suggesting that a lack of structure during initial group sessions tends to intensify participants' fears and leads to unrealistic expectations.

Goal setting is another important task of establishing a group identity. This includes helping group members establish personal goals as well as group purposes and goals. Leaders can assist participants in learning how to assess, monitor, and evaluate their goals. Leaders may teach clients to use self-monitoring or to explore critical events.

Stage 2: Managing Conflict and the Struggle for Control

When the group has become established, concerns are expressed about who is in charge, who administers the sanctions and rewards, and how much power a member has. Control needs may be expressed as a polarity in the form of need to be dominated or manipulated. Manipulations through both strength and weakness strategies become apparent. Attacks on the leader (often in the form of questioning his or her competence), blaming, and control struggles become evident at this stage.

During this early stage of development, it is important for leaders to create a climate in which participants can work through conflicts and confrontations openly. Participants can learn effective ways to recognize and manage their anxieties, constructively manage conflict, and share more responsibility for determining the group's direction.

Stage 3: Affection

When issues of control are resolved, affection concerns become prominent. Positive feelings, as well as hostility, are expressed to one another. Jealousies and pairings become evident. Again, polarities are involved as direct expressions of affection or avoidance of closeness. There is a heightened emotional expression generally as certain individuals in the group begin to show a greater willingness to risk.

This stage is considered the "working" stage of a group. Participants have established enough mutual trust to begin to explore and take action on significant problem areas. Group members are encouraged to take more responsibility in group leadership and in determining the kind of group help and feedback they desire from other participants.

Stage 4: Termination

In most groups this is a critical stage of development. For continuous groups, where members leave one at a time, it is a period where participants consolidate their learning and say their goodbyes. As groups terminate, they tend to resolve their affection, control, and inclusion needs in reverse fashion. First, personal feelings of loss and gain (positive and negative) are dealt with. Next, discussion often focuses on the leader and how the group members have rebelled against or complied with his or her methods. Finally, the group discusses the feelings of termination and their plans to apply what they've learned.

Termination generally elicits feelings of loss and depression, as well as some anxiety about separation. Members may collude to avoid talking about some of their grief issues. It is helpful for leaders to assist participants to develop a conceptual framework that will help them understand what they have learned in the group. Additionally, the leader can help members develop plans for how to integrate their learning into life following the group. Because some participants may leave the group with a desire for further counseling assistance, it is helpful to inform them of referrals about where they can continue counseling.

Sometimes a follow-up session can be planned several months after group termination. The follow-up session can be of value in discussing the group experience from a more distant perspective as well as the progress and difficulties participants have had in implementing what they have learned from the group.

It is also a time that the group leader can better evaluate through discussion or questionnaires either positive or negative effects of the group on participants.

STRATEGIES IN GROUP THERAPY

In group therapy, the leader can use all of the techniques described earlier in this volume. In addition, he or she must use other techniques that are unique to, or must be adapted to, group work. Some of the strategies and techniques mentioned are illustrative only. This topic is so broad and is developing so rapidly that intensive study and coleader training experience are necessary to become competent as a group facilitator.

Effective group work involves more than the knowledge of techniques. Techniques should be used when there are appropriate ways of clarifying the experiences of group participants. However, leaders must know how to work with the participants' experiences in a trained, knowledgeable, and caring manner. Lakin (1972) and Yalom (1975) suggest that in addition to academic training, group leaders should have experiences participating as group members, coleading groups with experienced leaders, observing, and being supervised by seasoned group leaders.

Psychodrama Techniques

Psychodrama utilizes various role-playing techniques to help clients apply playful acting out of their problems in a way that will increase their understanding of their conflicts. Role playing as a counseling technique often helps clients gain a better perspective of themselves and others. It can be used, for example, to practice social situations that are difficult for the client. Even when it is used in a group situation by qualified workers, emphasis should be placed on the fact that many complications can arise if it is not used properly. Bach (1954) warns of the possible traumatic effect of premature externalizing of threatening materials through role playing.

Some of the major types of psychodramatic procedures in a group therapy setting are described in more detail by Moreno (1959, 1983), Blatner (1973), and Leveton (1977).

T-Group Techniques

One of the primary contributions of training (T) groups has been to help participants understand their own decision-making processes. In an exercise described by Pfeiffer and Jones (1975), participants are set adrift on a sinking yacht far away from land. The group is given a list of 15 items and asked to consensually rank them in terms of their importance to survival. The group is then asked to discuss their experience, exploring patterns of leadership, conflict resolution, and decision-making processes.

Encounter Techniques

Encounter techniques are utilized to increase participant self-awareness. The "trust walk," for example, is used to expand sensory awareness and interpersonal trust. A participant is asked to guide a blindfolded partner by the hand or arm and take him or her on a sensory exploration walk. The guide is to protect the follower from any dangers of steps, trees, or walls and to persuade the partner to explore various smells and textures without using any words. Both partners reverse roles, then discuss their experiences. Another example of encounter exercises is where two partners sit back to back and have a conversation. The partners then process the experience of talking without having the visual cues available.

Gestalt Awareness

Gestalt group procedures are designed to intensify and clarify group members' awareness experiences. One set of exercises draws links between language and personality. For example, participants are told to personalize language, using "I statements." Leaders may help participants become aware of their use of language in discounting their experiences, such as, using language to deny their power to be capable, strong, and responsible. The use of the word "but" often discounts the speaker's preceding statement. To increase awareness of the power of language clients are asked to substitute the word "won't" for the word "can't." "I want" becomes substituted for "I need." "I choose to" replaces "I have to." Clients are asked to pay attention to the difference in their feelings as they alter their language patterns.

Emotional polarities also are explored by Gestalt techniques. In reversal techniques, clients are asked to enact a side of themselves that they rarely express. A person who always is "nice" is asked to say something "rude" to each person in the group in order to facilitate the integration of the individual's polarities. In the "topdog-underdog" conflict, a participant pairs up with another member. One person takes a "topdog" role in which he or she bullies and criticizes the other from a self-righteous position, telling the other how he or she should live. The "underdog" whines and makes excuses, saying he is trying to please but situations always interfere. After each person stays firmly in the role for 10 minutes, roles are reversed. Then each partner discusses the experience of feeling the power and authority of the "topdog" and the manipulative passivity of the "underdog."

Behavioral Techniques

Many of the behavioral techniques described in Chapter 7, such as modeling, coping skills training, relaxation, and problem-solving training, are also utilized in group therapy. One example of behavioral techniques is the use of behavioral rehearsal. In assertion training groups, participants describe situations in which they would like to become more assertive. Participants brainstorm ideas for how to handle the situation. Then group members are assigned roles to role play or rehearse the situation. Some participants may take the observer's role and the rehearsal is often videotaped for review and group feedback. The situation can be rehearsed repeatedly until the participant feels satisfied with his or her ability to behave assertively.

Dance and Art Therapy

Techniques from dance and art therapy are sometimes utilized in group therapy. Dance "mirroring" encourages body awareness, creative movement, and interpersonal empathy. Group members pair with a partner, for example. One takes the role of the leader, guiding the follower in various body movements, while maintaining eye contact. The follower tries to be a mirror image of the leader, following the leader's movements as closely as possible. Clay sculpting is an art therapy technique in which participants are asked to sculpt a representation of themselves, their family, their world, their problem, or the group and then share the results with other group members.

Interpretation Techniques

Usually after 40 or 45 minutes of the therapeutic hour have elapsed, the group leader or coleader often finds it propitious to make a summary interpretation of what has happened in the hour. We feel that this summary task is best performed by a coleader, rather than by the leader. The latter usually has a facilitative or management role and would find it difficult psychologically to perform both the summary interpretation and the facilitative role.

The intrepretation technique has been found helpful in giving the group a picture of what has happened during the hour. We have found the following types of summaries to be useful:

1. *"Theme" summaries:* Hobbs (1951) suggests that group therapy is much like a musical composition, in that there are certain "themes" that run through group conversation. The cotherapist identifies these themes in the summary. An example is: "Tonight we have been talking about competition. Sally and Jack see themselves as always running away from it. In the area of romance, Bill says he just gives up, or disposes of the possibility of winning. In interpersonal competition, we have decided that we have to define the problem clearly. This means defining the assets and liabilities of our competitors and then defining our own assets and liabilities. We then can decide on which techniques we ought to use. Doreen is competing now with another woman for her husband. One thing she can do better than this other woman is to be a good mother to her children and a good wife to her husband. She has decided this is one of her chief assets, which she can develop. We have also discussed the idea of 'shooting against our own par'—that is, competition with oneself is one of the best ways for improvement. This method doesn't hurt anybody in the process. Jim does this in his golf game—and we can do it here too."

2. *Individual analysis summaries:* Sometimes the discussions of a group do not center on a particular theme, but the individual group members discuss their own unique problems. The cotherapist then summarizes more individually, as for example: "Our discussion tonight has focused on four people, and I'd like to say something about each of them. We might call these people by certain pseudonyms.

"Alex here is Accepting Alex. He wants to be so accepting of everybody, because he has learned that this is what good psychologists do. But this is only half the story. Before we can really accept others, we first must learn to accept ourselves—both the negative and positive parts of ourselves. When Alex is able to do this completely, he'll not have trouble accepting others' positive and negative sides too.

"Doreen we might call Doormat Doreen. She has spent seventeen years being a doormat for her husband, and now she wants to change. She has been thinking that one way to do that is not to teach this year so that her husband will not have the money she makes to depend on. But Roberta and Sam are in agreement that a better way would be to continue teaching, since just sitting around might make her more depressed and tired than before. Roberta found that out in her own experience. Furthermore, we know that most of us get more tired from underwork than overwork. If Doreen then continued to teach, she could keep her own money and really be selfish for once in her life.

"Will we might call Un-Warm Uncle Will. He just doesn't want to admit he is warm, and yet Doreen has shown us that he really is. He doesn't want to be this way, and for the first time tonight has asked us to pull him down from his stand-offish position. He has humbled himself to do this, and I think we can help him."

3. *Interpersonal dynamic summaries:* Instead of focusing on the individual problems of clients, the therapist can describe the interpersonal dynamics of feelings which have been taking place in the hour. An example is: "We have had many feelings shown here tonight. Some of them have been obvious, others not so obvious. Pete and Ted have both expressed openly their warm feelings toward Connie. Jack has expressed hostility by saying that he doesn't like her because she is so pretty, that everyone likes her, and that rejection is good for such a person. But after analyzing this feeling we find that Jack is saying this because he fears that if he were to express his real feelings of warmth to Connie, she might reject him, so he takes the offensive instead by rejecting her first. But he finds that this isn't very satisfying, because it leaves him feeling, as he says, lousy."

These methods of interpretation may be combined in summarizing the session; they are presented separately above for purposes of clarity in exposition.

SUMMARY

We have presented group techniques to develop interpersonal as well as intrapersonal dimensions. Various models of groups have been described, such as therapy groups, growth groups, skill groups, stress debriefing groups, and actualization groups. We outlined general considerations for the organization of a group and discussed issues related to facilitator roles, selection of members, and group composition. Stages of group development with associated tasks were presented as a framework for understanding group process. Research related to group leadership and process has suggested the importance of leadership style, the use of multiple methods for facilitating client change, and the need for group evaluation.

It was suggested that the effective group facilitator must be familiar with the individual techniques presented in this book. In addition, certain supplementary group strategies were presented. Some of the techniques illustrated were drawn from various therapeutic approaches, such as encounter groups, T-groups, psychodrama, Gestalt therapy, behavioral therapy, and art and dance therapy.

CHAPTER 10

Couples and Family Therapy

Couples and family counseling have been closely tied with therapeutic psychology; however, each has a unique history (Allen, 1975; Broderick & Schrader, 1981). Couples, family, and sexual counseling grew out of different roots but have become amalgamated in practice over time. As psychologists increasingly provide services to couples and families, we believe it is important for psychologists to have a clear conception of couple and family functioning. Therefore, we are providing an overview of key concepts of marital and family functioning and their historical development. In this chapter we will highlight important concepts of marital and family therapy and provide an overview of strategies utilized in marital and family therapy. The reader may also wish to review the theoretical underpinnings of systems theories in Chapter 2.

HISTORICAL DEVELOPMENT

Couples Therapy

In the past, couples counseling was performed for the most part by physicians, lawyers, educators, clergy, and social workers in churches, public welfare agencies, family-service organizations, and as one aspect of a gynecological medical practice. Pioneers in marriage counseling include Dr. Emily Mudd, biologist Paul Poenoe, and Abraham and Hannah Stone who founded clinics in 1930. As late as 1950, over one-quarter of the members of the American Association of

Marriage and Family Counselors were gynecologists and an almost equal proportion were in other medical specialties.

Professional standards were developed for marriage counselors in 1949 by a joint committee of the American Association of Marriage Counselors (now the American Association for Marriage and Family Therapy) and the National Council on Family Relations. In 1963, California became the first of many states to pass a licensing law for marriage and family counselors.

The development of the marriage counseling profession paralleled changes in therapeutic modalities. In the 1940s, psychoanalytic therapy approaches began to recognize the value of conjoint therapy. Behavioral methods became applied to marital problems in the 1960s. Systems approaches were developed in the 1960s by researchers and therapists working with troubled families and marriages.

Family Therapy

The family therapy movement grew out of social work and psychiatry. Precursors to family therapy included Moreno's group psychodrama and influential writings of the 1930s and 1940s by authors such as Ackerman (1938), Richardson (1945), Bowlby (1949), and Dreikers (1949) describing conjoint family interviews. Family therapy approaches, such as Satir's conjoint approach (1964), gained wide acceptance in the 1960s. Within the counseling profession, there has been a growing interest in family counseling, not just as a technique but as a theoretical approach to counseling. The American Psychological Association has established Division 43, Family Psychology. The number of members of the American Association of Marriage and Family Therapy doubled between 1978 and 1986 (Maynard & Olson, 1987). The Association for Counseling and Development has also recently added a new division oriented toward marriage and family therapy.

Sexual Therapy

Sexual therapy practitioners were initially from the social hygiene movement or gynecologists. The work of Kinsey and his associates (1948, 1953) and later of Masters and Johnson (1966, 1970) provided sex counselors with a new set of scientifically documented facts regarding sexual behavior and the sexual response cycle. The research of Masters and Johnson led to the development of sexual therapy. Eventually, the American Association of Sex Educators and Counselors (now the American Association of Sex Educators, Counselors and Therapists) was established to certify qualified sex therapists.

Currently, practitioners of marital, sexual, and family therapy represent various helping professions, including psychology, mental health counseling, social work, nursing, pastoral counseling, psychiatry, and marriage and family therapy. Marital and family therapy have been increasingly utilized for intervention into a wide variety of clinical problems including affective disorders, alcoholism, sexual dysfunction, childhood behavior problems, and even obsessions and compulsions.

THEORETICAL APPROACHES TO COUPLES
AND FAMILY THERAPY

As the field of marriage and family therapy has integrated different historical roots, various theoretical approaches have been applied to the practice of marriage and family therapy. We will highlight only a few of the differences and similarities in approaches. We will elaborate more fully on the therapeutic process with couples and families based on key concepts that cross many theoretical lines. The principles for the synthesis of theoretical concepts and therapeutic interventions that we discussed in Chapter 7 are important to recall as we seek to develop an integrative marital and family therapy.

Psychoanalytic marital and family therapies tend to focus on the intergenerational aspects of client problems. In contrast to phenomenological, behavioral, and structural or strategic systems theories, psychoanalytic theories focus on the past. There is an emphasis on encouraging marital partners to work toward differentiation from their families of origin through insight or through actual encounters with their parents. Symptoms are often viewed as representative of unresolved losses or relationships with members of previous generations.

Psychoanalytic therapy also pays particular attention to the collusion of couples or family members in meeting unconscious needs. Analytically oriented therapists (as well as Bowenian systems therapists) believe that couples unconsciously choose marital partners who allow each partner to repeat familiar interactions from their own family of origin experiences. These marital choices, nevertheless, represent an unconscious attempt at finding intimate interpersonal conditions for individual growth.

Sager (1976, 1981) has described mate selection in terms of reciprocal unwritten, emotional "marital contracts." Sager discusses contracts in terms of three levels: *verbalized* (although not always understood by the partner), *conscious but not verbalized* (usually not verbalized out of fear of anger or disapproval), and *unconscious*, and often contradictory, expections, needs, and desires. Expectations in the marital contracts may be such things as having a panacea for the chaos and strife in one's life, insurance against loneliness, economic security, a mate to support one's career or family goals and many other possible spoken or unspoken desires. The unconscious level may include issues related to power and control needs, closeness–distance, contradictory active–passive impulses, child–adult conflicts, and gender identity conflicts. Sager has developed a typology of couples based on contracts. His treatment strategy involves helping couples become aware of their marital contracts and learning ways to meet one another's emotional needs.

Phenomenological therapists have focused on the here-and-now felt experiences of being in a marriage or family. In contrast to psychoanalytic therapies, they have a present-time focus. Their work has emphasized developing effective communications skills. Skills training and enrichment programs for couples, such as Guerney's Conjugal Relationship Enhancement Program, drew heavily on Rogerian influences as well as incorporating concepts from social learning theory. Important parenting skills programs such as Parent Effectiveness Training (Gordon, 1970) have been based on Rogerian assumptions and methods. Additionally, phenomenological therapists have developed a variety of creative experiential techniques, which have influenced pioneering systems therapists such as Virginia Satir and Fred and Bunny Duhl. Emotionally Focused Therapy (Greenberg & Johnson, 1988) exemplifies an experiential therapy that focuses on the expression and understanding of feelings in couples.

Behavioral therapists have emphasized the reciprocal balance of "giving" and "getting" within marriages. Behavioral therapists such as Neil Jacobsen, Richard Stuart, and Robert Weiss have utilized cognitive-behavioral as well as operant behavioral principles to provide couples with skills in identifying problematic behaviors and communication patterns and in resolving difficulties through problem solving, behavior change, and increased supportive and caring behaviors. In contrast to psychoanalytic theories, behavioral theories have paid little attention to intergenerational factors. Behavioral marital therapists view the immediate causes of marital strife as resulting from spouses' faulty efforts at behavior change that implicate the absence of specific relationship skills. Behaviorists, such as Patterson, have made strong contributions in the areas of parent training and classroom management of children. They have researched the systematic application of learning principles to behavior management.

Systems theories (except for those held by intergenerational theorists) view current problems as being maintained by current forces, not by the past. Systems therapists attend to issues of how leadership is shared, family roles, rules about communication, family structure, boundaries, coalitions, and the recursive patterns of communication that prohibit problem resolution within couples or families.

Intergenerational systems approaches, such as those described by Bowen, view healthy marital and family relationships as related to the individual's development of autonomy or differentiation from his or her family of origin. As clients individuate, they can view their marital partner as a person unto himself or herself with relatively little intrusion of past significant figures into their perception.

All approaches agree that marital and family conflict are the result of attempts to define the relationship between partners or family members. The explanations of the forces operating vary. Psychoanalytic therapists speak of shared collusions and multilevel contracts; systems therapists describe the implicit rules of the relationship or dysfunctional family structure; intergenerational systems theorists speak of fusion and the fear of individuation; phenomenological approaches point to inadequate communication skills; behaviorists speak of inequitable exchange of reinforcing behaviors between couples or ineffective reinforcement with children.

Despite differences across therapeutic approaches, agreement exists regarding goals in marriage and family therapy. In comparing various approaches to marital therapy, Gurman and Kniskern (1981) suggest that all approaches reveal a commonality of therapeutic goals in certain areas, such as (1) increased role flexibility; (2) resolution of presenting problems and decreased symptomatology;

(3) a more equitable balance of power; (4) open and clear communication; and (5) increased self-esteem. The current trend in family counseling is to view a family member's problems in the context of the family system, to focus on the present, and to emphasize the solution of the present problems rather than long-range goals for personal growth.

Gender and Ethnicity in Marital and Family Therapy

In the last decade, couples and family therapy came under criticism from feminists who felt that traditional women's roles within patriarchal families were reinforced in marital and family therapy (Carter, Papp, Silverstein, & Walter, 1988). Feminist family therapists assert that gender issues permeate all of marital and family therapy. Therapist biases lead women to be seen as being primarily responsible for childrearing and housekeeping, and as needing to support their husbands' careers by neglecting their own.

Family therapy often served as a forum for reinforcing the perception that women were incompetent and to blame for their children's difficulties. For instance, mothers were often seen by therapists as ineffective and overinvolved and in need of help from their peripheral but competent, rational husbands. Feminist therapists suggested that rather than blame mothers for their children's problems, therapists would better serve the family by helping them to examine and change the rules and roles that keep mothers overwhelmed and fathers disengaged. During the therapy process, fathers should be encouraged to become more involved with parenting because it is a father's responsibility as a parent, rather than because mothers are incompetent.

The problems being described by men and women in couples relationships frequently include conflicts between their perceived stereotypes of gender. The unacceptable feelings of one gender, for example, dependency in men, are projected to one's partner or inhibited through compensatory behaviors such as violence. Sheinberg and Penn (1991) have developed a set of "gender questions" for processing basic gender assumptions in therapy. These questions are used by a couple to explore the norms aspired to as well as the relational consequences for changing these norms. Examples include questions such as "If you were to show how angry you feel, how do you think your husband would feel and react? If you were to show how much you need protection, how do you think your wife would feel and react?" Additional questions concern the norms of the couple's parents and how those affected both the couple and their parents. Questions about the future address the potential for establishing new norms as well as altering how problems might continue. For instance, "If your fights with your daughter/son were about how to stay connected to each other rather than how to separate, would they be any different?"

Ethnicity has also challenged us to view marriage and family norms as varying across cultures. For example, Falicov and Karrer (1980) pointed out that in many cultures, the governing dyad in a family is not the husband or wife but rather an intergenerational dyad. It might be a husband and son in some cultures and a wife and son in others. Values related to parenting styles, family violence, open and expressive communication, and encouraging autonomy versus loyalty in children differ by culture and within cultures.

Although ethnicity leads us to be sensitive in accepting different family structures as normative for different cultures, it also raises theoretical and ethical difficulties for therapists. We must ask ourselves whether a normative belief or behavior pattern in another culture is necessarily healthy for family members. For example, families in other cultures are often more patriarchal than our own. Women and children particularly may be dominated or subjected to family violence. Should we accept this behavior because it is customary? Or do we need to adopt a position that there are some universal basic principles that determine a system's health or illness. Whether it is gender biases or other cultural biases, it is important for counselors to decide when they need to speak up rather than collude with an oppressive system.

As we described in Chapter 2, a related issue to gender and ethnicity is the experience of powerlessness that often accompanies lower socioeconomic status. Families from lower income levels often have additional differences that require counselors to reconceptualize these families and provide more outreach and support services. Such families have increased environmental pressures, often more isolation from social support, and more conflict between parents (typically mothers) and other relatives and adults who may criticize their parenting (Fulmer, 1988). These families may suffer from disorganization unless they have opportunities and resources that relieve them from the overwhelming responsibilities of maintaining households on insufficient emotional and financial resources.

KEY CONCEPTS IN MARITAL AND FAMILY THERAPY

We believe that many of the concepts described by marriage and family theorists can be subsumed under the concepts of *cohesion* and *adaptability* described by Olson and his colleagues (Olson et al., 1979, 1983) as the "Circumplex Model" of marital and family functioning. The Circumplex Model assumes that a marital or family system needs enough cohesiveness to give members a sense of identity and belonging and enough flexibility to balance family needs for change and stability.

Cohesion

Many marriage and family approaches place importance on the quality of affective involvement among family members. Olson et al. (1979) describe cohesion as the emotional bonding and the degree of individual autonomy that family members experience. There are several aspects to this definition: emotional bonding, coalitions, decision making, family boundaries, time, friends, interests, and recreation.

The cohesion dimension of a couple or family occurs along a continuum that lies between *enmeshment* at one extreme and *disengagement* at the other. Moderate or "balanced" levels of cohesion are considered to be most conducive to effective marital and family functioning and optimal individual development. For example, a family balanced on cohesion would have family members who are able to be alone at times (disengaged) and also are highly connected with their family (enmeshed), but do not stay at either extreme. Extreme family types are generally able to function only at that extreme and therefore have a smaller behavioral repertoire.

Family extremes on the cohesion continuum are associated with difficulties. At the enmeshed end of the continuum, boundaries between family members or between one subsystem and another are diffuse, resulting in emotional, intellectual, and/or physical overidentification with the family and limited autonomy. At the disengaged end of the continuum, boundaries are inappropriately rigid, underpinning an affective involvement that we would consider "lack of involvement." Thus, disengagement is characterized by low emotional bonding and high autonomy from the family. Minuchin and his colleagues described in *Families of the Slums* (Minuchin et al., 1967) how disengagement among family members prevented meeting children's developmental needs for supervision and support. Because of differences in cultural norms, it is possible for some families to operate at extremes of cohesion without problems. However, these extreme patterns are more problematic in the long run for families acculturated to the norms of American society.

The cohesion continuum should be seen within a developmental context. An integral part of the flexibility of a family system is its ability to make appropriate alterations in cohesion in accord with the developmental tasks that it faces. For example, family cohesion will be more connected in families with infants and more separated in families with adolescent children. A family may show dysfunctional enmeshment if an adolescent's increasing need for a sense of separate identity is not acknowledged and the family maintains a connectedness appropriate for younger children.

Within a well-functioning nuclear family, the family unit is strengthened by the formation of a solid coalition between the adult marital partners (Lewis et al., 1976). This coalition, as marital partners and parents, helps to maintain an appropriate boundary between parents and children by providing a clarity of the power structure and the generational lines. Strong marriages have been shown to have clear distributions of power and leadership, open and direct communication, and high levels of marital complementarity and need fulfillment. Power in the most competent family units is not arbitrary but is shared between the parents. The adults remain in charge but share leadership according to situational and developmental factors. Children's ideas are considered in family decisions.

Adaptability

The strength of a marital or family system is dependent upon its ability to change and show adaptability in its power structure, role relationships, and relational rules in response to situational and developmental stress. Flexibility is important if the family system is to meet adequately the developmental tasks of the family life cycle. Olson et al. (1979) describe elements of this dimension as leadership, control, discipline, roles, and rules. Adaptability also can be expressed along a continuum from overly flexible or *chaotic* systems to *rigid* systems which lack adequate flexibility.

Moderate or balanced levels of family adaptability seem optimal for marital and family health. This stress on the importance of the adaptability of structural relationships within normal families is borne out by the study of Lewis et al. (1976), where effective family functioning was associated with an adaptive flexibility of family structure. Low adaptability is characterized by system rigidity and resistance to change; extremely high adaptability verges on system chaos. Leadership is likely to be authoritarian at the rigid end of the continuum. In contrast, nobody takes charge among the chaotic couples and families.

The family system's adaptability has become an important consideration in therapy. It was once thought that the major therapeutic goal of marriage and family therapy was to make corrective changes in the family system in order to return it to a state of functional balance, as in the analogy of a thermostat that keeps the temperature within a prescribed range (Jackson, 1957). Recently, it has been suggested that the goals of therapy more appropriately involve pushing the marital and family system beyond its equilibrium to a point where it must accommodate by making substantial changes, thereby functioning at a new level (Dell, 1982; Elkaim, 1981).

Developmental Influences

Many marital and family therapists suggest that the family developmental cycle is a key component in understanding the family as a system (Haley, 1973; Solomon, 1973; Carter & McGoldrick, 1988). Family stress tends to be highest at the transition points between stages of the life cycle. Symptoms are most likely to appear in a family member when there is an interruption or dislocation in the unfolding life cycle signaling that the family is having difficulty moving through the transition to its next stage. Transitions ushering in new developmental epochs in couples or families may include normative events such as the birth of a child, a child entering school, a child leaving home, or paranormative events that modify the momentum of the family unit. Examples include miscarriages, relocations of household, illness, and changes of socioeconomic status. Such transitions require "second-order changes" or radical redefinitions and new behaviors for the family. Family transitions, however, at times can result in greater family cohesion and low disruption. For example, unexpected unemployment may draw family members together as a team to face forces that may be outside of their control.

The therapist's role is to help remobilize the family life cycle, so that normal developmental progress can continue. Minuchin (1974, p 60) states that if more therapists held a developmental perspective, "many more families who enter therapy would be seen as average families in transitional situations, suffering the pains

TABLE 10-1. THE STAGES OF THE FAMILY LIFE CYCLE. FROM CARTER & MCGOLDRICK (1980).

Family Life Cycle Stage	Emotional Process of Transition: Key Principles	Second Order Changes in Family Status Required to Proceed Developmentally
1. Between Families: The Unattached Young Adult	Accepting parent offspring separation	a. Differentiation of self in relation to family of origin b. Development of intimate peer relationships c. Establishment of self in work
2. The Joining of Families Through Marriage: The Newly Married Couple	Commitment to new system	a. Formation of marital system b. Realignment of relationships with extended families and friends to include spouse
3. The Family With Young Children	Accepting new members into the system	a. Adjusting marital system to make space for child(ren) b. Taking on parenting roles c. Realignment of relationships with extended family to include parenting and grandparenting roles
4. The Family With Adolescents	Increasing flexibility of family boundaries to include children's independence	a. Shifting of parent-child relationships to permit adolescent to move in and out of system b. Refocus on mid-life marital and career issues c. Beginning shift toward concerns for older generation
5. Launching Children and Moving On	Accepting a multitude of exits from and entries into the family system	a. Renegotiation of marital system as a dyad b. Development of adult to adult relationships between grown children and their parents c. Realignment of relationships to include in-laws and grandchildren d. Dealing with disabilities and death of parents (grandparents)
6. The Family in Later Life	Accepting the shifting of generational roles	a. Maintaining own and/or couple functioning and interests in face of physiological decline: exploration of new familial and social role options b. Support for a more central role for middle generation c. Making room in the system for the wisdom and experience of the elderly: supporting the older generation without overfunctioning for them d. Dealing with loss of spouse, siblings and other peers, and preparation for own death. Life review integration.

of accommodating to new circumstances." Carter and McGoldrick (1988) add that when normative stress intersects with transgenerational stress (i.e., unresolved family themes, triangles, losses from prior generations), there is a "quantum leap" in the anxiety engendered.

There are a variety of developmental schema to choose from when discussing the family life cycle. There are individual life-cycle descriptions by researchers such as Erickson, Levinson, Gould, and others. There are conceptualizations of marital life cycles such as those by Campbell (1980) and Schram (1979). Campbell's couple's life cycle includes five stages: (1) romance; (2) power struggle; (3) stability; (4) commitment; and (5) co-creation. Family life cycles vary by gender (Carter & McGoldrick, 1988), culture (Hines, 1988), and socioeconomic status (Fulmer, 1988).

While transitions in the family life cycle are described as relating to the presence of children, Carter and McGoldrick believe that most of the phases of the life cycle would also hold for family members who do not marry and/or who do not have children. Individuals who do not go through the child-oriented phases of the life cycle must still relate to their families and social networks on the issues other families go through. They still live within the context of previous generations, present family ties, and future generations.

FORMATS OF MARITAL AND FAMILY THERAPY

The marital and family therapist is faced with a variety of choices regarding treatment formats. Family therapists generally see families conjointly or in a combined format where subsystems are seen when considered appropriate. Marital therapists tend to use a variety of formats. Occasionally, marital issues are worked on through *individual therapy* with only one of the partners. We strongly discourage this practice. Gurman and Kniskern (1978) state that the reported negative therapeutic effects resulting from individual therapy for marital discord was twice (11.6 percent versus 5.6 percent) that of treatment formats in which both spouses were involved in one manner or another, through conjoint therapy, conjoint group, concurrent, or collaborative therapy. Moreover, the success rates of the formats of one-spouse versus both-spouses in treatment were, conversely, strikingly in favor (65 percent versus 48 percent) of the two-spouse approaches as an aggregate.

A second format involves *concurrent therapy with the same therapist.* The advantage to this approach is that the therapist can keep abreast of changes in either partner and their effects on the larger marital system. Confidentiality problems as well as lack of access to interactional patterns seem to be the major pitfalls of this approach.

A third format involves *concurrent therapy with different but collaborating therapists.* Although this approach may provide a broader perspective and may resolve the difficulty of the therapist holding secrets, the approach still intrudes upon the confidentiality of the therapists and often tends to get the therapists triangulated onto their clients' side. Lack of direct access to interactional patterns is also a major drawback.

Conjoint therapy tends to be utilized widely since the therapist has access to the clients' interactive patterns. The primary contraindication is the therapist's potential inability to prevent a spouse from utilizing the conjoint session for destructive purposes against his or her mate (Sager, 1966). *Couples groups* are also a useful treatment modality (Framo, 1973). The advantages include facilitative feedback and sharing among couples and the development of problem-solving skills as couples learn to help themselves and others.

PHASES OF MARITAL THERAPY

The phases of marital therapy parallel those for individually oriented therapy. An initial "joining" phase is followed by assessment and contracting, a change facilitation phase, and termination. Many of the skills and processes described in previous chapters apply to the practice of marital and family therapy. We will highlight some of the unique emphases and techniques utilized when working with couples and families.

The therapist's role throughout marriage and family therapy is to join the couple or family system as a participant-observer. The family needs to feel that the therapist understands them and is working with them and for them in a collaborative manner. Sometimes the therapist will act as a coach, a more distant expert, or an ally of a particular family member. Minuchin and Fishman (1981, p. 31) state, "Any technique (of joining) may be useful, depending on the therapist, the family, and the moment."

The therapist must be flexible enough to establish and maintain a focus in the session, guide treatment goals, and maintain a connection with each family member while avoiding becoming overly triangulated into conflict. The therapist also clarifies and expands communication among family members and, in this process, defines and clarifies the relationships among family members. Therapists often must challenge the assumptions, beliefs, and attitudes of couples and families about the nature of their problems and provide alternative problem definitions. The therapist takes an active role in stimulating family transactions, labeling, and interpreting transactions. Additionally, many therapists assign homework of various sorts.

Engagement Phase

During the engagement phase of therapy, the counselor must establish rapport and trust with the couple or family. In marital and family therapy, the counselor often needs to provide a rationale for conjoint treatment. Such a rationale usually includes the belief that the identified patient is best understood in the context of the whole couple or family. Couples and families often hold the belief that the symptom bearer has an individual internalized pathology. They expect the therapist to concentrate his or her efforts toward changing that person. The therapist, however, must explore the interpersonal transactions within the couple or family that lead to symptom formation.

Couples or families expect themselves to be able to talk about the problem that most concerns them, and for this reason starting with this problem is one of the most natural ways to begin an interview. As the counselor asks, "What problems have brought you to this session?" family members can begin to clarify and discuss the nature and course of their difficulties. Focusing on a particular problem and clarifying it, rather than simply gathering a list of all the different complaints, is a process that is helpful both to the therapist and clients. In the course of this discussion, the couple or family's problems may be redefined a number of times. This process may be facilitated by the therapist acting as a good problem solver: identifying, clarifying, and communicating problems.

It is important for the counselor to identify, validate, and support the family's past and present efforts at mastery of their problems, whether or not their attempts have met with success. In doing so, the therapist boosts the family's self-esteem and helps family members see one another in a more positive light. The therapist becomes an active neutral listener, helping each person tell his or her story. During this process, counselors will gather information about family structure and process. They note who talks to whom, who they find annoying, and of whom they feel protective.

Assessment Phase

The assessment process in marital and family therapy parellels the assessment process described for individuals in Chapter 6. However, there is a special emphasis on exploring and observing interpersonal transactions and patterns. Particular attention is given to the dimensions of cohesion, adaptability, and family development described previously.

Presenting Problem.   The therapist begins with learning about the presenting problem. The counselor asks for each person's experience of the presenting problem. The counselor tries to draw out each individual's personalized meaning of the problem as well as the effects of the family's previous attempts to resolve the problem. The therapist obtains a precise description of problematic behaviors and the sequence of events relative to the problems. Situational contexts of problematic behaviors are discussed, as are the reactions of others in the environment. Circular questions, as described in Chapter 6, are useful tools for drawing out a systemic understanding of the client's problems.

Comprehensive Picture of Family Functioning.   Once a description of the presenting problem has been established provisionally, the counselor seeks to build a comprehensive picture of family functioning. This includes information regarding elements of family cohesion and adaptability. Tools for building a comprehensive picture of family functioning may include interviews, psychological tests geared to family relationships (i.e., Caring Relationship Inventory, FACES, Family Environment Scales, PREPARE), and many of the intervention strategies described later in this chapter.

In exploring cohesion, the counselor seeks to find out the family unit's degree of enmeshment, disengagement, or balance. This information is often revealed through information about family members' independence, structure, boundaries, coalitions, amount of time, space, and friends shared alone or with other family members, and whether decisions tend to be made primarily individually (indication of disengagement) or always conjointly as a family unit (indication of enmeshment).

Adaptability is examined by exploring how rigid, chaotic, or balanced a family unit is in regard to assertion, control, negotiation, discipline, and rules.

For example, a rigid family may have authoritarian leadership with many explicit rules that are strictly enforced. In contrast, a chaotic family will show limited leadership, many implicit rules, and few explicit rules (which tend to be arbitrarily enforced). A comprehensive picture of family functioning may suggest a systemic function for the couple or family's difficulties.

Developmental History.   History taking can often provide valuable developmental background information for understanding how the couple or family's unique history influences their manner of experiencing and dealing with their current difficulties. Additionally, the history may provide clues to the systemic function of the "identified patients" difficulties. This history should provide a brief summary of each parent's family of origin with particular reference to each parent's relationship with his or her own parents and development. Genograms, described in Chapter 6, are a useful tool for organizing family histories.

A developmental history should include individual psychological development of family members as well as data about the history of the marriage and how the family has experienced each stage in the family life cycle. The nature of the presenting problems will provide clues as to what may be particularly relevant areas to discuss. For example, if the problem is about adolescent control issues, it may be particularly important to gather information about each parent's adolescence.

Blended or stepfamilies often have special difficulties related to including new members into the family and maintaining cooperative parental relationships between the divorced parents. Therapists should discuss the process of how the children were involved in the joining of two families and how well the new family's roles and boundaries as parents, couple, and children have been clarified.

Process Observation of Family Structure and Process.   In the process of gathering information about a couple or family's problems, the therapist assesses significant dysfunctional transactional patterns and structural problems. The counselor watches for evidence of problems in the expressive and regulatory aspects of the ongoing communication. These include interpersonal defenses such as triangulation or scapegoating in which a third family member (or lover, job, valued activity) becomes a source of conflict in a manner which detours conflict between two other family members. Family myths and projective identification are unconscious defensive processes in which unacceptable family roles or feelings are projected onto a family member who then acts them out. Persistent dysfunctional communication or distancing maneuvers tend to function in ways that maintain emotional distance within the family unit. The therapist is likely to experience personally some manifestation of these problems in the immediate therapy process.

Dysfunctional patterns often reveal important information about family subsystems and boundaries. Subsystems refer to a functional group involving two or more family members. Any one individual family member belongs to several different subsystems simultaneously. A functional subsystem may involve the children of a family as a sibling subsystem, the female subsystem, the parent subsystem, the marital subsystem, or another subsystem concerned with a particular family function. The therapist should explore how the boundaries between subsystems are maintained and whether they are rigid and impermeable, diffuse and ill defined, or permeable. Information about subsystems and their boundaries is often obtained by stimulating transactions between subsystems and exploring how well they maintain their function and boundaries within the therapist's office or in completing homework assignments. More will be said about these interventions when we discuss facilitation of marital and family changes.

Treatment Planning

Assessment involves stating a description and explanation of the problems that will be used as the basis for developing a therapeutic plan. This formulation links the family's surface behavior to identified dysfunctional family transactional patterns. Secondly, the therapist examines possible links between dysfunctional transactional processes, surface behavior, and the family's developmental history. Thirdly, the therapist asks what has precipitated the couple's or family's presenting concerns at this time. For example, consider the following:

Surface Behavior. The Johnson family's surface behavior includes poor communication between parents and their 16-year-old son, David. He and his parents have difficulty agreeing upon evening curfew limits, school grades, and use of the family car. Dad tends to be more lenient than Mom, and when David violates his parents' standards, Dad does not provide consequences. Mom tends to become highly upset with David. When David's father sees his wife upset, he becomes angry and punitive with David.

Dysfunctional Transactional Patterns. David becomes triangulated into his parent's marital difficulties. The couple holds the family myth that if they had to face their own differences without distraction from their son, David, the results would be catastrophic. The parents have disengaged marital and parental subsystems such that they rarely talk about their own differences or come to agreements about consequences for David's rules or rule violations.

Links between Surface Behavior and Developmental History. The family appears to have special difficulty with managing the family life-cycle stage of David's becoming an adolescent with new standards of independence. David's father's own adolescence was marked by anger and distance from his father. Dad came from a family where he had been triangulated into his own parents' conflicts. He had been in an alliance with his own mother in a protector role against his father. Dad is drawn into conflict with David as a way of protecting his wife, whom he views as emotionally vulnerable.

David's mother left home following unhappy high school years. She married out of high school but felt poorly prepared for survival in the community.

David's older brother left home at 17, following outbursts with his father. David's mother fears that David is now trying to become independent too quickly and is not preparing himself through his school work for survival in the world. The therapist speculates that David's mother becomes overly identified with David because of her own experience of leaving home ill prepared for life.

Both mother and father are inhibited in confronting one another or negotiating differences between themselves as a couple and as parents because of their own fears that close relationships lead to abandonment.

Current Factors Leading to the Presenting Problem.   David has recently gotten his driver's license and has assumed more independence. He has done poorly in school this year and cannot find a summer job. He has been spending more time at his older brother's apartment and does not want to spend time at home.

The formulation of a couple or family's problem clarifies the goals of treatment and the requisite changes that will be necessary to achieve these goals. In the previous example, several treatment goals are suggested:

1. The parents must function as a more effective parental subsystem. This will involve their learning to communicate better and negotiate about family matters.
2. David's parents must gain experience at negotiating with David over his desire to take more responsibility for his actions.
3. Both David and his parents should become more independent to decrease over-involvement in the family. Developing independence will require changing the triangulation pattern that is a feature of the family.
4. The marital subsystem must be strengthened in order to meet parental needs for closeness as David begins to separate from the family. David's parents will need to learn conflict resolution skills to overcome their marital distancing. They will have to face their fears of abandonment and having insufficient personal resources to face their own differences directly.

Generally, following an initial assessment phase, the therapist contracts with the couple or family for a particular number of sessions to focus on resolving particular issues. In marriage and family therapy, it is especially important to agree upon the format of therapy (conjoint or combined with individual) and discuss the nature of confidentiality. This is especially important if a combined format is utilized where the therapist is likely to see family members together and separately. The complex ethical, legal, and professional issues of marital and family therapy are discussed in detail by Huber and Baruth (1987).

FACILITATING MARITAL AND FAMILY FUNCTIONING

In marital and family therapy, a variety of interventions can be utilized, both for ongoing assessment purposes and to facilitate change. Interventions are intended to break dysfunctional interaction patterns, clarify problematic sequences of behavior, alter affective blocks, initiate cognitive restructuring, implement new transactional patterns, and mobilize external resources as required (Tomm & Wright, 1979). We will highlight a number of interventions related to developing balanced family cohesion and adaptability.

Interventions Promoting Cohesion

Cohesion-related interventions are aimed at establishing appropriate subsystem boundaries, clarifying coalitions, assisting decision making, increasing interpersonal empathy, and developing a family climate in which members are open to feedback from one another.

Fantasy and Imagery. Guided imagery and fantasy can be utilized in a manner similar to its use with individuals, as described in Chapter 7. Couples or families can be asked to image their ideal marriage and describe it to their partner. Or family members may be asked to visualize their difficulties in the form of a metaphoric image selected by the clients. The therapist asks the clients to visualize the image in detail and then to picture this image changing in some way. The therapist asks clarifying and guiding questions if the client feels blocked in change. By suggesting change is possible, family members' "metaphoric minds" often develop creative solutions to difficulties. Such difficulties can then be processed and discussed by family members.

Imagery can also be used to enhance memory of positive past experiences. The counselor can guide family members as they seek to remember experiences from the past that may help them reach current goals. For example, as a couple desires to increase the caring between them, the counselor might ask them to visualize experiences of such caring at various stages of their marriage. These memories can then be used to help formulate a behavioral description of what it means when they say they want more caring from their partner.

Sculpting. Family sculpting (Papp, 1973) involves asking a couple or family member to physically position themselves and other family members into a formation which metaphorically represents the family relationships. The family member may then reposition family members to represent an ideal image of the family. While remaining in their positions, the therapist may ask family members to describe their experience in the formation. Sculpting can metaphorically represent various aspects of a relationship system: closeness/distance, splits and alignments, the experience of being one up or one down in reference to another—all aspects not usually elicited by verbal reports. Nonverbal exercises such as sculpting often help family members become more aware of hidden system dynamics.

Boundary Setting. Boundary setting is a process within a couple relationship or family intended to differentiate family subsystem boundaries to make room for flexibility (Minuchin & Fishman, 1981). Boundary setting generally involves building "walls" between people to establish separation or "bridges" to allow more permeable boundaries and connection.

Many boundary-setting strategies are available to demarcate and encourage strengthening of subsystem boundaries. Spatial arrangements, such as seating the parents next to each other or moving chairs farther apart, created boundaries. Monitoring communication so that only one person speaks at a time can help an enmeshed couple or family create a permeable but more rigid boundary establishing each person's individuality. Encouraging a longer duration of dialogue between a distant parent and child can strengthen a weak subsystem. Or, the therapist can block triangulation in conflict resolution by keeping a third person from becoming involved in disputes between two others. For example, the therapist is sometimes triangulated into an unwanted marital coalition by one person (A) speaking to the therapist about the spouse (B) rather than directly to their spouse (B). The therapist can (1) continue looking at person A rather than at B while A speaks; and (2) tell A to speak to, not about B; or (3) ask A how he or she feels about it; or (4) address a comment about A to B (Sluzki, 1978). These maneuvers establish a rule that the couple must speak for themselves and deal directly with their spouse. Other boundary-setting activities might involve family tasks such as estabishing rules regarding an adolescent's need for privacy (i.e., "knocking before entering bedrooms"). Additional examples are assigning an underinvolved father the task of helping his son with his homework, teaching the boy how to play soccer, or controlling the boy when he misbehaves.

Unbalancing. Unbalancing the family hierarchy is a structural technique (Minuchin & Fishman, 1981) achieved by the therapist using his own authority to ally himself with a family member or subsystem to challenge the family structure. For example, in a family with a strong mother-child coalition and a peripheral father, the therapist might insist that the father be in charge of parenting the identified patient child "in order to relieve the exhausted mother." Such an unbalancing move is intended to challenge the family structure by creating more proximity of the father with the mother and child and more distance between mother and child. Father is placed into an executive position in respect to the child and reenters a parental subsystem with the mother.

Complementarity. The therapist attempts to make explicit the style of living together that the family has evolved, labeling the *reciprocity of behavior and emotion* within the family system. Minuchin and Fishman (1981) describe an enmeshed family in which, as a youngster sneezes, the mother hands the father a handkerchief for him, and the sister looks in her purse for a handkerchief. The therapist says, "My goodness, look how one sneeze activates everybody. This is a family that makes helpful people." In this intervention, the therapist begins to identify how each family's behavior or "dance" is rule governed and how these rules are an important aspect of the family's problems.

Caring Days. Stuart (1980) has developed a "caring days" strategy for increasing a couple's expectations of positive therapy outcome as well as to build a sense of commitment to their marriage. The technique is based on the premise that positive actions are likely to induce positive reactions, first in the attitudes of others, and then in their behavior. On specific caring days, couples are asked to act "as if" they cared for one another even though they will not experience these feelings until they have changed their behavior. Each partner is asked to list at least 18 specific, small, positive behaviors that his or her partner could do as a means of showing that he or she cares for the other. For example, items might include, "Ask me about my day at work," "Hold my hand when we go for walks," or "Call me during the day." On specified caring days during the week, each spouse is expected to emit at least five of the caring behaviors on his or her partner's list irrespective of whether the other has made similar gestures.

Sexual Therapy. Sexual problems are among the more common complaints of couples entering marital counseling. Primary sexual problems in either or both partners may give rise to other relationship stresses or may result from problems in the spouses' marital interaction. While there are unique elements in the various sexual dysfunction approaches, they all share goals of (1) reduction of performance anxiety (often through graduated sexual tasks and cognitive behavioral strategies), (2) sex education, (3) skill training in communication and sexual technique, and (4) attitude change procedures (Heiman, LoPiccolo, & LoPiccolo, 1980). Discussion of specific strategies is beyond the scope of this chapter, but an overview of treatment approaches can be found in Heiman, et al. (1980), Kaplan (1974), and Stuart (1980).

Interventions Promoting Adaptability

Strategies aimed at increasing family adaptability focus on developing clear and flexible family leadership, discipline, roles, rules, and communication.

Communication Rules. Couples and families must develop the ability to express themselves as well as to hear and understand others. Stuart (1980) has suggested communication training in five areas: listening, measured self-expression, selective request making, provision of positive and corrective feedback, and clarification of intended meanings. Each of the first skills is a prerequisite for those that follow. Practice of the skills using both nonverbal and verbal expression of feelings and ideas can help family members learn about other members' desires and is a prerequisite to being able to negotiate behavioral changes.

Problem Solving and Negotiation. Couples and families can be taught to make agreements to change some of their patterns of interaction. In negotiation, each person agrees to make any of several changes while the other is expected to do the same. Stuart (1980) has listed four steps to negotiating agreements. First, each person is asked to list his or her *positive* and *specific* requests for change in the other's *behavior.* Secondly, each spouse or child is asked to rephrase the other's request to clarify his or her meaning. Thirdly, the parties should be asked to write their requests in the form of a contract to build some accountability into their reciprocated requests for change. Finally, the parties are asked to put the contract into action, making note of their own and the other's efforts to abide by its terms. Renegotiation of the contract can be an ongoing process.

Powergram. The powergram (Stuart, 1980) is a method for clarifying the power balance in a marital relationship. Decisions in a marriage may be made along a continuum of power balance, which will vary for different couples and for different types of decisions. Some decisions might be made separately by each spouse; some might be made by each spouse upon consultation with the other; and some might be joint efforts. Couples are asked to read over a list of areas in which couples commonly make decisions (i.e., how many hours the husband works, what job his wife takes, how to spend money, how and when to pursue interests). Couples are asked to identify how they believe decisions are made currently and then to indicate how, ideally, they would like decisions in the different areas to be made. The therapist then helps them compare notes and negotiate desired changes.

Enactment. Enactment is described by Minuchin and Fishman (1981) as a technique "by which the therapist asks the family to dance in his presence." It is a method by which the therapist challenges the family's definition of the problem. The initial presenting problem becomes repeatedly redefined and its transactional significance is made more apparent.

Enactment occurs in three stages. First, the therapist allows the family members to interact spontaneously with each other in his or her presence, to experience the family reality as they describe it. This enactment permits aspects of the family's functioning to become manifest. In the second stage of enactment, the therapist can elicit transactions to test hypotheses about how the couple or family patterns contribute to the presenting symptoms. Family members can become more aware of the effects of their behavior on others and how symptoms reflect systemic processes rather than residing within the identified patient. Then, in the third stage, the therapist can suggest alternative transactions to develop a new communication pattern that helps the couple or family resolve its differences.

Focus. Focus is a technique described by Minuchin and Fishman (1981) in which the therapist explores one family theme in depth. In contrast to gathering family history and description, focus relates to the process of change. Minuchin and Fishman describe a multiproblem family, which is characterized by pervasive hopelessness. The family reality focuses on its deficits. The mother and outside agencies lump all the children together as one mass of problems. Since the mother and social welfare institutions emphasize only the family's deviancy, the therapist determines to focus therapy on another aspect of reality—the elements of competence within the family. The goal of the therapist is to pull the family members away from their insistence on negatives and move them toward actualizing their competence. In so doing, he helps the family reframe their reality or view of themselves. Such reframing leads to alternative ways of dealing with their problems.

Intensity. Increasing emotional intensification is another strategy for achieving marital or family changes (Minuchin & Fishman, 1981). It is often at a point of closeness or conflict that a couple or family reverts to a transactional pattern that will lower affective intensity and prevent a change from occurring in the relationship system. Intensifying the affect at such a point in a session can lead the couple or family into a new pattern of communication. Intensification can occur through enactment, by exploring and interpreting an affective issue, by repeating a message to the family, or by reducing physical distance between family members. Increased intensity allows the system to reach an affective "threshold of resolution" in which people can speak honestly and work out disagreements with other family members. When families lower affective intensity prematurely, they fail to reach this resolution threshold and end up fighting repetitively without resolution.

Challenging the Family Reality. All people strive to make sense of their experience. Depending upon the way we label our experiences, we can facilitate or inhibit our constructive action. We formulate expectations of how others will treat us based upon the way we label their behavior.

Weakland et al. (1974) suggest that clients can be helped to change their framework for understanding their difficulties. By "reframing" behavioral patterns, the therapist can offer new ideas that challenge the couple's or family's own world view. Reframing can be accomplished in various ways. In Chapter 9, we discussed positively connoting behavior as a method of reframing a problem. For example, "anger" is reframed as "concern" or someone's symptom becomes an act of "kindness and goodwill." At other times, a symptom may need to be "inflated" into something bigger as a means of reframing the problem. Teaching complementarity is one way that an individual's behavior becomes framed as a relational pattern that is triggered by another's behavior. Focusing can be a way of reframing a family's focus on incompetence toward a view of themselves as competent.

RESEARCH IN MARITAL AND FAMILY THERAPY

Marriage and family therapy outcome research seeks information regarding the effectiveness of a particular treatment strategy. Reviewers of outcome research (Pinsof, 1981; Jacobson, 1978, 1991) have difficulty determining the effects of marital and family therapy because of the complexity of the variables involved. Much of the available research has focused on developing complex coding systems to explore patterns of the therapist's and client's behaviors. The findings suggest only a few conclusions based on quantitative research.

First, data support marital and family therapy approaches as effective treatments. Most quantitative research on marital and family therapy has investigated behavioral therapy. The available evidence tentatively suggests that behavioral exchange programs, when they include either communication, problem-solving training alone, or communication training plus behavioral exchange, are an effective treatment for marital problems (Hahlweg & Markman, 1988). In a comparative study with behavioral marriage therapy, it was found that insight therapy was perhaps even more effective at a four-year follow-up (Snyder, Wills, & Grady-Fletcher, 1991). There is also evidence of the effectiveness of Emotionally Focused Therapy (Greenberg & Johnson, 1988). Systems therapy has not received as much quantitative investigation, in part because these theories are relatively general and lack adequate microtherapy constructs or a "hypothesis map" that can function as a guide to family therapy process research.

Marital research is particularly difficult because of the problems in locating variability in the treatments. There is a need to measure therapist variability in terms of competence and adherence to treatment manuals. Also, the goals of treatment vary. Some measure behavioral change, while others emphasize mutual acceptance and understanding as desirable outcomes. Outcome variance is related to a complex array of therapist, client, interactive, and technique variables that are difficult to isolate. Gender influences represent a major area that has received little research attention.

Research progress is more likely to come from new strategies such as within-model comparisons, comparisons of specific components, and consideration of how mini-interventions might affect a specific process. Task analytic research offers some promise by identifying important moments in interactional sequences, generating hypotheses about what the mechanisms are that make that segment important, coding the interaction, and predicting based on that model. Also, comparing high-change with low-change sequences can help identify important elements of effectiveness.

Across numerous studies it has been found that various family therapies are more effective than individual psychotherapy when family-related issues and problems are at the heart of the presenting problem (Gurman & Kniskern, 1981). Conjoint couples therapy is clearly superior to individual therapy for problems presented as marital difficulties; in addition, negative outcomes accrue from individual treatment of marital problems twice as often as in conjoint treatment (Gurman & Kniskern, 1978).

DIVORCE COUNSELING

Clinical intervention for divorcing couples focuses on helping the couple come to a decision about their marriage, grieve their emotional pain, and, when children are involved, reduce the intensity of the divorcing process so that parenting functions can be maintained while marital relationships are dissolving. Identification of patterns of attachment and the part each individual plays is critical.

Resolution of personal loss and grief without projection of responsibility onto others is important.

Kessler (1975) has described a six-stage process model of divorce, from recognition of the marital discord through separation and divorce. Her model is similar to Kubler Ross's stages (1969) in the grieving process. Stages 1 and 2 compose the "pre-divorce deliberation period." Stage 1, *disillusionment,* involves recognition of feelings of dissatisfaction and alienation at a time when the couple quarrels and perhaps seeks therapy. The second stage, *erosion,* involves anguish, ambivalence, and a sense of personal inadequacy. It is characterized by ambivalent behavior of alternately withdrawing and attempting to win back affection. Stages 3 and 4 are the "during-divorce litigation period" in which the divorcing individuals experience depression, anger, confusion, sadness, and loneliness. Stage 3, *detachment,* represents a bargaining and mourning stage. During stage 4, *physical separation,* a physical separation occurs and divorce papers are filed. Couples at this stage must tell friends and relatives. Stages 5, *second adolescence,* and 6, *hard work,* compose the "post-divorce re-equilibration" period in which the divorcing parties experience renewed optimism, excitement, and self-worth mixed with resignation that their former marriage is over. The task of the final stage is to integrate what has been learned through the divorce process. The stages of divorce do not occur in an invariant sequence but shift back and forth with alternating highs and lows and movement forward and backward.

Various authors (Peck & Manocherian, 1988; Vines, 1979; Beal, 1980) have highlighted the importance of developmental issues affecting the divorce process. Shifts in both the individual life cycle and family life cycle are associated with divorce. The impact of divorce on family members will also be influenced by the family life-cycle stage at the time of divorce. Knowing an individual's developmental issues at the time of marriage and divorce may lead to a better understanding of the client's needs and frustrations. For example, if a man marries directly out of high school, it may be that he has transferred family separation issues from his parents onto his spouse. Or if people are feeling stagnant at midlife, they may consider divorce as a major rebuilding of their life structure. Such patterns may also represent a characteristic "emotional cut-off" pattern in families appearing through many generations. Helping divorcing individuals explore the larger context of their decision can often provide new perspectives and new options for achieving the desired life and relationship goals.

The impact of divorce on children will depend on many factors. These factors include the intensity of the emotional attachment and conflict between parents and the degree to which the child is the focus of the family emotional processes. Beal (1980) has described differing effects of divorce on children depending on their ages. An evaluation by Lamb (1977) led him to conclude that children of divorced parents are more at risk for psychological damage than are children of intact families. However, this may only be true if the intact family is functioning reasonably well together. His second conclusion is that there are no *universal* effects of divorce. In fact, there is a wide diversity of outcomes for children.

Counselors can provide services at various stages of the divorce process. Counselors can provide therapy to couples and individuals contemplating divorce. During the separation process, trained therapists can function as mediators to resolve differences related to custody, money, property, and further relationship. Therapists can serve postdivorce individuals through support networks such as recovery groups or divorce lifelines. Therapists can also help couples develop rituals to help end their marriage. Bach (1974) describes such an "unwedding" group ritual in which a person in a clergy role unties a couple's clasped hands, has the couple return their rings, and pronounces them "unwed." Friedman (1988) has described the importance of rituals at nodal points in the family life cycle.

SKILL-TRAINING PROGRAMS
FOR COUPLES AND FAMILIES

It is difficult to draw a boundary that clearly distinguishes skill-training programs from therapy. The relatively structured nature of skill-training programs stands in contrast with the relatively unstructured nature of therapy. Skill-training programs also tend to be shorter than most therapies. L'Abate (1981) adds that therapy models generally seem to stress the ambivalence that its recipients have about change more than skills approaches. Skill-training programs, in addition, usually emphasize therapist or leader-generated agendas for sessions, while therapy usually involves therapist interventions that are more immediately responsive to felt client needs of the moment. He adds the analogy that "therapy may be to skills programs as teaching learning disabled children is to normal classroom education" (p. 634).

Skill-training programs are most appropriate as prevention measures with well-functioning or semifunctioning nonclinical couples and families. These clients may still need some help in specific areas of functioning, may wish the support of other families, or may wish to review principles related to enhancing couple and family relationships. Couples who need therapy rather than skill training should be screened in a preprogram interview.

Skill-training programs can be classified according to a family life-cycle sequence: (1) premarriage training; (2) marital; (3) parenthood (4) total family, and (5) divorce mediation (L'Abate, 1981).

Premarriage Programs

Most group premarriage programs emphasize development of skills in conflict resolution, negotiation, decision making, and communication about issues such as role expectations, sexuality, and money. The format of premarriage programs often involves minilectures regarding topics by the group leader, followed by an experimental exercise related to the topic. For example, following a mini-lecture about money, the group facilitator might pass out a sample budget sheet to the participants and have them rank how they would choose to spend money in various categories. Couples would then compare their responses with those of their partners and discuss similarities and differences. Occasionally, a group format is combined with a joint session between each couple and counselor to discuss results from psychological tests related to marital relationships.

While L'Abate found little long-range follow-up data on the effectiveness of premarital programs, an often unspoken goal is to provide an enjoyable counseling experience such that clients may consider counseling at a later time if problems develop. Sometimes a one-year follow-up visit with a counselor is included as a component of the premarriage program.

Marital Programs

Many of the marital skill-training programs share common characteristics of (1) emphasizing open and direct exchange of feelings without emotional putdowns; (2) assumption of personal responsibility for whatever is said and done in the marriage; (3) clarification and differentiation of feelings as being different from thoughts and actions; and (4) increased awareness of options available to build a marriage. Among the major programs are the Couples Communication Program, Relationship Enhancement Program, Marriage Encounter, and structured enrichment programs that teach fair fighting, assertiveness, and problem solving.

The Couples Communication Program (Miller, Nunnally, & Wackman, 1977) is one of the oldest and most researched marital skills programs. The major skills emphasized are awareness, which enables partners to understand their rules of interaction, and communication skills, which allow them to change past rules and interaction patterns. The program attempts to help couples become more aware of their own contributions to their marital interaction and to increase each couple's capacity for clear, direct, open communication regarding their relationship. Groups of five to seven couples meet with one or two certified instructors for three-hour sessions one night a week for four weeks. Couples use a workbook and a textbook. They are taught skills in communication and given the opportunity to practice specific skills each week. Wampler (1982) reviewed 19 studies of the Couples Communication Program and found that the program had an immediate positive effect on communication behavior and relationship satisfaction. An 18–20-week follow-up study (Joanning, 1982), however, showed that couples did not continue to incorporate the communication skills into their repertoire. It appears that couples may need more opportunity to develop skills or may need follow-up booster sessions to maintain their skills. Or, it may be that enrichment programs emphasizing clear communication may open up some awareness of relationship difficulties and that couples return to pretreatment communication as a way of avoiding conflict.

The Association of Couples for Marriage Enrichment (ACME) is a national organization composed of married couples with the primary goal of developing and maintaining effective support systems for marriage enrichment. ACME has sponsored weekend retreats, couples support groups, or enrichment workshops to enhance couples' efforts to support one another in marriage.

Marriage Encounter is a 44-hour program designed for weekend retreats and is usually under the auspices of religious organizations. Leader couples give short talks related to themes such as "I," "We," "We-God," and "We-God-World." Couples are given questions for reflection and dialogue. Questions generally help couples share positive aspects of their relationship with one another. Couples then discuss their plan for commitment to one another, their families, and the world. After the weekend is over, couples are urged to join various follow-up programs to provide support. Although there is a paucity of outcome research on Marriage Encounter, L'Abate (1981) found support for Marriage Encounter as a method of teaching couples how to share feelings and to communicate on a deeper level. Studies by Doherty and his associates (1978, 1986) suggest that about one in ten couples feel negatively affected by the weekends. The most frequently cited complaint was that the couple's expectations were unmet and they became more frustrated with their marriages following the weekends.

Parenting Programs

Parenting programs show more similarity to therapy than other types of skill-training programs. They tend to teach a variety of childrearing and child-management approaches based primarily on Adlerian, behavioral, and humanistic approaches. Examples of parenting programs include Parent Effectiveness Training (PET), Patterson's social learning approach, Behavioral Parent Training, and Adlerian-based programs such as Active Parenting. Parent training programs focus on teaching parents principles of appropriate reinforcement, communication skills, and problem-solving skills.

The evidence of effectiveness of parenting programs in meeting their specified goals remains unclear. For example, Gordon's PET program, which teaches skills in active listening and negotiation with children, has not been shown clearly to improve communication and problem solving. In their review of research, Rimm and Markle (1977) concluded that it is difficult to evaluate the effectiveness of PET because outcome studies generally showed inadequate methodology. Gordon and Davidson (1981), in reviewing the literature on behavioral parenting programs, conclude that they are an effective intervention for discrete, well-specified behavior problems. In cases of more complex dysfunctional behavior, the research is encouraging but not conclusive. The "Tough Love" program (Neff, 1984) is targeted at families where children appear out of control. Parents are involved in peer support groups who help them to find short-term alternative living situations for their children when necessary and coach parents in negotiating and contracting with their children. More research needs to evaluate this approach.

Family Enrichment

Family education programs are intended as a preventive approach to produce change before serious problems develop. Family enrichment has included formats such as family clusters or family education programs. Typically, all forms of family education involve groups of families in weekly discussions, lectures, experiential exercises, or weekend retreats. The purpose of these groups is to strengthen communication within families, provide mutual support among families, and to provide children and adults with the opportunity to gain new perspectives about their own relationships through contact with other families. Although family education has traditionally been utilized with nonclinical families, a recent trend involves greater use of family education as an adjunct to family therapy with clinical families (Carnes, 1981; L'Abate, 1977). In their meta-analysis of premarital, marital, and family enrichment programs, Giblin et al. (1985) found that enrichment programs showed greater effects with distressed populations than with nondistressed populations. These effects may, in part, be attributable to ceiling effects of instruments which are not sensitive to changes of healthy couples or families.

One example of a family enrichment program, *Understanding Us*, is based on the Circumplex Model described in this chapter. Families in the *Understanding Us* program meet for four weekly meetings with six to eight other families to apply concepts of cohesion and adaptability to their own families through discussion and experiential exercises. Participants discuss how their family leadership, rules, and problem-solving styles reflect their family's flexibility. The family's use of time, space, friendship, and recreational patterns are discussed in relation to the degree of autonomy family members experience. Abrego (1981) found that participants in both the *Understanding Us* program and an alternate family education program placed greater value on autonomy within their families after participating in the education programs. Families also showed a trend toward spending a greater proportion of time together, greater role flexibility, and family assertiveness over the treatment and follow-up periods. Generally, family enrichment programs show fewer positive effects than marital or parent-child dyad programs (Giblin et al., 1985).

Divorce Mediation

Coogler (1978) developed divorce mediation to assist divorcing couples in working out divorce settlement issues related to child support, custody, alimony, and the division of property according to a time-limited framework and a contractual agreement. Under marital mediation, arbitration rules are given to the couple, which help them define issues that must be resolved for settlement. Procedual methods are followed for collecting information. On the basis of this information, the couple is helped to resolve their differences.

Reviews of divorce therapy and mediation (Sprenkle & Storm, 1983; Emery & Wyer, 1987) indicate that mediation shows considerable advantages over the traditional adversary method of resolving the same kind of dispute. It appears to result in a higher rate of pretrial agreements, a higher level of satisfaction with the mediated agreements than with those imposed by courts, a reduction in the amount of litigation following final orders, an increase in joint custody arrangements and a decrease in public expenses. Divorce mediation appears least effective for couples with a range of highly disputed economic and child-related issues, poor communication, and for couples in which one partner did not wish to divorce.

SUMMARY

In this chapter we have addressed the application of therapeutic psychology to counseling couples and families. We discussed key concepts of family cohesion, adaptability, and development in understanding marital and family patterns.

The process of marital and family therapy parallels that of individual therapy in its emphasis on engagement, assessment, intervention, and termination stages. However, marital and family assessment pay particular attention to the links between presenting problems and dysfunctional interaction patterns. Developmental knowledge provides an important context for understanding symptom onset and formation. A variety of marital and family techniques were described, such as sculpting, boundary setting, and caring days.

Special types of marriage and family therapy, such as divorce therapy and skill-training programs, were described. Research indicates that these programs are promising. The complexity of measuring marital and family interactions has led to a paucity of research in the field. The challenge to theorists is to develop more researchable hypotheses to test which types of therapy or training programs will be most effective with couples and families with different kinds of problems.

CHAPTER 11

Counseling for Career Transitions

Choosing a satisfying life style is one of the principal developmental tasks of life. In terms of our actualizing model, it involves all levels of awareness in the person, from values clarification at the core level, analysis of basic styles of functioning, and development of effective decision-making methods at the actualizing level. This life-style choice incorporates what was once called vocational planning, but now this choice includes a much broader range of choices covering the type of community life, the desired family structure, avocational activities, as well as the range and kinds of friendships and partnerships.

Career planning packages and programs put careers in the context of life planning over the entire age spectrum. Bolles's self-help manuals (1978, 1991) stress a process of balancing and getting out of what he calls the three boxes of life—work, education, and retirement. Bolles uses the box metaphor to describe the compelling quality of each of these three life conditions and how people must struggle to free themselves. His manuals are examples of how a person makes the complex series of choices leading to a satisfying life and work plan. While these types of materials are useful checklists to make people aware of what they need to know and do to plan their lives, we know of no evidence that makes the do-it-yourself workshop approach superior to consultations with career counseling specialists. The complexities of the life decision-making and planning process and the technical resources needed are such that a counseling relationship appears a necessity to us.

Life planning is considered an integrated process involving many values and choices. This state of affairs offers a great challenge to actualizing counseling and therapy to provide a range of counseling methods and the most appropriate kind of relationships to help people make responsible choices and plans to sustain them for their lifetimes. Life-style counseling, combined with group experiences where values are explored, strengths and skills are inventoried, problems are examined, and plans are formulated, offers such a comprehensive approach.

The social consequences of career choices are considerable. The principal values of professional career counseling services to society are the discovery, utilization, and conservation of human talent as a humanistic goal. Appropriate career choice is especially significant in view of the multiple career transitions people now make during a lifetime to keep up with rapid changes on the job scene, as well as to match their career to their evolving life style. Career planning for the disabled is wise social policy also.

Counseling cannot become an instrument of national policy, however, since this would violate our values about freedom of choice. Therapeutic psychology seeks to help clients become aware of their assets, limitations, and opportunities in all possible areas so that they will make wise choices and will use their unique talents if they care to do so. We believe that when individuals know their talents and use them in ways of their own choosing, the effects ultimately will be best for the society in which they live. In addition, counseling serves broad social purposes through helping individuals overcome obstacles to effective learning and achievement by means of rehabilitative planning and action.

COUNSELING FOR CAREER TRANSITIONS

Career choice has been regarded historically as *vocational guidance*—a process of helping the client to choose, prepare for, and succeed in a given occupation. This process was centered around counseling, which consisted largely of examining data about the client and looking over the occupational possibilities to find a specific career goal, at which point an educational plan was formulated to reach that goal.

More recently, there has been a change in the perception of the significance and scope of career guidance. First, career development is considered a continuous process over the life span. Career development theories now examine career choice and adjustment through adult years rather than focusing primarily on adolescent career decisions. Secondly, career is more broadly conceptualized as the pattern of activities and experiences that make up a lifetime of work, learning, and leisure. The term includes occupational and educational choices and patterns as well as other aspects of a person's life such as personal and social behaviors, skills, social responsibilities, and leisure activities. The individual's occupational career and other life roles cannot be separated in the career counseling process. Thirdly, career counseling has broadened from the concept of choosing an occupation and adjusting to the work environment to learning to cope with a spectrum of career transitions. These transitions are defined as "an event or nonevent that results in a change in assumption about oneself and the world and thus requires a corresponding change in one's behavior and relationships" (Schlossberg, 1981, p. 5). This definition acknowledges that for many people, career counseling may deal with issues such as stress from the lack of change in one's work or the loss of a life dream. For example, Rosenbaum (1979) suggests that promotion chances in organizations increase until age 35 to 40 and then decline, thus precipitating midlife crises for many individuals. O'Neil and Fishman (1986) have identified 21 major career transitions for men related to career choice, advancement, job change, work conflicts, "peaking," loss of meaning, and retirement.

Career counseling is a task of therapeutic psychology. Vocational psychology cannot be singled out as a special branch of counseling and psychotherapy, largely because career counseling must be accomplished in the context of the individual's total life style and in relationship to his or her subculture. Optimally effective career counseling, therefore, cannot be an isolated and mechanical process of matching people and jobs.

Career counseling goals can be construed in several ways. A primary goal of career counseling is to help clients view themselves as having the ability to make their own choices about their life direction. We believe it is important to help clients to understand their choices and decisions as occurring within a broad, developmental context. Additionally, individuals can be helped to make choices and plan their careers by increasing their knowledge about themselves, the work environment, and other factors influencing career decisions. These factors include family expectations and values, gender role expectations, community influences, reinforcement received from previous career-related activities, the economic and social conditions of the society, and other influences outside the individual. Clients also need access to information related to implementing job search, career enhancement, and life-style change. Counselors should assist clients in considering the impact of career and job choices on other life roles. Finally, counselors can help clients develop coping skills for anticipating and managing career transitions.

Therapeutic psychology is uniquely suited to accomplish this broad goal of effective planning for career transitions. The strategies described in earlier chapters, plus some special tools uniquely suited to career planning, are the principal requirements for effective career planning. Career choice, from the research results reported to date, is not a strictly rational process. Neither is it a process of decision making on the basis of a few interviews with a counselor. Research supports the idea that decisions are the product of a long series of life experiences and learnings that come to a focus in the interviews with the counselor.

THEORETICAL FOUNDATIONS OF CAREER DEVELOPMENT

To understand the process of career development, the interwoven contributions of career choice, adult development, and family development theories need to be examined. Levinson (1980) offered a tapestry as being a useful metaphorical image of adulthood. Each person's life is like a huge tapestry threaded by inter-related roles around occupation, friendships, career networks, family relationships, and leisure activities. The meaning of each thread or role depends on its place in the total design of the tapestry. Adult development research and theories have focused on different aspects of this tapestry. Some, such as Levinson and associates (1978), Erikson (1963), and Gould (1978) have studied the tapestry over time. Super (1957, 1990) Shein (1978), and Holland (1985) focused primarily on the single-career thread of the tapestry. Carter and McGoldrick (1988) have pointed to the importance of the family life cycle. Still others, such as transition theorists Schlossberg (1981, 1984), Hopson and Adams (1977), and Pearlin and Schooler (1978), described individual responses to major life transitions. Each perspective illuminates a particular aspect of human development, yet each is incomplete in itself. For this reason, we will highlight major career development theories and then discuss contributions from other developmental perspectives that provide a useful context for understanding career development.

Career Development Theories

Various career development researchers have focused on the importance of developmental career stages. Their theories "specify that individual development proceeds through a series of stages, each of which requires the mastery of developmental tasks and/or resolution of developmental issues unique to that stage. Movement to subsequent stages is viewed as contingent upon the satisfactory completion or resolution of previous stages" (Campbell & Heffernan, 1983).

Super's (1957, 1990) writings provide the core assumption of most developmental theorists. He described career development as an evolutionary process occurring over the life span. Super's theory emphasizes that as an individual moves through the life cycle, each stage of that cycle calls for a different kind of vocational behavior. Adolescence is a period of preparation in which the individual crystalizes his or her ideas about appropriate work and makes relevant educational choices. During the late teens and early twenties, young adults must narrow their vocational directions and begin to implement a vocational preference by completing appropriate training and entry employment. After a young adult becomes established, the task of middle age is to stabilize and consolidate one's career. The final stage of career development is retirement, although it is considered increasingly as an opportunity for a new or continued career.

Many writers have further elaborated on developmental ideas. Jepson (1990) and Crites (1981) have provided important elaboration on the developmental counseling process. Shein's (1978) list of career-related developmental tasks for early and middle adulthood involves primarily career entry and advancement in the early and middle years. Then career decline or voluntary renewal characterizes later middle age. The final tasks are disengagement from work-related satisfactions and finding new sources of fulfillment.

Campbell and Heffernan (1983) have adapted Super's developmental tasks and applied them to individuals involved in mid-career transitions. Mid-career adults as well as young people encounter the "preparation" tasks of career development. These tasks involve decisions regarding vocational direction and implementing the choices. Mid-life workers must also complete establishment tasks that involve becoming oriented and adapted to the organizational environment. Additional tasks are establishing harmonious relationships with coworkers, learning the requirements of the position, and demonstrating one's competence. In this stage, individuals need to examine their job satisfaction, consider advancement opportunities, and develop future career plans. To manage careers satisfactorily, individuals must be able to succeed at "maintenance stage" career tasks that involve adjusting to changing organizational needs as well as reevaluating work performance goals. Problems with any of these tasks might lead to mid-life career change.

A second major career theory, Holland's theory (1985), emphasizes the importance of congruence or fit between one's personality pattern and demands of the work environment. Holland suggests that an individual most resembles one of six types of people: realistic, investigative, artistic, social, enterprising, or conventional. In the same way, work environments may also resemble these six types. Each work environment is dominated by a given type of personality. For example, social environments are dominated by social personalities, realistic environments by realistic personalities, and so on. Individuals search for work environments that will let them express their personalities and reward them for their skills and values. Environments search for people who are congruent with their dominant type through friendships and recruiting practices.

Holland believes that lack of congruence or fit between people and their work environment is the primary factor accounting for career change. He states that stable career patterns are most likely to occur when one's work environmental patterns resemble one's personality pattern. When these patterns are congruent, the person receives selective reinforcement for her or his successful performance of tasks or activities the individual considers important. A discrepancy between one's personality pattern and work environmental pattern, however, results in career dissatisfaction. This dissatisfaction is resolved by changing oneself, restructuring one's current work environment, or changing careers. Holland also suggests that an undifferentiated or inconsistent personality pattern can also contribute to a poor fit with one's work.

Gottfredson (1981) has added the notion that attraction to a particular occupation is primarily a function of its fit with one's gender self-concept (suitably masculine or feminine) and one's need for social class or prestige. These primary requirements for a job take precedence over interest level, which is secondary to gender and prestige attitudes as a basis for career selection and development. An important implication is that an individual is likely to make compromises in career choices based primarily on the career's fit with one's own gender-role attitudes and prestige levels. Clients who exhibit rigid gender-role attitudes or low expectations of job prestige because of sociocultural influences are likely to seek a limited range of career choices that fit with their modest self-expectations.

Social learning theorists (Krumboltz, Mitchell, & Jones, 1976; Krumboltz &

Nichols, 1990) have emphasized career choice as a process involving instrumental and associative learning. Choices evolve as individuals are rewarded for activities in which they succeed. Also, exposure to occupations and how others view those occupations shapes a person's self-concept and attitudes toward occupations. Through self-observations about one's interests, abilities, and occupations, individuals form beliefs that become the basis for career-relevant activities. Role models are particularly important factors in shaping an individual's development of abilities, preferences for activities, emotional response to careers, and implementation of career development behaviors. Individuals living in an environment with high unemployment and limited job opportunities may have restricted role models and opportunities and, thus, limited knowledge of the world of work. The impact of limited career aspirations for women and ethnic minorities is of particular importance, because the Bureau of Labor Statistics estimates that by the year 2000, the labor force is expected to grow 18 percent. Women and minorities will account for 90 percent of this growth.

In the past decade there has been a convergence in these theories of career development (Osipow, 1990; Walsh, 1990). Each of the major theories we have discussed provides an explanation of the development of self-knowledge, career choice, development, and satisfaction. Overlap in these theories occurs in many areas. For instance, Super's idea of self-concept is similar to the social learning notion of self-observation generalizations. All of these theories agree that individuals refine self-concepts over time with learning. They stress that individuals seek to find a fit between the actual world of work and their view of themselves. The works of Gottfredson (1981) and Betz and Fitzgerald (1987) have addressed particular issues of women in career development theory. Krumboltz and Nichols (1990) have suggested that Living Systems Framework (Ford, 1987) may provide an important cognitive meta-theory for integrating social learning theory into a broader theoretical context for understanding career development.

Contributions of Adult and Family Developmental Theories

Counselors should not isolate career problems from other developmental issues. O'Neil, Fishman, and Kinsella-Shaw (1987) suggest that for many people, such as dual-career couples, one's gender, friendship, spouse, parental, and leisure life roles are not simply complementary but central to maintaining careers and are intertwined with career decisions. Many family developmental factors such as timing of a marriage and childbearing are closely related to career factors such as career promotions, satisfactions, and salience. These various life roles and developmental tasks may come into conflict with career development needs or may enhance career development. Career development theories have not addressed how career development is part of the larger process of change and growth over the life span. Nor has adequate research indicated how career development issues, such as career changes or productivity patterns, are related to satisfaction or distress in other life roles.

There seems to be a continuum on which developmental issues and career development are intertwined. For some individuals, career decisions represent attempts to cope with other developmental tasks. For example, Lopez and Andrews (1987) consider college students' career indecision as often representing a failure in family transformation at the time students need to be separating from their families. They suggest that various family processes contribute to career indecision. Sometimes the student is triangulated into a cross-generational parental coalition, a pattern frequently correlated with family dysfunction and with the presence of marital conflict. At other times the students appear to be enmeshed with parents such that the career indecision provides the family with a vehicle for postponing an important family transformation of young adult separation. Ulrich and Dunne (1986) have described how multigenerational family themes affect career development. Osherson (1980) and Abrego and Brammer (1992) have described mid-life career change within a broad developmental context. At the other end of the continuum, some individuals' career development issues seem primarily linked more to specific job-related factors such as a poor relationship with supervisors.

For many people, career development goals involve attempts to find a better fit between one's self identity and a work environment that provides an opportunity for integrating dreams and goals. Individuals must be able to express their values and interests and play roles and perform activities that they deem appropriate for themselves. For example, for some people at mid-life, career transitions may be attempts to cope with the discrepancy between the anticipated self of young adulthood and the perceived self at mid-life. This discrepancy may precipitate or be precipitated by a career change and will result in an experience of loss and grief.

When career decisions become strategies for coping with developmental issues, they can be either growth oriented or may represent a retreat. They become growth oriented when they offer an opportunity to integrate more of one's total personality into one's life style. This kind of career decision enables the individual to manage better other life-span developmental tasks. Career decisions can also represent a retreat from facing fearful developmental issues and may prematurely foreclose important developmental tasks.

The process of coping successfully with career transitions is facilitated by broad, flexible coping skills for managing life transitions, and career transitions in particular. Metaphorically, it is useful to think of coping strategies as "tools in a tool box" or "arrows in a quiver." If something must be fixed or a bull's-eye must be hit, there will be more possibilities of success than with only one tool or arrow.

PROCESS OF CAREER COUNSELING

Career counseling follows a series of phases parallel to those we have described in previous chapters. The counselor needs to gather a comprehensive picture of how the client's decisions about work are understood within the context of other life roles and developmental issues. Then further appraisal is concerned with gathering more specific work-related information. Crites (1981) suggests that the counselor must do a vocational differential diagnosis to determine which interview techniques and tests should be used and how to introduce occupational information. Overall, career counseling seems to deal with several categories of information: (1) self-assessment of one's goals, values, and abilities related to work, (2) gathering information about occupations, employers, and work environments, and (3) skills in decision making and implementation of strategies for job search, career enhancement, and life-style change.

The counselor's approach to career counseling will probably be related to the life stage of the client. Intervention takes a different form for an adolescent than for someone at mid-life. During school years there is more emphasis on career education and exposure to a range of occupational environments. Many schools provide opportunities for students to experience various work environments through cooperative education approaches where students can have actual work experiences in the field. There may also be a greater emphasis on identification of values and development of self-knowledge based on test results. For adults, the counselor may make greater use of the individual's previous work and life experience to identify enjoyable skills and important values. For all age groups there has been a trend toward less reliance on psychometric methods and more reliance on promoting behaviors that might be useful in skill development and implementation.

Assessment of Presenting Problems

Career counselors encounter a wide range of presenting problems in their work. These presenting difficulties deal with clients' lack of career knowledge, decisional problems, anxiety over the need to make a good decision, and skill deficits in implementing potentially satisfying decisions. Presenting problems may concern making an initial career choice, dealing with on-the-job difficulties, or implementing a career change.

Several writers have developed taxonomies describing career problems. Campbell and Cellini (1981) identified a taxonomy of career problems that includes problems in decision making, problems in implementing career plans, problems of an organizational or institutional nature, and problems related to adaptation into an institution. Louis (1980) developed a typology of career transitions that includes interrole and intrarole categories.

Interrole transitions involve taking on a new and different career role. An example of career *entry transition* is a homemaker entering a new job in business. *Interprofessional transitions* involve shifting from one profession to another. A less radical career change occurs when a person transfers from one department to another within the same organization, termed an *intraorganizational transition*. The final interrole transitions in Louis's typology are the *exit transitions*, which may be voluntary exits such as child-care leaves and sabbaticals or involuntary terminations.

Intrarole transitions involve an individual's internal change of attitude without altering the job role externally. Some employees want change but do not want to change organizations or job roles because of personal constraints (e.g., loss of pension plans). Pearlin and Schooler (1978) found that these dissatisfied employees coped with work frustrations by changing their attitudes. One such coping mechanism was the use of positive comparisons such as "count your blessings" or "we're all in the same boat." Current frustrations may then be evaluated as being an improvement over the past or as a forerunner of an easier future. "Selective ignorance" was a second method for attending to the positive qualities of the experience. A third strategy for changing the meaning of one's work was to change one's hierarchy of priorities, devaluing unavailable rewards and substituting others (e.g., devaluing money and intrinsic work reward and valuing rewards extrinsive to work). Whereas career decisions typically are active strategies to cope with career frustrations, these strategies represent more subtle forms of career change. It is possible for individuals to cope with career crises by changing the internal meaning of their work rather than the actual job itself. In summary, there is a range of presenting career transitions ranging from transitions involving role changes to transitions in which only the meaning of one's work is altered.

Comprehensive Picture

As we have discussed in previous chapters on assessment, it is important to develop a comprehensive picture of client functioning. Learning about satisfactions and dissatisfactions in other life roles and about styles of coping with previous transitions can help the counselor and client explore the strengths and weaknesses in coping skills. This information is useful also in making a mutual assessment of whether this transition is primarily a career transition or reflects other developmental issues. Many career decisions, such as career change, represent conflicts between one's professional development and personal developmental tasks, or transition points in the life cycle of a significant other, or transitions in the family life cycle.

In assessing the work-related difficulties of the client, Crites (1981) and Fitzgerald (1986) suggest a vocational appraisal that includes a personal appraisal (present status and functioning, developmental history), problem appraisal, and a prognostic appraisal related to successful vocational counseling and vocational adjustment.

Vocational appraisal involves gathering information in numerous areas. The counselor seeks to classify the client's difficulties within one of the available taxonomies. Are the difficulties related to preparation, establishment, maintenance, or disengagement tasks? Additionally, the counselor assesses the client's involvement in the decision-making process. How does he or she perceive occupations? What are her or his beliefs about the importance of work in relation to other life roles? What are the client's needs, values, and aptitudes? What is the cognitive style of the client? Does the client use "either-or" thinking? What is the relationship of the client's personality to his or her decision process? How knowledgeable is the client about work environments? How are gender-role conflicts and expectations manifested in the career decision? We will discuss special methods of assessment, such as testing and skills analysis, later in this chapter.

The counselor also seeks information that will help determine the most effective counseling approach. What are the client's expectations for the counseling process? Would the client relate well to an individual counselor and talk openly in an interview? Would this client respond better to tests, interactive computer programs, or a career group counseling approach? Does the client have the assertiveness to interview people in order to gather job information?

Developmental Perspective

In addition to the general developmental history we describe in our Chapter 6 discussion of assessment, there are particular areas that the career counselor must attend to. As we have mentioned, career transitions should be viewed in relation to earlier life history and long-range implications. Additionally, career transitions should be viewed as possibly intertwined with other developmental events occurring simultaneously. These might include divorce, the death of a parent, or children entering school or leaving home. For some individuals, career transitions involve a strategy of coping, a developmental task such as individuation, or becoming more of a "whole person." Such a person may be searching for ways to become more generative, nurturing, or independent.

Other developmental information is more directly related to vocational expectations. What were the client's family models of career? What were the family attitudes toward the role of men and women? How was the client encouraged to develop career interests and reinforced for vocational planning and pursuits? What were early interests and abilities? What were early vocational choices and plans and how have these changed over time? How have subsequent career experiences shaped the client's expectations about work?

Systemic Function

Career decisions often have important systemic factors that influence the nature of the client's decisions or the ability to make a decision. Systemic factors in career decisions include the role played by the individual's significant others in the client's career decisions. What are the implications of decisions on one's parents, marriage, or children? What other factors, such as financial resources, organizational influences (i.e., policies, pension programs, politics), play a role in career planning?

Gender Roles and Career Counseling

Gender role is an important factor for both men and women in determining the nature, quality, and direction of career decisions. Gender roles are "behaviors, expectations and role sets defined by society as masculine or feminine that are embodied in the behavior of the individual man or woman and culturally regarded as appropriate to men or women" (O'Neil & Fishman, 1986). These roles are learned through socialization. They are likely to change with the demands of different phases of the life cycle. Gender roles often conflict with important values related to career decisions and may lead to negative consequences or impacts on the client or others. This gender-role conflict can be experienced as cognition, affect, behavior, or a phenomenon outside of our awareness. One potential negative outcome of gender-role conflict is role restriction or devaluation of others or oneself.

Socialization patterns in society can create prescriptions for male and female roles that discourage men and women from developing and implementing certain abilities, interests, and personality characteristics. Additionally, these patterns effectively bar individuals of both sexes from participating in certain occupations or occupational environments. Thus, both the personal and environmental components of Holland's matching model may be distorted by the expectations and requirements of sex roles.

Female gender-role prescriptions often create conflict between various life roles, impact the decision-making process, and limit the range of career choices perceived by women. There is typically a home versus career role conflict. Many women are socialized to expect that all women should engage in childrearing and that childrearing is either antithetical to or should take precedence over career development. Fitzgerald (1986) suggests that many traditional women may not actually progress through Super's stage of career exploration, nor successfully crystalize and specify a choice. Rather, female exploration may actually be pseudoexploration, as women await marriage. True vocational development may occur later, when childrearing duties have been largely completed. In addition to expectations regarding childrearing, many women are not socialized toward independence by their parents, schools, or spouses. They are likely to be more indecisive and anxious about making decisions. Women may have limited academic backgrounds in science and math or be especially anxious about achievement in areas not traditionally considered as "feminine." As women enter the labor force following childrearing, they often have low self-confidence and assertiveness. Their decision-making process is further complicated by the existence of discrimination in selection, promotion, and compensation, sexual harassment in the work place, and other factors. There are often negative consequences from significant others or coworkers as women seek to escape gender-role restrictions and consider nontraditional careers.

O'Neil and Fishman (1986) have described parallel processes of gender-role conflicts for males. They suggest that males are socialized by families, schools, peers, and often their spouses to value that "(a) men are superior to women and masculinity is superior to femininity; (b) power, control, and dominance are essential to prove one's masculinity; (c) emotions, feelings, vulnerability and intimacy are to be avoided because they are feminine; (d) career and economic successes are measures of one's masculinity," (p. 139). Men are taught to be competitive, achievement oriented, and competent. Manhood is measured by success, achievement, and career ascendancy. Work becomes a man's primary way to define self-worth. When some men marry they may expect exclusive right to the breadwinner or career role unless it is economically necessary for their wives to work. These beliefs devalue both women and men by denying the importance of expressing a full range of emotions and behaviors. Men are less likely to value expressions of emotional vulnerability and interdependence and to participate in nonwork-related roles such as leisure or parenting (Levant, 1992).

While women's career development suffers more than men's from sex-role attitudes and discrimination, deviation from male gender-role expectations can produce self-devaluation or negative consequences from others. O'Neil and Fishman state that men may experience fear of failure, low self-esteem, and emotional crises when faced with strong work competition or unsuccessful attempts to gain achievement, power, and success. Fearing emasculation, some men work so hard to demonstrate success that they neglect important relationships with spouses, friends, and children. All of these stresses can culminate in overwork, fatigue, and marital discord, posing serious threats to the man's physical and psychological health.

An important task for women and men making career decisions is to gain an understanding of how gender-role socialization impacts career decision making. These include recognizing experiences of gender-role conflict and evaluating the personal costs and benefits from decisions to deviate from gender-role expectations. The "Born Free" program (Hansen & Keierleber, 1978) represents an organizational intervention designed to help educators perform a systems analysis of their own institutional programs in order to reduce career-related sex-role stereotyping.

The counselor must attempt to integrate a complex amount of data to determine how the presenting career problems are related to the client. After summarizing this information, the counselor and the client must select a focus for counseling and determine appropriate strategies for facilitating career development.

STRATEGIES FOR FACILITATING CAREER DEVELOPMENT

Career counseling services can be delivered in a variety of formats. These include one-to-one counseling, workshops, group guidance, curriculum, telephone service, self-help materials, and the computer. Generally, service delivery is enhanced by using a combination of modalities. Goals for career counseling include improvement in decision-making skills, career maturity, quality of vocational choices, employment seeking skills, job performance and satisfaction, and general skills related to coping with life transitions.

Basic Transition Coping Skills

Flexible coping skills for coping with life transitions are important to individuals involved in career transitions. While not representing a comprehensive listing of coping skills, the taxonomy described by Brammer and Abrego (1981)

TABLE 11-1. LEVEL 1 BASIC COPING SKILLS FOR MANAGING TRANSITIONS.

1. *Skills in perceiving and responding to transitions.*
    1.1 The person mobilizes a personal style of responding to change. He or she—
       1.11 Accepts the proposition that problematic situations constitute a normal part of life and that it is possible to cope with most of these situations effectively. (Perceived control over one's life)
       1.12 Recognizes the importance of describing problematic situations accurately. (Problem definition)
       1.13 Recognizes the values and limitations of feelings as cues to evaluate a change event. (Feelings description)
       1.14 Inhibits the tendency either to act impulsively or to do nothing when confronted with a problematic situation. (Self-control)
    1.2 The person identifies his or her current coping style. (Style of responding to change)
2. *Skills for assessing, developing, and utilizing external support systems.*
    2.1 The person can assess an external support system. He or she can—
       2.11 Identify his or her emotional needs during times of transition.
       2.12 Identify people in his or her life who provide for personal needs.
       2.13 Describe a personal support network in terms of physical and emotional proximity.
    2.2 The person can develop a personal network. He or she can—
       2.21 Seek sources (groups, organizations, locales) of potential support persons.
       2.22 Apply social skills to cultivate persons to meet identified needs.
    2.3 The person can utilize an established support network. He or she can—
       2.31 Develop strategies for spending time with persons considered most helpful.
       2.32 Apply skills for utilizing persons in his or her network when a transition is anticipated or arrives.
3. *Skills for assessing, developing, and utilizing internal support systems.*
    3.1 The person can assess the nature and strength of positive and negative self-regarding attitudes. He or she can—
       3.11 Identify personal strengths.
       3.12 Identify negative self-descriptive statements as well as the assumptions and contextual cues which arouse such statements.
    3.2 The person can develop positive self-regard attitudes. He or she can—
       3.21 Affirm personal strengths.
       3.22 Convert negative self-descriptions into positive descriptive statements when the data and criteria so warrant.
    3.3 The person can utilize his or her internal support system in a transition. He or she can—
       3.31 Construe life transitions as personal growth opportunities.
       3.32 Identify tendencies to attribute personal deficiencies as causative factors in distressful transitions.
4. *Skills for reducing emotional and physiological distress. He or she is able to—*
    4.1 Practice self-relaxation responses.
    4.2 Apply strategies to control over-stimulation/under-stimulation.
    4.3 Express verbally feelings associated with his or her experience of transition.
5. *Skills for planning and implementing change.*
    5.1 The person can analyze discrepancies between existing and desired conditions.
    5.2 The person exercises positive planning for new options. To the best of his or her abilities, the person—
       5.21 Thoroughly canvasses a wide range of alternative courses of action.
       5.22 Surveys the full range of objectives to be fulfilled and the values implied by the choice.
       5.23 Carefully weighs whatever he or she knows about the cost and risk of negative consequences that could flow from each alternative.
       5.24 Searches intensely for information relevant to further evaluation of the alternatives.
       5.25 Utilizes feedback to reassess his or her preferred course of action.
       5.26 Reexamines the positive and negative consequences of all known alternatives.
       5.27 Makes detailed provisions for implementing or executing the chosen course of action including contingency plans.

5.3 The person is able to implement successfully his or her plans. He or she can—

    5.31   Identify stressful situations related to implementing goals.

    5.32   Identify negative self-statements which interfere with implementing plans.

    5.33   Utilize self-relaxation routines while anticipating the stressful implementations of plans.

    5.34   Utilize self-rewards in goal attainment.

    5.35   Identify additional skills needed to implement goals (e.g., anxiety management, training in assertiveness, overcoming shyness).

---

represents some basic skill clusters that can be utilized by clients across a variety of transitions. (See Table 11-1.) We will briefly describe these skill groups and then discuss some more specific career-related coping skills.

Skills in Perceiving and Responding to Transitions. These skills relate to a person's perceptions and responses to transitions. Perceptions toward change have an important relationship to how people interpret, and, in turn, experience events. Two important beliefs are: (1) the acceptance of problematic situations as a normal part of living and (2) a belief that each person has a variety of strengths and resources that help him or her to cope with most of these situations effectively. An individual holding these beliefs gains an increased sense of self-control and self-esteem. Threats are not perceived as overwhelming.

These beliefs can be assessed by exploring the client's reactions to previous life transitions. In this discussion, the counselor can validate the individual's strengths and coping skills. This is particularly important for individuals experiencing involuntary transitions, such as layoffs, where they may doubt their ability to cope with or survive the situation. Clients can be asked to write an autobiography describing their life course with special emphasis on the coping skills that have been useful to them in the past. This assignment can help instill a greater sense of having some choice about the eventual outcome of their current transitions. Sometimes information, such as readings, about developmental transitions as a normal part of life can also be useful.

Several other important coping skills are included in the first category. These skills relate to an individual's initial response to threat. They include describing threats accurately, recognizing the role of feelings in appraising a situation, and inhibiting both impulsiveness and passivity. These skills in responding to transitions allow individuals to gain awareness of how they think, feel, and behave when confronted with problematic situations. People's reactions are important clues about transitions that signal a need to heed other data from the environment. Inhibiting impulsiveness or passivity allows a person time to appraise a problem situation accurately and to construct a proactive and reasoned coping response (Kahana & Kahana, 1976).

Various techniques can be utilized to develop these skills in responding to transitions. Sometimes it is useful to help a client describe a situation in detail, using specific behavioral language in order to identify the most problematic issues and how the client thinks and feels in those situations. It may also be helpful for people to clarify their response to a transition by keeping a journal describing their emotional highs and lows. Some people may have difficulty understanding their feelings and thus are unable to use their feelings as cues. Self-monitoring of feelings could be assigned during different times of the day and a list of feeling words provided as an aid to identifying possible feelings.

Skills for Assessing, Developing, and Utilizing External Support Systems.   Individuals in transition often need extra sources of emotional support during times of change. Skills for assessing, developing, and utilizing an external social support network involve identifying one's emotional needs and then seeking specific people to serve in one's support network. This search results in intentionally planning to spend time with people who provide support, or increasing the supportive quality of present relationships.

People often expect all of their support to come from a few people—typically a spouse or close friend. We urge clients to expand their social networks to include a variety of people, including some of the types described by Hopson and Adams (1977): (a) whom we can depend on in a crisis, (b) with whom to discuss concerns, (c) whom we can feel close to, (d) who can help us feel competent and valued, (e) who can give us important information, (f) who will challenge our stereotyped thinking, and (g) with whom we can share good news and feelings.

Counselors can help clients assess their support needs by asking them to list people in various categories, or to pictorially represent them, using a method described by Waters and Goodman (1981). Sometimes key support people such as family members can be included in the counseling. Individuals may be able to change the quality of support by renegotiating such expectations.

People in career transitions who lack a support network, such as those who have made geographic moves and have left friendships in another community, may need to participate in formalized support groups, generally consisting of individuals also involved in career transitions. Other groups, organized around various interests, provide support as a secondary benefit. These include groups where members share common interests in the outdoors, dancing, religious faith, or a variety of avocations.

Skills for Assessing, Developing, and Utilizing Internal Support Systems.   Internal support refers to "self-messages"—messages people give themselves about how they experience a transition. This internal self-talk provides critical or supportive messages during a transition. These internal thoughts and mental images allow people to remember and use past experiences in their current decisions and plans. However, their thoughts could function as "self-defeating instructions" also. Clients may unduly hamper themselves by fears of failure, low self-esteem, or inability to cope with frustration.

Many of the cognitive-behavioral strategies described in Chapter 7 can be utilized to help clients become more internally supportive. One strategy is to teach clients about cognitive distortions that lead them to feel discouraged, depressed, and frustrated. Clients may catastrophize their job circumstance, disqualify their positive attributes, or think in ways that increase their fears and limit their positive responses to career transitions. People can learn to recognize these distortions in their own thinking and substitute a rational alternative to these thoughts.

Skills for Reducing Emotional and Physiological Distress. Selye (1974) stated that stress is a normal condition of meeting changes and threats with adaptive responses. Stress involves physiological changes (general adaptation syndrome) that may be experienced as either anxiousness (distress) or as pleasure (eustress). The task for each person is to find the optimum amount of stressful stimulation that is exhilarating and energizing and yet that maintains a feeling of relaxation and flow. Each person also must seek a balance between alternating periods of stress and quietness. Skills in this fourth group of coping skills are intended to manage the stress effects often associated with transition.

Counselors can help individuals in career transitions to assess their responses to stress by discussing physiological, cognitive, emotional, and behavioral signs of distress. It is useful to elicit the methods the person has used previously to manage stress. He or she may have some useful methods of managing stress that are not being used at this time but that could be reactivated. Many of the strategies mentioned in Chapter 7, such as muscle relaxation exercises, meditational breathing, cognitive restructuring, stress inoculation, and setting priorities, are representative of these strategies.

It is important to note that not all approaches to stress management necessarily involve reducing stress. Some individuals lack sufficient stimulation to feel comfortable. Employees who are distressed because they lack occupational promotion, for example, may need to increase their activity level in order to manage stress.

Skills for Planning and Implementing Change. Personal transitions usually are accompanied by a desire to reassess one's current life style and to plan strategies for responding to the change constructively. Because of the importance of making effective decisions during transitions, some of the decision-making and implementing skills required have been specified.

Transitional decisions differ from routine life decisions because they involve the risk of suffering further loss. As a result of perceiving the potential risks, many people feel overwhelmed and experience acute choice conflict. This conflict is characterized by feelings of anxiety, hesitation, vacillation, and uncertainty. These feelings also may be accompanied by self-blame or a desire to escape from the situation (Lazarus, 1977).

Although there are various styles of decision making, skills in rational decision making are emphasized. According to Janis and Mann (1977), people who cope well under stressful conditions tend to utilize rational decision-making skills. In contrast, poor decision making often leads to regrettable outcomes, such as feelings of helplessness or disappointment and increased expectations of vulnerability.

Counselors can help individuals assess their decision-making skills by exploring previous decisions they felt were made effectively. From reexamining past experience, people can clarify their typical decision-making styles, beliefs about risk taking, and abilities to implement plans.

Decison-making skills can be learned through various methods. Workbooks, such as those of Loughary and Ripley (1976), provide structures for applying rational decision-making skills to career decisions. Computer programs, such as SIGI and DISCOVER, can be useful in clarifying trade-offs in contrasting career choices. Visualization can be used to imagine oneself implementing divergent career choices. Self-management skills such as using self-rewards for attaining goals can be practiced as one takes action to explore career alternatives.

Career Development Coping Skills

In addition to general transition coping skills, individuals in career transitions often need specific career development coping skills. These skills can be grouped as skills in self-assessment, gaining occupational and work environment information, and conducting a job search.

Category 1: Self-Assessment Skills.   Self-assessment skills involve the ability to identify one's goals, values, and abilities related to work. Career goals generally are based on analysis of skills and values. One's career skills and values are usually assessed by reviewing previous accomplishments, present interests, and future dreams. Many writers have described approaches to identifying values and skills. Bolles (1991), Haldane (Germann & Arnold, 1980), Crystal and Bolles (1974), and Brammer and Humberger (1984) systematically reviewed life accomplishments, describing each accomplishment and then clustering skills that clients enjoyed. Loughary and Ripley (1976) provided workbook exercises for identifying values and abilities. Forster (1985) utilizes repertory grids based on Kelly's personal construct theory to analyze important career-related values.

Career skills are usually divided into three categories: self-management skills, transferable skills, and specific knowledge skills. *Self-management skills* refer to personal attributes or traits describing a person's style of responding to problems and demands. These skills can be of significant importance to success in various occupations. They include attributes such as being dynamic, versatile, responsible, perceptive, concerned, compassionate, candid, sensitive, reliable, warm, open-minded, and outgoing. Self-management skills can be identified from checklists based on autobiographies, interpersonal feedback, and certain psychological tests.

Transferable "functional" skills can be utilized across a variety of occupations. These skills include communication, managing, reporting, planning, organizing, coordinating, leading, delegating, and instructing. They can be clustered in various ways, such as data/people/things, or into Holland's categories. Transferable skills can be analyzed using materials developed by Bolles (1991), Crystal and Bolles (1974), and Haldane (Germann & Arnold, 1980).

Specific knowledge skills are the least transferable. They include specific knowledge or procedures that are useful in one field of work but are not always transferable to other occupations. A nurse's knowledge of anatomical terms, for example, would be a specific knowledge skill with limited transferability to other career fields. Specific knowledge skills are most often learned through formal education.

Category 2: Skills in Learning about Occupations, Employers, and Work Environments. Once clients have identified their category 1 career skills, they then need to gather information about occupations, employers, and work environments. The *Occupational Outlook Handbook,* the *Dictionary of Occupational Titles,* and professional or trade journals can provide useful occupational information. Additional occupational information, as well as information about specific employers or work environments, can be learned by networking and establishing personal contacts in organizations of interest. These personal contacts can then be interviewed for career information. A Department of Labor study reported that 54 percent of jobs are found through friends and relatives and another 31 percent are found through direct contacts. Only 5 percent are found through ads and 9 percent are found through a combination of school placement, state employment services, and private placement agencies (U.S. Department of Labor, 1981).

Category 3: Skills in Job Search, Career Enhancement, and Life-Style Change. When an individual has targeted an occupational role, potential employer, and work environment in which to utilize her or his skills, the next step involves implementing one's decision. At this stage, it is often important to develop job search or career enhancement skills. Interviewing and writing resumes are particularly important. For individuals who remain in the same job organization, other skills may be useful for career transfer or advancement. For example, taking an advanced management course might enhance chances of obtaining a promotion. Skills for interviewing and writing resumes have been described by Bolles (1991) and Brammer and Humberger (1984). Counselors can assist clients by role playing interviews and reviewing resumes.

Use of Tests in Career Counseling

Use of vocational inventories and tests can enhance career counseling. Career inventories can provide an added perspective on work interests, abilities, personality characteristics, and decision-making processes. Crites (1984, 1986) has reviewed career assessment instruments. Tests measure areas such as ability, intelligence, achievement, reading, aptitude, vocational interests, work needs and satisfaction, and personality characteristics.

Ability tests are utilized to measure general intelligence, achievement, reading, or specific aptitudes. Examples of ability tests used in career counseling are intelligence tests such as the Wechsler Adult Intelligence Scales-Revised (WAIS-R), the Revised Army Beta Examination (Beta-II), and the Wonderlic Personnel Test. Intelligence tests tend to be utilized to assess a general level of intelligence and to estimate a probable level of occupational attainment. Because there are a wide range of factors associated with levels of occupational attainment, intelligence tests have only modest vocational validity. Intelligence tests or achievement tests are sometimes used in decisions about whether remedial education is indicated before proceeding with a job search. Aptitude tests, such as the General Aptitude Test Battery (GATB) and the Employee Aptitude Survey (EAS), provide measures of variables such as verbal reasoning, numerical ability, spatial visualization, and visual speed and accuracy. Counselors can relate the client's aptitudes to a larger occupational aptitude pattern database of occupations clustered according to specific aptitudes required.

Vocational interest tests assess interests and compare client responses to the responses of successful individuals in various occupations. These tests are useful for people who want to confirm or "reality test" their expressed interests or to explore areas of interest similarity. Some of the widely utilized interest inventories of professional or white collar occupational levels include the Strong Campbell Interest Inventory (SCII) and the Kuder Occupational Interest Survey (KOIS). At the nonprofessional or semiskilled occupational levels, the Career Assessment Inventory (CAI) is often used. Another instrument, the Self-Directed Search, was developed by Holland and is designed to be a self-administered, self-scored, and self-interpreted instrument revealing a summary Holland code which the user can use to explore occupations in the Dictionary of Occupational Titles.

Other vocational instruments measure "career maturity" or the individual's mastery of the vocational tasks appropriate to their age level. The Career Maturity Inventory and The Career Development Inventory are examples of this type of instrument. The Career Development Inventory, based on Super's theory, identifies how the individual is aware of the need for career decision making, accepts responsibility for choice and planning, and uses resources in obtaining occupational information.

Personality inventories have been applied to assessing personality in the work environment. They can be helpful in the client's self-assessment process by identifying and clarifying personality characteristics and self-management skills. Examples of personality instruments utilized in career counseling are the California Psychological Inventory, the Edwards Personal Preference Schedule, and the Myers-Briggs Type Indicator.

Computer Utilization in Career Planning

Computer-based counseling systems fall along a continuum from those that primarily provide career information to those that are oriented toward counseling and guidance. Increasingly, systems are being developed that provide both information and guidance.

Guidance systems such as SIGI Plus and DISCOVER, that emphasize information specialize in the development of local labor market information. The computer can be used to present occupational information in an objective, non-biased way. Additionally, it can be updated more quickly than printed information.

Guidance systems provide self-assessment instruments such as interest inventories, values inventories, and ability rating scales at the computer terminal. Additionally, guidance systems use the computer to teach career development concepts such as clarification of values, organization of the work world, the decision-making process, job seeking skills, and life/career stages. Organization of self-data from the computer is used to provide a list of occupational titles for exploration. Further, the computer may be used to show the user the overlap or inconsistency between or among interests, values, and abilities.

Computers have made significant contributions to the client's acquisition of self-data and the translation of self-data into occupational alternatives. Computerized systems have also been useful in providing information about identified occupations and related educational programs. They have assisted clients in developing decision-making skills and implementing choices. As technological advances become more widely utilized, we can expect more sophisticated computerized career counseling systems. Videodisks and video cassettes, combining sound and video, will provide clients with a closer examination of actual work settings and tasks than does reading information about work environments (Harris-Bowlsbey, 1992).

Research on the effectiveness of computerized career guidance systems is still in preliminary stages (Rayman, 1990). However, computers have not replaced the need for counselors. One study by Garis and Harris-Bowlsbey (1984) comparing the use of the DISCOVER program with individual use of career counseling found that the combined DISCOVER and counseling treatment produced stronger effects upon career planning progress than either of its components used separately.

TARGET POPULATIONS AND SETTINGS

Dual-Career Couples

Increasing numbers of men and women are choosing simultaneously to pursue careers and maintain a family life. There is a continuum of varying commitment each spouse brings to his or her work. Gilbert and Rachlin (1987) have drawn the distinction between dual-earner couples and dual-career couples. The dual-career couples are often more highly committed to their careers and are not working solely for economic reasons. They often demand more of themselves in relation to their work and may experience more stress because each spouse's career is considered equally important. Many of these couples find themselves ill prepared for the changes required in their functioning as a couple. There is often a blurring of the traditional division of roles. As a result, family work tasks must be reassigned.

The dual-career life style involves the coordination, balance, and integration of career and family roles for each spouse individually and as a couple. O'Neil, Fishman, and Kinsella-Shaw (1987) describe potential dilemmas for dual-career couples in relation to career development, gender-role conflicts, and marital roles. Many of these dilemmas involve deviating from socially expected patterns in relation to these roles. Additionally, just as career and family development life cycles often conflict for individuals, the complexity of potential conflicts and dilemmas increases substantially when each spouse is highly committed to career and family life.

Counselors providing services to dual-career couples must help couples deal with the complexity of their situation. Hazard and Koslow (1986) suggest that conjoint counseling is the preferred mode with dual-career couples. Counselors can be helpful in clarifying some of the normative dilemmas that dual-career couples face. It is especially important to assess the impact of career transitions on family life and the effects of family life on career transitions. Counselors can help couples communicate clearly and negotiate the sometimes conflicting aspects of combining a commitment to career and family life. Couples can be encouraged to increase role clarity and communicate role expectations more directly. Additionally, it is important to help spouses find ways to show mutual support and commitment to their spouses.

Preretirement Planning

Increases in the numbers of upper-middle-aged people and removal of mandatory retirement regulations make retirement planning a complex process. At the same time that the number of people becoming eligible for retirement is increasing, there are also increasing possibilities for and acceptance of early retirement. This has often resulted in a fourth of the work force being eligible for retirement in many organizations (Parnes, 1981).

The abundance of studies on retirement satisfaction also indicates how individualized the process of planning for retirement must be. For example, some people thrive on an activity theory of retirement, where they must remain in meaningful activity, sometimes related to their former employment. Others prefer to be totally disengaged from any meaningful work and want to enjoy protracted leisure. Then, there are the mixtures in between.

Merikangas and Fretz (1986) suggest that many people have negative perceptions of retirement based on myths such as the following:

1. Most people find retirement less enjoyable than they expected.
2. The most difficult time to adjust to retirement is during the first few months.
3. Happiness in retirement is strongly related to the amount of retirement income.
4. Persons who are retired are less healthy than persons in the same age group who are still working.
5. Retirees are more likely to die prematurely than persons still working.

6. Persons who are workaholics most often have the hardest time adjusting to retirement.
7. The majority of retirees engage in paid work.
8. Most retirees move to another state sometime during their retirement.
9. Marital problems usually increase during retirement.
10. Retirees generally have more interactions with their immediate family (e.g., children, siblings) than persons the same age who are still working.
11. Retirees generally have fewer friends and social relationships than similarly aged persons who are still working.

Merikangas and Fretz (1986, p. 221) state, "The primary task counselors in organizations face is creating an environment in which individuals can understand the authentic rather than mythical issues of retirement living." The objective is to prepare the individual to pass through the retirement transition equipped with clear values and a life direction. Retirement programs focus on the individual's needs for information, social support, and a structure for individualized planning. Programs are generally offered at a "remote phase" of preretirement during which the employee is just becoming aware of approaching retirement eligibility and at a "near phase" closer to retirement.

Workshops on preparing for and managing retirement include topics that ease the transition trauma and the documented retirement fears, as well as maximize anticipated satisfaction. Common topics are financial planning, emotional preparation, meaningful use of leisure, health maintenance, and continuing education.

Career Education and Educational Planning

Counselors in educational settings often provide career planning assistance to students through career education programs that attempt to bridge the separation of the educational and the nonacademic worlds of work. Students at high schools and colleges generally have the option of attending career classes that include field observations and interviews with people in different occupations, small group discussions, values clarification exercises, job research papers, and self-analysis through standardized interest tests, interactive computer programs, and personal reflection. Studies by Trebilco (1984) and Remer and associates (1984) found that life-planning courses aided students in their career decision making and produced more crystalized vocational self-concepts. School counselors may also provide leadership in "cooperative education" programs, which place students in work roles designed as internship experiences for students. Counselors may meet with students on a weekly basis to discuss their learning experiences as they enter an unfamiliar work culture.

Educational counseling consists of counseling assistance related to educational planning and development of study skills. A primary goal of educational counseling is the development of student's self-efficacy and its application toward academic persistence and achievement (Lent, Brown, & Larken, 1987; Brown, Lent, & Larken, 1989). Educational counseling helps students make decisions related to issues such as selecting training institutions, predicting success in training and education, financing training, and developing skills for entry into training institutions. Educational planning is most often conducted through a combination of individual and group formats in high schools and colleges. Sometimes students are enrolled into programs such as "developmental assistance programs" in order to develop skills such as knowledge of test-taking, note-taking, understanding the "nuts and bolts" of how to use libraries and other educational services, and interpersonal skills in assertiveness.

Rehabilitation Counseling

Rehabilitation is a process of restoring clients with disabilities to the fullest possible usefulness to themselves and society. The concept of rehabilitation has been broadened from the original concept of physical and mental disabilities to include the culturally deprived and the socially handicapped, such as released prisoners. Counseling plays a vital part in this rehabilitation process. Vocational placement and adjustment have traditionally been primary goals of rehabilitation counseling. However, more attention is now given to helping individuals actualize their potential across a variety of life roles. Counseling techniques for handicapped persons are little different from counseling for the able bodied. Occupational distribution of the disabled is roughly similar to that of persons who are not disabled. Rehabilitation counselors are employed by state departments of vocational rehabilitation, hospitals, vocational schools, sheltered workshops, and in private consulting groups that contract with government agencies.

Rehabilitation counselors are increasingly concerned with transitions of the disabled over the life span. Examples of such issues include transitions of adolescents with chronic illnesses and disabilities (Davis et al., 1985), school to work transitions of the disabled (Szymanski & Danek, 1985), and counseling individuals who become disabled at mid-life (Power, Hershenson, & Schlossberg, 1985). As the average age of the population increases, programs are adapting rehabilitation programs to older persons (Kivnick, 1985; Finnerty-Fried, 1985; Myers, 1985). Clients who are members of ethnic minority groups, particularly women, often experience differential rehabilitation needs because of their status of less power in society.

Mid-Life Career Change

The nature and extent of mid-life career change are complex and not well researched. In reviewing studies of mid-life career change, Waltz (1978) suggested that as many as 25 percent of men and 30 percent of business managers between the ages of 35 and 55 are involved in career changes and experience major personality and behavior changes. Because many current research studies include only men, it is difficult to estimate the number of women making mid-life career changes.

As we have mentioned earlier, there are multiple reasons people have for making mid-life career changes. Many of the reasons may result from transition in other life roles or conflicts over developmental issues that lead to new goals, the desire to satisfy higher-level needs, and the desire for new purposes and aspirations. Other motivations will result from the work itself. Sinick (1977) listed a variety of motivations, including excessive work pressure, low earnings, incongruence with vocational interests, dead end in advancement, and a disproportion between prescribed and discretionary duties.

Abrego and Brammer (1992) described a number of factors affecting personal reactions to mid-life career change. Factors included motivation (whether voluntary or involuntary), predictability of the transition, support, perceived control over the transition, and the ability to manage anxiety. Typical reactions involve a grief process involving phases of shock, minimization, self-doubt, letting go, testing new options, making sense of the experience, and integration and renewal.

Counseling mid-life career changers is a complex process to determine the relation between career roles and other life roles and tasks. Counseling goals are aimed at helping the clients to (1) assess their values, abilities, and interests; (2) enhance their general coping and career decision-making skills; and (3) implement choices where more of their self-concept can be expressed in their life styles.

Counseling services for mid-life career changers take a variety of forms. Many private services exist for comprehensive career planning help. A growing number of larger businesses are adding programs called outplacement, inplacement, career counseling, and management succession to their human resource management offices. These career planning programs help employees plan long-term career development within the organization. Examples of institutional programs for mid-life career changers are described by Abrego and Brammer (1992).

RESEARCH IN CAREER COUNSELING

Outcome research regarding the effectiveness of career counseling is promising. Spokane and Oliver (1983) used a meta-analysis procedure to evaluate career counseling outcome studies and reported that clients who received any kind of career counseling intervention were better off afterward than more than 80 percent of clients receiving no treatment. Career counseling is difficult to evaluate because it is such a complex process with effects that may not become apparent for a long time. Further research needs to examine how different types of treatments (e.g., decision training) show differential effectiveness on specific outcome measures (e.g., information seeking). Fretz (1981) challenges counselors to indicate the characteristics of the clients served, specify the instruments used, and describe how the counseling outcome is measured. Counselors must also fully describe treatment interventions and discuss the relationship among treatment components. Career research is reviewed annually in the *Journal of*

Vocational Behavior. Additionally, extensive reviews were published in the *Annual Review of Psychology* in 1981, 1984, 1987, and 1990.

Much additional research must be done on career transitions of adults. This research will need to explore how different counseling interventions may be more useful for individuals at different developmental periods of the life cycle. Much more exploration needs to examine the interplay of career and other important life roles and how career transitions are related to the larger process of change and growth during all phases of the life cycle. Research might also explore the meaning of work beyond providing a livelihood as well as indicating how individuals can integrate and express new self-potentialities as they mature in adulthood.

SUMMARY

We have described career development within a broad transitions framework. Career transitions integrate personality growth over the life cycle in a variety of interwoven life roles such as job, marriage, family, and leisure. We have examined the contributions of career development, adult development, and family development theories in understanding the complex nature of career transitions.

We applied our assessment process, described in previous chapters, to career transitions. Emphasis was given to some of the unique aspects of career assessment such as the use of career problem taxonomies and the important aspect of gender-role expectations.

In planning counseling interventions for career transitions, we emphasized the importance of developing generic coping skills as well as specific career-related coping skills. These specific skills include skills related to self-assessment; skills in learning about occupations, employers, and work environments; and skills in job search, career enhancement, and life-style change. Contributions of psychological testing and computerized systems to the counseling process were discussed.

Specific target groups for career transition counseling were described. These included special issues related to dual-career couples, preretirement, career education and educational planning, rehabilitation counseling, and mid-life career change. Research implications in career counseling were described.

CHAPTER 12

Applications of Therapeutic Psychology to Special Populations and Work Settings

Therapeutic psychology is finding applications in a wide array of settings. The purpose of this chapter is to describe how therapeutic psychology is applied among special populations and work settings. We have limited our discussion to several selected target groups and work settings. In these discussions, we hope to apply important principles and concepts described in previous chapters.

Therapeutic psychologists must become aware of the unique concerns of specific groups of clientele while recognizing the many individual differences within these groups. We have focused our discussion on therapeutic issues related to gender, health, multicultural settings, and aging. Society's changing sex roles, for example, have heightened our awareness of how gender issues influence one's sense of personal identity and determine counseling issues raised by our gay and lesbian clients. As ethnic-minority populations increase, people have become more aware of the need for effective cross-cultural counseling methods. Therapeutic psychologists recognized that methods developed for white middle-class clients, for example, were not appropriate for many ethnic-minority clients. Because the population is aging so rapidly, therapeutic psychologists are addressing the concerns of these older adults and their families.

SPECIAL POPULATIONS

Counseling Women and Men

As society changes, men and women are reevaluating their sex roles and new gender definitions are emerging. Many women and men have evaluated their customary sex roles as "hazardous to their health" or simply incompatible with developing a satisfying life style. For example, many of the conflicts described in Chapter 11 regarding career development and dual-career families are intertwined with gender-role issues. Although there are unifying themes to role norms of either sex, variations of sex-role expectations occur along lines of race and social class. Gender roles prescribe the range and parameters of behavioral repertoires that each individual learns. Success and failure in a variety of developmental tasks often are perceived, both by the individual and her or his emotional environment, in terms of adherence to or deviation from gender-role norms. For example, many women and men in nontraditional occupations experience ridicule for their career choices. Thus, these gender-role issues have important implications for counselors working with clients who want to maximize their personal growth.

Gender-Role Themes.   Female socialization patterns strongly influence a woman's vocational goals, interpersonal relationships, sexuality, and self-efficacy. Brown (1986) has summarized popular notions about how female socialization affects white middle-class women. She states that

> a "good" woman is marked by a focus on interpersonal relationships, nurturance, compliance, avoidance of conflict and expression of anger. She will probably be concerned about her appearance, particularly her weight. She is likely to have some kind of clear vocational goal but equally as likely to devalue that goal in relationship to prospective marriage and parental roles. The good woman will be equally ambivalent sexually, wishing to be sexually attractive to others but uncomfortable with her sexual interest and assertiveness.(p. 244)

Brown further suggests that this socially defined woman will tend to see herself responsible for interpersonal success. She will not be likely to perceive herself, however, as the reason for her vocational or her noninterpersonal success, but rather will attribute her success to luck, hard work, or the ease of the task. Consequently, her self-esteem, sense of efficacy, and perceived competency may be shaky, while her need to please others will be high. She often will give the power for execution of major life decisions to significant others in the service of pleasing them. The good woman thus is expected to plan her life around a center consisting of interpersonal relationships. The resulting dependency may be highly valued as evidence of her love and loyalty.

According to Brown, women who deviate from these norms are likely to be penalized and stigmatized in a variety of ways. Women who violate gender-role norms on use of overt power, for example, often receive derogatory labels such as domineering or pushy. Women who choose nontraditional occupations or who don't fit female stereotypes of beauty may be labeled pejoratively. It is essential for counselors to understand that many of the concerns brought to counselors by female clients are related to gender-role conflicts.

Levant (1992) and O'Neil (1981) suggest that men are socialized to use power, control, and competition to validate their masculinity. Additionally, men show restricted emotional expression so that they have difficulty expressing feelings openly, giving up emotional control, and being vulnerable to self, others, and new experiences. Male patterns contribute to difficulties in interpersonal relationships, work life, and home and family life.

The male socialization process impacts on men's ability to relate to women and to other men. To compensate for their expressive limitations, many men overdevelop cognitive rationalistic patterns of communication that emphasize objective information, task orientation, and outcomes. However, when used exclusively, this style may be restrictive in interpersonal relationships, since women often see this approach to communication as impersonal or they see men using it to maintain control of the relationship. In contrast, women are socialized toward the expressive level of communication and are more effective at using expressive communication in interpersonal conflicts and situations. Since women are believed to be more aware of the subjective, expressive aspect of the messages, they tend to use this information to effect desired changes in their relationships. Many women have not been socialized to compete with men in male-patterned communications and are sometimes unsure about how to be assertive, express themselves, and use their expressive skills. Under these circumstances, the potential for miscommunication and misunderstanding is usually high. Men and women become polarized into dichotomous roles of "the head" and "the heart." Both types of communication patterns are necessary for a fully functioning human relationship.

Men's socialization toward competitiveness and power also inhibits interpersonal relationships with other men. To validate one's masculinity, men have to prove themselves continuously in their various life roles. To be successful men must compete against other men and women and become interpersonally distant and invulnerable to other male competitors. Many men's drive for achievements, such as career accomplishments, are considered important to masculinity and thus prohibit time for other male friendships.

Male sexuality, also a product of the masculine socialization process, is oriented toward performance and outcome. Sexuality is valued as proof of masculinity as symbolized in power and control. Often sexuality is separated from love and intimacy. Zilbergeld (1978) and O'Neil (1981) have described common themes that shape men's sexual attitudes and behaviors in ways that produce interpersonal distance during sex and sometimes sexual dysfunction. Examples are:

1. Sex is a performance.
2. All physical contact must lead to sex.
3. A man must orchestrate sex to show control, dominance, and power.
4. A man always wants and is always ready to have sex.
5. Sex equals intercourse.

These masculine myths separate sexuality from emotional intimacy. Rather than being an *intimate and playful communication process,* sex becomes a goal-oriented performance that then becomes a measure of a man's identity. These attitudes about sex restrict sexual pleasure to intercourse at the expense of other types of pleasuring and communication.

Male attitudes about home life also are influenced by socialization patterns. Men are often taught that women have instinctual drives to nurture children and know innately more about childrearing than men. Therefore, fathering is of secondary importance. Although active fathering may be considered to have some importance, it is regarded as impractical because of the belief that men are supposed to be the family breadwinners. Difficulties in fathering are exacerbated by defining male worth exclusively in terms of work and career success. Some men learn that the home and family is another outlet to exert power and control as a measure of masculinity. This leads men to treat their sensitive-interpersonal conflicts at home in the same impersonal manner in which they manage conflicts at work.

Counselors working with men can help them to examine the degree to which restrictive emotionality and control and power issues, as well as other gender-role conflicts, limit their self-actualization. Groups designed especially for men offer opportunities to understand and release their cumulative anger, especially toward their fathers. They find intimacy and love in the male group in ways they never experienced with their fathers. Awareness of primitive yearnings for acceptance and meaning are approached through rituals, poetry, rhythms, and campfire comraderie. They can face their vulnerability and look behind their masks of dominance, power, and bravado.

Assessment and Treatment Issues Related to Gender Role.

We have discussed previously in Chapter 6 how gender role can become an important factor in assessment. Gender-role themes provide a rich source of data for generating hypotheses and understanding clients. Knowledge of gender-role themes can free the counselor from limiting sex-role stereotypes. Often what might be considered pathology from one perspective might be seen as more normal by a counselor who is informed about gender-role issues. For example, Smith and Siegel (1985) have commented on the variety of means to express *covert* power that are available to women who are operating within the constraints of the feminine gender role and on the creativity and skillfulness demonstrated by such women. Survivors of sexual assault and battering, for example, may choose resourceful strategies, rather than becoming passive, compliant victims.

Gender can be an important issue in psychological testing and should be built into our assessment framework. As we discussed in Chapter 6, most test instruments are biased or deficient where gender-role analysis is concerned.

Women and men at different life stages have differential experiences and perceptions of themselves based on gender-role issues. For instance, compliance with gender-role expectations for women can be a catalyst for serious depressive episodes in middle adulthood. During middle age the rewards of compliance to gender-role socialization often diminish or disappear.

It is important for counselors to help their clients understand that appropriate gender-role behaviors may be normative, yet serve as barriers and obstacles to an individual's goals for change. These attitudes and behaviors may be sources of pain and distress that have gone unchallenged because of their roots in highly valued roles in the dominant culture.

In assessing gender-role expectations, Brown (1986) suggests it is important for counselors and clients not only to know what the lessons of gender were developmentally, but also to understand how they were learned and what meaning was given to that learning experience. Gender-role assessment seeks to understand questions such as, "What did it mean to grow up female or male?" "What lessons did the client learn about gender issues?" "Were these learnings direct or indirect?" "What experience did the client have with individuals who deviated from gender roles?" "What were the consequences of such deviations from traditional gender roles?"

Contextual data is important to understand the influence of socialization. Culture is an especially potent determining variable. Factors include age cohort, religious background, family history in regard to ethnicity and participation in ethnic culture, family roles of women and men, class backgrounds and education of parents, wantedness of children, and how gender was a variable in the wantedness of any given child.

Subtle indices of gender-role compliance and deviation include information about how major life decisions were made, and by whom; vocational and avocational interests; how conflict was handled by the client; how dependency needs were identified and expressed; and how the client related to her or his body in terms of health and attractiveness. Routine questions regarding the client's relationship with food are another mode of subtly assessing gender-role issues, since disordered eating behaviors in women appear to be strongly related to compliance with feminine gender-role norms. Assessment of past sexual and physical abuse, including sexual harassment or verbal degradation as well as rape or battering, provides information about clients' interpretation of gender membership and gender-role compliance.

Gender-role assessment provides important knowledge for the counselor and offers clients potential self-awareness and empowerment. The client who can comprehend how he or she is strengthened or sabotaged by gender-role issues and is aware of how she or he is like other women and men in these ways is likely to feel less alienated and more powerful and confident.

Although there has been much professional debate about the necessity for counselors having special skills to work with women, there is general agreement that women have unique concerns. The Counseling Psychology Division of the American Psychological Association produced a widely used statement, "Principles Concerning the Counseling and Therapy of Women" (1979, 1992). This report describes the special knowledge, skills, and attitudes important to counseling specific subgroups of women. Examples include being sensitive to circumstances where it is more desirable for a woman client to be seen by a female or male counselor, using nonsexist language in counseling, and being knowledgeable of verbal and nonverbal process variables, particularly with regard to power in the relationship, as these affect women in counseling.

Counseling with Lesbians and Gay Men

In Chapter 1, we suggested that the current paradigms of counseling theory are challenged by issues of gender, cultural diversity, and empowerment of oppressed groups. All of these issues are encountered in the counseling needs of sexual minorities. It is estimated that approximately 10 to 15 percent of the United States population are sexual minorities. Lesbians, gay men, and bisexuals are found in every race, class, age cohort, and geographic area. In this section, we will highlight some of the unique counseling needs faced in this population. It is important for counselors to remember that many of the needs of gay and lesbian clients are the same as those of nongay clients, in spite of the stereotype that their needs must be related to their sexual orientation.

Many of the unique difficulties experienced by gay and lesbian clients result from their lack of acceptance by majority society. Their counseling needs often include development of sexual identity, healing from shame, and developing a positive self-identity in a hostile social context. Gay men and lesbians also experience a unique situation among oppressed groups, in that they are usually reared in nongay families in which emotional support needed for accepting and affirming a gay or lesbian identity is absent. The fear and prejudice that characterize reactions to gay people by family, friends, and society is termed homophobia. Lesbians and gay men grow up learning the same negative attitudes toward same-sex feelings and behavior that nongays do. They often internalize homophobic attitudes that they must overcome to accept their sexual orientation. Internalized homophobia thus further complicates an already complex process of self-definition. By living in a primarily heterosexual society, gay people also face heterosexual bias that sanctifies nongay norms and devalues gay experience as inferior or insignificant.

Gay identity development is sometimes referred to as "coming out" (of the closet). The experience of gay identity development varies considerably depending on many factors, such as gender, race, ethnicity, social class, age, religion, and geographic location. In this process, the individual must confront negative social attitudes as well as one's own internalized homophobia. Often there are few resources such as role models, support systems, or legal protections to nurture the process of developing a positive self-identity.

Development of a positive self-identity involves complex decisions and emotional risks. For example, coming out to families within racial communities often results in rejection and loss of one's primary ethnic identification and community. In career decisions, gays and lesbians must consider whether they want to work in occupations or work settings in which their sexual orientation must be hidden to prevent overt or covert discrimination. Role models for couple and family relationship decisions, such as whether to parent either within a relationship or as single parents, may be lacking. Other relationship decisions, such as questions of monogomy, may be open to question because of their basis in heterosexual norms. Many gay and lesbian clients express spiritual questions about their lives and yet feel disenfranchised by majority religious organizations.

Many majority members disapprove of gay life styles and think they should be barred from inclusion in society, particularly from positions of responsibility. Social, legal, and religious discrimination interacts with sexism and racism. Examples of discrimination include lack of support for legalization of marriage for gay and lesbian couples, and tolerance of abuse. Studies suggest that as many as 92 percent of gay men and lesbians report being targets of verbal abuse or threats and well over one-third are survivors of violence related to their gayness (Herek, 1989).

Although not a gay disease, AIDS has tremendously affected the gay experience. Partners must be questioned about previous sexual partners and experiences. Grief and loss have touched most in the community. Individuals must struggle with the decision of whether to take the HIV antibody test.

Gay and lesbian clients often encounter difficulties in the mental health system. The Final Report of the Task Force on Bias and Psychotherapy with Lesbians and Gay Men (Garnets, Hancock, Cochran, Goodchilds, & Peplau, 1991) gave specific examples of overt and covert heterosexual bias in counseling gays and lesbians. Examples included bias in diagnosis and treatment by attributing clients' problems to their sexual orientation without exploring the symptoms and sources of current distress, treatment of intimate relationships without sensitivity to the sexual issues and norms in the gay community, and inadequate expertise and professional training.

It is of vital importance for mental health professionals to develop the attitudes, knowledge, and skills needed to work with gay and lesbian clients. A number of authors (Clark, 1987; Fassinger, 1991; Shannon & Woods, 1991) have outlined specific guidelines for implementing affirmative counseling of gay men and lesbian women. Their recommendations include the following:

1. Feel comfortable with your own sexuality. Don't jump to conclusions based on stereotypes. Seek to rid yourself of homophobic feelings or they will become blind spots in your counseling with gay and lesbian clients.
2. Carefully consider the decision to enter into a contract to eliminate gay feelings and behaviors in your client. Willingness to enter into such a contract implies that homosexuality is pathological and undesirable. Many clients who ask for change are really asking for acceptance.
3. Support consciousness-raising efforts. Encourage clients to establish a gay support system. Become knowledgeable about resources and make them available. Sources of information include APA Division 44 (Society for the Psychological Study of Lesbian and Gay Issues) and special issues of *The Counseling Psychologists* (Fassinger, 1991) and the *Journal of Counseling and Development* (1989).
4. Help clients free themselves of stereotypes and negative conditioning and help them to develop a personally relevant value system about what it means to be gay.
5. Desensitize shame and guilt surrounding homosexual thoughts, feelings, and behaviors by encouraging discussion of gay experiences and showing affirmation for the client.

6. Educate yourself about gay life styles and concerns and be familiar with gender-specific socialization theories as well.

7. Understand the interaction of other kinds of diversity (e.g., ethnic, gender, age, disability, socioeconomic, religious, geographical) with the development and maintenance of a positive gay identity. Be aware that the identity development process and preservation of healthy life styles differ widely within the gay and lesbian population and adjust your therapeutic interventions accordingly.

8. Be familiar with the treatment of addictive behaviors such as alcohol abuse and eating disorders, which are fairly common in the gay and lesbian community and often masked by other presenting issues.

9. Acquire knowledge and training in AIDS-related issues and death and dying. Accurate information about safe-sex practices should be given in a nonjudgmental manner. Be familiar with "duty to warn" ethics.

10. Be particularly sensitive to ethical issues such as confidentiality and, for gay and lesbian therapists, the difficulties inherent in providing mental health services within one's own community of social support.

11. Any counseling approach should be carefully examined for inherent bias against sexual minorities.

ETHNIC DIVERSITY

As populations become more ethnically diverse, increased attention must be given to how counseling interventions could be tailored to the needs of these groups. As we indicated in earlier chapters, these treatment interventions are likely to be most effective when they are consistent with the expectations and cultural backgrounds of clients. A cultural match means that the therapist is better able to understand and assess the unique ethnic problems and situation of the client in a sensitive manner. Also, the counselor can use language or concepts that are within the world view or experience of the client, so that the culturally consistent therapy becomes more comprehensible and acceptable to the client. In contrast, difficulties in cross-cultural counseling arise in situations where the counselor and client do not share a cultural definition of the situation. Many clients fail to use psychotherapeutic services, prematurely terminate treatment, or fail to show positive outcomes when treatment approaches are culturally inconsistent with the background and expectations of clients (Sue & Morishima, 1982). Thus, it is important for counselors to be aware of ethnicity and to incorporate that awareness into practice.

Counselors cannot become specialists on all cultures of the world, but they can become aware of the range of social values and behaviors and they can learn much about their client's particular ethnic groups. At the same time it is important to recognize the wide range of individual differences existing within each particular ethnic group, so that counselors do not assume that an intervention tailored to a particular ethnic group will be suited to all individuals within that ethnic group.

The perceptions and behaviors of ethnic minority groups are a function of the interactions among cultural patterns, personal values, and social institutions of the larger society. This cultural context determines the nature of stressors, the manifestation of symptoms, the course of the client's difficulties, and response to treatment (Smith & Vasquez, 1985).

Individual and collective history affect problem generation and solutions. The collective history of a group that may include slavery, an immigrant experience, the Holocaust, or flight from civil war or revolution affects each individual in that group uniquely. Traditions and past discrimination may generate problems in the present that must be addressed in the present if the family member is to return to appropriate functioning. For example, an Italian family that carries on a tradition of "caring for our own" may resist treatment for a seriously ill family member.

Ethnicity can be a source of cohesion, identity, and strength as well as a source of strain, discord, and strife. Ethnic factors associated with family, rituals and celebrations, language, and social institutions provide a source of support for many members of ethnic groups. It is important for counselors not to assume that assimilation into the dominant culture is a goal for ethnic-minority clients, because assimilation often means losing one's positive sense of ethnic identity.

Although it is important to recognize the value of history, customs, and beliefs at the individual and institutional level, one must realize that racism exists in the present and influences the daily life of ethnic minority populations. Individuals often internalize these negative and stereotypic images society holds of them, resulting in restricted views of themselves and reduced quality of interpersonal relationships. Personality and recent life experience serve as filters determining which facets of ethnic history and identity will remain an integral part of a person's functioning, which will be forgotten, and which will be consciously rejected. Counselors have special responsibility to reach out to and attend to the individual consequences of racism, poverty, and discrimination.

The route to a counselor affects problem definition and kind of intervention. Routes vary along a continuum from totally coercive, when clients are assigned by the courts, to totally voluntary, when individuals decide for themselves that there is a need for professional assistance. Persons at the coercive end of the continuum are more likely to have their problems defined for them by social institutions and will likely be members of ethnic-minority groups with low incomes. Voluntary clients are more likely to be of middle income and members of more mainstream ethnic groups.

Counseling interventions must be adapted in accord with the particular needs and dispositions of various ethnic groups. Conveying respect may have different effects on ethnic groups. Direct eye contact may be considered shameful or a sign of disrespect by certain Asians and American Indians. The client who avoids eye contact and resists the invitation of the counselor must not be accused immediately of resisting or being pathological.

Leininger (1985) has described a multicultural approach to counseling based on the concept of *transcultural caring*. She considers care as being essential for human growth and well-being. Care components such as compassion, empathy, love, concern, presence, trust, support, succorance, nurturance, protection, and others can be identified through ethnographic study of cultures. For example, she considers alleviating stress, discomfort, and anxiety as well as providing comfort to self and others as key care constructs for middle-class Anglo-Americans. In contrast, key care constructs for Philippine-Americans include harmonious relationships with others (especially among Philippine family members), silence, respect for elders and those in authority, reciprocity, and generosity. Vietnamese in the United States view family sharing as the key concept of care.

Transcultural care constructs are utilized in therapy according to three major principles. First, the therapist preserves the cultural-care construct by recognizing that it is helpful and thus seeks to retain the construct in counseling. The second principle, cultural-care accommodation, means that the therapist makes special efforts to include old and new care features into the therapy. For instance, the Sioux Indian culture values respect for elders and maintains silence until the elder man has spoken. So, the therapist might acknowledge and show respect to elders, permit them to speak first, and then may include the Anglo greeting of "Hello." The third principle, cultural-care repatterning, means that once care values are identified, the therapist works with the client to repattern care values so that the best of professional manners and folkways fit together meaningfully. This requires in-depth understanding of the culture, clear perception of desired changes, and an acceptable strategy plan for integrating specific care constructs into a new pattern for the client.

Atkinson (1983) reviewed literature related to ethnic similarity and counseling outcome to answer the question, "Should clients be served by counselors of similar ethnicity who might better understand their clients' problems, serve as role models for their clients, and resolve their client's difficulties?" Certain cross-cultural counselors believe that culturally sensitive counselors should be able to transcend cultural differences between themselves and their clients. Other counselors believe it is in the client's best interests to be counseled by an individual of similar ethnic background. Atkinson found that blacks prefer racially similar counselors and that for many blacks, utilization of counseling services may be a function of the availability of black counselors. However, the lack of replication with other groups (American Indians and Hispanics) and evidence of within-group differences for blacks suggest that preference for an ethnically similar counselor is not universal. The research reviewed suggests there is very little carry-over from preference for counselor ethnicity to more direct evidence of counseling effectiveness. Research on counselor bias, counseling process, and counseling outcomes is for the most part evenly divided between studies finding an ethnic similarity effect and those finding no such effect. Factors other than membership-group similarity appear to be operating in the counseling relationship.

In working with clients from ethnically diverse groups, therapeutic approaches should be assessed for their effectiveness and potential side effects. Intervention strategies that match the culture or life style of the client should be considered. When devising nontraditional strategies, knowledge of the client's culture, experience with members of an ethnic-minority group, and the advice of supervisors or consultants knowledgeable about the client's culture or life style are important (Sue, Akutsu, & Higashi, 1985).

OLDER ADULTS

As our population ages, the need for counselors to work with the elderly increases dramatically. While many of the basic helping skills for counseling the elderly are the same as for other populations, adaptations must be made that take into account the broader life experiences of older people. They are more likely to have sensory deficits, mobility limitations, and other losses. Counselors are in an important position to focus on preventive work with older adults and their families since many transitions of the elderly can be anticipated. Key goals are to enable older clients to assess their resources and deficits, to plan for changes, and to enable clients and their families to cope with the transitions of aging.

Counseling services to older persons are provided in a variety of settings. *Community mental health centers* provide specialized services such as diagnostic treatment, liaison, and follow-up services. *Adult day care* serves functions of prevention, attention, self-sufficiency, and extended family stability. Adult day care provides respite care for older persons in a center as an alternative to nursing home placement. A variety of health and social services may be provided in these settings, including nursing care; physical, speech, and occupational therapy; nutrition; recreation; and socialization. Use of adult day-care centers enables families to maintain frail elderly members in the home while being free to carry on their own normal jobs and living tasks. *Long-term care facilities* (such as nursing homes) incorporate intervention strategies such as structured group interaction, social interaction, social skills acquisition, companionship therapy, and prescribed physical activity. *Shared housing* allows many older adults to combine the companionship of cooperative living with other seniors. *Community social service agencies* have life-development groups that have a preventive focus, coping groups that emphasize support, and socialization groups that add to the quality of life. *Senior centers* provide opportunities for socialization and education. *Religious organizations* provide a variety of services including discussions of spirituality in the later years and programs that bring together older adults with younger generations.

Often, the counselor's initial task is to assist the older client in differentiating the normal aging process from pathological processes. Although development continues throughout the life span, the pace of development varies both across individuals and within the same individual. The normative changes of aging can be viewed as life transitions with interrelated biological, psychological, environmental, and social/cultural factors (Smyer, 1983). Transitions include career changes, retirement, changes in family status (marriage, divorce, parenthood, grandparenthood), geographical moves, and changes in health status.

A careful assessment is important because so many personal factors are interrelated. For example, physiological problems may become interwoven with emotional difficulties. Memory loss and anxiety can have physiological bases or be drug related. It is important to do psychological assessment in conjunction with neurological and medical evaluations. Users of psychological tests must recognize that many tests have item content that is inappropriate for the elderly and lack normative data for older adults.

A primary goal of counseling is to help older clients maintain independence and control. Actual as well as feared losses, such as jobs, roles, spouses, or significant others, are often major issues. One difference in counseling older clients is that they have lived longer and have more life experience that can be utilized in counseling. Older adults can often use their experience to access memories of times in which they utilized effective coping skills and decision making. It should be remembered that many older people hesitate to seek counseling assistance because, to them, mental health services have a negative association. It is for these reasons that counselors must not only know the problems of older adults but must also be familiar with the major social theories of aging and their implications. Fry (1992) for example, has reviewed these theories of aging and has identified the principal ones as *disengagement,* or gradual voluntary severance from society; *abandonment,* or neglect and loss of status; and *activity,* or staying physically and mentally active. Counselors must make accurate assessments of the older adult's preferred lifestyle and what gives her or him primary life satisfactions. These preferences then must be placed against the mirrors of health, energy, stamina, and available personal resources.

Group work is often particularly valuable with older adults since groups provide an opportunity to learn that others have similar life experiences and feelings. Groups also allow the teaching of social skills. This opportunity may be especially important for widowed persons whose spouses had made all social arrangements, older people who have moved to a new environment, or for those whose long-term support system has dwindled through death or relocation. Thus, groups serve as an antidote for loneliness and an opportunity for increasing self-esteem. Groups are not advisable, however, for people who are too disoriented to participate by taking turns or following conversations.

Various types of counseling groups are used with the elderly. *Enrichment groups* are designed to enhance members' self-esteem and communications skills. *Assertion training groups* assist older adults to initiate friendships as well as cope with bureaucracies involved in obtaining services. *Groups for children of aging parents* provide information about the aging process that can help children better understand their parents and become familiar with community resources. Groups for children of aging parents also give family members an opportunity to understand and express feelings they have about their changing relationship with their parents. *Self-help groups* generally are organized around common problems or transitions. Examples are groups for widows and groups for patients with common illness such as cancer, diabetes, or Alzheimer's disease. Many self-help groups are facilitated by peer counselors.

Elders are being trained increasingly as peer counselors. They serve as role models for successful aging, not only in their ability to cope with problems and losses, but also in their willingness to take on new roles and responsibilities. People of the same age have lived through the same historical period and may have shared similar types of experiences. This condition often leads to a similarity in values and language and makes communication between helpers and helpees easier than between cross-generational helpers.

A variety of specialized counseling techniques has been found to be particularly useful with older people. The *life review* involves helping older people reminisce about their life recollections and memories. Life reviews can be conducted individually, in a family setting, or in counseling groups. Fantasy, photographs, and mementos of earlier experiences, such as music and newspapers, are utilized to help elicit a person's memories of life experiences.

Life reviews are based on assumptions about the developmental needs of older adults. Butler and Lewis (1977), for example, postulate the universal occurrence of an inner review of one's life in older people that accounts for the increased reminiscence at this stage of life. It is characterized by a progressive return to consciousness of past experiences, in particular the resurgence of unresolved conflicts that can now be surveyed and reintegrated. Thus, life reviews provide an opportunity for people to resolve past conflicts and for those in a crisis to get in touch with previously used coping skills. These life reviews may bring unresolved issues to awareness and thus may be painful. In view of this possibility, life review groups should be conducted by trained counselors.

Reminiscence relates to Erikson's final developmental task, which involves the choice between integrity and despair. Integrity conveys an acceptance of one's life as having been meaningful. In Butler's view, the life-review process is stimulated by the realization of approaching death. Therefore it is much more common among older people, but also occurs among younger people who are anticipating death.

Reality orientation is a technique employed in institutional settings with confused patients. The purpose of reality orientation is to reverse or halt the confusion, disorientation, social withdrawal, and apathy so characteristic of the institutionalized elderly. It involves client recall, the repetition and learning of basic facts, such as their names, the place, time of day, date, day of the week, and the time of the next meal.

Milieu therapy is a technique for modifying the environment to provide facilitative conditions for treatment. Milieu therapy creates a situation in which the physical and social structure of the treatment unit is involved as part of the therapeutic process. This process is facilitated by making the physical facility take on a more homelike and less institutional atmosphere. In this setting, the role of the staff is to help patients maximize their growth potential for all kinds of interactions and activities. A major aim is to encourage patients to try new skills in a safe environment with the hope that this will increase self-esteem. It incorporates a focus on gaining independent living skills to resume useful, meaningful, and productive lives. In milieu therapy settings, patients are given many more responsibilities than is usually the case with institutionalized persons. The expectation is that participation in decision making will increase trust and respect between patient and staff.

Remotivation is a technique to encourage moderately confused elderly patients to take a renewed interest in their surroundings by focusing their attention on the simple objective features of everyday life that are unrelated to the clients' emotional difficulties. Typically, remotivation involves structured programs of discussion that use pictures, music, or other objects to stimulate reactions and discussions. Topics might focus on vacations, gardening, sports, and pets. Through such topic-related discussions, group members are encouraged to talk about themselves.

The emphasis of many community-based programs is to increase support systems for the elderly. Because retirement and the aging process bring a loss of status for many older adults in our society, many efforts are made to provide opportunities for the elderly to share their experiences with one another as they continue to seek ways to pursue growth and independence in the later years.

WORK SETTINGS

Schools and Colleges

Counseling services in school and college settings have traditionally emphasized educational and career planning and short-term therapy. Even though school counselors are preoccupied with problems of teen suicide, drug abuse, and truancy, there is currently a renewed interest in developing preventive counseling and consulting services targeted toward groups not yet experiencing significant problems. These preventive approaches can reach a wider range of clients than remedial services and promote life-skills development through consultation, curricular interventions, and preventive outreach programs. We wish to highlight these preventive measures in our discussion of counseling in school and college settings.

Traditional school guidance specialists (counselors, school psychologists, social workers) have emphasized one-to-one counseling related to personal, educational, and career-related concerns. Although many of these services have been effective, they tend to have low visibility in the school community. Consequently, the numbers of guidance specialists in the schools have been reduced as funding of school districts has decreased. Additionally, the role of guidance specialists has changed, reflecting the need to become more visible and provide services to more students. The shift taking place is away from a remedial service model toward a prevention model of counseling. We wish to emphasize that elements of both models are important in a comprehensive guidance program. The remediation of one child's needs in a classroom situation can be considered to be preventive for the balance of the children.

In the remedial service model, emphasis is placed on providing services to students with existing problems. There are various reasons why counselors adopt a remedial model. First, students with existing problems tend to command more attention than students who manifest no apparent problems. The sense of urgent need they convey is much more compelling than the need for primary preventive services. Second, techniques for therapeutic or remedial intervention were developed earlier and are better understood than preventive interventions. Third, counseling people who have problems is the reason most counselors entered their profession, so that in providing remedial services, counselors are engaged in activities they enjoy. Preventive efforts rely more on educational methods such as information sharing and self-assessment to energize change than on using typical counseling strategies to build a therapeutic alliance. Many counselors have not received training in design and delivery of these new preventive approaches.

Drum (1984) notes that resistance to preventive measures also comes from consumers. Students generally are less motivated to change than the typical one-to-one client. Whereas individual counseling clients have generally assumed ownership of their problems and seek to be partners in the change process, those who deny or question their susceptibility to particular problems are likely to have lower motivation to change.

It is becoming increasingly clear that the more traditional methods of individual, family, or group counseling are unlikely to reach a significant proportion of the school population. A preventive model promotes healthy physical, social, and biological environments and personal social growth of all individuals in order to reduce the incidence of physical, mental, emotional, or social impairment. Prevention is also closely tied to a developmental understanding of individuals. It seeks to target the development and nurturance of academic and social skills that will prevent the development of maladaptive responses to transitions of school-age children and their families. As Danish, Smyer, and Nowak (1980) pointed out, primary prevention goals may be achieved either by eliminating the causes of dysfunction or by promoting psychosocial health through development of positive competencies.

Schools are an ideal context for primary preventive interventions that are educational activities targeted to large groups and intended to prevent dysfunction before it occurs (Alpert, 1985). Students are experiencing a variety of stressful developmental tasks and transitions. Additionally, schools are the one place in our society where virtually everyone can be reached by helping professionals. Primary preventive interventions can reduce the likelihood that students and their families will develop difficulties as they pass through the many transitions of the school years. Primary prevention techniques may assist students to learn more effectively, to attend school more often, and to relate more effectively with others. From a teacher's or parent's point of view, primary prevention efforts may make it easier to teach and to live with children.

Interventions need to be designed to benefit people at different stages of readiness to change. According to a change model developed by Prochaska and DiClemiente (1982), people can be classified as being at one of four possible stages of readiness for change: precontemplation, contemplation, action, or maintenance. Drum (1984) has adapted these stages to planning preventive interventions. At the *precontemplation* stage, people lack awareness of their problems or the likelihood that they even have a problem or that they are at risk. In the *contemplation* stage, the person is aware of an existing difficulty or is seeking to understand some aspect of his or her life. Though the person may have some urge to change at this stage, he or she usually exhibits no noticeable commitment to such a change.

In the *action* stage, people are actively attempting to make changes that will prevent a problem from developing or are overcoming some existing difficulty. Even though the desired change may not have been achieved, external sources of assistance (information, decision-making strategies, workshops, counseling) can still be beneficial. A person in the *maintenance* stage has made the desired change and is seeking to stabilize the progress he or she has achieved. People who seek assistance in this stage do so largely to prevent relapse or to strengthen their gains.

An emerging role for the school guidance specialist is that of consultant involved with the entire educational process. This preventive consultation is provided both on an individual and group basis to administrators, teachers, parents, and committees. It requires strong administrative support. The school counselor works with administrators and teachers to formulate goals, such as increased test scores, reduced disciplinary problems, and improved teacher morale. Counselors provide group consultation to teachers on issues related to motivating students, managing misbehavior, teaching interpersonal skills, and instituting effective disciplinary programs. Additionally, counselors may be consulted regarding how to incorporate effective education into classroom curricula. These consultation efforts can free counselors from spending so much time in responding to crisis-oriented referrals from teachers. Parent-training programs, as described in Chapter 10, are an additional way for counselors to have an impact on the school environment. Such programs can provide parents with emotional support from other parents and suggest strategies for dealing with the common developmental challenges that families experience during the school years.

The guidance specialist consultant who teaches communication skills to groups of teachers, behavior management skills to groups of parents, and interpersonal problem-solving skills to class-sized groups of children is highly visible. The number of students who can be reached effectively is much greater than through remedial services.

Assessment, an important component of prevention efforts, helps to identify children who are likely to develop academic deficits or personal problems and who might benefit from enhanced psychological support. Barclay (1984) has described a computerized assessment system for elementary school students utilizing self-report data, peer nominations, teacher judgments, and achievement data. Such information can be utilized in conjunction with research findings about which students are likely to benefit most from selected interventions.

Prevention efforts can often be implemented through psychological education. Psychoeducational approaches include direct training and education of clients in psychological skills, developing programmed instruction materials for training purposes, and developing instructional media programs. In his review of psychological education, Watkins (1985) notes that psychoeducational treatments have been used effectively to improve interpersonal skills and general coping skills, increase assertiveness and study skills, reduce anxiety, as well as treat a variety of behavioral medicine concerns. In psychological education, the therapeutic psychologist relates to the trainee as a teacher. This role is often more cognitively oriented and less personal than is psychotherapy. The psychoeducational approach is skill oriented and usually time limited.

School counselors have integrated psychological education into school curricula. Morgan (1984) described a K–6 guidance curriculum intended to foster student self-esteem, effective interpersonal skills, and self-responsibility. The curriculum varied according to the developmental level of students. It was taught by teachers who received training by guidance specialists through in-service training, workshops, and continuing education classes. The curriculum included eight major skill areas:

1. Decision making
2. Causes of behavior
3. Awareness of feelings
4. Listening
5. Cooperation and conflict
6. Understanding the meaning of values
7. Occupational/educational decision making
8. Classroom management strategies (intended for teachers)

Evaluation of the student response to the curriculum suggested that students were increasing their affective skill levels. Similar efforts to enhance curriculum through psychological education can also be made in upper-grade levels. Curricula in high school may include many of the same topics but will be dealt with in a new level of sophistication. More attention may be given to topics of concern to high school students, such as dating, sexuality, AIDS, substance abuse, suicide, career planning, and personal identity.

One example of a successful prevention program aimed at junior high school students' smoking behavior has been described by Thoreson and Eagleston (1985). The program used a cognitive social learning model to modify students' smoking behavior and "inoculate" students against environmental and cognitive demands to start smoking. High school students guided seventh graders to resist personal and social pressures to smoke. These high school students conducted seven skill sessions dealing with resistance to cigarette smoking. From the seventh to tenth grades, smoking among students in the treatment program had increased by only 5 percent compared to 17 percent for students in the control group.

Programs focused on prevention themes are offered on college and university campuses. These programs are based on the assumption that certain incomplete developmental tasks may form the basis for later life problems. Thus, by helping students to address their unfinished developmental tasks, future problems can be prevented.

In contrast to preventive programs in public schools, colleges face unique challenges in gaining access to students, since many students may not choose to participate in the programs. Because preselection of participants is seldom feasible in preventive programming, each workshop or panel must be designed to accommodate participants at dramatically different stages of readiness for change. A college counseling outreach program, described by Drum (1984), emphasizes a global theme of "Transitions." This outreach program focused on three major types of changes: roles, relationships, and self. Interventions were designed to benefit people at different stages of readiness for change. Follow-up opportunities were made available to students who wished to pursue personal change through individual or group counseling.

On the college campus, a theme-focused prevention program must be timed to correspond with the emergence of students' ability to profit from assistance. Timing of the prevention offering is important since such offerings compete with other campus activities, such as midterm and final examinations. Location of programs is important also in order to be visible and attractive to large numbers of students.

A major trend in school and college counseling has been toward proactive preventive programming. These programs should be designed to help participants personalize information and to meet the needs and developmental level of the consumer. As with counseling, preventive programs must be goal focused in order to give coherence to the effort. The intervention must be targeted to people who are at risk to the problem being addressed. Preventive programs must involve an assessment of need that helps the counselor decide which type of intervention is likely to be most effective for the particular target group. There should be a method of evaluating program effectiveness.

Business and Industry

An increasing number of mental health specialists are finding roles in business and industry, predominantly as consultants but also as employees in human resource management, organizational development and training, employee assistance programs, and program evaluation. In human resources departments, the therapeutic psychologist may function in a variety of roles, such as developing counseling programs related to career development within the organization. Counseling involves programs related to either individual or institutional processes (Gutteridge & Otte, 1983). *Individual processes* are intended to respond to individual needs, such as occupational choice, career self-development, developing management skills, helping employees manage geographic and role transitions, and preretirement planning. Cairo (1986) interpreted the goals of career-planning programs broadly when he stated that "one of the desired outcomes of career planning is to prepare persons to respond effectively to changing circumstances by applying their competencies to whatever opportunities are available." He cautions that career development should not be concerned entirely with advancement, since many organizations may not be expanding and hence promotions may not be available. Some individuals may be at a career plateau, where the likelihood of additional hierarchical promotion is very low. Career-planning goals may include anything from making horizontal transfers, entering a different type of work, and using leisure time more effectively to managing dual-career family situations. Such activities may not lead to promotion but might enhance overall career satisfaction or general quality of life.

Institutional processes are concerned primarily with problems such as recruitment and selection, human resource allocation, assessment and evaluation, and training and development. These processes also involve consultation with managers and supervisors about personnel who are not performing in desired or expected ways. Other roles in which psychologists also become involved include surveying employee attitudes regarding benefit programs, assessment of skills in leadership, decision making and planning, suitability for transfer, or safety. Efforts to increase safety in high-stress or high-risk jobs include informing workers on the effects of stress, alcohol, and illegal drug use on safety performance. Values, psychological defenses, and risk taking are investigated as important psychological aspects of safety behavior.

Career planning programs need to take into account employees' diverse career development needs. Campbell and Cellini's (1981) diagnostic taxonomy of adult career problems included four common types: problems related to career decision making, implementing career plans, organizational performance, and organizational adaptation. Some employees may need values and skills assessment, while others may need information about career paths, job requirements, and training resources that will help employees identify and reach objectives.

Some employees may desire skills to improve work performance or adjust to their work environment. An important role of the career counselor in industry is to help such employees develop and improve their work-related skills. Methods for assessment of work-related skills include tests, work simulations, or structured learning exercises. Counselors help employees with career counseling and finding the training resources they need to improve their skills and extend their career opportunities. Some firms encourage employees to learn other jobs in the company through in-house educational programs or through tuition refunded courses at educational institutions in the community.

For professional, managerial, and technical employees who are terminated because they do not measure up to performance standards, outplacement counseling services are provided. Usually the company will provide the cost of an extensive counseling series, called outplacement counseling, to help the person examine career goals and engage in a job search.

Training opportunities for counselors within industry involve teaching psychological skills related to supervision and management, team building, conducting effective meetings, performance appraisal, creative problem-solving, and effective discipline. While many companies develop training programs in house, most rely on outside consultants to meet their specialized training needs.

The development of Employee Assistance Programs (EAPs) has represented one of the most visible and effective interventions by psychologists, social workers, and physicians in business and industry. Although EAPs focus primarily on alcoholism and chemical dependency, the primary purpose of many programs is to provide assistance with psychological, family, legal, and financial difficulties. The key functions of EAPs are prevention as well as early identification and treatment of employee problems. Corporate motivation to establish such programs is economic as well as humane in that employee problems impact on safety, performance, waste, medical, absenteeism, and replacement training costs. Research supporting the cost effectiveness of EAPs has been summarized by Toomer (1983).

Psychological counselors working within business and industry face unique ethical dilemmas (Toomer, 1983) due to their conflicting roles and functions. The psychologist in industry usually serves multiple functions: consultant to management, forensic psychologist in court, psychotherapist with an employee, or expert with knowledge of selection testing and EEO laws. In industrial settings, conflicts arise when psychologists provide professional services to clients and, simultaneously, function as members of a profit-making organization. The salaries of both client and mental health professional are paid by the organization, resulting in greater potential influence over the actions of counselors than is present in other service settings. Counselors in business settings must consider their unique roles and, after choosing among their conflicting ethical responsibilities concerning confidentiality, determine who their client is and clarify their dual relationships with clients.

Health Care

Health professionals are rediscovering the wisdom that health and well-being are highly related to personal life style. They are also becoming acutely aware that epidemic diseases, such as acquired immunodeficiency syndrome (AIDS), are threatening the life style of millions potentially. This term conjures up images of fear, despair, hopelessness, and finally loneliness and death. AIDS affects all levels of society. Although it is basically a physical health problem, the counseling implications for people with AIDS or the HIV positive virus findings are enormous (Kain, 1989). Counselors are key people in promoting empowerment, hope, and tools for leading a meaningful life in the state of crisis. The sense of loss and consequent mourning and depression demand the best that counselors can offer in the way of support, information, networking, and acceptance. Kain's manual on counseling AIDS patients is a desk tool for all helping professionals. Kain summarizes the following guidelines for counseling AIDS patients:

1. Focus on the positive, less fatalistic features of the illness.
2. Emphasize the healing power of hope and caring.

3. Assist them to reconnect with a support system.
4. Teach ways to gain control of their illness and their lives.
5. Assist them to reduce their victim mindset.
6. Advocate for the needs and rights of AIDS patients and reaffirm the belief in the dignity and worth of all people. (p. 20)

Current conceptions of health are influenced by a holistic view of humankind that considers mind and body to be mutually interdependent (Capra, 1982). Mental operations are considered to be coequal with physiological factors in all illness. Psychosomatic illness thus becomes the province of all health care professionals. Additionally, people are understood in context with other living systems so that health is considered in the context of how people live in their particular environments. This new broader conception of health is reflected in more wideranging interdisciplinary work. For example, researchers in psychoneuroimmunology are exploring how cognitive and behavioral processes influence the body's immune system and, hence, the body's susceptibility to diseases. Ironically, this emerging view of health is similar to the Hippocratic tradition of 400 b.c., in which health reflected a state of balance among environmental influences, ways of life, and the various components of human nature. Within that tradition, illness is likely to occur when a person is out of synchrony with himself or herself and the surrounding world. The emerging model of health emphasizes achievement of maximum wellness through balance in work and relationships, as well as an internal balance of body, mind, and spirit.

One's conceptual model of health influences the type of treatment selected. Thoreson and Eagleston (1985) suggest that health care in the United States reflects a narrow biomedical disease model. They state, "Health care in the United States is based primarily on treating acute, well-advanced (and often terminal) disease processes (often in hospitals), using an infection/disease paradigm." This paradigm emphasizes the role of the physician in observing signs, evaluating symptoms, and applying an accurate diagnostic label. Thoreson and Eagleston suggest that contemporary "health care" is a misnomer and might more accurately be described as "disease care" since it ignores efforts to improve health and prevent disease.

The biomedical model of health may also create psychological problems. Critics suggest that it leads to the dehumanization of health care due to overreliance on technology and overspecialization of health care providers. Also, it promotes the impression that health maintenance is the responsibility of the health care provider rather than the patient. It acknowledges the primacy of physical factors in disease and does not address the social, psychological, and behavioral dimensions of health in terms of etiology, prevention, and treatment.

The emerging model of health does not associate the causes of poor health and serious disease processes with a single infectious microbe, but instead links poor health to many factors, particularly behavioral and cognitive habits along with specific social and physical environments. Matarazzo (1984) argues that "behavioral pathogens," meaning high-risk behaviors that are harmful to health, such as excessive alcohol use, chronic distress, cigarette smoking, and overeating, have been sorely neglected compared to microbial pathogens. He also acknowledges that we are slowly learning to appreciate the scientific and the clinical value of what he terms "behavioral immunogens," defined as specific health-related behaviors that can reduce the risk of disease as well as enhance health and perhaps contribute to quality of life. In this wellness model, good health is more than the absence of specific diseases, and the model recognizes the reciprocal and dynamic influences of the social and physical environment, cognition, behavior, physiology, and genetic contributions (Matarazzo, 1984).

This philosophy of health stresses individual responsibility for maintaining good health and that good health is the social responsibility of the family and community. The health professional is a *therapeutic partner* or consultant to the patient. Individual health must be viewed as a relative state within a given social and cultural context. For example, health and disease processes may fluctuate in response to perceived demands to function effectively in familial and occupational roles within one's cultural milieu.

In the United States during the past century, health problems have shifted from being attributable primarily to infectious diseases toward diseases where the risk factors are not infectious agents. Instead, the risk factors are often behaviors of people or characteristics of demanding situations. Similarly, chronic disease is no longer considered to be tied directly to one specific infectious agent but rather to a complex interplay of individual and environmental factors patterned over time. In chronic conditions, the human organism as a system seems to break down gradually in the presence of many probability (or high-risk) factors that relate to the disease process. For example, the statement that cigarette smoking is a risk factor in heart disease prompts one to inquire about the causes of smoking. Similarly, chronic stress or hypertension that have their own antecedents that place someone at risk. An important function of the health psychologist is to help clients assess the meaning of risk information and then make appropriate choices.

Evidence is mounting that an individual's thoughts and feelings are associated with health and disease. Thoreson and Eagleston (1985) reviewed several longitudinal studies with adults which associated seven health practices with longevity. These health behaviors were:

- Ate breakfast almost every day
- Rarely or never ate between meals
- Slept 7 to 8 hours daily
- Maintained normal weight adjusted for height, age, and sex
- Never smoked cigarettes
- Avoided alcohol or used alcohol moderately
- Had regular physical activity

These seven illustrative health practices were significantly associated with lower death rates, even when socioeconomic level and physical health status of subjects at the beginning of the study were considered. Another study by Berkman and Syme (1979) examined the social network levels of subjects, particularly their marital status, number and frequency of contact with close friends and relatives, and membership in church and other groups. Over a 9½ case-year period the incidence of death from all causes was associated with level of social network. In general, people with fewer social contacts were found to have substantially higher death rates. These relationships between social support and death were found to be independent of initial physical health status, socioeconomic status, use of preventive health services, and risk factors, such as smoking, alcohol use, physical activity level, and obesity.

Psychologists are becoming involved increasingly in health-related interventions. These interventions are aimed toward the promotion and maintenance of good health through development of healthy habits and life styles, including increased exercise, social support, and attention to nutrition. Other interventions attempt to prevent and treat disease through changing unhealthy behaviors, especially those that may be associated with chronic diseases and health problems, such as cigarette smoking, alcohol and chemical dependency, and failure to use seat belts. Diseases in which counselors might be involved in collaborative interventions include hypertension, headaches, breast and skin cancer, diabetes, and sleep disorders. Habits related to alcohol and substance abuse, stress, eating disorders, insomnia, medical compliance, smoking, obesity, sexually transmitted diseases, and eating disorders represent conditions in which counselors could apply psychological knowledge within a comprehensive treatment program. Additionally, psychologists can apply a holistic understanding of disease processes such as cardiovascular problems or AIDS in community-wide efforts at promoting safe health practices and changing health-related behaviors.

Thoreson and Eagleston (1985) describe an intervention program designed to alter the stressful Type A behavior pattern identified as a major risk factor for coronary heart disease. This pattern of behavior has cognitive, behavioral, physiological, and environmental concomitants. Subjects were people who had already suffered at least one myocardial infarction. The treatment, based on a cognitive social learning model, focused on how to alter cognitive, behavioral, environmental, and physiological factors related to the Type A behavior pattern. Techniques included teaching clients to apply appropriate cognitive self-talk, perform mental relaxation, build interpersonal skills, reduce hurried physical activity, alter environmental factors likely to elicit unnecessary arousal, and learn about the biochemical processes in chronic stress. When compared with a group led by cardiologists focused on diet, exercise, adherence to medication, and new developments in cardiovascular physiology, the behavioral counseling group had 44 percent fewer recurrences of myocardial infarctions within the first 36 months of the research study.

Counselors also play a significant role in drug and alcohol treatment. This form of health psychology, known as substance abuse counseling, refers to counseling persons who suffer from the psychological and physiological effects of alcohol and drug abuse. Counseling approaches generally include educational, vocational, medical, family, and psychological facets of treatment. Most treatment programs include an aftercare follow-up group and suggest involvement in Alcoholics Anonymous or Narcotics Anonymous to prevent relapse. Research (Vaillant, 1983) indicates that psychotherapy is ineffective as the main treatment for active alcoholism. Clients with severe alcohol problems will do anything to solve their problem except not drink. Psychotherapy conducted with individuals in abstinence-based recovery, as opposed to those in active alcoholism, is very useful as an aftercare support. There is an increasing interest in how to help clients prevent relapse and maintain sobriety (Marlatt & George, 1984; Marlatt & Gordon, 1984).

As the emerging model of health places more responsibility on individuals and communities for health maintenance, it is likely that health psychologists will play an increased role in formulation of health education and health policies. The aim of health education will be to help people understand how their behavior and their environment affects their health and to teach them how to maintain health in their daily lives. Health policies established by governments and organizations will attempt to prevent health hazards from being generated. Ultimately, it seems likely the health care delivery system itself will need to change and expand to meet the requirements of a holistic understanding of health.

Private Practice

Private practice can represent a great personal challenge to the therapist as well as a source of satisfaction. Therapists considering private practice often fear that they will have an empty schedule, experience loneliness and isolation, or get bored or depressed by the emotional drain from continually counseling people. However, some private therapists learn how to fill their appointment schedules, see the clients they want to see, make the practice fun, and become personally and professionally stimulated by their work.

Private practitioners must maintain optimism about the ability of people to change in order to survive as therapists. Therapists need to be open to helping their clients learn to experience life, work toward their desired goals, and survive when life does not work out the way they would like. However, it is easy for therapists to become discouraged by the low frequency of improvement among their clients. It can sometimes seem like the successful clients leave while those who fail to make changes return and provide reminders of the therapist's fears of incompetence. The therapist must be able to recognize his or her contributions to change as well as limitations related to other factors in clients' lives that limit treatment outcomes.

One of the initial tasks of the therapist is to build a practice. The paradox here is that the most referrals go to the therapist who is seeing the most clients. The lesson is that most therapists need to market their services. Many will visit school counselors, nurses, doctors, or domestic attorneys—people who do not practice therapy but see people with problems. Sometimes a beginning therapist will get referrals from a seasoned therapist whose schedule is full. Other therapists participate in organizations or activities that help them get known in the community. They may give public talks, media interviews, or become active in professional or civic groups. Some therapists build a practice by specializing. It may be useful to specialize in a type of client that other therapists may not want to see or be trained to deal with, such as eating or substance abuse disorders or difficult family situations.

Most therapists must learn to operate their practice as a business. Few therapists have been trained in graduate school about the business aspects of operating a private practice. They may need to find the professional legal and accounting resources they need in order to operate a small business.

One of the personal challenges for therapists is to learn to deal with their attitudes toward money. Many are not sure that it is respectable to ask people who are in pain to pay while the therapists are enjoying their work. Paying a fee for service can help equalize the client's power in a therapeutic relationship and yet may challenge the counselor's need to be a giver. As with many issues in therapy, dealing with money has many layers of meanings. In addition to the need for the therapist to obtain a fair fee for service, there are the symbolic meanings of money attached to financial transactions between client and therapist. Thus, fees, payment structures, and management of payments assume therapeutic significance.

Another challenge to building a practice is to maintain the humanistic and caring impulses that create a climate for therapeutic change. Millon and associates (1987) warn that for established clinicians, the prerequisites of financial comfort and professional recognition can eclipse the humanitarian desires to provide therapy. Established therapists begin to advise clients who are less interesting or are poor to seek treatment at more affordable therapeutic groups or at publicly supported agencies.

As they put immense energy into building and expanding a practice, there is a danger that therapists can become so absorbed by their professional paths that they may stop listening to their own "personal drumbeat" and lose their personal self. Freudenberger and Robbins (1979) refer to the "ironic paradox" that many clients seem to live more fully than their therapists, who become overly controlled, objective, and professional in their stance toward all relationships.

Therapists must become knowledgeable about changes in the health care industry that may impact their role as independent practitioners. These include such things as the increase in mental health services contracted by businesses to employee assistance contractors, preferred provider organizations, and health maintenance organizations. Independent practitioners may want to consider becoming providers within a group that contracts with businesses. Changes in insurance reimbursement and coverage may also affect independent providers.

Other changes in the marketplace include the rise of competing professionals within the mental health field. There is often a large overlap in the types of private clients seen by psychiatrists, psychologists, nurses, social workers, and mental health counselors. The pressure of this competition can be stressful for psychologists who do not want to compare themselves or be compared to others by their clients. However, there is pressure from clients who are paying high fees for the services they receive to have high expectations from the professional they see. They may challenge the therapist or terminate therapy if they become disappointed in their progress.

Therapists in private practice must also find ways to deal with personal isolation and professional growth. Working for the most part without a secretary or receptionist, the independent practitioner faces a day devoted to a world of symbols and intense relationships shared in a secluded setting. The private transactions of solo clinicians deprive them of opportunities for obtaining affirmation. The therapist role can seem ambiguous, unreal, and may assume a ritualized quality. There are often fewer opportunities for professional consultation with colleagues than in institutional practice settings. Therapists in private practice may have to be more intentional in scheduling times with colleagues both for personal and professional renewal. Independent practitioners may wish to become more involved in professional association activities, organize a peer consultation group that meets on a regular basis, and participate in various continuing education experiences.

Therapists who enjoy private practice express the feeling of being honored at having clients choose them to share their life experience. Additionally, many private practitioners like the independence of self-employment. They enjoy the personal growth challenges that accompany the experience of being therapists. Most learn ways to diversify their work to find new creative edges and avoid stagnation and isolation.

SUMMARY

In this chapter we have described the applications of therapeutic psychology to various client groups and work settings. Particular attention was devoted to the concerns of gender issues in counseling as well as treating cross-cultural clients and older adults. While many of the techniques described in previous chapters apply to counseling individuals within these populations, we believe that therapy must be tailored to the unique needs of men and women, ethnic-minority clients, and older adults.

Applications of therapeutic psychology to several different work settings were described. Although many therapeutic strategies overlap across settings, we suggested some of the unique challenges and opportunities available for therapists within business and industry, health care, educational settings, and private practice. Particular emphasis was placed on the role of the counselor as consultant and developer of prevention programs. Additionally, we described the need for counselors in different work settings to work closely with colleagues from other disciplines.

CHAPTER 13

Counseling and Human Values

The question, "What am I going to do with my life?" is raised frequently in actualizing counseling and psychotherapy. It comes in the form of choices of life style or of value conflict. Terms such as *human revolution, human potential,* and *human intentionality* put basic questions of purpose and meaning in an urgent social context. These questions became problems for therapists when psychotherapy in recent years shifted from earlier preoccupation with relief from psychological pain and disorder to questions of meaning and purpose.

The main purpose of this chapter is to examine the place of basic human values in counseling and how counselors and psychotherapists manage value-choice issues. We will consider the nature of values development, the impact of counselor and client values in psychotherapy, transcendent values and psychotherapy, and how counselors can help clients develop more sophisticated decision-making skills regarding values decisions.

Psychology as a science and a profession has a long history of concern about values, including the value assumptions underlying science itself (Worthington, 1989; Sperry, 1988; Bergin, 1991). The term *value* in this context is defined as a firm belief in the worth of an idea or feeling. The philosophical problem of the absoluteness or relativity of values will be treated only incidentally. We will focus on subjective values.

It is a truism that counselors deal with fundamental problems of actualized living, namely loving, becoming a person able to balance one's own independence and dependence on others, handle normal guilt, and gain a mature perspective on the frustrating and tragic incidents of everyday life. Increasingly clients bring complex value dilemmas related to issues such as the right to die, abortion, sexual expression, abuse, and suicide. We are aware of the difficulties in approaching the topic of values in the context of therapeutic psychology. This chapter is offered as a starting point for the student who may not have done much previous reading or thinking about the numerous value problems confronting client and counselor.

THE DEVELOPMENT OF VALUES AND MEANING

Developmental Research

As we have described in previous chapters, developmental researchers have made us aware of specific dimensions of our growth as moral selves and constructors of meaning and identity. Generally, these writings help us to see that development of human wholeness requires a balance between responsibility and care for others, on the one hand, and regard and care for self, on the other. For this balancing of self-determination and caring for others, we need qualities of connectedness, intimacy, love, and a principled commitment to justice, as well as a strong sense of self.

Although developmental researchers have described personality growth over the life span, few have addressed the process by which individuals construct personal meaning (Worthington, 1989). Erik Erikson acknowledges the importance of a religious or philosophical world view for expressing and grounding the conviction that life has meaning, but he does not in any consistent or comprehensive way focus on the role of ultimate values—or the development of such values—in our life cycles. Daniel Levinson has little to say about core values or beliefs in his studies of middle age. Carol Gilligan's work, like that of Kohlberg, tends to deal with moral development primarily in terms of moral perception and judgment. She and her colleagues have given little explicit attention to the meanings and images by which their respondents shape their responses and initiatives in life.

In Worthington's (1989) review of development of religious faith across the life span, he identified seven different models of faith development. We will present only one for illustration—Fowler's. His developmental model, in our opinion, is the most explicit. We will also attempt to make distinctions among faith, values, morals, and beliefs.

James Fowler and his colleagues (1981, 1984) have been researching how people develop their faith. Fowler believes that faith is a universal human experience. We live by forming and being formed in images and dispositions toward life's ultimate conditions. Fowler's research focuses on how we construct these guiding images of existence and shape our lives in relation to ultimate values. These visions center in causes, persons, or goals that promise to give our lives meaning. While in the past ultimate meaning was addressed in religious terms, modern history has been marked by the rise of scientism, pluralism, and humanism. It is important for counselors to understand the nature of ultimate meaning for our clients and to examine how such values influence their motivations and choices. Gerkin suggests that many persons suffer from distorted images or breakdown of meaning in their lives. They desire a counselor who will help them find new perspectives on their lives by acting as "an interpreter who offers a new possibility of meaning" (1984, pp. 53–54).

We have come to recognize that development of one's faith and the struggle for integrity may take forms and directions other than institutional religion. Paul Tillich (1957) referred to faith as "ultimate concern." The values toward which we focus our lives and which we prize most deeply comprise our faith. For example, we may be concerned with jobs, health, family, wealth, or spirituality. Our ultimate "gods" may not be particularly religious but may include secular forms and objects of faith, such as success, social standing, and economic power. We may value secular communities of faith, such as civil rights groups, with whom we associate because they share similar values and visions with us. Each person or small subculture struggles to form and maintain a shelter of shared values and life style that will provide protection against the quicksand of meaninglessness and aloneness. Fowler (1984) notes that

> for many, narcotization is the solution—the forgetting, the ignoring, or the escape through consumption or distraction from the burdens of our finite vulnerability. Or in the form most favored by a culture that believes its own distorted myths of individualism, there is the effort, through the acquisition of stuff, power, or 'securities,' or through achievements or relationships to negate our vulnerability and to outfox fate. (p. 51)

Faith Development Theory

Fowler and his colleagues have described a general pattern of developing a sense of ultimate meaning, which parallels certain developmental patterns in the domains of cognitive, psychosocial, and moral growth. Fowler's seven stages, which try to describe uniform and predictable ways of being in faith, are not primarily matters of the *contents* of faith. They do not suggest that a person goes through a succession of world views and adopts particular value systems. Rather, they try to identify and communicate differences in the *styles,* the *operations of knowing and valuing,* that constitute development of faith.

In Fowler's theory, movement from one faith to another is not analogous to climbing stairs or a ladder but is rather a successive progression of more complex, differentiated, and comprehensive modes of knowing and valuing. Shifts in faith development can be experienced as personally disconcerting because one's very life meanings and identity are at stake in faith stage transitions.

The initial stage of faith, *primal faith,* begins as the infant learns the first rhythms of intimacy in the give and take of learning about what Erikson terms "basic trust." Primal faith is a confidence that significant others and the environment will welcome the child and offset his or her profound vulnerability. The quality and consistency of primary care givers constitutes the infant's first experiences of trust and mistrust in ourselves and others. These primal images of self-other become present in the images of God that take more conscious form by the fourth or fifth years of life (Rizzuto, 1979).

The second stage of faith, termed *intuitive-projective faith*, occurs between the ages of two and six or seven. As language begins to mediate the child's experience with the world, the child is able to reflect about himself or herself and the world. The child encounters newness in the world daily with an active, inquiring mind. The child's understanding of the world occurs primarily through perception, feelings, and imaginative fantasy. Stimulated by experience and by stories, symbols, and examples from their significant others and environment, children form deep and long-lasting images that hold together their worlds of meaning and wonder. The child's lively imagination grasps the world, endeavoring to give it unity and sense. Through the imagination, the child gains powerful identifications and aspirations as well as sources of guidance and reassurance. Faith is based on intuitive-projective interpretations of the stories and symbols the child encounters through such things as fairy tales, television, and the messages of significant others.

The third stage of faith development, *mythic-literal faith*, begins at about the time a child starts primary school and continues until about age 12. Children at this age have developed concrete-operational thinking. Stable categories of space, time, and causality make the child's constructions of experience much less dependent on feeling and fantasy. The world becomes more linear, orderly, and predictable. Children at this stage routinely take the perspectives of others on matters of mutual interest, and they recognize others' perspectives as different from their own. Their thinking about what is right and wrong, good and evil, is based on a sense of reciprocal fairness. They learn that good actions are rewarded and bad are punished. People are often defined by their roles and actions. Because the child does not have the ability to reflect on his or her overall direction or meaning, faith becomes a matter of reliance on the stories, rules, and implicit values of his or her family's sense of meanings. There is a concreteness and literalness in the appropriation of these beliefs.

Stage four, *synthetic-conventional faith*, appears in conjunction with the formal operational mind typically developed during adolescence. Formal operational thinking makes possible the generation and use of abstract concepts and ideals and the ability to see ourselves as others see us. There is a new "self-consciousness" in adolescence that involves new awareness of and interest in the emotions, ideas, and experiences of oneself and others. The term "synthetic" refers to the integration of our self-reflections into a unified sense of the meaning of life and a personal identity. This faith is conventional in that the world view is a synthesis of belief and value elements that are derived from one's significant others. For example, although one may hold strong and sustaining religious or other beliefs, the authority for these beliefs still lies principally with one's parents or peer group. Although this synthesis of ultimate meaning is personalized, deeply felt, and strongly held, it has not yet become an object of self-critical reflection and inquiry. Fowler believes that most adults move through the life cycle at this stage of faith development, holding a set of tacitly held, strongly felt, but largely unexamined beliefs and values.

Fowler's fifth stage of faith, *individuative-reflective faith,* involves a more critical choosing of one's beliefs, values, and commitments. What were previously tacit and unexamined convictions and beliefs must now become matters of more explicit commitment and accountability. At this stage, the person is no longer so dependent on others' perceptions of him or her and is able to fashion meaning based on more personalized reflection of one's life experience. Movement to this stage is often precipitated by a personal crisis of meaning associated with leaving home emotionally or physically. For example, a college freshman may encounter world views quite novel from any to which he is accustomed, which cause him to reevaluate the basis of his or her own beliefs. People at this stage consider the expectations, advice, and counsel of others but ultimately choose their beliefs and take responsibility for their choices. The individual may sometimes reaffirm values and commitments held previously or may choose to pursue new directions, life commitments, and communities.

Fowler's sixth stage, *conjunctive faith,* emerges for some people at mid-life. It involves the integration of apparent contradictions in our experience of ourselves, society, and ultimate reality. During this stage, there is an awareness of certain patterns of our behavior that we may never be able fully to change and the polar tensions in one's life: the polarities of being both old and young, masculine and feminine, constructive and destructive, and having both a conscious and a shadow self. Conjunctive faith comes to cherish paradox and the apparent contradictions and to move beyond either/or thinking about ourselves or the world. Conjunctive faith combines deep particular commitments while maintaining an openness to the truth of other traditions. It combines loyalty to one's own primary communities and a desire to learn and appreciate what can be learned from other belief traditions.

The seventh stage, *universalizing faith,* is marked by an unusual self-transcendence and love or solidarity with all others. Fowler considers persons such as Gandhi, Martin Luther King, Jr., and Mother Teresa of Calcutta as representative of this stage. Such persons have an enlarged vision of justice and, through example or teaching, call us to a wider, less self- or group-centered faith. Fowler does not consider it likely that many people will experience this stage of faith because it involves a degree of negation of self-interest that is not likely to happen without a personal subordination to oneness with "the Transcendent." Because of the religious nature of this stage of faith, it is not considered as universal as the previous six stages.

Fowler's model of faith development describes a process of differentiation in which the individual moves from being embedded in the perspectives of his or her own immediate significant others and traditions toward a stance of greater moral empathy with the values of others, while at the same time deriving a more self-reflective set of values. One's concern for others becomes more inclusive and less self- or group-referenced ethic. This faith development is not intended to describe merely *belief* but is meant to reflect an *active commitment* of the total person. Faith is constantly growing along with other dimensions of our lives. It will involve doubts, confusion, turmoil, and changes over time as old levels of faith die and more adequate ones arise.

Implications of Fowler's Model for Counseling

Fowler's stages describe in formal terms the structural features of faith as a way of construing, interpreting, and responding to the factors of ultimate concern in our lives. His model offers developmental principles for a spiritual frame of reference in counseling theory. By focusing on the form of faith, Fowler's theory helps us recognize challenges to our own ultimate meaning and ways to support others' pilgrimage of creating meaning throughout the life cycle. As therapists, the model challenges us to continually reexamine our own tacitly held beliefs and to view this process as a life-long pilgrimage of consciously being aware of the values we live by. It encourages us to consider subtle ways that we are influenced by early images of ultimate meaning as well as development of our own conflicting emotional polarities. Counselors must become cognizant of their own processes of moral and ethical decision making because of the ways that they might affect the therapeutic process. Fowler's model also suggests that we must be attuned to our client's *process* of developing a spiritual base rather than simply the *content* of their values and beliefs. As we help our clients to reexamine their guiding values and commitments, we can also expect that movement to new stages of faith development may be experienced as disruptive, frightening, or threatening to their basic identity.

Fowler's model would help clients become aware of the differences between extrinsic and intrinsic religious orientations. Extrinsically oriented people use their religious commitments as a means of obtaining status, power, or security—a kind of "insurance policy." Intrinsic motivation, on the other hand, internalizes their beliefs so that they live by them in spite of external pressures and crises. A developmental approach, such as Worthington's (1989), also focuses on faith issues at different stages in life. Children, for example, must come to terms with the finality of death and develop their concept of God.

THE INFLUENCE OF VALUES IN PSYCHOTHERAPY

With the resurgence of interest in values among helping professionals has come much controversy over how assertive the counselor should be in advocating certain values. There is general agreement that the transmission of personal values is unavoidable in the close psychotherapeutic relationship. Sullivan (1953) recognized long ago that therapists' personal values and attitudes toward life influence their professional work as much as their skills and training.

The basic issue is how to advocate values to the client's advantage without risking the client's vulnerability through abuse of the therapist's power. It is a delicate balancing act, that to others appears to be "waffling" on the value issue. It is really the therapist struggling between advocacy of therapeutic values and infringing on the client's autonomy to decide value issues for him or herself. Therapists want to avoid being labeled "secular high priests" or moralists (London, 1986), even though they freely admit to influencing client values by letting them know how they can make their lives more meaningful. In American society, where the physician cannot deal effectively with symptoms and the priest is not always credible for dealing with problems of living, the psychotherapist is looked upon increasingly as the arbiter and linkage between the two.

Bergin (1991) argues that a noncommittal strategy doesn't work, because even silence sometimes is construed as consent. He claims that therapists must be open and honest about their views on alternative courses of action for clients. Sometimes therapists may watch clients make bad decisions, but they need to learn from the consequences. Yet there comes a time when it is desirable to offer our considered opinions. We collaborate with clients in setting goals and evaluating the efficacy of outcomes, but we try to honor their right to make their own decisions without too much influence. This is true especially in difficult life decisions such as abortion, suicide, and sexual behavior. This view is a value position in itself.

Part of the therapist's decision on how much to advocate mental health values rests on his or her views on relativity versus universality. Are there laws that regulate human behavior like the physical laws of the universe? Many therapists argue that there are universal principles that must be supported with vigor and courage. An example is the belief that human life is sacred. Even if it is difficult for the therapist to convey strong conviction on some values that may be controversial, it is essential to endorse these universal values strongly to give clients the courage to act upon them. In the next section, more specific attention will be given to these issues of values in psychotherapy.

Bergin (1980, 1991) has proposed six important theses regarding the influence of values in psychotherapy.

1. Values are an inevitable and pervasive part of psychotherapy. Values regarding the direction of client change may differ from the perspective of the client, the counselor, and the community systems in which the client and/or therapist participate. The priorities for client change and the criteria for measuring change are determined on the basis of value choices. Worthington (1989) and Worthington and Scott (1983) state that counselors influence clients' beliefs by the goals they lead clients to select. Their data suggest that counselors guide clients subtly toward or away from religious values through their problem definition and selection of goals for counseling.

Therapeutic techniques themselves are not value free. All therapeutic interventions involve implicit value orientations. For example, studies evaluating Carl Rogers's person-centered therapy (Murray, 1956; Truax, 1966) showed that Rogers systematically rewarded and punished expressions that he liked and did not like in the verbal behavior of his clients. His values subtly regulated the structure and content of therapeutic sessions as well as their outcomes.

Ethical standards alone cannot form an adequate basis for making value decisions in therapy. Given the unique contexts in which moral choices arise, ethical standards can neither tell counselors what to do in each specific situation nor explain why a counselor should choose a particular strategy. Codes are seldom a sufficient guide to choice regarding the many complex issues related to competence, selection of goals and means, and assessment of intended and unintended effects, that arise through selecting therapeutic interventions with clients.

2. Not only do theories, techniques, and criteria reveal pervasive value judgments, but outcome data comparing the effects of diverse techniques show that nontechnical, value-laden factors pervade professional change processes. Studies comparing different approaches to psychotherapy reveal few differences in affects attributable to therapeutic technique's (Smith, Glass, & Miller, 1980). This suggests that nonspecific or personal variables account for much of the client's change. If the core ingredients of psychotherapeutic change involve nonspecific factors, then change seems to be heavily influenced by personal traits and beliefs of the client and therapist. This raises unanswered questions about what belief factors tend to be therapeutic and how client versus therapist disagreement over values and beliefs impact therapeutic outcome.

Since the therapist and client both bring value assumptions to the counseling process, it is essential for counselors and clients to reflect upon and dialogue about questions such as, "Why take this approach? What purpose does it serve? What is the probable outcome? How does this approach benefit the client?" Explanations of why a particular approach is considered beneficial (beneficial for what, whom, when and under what circumstances) often reveal important value dimensions of the therapist.

3. Several broad classes of values are dominant in the mental health professions. Counselors should become aware of how their personal values about "ultimate concern" may clash with other belief systems. Such differences will lead to differing assumptions about what constitutes "the good life." In describing value systems of therapists, Bergin (1980, 1991), Walls (1980), and Ellis (1980) contrast three classes of values (see Table 13-1). Although there is some overlap and agreement among the systems, they illustrate how personal value systems also conflict.

Bergin's description of theistic values draws on prominent themes from religious traditions that he believes may be positive additions to clinical thinking. Theistic values are based on the axiom that God exists, that human beings are the creations of God, that there are unseen spiritual processes by which the link between God and humanity is maintained, and that there is a transcendent organizing influence in the universe. This approach, beginning with faith in God, assumes that spiritual conviction gives values an added power to influence life.

Bergin (1980), states that as a psychologist he does not intend to support organized religion in general but rather the themes from religious life that are most health producing. He cautions that religious faith operates at multiple levels. "It has social structure aspects that are sociological; it influences specific forms of small-scale interaction, such as child-rearing practices in families; it operates in the cognitive domain to provide interpretive schemas for life experience and values as regulators of conduct; and it provides emotional experiences of ecstasy, oneness, insight, and conviction" (Bergin, 1980, p. 648). Because of its complexity it is possible for religious faith to be beneficial to people in mental health terms or to become incorporated in harmful ways.

Bergin (1991) reviewed studies on values in the 10-year period since his 1980 review. This survey included his own studies with Jensen (Jensen & Bergin, 1988; Bergin & Jensen, 1990) where they asked a large sample of mental health professionals for their views on values and religion. They were surprised at the high level of consensus on 10 value themes that they would advocate for clients also. Examples were having a sense of identity and feelings of worth; being sensitive, nurturant, and trusting; and having self-control and personal responsibility.

Walls's value descriptions are termed "clinical-humanistic" and are based upon traditions of pragmatism and humanistic idealism. Clinical pragmatism implements the values of the dominant social system. It is centered on diminishing pathologies as defined by the client and therapist. Humanistic idealism emphasizes goals of change such as flexibility and self-exploration; independence; active goal orientation with self-actualization as a core goal; human dignity and self-worth; interpersonal involvement; truth and honesty; happiness; and framework or philosophy by which one guides one's life.

Ellis's concepts are similar to Walls's description of "clinical-humanistic." However, Ellis considers himself a "probabilistic atheist" who believes that since there is an exceptionally high probability that no gods or superhuman entities of any kind exist, we had better assume that they do not and live our lives according to this assumption. His "clinical-humanistic-atheistic" views provide a stronger contrast to theistic views than those described by Walls.

4. There is a significant contrast between the values of mental health professionals and those of a large proportion of clients. Therapists must take into account possible discrepancies between their values and those of their clients. Bergin (1980) suggests that the beliefs of mental health professionals are not very harmonious with those of the subcultures with which they deal, especially as they pertain to definitions of moral behavior and the relevance of moral behavior to societal integration, familial functioning, prevention of pathology, and the development of self. A potential danger of these differences is that conflict over values may lead to a poor therapeutic outcome. Clients may fear having their values changed or being misunderstood by their counselor. For example, Worthington and Scott (1983) identified six fears of conservative Christian clients that led to distrust of secular counselors. If value differences are unrecognized by the client and therapist, the client may become inculcated with the therapist's values without the awareness of either therapist or client. There is some research evidence showing that when counseling is effective, clients change their values in the direction of their counselor's values (Welkowitz, Cohen, & Ortmeyer, 1967; Beutler, Jobe, & Elkins, 1974). Beutler and his colleagues (1979) found that clients report more improvement when they change values to be more like their counselor's.

Kluckhohn and Strodtbeck (1961) studied the core values of individuals

TABLE 13-1. COMPARISON OF THREE VALUES IDEOLOGIES.

Theistic (Bergin, 1980)	Clinical-Humanistic Values	Clinical-Humanistic-Atheistic
God is supreme. Humility, acceptance of (divine) authority, and obedience (to the will of God) are virtues.	Humans are supreme. Individual freedom and responsibility form the basis for a cooperative society that recognizes each person's legitimate claims and obligations. Authority is derived from rational principles of justice.	No one and nothing is supreme. To aggrandize or rate the self is to be disturbed. A balance between autonomy and living cooperatively with others and a balance between rejecting and overconforming to external authority are virtues.
Personal identity is eternal and derived from the divine. Relationship with God defines self-worth.	Identity is defined by individuals according to self-chosen values. Self-worth is defined by one's relation to those values.	Personal identity is ephemeral and mortal. Relationships with others often provide increased happiness but never define self-worth. Nothing does. Self-worth, self-esteem, or rating one's "self" globally is a (theological) mistake, leading to disturbance. Self-acceptance can be had for the asking, independent of any god or human law.
Self-control in terms of absolute values. Strict morality. Universal ethics.	Self-expression in terms of universal values at the highest stages of development. Transcendent values are translated into laws, mores, and roles that allow those at different developmental stages to function cooperatively.	Self-expression in terms of relative values. Flexible morality. Situation ethics.
Love, affection, and self-transcendence are primary. Service and self-sacrifice are central to personal growth.	Self-actualization includes commitment to values that transcend personal needs and the ability to be motivated by socially relevant goals	Personal desires and self-actualization are to be sought within a social context. Increasing self-satisfaction, including social satisfaction and love, is central to personal growth.
Committed to marriage, fidelity, and loyalty. Emphasis on procreation and family life as integrative factors.		Choice of no marriage, conventional marriage, or open marriage. Emphasis on sex gratification with mutually chosen partners, with or without long-term responsibilities. Family life optional; often desirable but not necessary for health and happiness.
Personal responsibility for own harmful actions and changes in them. Acceptance of guilt, suffering, and contrition as keys to change. Restitution for harmful effects.	Individuals are responsible for their own actions and roles in society.	Personal responsibility for own harmful actions and changes in them. Maximizing responsibility for harmful and immoral acts and minimizing guilt (self-damnation in addition to denouncing one's acts). No apology or "cop-out" for effects of one's ethical behavior. Restitution for harmful effects.

Forgiveness of others who cause distress (including parents) completes the therapeutic restoration of self.

Forgiveness of others is based on the understanding of the difficulties of being human.

Forgiveness of others who cause needless distress (including parents) but no condonation of their acts. Unconditional acceptance or positive regard for all humans at all times, but clear-cut condemnation of their immoral behavior. Acceptance of self helped by unconditional acceptance of others.

Knowledge involves a conscientious effort to understand reality, which ultimately rests on faith. Meaning and purpose require that reason, intuition, emotion, and compassion operate harmoniously.

Adapted from Bergin, A. E. (1980). Psychotherapy and Religious Values, *Journal of Consulting and Clinical Psychology, 48* (1), p. 100; Walls, G. B. (1980). Values and Psychotherapy: A Comment on "Psychotherapy and Religious Values," *Journal of Consulting and Clinical Psychology, 48* (5), p. 641; and Ellis, A. E. (1980). Psychotherapy and Atheistic Values: A Response to A. E. Bergin's "Psychotherapy and Religious Values," *Journal of Consulting and Clinical Psychology, 48* (5), p. 636. Copyright 1980 by the American Psychological Association. Adapted by permission of the authors.

across cultures in an effort to develop a schema for organizing human values. These categories for understanding values, beliefs, and attitudes regarding people, their nature, the relationship between people and nature, and time and activity perspectives provide a useful framework for understanding the complexities of value orientations and have utility for assisting counselors in understanding themselves and their clients from different value systems. Ibrahim (1985, p. 629) has summarized these categories in Table 13-2. Ibrahim suggests that lack of understanding of one's own and one's clients' world views results in frustration and anxiety for both the counselor and client because the goals and processes considered appropriate by the therapist may be antithetical or meaningless to the client. In this sense, all counseling relationships should be considered as "cross-cultural" because it is important for the therapist to determine and work within (and perhaps help expand and edit) the client's value system.

5. *It is honest and ethical to acknowledge that we are implementing our own value systems via our professional work and to be more explicit about what we believe while also respecting the value systems of others.* Bergin suggests that we should be open with our clients about our belief systems so that clients can then decide whether possible differences in belief might be a difficulty in therapy. Many of us disregard our important role as value agents in therapy and see our work only as based on scientific technologies.

When counselors realize that their training, professional experience, or life experience is inadequate to deal with a client's problems, it is important to refer the client to another counselor. Occasionally a counselor will have strong countertransference toward a client's values such that it is difficult to accept the client

TABLE 13-2.   THE FIVE EXISTENTIAL CATEGORIES AND RANGE OF VARIATIONS.

Human Nature
How is human nature defined and characterized?
(a) Bad: Human nature is bad or evil.
(b) Good and Bad: Human nature is a combination of good and bad.
(c) Good: Human nature is good.
Human Relationships
How are human relationships defined?
(a) Lineal-Hierarchical: Ordered positional succession within the group, continuity through time and primacy of group goals.
(b) Collateral-Mutual: Primacy is given to goals and welfare of lateral extended groups.
(c) Individualistic: Primacy is given to individual goals.
People/Nature
What is the relationship of people to nature?
(a) Harmony: People and nature coexist in harmony.
(b) Subjugation and Control: People can subjugate and control nature.
(c) Power of Nature: Nature is powerful and controls people.
Time Orientation
What is the temporal focus of human life?
(a) Past: There is a focus on the past.
(b) Present: There is a focus on the present.
(c) Future: There is a focus on the future.
Activity Orientation
What is the modality of human activity (i.e., self-expression)?
(a) Being: There is a preference for activities that provide spontaneous expression of the self.
(b) Being-Becoming: There is an emphasis on activities that have as their goal development of all aspects of the self as an integrated being.
(c) Doing: There is a preference for activities that result in measurable accomplishments by external standards.

From Ibrahim, F. (1985). Effective cross-cultural counseling and therapy: A framework, *The Counseling Psychologist, 13* (4), p. 629, Table adapted in part from Green, L. and Haymes, M. (1973) in *Journal of Youth and Adolescence, 2,* 213–231 and Kluckhohn and Strodtbeck (1961). Variations in Value Orientations, Evanston, IL: Row, Peterson. Reprinted by permission of Sage Publications, Inc., and Plenum Publishing Corporation.

without needing to "clear up" or "reform" the client's thinking. At other times, the counselor may have such a different life experience that it is difficult to empathize or understand the client's experience. Sometimes, it may appear that the client might work better with a therapist with different professional training, such as a pastoral counselor, who might better understand the client's religious problems and provide more adequate information or interpretation. If the counselor finds that he or she is doing violence to his or her own or the client's belief system, the counselor then must face the issue frankly and refer.

6. It is our obligation as professionals to translate what we perceive and value intuitively into something that can be openly tested and evaluated. Bergin suggests that we recognize that many of our values are personal and subjective and are shaped by the culture with which we are most familiar. We should let them influence our professional work only to the extent that we can openly justify them. He suggests that we put our values to the test as research hypotheses. For example, he suggests that we research testable hypotheses such as "Disturbances in clinical cases will diminish as these individuals are encouraged to adopt forgiving attitudes toward parents and others who may have had a part in the development of their symptoms," or "Teaching clients love, commitment, service, and sacrifice for others will help heal interpersonal difficulties and reduce intrapsychic distress."

INCREASING CLIENT ETHICAL-MORAL BEHAVIOR

Client Dependence

Counselors are often put in a difficult position when clients expect more than help in gaining awareness, changing behavior, or receiving comfort. Many clients, in effect, beg counselors to tell them how to live, what kinds of persons they should be, how they can meet the vicissitudes and seeming meaninglessness of life. Frequently, clients expect counselors to relieve them of basic anxieties such as fear of nonbeing or death.

As indicated earlier, we are not proposing that counselors set themselves up as authorities on such questions, nor that they should yield to client demands for answers to basic questions by giving their personal philosophies. We believe the counselor's role is to help clients develop more functional processes for making value decisions based on reflection of the clients' ultimate values.

In the actualizing counseling model, the valuing process takes place primarily in the core of the person, with rational decision making largely an actualizing level function. In Fowler's terms, we are helping people move from synthetic-conventional faith toward a more individuative-reflective or conjunctive faith stage. This suggests that the person should look inward toward the core for value guidelines. He or she thus becomes "inner-directed" rather than "outer-directed." Outer-directed persons seek answers for value questions largely outside of themselves in codes and dogmas. They value expert opinion on these matters; so they look to authority and tradition for answers to difficult life questions. They attempt to please others through manipulative behaviors and operate largely at a rational facade level. One goal, then, of the actualizing process is to encourage people to look within for cues and guidelines and to learn to trust what they uncover from their core being. This does not mean turning inward for answers exclusively but to find the best balance between inner and outer criteria. The actualizing model offers a wide spectrum of methods to deal with this search for awareness and inner support as well as for decision-making skills in making value choices.

The process of learning, projecting, and incorporating values into a more differentiated belief system and philosophy of life, as we see it, is diagrammed in Figure 13-1. The beliefs in the core level (a) are learned during the growing-up process from values held by parents and others close to the person. These internalized external values (b) are reperceived later as external to the person since they are projections of previously learned values.

During this projection process (c), the core and the rational processes of the

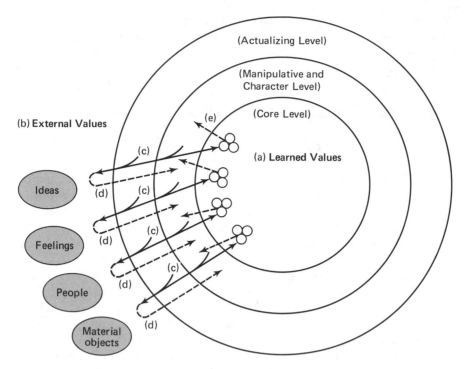

FIGURE 13-1 The Process of Developing a Philosophy of Life.

actualizing level modify the projected values so that there is no one-to-one relationship between the core values and the projected values. For example, people may project their security value system to external objects in such a way that they build their security around a bank account, a family member, or an ideology. Tennyson and Strom (1986) have suggested that the reasoning skills and dispositions related to ethical development are acquired best through critical self-reflection and dialogue with significant others about common problems.

The Counseling Tasks

The main task of the counselor is to help the client move through the steps of Figure 13-2. The first tasks are to encourage clients to *examine their implicit core values* and beliefs and to *be aware of how they are projecting* these core values and beliefs onto other persons and objects (Step a). Specific cognitive skills described in earlier chapters are problem definition, setting goals consonant with values, developing strategies to achieve goals, analysis of probable consequences of specific behaviors, and seeking new information.

The skills cited above also lead into the second step (b)—*clarification and evaluation of one's values.* This includes an analysis of the cultural context for the anticipated action and a redefinition of the central problem. This step includes

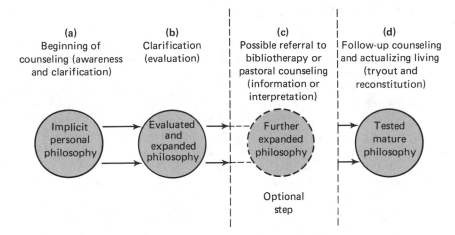

(a)	(b)	(c)	(d)
Beginning of counseling (awareness and clarification)	Clarification (evaluation)	Possible referral to bibliotherapy or pastoral counseling (information or interpretation)	Follow-up counseling and actualizing living (tryout and reconstitution)

FIGURE 13-2 The Role of Therapeutic Counseling in Value Problems.

awareness of the emotional attachments to these values. This clarification step will reveal contradictions, distortions, discrepancies, and hidden meanings behind decisions. Clients will be more aware of whether or not their problem-solving processes are consistent with their evolving values. Research by Fowler (1981) and Kohlberg (1981) suggests that development in thinking about moral situations is more than learning rules or laws. Their critical thinking skills will very likely reduce their dependence on external authority and avoid the tyranny of overdependence on their core values and beliefs. Questioning strategies described in Chapter 6 would be helpful in clarifying value decisions. For example, a counselor might ask clients to recall a decision that was or was not consistent with what they would want for themselves or for their loved ones. They could also be asked which alternative would produce the least amount of harm toward themselves or others. What people think they should do morally is not always what they decide to do. Research suggests that behaving according to one's morals and values is influenced largely by the strength of commitment to a value position, self-confidence, and self-efficacy (Rest, 1983).

If the processes cited above do not work, or the requisite skills are not present, an optional step (c) may be indicated. This could include *referral* to another type of counselor, such as pastor, physician, abuse counselor, or confrontation group experience. In some cases this would include the criminal justice system or similar experience coercing self-confrontation on values, or at least opening the possibilities for feeling remorseful or guilty.

The goal is to reach step d—the development of a tested and trusted value and belief system. The client reaching this point has the capacity for moral responsibility and the strength of character to act in ways consistent with his or her mature values. An optional following step might be to check one's emerging values with others to check for consensus. People do not build their value structures in a social vacuum.

Coping with Guilt

Guilt has two basic meanings. One is a kind of existential guilt for not living up to one's potential. It is experienced as a vague sense of "wrongness" accompanied by a string of "shoulds." "I should be doing something better or different," for example. The second type of guilt is feeling distressed over a specific act that is at variance with one's core values. The consequence often is awareness of feeling inadequate or a failure. Breaking social rules about lying, cheating, or stealing are examples. According to May (May, Angel, & Ellenberger, 1958), guilt is best understood if a differentiation is made between normal and neurotic guilt. Normal guilt is universal and is of three basic types: guilt against one's self for not fulfilling one's potentialities; guilt against one's fellow humans for not meeting their needs; and guilt against nature or God and a feeling of separateness or alienation therefrom. Neurotic guilt is defined as unaccepted and repressed normal guilt. Therapy, therefore, consists of assisting the client to accept and face his or her neurotic guilt and to turn it into normal guilt. This is in sharp contrast to the view that therapy should water down, expunge, or neutralize guilt entirely. While this subject is too vast to discuss adequately here, we wish to summarize the general steps counselors take to assist clients with their feelings of guilt. Since it is the guilt feeling that drives the client to seek counseling, we agree with May and colleagues above that the counselor should not try to help the client remove the guilty feelings entirely. The recommended steps are as follows:

1. Admit what the client has done to feel guilty and assess the type of guilt, as discussed above, that may be present.
2. Help the client to become aware of how his or her behavior has helped or hindered achieving goals or satisfying needs.
3. Help the client cut through the rationalizations, denials, and projections. This is the beginning of taking responsibility for his or her own behavior.
4. Assist clients to express normal feelings of guilt for admitted self-defeating behaviors and violation of their values. Thus, they can see the possibilities of closing the gap between their present self-image and their behavior.
5. Discuss how clients might change their behavior to reduce present and future guilt and suffering.

The steps outlined above suit the usual normally guilty client. There are distorted forms of guilt that require extensive psychotherapy. Examples are the overdeveloped conscience, projected blame, extreme need for self-punishment, or pharisaical self-righteousness.

PSYCHOTHERAPY AND TRANSCENDENT VALUES

Another purpose of this chapter is to examine some of the relationships between therapeutic psychology and religious issues. Religion includes any set of beliefs, symbols, or rituals that interpret human experience (past, present, and future) in a transcendental fashion. Thus, spirituality involves a person's experience of dimensions of power, love, and meaning transcendent to the world of sensory reality. Transcendent experiences may be "peak" or mystical experiences of higher consciousness, such as those reported by survivors of clinical death (Ring, 1984). In therapeutic psychology, we seek an understanding of how clients integrate transcendent experiences into their lives and how their behavior is congruent with their transcendent beliefs.

We prefer Wrenn's description of the two approaches: "Religion and psychology complement each other. Psychology contributes to an understanding of the nature of self and of one's relationships with others, religion to an understanding of the meaning and purpose in life, and the significance of these same relationships. Both may contribute to more effective living" (1958, p. 331).

In the psychological literature generally, there has been an awakening interest in philosophical problems underlying the psychological study of persons. Bergin (1980, p. 96) has noted that

> the emergence of studies of consciousness and cognition, which grew out of disillusionment with mechanistic behaviorism and the growth of humanistic psychology, has set the stage for a new examination of the possibility that presently unobservable realities—namely, spiritual forces—are at work in human behavior . . . Although there has always been a keen interest in such matters among a minority of thinkers and practitioners (Allport, 1950; James, 1902; Jung, 1958; Mowrer, 1957; the pastoral counseling field, etc.), they have not substantially influenced mainstream psychology (p. 95). Bergin believes the present phenomenon has all the aspects of a broad-based movement with a building momentum. Carl Rogers (1973, p. 386) also challenged us to consider other dimensions of human reality, stating, "There may be a few who will dare to investigate the possibility that there is a lawful reality which is not open to our five senses; a reality in which present, past, and future are intermingled, in which space is not a barrier and time has disappeared. . . . It is one of the most exciting challenges posed to psychology."

Psychologists' interest in spiritual matters is indicated also by an increase in transcendental meditation, the organization and rapid growth of the American Psychological Association's Division 36 (Psychologists Interested in Religious Issues), the Association for Religious and Value Issues in Counseling, and the publication of new journals with overtly spiritual contents, such as the *Journal of Judaism and Psychology, Journal of Transpersonal Psychology*, the *Journal of Theology and Psychology*, and *Counseling and Values*. Transpersonal psychologists (Tart, 1975; Wilber, 1979, 1983; Boorstein, 1980) have sought to expand psychological inquiry into the farther reaches and altered states of human consciousness. They have studied meditation, trance, and mystical experiences found in many religious traditions. This interest is also manifested by the publication of religious psychologies by academicians such as Jeeves (1976), May (1982a, 1982b), Collins (1977), Peck (1978), and Myers (1978). Additionally, the value of therapy and the values that pervade its processes have become topics of research (Bellah et al., 1985; Lowe, 1976; London, 1986; Szasz, 1978; Watts, 1961; Bergin, 1991).

Psychological counselors have been reluctant to face the possibility that they might have functions and responsibilities that could be termed broadly as *religious*. This reluctance has been due to their cautious empirical tradition, basic philosophical differences between social science and theology, alleged emotional extremism, and hypocrisy in some organized religious behavior. The counselor's own spiritual ignorance or conflict has been an additional barrier. More psychological counselors are recognizing, however, that religious sentiments and feelings are powerful positive or negative motives in their clients' lives.

Traditionally, psychology has been biologically oriented. The early models and scientific procedures of the late 19th century were based on physiology and physics. Darwinian philosophy had considerable influence on behavioral psychologists' view of humankind as a continuation of the animal world, subject to the same natural laws. Early American psychology added a functional note to the biological models imported from Germany. There was a very strong effort to divorce psychology from its earlier philosophical roots and to make the understanding of behavior a strictly scientific venture.

We do not advocate a return to rationalistic and other philosophical methods as a substitute for careful observation and rigorous experimentation. Psychology as a science must remain firmly planted in scientific methods and critical thinking. We are in accord, however, with the trend in psychological services to examine the methods and assumptions of psychology in regard to their adequacy for understanding basic human problems and helping people to deal with them more effectively. We must be careful not to make premature and unrealistic demands on such an infant endeavor as therapeutic psychology.

The assumption that it is necessary to go beyond empirically validated psychological methods in helping clients with value problems puts the therapeutic psychologist squarely in the area of traditional religious concern. Here again, the history of psychology at some points has run counter to formal religion. Psychologists looked with suspicion on colleagues who had any strong personal religious beliefs. They were automatically suspect because of the assumed interference these beliefs had with an attitude of objectivity so necessary for their profession.

Jung's attitude toward religion, contrary to Freud's, was that the client's present belief system should be used in such a way that it would hasten his or her recovery of mental health. Jung is reputed to have advocated finding God within experience as part of the individuation process (Glover, 1950). The "God within" the racial unconscious of the Jungian system is then equated by many persons with a transcendental "God without." Jung admits that it is not the business of the psychologist to establish or even investigate objective truth regarding the existence of God. He states, furthermore, that neither is it the psychologist's business to construct a pseudoreligion out of primitive yearnings or myths. Jung tried to stay close to empirical facts in this realm and to concentrate on the oak rather than on the acorn (1933).

Interdisciplinary Relationships

As we mentioned previously in our discussion of "ultimate concern," it seems that one must recognize that religious faith and psychological concepts are not mutually exclusive. One must not assume that either religious concern or psychological interpretation is the total solution to, or explanation of, humanity's problems. Many people put this proposition into the form of an uncomfortable dichotomy. They feel inclined either to reject psychological interpretations and explanations of behavior or to reject their religious belief system. There seems to be a third position for confused clients. This view is that there is considerable overlap and common bases of interest as well as conflict between the psychological and theological views of personal reality. For example, the value systems might agree on the importance of love, balancing autonomy and conformity, developing one's personal potential, developing personal responsibility, and commitment to human rights and social justice. One should recognize these points of overlap and conflict, then look assiduously for areas where the meanings are congruent and seem to give greater combined insight into human existence and the solution of human problems.

The research literature that studied correlations between religion and mental well-being is contradictory and ambiguous. The failure to differentiate the diverse contents and processes of religious life has resulted in divergent results. It appears that there are benevolent aspects of religious experience as well as factors that can be detrimental to certain individuals. It is difficult to judge these factors without comparing similar characteristics in nonreligious persons. Many of the characteristics thought to be detrimental (such as dogmatism, incongruence, irrationality, and hypocrisy) from religious persons are attributions that may also prove detrimental in evaluating nonreligious persons with similar characteristics. Bergin (1991) reviewed the research on the relationship between religiosity and mental health problems. The evidence is conflicting, but Bergin did not find a correlation between religion and mental illness.

Integrating Psychological and Religious Approaches to Counseling

A variety of examples of integration of psychological and religious approaches can be found. They include therapists practicing from Eastern, Western, and noninstitutional religious traditions. Worthington (1986) has identified three competing views about what constitutes use of religious counseling techniques. Proponents of the first view suggest that any secular technique used in counseling can be "religious" since it can promote the client's growth within a religious counseling context. Lovinger (1979, 1984), writing from a psychoanalytic position and a Jewish perspective, describes use of secular techniques with religious clients. Noble (1987) suggests that the aftermath of peak or mystical experiences often involves a grief and loss reaction parallel to adjusting to a major life crisis. Many techniques utilized to work through disequilibrium and loss can be employed in helping clients integrate a transcendent experience into their lives.

A second view tends to adapt techniques to fit a religious belief system or utilize religious practices in a therapeutic way. McGuire (1980) draws on Buddhist tradition utilizing techniques of meditation, koans (paradoxes), and assuming the role of a Buddhist master in an attempt to "shock the disciple out of the patterns of thought and rationality that hold the individual in bondage" (p. 583). Morita therapy (Reynolds, 1976; Ishiyama, 1986), a treatment which encourages anxious clients to relinquish self-control, is congruent with Taoistic and Zen Buddhist perspectives on life. Khan (1982) introduces Sufi concepts of personal transformation into counseling and psychotherapy. Strong (1980), from a Christian tradition, recommends prayer, confession, forgiveness, and encouragement to the client to behave more positively in the future.

A third view adapts secular theories to be compatible with religious assumptions. Counseling techniques may utilize religious content and be used to strengthen the client's faith as well as alleviate distress. For example, Crabb (1977), Worthington (1982, 1989), and Miller and Martin (1988) have integrated cognitive-behavioral techniques and spiritual approaches to change. Maloney (1980) and Lawrence (1983) have adapted transactional analysis to Christian assumptions. Collins (1980) describes a variety of approaches toward adapting secular theories to religious assumptions. Much of the writing on psychology and religious integration in the United States reflects our country's primary Hebraic-Christian heritage. However, as our population becomes more religiously diverse, there are likely to be increased writings reflecting psychology's integration with other religious traditions.

We would like to examine two examples of integrative counseling approaches in more depth—Yogic and Christian. There are many others, (for example, Hebraic, Buddhist, Islamic, Shinto, and Animist), but space does not permit more than two examples. Yoga psychology (Rama, Ballentine, & Ajaya, 1976; Ajaya, 1983) approaches psychotherapy from Eastern yogic traditions. The integrative approach of pastoral counselor Merle Jordan (1986) patterns an understanding of the therapeutic process on key Christian theological concepts. Both therapies integrate therapeutic interventions of behavioral, psychoanalytic, phenomenological, and systems approaches with transcendent religious assumptions. These approaches illustrate how therapists might help clients to deal with distortions of religious understandings from within the context of the client's own religious tradition.

Yogic Psychotherapy.   Yogic psychotherapy is based on a variety of Hindu religious writings such as the Vedic, the Upanishads, and the Gita. Its philosophy emphasizes the evolution of mental and physical consciousness. In much the same way that an environmentalist would be concerned with restoring a polluted lake to its natural state of purity and equilibrium, the yoga therapist is interested in leading a person from the experience of inner disturbance or pollution to the pure consciousness of equilibrium and tranquility.

True self-realization is found through processes of self-mastery and purification. Growth and evolution toward higher consciousness consist of discarding false beliefs and assumptions and recognizing what one's identity is and always has been. At the highest levels of consciousness, the individual experiences a transpersonal unity of consciousness with others but does not lose his or her own personal identity. One can also differentiate between an identity based on role identification and one's true or core self.

A fundamental tenet of yoga therapy is that there is body-mind-spirit integration. Purification must be holistic. The therapist utilizes yogic training in self-awareness and self-regulation of the body. In the progression toward greater consciousness, each step builds on the previous level of mastery and works in synergy toward greater self-mastery.

Self-mastery helps the client learn to live at higher levels of consciousness. The individual progresses through different centers of consciousness (chakras). The initial phase of yoga therapy consists of purifying the person from body toxins it cannot assimilate and thoughts that do not reflect the true underlying reality. This phase of therapy often incorporates body work because this provides a concrete experience of self-control. For example, the yoga therapist might assign a diet of particular food categories intended to elicit desired emotional outcomes. Some foods are thought to create restlessness and disturbance, others to create lethargy and dullness, and still others to lead to a peaceful, joyful, relaxed yet energetic state. Hatha yoga would be used to break down bodily "character armor" and emotional blocks that accompany characterological muscle tension. Posture is viewed as an expression of psychological states. By practicing different postures, the client brings forth new emotional expression. Hatha yoga also helps increase relaxation and reduce anxiety and psychosomatic complaints through releasing repressed emotionality.

Habit control is an important element of self-mastery. In learning new habits, the client does not concentrate on the undesirable habit. Rather, she or he turns attention to establishing a more desirable habit in its place. By repeatedly engaging in a new behavior that is incompatible with and antithetical to the undesirable habit, the old behavior pattern is extinguished.

The next step in the progressive path toward total self-mastery focuses on work with breathing practices, which can lead to control of the energy that underlies all physical and mental activity. Through yoga, one learns to consciously alter one's breathing patterns and thus enhance one's emotional state. In yoga therapy, the energy system is something of a cross between Freud's concept of "libido" and Reich's more physical "orgone" energy. The development and exploration of higher states of consciousness demand higher levels of energy. Through yoga and breathing exercises, clients learn to better channel their energy in ways that help conserve and restore energy. The client learns to regulate sensory input so that information from the sensory organs does not distract the mind from observation of itself.

During the final steps of yoga therapy the student learns increased mental concentration. As one's behavior, body, energy, and senses have been mastered, the student becomes ready to focus attention toward directing and controlling the thoughts that come before the mind and distract it. This work is achieved through raja yoga to develop concentration and a deep contemplation, known as samadhi, the highest state of consciousness.

Meditation may be used to help disentangle the client from distractions and worries. Raja yoga purification often involves meditation on principles concerned with *interpersonal relations,* such as noninjury, nonlying, and nongreed, and *internal purification* such as contentment, austerity, and self-study.

Nonattachment, a key concept in yoga therapy, refers to maintaining objectivity rather than becoming emotionally engulfed by situations. Nonattachment is facilitated by assuming responsibility for one's Karma. The notion of Karma suggests that we create or place ourselves into a particular situation because it is the best possible learning experience for us at that time. There are no good and bad experiences. Rather, every experience has an equal potential for helping us to learn and develop.

In yoga therapy, the psychotherapy itself usually focuses on the psychological and spiritual concerns of the client. The therapist may meet with a client individually, or may meet with a couple or with a family. The yoga therapist may choose from a wide array of therapeutic interventions. If he or she has the resources of an ashram, or residential community, there may be opportunity for regular practice in each aspect of yoga therapy including diet, hatha yoga postures, breathing, meditation, solitude, self-study, and ego transcendence. There is also a chance to deal with projections and transference in interpersonal relations. Often, a client working with a yoga therapist has been learning hatha yoga, correct breathing, meditation, and other yogic techniques in classes and is practicing each day outside of the therapy session.

Psychotherapy in the Christian Tradition. Pastoral psychotherapy in the Christian tradition is built on Christian premises that a personal, loving God offers forgiveness and reconciliation to heal a relationship broken by human worship of other idols. Jordan describes his approach as "incarnational" in that an accepting counselor becomes a paradigm of God's grace in accepting people even when they are unacceptable. Jordan (1986, p. 70) states,

> Theologically, one might say that God created the children of the earth to be loved and confirmed in all their uniqueness and realness. The nature of God's love is to affirm each person's unique identity and to provide a holding, caring environment for each, that each might blossom in his or her own special way. The therapeutic process is in many ways a corrective to faulty child-rearing practices, with the counselor mediating more of the nature of the divine parent who can love the individual into his or her true and authentic self. The false self and neurotic adaptations can then be surrendered, because self-destructive personality sacrifice is not required by the Eternal Heart.

Although it is not essential in Jordan's approach to utilize Christian language, the therapist may use overt Christian language, religious practices, or rituals and can adapt secular techniques to serve the counseling purposes.

Jordan views his approach as representing an "encounter between gods." This encounter is a confrontation with the psychic structures, forces and images that masquerade as God but that represent an unhealthy idolatry. Jordan terms his approach as "clinical or operational theology" because he draws upon the implicit religious story by which a person is living.

Jordan believes that self-concept always goes hand-in-hand with one's concept of ultimate authority. A person is largely defined by what he or she places at the center and ground of his or her personality. Distorted and false perceptions of ultimate authority become directly linked with erroneous definitions and beliefs about one's self, one's identity, and one's worth. False authority images, termed *idolatry*, are usually derived from developmental experiences with one or more parental figures and are projected onto God (as in Fowler's first three faith development stages). This idolatrous view of ultimate reality becomes directly related to one's self-image. The experience of affirming parents, and thus a loving God, for example, fosters a more positive self-concept than that of critical parents whose projection becomes a weak, impotent, or judgmental God who doesn't empower and affirm.

In order to survive in the symbolic world governed by a false ultimate authority, an individual has to construct a second idolatry around the self. This second idolatry is a reaction to the first idolatrous misperception of the nature of God. It can be thought of as a defensive *strategy of salvation,* or an attempt to provide one's own rescue in the face of a negative view of reality. These "salvation" attempts might involve many possible patterns: using repression, depression, and somatic symptoms to crucify part of one's personality, offering some kind of good works (becoming a submissive care giver) to pacify and maintain a relationship with the perceived god, or efforts to overthrow idolatrous authority by engaging in acting out and rebellious behaviors.

A *covenant* of invisible loyalty often binds the person and the idol. This includes an unconscious set of rules to live by. The covenant can be considered as similar to the script messages of transactional analysis. Examples of covenant rules are, "You have to be nice all the time. You have to work hard every minute or you are not worthwhile. You can never love anyone but me." In actualization therapy, these are messages within the core of the person.

The teachings, values, and beliefs transmitted by the idol are referred to as *secular scriptures* since they are experienced as divine truth even though they are destructive lies. These are injunctions and shoulds, similar in nature to Ellis's irrational beliefs or the cognitive distortions discussed in cognitive-behavioral psychology. They often include value statements about how feelings such as sadness, anger, and joy are wrong and unacceptable. The ongoing dialogue between the client and the idol is referred to as *secular prayer.* Secular prayers often express desires to be able to avoid pain, fear, vulnerability, and risk.

The therapist will borrow interventions from object relations theory, cognitive-behavioral psychology, person-centered, Gestalt, and family systems theory to challenge and confront idolatrous covenants, secular scriptures, and prayers while maintaining an accepting stance with the client. The therapist may also use Biblical stories or references to challenge the client's idolatrous covenants and encourage development of a new covenant. Whether or not the therapist uses religious language per se, it is intended that the client will have an *experience* of God's personal love through the person of the therapist. It is hoped that over time the client will gain a new perception of ultimate authority and will develop a genuine hope in a loving God.

Transcendent approaches to psychotherapy, such as those described above, seek to integrate therapy with a consciousness which transcends the individual. For example, in Eastern religious psychologies, counseling aims toward helping the client experience unity with a transpersonal consciousness. In Christian psychotherapy, the individual is asked to draw upon the mystery of God's love which is present as the "depth" or "horizon" backdrop of all human experience. As in Fowler's developmental model, individuals within these faith traditions mature through a process of differentiation in which they show greater empathy with others while at the same time derive an increasingly self-reflective set of values.

When it comes to values derived from contact with the ultimate mystery of the universe, religions are united by shared values of deep concerns for faith, meditation, simplicity, humility, gratitude, and service. "Faith," the personal experience of the transcendent, unites individuals across religious boundaries. "Beliefs," the intellectual expression of transcendent experience, involve significant points of difference. In psychotherapy with religious clients, there may be unified emphases on values and experiences across religious traditions; yet counselors will need to integrate their approaches with differing belief systems.

Considerations in Counseling Religious Clients

In serving religious clients it is important for therapists to consider the differences within groups of religious clients and not treat religious clients uniformly. Worthington (1986) suggests differentiation must be made by (a) religion (e.g., Christian, Jewish, Hindu, Moslem); (b) denominational affiliation (e.g., Catholics differ from Baptists, Orthodox Jews differ from Reformed or Conservative Jews); (c) commitment (e.g., religious people differ according to their commitment to devotional practices, theological beliefs, dogma of the church, religious behavior, and the degree to which religion is included in daily life); and (d) individual values, especially attitudes toward human authority, authority of sacred writings, and tolerance of different opinions and life styles.

In working with religious clients, it is important to remember it is on *persons* and not religion that we ought to focus. Religions are cumulative traditions with many elements: laws, rituals, myths, symbols, priesthoods, and doctrines. We can study all these things and yet miss an understanding of the person who lives within the tradition. Fischer and Hart (1986) suggest we must ask ourselves questions such as, What does it feel like to be a Jew, a Buddhist, or a Muslim? How does one view the universe, oneself, other people, the transcendent? What does one make of relationships, death, sexuality, and work? How does one express life's deepest values? How does one conduct oneself in the world? As we ask these questions of individuals, we begin to understand the individual's experience of the transcendent.

Teams of therapists representing both differing values and mental health disciplines can be useful in providing an interdisciplinary point of view in which professionals can work together. Each professional can provide a distinct but overlapping view of the client's difficulties as well as suggestions for possible treatment interventions. Religious clients often have a problem of overcoming their fear of secular counselors. They fear that either they will be misunderstood and considered naive or their faith will be threatened (Worthington, 1989).

Additionally, churches, synagogues, and other faith communities can be enhanced by actualizing groups. A church, synagogue, or temple traditionally has been a community of people enhancing one another's growth, but critics of highly institutionalized churches feel that this *koinonia,* or fellowship of persons, has been lost. The actualizing approach described in this and previous chapters is one way to recapture the spirit. Actualization groups conducted by ministers, understanding therapeutic psychologists, and/or experienced lay leaders can provide a vehicle for members to experience the rewards of peace, joy, and a renewed sense of community and commitment. Participants have possibilities for reexamination of their values, rediscovery and enhancement of their human dignity and worth, and respect for the "thou-ness" of others. Actualization groups in churches are more, therefore, than conventional encounter groups. Many of the foundations of small group community as part of a larger faith community are described by Peck (1987). Mowrer's "integrity groups" (1964) were efforts to repair damaged relationships through a kind of expiation process that involved confession of one's transgressions. In this sense they were similar to Alcoholics Anonymous groups. Mowrer, a psychologist, used theological language to explain the process of recovery from conflict and guilt.

Mowrer (1964) has shown that the original Christian church was a small group movement. The faithful would meet secretly in caves to discuss their mutual concerns. The modern church and other spiritual communities must revitalize the spirit of the small group sharing if they are to remain relevant for modern persons. It is our thesis that the actualizing process is a way to recapture this spirit. Efforts in this direction are the marriage enrichment programs of several denominations.

Introduction of the actualizing process through group techniques has produced results in several church-affiliated studies. Reddy (1972) has reported the effects of a five-day residential human relations training program for 40 interdenominational missionaries preparing for foreign service. He found significant increases in self-actualizing behaviors as defined by the POI. Knapp and Fitzgerald (1973) showed gains in actualizing behaviors with the Navy Chaplain Corps in an eclectic transgenerational workshop program with navy personnel. This program was established with the particular objective of building an increased sense of community among those persons whose feelings of alienation had led to such unsatisfactory behavioral expressions as drug abuse or alcohol addiction. Again, results from administration of the POI before and after the workshop demonstrate the positive effectiveness of programs of this type. Life-review programs, where older adults in particular review their lives in terms of paths chosen, fulfilled and unfulfilled aspirations, and potentials to be realized are potent vehicles for spiritual growth. Through such experiences, conducted by trained and sensitive clergy, participants had the opportunity to reexamine their personal values, to rediscover and enhance their dignity and worth, and to regain their respect for others.

GROWTH POTENTIAL IN CONFRONTING VALUES PROBLEMS

Confronting complex values decisions can be very difficult for clients and therapists. As each of us moves along our own faith development pilgrimage, there are many valleys, peaks, and frequent feeling that we have lost the trail completely. Kunkel (1954) has developed a point of view on handling real or projected values crises, which is beneficial for the therapeutic psychologist. Kunkel's thesis is that people learn to face larger crises in life by a process of meeting minor life crises from early childhood on through development. He sees human life as one "unending chain of crises" (1954, p. 150). Old thoughts, feelings, and behavior patterns are disrupted and discarded for new patterns required by the crises. Current life transition theory supports this idea that people can and do learn much from facing life crises (Brammer & Abrego, 1981; Brammer, 1991). The feelings of creativity and confidence that come out of a crisis solution constitute an important part of personality growth. Client experience of crisis, desperation, and helplessness is the prelude to critical examination and transformation of their life style. Suffering is regarded as a facilitative force in their growth.

Crises require judgments and, usually, bring out strengths in judgment the person did not realize before the crisis. The process of making value judgments that propel people forward in their mastery of life draws on many positive elements of personality and demands a high level of functioning. Each life crisis of values and meaning has a rich potentiality for building additional personal strength.

What can be said about the person who does not respond positively to crises and ends with feelings of inadequacy, failure, and incapacity to meet crises? The whole problem of the client's life style, creative potential, life philosophy, and religious outlook must be considered in a counseling relationship. Through counseling, clients may become more aware of their defenses and their problems of developing spiritual strength for meeting life crises. An example is the situation in which a client projected onto God certain expectations of the help provided by his mother. When the crisis came and mother was not nearby to nurse his hurt, he blamed God, who had become equated psychologically with mother. He began to see that his inadequacies in meeting life demands and crises were rooted in his own immaturity and fear of psychological and spiritual creativity. The therapeutic psychologist thus utilizes the life crisis to help the client become more aware and to make changes in outlook and behavior.

A critical factor in achieving these growth objectives, as indicated so many times in this volume, is the growth relationship itself. The opportunity to face feelings of doubt, inadequacy, insecurity, and defeat in the presence of a counselor in relationship is what seems to us to be the primary factor in drawing forth a client's new powers to meet life's challenges. This discovery of feelings of confidence and creative power is what Kunkel has called the "miraculous center of every constructive crisis" (1954, p. 163). The alternatives to this creative experience are continued feelings of discouragement, defeat, and emptiness, often leading to personality deterioration.

SUMMARY

In the science and profession of psychology, keen interest is being exhibited in problems of value. This chapter included a discussion of a theory of faith development over the life span. The counselor was described as someone who could enhance more complex and differentiated ethical thinking and behavior in clients. A process for helping clients become aware of value choices, weigh alternatives, and act on their beliefs was described. The problem of guilt arising through value decisions was addressed.

We considered particular ways in which values become intertwined with the process of counseling. Counseling is a value-laden process and it is imperative for counselors to become sensitized to the value implications in therapy and to be clear with themselves and their clients about their beliefs.

There is increased interest among professional counselors in spiritual dimensions of counseling. Several ways of integrating psychological and spiritual dimensions in therapy were described. Community building through small faith sharing groups was encouraged as a means for clarifying and enhancing values.

CHAPTER 14

Professional Counseling and Psychotherapy

Therapeutic psychology represents a body of knowledge that gathers its data from various related professions. This chapter describes various professional disciplines and the current status and trends in therapeutic psychology. We hope that it will provide the student with a broader understanding of the relatedness and uniqueness of the helping professions as well as the current professional trends that are impacting all disciplines.

PROFESSIONAL GROUPS ASSOCIATED WITH THERAPEUTIC PSYCHOLOGY

Therapeutic psychology has its roots in many disciplines. The following historical sketch covers the development of therapeutic psychology as a socially responsible service and illustrates how selected human service fields are related to therapeutic psychology.

Counseling Psychology

Counseling psychology is a psychological speciality in which practitioners help others improve their well-being, alleviate their distress, resolve their crises, and increase their ability to solve problems and make decisions. Counseling psychologists enable and facilitate psychological growth and development by helping others better use existing resources and skills, or by guiding them in developing new ways to help themselves.

Counseling psychologists apply systematic, research-based approaches to help themselves and others understand problems and develop potential solutions to them. Problems which lead people to seek the services of the counseling psychologist arise from environmental influences or from specific conflicts between or within persons or groups. The problems may be vocational, educational, emotional, social, health-related, or developmental in nature. (Division 17, American Psychological Association, 1984)

Counseling psychology seems to be moving closer to clinical psychology as this latter specialty concerns itself more with personal assets and less with behavior pathology. Training programs often use the title *professional-scientific* or *professional psychologist* to blur the distinctions further.

The Educational Testing Service (ETS), under contract with the American Association of State Psychology Boards, conducted a major job analysis of licensed psychologists in the United States (Rosenfield, Shimberg, & Thornton, 1983). The ETS study found relatively few differences among psychologists' training and job functions in various work settings, thus supporting the view that the four major specialties (i.e., clinical, counseling, school, and industrial/organizational) do not differ substantially from one another. Fitzgerald and Osipow's (1986) later survey found that most counseling psychologists are employed primarily in academic settings. The second most common form of employment was in direct service in health care and independent practice. When actual work settings and work behaviors were examined, the data suggested that counseling psychologists were involved primarily in counseling and secondarily in teaching and research. The researchers concluded that counseling psychology appears to be an increasingly applied specialty. Second, career counseling appears to be diminishing as the traditional foundation for the discipline. Finally, few empirical bases on which to distinguish counseling psychologists from their colleagues in clinical psychology on training or service delivery were found. These findings add credence to our earlier assertion that counseling and clinical psychology are converging rapidly.

The outlook generally appears optimistic about the continuing need for counseling psychologists. Their flexible, open approach to meeting client needs in a variety of settings and their emphasis upon improving client functioning and personal decision-making skills are needed in the current climate of preoccupation with mental illness and irresponsible behavior. Primary prevention of mental health problems is a key function of the counseling psychologist. Kagan called the counseling psychologist "mental health's primary care worker" (Kagan, 1977). Current American and Canadian health policy, as reflected through government agencies, stresses the prevention of mental and physical illness. Counseling psychologists are in the front of this crusade for promotion of healthful living.

The vitality of a profession must be judged also on how it deals with issues of social justice and equality. The Division of Counseling Psychology as well as the American Psychological Association have had active task groups working on women's issues, child and elder welfare, and minority concerns. An example is "Cross-Cultural Counseling Competencies" (Sue, 1981).

Counseling psychologists also have taken a strong lead in developing counseling programs for women. Three special issues of *The Counseling Psychologist* have been devoted exclusively to counseling women. The APA Counseling Psychology Division's Committee on Women developed "Principles Concerning the Counseling and Therapy of Women" (1979) with a revision in press (1992). Not only were these principles endorsed by the entire membership of counseling psychologists but they were adopted by other human service groups. A task force of the same committee produced a special report on "Models of Training Counselors of Women" (Johnson & Richardson, 1981). This report deals with the special problems created when most consumers of counseling and therapy services are women and most service providers are men. The report points up the need to reduce male bias and raise the consciousness of male counselors about the special concerns of women.

The APA's Division on Counseling Psychology is working continuously on defining counseling psychology and roles for counseling psychologists. The identity and future of counseling psychology have been examined and clarified through a series of three national conferences, the most recent of which was the Georgia National Conference for Counseling Psychology (1988). Whiteley and others (1980, 1984) have documented historical trends and future directions for the profession.

Other occupational designations for counselors have been made. It is quite apparent that the term *counselor* must be preceded by an adjective to be meaningful, since so many persons with differing skill levels claim to do "counseling." Other terms have been suggested to describe the psychological counseling function—clinical counselor, psychological counselor, psychotherapeutic counselor, community counselor, and psychosocial educator. Employment service, substance-abuse, multicultural, rehabilitation, family, and gay/lesbian are additional titles of counselors serving specific populations.

Clinical Psychology

Clinical psychology grew largely out of intelligence testing efforts from 1912 to 1930. Clinical psychology and counseling psychology have much in common, since both use case study methods, evaluation instruments, and psychotherapeutic interviewing techniques. A comparison of survey responses by both counseling and clinical psychologists (Watkins, Lopez, Campbell, & Himmell, 1986) found areas of difference and convergence among the two groups. Both groups tended to be oriented toward clinical practice. Counseling psychologists were employed more in higher education, while clinical psychologists were more frequently employed in health care settings. Both groups were involved increasingly in independent practice. Both counseling and clinical psychologists identified their theoretical orientation as eclectic. However, clinical psychologists more frequently endorsed a traditional analytic/dynamic theoretical orientation whereas counseling psychologists more frequently endorsed a cognitive or person-centered orientation.

Clinical psychology has had its periodic training and role-definition conferences similar to those of counseling psychology. Boulder, Miami, Chicago, and Vail have been locations for crucial conferences of leaders in the education of clinicians. These conferences have reflected a growing shift from almost exclusive concern about responsibility to the individual client to a much more widespread concern about responsibility to the broader community and public interest. Clinical psychology has specialty standards comparable to those of counseling psychology and credentialing programs for practitioners similar to those of counseling psychologists.

Psychiatry

Psychiatry, a third psychotherapeutic counseling specialty, is difficult to distinguish functionally from other counseling specialties. The obvious distinction is one of differential training—the psychiatrist having an M.D. degree and the psychologist generally having a Ph.D. Medical therapies used in the treatment of severe emotional conditions contribute other clear distinctions. Prescriptions of drugs, for example, can be done only by psychiatrists, although at this writing limited prescription authority for psychoactive drugs is under active consideration by psychologists.

Another approach to differentiating forms of therapeutic help is to look at traditional professional roles and responsibilities. Figure 14-1 shows the great overlap that exists between psychology and psychiatry, as well as some of the unique functions of medical therapists on the extreme left and of psychologists and counselors on the extreme right. The reeducative or psychotherapeutic functions shared by both groups are listed in the middle with factors to be considered in determining responsibility for psychotherapy.

There are psychiatrists who claim that all psychotherapy is medicine and would crowd counselors and clinical psychologists to the extreme right of Figure 14-1. Some psychologists and educators would do the same for physicians. We feel there are logical and practical reasons for sharing responsibility in psychotherapy, especially with the growing emphasis upon holistic health and the prevention of disease through altered life styles. The answer, in our opinion, lies in making carefully defined distinctions around the middle transitional area of Figure 14-1. The criteria of depth, training, experience, responsibility, and institutional setting should determine who does psychotherapy and to what degree.

Counselors and psychotherapists cannot escape the reality of medical responsibility. The physician has legal responsibility for care, which has life or death implications for the individual. From one point of view, this concept embraces all of life's activities. From another view, the psychiatrically trained physician's responsibility covers psychotherapy mainly to the point where the problem becomes one of ignorance or learning rather than one of illness. Fine distinctions between ignorance and illness, however, become very vague in practice. Szasz (1960) created considerable controversy the past three decades with his emphasis upon severe emotional problems as disorders of learning and perception rather

FIGURE 14-1. THERAPY CONTINUUM BETWEEN MEDICINE AND PSYCHOLOGY.

Psychiatry and Neurology (Medicine)		*Counseling—Clinical (Psychology)*
Treatment of severe dysfunction, involving, for example: Psychosurgery Electro-shock Clinical pharmacology Vitamins	Psychotherapy or reeducation Criteria applied to determine the locus of responsibility in a medical or psychological therapist *Therapist factors:* Amount of training in psychotherapy Experience in psychotherapy Diagnostic skill and knowledge of psychotherapy Amount of therapeutic responsibility delegated by the institution Type of institutional setting (hospital or school) Legal restrictions *Patient or client factors:* Depth of involvement in the personality Rigidity of defense structure Strength of the ego and other personality resources Somatic involvement Incapacitating nature of the symptoms Nature of therapeutic goal	*Planning and problem solution, involving, for example:* Diagnostic and predictive psychological tests Informational resources Interpretation of data *Learning difficulties, involving:* Remedial techniques Diagnostic psychological tests *Feeling problems, including:* Working through situational anxiety, hostility, ambivalence, and their nonincapacitating, nonimbedded symptoms Case studies and descriptions of personality functioning through use of psychometric tests

than illness in the traditional medical meaning. Szasz, a physician, certainly recognizes that there are brain diseases that affect behavior profoundly. He objects to the mental illness idea that all disorders of thought and feeling are related to some neurological defect. Problems of living, from this viewpoint, are reduced to a biochemical process that will be discovered ultimately. Such difficulties in everyday living, or differences in belief or value causing personal problems, are then by definition "mental illnesses" because they differ little from analogous bodily disease. Szasz argues that this view is erroneous because it confuses a *defect* correlated with a lesion in the central nervous system with a *belief*, a learned behavior. Szasz also emphasizes the role of social value norms in making judgments about who is deviant or "sick."

Finally, the concept of *personal responsibility* for one's behavior enters this controversy. If people believe they cannot function because they are "sick," they relieve themselves of responsibility for their behavior. If they believe, on the other hand, that their beliefs and choices determine their behavior, then they carry the awesome burden of responsibility for their actions. The relationship of personal attitudes to physical illness, while controversial, illustrates the role of personal responsibility. The Simontons (1978), for example, cite the role of psychological methods in the treatment and prevention of cancer. Cousins's personal document on how he took responsibility for dealing successfully with his illness, diagnosed as terminal, indicates the power of psychological methods (1979, 1989). This issue of personal responsibility is critical in dealing with criminal behavior also.

Perls (1969b), also a psychiatrist, expresses his disillusionment with the medical model of sickness or wellness. Perls emphasizes the person who has experienced problems of living and uses self-defeating manipulative patterns. Similarly, Glasser (1965), who is also a physician, stresses the therapist's role of teaching clients more responsible, self-controlled, and self-fulfilling behavior. He emphasizes how this learning approach is incompatible with a conventional conception of mental illness.

Psychotherapeutic counseling involves helping the individual whose learning is incomplete or who has more or less conscious conflicts that have as their accompaniment so-called normal anxiety. This, of course, places a severe burden on the counselor to distinguish "normal" from "pathological," but this recognition of pathology and therapeutic limitations has become part of the psychologist's professional training. It is important for any professional group to realize that it cannot be all things to all people and to practice only in its areas of demonstrated competence.

Clinical Social Work

Psychiatric or clinical social work, a fourth counseling specialty, also is difficult to distinguish from psychology in terms of psychotherapeutic function. Many practitioners of this professional group, especially those in private practice, feel they are doing psychotherapy in the formal sense. One principal difference, however, is the training route. Social workers generally complete a two-year graduate program, including a year of supervised agency work, leading to a master's degree in social work. Clinical social workers function, as do clinical psychologists, on health care teams, although many go into private practice. In clinics they specialize in the intake process, deal with other agencies, work with families, and collect psychiatric histories. Social workers, by tradition and training, have had responsibilities for family counseling services, although they perform counseling roles in many types of community agencies.

Mental Health Counseling

Mental health counselors have emerged as a major force in recent years. These professionals are employed in a broad range of employment settings, although their primary locale is the community mental health center. Their professional organization, the American Mental Health Counselors Association, is the largest affiliate division of the American Counseling Association. Mental health counselors are licensed or certified in many states. Mental health counselor education programs have an accreditation procedure developed through the Council for Accreditation of Counseling and Related Educational Programs (CACREP). In addition, mental health counselors have their own academy of professional practice.

School Counseling

A fifth counseling specialty, educational counseling, differs from other specialties largely on the basis of breadth of training and experience required. School counselors deal with a wide variety of educational problems close to the areas of teaching and administration, in addition to working with the personal counseling problems of children and adolescents.

Levels of service is a significant concept in school counseling. Three general counseling levels are identifiable on the basis of differences in training, competence, and counseling time. These are functional levels, not status differentials. On the first level is the educational counselor whose professional roots are mostly in teaching and who may be doing part-time counseling largely of the educational planning type. This counselor primarily gives information and suggestions. The counselors on this level are frequently called "advisers."

At the second level is the counselor whose professional affiliation is primarily in education and who generally has a master's degree or special training in counseling. This counselor deals with most school counseling problems, ranging from giving simple information on college requirements, through vocational planning and social conduct, to dealing with the more emotionally involved problems concerned with maturation. School counselors suffer from a severe identity problem, since the historical educational guidance model does not meet their needs. Since school counseling deals with the kinds of developmental problems described under counseling psychology, it appears that this model holds hope for the school counseling specialist.

The counselor on the third level is the counseling or clinical psychologist, described earlier in this chapter. School or college counselors on this level generally have experience in educational positions; but their primary graduate professional education has been psychology, psychiatric social work, or medicine.

Psychosocial Nursing

Psychosocial nursing, sometimes designated psychiatric nursing, is a health care specialty with a strong clinical counseling component. Special areas of counseling focus are death and dying, stress management, life-style change, family counseling, and geriatrics. While working mainly in health care agencies, many persons trained in this specialty go into private counseling practice, especially the more specialized nurse practitioners.

Pastoral Psychology

Ministers have been counseling their parishioners for years. There was a growing historical emphasis on clinical training for the clergy to do psychological counseling. Increasingly, seminarians have taken clinical internships in counseling agencies. Many churches offer extensive counseling on marriage, divorce, widowhood, drug abuse, and family problems in line with their traditional community helping services. The American Association of Pastoral Counseling has procedures for certifying individuals on the basis of their clinical and behavioral science education plus supervised clinical training leading to fellow and diplomate status. In addition, the association has an accrediting process for preparation programs. In Chapter 13 we described some of the specialized concerns with which all secular and religious counselors must come to grips as they deal with clients who have moral and spiritual value problems.

Marriage and Family Therapy

While general counseling and clinical psychologists work with couples and families extensively, a specialty has emerged with its own professional organizations, journals, and licensing in a growing number of states. Marriage and family therapists come from many of the human service professions as well as specifically accredited marriage and family therapy degree programs. Many of these professionals belong to the American Association for Marriage and Family Therapy. This association has an elaborate process for certifying individuals for clinical membership and an accrediting procedure for preparation programs. Their functions were described in Chapter 10.

Rehabilitation and Employment Counselors

With considerable national emphasis on solutions to problems of disabled and underprivileged citizens, counseling has become a central helping function. Vocational rehabilitation counselors, working in state rehabilitation offices, hospitals, and private agencies with the physically and emotionally disabled, have had their functions increased by law to include mentally, socially, and economically disabled clients. Rehabilitation counselors are needed to serve the 10 percent of the American population that is in some way disabled.

An increasing role is emerging for counselors involved in rehabilitating substance abusers. Private industry has found it profitable to establish employee assistance programs whose role is to assist employees with employee health concerns. One of the primary roles of counselors within these programs is to help employees with alcohol and other drug-related problems. Hospital and outpatient drug rehabilitation programs have become widespread and many rehabilitation counselors specialize in drug-abuse-related counseling.

In similar fashion, recent labor and economic opportunity legislation has created expanded roles for employment and career counselors, who traditionally have been concerned primarily with placement problems. With fast-changing economic conditions, many persons need counseling connected with retraining and upgrading of job skills, and planning for retirement. Inflationary pressures mean people will be working well beyond usual retirement age and often in new careers. Many industries have begun programs within their organizations to provide career counseling to their employees who wish to upgrade their skills, change jobs, or cope with being fired or laid off from work.

TRENDS IN THERAPEUTIC PSYCHOLOGY

This chapter deals with five trends in the practice of therapeutic psychology: (1) insistence on accountability and competence; (2) an emphasis on new research methodologies in counseling; (3) broadening roles and work settings for counselors; (4) clarification of counseling goals and values and emphasis on self-help; and (5) skills training and prevention.

Trend I: Accountability and Ethical Behavior

The prevalence of the term *accountability* indicates the concern of professional helpers, their clients, and their agencies about responsibility and productivity. Counselors recognize the necessity to strive for improved competency, evaluation of expected outcomes, and cost effectiveness. When agencies tighten their budgets on human services, we are pressed harder than ever to show that our efforts help clients and agencies reach their goals efficiently as well as effectively. Efforts to increase accountability have focused on strengthening professional practice standards, continuing education requirements, and outcome research on the effectiveness of counseling.

Training Sequences and Standards for Psychological Services. Professional accountability has led professional associations to take a closer look at training experiences and practice standards for providers of psychological services. Professional groups such as the American Psychological Association, the American Counseling Association, and the American Association for Marriage and Family Therapy have published recommended training standards for their professions. These training programs are superimposed generally on a basic background of behavioral sciences and general education. In psychology, early graduate years contain further generic training in general psychology, experimental methods, statistics, measurement, human development, physiology, social psychology, personality theory, and behavior pathology. Advanced training leading to a doctoral degree should contain, according to the American Psychological Association's *Accreditation Handbook* (1990), additional work in appraisal, internship, professional issues, and research.

Each professional association stresses the need for graduate internship training to give supervised experience in therapeutic psychology as well as to enable the student to synthesize many fragments of information from previous courses and learning experiences. The National Conference on Internship Training in Psychology (APIC, 1987) reaffirmed the importance of internship training for professional psychology. The conferees recommended continuation of a two-year doctoral internship—one a predoctoral year.

The American Psychological Association has published generic guidelines for the providers of psychological services (APA, 1987). To supplement these basic statements, specialty standards, as mentioned earlier, have been developed in counseling, clinical, industrial, and school psychology. These documents provide general principles, definitions of providers, accountability principles, and guidelines for practice. Standards statements supplement previously published APA ethics statements and are used by APA committees on program accreditation, service agencies, and third-party insurers.

The Association for Counselor Education and Supervision, a division of the American Counseling Association, has developed a statement of standards for counselor education over the last 20 years. Most recently, it has developed and applied accreditation procedures for master's and doctoral programs in counselor education under these standards (AACD, 1990). Entry-level programs may receive accreditation in the areas of student personnel services, school counseling, and community agency counseling. Accreditation has promoted greater clarity of purpose and standardization in preparation programs, which in turn seems to have led to greater credibility within and beyond the field of counseling. Similarly, the American Association for Marriage and Family Therapy has an elaborate credentialing process for individuals and training programs.

Most counselor training programs have established a competency base which looks at counselor performance as related to counseling outcomes and specific competencies. These competencies are assessed before training to establish baseline achievement and prescribe training events to establish minimum performance competencies. Competencies are reassessed at the end of training to ascertain achievement of minimum performance. Specified counselor behaviors in a competency program, especially when tied to client outcomes, clarify expectations and role definitions of counselors.

Professional associations have attempted to strengthen professional accountability through reexamining training sequences and practice standards for providers of psychological services. For example, in the field of psychology, there has been debate about whether training in applied psychology should become more specialized or by primarily generic, with specialization occurring during postdoctoral training experiences. Supporters of generic training believe that few differences exist among the specializations within psychology. They also cite recent surveys showing a close similarity among functions of counseling and clinical psychologists in psychology practice. Additionally, the current model of training is organized to accredit training programs in only three specialties: clinical, counseling, and school psychology. Procedures are being developed to accredit new specializations, such as family, neuropsychology, and forensic psychology.

Generic training supporters believe that students wishing to become applied psychologists should all undertake similar graduate programs, completing coursework in core areas such as biological basis for behavior, learning and human development, personality, social psychology, measurement, and research design. Specialization into clinical, counseling, school, or others would follow completion of a core graduate degree in professional psychology. They believe this new training model would provide recognition and opportunities for better training of new specialists in applied psychology.

Others believe there are advantages in distinguishing among clinical, counseling, school, and other specialties. Through recognizing uniqueness, they argue, it is possible to allow each specialty to tailor its training throughout a graduate program to meet its own training needs. Many similar core classes would be taken, but specialization would be built into a student's program from the beginning of the student's training. Implementing the proposed curriculum changes would require an overhaul of current accreditation practices.

A related debate revolves around the basic "scientist-practitioner" training model used in applied psychology. Many psychologists voice the opinion that a model that tries to produce good researchers and clinicians produces neither very well. Critics suggest that new training tracks be made that separate training programs for clinical researchers and clinical practitioners. Researchers might follow a Ph.D. program while practitioners would go through a doctor of psychology (D.Psy.) program emphasizing skill in clinical practice. Fox and associates (1985) have proposed a series of such curriculum changes. Curriculum changes leading toward a doctor of psychology degree have been developed in accordance with a "practitioner-scholar" model. This model emphasizes both effective professional functioning and the ability to apply research results and skills to the solution of professional problems. Resolution of this training issue involves reducing the larger tensions that exist between psychological practitioners and academic psychologists.

Professional Societies, Publications, and Codes of Ethics. Professional societies provide dedicated efforts to bring accountability to the counseling profession. In psychology, for example, the American Psychological Association is one group whose object is "to advance psychology as a science, as a profession, and as a means of promoting human welfare" (1954). The American Counseling Association is another professional association dedicated to the improvement of counseling services. Societies promote counseling through encouraging research, professional advocacy in legislative issues, publishing professional journals, and establishing codes of ethics.

Some of the representative publications of help to counselors and psychotherapists are the *Journal of Counseling Psychology*, the *Journal of Clinical and Consulting Psychology*, the *Journal of Counseling and Development*, *American Psychologist*, *The School Counselor*, *The Counseling Psychologist*, *Psychotherapy: Theory, Research and Practice*, the *Journal of Marriage and Family Therapy*, and the *Journal of Applied Behavioral Science*.

Codes of ethics are a major contribution of professional societies. The opening statement in the APA *Ethical Standards of Psychologists* is, "Psychologists respect the dignity and worth of the individual and honor the preservation and protection of fundamental human rights" (1990, p. 1). Psychotherapeutic counseling, being a welfare service, is faced with ethical practice problems. Until codes were formulated, there were few guides for determining unethical practices. The presence of a well-defined code and tradition of ethical practice is a distinguishing mark of a profession.

The APA code of ethics is under continuous revision. Additionally, the *Casebook on Ethical Principles of Psychologists* (APA, 1987a) is updated continually as a guide to implementing ethical standards. The APA Committee on Professional Standards publishes several cases a year in the four specializations of clinical, counseling, school, and industrial psychology under the title *Casebook for Providers of Psychological Service* (1987c). This periodic collection of cases illustrates current issues in ethics and standards of practice. The Committee on Ethical Practices of the American Counseling Association (1988) has published a similar revised code. While some of the code principles reflect timeless human values, these codes reflect professional and social values of the surrounding culture, hence the need for continuous revision.

Certification and Licensing.   Although many professionals believe licensing protects the consumer, others believe that consumer protection could be strengthened by other measures. A license primarily assures the public that a practitioner has completed a formal academic program, has been supervised for a set number of clinical hours, and may have passed a written or oral exam related to clinical practice. Critics of licensing (Wellner, 1976, 1978) note that the American Psychological Association's Task Force on Education and Credentialing found that individuals functioning as licensed psychologists received training in almost two dozen different kinds of academic programs and carried 18 distinguishable terminal degrees. This diversity of training experience may be both confusing to the public and also may signify a lack of consistency in psychology training. Additionally, critics of licensing argue that the objective, multiple-choice examination given routinely in most states does not measure competence for practice (Fox et al., 1985).

Several suggestions have been made to strengthen the consumer protection intent of professional licensing. The diversity of training can be simplified by licensing only individuals from accredited programs, as the APA proposes should be done by 1995. It also has been suggested that licensing exams should be expanded to assess competency in the delivery of professional services, knowledge of legal and ethical responsibilities as practitioners, and familiarity with the broad social and cultural pressures that inevitably shape clinical practice. Therapists' disclosures of information about their practices, training, theoretical orientation, and professional experience are required by state licensing laws. These disclosure statements include the practitioner's professional qualifications, conditions for practice (such as ethics, hours, and confidentiality), and principles of client protection.

Continuing Education.　　Continuing education to update knowledge and skills is required by most states and professional bodies that license or certify counselors. Organizations such as the National Board for Certified Counselors and the American Association for Marriage and Family Therapy require continuing education hours for continued membership. Most states require continuing education for psychologists and other licensed human service professionals. Continuing education usually takes a variety of forms, including formal coursework, attending professional workshops, receiving clinical supervision, and participation in professional conferences.

Trend II: Methodological Diversity in Counseling Research

Psychotherapy research has been a priority in the counseling field since the late 1950s. In recent years, for example, there has been a trend toward closer scrutiny of the effectiveness of psychotherapy. This new emphasis toward accountability has come from within the field of psychology as well as from an increasingly well-educated and well-informed consumer population, media reporters, and policymakers. Policy debates related to whether psychotherapy should be covered under health care financing programs have stimulated more applied research concerned with the efficacy as well as comparative costs and outcomes. Increasingly, the courts have turned to the behavioral sciences for professional views on issues related to child custody, neuropsychology, and many other legal matters. At the same time, according to psychotherapy researcher Hans Strupp (1986, p. 121):

> There has been a veritable explosion of therapeutic approaches and techniques into the hundreds ranging from "traditional" psychotherapy (based on psychodynamic principles) to various forms of behavior therapy (Harper, 1975). These burgeoning psychological techniques are being practiced by a diverse and growing cadre of helping professionals. "Therapy" has become a household word, and its consumers are legion. Psychotherapy has become a billion-dollar industry (Klerman, 1983), lacking clear boundaries, with hazy quality control and relatively vague ethical standards.

In the future, it is likely that psychotherapy research will become more sophisticated and methodologically open. For many years it seemed as though counseling research was divorced from clinical practice. The focus of research tended to be either on units of the counseling process, which in isolation seemed too small to have clinical significance, or too large, as in outcome research, to have a clear understanding of how to integrate the findings into clinical practice. Currently, there is an atmosphere of creativity and openness to new research strategies.

A major trend in psychotherapy research has been to shift the research emphasis from comparative outcome studies of different schools of therapy to examining the processes occurring within psychotherapy. As it was discovered that methods espoused by different theories were practiced so differently by different practitioners, there came a problem of methodological control in comparative studies of different psychotherapies. These concerns resulted in an effort to operationally define and standardize treatments. Treatment manuals soon appeared for various forms of therapeutic approaches. The first major test of manual-driven therapies was the NIMH Collaborative Study of Depression (Elkin et al., 1985). These methodologies have been extended to compare the manualized treatments to the study of specific subgroups of subjects, such as those with concomitant depression and marital problems, anxiety disorders, and the depressed elderly.

In spite of the advances of treatment manuals, these outcome studies continue to be criticized for various reasons. Persons (1991) and Schacht (1991) argue that current approaches to outcome research poorly represent current models of psychotherapy because traditional research assessment is standardized, atheoretical, and conceptually separated from treatment. Outcome studies have not carried out a theoretically derived psychological assessment of the client's difficulties. Assessment is standardized based on atheoretical diagnostic criteria. A difficulty of this approach is that outcome studies ignore the link between assessment and treatment described in the theory. Treatments are not derived from a diagnosis that is based on the theoretical approach being evaluated.

In many outcome studies, treatment is standardized rather than individualized. This application of a standard, multicomponent package is incompatible with the approach to clinical problems described by current theories of psychotherapy. They perpetuate one of the key problems we have described in this text, that is, how to match specific treatment interventions with the particular needs of clients. The intention of most counseling theories is not to prescribe a standard multicomponent intervention for all clients with a particular problem.

Disagreement on appropriate outcomes is also a problem. Some theories suggest that acceptance or understanding may be as important outcomes as behavior change. This is particularly important in marital therapy outcomes.

Jacobson (1991) has suggested that there is a similarity of technique in different counseling approaches even though the theories have different understandings of how those techniques work. It is likely that the essential similarities carry more weight in accounting for outcome variances than do the differences in theoretical approach. These criticisms of past psychotherapy research form the basis of complaints by practitioners that psychotherapy research is divorced from the realities of daily practice.

New research strategies are being suggested to overcome these criticisms and make psychotherapy research more relevant for clinicians. Several suggestions have been made to improve on the use of therapy manuals in research. Jacobson (1991) proposes evaluating therapist competence, which is missing from most treatment manuals. This process would rule out the differences between treatments that are confounded by differential therapist competence.

Persons (1991) has proposed a case formulation approach to study psychotherapy in closer relation to its theoretical underpinnings. In this approach, the counseling provider formulates treatment hypotheses and individualizes a treatment plan based on a particular psychotherapeutic approach under study. This assessment is reviewed by judges for the sake of reliability and the therapist's behavior during assessment and treatment are described in a written protocol based on the psychotherapeutic model itself.

If a researcher wishes to conduct a comparative study, for example, of cognitive behavior therapy and brief psychodynamic treatment for clients with depressive symptoms, the clients would first be randomly assigned to treatment conditions. Then, in each condition, the therapist would carry out an individualized assessment and treatment, using methods described in the assessment-plus-treatment protocol for the particular condition. Outcomes could be compared in an idiographic way. Each client would have a different set of problems assessed with a different set of measures. Within-group pre- and posttreatment comparisons are made and group comparisons are made by comparing proportions of subjects who changed across treatment approaches.

Another promising direction is to consider intramodel comparisons. Many possibilities exist for such comparisons. Researchers could pursue a component analysis of mini-interventions at different points in therapy or examine specific interventions intended to affect a specific process, such as facilitate client decisions in a particular stage of therapy. Matching clients who have similar impairments can be used as a method to test the hypothesis that people will respond more favorably if the treatment they receive is matched with their impairment. For example, clients with a combination of depression and marital difficulties would get a different treatment from subjects showing depression but not marital distress.

The task analytic approach described by Rice and Greenberg (1984) involves identifying important moments or sequences in psychotherapy and then generating hypotheses about the nature of the mechanisms that seem important to these segments. A coding system can be developed to measure these processes and they can be used to investigate counseling interventions in a predictive way. A variation on this approach is to analyze the differences in sessions for a particular problem, such as depression, rated by therapists and clients as "high change" versus "low change," in order to discriminate therapy sessions by important patterns of therapist and client behavior. The ability to identify factors that predict intermediate outcomes in therapy contribute to revised conceptualizations of the change process.

Much recent attention has been given to the promise of qualitative research in counseling (Hoshmand, 1989; Polkinghorne, 1991). These strategies involve naturalistic and ethnographic methods that have traditionally been utilized in anthropology and sociology. Examples include archival research, ethnographic observation, qualitative interviews, and critical incidents. These methods may be used for theory generation and testing. One illustration of this approach is the use of "grounded theory" methods in research on clients' experience of psychotherapy (Rennie, 1984; Rennie, Phillips, & Quartaro, 1988). By obtaining descriptive data from clients under tape-assisted recall, meta-cognitions regarding the client's and the therapist's operations were revealed. The meanings that emerged from these subjects suggested a phenomenon of "client agency," which then became subject to further research.

Increasing diversity of research also results when questions are posed from new vantage points. As we have discussed in this text, new counseling theories need to be developed "from the people" as opposed to "for the people." We need to ask research questions from different perspectives—particularly viewpoints that have not been listened to well. These include feminist, cross-cultural, gay and lesbian, and other minority perspectives.

Trend III: New Roles and Work Settings for Counselors

Various forces from both within and outside of psychology have brought about a variety of new roles for counselors. National census data (Stapp, Tucker, & VandenBos, 1985) indicate that many psychologists at both the master's and doctoral levels are involved in several different kinds of activities: research, teaching, clinical service, and administrative work. Work settings are diverse and include universities, schools, independent practice, business and government, labor unions, hospitals, and mental health clinics. Many psychologists are becoming new specialists in areas such as forensic psychology, sports psychology, family psychology, neuropsychology, health psychology, and career development. Counselors have responded with creativity to demographic changes that have led to lower university enrollments and thus fewer academic positions for psychologists. Increased growth in knowledge about behavioral medicine has led many psychologists to specialize in health psychology. Many of these counselors have become providers within the growing number of health maintenance organizations, preferred provider organizations, and business employee assistance programs to develop wellness, career development, and stress management programs.

Trend IV: Goals, Values, and Self-Help

Another prominent trend discernible in psychotherapeutic counseling discussions is that of increasing clarification of the goals and purposes of counseling. There has been a pronounced movement from preoccupation with process to a focus on outcomes. This trend naturally takes a tack into the realm of values and concern about what outcomes are desirable.

The change in emphasis from the solution of immediate manifest problems the client may have, such as choosing a career goal or relieving momentary situational anxiety, to more long-range goals is very apparent. An example of a long-range, generalized goal is the reinforcement of the self-directive capacities of clients that make them better able to solve their problems in the future without help. Self-help is a strong social trend, with groups forming daily to cope with some special need, such as grieving, readjustment after divorce, single parenting, family abuse, and recovering from alcoholism. One key counseling goal is to help clients learn skills that will enable them to cope with future problems by themselves. Self-help approaches give deprived groups new ways of dealing with their problems and reaching out to others for mutual help.

Counselors with concerns about values tend to become involved in social issues such as protection of civil rights for all populations, peace and war, status of women, protection of the environment, reduction of poverty, and protection of children. All in society must be able to take advantage of the opportunity structure of society with respect to housing, welfare, education, and employment. This help has included teaching how to search for political power. For example, in recent years the trend among American ethnic minorities has been less toward assimilation and more toward enhancing ethnic distinctiveness through cultural revitalization and group involvement in the political process. In the African-American population, this cultural reawakening has taken the form of learning about Africa (and sometimes Islam), with the adoption of African names and observance of folk festivals. More significant in terms of political power has been the rise to prominence of Cubans in Florida and those with Hispanic names elsewhere in the country. These groups have been transformed into sociopolitical systems demanding recognition from the larger society.

Trend V: Emphasis on Prevention and Skills Training

A trend toward prevention models of mental health and away from what Albee (1982) refers to as the "defect model" of mental health has occurred in recent years. The defect model explains personal problems by finding a defect or a conflict inside the individual to account for his or her dysfunctional behavior. The prevention approach emphasizes the development of strengths, such as assuming personal responsibility for health, making life-style changes, and creating less stressful and more humane environments. Prevention emphasizes a variety of strategies for increasing the coping skills and community support for individuals who are vulnerable to stress. Strategies may involve local media campaigns, educational efforts, and development of mutual aid and self-help programs.

A variety of research reviews have demonstrated the effectiveness of prevention programs in eliminating or reducing the incidence of later mental health problems (Kessler & Goldston, 1986; Lorion & VandenBos, 1990; Price, Cowen, Lorion, & Ramos-McKay, 1988). Examples are programs to reduce alcohol and drug abuse, decrease absenteeism, increase foster care programs in place of orphanages for children and enhance education on sexuality and health issues, such as prevention of AIDS. Efforts to teach effective coping skills in anticipation of life transitions, such as retirement, have also been part of the prevention approach. Brammer and Abrego (1981) have described a variety of self-help and psychological education programs for teaching coping skills related to life transitions.

Political action and social change may be necessary in many primary prevention programs. Prevention programs with refugee populations suggest that the size of the refugee group targeted for primary prevention is directly related to the probability that political action and social change will be needed as part of the intervention. For example, Garcia-Peltoniemi, Jaranson, and Teter (1989) describe a primary prevention program that was initially conceived to address the needs of all refugees in a small Texas border community. It then grew to include all refugees in the Rio Grande area of all of Texas and finally to encompass all Hispanic refugees in the United States. As the program expanded, the necessity for political action increased greatly. This interrelationship of prevention and social change is highlighted in the *Declaration of Human Rights and Mental Health* of the World Federation for Mental Health.

SUMMARY

This chapter has included a description of the many professional groups associated with therapeutic psychology. Similarities and differences among approaches of professions such as clinical psychology, counseling psychology, mental health counseling, psychiatry, and marriage and family therapy were discussed. Five professional trends were discussed emphasizing accountability, research, new roles and work settings, values concerns, and an emphasis on prevention and skills training.

References

ABREGO, P. (1981). An evaluation of the effects of a family life education program on marital and family relationships. Unpublished doctoral dissertation, University of Washington.

ABREGO, P., & BRAMMER, L. (1992). Counseling adults in midlife career transitions. In Z. B. Leibowitz & H. D. Lea (Eds.), *Adult Career Development: Concepts, Issues and Practices* (2d ed.). Alexandria, VA: American Association for Counseling and Development.

ACKERMAN, N. W. (1938). The unity of the family, *Archives of Pediatrics, 55,* 51–62.

AJAYA, S. (1983). *Psychotherapy East and West: A Unifying Paradigm.* Honesdale, PA: Himalayan Institute.

ALAGNA, F., WHICHTER, S., FISCHER, J., & WICAS, E. (1979). Evaluative reaction to interpersonal touch in a counseling interview. *J. Counsel. Psychol., 26,* 465–472.

ALBEE, G. W. (1982). Preventing psychopathology and promoting human potential. *American Psychologist, 37,* 1043–1050.

ALEXANDER, F., & FRENCH, T. M. (1946). *Psychoanalytic Therapy.* New York: Ronald Press.

ALLEN, T. (ED.). (1975). Marriage and family counseling. *Counseling Psychologist, 5,* 1–136.

ALLMON, D. (1981). Verbal reexpression: its effects in social interaction. Unpublished doctoral dissertation. University of Washington.

ALLPORT, G. W. (1955). *Becoming: Basic Considerations for a Psychology of Personality.* New Haven: Yale Univ. Press.

—— (1950). *The Individual and His Religion: A Psychological Interpretation.* New York: Macmillan.

—— (1937). *Personality: A Psychological Interpretation.* New York: Holt.

ALPERSON, B. L., ALPERSON, E. D., & LEVINE, R. (1971). Growth effects of high school marathons. *Experimental Publications System 2,* Ms. No. 369–56.

ALPERT, J. (1985). Change within a profession: Change, future, prevention and school psychology. *American Psychologist, 40,* 1112–1121.

AMERICAN ASSOCIATION FOR COUNSELING AND DEVELOPMENT. (1990). *Accreditation Procedures Manual for Counselor Education.* Washington, DC: American Personnel and Guidance Association.

—— (1988, March). Ethical standards (1981 revision). *Journal of Counseling and Development, 67,* 4–8.

—— (1979). *Counseling the Aged: A Training Syllabus for Education.* Washington, DC: American Personnel and Guidance Association.

—— (1978). Responsibilities of users of standardized tests, *Guidepost,* 5–8.

AMERICAN EDUCATIONAL RESEARCH ASSOCIATION, AMERICAN PSYCHOLOGICAL ASSOCIATION, & NATIONAL COUNCIL ON MEASUREMENT IN EDUCATION. (1985). *Standards for Educational and Psychological Testing.* Washington, DC: American Psychological Association.

AMERICAN PERSONNEL AND GUIDANCE ASSOCIATION. (1981). *Counseling Older Persons: A Training Man-*

ual for Para-professionals. Washington, DC: American Personnel and Guidance Association.

AMERICAN PSYCHIATRIC ASSOCIATION. (1987). *Diagnostic and Statistical Manual of Mental Disorders* (3d ed., rev.). Washington, DC: Author.

AMERICAN PSYCHOLOGICAL ASSOCIATION. (1992). APA continues to refine its ethics code. *APA Monitor,* 23(5), 38–42.

—— (1990a). *Accreditation Handbook.* Washington, DC: Author.

—— (1990b). *Ethical Standards of Psychologists.* Rev. ed. Washington, DC: American Psychological Association.

—— (1990c). Ethical standards for psychologists. *American Psychologist, 45,* 390–395.

—— (1987a). *Casebook on Ethical Principles of Psychologists.* Washington, DC: Author.

—— (1987b). General guidelines for providers of psychological services. *American Psychologist, 42,* 712–723.

—— (1987c). *Casebook for Providers of Psychological Services.* Washington, DC: American Psychological Association.

—— (1981). Specialty guidelines for the delivery of services. *American Psychologist, 36,* 639–681.

—— (1954). *Psychology and Its Relations with Other Professions.* Washington, DC: American Psychological Association.

AMERICAN PSYCHOLOGICAL ASSOCIATION, Division 17, Counseling Psychology. (1984). *What Is a Counseling Psychologist?* Washington, DC: Author.

—— (1978). Principles concerning the counseling and therapy of women, *Counseling Psychologist, 8,* 21. Revised edition in preparation for 1993.

ANSBACHER, R., & ANSBACHER, H. (1956). *The Individual Psychology of Alfred Adler.* New York: Basic Books.

APIC (ASSOCIATION FOR PSYCHOLOGICAL INTERNSHIP CENTERS). (1988). *Proceedings of the National Conference on Internship Training in Psychology* (Gainesville, Florida). Washington, DC: American Psychological Association.

ASPY, D. N. (1975). Empathy. *The Counseling Psychologist, 5,* 10–14.

ASSAGIOLI, R. (1965). *Psychosynthesis.* New York: Viking Press.

ASSOCIATION FOR SPECIALISTS IN GROUP WORK. (1980). *Ethical Guidelines for Group Leaders.* Falls Church, VA: Author.

ATKINSON, D. R. (1983). Ethnic similarity in counseling psychology: A review of research. *The Counseling Psychologist, 11,* 79–92.

—— (1966). The marathon group: intensive practice of intimate interaction. *Psychological Reports, 18,* 995–1002.

BACH, G. R. (1954). *Intensive Group Psychotherapy.* New York: Ronald Press.

BANDLER, R., & GRINDER, J. (1975). *The Structure of Magic.* Palo Alto, CA: Science and Behavior Books.

BANDURA, A. (1984). Recycling misconceptions of perceived self-efficacy. *Cognitive Therapy and Research, 8,* 231–255.

—— (1977). *Social Learning Theory.* Englewood Cliffs, NJ: Prentice-Hall.

—— (1971). Psychotherapy based upon modeling principles. In A. E. Bergin & S. L. Garfield (Eds.), *Handbook of psychotherapy and behavior change: An empirical analysis.* New York: Wiley.

—— (1969). *Principles of Behavior Modification.* New York: Holt, Rinehart & Winston.

BANDURA, A., & ADAMS, N. E. (1977). Analysis of self-efficacy theory of behavioral change. *Cognitive Therapy and Research, 1,* 287–310.

BARAK, A., & LA CROSSE, M. (1975). Multidimensional perception of counselor behavior. *J Counsel. Psychol., 22,* 471–476.

BARBER, T., SPANOS, H., & CHAVES, J. (1976). *Hypnosis, Imagination, and Human Potentialities.* Elmsford, NY: Pergamon Press.

BARCLAY, J. R. (1984). Primary prevention and assessment. *The Personnel and Guidance Journal,* 475–479.

BEAL, E. W. (1980). Separation, divorce, and single-parent families. In E. A. Carter & M. McGoldrick (Eds.), *The Family Life Cycle: A Framework for Family Therapy.* New York: Gardner Press.

BECK, A. T. (1976). *Cognitive Therapy and the Emotional Disorders.* New York: International Universities Press.

BECK, A. T., RUSH, A. G., SHAW, B. F., & EMERY, G. (1979). *Cognitive Therapy of Depression.* New York: Guilford.

BECK, J. T., & STRONG, S. R. (1982). Stimulating therapeutic change with interpretations: A comparison of positive and negative connotation. *Journal of Counseling Psychology, 29,* 551–559.

BEERS, T., & FOREMAN, M. (1976). Intervention patterns in crisis interviews. *J. Counsel Psychol., 23,* 87–91.

BEITMAN, B. D. (1987). *The Structure of Individual Psychotherapy.* New York: Guilford.

BELL, L., & BELL, D. (1982). Family climate and the role of the female adolescent: Determinants of adolescent functioning. *Family Relations, 31,* 519–527.

BELLACK, A. S., & HERSEN, M. (1978). Chronic psychiatric patients and social skills training. In M. Hersen & A. S. Bellack (Eds.), *Behavior Therapy in the Psychiatric Setting.* Baltimore, MD: Williams and Wilkins.

BELLAH, R., MADSEN, R., SULLIVAN, W., SWIDLER, A., & TIPTON, S. (1985). *Habits of the Heart.* Berkeley: University of California Press.

BENSON, H. (1975). *The Relaxation Response.* New York: Avon.

BENSON, P. (1984). Informed consent: Drug information disclosed to patients prescribed antipsychotic medication. *Journal of Nervous and Mental Disease, 172,* 642–653.

BENTLER, L., JOBE, A., & ELKINS, D. (1974). Outcomes in group psychotherapy: Using persuasion theory to increase treatment efficacy. *J. Consult. and Clin. Psychol., 42,* 547–553.

BERGER, M. (1970). *Videotape Techniques in Psychiatric Training and Treatment.* New York: Brunner/Mazel.

—— (1968). The use of video tape with psychotherapy groups in a community mental health program. Paper delivered at the American Group Psychotherapy Conference, January 1968.

BERGIN, A. E. (1991). Values and religious issues in psychotherapy and mental health. *American Psychologist, 46,* 394–403.

—— (1980). Psychotherapy and religious values. *Journal of Consulting and Clinical Psychology, 48,* 95–105.

BERGIN, A. E., & JENSEN, J. P. (1990). Religiosity of psychotherapists: A natonal survey. *Psychotherapy, 27,* 3–7.

BERGIN, A. E., & SUINN, R. M. (1975). Individual psychotherapy and behavior therapy. *Annual Review of Psychotherapy, 26,* 509–556.

BERGMAN, D. V. (1951). Counseling method and client responses. *J. Consult. Psychol., 15,* 216–224.

BERKMAN, L., & SYME, E. L. (1979). Social networks, host resistance, and mortality: A nine year follow-up study of Alameda County residents. *American Journal of Epidemiology, 109,* 186–204.

BERNE, E. (1961). *Transactional Analysis.* New York: Grove Press.

BERZON, B., & SOLOMON, L. (1966). The self directed therapeutic group: three studies. *J. Counsel. Psychol., 13,* 491–497.

BETZ, N. E., & FITZGERALD, L. F. (1987). *The Career Psychology of Women.* New York: Academic Press.

BEUTLER, L. E. (1983). *Eclectic Psychotherapy: A Systematic Approach.* New York: Pergamon.

—— (1982). Convergence in counseling and psychotherapy: A current look. *Clinical Psychology Review, 1,* 79–101.

—— (1979). Values, beliefs, religion and the persuasive influence of psychotherapy. *Psychotherapy: Theory, Research and Practice, 16,* 432–440.

BEUTLER, L. E., & CLARKIN, J. F. (1990). *Systematic Treatment Selection.* New York: Brunner/Mazel.

BEUTLER, L. E., JOBE, A. M., & ELKINS, D. (1974). Outcomes in group psychotherapy: Using persuasion theory to increase treatment efficiency. *Journal of Consulting and Clinical Psychology, 42,* 547–553.

BLACK, J. D. (1952). Common factors of the patient-therapist relationship in diverse psychotherapies. *J. Clin. Psychol., 8,* 302–306.

BLANCK, G., & BLANCK, R. (1968). *Ego Psychology: Theory and Practice.* New York: Columbia University Press.

BLATNER, H. A. (1973). *Acting-in: Practical applications of Psychodramatic Methods.* New York: Springer.

BLOCHER, D. H. (1966). *Developmental Counseling.* New York: Ronald Press.

BOLLES, R. N. (1991). *What Color Is Your Parachute?* Berkeley, CA: Ten Speed Press.

—— (1978). *The Three Boxes of Life.* Berkeley, CA: Ten Speed Press.

BOORSTEIN, S. (ED.). (1980). *Transpersonal Psychotherapy.* Palo Alto, CA: Science and Behavior Books.

BORDIN, E. S. (1975). The generalizability of the psychoanalytic concept of the working alliance. *Psychotherapy: Theory, Research and Practice, 16,* 252–260.

—— (1955). *Psychological Counseling.* New York: Appleton-Century-Crofts.

BOSZORMENYI-NAGY, I., & SPARK, G. (1973). *Invisible Loyalties: Reciprocity in Intergenerational Family Therapy.* New York: Harper & Row.

BOWEN, M. (1978). *Family Therapy in Clinical Practice.* New York: Jason Aronson.

BOWLBY, J. (1988). *A Secure Base.* New York: Basic Books.

BOWLBY, J. (1949). The study and reduction of group tension in the family. *Human Relations, 2,* 123–128.

BRAMMER, L. (1993). *The Helping Relationship: Process and Skills.* 5th ed. Englewood Cliffs, NJ: Prentice-Hall.

BRAMMER, L. M. (1991). *How to Cope with Life Transitions: Managing Personal Change.* Washington, DC: Hemisphere.

—— (1983). Counseling theory and the older adult. *The Counseling Psychologist, 12,* 29–38.

BRAMMER, L., & ABREGO, P. (1981). Intervention strategies for coping with transitions. *J. Counsel. Psychol., 9,* 19–36.

BRAMMER, L., & HUMBERGER, D. (1984). *Inplacement and Outplacement Counseling.* Englewood Cliffs, NJ: Prentice-Hall.

BRANAN, J. M. (1967). Clients reaction to counselor's use of self-experience. *Pers. and Guid. J., 45,* 568–572.

BRIM, O. (1977). Theories of the male midlife crisis. In N. Schlossberg & A. Entine (Eds.), *Counseling Adults.* Pacific Grove, CA: Brooks/Cole.

BRODERICK, C. B., & SCHRADER, S. S. (1981). The history of professional marriage and family therapy. In A. S. Gurman & D. P. Kniskern, *Handbook of Family Therapy.* New York: Brunner/Mazel.

BRODY, E. (1990). Mental health and world citizenship: Sociocultural bases for advocacy. In W. H. Holtzman & T. H. Bornemann (Eds.), *Mental Health of Immigrants and Refugees.* Austin, TX: Hogg Foundation for Mental Health, University of Texas.

BROWN, G., & HARRIS, T. (1978). *The Social Origins of Depression.* New York: Free Press.

BROWN, J. F. (1940). *Psychodynamics of Abnormal Behavior.* New York: McGraw-Hill.

BROWN, L. S. (1986). Gender-role analysis: A neglected component of psychological assessment. *Psychotherapy, 2,* 243–248.

BROWN, S. D., LENT, R. W., & LARKIN, K. C. (1989). Self efficacy as a moderator of scholastic aptitude-academic performance relationships. *Journal of Vocational Behavior, 35,* 64–75.

BRY, A., & BAIR, M. (1978). *Directing the Movies of Your Mind: Visualization for Health and Insight.* New York: Harper & Row.

BUGENTAL, J. F. T. (1987). *The Art of the Psychotherapist: Subtle Skills of the Life Changing Enterprise.* New York: Norton.

———— (1981, 2d ed). *The Search for Authenticity; an Existential-Analytic Approach to Psychotherapy.* New York: Holt, Rinehart & Winston.

———— (1963). Humanistic psychology: A new breakthrough. *American Psychologist, 18,* 563–567.

———— (1952). Psychological interviewing. Unpublished manuscript.

BUTCHER, J. N. (ED.). (1987). *Computerized Psychological Assessment.* Hillsdale, NJ: Lawrence Erlbaum.

BUTCHER, J. N., KELLER, L. S., & BACON, S. F. (1985). Current developments and future directions in computerized personality assessment. *Journal of Consulting and Clinical Psychology, 53,* 803–815.

BUTLER, R. (1975). *Why Survive? Being Old in America.* New York: Harper & Row.

BUTLER, R., & LEWIS, M. L. (1977). *Aging and Mental Health* (2d ed.). St. Louis, MO: Mosby.

CAIRO, P. (1986). Career planning and development in organizations. In Z. B. Leibowitz & H. D. Lea (Eds.), *Adult Career Development: Concepts, Issues and Practices.* Alexandria, VA: American Association for Counseling and Development.

CAMPBELL, R. E., & CELLINI, J. V. (1981). A diagnostic taxonomy of adult career development problems. *Journal of Vocational Behavior, 19,* 185–190.

CAMPBELL, R. E., & HEFFERNAN, J. (1983). Adult vocational behavior. In W. B. Walsh & S. Osipow (Eds.), *Handbook of Vocational Psychology.* Hillsdale, NJ: Erlbaum.

CAMPBELL, S. (1980). *The Couple's Journey.* San Luis Obispo, CA: Impact Press.

CAPRA, F. (1982). *The Turning Point.* New York: Bantam Books.

CARKHUFF, R. (1969). *Helping and Human Relations.* New York: Holt, Rinehart & Winston.

CARKHUFF, R., & TRUAX, C. (1966). Toward explaining success and failure in interpersonal learning experiences. *Pers. and Guid. J., 44,* 723–728.

CARNES, E. F. (1949). Counselor flexibility: Its extent, and its relationship to other factors in the interview. Unpublished doctoral dissertation, Ohio State University.

CARNES, E. F., & ROBINSON, F. P. (1948). The role of client talk in the counseling interview. *Educ. Psychol. Measmt., 8,* 635–644.

CARNES, P. (1981). *Understanding Us: Instructor's Manual.* Minneapolis, MN: Interpersonal Communications Programs, Inc.

CARROLL, L. J., & YATES, B. T. (1981). Further evidence for the role of stimulus control training in facilitating weight reduction after behavioral therapy. *Behavior Therapy, 12,* 287–291.

CARTER, E., & McGOLDRICK, M. (1988). The family life cycle and family therapy: An overview. In E. Carter & M. McGoldrick (Eds.), *The Family Life Cycle: An Overview for Family Therapy* (2d ed.). New York: Gardner Press.

CARTER, B., PAPP, P., SILVERSTEIN, O., & WALTER, M. (1988). *The Invisible Web: Gender Patterns in Family Relationships.* New York: Guilford.

CASAS, J., FURLONG, M., & CASTILLO, S. (1980). Stress and coping among university counselors: a minority perspective. *J. Counsel. Psychol., 27,* 364–373.

CASHDAN, S. (1988). *Object Relations Therapy.* New York: Norton.

CAUTELA, J. R. (1976). The present status of covert modeling. *Journal of Behavior Therapy and Experimental Psychiatry, 6,* 323–326.

CAUTELA, J. R., & UPPER, D. (1976). The behavioral inventory battery: The use of self-report measures in behavioral analysis and therapy. In M. Hersen & A. S. Bellack (Eds.), *Behavioral Assessment: A Practical Handbook.* New York: Pergamon Press.

CHANCE, E. (1958). Measuring the anticipations of therapists about their patients. Unpublished paper.

CHEATHAM, H. (1990). Empowering Black families. In H. Cheatham & J. Stewart (Eds.), *Black Families* (pp. 373–393). New Brunswick, NJ: Transaction.

CHEEK, D. (1976). *Assertive Black . . . Puzzled White.* San Luis Obispo, CA: Impact Press.

CLAIBORN, C. D. (1979). Counselor verbal intervention, non-verbal behavior, and social power. *Journal of Counseling Psychology, 26,* 378–383.

CLAIBORN, C. D., WARD, S. R., & STRONG, S. R. (1981). Effects of congruence between counselor interpretations and client beliefs. *Journal of Counseling Psychology, 28,* 101–109.

CLARK, D. (1987). *The New Loving Someone Gay.* Berkeley, CA: Celestial Arts.

COHEN, A. M., & SMITH, R. D. (1976). *The Critical Incident in Growth Groups: Theory and Technique.* La Jolla, CA: University Associates.

COHEN, R. C. (1947). Military group psychotherapy. *Mental Hygiene, 3,* 94–103.

COLLINS, G. R. (1980). *Helping People Grow.* Santa Ana, CA: Vision House.

———— (1977). *The Rebuilding of Psychology: An Integration of Psychology and Christianity.* Wheaton, IL: Tyndale House.

COLLINS, R. (1977). Counseling interventions and cognitive psychology: reactions to programs for social-cognitive growth. *Counsel. Psychologist, 6,* 15–17.

COLON, F. (1980). The family life cycle of the multiproblem poor family. In E. Carter & M. McGoldrick (Eds.), *The Family Life Cycle: An Overview for Family Therapy.* New York: Gardner Press.

COMBS, A. W. (1969). *Florida Studies in the Helping Professions.* Gainesville, FL: University of Florida Press.

COMBS, A. W., & AVILA, D. L. (1985). *Helping Relationships: Basic Concepts for the Helping Professions.* Boston: Allyn and Bacon.

COMMITTEE ON PROFESSIONAL STANDARDS (1986). Casebook for Providers of Psychological Services. *American Psychologist 1986, 41,* 688–693.

COOGLER, O. J. (1978). *Structured Mediation in Divorce Settlement.* Lexington, MA: Lexington Books.

COREY, G. (1986). *Theory and Practice of Counseling and Psychotherapy* (3d ed.). Pacific Grove, CA: Brooks/Cole.

———— (1981). *Theory and Practice of Group Counseling.* Pacific Grove, CA: Brooks/Cole.

COREY G., COREY, M., & CALLAHAN, P. (1979). *Professional and Ethical Issues in Counseling and Psychotherapy.* Belmont, CA: Wadsworth.

CORMIER, W. H., & CORMIER, L. S. (1985). *Interviewing Strategies for Helpers* (2d ed.). Pacific Grove, CA: Brooks/Cole.

COTTLE, W. C., & LEWIS, W. W., JR. (1954). Personality characteristics of counselors: II. Male counselor responses to the MMPI and GZTS. *J. Counsel. Psychol., 1,* 27–30.

COUNCIL FOR ACCREDITATION OF COUNSELING AND RELATED EDUCATIONAL PROGRAMS. (1986). *Accreditation Procedures Manual.* Gainsville, FL: American Association for Counseling and Development.

COUNCIL OF THE NATIONAL REGISTER OF HEALTH SERVICE PROVIDERS IN PSYCHOLOGY. (1983, July). *Register Report* (No. 18).

COUSINS, N. (1989). *Head First: The Biology of Hope.* New York: Dutton.

———— (1979). *Anatomy of an Illness.* New York: Norton.

COWEN, E. (1977). Baby-steps toward primary prevention. *American Journal of Community Psychology, 5,* 1–22.

CRABB, L. J. (1977). *Effective Biblical Counseling.* Grand Rapids, MI: Zondervan.

CRASINECK, H. B., & HALL, J. A. (1975). *Clinical Hypnosis: Principles and Application.* New York: Grune & Stratton.

CRIDER, B. (1946). The hostility pattern. *J. Clin. Psychol., 2,* 267–273.

CRITES, J. O. (1986). Appraising adults' career capabilities: Ability, interest, and personality. In Z. B. Leibowitz & H. D. Lea (Eds.), *Adult Career Development: Concepts, Issues and Practices.* Alexandria, VA: American Association for Counseling and Development.

———— (1984). Instruments for assessing career development. In N. C. Gysbers & Associates, *Designing Careers.* San Francisco: Jossey-Bass.

———— (1981). *Career Counseling: Models, Methods, and Materials.* New York: McGraw-Hill.

CROSS, D., SHEEHAN, P., & KAHN, J. (1982). Short- and long-term follow-up of clients receiving insight-oriented therapy and behavior therapy. *Journal of Consulting and Clinical Psychology, 50,* 103–112.

CRYSTAL, J. C., & BOLLES, R. N. (1974). *Where Do I Go from Here with My Life?* Berkeley, CA: Ten Speed Press.

CURRAN, C. A. (1944). Structuring the counseling relationship: A case report. *J. Abnorm. Soc. Psychol., 39,* 189–216.

D'ALELIO, W. A., & MURRAY, E. J. (1981). Cognitive therapy for test anxiety. *Cognitive Therapy and Research, 5,* 299–307.

D'ZURILLA, T. J., & GOLDFRIED, M. (1971). Problem solving and behavior modification. *J. Abnormal and Social Psychol., 78,* 107–126.

D'ZURILLA, T. J., & NEZU, A. (1982). Social problem solving in adults. In P. C. Kendall (Ed.), *Advances in Cognitive-Behavioral Research and Therapy* (Vol. 1). New York: Academic Press.

DANISH, S. J., SMYER, M. A., & NOWAK, C. A. (1980). Developmental intervention: Enhancing life-event processes. In P. B. Baltes & O. G. Brim, Jr. (Eds.), *Life-Span Development and Behavior* (Vol. 3). New York: Academic Press.

DAVIS, S. E., ANDERSON, C., LINKOWSKI, D. C., BERGER, K., & FEINSTEN, C. F. (1985). Developmental tasks and transitions of adolescents with chronic illnesses and disabilities. *Rehabilitation Counseling Bulletin, 29,* 69–80.

DAY, R., & SPARACIO, R. (1980). Structuring the counseling process. *Pers. and Guid. J., 59,* 246–251.

DEFFENBACHER, J. L. (1986). A cognitive-behavioral response and a modest proposal. *The Counseling Psychologist, 13,* 261–270.

DELL, P. F. (1982). Beyond homeostasis: Toward a concept of coherence. *Family Process, 21,* 21–41.

DEMILLE, R. (1973). *Put Your Mother on the Ceiling.* New York: Penguin Books.

DE SHAZER, S. (1988). *Clues: Investigating Solutions in Brief Therapy.* New York: Norton.

DEVORE, W. (1985). Developing ethnic sensitivity for the counseling process: A socialwork perspective in P. Pederson (Ed.), *Handbook of Cross-Cultural Counseling and Therapy,* Westport, CT: Greenwood Press.

DOHERTY, W. J., LESTER, M. E., & LEIGH, G. (1986). Marriage encounter weekends: Couples who win and couples who lose. *Journal of Marital and Family Therapy, 12,* 49–61.

DOHERTY, W. J., McCABE, P., & RYDER, R. G. (1978). Marriage encounter: A critical appraisal. *Journal of Marriage and Family Counseling, 4,* 99–106.

DOLLARD, J., & MILLER, N. (1950). *Personality and Psychotherapy.* New York: McGraw-Hill.

DOWD, E. T., & MILNE, C. R. (1986). Paradoxical interventions in counseling psychology. *Counseling Psychologist, 14,* 237–282.

DREIKERS, R. (1949). Counseling for family adjustment. *Individual Psychology Bulletin, 7*, 119–137.

DRUM, D. J. (1984). Implementing theme-focused prevention: Challenge for the 1980s. *The Personnel and Guidance Journal, 62*, 503–513.

DUCKWORTH, J. (1990). The counseling approach to the use of testing. *The Counseling Psychologist, 18*, 198–204.

EDELSTEIN, B. A., & EISLER, R. M. (1976). Effects of modeling and modeling with instructions and feedback on the behavioral components of social skills. *Behavior Therapy, 7*, 382–389.

EDELWICH, J., & BRODSKY, A. (1980). *Burn-out.* New York: Research Press.

EFRAN, J. S., LUKENS, M. D., & LUKENS, R. J. (1990). *Language, Structure, and Change.* New York: Norton.

EGAN, G. (1976). *Interpersonal Living.* Pacific Grove, CA: Brooks/Cole.

EHRLICH, R., D'AUGELLI, A., & DANISH, S. (1979). Comparative effectiveness of six counselor verbal responses. *J. Counsel. Psychol., 26*, 390–398.

EISLER, R. M., FREDERIKSEN, L. W., & PETERSON, G. L. (1978). The relationships of cognitive variables to the expression of assertiveness. *Behavior Therapy, 9*, 419–427.

ELKAIM, M. (1981). Non-equilibrium, chance and change in family therapy. *Journal of Marital and Family Therapy, 7*, 291–297.

ELKIN, I., PARLOFF, M. B., HADLEY, S. W., & AUTRY, J. H. (1985). The NIMH Treatment of Depression Collaborative Research Program: Background and research plan. *Archives of General Psychiatry, 42*, 305–316.

ELKINS, R. L. (1980). Covert sensitization treatment of alcoholism: Contributions of successful conditioning to subsequent abstinence maintenance. *Addictive Behaviors, 5*, 67–89.

ELLIS, A. (1984a). Rational-Emotive Therapy. In R. Corsini (Ed.), *Current Psychotherapies* (3rd ed., pp. 162, 196–238. Itasca, IL: Peacock.

―――― (1984b). *Rational-Emotive Therapy and Cognitive Behavior Therapy.* New York: Springer.

―――― (1980). Psychotherapy and atheistic values: A response to A. E. Bergin's "Psychotherapy and Religious Values." *Journal of Consulting and Clinical Psychology, 48*, 635–639.

―――― (1977). Psychotherapy and the value of a human being. In A. Ellis & R. Grieger (Eds.), *Handbook of Rational-Emotive Therapy* (pp. 99–112). New York: Springer.

―――― (1962). *Reason and Emotion in Psychotherapy,* New York: Lyle Stewart.

―――― (1955). New approaches to psychotherapy. *J. Clin. Psychol.,* Monograph Supplement, 11.

ELLIS, A., & GRIEGER, R. (1977). *Handbook of Rational-Emotive Therapy.* New York: Springer.

EMERY, R. E., & WYER, M. M. (1987). Divorce mediation. *American Psychologist, 42*, 472–480.

EPSTEIN, L. (1977). The therapeutic function of life in the countertransference. *Contemporary Psychoanalysis, 13*, 442–461.

ERDMAN, H. A., & FOSTER, S. W. (1986). Computer-assisted assessment with couples and families. *Family Therapy, 13*, 23–40.

ERIKSON, E. H. (1963). *Childhood and Society* (2d ed.). New York: Norton.

EYSENCK, H. (1952). The effects of psychotherapy: An evaluation. *J. Consult. Psychol., 16*, 319–324.

FALICOV, C., & KARRER, B. (1980). Cultural variations in the family life cycle: The Mexican-American family. In E. Carter & M. McGoldrick (Eds.), *The Family Life Cycle: An Overview for Family Therapy.* New York: Gardner Press.

FASSINGER, R. E. (1991). The hidden minority: Issues and challenges in working with lesbian women and gay men. *The Counseling Psychologist, 19*, 157–176.

FIEDLER, F. E. (1951). Method of objective quantification of certain countertransference attitudes. *J. Clin. Psychol., 7*, 101–107.

―――― (1950). A comparison of psychoanalytic, nondirective, and Adlerian therapeutic relationships. *J. Consult. Psychol., 14*, 436–445.

FIFE, A. R. (1975). A study of hypnosis using varied pretrance training. Unpublished doctoral dissertation, Brigham Young University.

FINNERTY-FRIED, P. (1985). Adapting rehabilitation counseling for older persons. *Rehabilitation Counseling Bulletin, 29*, 136–142.

FISCHER, K. R., & HART, T. N. (1986). *Christian Foundations: An Introduction to Faith in Our Time.* Mahwah, NJ: Paulist Press.

FISHER, A., & PAVEZA, G. (1975). The relationship between theoretical orientation and therapist's empathy, warmth and genuineness. *J. Counsel. Psychol., 22*, 399–403.

FITZGERALD, L. (1986). Career counseling women: Principles, procedures and problems. In Z. B. Leibowitz & H. D. Lea (Eds.), *Adult Career Development: Concepts, Issues and Practices.* Alexandria, VA: American Association for Counseling and Development.

FITZGERALD, L., & OSIPOW, S. H. (1986). An occupational analysis of counseling psychology: How special is the specialty? *American Psychologist, 41*, 535–544.

FLEMMING, W. M., & ANDERSON, S. A. (1986). Individuation from the family of origin and personal adjustment in late adolescence. *Journal of Marital and Family Therapy, 12*, 311–315.

FLEURIDAS, C., NELSON, T. S., & ROSENTHAL, D. M. (1986). The evolution of circular questions: Training family therapists. *Journal of Marital and Family Therapy, 12*, 113–128.

FLOWERS, J. V., & BOORAEM, C. D. (1980). Three studies toward a fuller understanding of behavioral group therapy: Cohesion, client flexibility and outcome generalization. In D. Upper & S. M. Ross (Eds.), *Behavior Group Therapy.* Champaign, IL: Research Press.

FONG, M. L., & COX, B. G. (1983).   Trust as an underlying dynamic in the counseling proceeds: How clients test trust. *Personnel and Guidance Journal, 62*, 163–166.

FORD, D. H. (1987).   *Humans as Self Construcing Living Systems: A Developmental Perspective on Personality and Behavior.* Hillsdale, NJ: Erlbaum.

FORD, M. E., & NICHOLS, C. W. (1987).   A taxonomy of human goals and possible applications. In Ford, D. M., & Ford, M. E. (Eds.), *Humans as Self Constructing Living Systems: An Overview* (pp. 289–311). Hillsdale, NJ: Erlbaum.

FORSTER, J. (1985).   Investigating personal goals using personal construct theory and grid methods. In A. Landfield & F. Epting (Eds.), *Anticipating Personal Construct Psychology.* Lincoln: University of Nebraska Press.

FOWLER, J. (1984).   *Becoming Adult, Becoming Christian.* San Francisco: Harper & Row.

———— (1986).   Faith and the structuring of meaning. In C. Dystra & S. Parks (Eds.), *Faith Development and Fowler.* Birmingham, AL: Religious Education Press.

———— (1981).   *Stages of Faith: The Psychology of Human Development and the Quest for Meaning.* San Francisco: Harper & Row.

FOWLER, R. A. (1985).   Landmarks in computer-assisted psychological assessment. *Journal of Consulting and Clinical Psychology, 53*, 748–759.

FOX, R. E., KOVACS, A. L., & GRAHAM, S. R. (1985).   Proposals for a revolution in the preparation and regulation of professional psychologists. *American Psychologist, 40*, 1042–1050.

FRAMO, J. L. (1981).   The integration of marital therapy with sessions with family of origin. In P. Gurman & D. Kniskern, *Handbook of Family Therapy.* New York: Brunner/Mazel.

———— (1973).   Marriage therapy in a couples group. In D. A. Bloch (Ed.), *Techniques of Family Psychotherapy: A Primer.* New York: Grune & Stratton.

FRANK, J. D., & FRANK, J. B. (1991).   *Persuasion and Healing* (3d ed.). Baltimore, MD: Johns Hopkins University Press.

FRANKL, V. E. (1967).   *Psychotherapy and Existentialism: Selected Papers on Logotherapy.* New York: Simon & Schuster.

———— (1946).   Ärtzliche Seelsorge. Vienna: Franz Deuticke Verlag.

FREMONT, S., & ANDERSON, W. (1986).   What client behaviors make counselors angry? An exploratory study. *Journal of Counseling and Development, 65*, 67–70.

FRETZ, B. R. (ED.). (1986).   Research training in counseling psychology. *The Counseling Psychologist, 14*, 1–231.

———— (1981).   Evaluating the effectiveness of career interventions. *Journal of Counseling Psychology, 28*, 77–90.

FRETZ, B. R., CORN, R., TUEMMLER, J. M., & BELLET, W. (1979).   Counselor nonverbal behaviors and client evaluations. *Journal of Counseling Psychology, 26*, 304–311.

FREUD, S. (1935).   *A General Introduction to Psychoanalysis.* New York: Liveright.

FREUDENBERGER, H. J., & ROBBINS, A. (1979).   The hazards of being a psychoanalyst. *Psychoanalytic Review, 66*, 275–296.

FRIEDMAN, E. H. (1988).   Systems and ceremonies: A family view of rites of passage. In B. Carter & M. McGoldrick (Eds.), *The Changing Family Life Cycle: A Framework for Family Therapy* (2d ed., pp. 545–578). New York: Gardner Press.

FROMM, E. (1957, March).   Man is not a thing. *Saturday Review*, 9–11.

———— (1956).   *The Art of Loving.* New York: Harper & Row.

———— (1950).   *Psychoanalysis and Religion.* New Haven: Yale University Press.

———— (1947).   *Man for Himself.* New York: Farrar and Rinehart.

———— (1941).   *Escape from Freedom.* New York: Farrar and Rinehart.

FRY, P. S. (1992).   Major social theories of aging and their implications for counseling concepts and practice. *The Counseling Psychologist, 20*, 246–329.

FRY, P., & CHARRON, P. (1980).   Effects of cognitive style and counselor-client compatibility on client growth. *J. Counsel. Psychol., 27*, 529–538.

FUHRIMAN, A., & BURLINGAME, G. M. (1990).   Consistency of matter: A comparative analysis of individual and group process variables. *The Counseling Psychologist, 18*, 6–63.

FUKUYAMA, M. (1990).   Taking the universal approach to multicultural counseling. *Counselor Education and Supervision, 30*, 6–17.

FULMER, R. (1988).   Lower-income and professional families: A comparison of structure and life cycle process. In B. Carter & M. McGoldrick (Eds.), *The Changing Family Life Cycle: A Framework for Family Therapy* (2nd. ed., pp. 545–578). New York: Gardner Press.

GAMSKY, N. R., & FARWELL, G. F. (1966).   Counselor verbal behavior as a function of client hostility. *J Counsel. Psychol., 13*, 184–190.

GARCIA-PELTONIEMI, R. E., JARANSON, J., & TETER, H. (1989, November).   The mental health needs of Central American victims of organized violence in the United States: The Rio Grande Community Training Project. Paper presented at the Second International Conference of Center, Institutions and Individuals Concerned with the Care of Victims of Organized Violence, San Jose, Costa Rica.

GARDNER, J. (1965).   *Self-Renewal.* New York: Harper & Row.

GARFIELD, S. (1981).   Psychotherapy: a forty-year appraisal. *Amer. Psychologist, 36*, 174–183.

———— (1979).   *Psychotherapy: An Eclectic Approach.* New York: Wiley.

GARFIELD, S. L. (1989). *The Practice of Brief Psychotherapy*. New York: Pergamon Press.

—— (1986). Research on client variables in psychotherapy. In S. L. Garfield and A. E. Bergin, *Handbook of Psychotherapy and Behavior Change* (3d ed.). New York: Wiley.

GARFIELD, S. L., & KURZ, R. A. (1977). A study of eclectic views. *Journal of Consulting and Clinical Psychology, 45*, 78–83.

—— (1975). Clinical psychologists: A survey of selected attitudes and views. *Clinical Psychologist, 28*, 4–7.

GARIS, J., & HARRIS-BOWLSBEY, J. (1984). *DISCOVER and the Counselor: Their Effects upon College Student Career Planning Progress*. Iowa City, IA: American College Testing Program.

GARNETS, L., HANCOCK, K. A., COCHRAN, S. D., GOODCHILDS, J., & PEPLAU, L. A. (1991). Issues in psychotherapy with lesbians and gay men. *American Psychologist, 46*, 964–972.

GAWAIN, S. (1982). *Creative Visualization*. New York: Bantam.

GAZDA, G. (1978). *Group Counseling: A Developmental Approach*. New York: Allyn & Bacon.

GAZDA, G. M., ASBURY, F. S., BALZER, F. J., CHILDERS, W. C., & WALTERS, R. P. (1977). *Human Relations Development* (2d ed.). Boston: Allyn & Bacon.

GELSO, C. (1979). Gratification: a pivotal point in psychotherapy. *Psychotherapy, Research, and Practice*, 276–281.

GELSO, C. J., BETZ, N. E., FRIEDLANDER, M. L., HELMS, J. E., HILL, C. E., PATTON, M. J., SUPER, D. E., & WAMPOLD, B. E. (1988). Research in counseling psychology: Prospects and recommendations. *The Counseling Psychologist, 16*, 385–406.

GELSO, C. J., & CARTER, J. A. (1985). The relationship in counseling and psychotherapy-components, consequences and theoretical antecedents. *The Counseling Psychologist, 13*, 155–243.

GENDLIN, E. (1986). *Let Your Body Interpret Your Dreams*. Wilmette, IL: Chiron Publications.

—— (1978). *Focusing*. New York: Everest House.

—— (1962). *Experiencing and the Creation of Meaning*. New York: Free Press.

GEORGIA CONFERENCE FOR COUNSELING PSYCHOLOGY (1988). *The Counseling Psychologist, 16* (whole July issue).

GERKIN, C. (1984). *The Living Human Document*. Nashville: Abingdon Press.

GERMANN, R., & ARNOLD, P. (1980). *Bernard Haldane Associates' Job & Career Building*. Berkeley, CA: Ten Speed Press.

GIBB, J. R. (1971). Sensitivity training as a medium for personal growth and improved personal relationship. In G. Egan (Ed.), *Encounter Groups: Basic Readings*. Belmont, CA: Wadsworth.

GIBLIN, P., SPRENKLE, D. H., & SHEEHAN, R. (1985). Enrichment outcome research: A meta-analysis of premarital, marital and family interventions. *Journal of Marital and Family Therapy, 11*, 257–271.

GILBERT, L. A. (1987). Female and male emotional dependency and its implication for the therapist-client relationship. *Professional Psychology: Theory, Research, and Practice, 18*, 555–561.

GILBERT, L. A., & RACHLIN, V. (1987). Mental health and psychological functioning of dual-career families. *The Counseling Psychologist, 15*, 7–49.

GILLIGAN, C. (1982). *In a Different Voice: Psychological Theory and Women's Development*. Cambridge: Harvard University Press.

GLADSTEIN, G. (1977). Empathy and counseling outcome: an empirical and conceptual review. *Counsel. Psychologist, 6*, 70–77.

GLASSER, W. (1965). *Reality Therapy*. New York: Harper & Row.

GLAZER, S. H. (1956). An open-ended questionnaire for precounseling orientation. *Vocational Guid. Quart., 5*, 15–17.

GLOVER, E. (1950). *Freud or Jung*. New York: Norton.

GOLDFRIED, M. (1980). Toward the delineation of therapeutic change principles. *American Psychologist, 35*, 991–999.

GOLDFRIED, M. R. (Ed.), (1982). *Converging Themes in Psychotherapy*. New York: Springer.

—— (1980). Toward the delineation of therapeutic change principles. *American Psychologist, 35*, 991–999.

—— (1971). Desensitization as training in self-control. *Journal of Consulting and Clinical Psychology, 37*, 228–234.

GOLDFRIED, M. R., & DAVISON, G. C. (1976). *Clinical Behavior Therapy*. New York: Holt, Rinehart & Winston.

GOLDFRIED, M. R., & PADAWER, W. (1982). Current status and future directions in psychotherapy. In M. R. Goldfried (Ed.), *Converging Trends in Psychotherapy*. New York: Springer.

GOLDMAN, R. K., & MENDELSOHN, G. A. (1969). Psychotherapeutic change and social adjustment: A report of a national survey of psychotherapists. *J. Abnorm. Psychol., 74*, 164–172.

GOLDSTEIN, A. P., & MYERS, C. R. (1986). Relationship-enhancement methods. In F. H. Kanfer & A. P. Goldstein (Eds.), *Helping People Change* (3d ed.). New York: Pergamon Press.

GOLDSTEIN, K. (1940). *Human Nature in the Light of Psychopathology*. Cambridge: Harvard University Press.

GOMES-SCHWARTZ, B., HADLEY, S. W., & STRUPP, H. H. (1978). Individual psychotherapy and behavior therapy. *Annual Review of Psychology, 29*, 435–471.

GOOD, G. E. (1992). Counseling psychologists in hospital/medical settings. *The Counseling Psychologist, 20*, 67–74.

GOOD, G., GILBERT, L., & SCHER, M. (1990). Gender aware therapy: A synthesis of feminist therapy and knowledge about gender. *Journal of Counseling and Development, 68,* 376–380.

GORDON, D. (1978). *Therapeutic Metaphors.* Cupertino, CA: Meta Publications.

GORDON, S. B., & DAVIDSON, N. (1981). Behavioral parent training. In A. S. Gurman & D. P. Kniskern (Eds.), *Handbook of Family Therapy.* New York: Brunner/Mazel.

GORDON, T. (1970). *Parent-Effectiveness Training.* New York: Peter H. Wyden.

GOTTFREDSON, L. S. (1981). Circumscription and compromise: A developmental theory of occupational aspirations. *Journal of Counseling Psychology, 28,* 545–579.

GOTTSEGAN, G., & GOTTSEGAN, M. (1979). Countertransference—the professional identity defense. *Psychotherapy: Theory, Research, and Practice, 16.*

GOULD, R. (1978). *Transformation: Growth and Change in Adult Life.* New York: Simon & Schuster.

GRATER, H. A. (1964). Client preference for affective or cognitive counselor characteristics and first interview behavior. *J. Counsel. Psychol., 11,* 248–250.

GRAVES, J. R., & ROBINSON, J. D. (1976). Proxemic behavior as a function of inconsistent verbal and nonverbal messages. *Journal of Counseling Psychology, 23,* 333–338.

GREEN, L. L., & HAYMES, M. (1973). Value orientation and psychosocial adjustment at various levels of marijuana use. *Journal of Youth and Adolescence, 2,* 213–231.

GREENBERG, L. S. (1986). Change process research. *Journal of Consulting and Clinical Psychology, 54,* 4–9.

———— (1983). Toward a task analysis of conflict resolution in Gestalt therapy. *Psychotherapy: Theory, Research, and Practice, 17,* 143–152.

———— (1979). Resolving splits: Use of the two-chair technique. *Psychotherapy: Theory, Research, and Practice, 16,* 316–324.

GREENBERG, L., & HIGGINS, H. M. (1980). Effects of two-chair dialogues and focusing on conflict resolution. *Journal of Counseling Psychology, 27,* 221–224.

GREENBERG, L. S., & JOHNSON, S. M. (1988). *Emotionally Focused Therapy for Couples.* New York: Guilford.

GREENBERG, L., & WEBSTER, M. C. (1982). Resolving decisional conflict by Gestalt two-chair dialogue: Relating process to outcome. *Journal of Counseling Psychology, 29,* 468–477.

GREIST, J. H., GUSTAFSON, D. H., STAUSS, F. F., ROWSE, G. L., LAUGHREN, T. P., & CHILES, J. A. (1973). A computer interview for suicide risk prediction. *American Journal of Psychiatry, 130,* 1327–1332.

GREIST, J. H., KLEIN, M. H., VAN CURA, L. J., & ERDMAN, H. P. (1975). Computer interview questionnaires for drug use/abuse. In D. J. Lettieri (Ed.), *Predicting Adolescent Drug Use: A Review of Issues, Methods and Correlates.* Washington, DC: U.S. Government Printing Office.

GURMAN, A. S., & KNISKERN, D. P. (1981). Family therapy outcome research: Knowns and unknowns. In A. S. Gurman & D. P. Kniskern, *Handbook of Family Therapy.* New York: Brunner/Mazel.

———— (1978). Research on marital and family therapy: Progress, perspective and prospect. In S. Garfield & A. Bergin (Eds.), *Handbook of Psychotherapy and Behavior Change* (2d ed.). New York: Wiley.

GUTTERIDGE, T. G., & OTTE, F. L. (1983). Organizational career development: What's going on out there? *Training and Development Journal, 37,* 22–26.

HAAGA, D. A., & DAVISON, G. C. (1986). Cognitive change methods. In F. H. Kanfer & A. P. Goldstein (Eds.), *Helping People Change.* New York: Pergamon Press.

HADLEY, S., & STRUPP, H. (1976). Contemporary views of negative side effects in psychotherapy. *Archives of General Psychiatry, 33,* 1291–1302.

HAFNER, J., & MARKS, I. M. (1976). Exposure in vivo of agorophobics: the contributions of diazepam, group exposure, and anxiety evocation. *Psychological Medicine, 6,* 71–88.

HAHLWEG, K., & MARKMAN, H. J. (1988). The effectiveness of behavioral marital therapy: Empirical status of behavioral techniques in preventing and alleviating marital distress. *Journal of Consulting and Clinical Psychology, 56,* 440–447.

HAHN, M. E., & MCLEAN, M. S. (1950). *General Clinical Counseling.* New York: McGraw-Hill.

HALEY, J. (1977). *Problem-Solving Therapy.* San Francisco: Jossey-Bass.

———— (1973). *Uncommon Therapy: The Psychiatric Techniques of Milton H. Erickson.* New York: Norton.

HANSEN, L. S., & KEIERLEBER, D. L. (1978). BORN FREE: A collaborative consultation model for career development and sex-role stereotyping. *Personnel and Guidance Journal, 56,* 395–399.

HARE-MUSTIN, R. T., & MARACEK, J. (EDS.). (1990). *Making a Difference: Psychology and the Construction of Gender.* New Haven: Yale University Press.

HARLOW, H. F. (1958). Nature of love. *American Psychologist, 13,* 673–685.

HARPER, R. A. (1975). *The New Psychotherapies.* Englewood Cliffs, NJ: Prentice-Hall.

HARRIS-BOWLSBEY, J. (1992). Systematic career guidance and computer-based systems. In Z. B. Leibowitz & H. D. Lea (Eds.), *Adult Career Development: Concepts, Issues and Practices* (2d ed.). Alexandria, VA: American Association for Counseling and Development.

HART, J. T., & TOMLINSON, T. M. (EDS.). (1970). *New Directions in Client-Centered Therapy.* Boston: Houghton Mifflin.

HARTSOUGH, D. M., & MYERS, D. G. (1985). *Disaster Work and Mental Health: Prevention and Control of Stress Among Workers.* Washington, DC: NIMH, Center for Mental Health Studies of Emergencies.

HAVIGHURST, R. J. (1953). *Human Development and Education.* New York: Longmans.

HAZARD, L. B., & KOSLOW, D. (1986). Conjoint career counseling: Counseling dual-career couples. In Z. B. Leibowitz & H. D. Lea (Eds.). *Adult Career Development: Concepts, Issues and Practices.* Alexandria, VA: American Association for Counseling and Development.

HEATH, D. H. (1991). *Fulfilling Lives: Paths to Maturity and Success.* San Francisco: Jossey-Bass.

HEFFERNAN, T., & RICHARDS, C. S. (1981). Self-control of study behavior: Identification of natural methods. *Journal of Counseling Psychology, 28,* 361–364.

HEIMAN, J. R., LoPICCOLO, L., & LoPICCOLO, J. (1980). The treatment of sexual dysfunction. In A. S. Gurman & D. P. Kniskern, *Handbook of Family Therapy.* New York: Brunner/Mazel.

HEINE, R. W. (1950). An investigation of the relationship between change in personality from psychotherapy as reported by patients and the factors seen by patients as producing change. Unpublished doctoral dissertation. University of Chicago.

HELLER, K., DAVIS, J. D., & MYERS, R. A. (1966). The effects of interviewer style in a standardized interview. *J. Consult. Psychol., 30,* 501–508.

HEPPNER, P. P. (1990). Problem solving and cognitive therapy. *Journal of Cognitive Psychotherapy, 4,* 243–246.

HEPPNER, P. P., & KRAUSKOPF, C. J. (1987). An information processing approach to personal problem solving. *The Counseling Psychologist, 15,* 371–447.

HERBERT, D. L., NELSON, R. O., & HERBERT, J. D. (1988). Effects of psychodiagnostic labels, depression severity, and instruction on assessment. *Professional Psychology: Research and Practice, 19,* 496–502.

HEREK, G. M. (1989). Hate crimes against lesbians and gay men: Issues for research and policy. *American Psychologist, 44,* 948–955.

HERINK, R. (1980). *The Psychotherapy Handbook: The A to Z Guide to More Than 250 Different Therapies in Use Today.* New York: New American Library.

HERSEY, P., & BLANCHARD, K. H. (1977). *Management of Organizational Behavior: Utilizing Human Resources* (3d ed.). Englewood Cliffs, NJ: Prentice-Hall.

HERSON, M., EISLER, R. M., MILLER, P. M., JOHNSON, M. B., & PINKSTON, S. G. (1973). Effects of practice, instructions and modeling on components of assertive behavior. *Behaviour Research and Therapy, 11,* 443–451.

HERZBERG, A. (1945). *Active Psychotherapy.* New York: Grune & Stratton.

HILL, C. E., & GORMALLY, J. (1977). Effects of reflection, restatement, probe, and nonverbal behaviors on client affect. *J. Counsel. Psychol., 24,* 92–97.

HILL, C. E., SIEGELMAN, L., GRONSKY, B. R., STURNIOLO, F., & FRETZ, B. R. (1981). Nonverbal communication and counseling outcome. *Journal of Counseling Psychology, 28,* 203–212.

HILL, C., TANNEY, M., LEONARD, M., & REISS, J. (1977). Counselor reactions to female clients: Type of problem, age of client, and sex of counselor. *J. Counsel. Psychol., 24,* 60–65.

HILLENBERG, J. B., & COLLINS, F. L., JR. (1982). A procedural analysis and review of relaxation training research. *Behaviour Research and Therapy, 20,* 251–260.

HINES, P. M. (1988). The family life cycle of poor Black families. In B. C. Carter & M. McGoldrick (Eds.), *The Changing Family Life Cycle* (2d ed., pp. 513–544). New York: Gardner Press.

HOBBS, N. (1951). Group-centered psychotherapy. In C. R. Rogers (Ed.), *Client-Centered Therapy.* Boston: Houghton Mifflin.

HOFF, L., & MILLER, W. (1980). *Marriage Enrichment: Philosophy, Process, and Program.* Bowie, MD: Charles Press.

HOFFMAN, L. (1981). *Foundations of Family Therapy: A Conceptual Framework for Systems Change.* New York: Basic Books.

HOLLAND, J. (1985). *Making Vocational Choices: A Theory of Careers* (2d ed.). Englewood Cliffs, NJ: Prentice-Hall.

HOPSON, B., & ADAMS, J. (1977). Toward an understanding of transition. In J. Adams & B. Hopson (Eds.), *Transition: Understanding and Managing Personal Change.* Montclair, NJ: Allenhald & Osmund.

HORNEY, K. (1950). *Neurosis and Human Growth.* New York: Norton.

—— (1942). *Self-Analysis.* New York: Norton.

—— (1937). *The Neurotic Personality of Our Time.* New York: Norton.

HOROWITZ, M., MARMAR, C., KRUPNICK, J., WILNER, N., KALTREIDER, N., & WALLERSTEIN, R. (1984). *Personality Styles and Brief Psychotherapy.* New York: Basic Books.

HOROWITZ, M. J., MARMAR, C., WEISS, D. S., DeWITT, K., & ROSENBAUM, R. (1984). Brief psychotherapy of bereavement reactions: The relationship of process to outcome. *Archives of General Psychiatry, 41,* 438–448.

HOSHMAND, L. L. S. (1989). Alternative research paradigms: A review and teaching proposal. *The Counseling Psychologist, 17,* 3–79.

HOVESTADT, A. J., ANDERSON, W. T., PIERCY, F. P., COCHRAN, S. W., & FINE, M. (1985). A family of origin scale. *Journal of Marital and Family Therapy, 11,* 287–298.

HOWARD, G. S., NANCE, D. W., & MYERS, P. (1986). Adaptive counseling and therapy: An integrative eclectic model. *The Counseling Psychologist, 14,* 363–442.

HOWARD, K. I., KOPTA, S., KRAUSE, M., & ORLINSKY, D. (1986). The dose-effect relationship in psychotherapy. *American Psychologist, 41,* 159–164.

HUBER, C. H., & BARUTH, L. G. (1987). *Ethical, Legal, and Professional Issues in the Practice of Marriage and Family Therapy.* Columbus, OH: Merrill.

IBRAHIM, F. (1985). Effective cross-cultural counseling and therapy: A framework. *The Counseling Psychologist, 13,* 625–638.

INGHAM, H. V., & LOVE, L. R. (1954). *The Process of Psychotherapy.* New York: McGraw-Hill.

ISHIYAMA, F. I. (1986). Morita therapy: Its basic features and cognitive intervention for anxiety treatment. *Psychotherapy, 23,* 375–381.

IVEY, A. E. (1986). *Developmental Therapy.* San Francisco: Jossey-Bass.

——— (1980). Counseling 2000: Time to take charge. *The Counseling Psychologist, 8,* 12–16.

——— (1979, June). Cross-cultural counseling and psychotherapy: foundations, evaluation, and training. Paper delivered at University of Hawaii Conference on Cross-Cultural Counseling. Honolulu, Hawaii.

IVEY, A. E., & AUTHIER, J. (1978). *Microcounseling* (2d ed.). Springfield, IL: Charles C. Thomas.

IVEY, A. E., & GLUCKSTERN, N. (1976). *Basic Influencing Skills: Participant Manual.* North Amherst, MA: Microtraining Associates.

——— (1974). *Basic Attending Skills: Participant Manual.* North Amherst, MA: Microtraining Associates.

IVEY, A. E., IVEY, M., & SIMEK-MORGAN, L. (2d ed.). (1991). *Counseling and Psychotherapy: A Multicultural Perspective.* Boston: Allyn & Bacon (3d ed. in press, 1992).

IVEY, A. E., & SIMEK-DOWNING, L. (1986). *Counseling and Psychotherapy: Skills, Theories, and Practice.* Englewood Cliffs, NJ: Prentice-Hall.

JACKSON, D. D. (1957). The question of family homeostasis. *Psychiatric Quarterly Supplement, 31*(1), 79–90.

JACOBSON, E. (1964). *Anxiety and Tension Control.* Philadelphia: Lippincott.

——— (1938). *Progressive Relaxation* (2nd ed.). Chicago: University of Chicago Press.

JACOBSON, N. S. (1991). Toward enhancing the efficacy of marital therapy and marital therapy research. *Journal of Family Psychology, 4,* 373–393.

——— (1981). Behavioral marital therapy. In A. S. Gurman & D. P. Kniskern, *Handbook of Family Therapy.* New York: Brunner/Mazel.

——— (1978). A review of the research on the effectiveness of marital therapy. In T. J. Paolino, Jr. & B. S. McCrady (Eds.), *Marriage and Marital Therapy.* New York: Brunner/Mazel.

JAHODA, M. (1958). *Current Concepts of Positive Mental Health.* New York: Basic Books.

JAMES, W. (1902). *The Varieties of Religious Experience.* Garden City, NY: Doubleday.

JANIS, I., & MANN, L. (1977). *Decision Making: A Psychological Analysis of Conflict Choice and Commitment.* New York: Free Press.

JARVIK, L. (1978). *Aging into the 21st Century.* New York: Garden Press.

JEEVES, M. (1976). *Psychology and Religion: The View Both Ways.* Downers Grove, IL: Intervarsity Press.

JENSEN, J. P., & BERGIN, A. E. (1988). Mental health values of professional therapists: A national interdisciplinary survey. *Professional Psychology: Research and Practice, 19,* 290–297.

JEPSON, D. A. (1990). Developmental career counseling. In W. B. Walsh & S. H. Osipow (Eds.), *Career Counseling: Contemporary Topics in Vocational Psychology.* Hillsdale, NJ: Erlbaum.

JOANNING, H. (1982). The long term effects of the couple communication program. *Journal of Marital and Family Therapy, 8,* 463–468.

JOEL, W., & SHAPIRO, D. (1950). Some principles and procedures for group psychotherapy. *J. Psychol., 29,* 77–88.

JOHNSON, M., & RICHARDSON, M. (1981). *Models of Training Counselors of Women.* Mimeographed report of Division 17, Committee on Women Task Force on Training for Counseling Women.

JOHNSON, W. (1946). *People in Quandaries.* New York: Harper.

JORDAN, M. (1986). *Taking on the Gods.* Nashville: Abingdon Press.

JOSLIN, L. C. (1965). Knowledge and counseling competence. *Pers. and Guid. J., 43,* 790–795.

JUNG, C. G. (1958). *The Collected Works: Vol. 11. Psychology and Religion: West and East.* New York: Pantheon Books.

——— (1933). *Modern Man in Search of a Soul.* New York: Harcourt, Brace.

KAGAN, N. (1977). Presidential address to division of counseling psychology. *Counsel. Psychologist, 7,* 4–9.

KAHANA, E., & KAHANA, B. (1976). *Strategies of Adaptation in Institutional Settings.* NIMH Grant Report. Detroit: Elderly Care Research Center.

KAIN, C. (1989). *No Longer Immune: A Counselor's Guide to AIDS.* Alexandria, VA: American Association for Counseling and Development.

KANFER, F. H., & GAELICK, L. (1986). Self-management methods. In F. H. Kanfer & A. P. Goldstein (Eds.), *Helping People Change.* New York: Pergamon Press.

KANFER, F. H., & GOLDSTEIN, A. P. (1986). *Helping People Change* (3d ed.). New York: Pergamon Press.

KANTOR, D., & NEAL, J. H. (1985). Integrative shifts for the theory and practice of family systems therapy. *Family Process, 24,* 13–30.

KAPLAN, H. S. (1974). *The New Sex Therapy.* New York: Brunner/Mazel.

KAROLY, P., & KANFER, F. A. (EDS.). (1982). *Self-Management and Behavior Change.* New York: Pergamon Press.

KEEFE, F. J., & BLUMENTHAL, J. A. (1980). The life fitness program: A behavioral approach to making exercise a habit. *Journal of Behavior Therapy and Experimental Psychiatry, 11,* 31–34.

KEGAN, R. (1982). *The Evolving Self.* Cambridge: Harvard University Press.

KENDALL, P. C., & HOLLON, S. D. (EDS.). (1981).

Assessment Strategies for Cognitive-Behavioral Interventions. New York: Academic Press.

KERNBERG, O. F. (1980). *Internal World and External Reality.* New York: Jason Aronson.

KERR, M. E. (1981). Family systems theory and therapy. In A. S. Gurman & D. P. Kniskern (Eds.), *Handbook of Family Therapy.* New York: Brunner/Mazel.

KESSLER, M., & ALBEE, G. (1975). Primary prevention. *Annual Review of Psychology, 26,* 557–591.

KESSLER, M., & GOLDSTON, S. E. (EDS.). (1986). *A Decade of Progress in Primary Prevention.* Hanover, NH: University Press of New England.

KESSLER, S. (1975). *The American Way of Divorce.* Chicago: Nelson-Hall.

KHAN, P. (1982). *Introducing Spirituality into Counseling and Therapy.* Lebanon Springs, NY: Omega Press.

KIESLER, D. J. (1966). Some myths of psychotherapy research and the search for a paradigm. *Psychological Bulletin, 65,* 110–136.

KILBURG, R. R., NATHAN, P. E., & THORESON, R. W. (1986). *Professionals in Distress.* Washington, DC: American Psychological Association.

KINSEY, A. C., POMEROY, W., MARTIN, C., & GEBHARD, P. H. (1953). *Sexual Behavior in the Human Female.* Philadelphia: Saunders.

_____ (1948). *Sexual Behavior in the Human Male.* Philadelphia: Saunders.

KIVNICK, H. Q. (1985). Disability and psychosocial development in old age. *Rehabilitation Counseling Bulletin, 29,* 123–135.

KLEIMAN, J. I. (1981). Optimal and normal family functioning. *American Journal of Family Therapy, 9,* 37–44.

KLEIN, M. (1975). *Envy and Gratitude and Other Works, 1946–1963.* New York: Delacorte Press.

KLEINMAN, A. (1988). *Rethinking Psychiatry.* New York: Free Press.

KLERMAN, G. L. (1983). The efficacy of psychotherapy as the basis for public policy. *American Psychologist, 38,* 929–934.

KLUCKHOHN, F. R., & STRODTBECK, F. L. (1961). *Variations in Value Orientations.* Evanston, IL: Row, Peterson.

KNAPP, R. R., & FITZGERALD, O. R. (1973). Comparative validity for the Personal Orientation Inventory. *Educ. Psychol. Measmt., 33,* 971–976.

KOHLBERG, L. (1981). *The Philosophy of Moral Development.* San Francisco: Harper & Row.

KOHUT, H. (1984). *How Does Analysis Cure?* Chicago: University of Chicago Press.

_____ (1977). *The Restoration of the Self.* New York: International Universities Press.

_____ (1971). *The Analysis of the Self* (The Psychoanalytic Study of the Child, Monograph No. 4). New York: International Universities Press.

KORNBERG, M., & CAPLAN, G. (1980). Risk factors and prevention intervention in child psychopathology: A review. *Journal of Prevention, 1,* 71–133.

KRASNER, L., & ULLMAN, L. (1965). *Research in Behavior Modification.* New York: Holt, Rinehart & Winston.

KRUMBOLTZ, J. (1966). Behavioral goals for counseling. *J. of Counsel. Psychol., 3,* 153–159.

KRUMBOLTZ, J. D., MITCHELL, A., & JONES, G. B. (1976). Social learning theory and career development. *The Counseling Psychologist, 6,* 71–81.

KRUMBOLTZ, J. D., & NICHOLS, C. W. (1990). Integrating the social learning theory of career decision making. In W. B. Walsh & S. H. Osipow (Eds.), *Career Counseling: Contemporary Topics in Vocational Psychology.* Hillsdale, NJ: Erlbaum.

KUHN, T. S. (1977). *The Essential Tension: Selected Studies in Scientific Tradition and Change.* Chicago: University of Chicago Press.

KUNKEL, F. (1954). Growth through crises. In S. Doniger (Ed.), *Religion and Human Behavior.* New York: Association Press.

L'ABATE, L. L. (1981). Skill training programs for couples and families. In A. S. Gurman & D. P. Kniskern (Eds.), *Handbook of Family Therapy.* New York: Brunner/Mazel.

_____ (1977). *Enrichment: Structured Interventions with Couples, Families and Groups.* Washington, DC: University Press of America.

LACKS, P., BERTELSON, A. D., SUGERMAN, J., & KUNKEL, J. (1983). The treatment of sleep-maintenance insomnia with stimulus-control techniques. *Behavior Research and Therapy, 21,* 291–295.

LAKIN, M. (1972). *Interpersonal Encounter: Theory and Practice in Sensitivity Training.* New York: McGraw-Hill.

LAMB, M. E. (1977). The effects of divorce on children's personality development. *Journal of Divorce, 1,* 163–174.

LAMBERT, M., DeJULIO, S., & STEIN, D. (1978). Therapist interpersonal skills: Process, outcome, methodological considerations and recommendations for future research. *Psychological Bulletin, 85,* 467–489.

LANGS, R. J. (1974). *The Technique of Psychoanalytic Psychotherapy* (Vol. 2). New York: Jason Aronson.

LANKTON, S. R., & LANKTON, C. H. (1983). *The Answer Within: A Clinical Framework of Ericksonian Hypnotherapy.* New York: Brunner/Mazel.

LARSON, D. (1967). In support of technical eclecticism. *Psychological Reports, 21,* 415–416.

LAWRENCE, C. (1983). Redecision and repentance: Reframing redecision work for the religious client. *Transactional Analysis Journal, 13,* 158–162.

LAZARUS, A. (1982). *Personal Enrichment Through Imagery.* Workbook [Audiotape]. New York: BMA Audio Cassettes.

_____ (1981). *The Multimodal Life History Questionnaire.* The Multimodal Therapy Institute.

_____ (1976). *Multi-Modal Behavior Therapy.* New York: Springer.

_____ (1971). *Behavior Therapy and Beyond.* New York: McGraw-Hill.

LAZARUS, R. (1979). Positive denial: the case for not facing reality. *Psychology Today, 17,* 44–60.

LAZARUS, R. S. (1977). Cognitive processes in emotion and stress. In A. Monat & R. S. Lazarus (Eds.), *Stress and Coping: An Anthology.* New York: Columbia University Press.

LEARY, T. (1957). *Interpersonal Diagnosis of Personality.* New York: Ronald Press.

LEBOW, J. L. (1987). Developing a personal integration in family therapy: Principles for model construction and practice. *Journal of Marital and Family Therapy, 13,* 1–14.

LEININGER, M. M. (1985). Transcultural caring: A different way to help people. In P. Pedersen (Ed.), *Handbook of Cross-cultural Counseling and Therapy.* Westport, CT: Greenwood Press.

LENT, R. W., BROWN, S. D., & LARKIN, K. C. (1987). Comparison of three theoretically derived variables in predicting career and academic behavior: Self efficacy, interest congruence, and consequence thinking. *Journal of Counseling Psychology, 34,* 293–298.

LESSER, W. M. (1961). The relationship between counseling progress and empathic understanding. *J. Counsel. Psychol., 8,* 330–336.

LEVANT, R. F. (1992). Toward the reconstruction of masculinity. *Journal of Family Psychology, 5,* 379–402.

LEVETON, E. (1977). *Psychodrama for the Timid Clinician.* New York: Springer.

LEVINSON, D. J. (1980). Toward a conception of the adult life course. In N. Smelser & E. Erikson (Eds.), *Themes of Work and Love in Adulthood.* Cambridge: Harvard University Press.

LEVINSON, D., DARROW, C., KLEIN, E., LEVINSON, M., & McKEE, B. (1978). *The Seasons of a Man's Life.* New York: Knopf.

LEWIS, J., BEAVERS, W. R., GOSSETT, J. P., & PHILLIPS, V. (1976). *No Single Thread.* New York: Brunner/Mazel.

LIEBERMAN, M. A. (1980). Group methods. In F. H. Kanfer & A. P. Goldstein (Eds.), *Helping People Change* (2d ed.). New York: Pergamon Press.

LIPKIN, S. (1954). Clients' feelings and attitudes in relation to the outcomes on client-centered therapy. *Psychol. Monogr., 68,* 372.

LIPSKY, M. M., KASSINOVE, H., & MILLER, N. (1980). Effects of rational-emotive therapy, rational role reversal, and rational-emotive imagery on the emotional adjustment of community mental health center patients. *J. Consult. and Clin. Psychol., 3,* 366–374.

LITTLE, L. M., & CURRAN, J. P. (1978). Covert sensitization: A clinical procedure in need of some explanations. *Psychological Bulletin, 85*(3), 513–531.

LONDON, P. (1987, April). Address to the Society for the Advancement of Psychotherapy Integration, Harvard University.

——— (1986). *The Modes and Morals of Psychotherapy* (2d ed.). Washington, DC: Hemisphere.

LOPEZ, F. G., & ANDREWS, S. (1987). Career indecision: A family systems perspective. *Journal of Counseling and Development, 65,* 304–307.

LORION, R. P., & VANDENBOS, G. (1990). Recent advances in the prevention of psychological disorders. *Hospital and Community Psychiatry, 41,* 735–736.

LOUGHARY, J., & RIPLEY, T. (1976). *Career and Life Planning Guide.* Chicago: Follett.

LOUIS, M. (1980). Career traditions: Varieties and commonalities. *Academy of Management Review, 5,* 329–340.

LOVINGER, R. J. (1984). *Working with Religious Issues in Therapy.* New York: Jason Aronson.

——— (1979). Therapeutic strategies with "religious" resistances. *Psychotherapy: Theory, Research and Practice, 16,* 419–427.

LOWE, C. M. (1976). *Value Orientations in Counseling and Psychotherapy: The Meanings of Mental Health* (2d ed.). Cranston, RI: Carroll Press.

LOWEN, A. (1972). *Training Manual in Bioenergetics.* Unpublished manuscript.

——— (1967). *Betrayal of the Body.* New York: Macmillan.

LUBORSKY, L. (1984). *Principles of Psychoanalytic Psychotherapy: A Manual for Supportive-Expressive Treatment.* New York: Basic Books.

LUBORSKY, L., CHANDLER, M., AUERBACH, A., COHEN, J., & BACHRACH, H. (1971). Factors influencing the outcome of psychotherapy: A review of the quantitative research. *Psychological Bulletin, 75,* 145–185.

LUBORSKY, L., CRITS-CHRISTOPH, P., ALEXANDER, L., MARGOLIS, M., & COHEN, M. (1983). Two helping alliance methods for predicting outcome of psychotherapy. *Journal of Nervous and Mental Disease, 171,* 480–491.

LUBORSKY, L., SINGER, B., & LUBORSKY, L. (1985). Therapist success and its determinants. *Archives of General Psychiatry, 42,* 602–611.

LUBORSKY, L., SINGER, B., & LUBORSKY, L. (1975). Comparative studies of psychotherapies. *Archives of General Psychiatry, 32,* 995–1008.

LUBORSKY, L., & SPENCE, D. P. (1978). Quantitative research on psychoanalytic therapy. In S. Garfield & A. Bergin (Eds.), *Handbook of Psychotherapy and Behavior Change* (2d ed.). New York: Wiley.

MAEDER, T. (1989). Wounded healers. *The Atlantic Monthly, 52,* 37–42.

MAGDEN, S., & SHOSTROM, E. Unpublished paper presented to annual meeting of American Psychological Association, New Orleans, 1974.

MAHLER, M., PINE, F., & BERGMAN, A. (1975). *The Psychological Birth of the Human Infant.* New York: Basic Books.

MAHONEY, M. (1979). Cognitive and noncognitive views in behavior modification. In *Trends in Behavior Therapy.* P. Sjoden and S. Bates. (Eds.), New York: Plenum Press.

—— (1974). *Cognition and Behavior Modification.* Cambridge, MA: Ballinger.

MAHONEY, M. J. (1991). *Human Change Processes: The Scientific Foundations of Psychotherapy.* New York: Basic Books.

MALONEY, H. N. (1980). Transactional analysis. In G. R. Collins (Ed.), *Helping People Grow.* Santa Ana, CA: Vision House.

MARLATT, G. A., & GEORGE, W. H. (1984). Relapse prevention: Introduction and overview of the model. *British Journal of Addictions, 79,* 261–273.

MARLATT, G. A., & GORDON, J. R. (1984). *Relapse Prevention: Maintenance Strategies in Addictive Behavior Change.* New York: Guilford Press.

MARZIALI, E. A. (1984). Three viewpoints on the therapeutic alliance: Similarities, differences and associations with psychotherapy outcome. *Journal of Nervous and Mental Disease, 172,* 417–423.

MASLACH, C. (1978). The client role in staff burnout. *J. of Social Issues, 34,* 11–124.

—— (1976). Burned out. *Human Behavior, 5,* 74–78.

MASLOW, A. H. (1970). *Motivation and Personality* (2d ed.). New York: Harper & Row.

—— (1966). *The Psychology of Science.* New York: Harper & Row.

MASTERS, M. A. (1992). The use of positive reframing in the context of supervision. *Journal of Counseling and Development, 70,* 387–390.

MASTERS, W. H., & JOHNSON, V. E. (1974). *The Pleasure Bond.* Boston: Little, Brown.

—— (1970). *Human Sexual Inadequacy.* Boston: Little, Brown.

—— (1966). *Human Sexual Response.* Boston: Little, Brown.

MATARAZZO, J. (1984). Behavioral immunogens and pathogens in health and illness. In C. Scheirer & B. Hammond (Eds.), *Psychology in Health* (Master Lecture Series, Vol. 3). Washington, DC: American Psychological Association.

MATHENY, K. B., AYCOCK, D. W., PUGH, J. L., CURLETTE, W. L., & SILVA CANELLA, K. A. (1986). Stress coping: A qualitative and quantitative synthesis with implications for treatment. *The Counseling Psychologist, 14,* 499–549.

MATURANA, H. R., & VARELA, F. J. (1987). *The Tree of Knowledge: The Biological Roots of Human Understanding.* Boston: Shambala.

MAURER, R. E., & TINDALL, J. H. (1983). Effect of postural congruence on client's perception of counselor empathy. *Journal of Counseling Psychology, 30,* 158–163.

MAY, G. (1982a). *Care of Mind/Care of Spirit.* New York: Harper & Row.

—— (1982b). *Will and Spirit.* New York: Harper & Row.

MAY, R. (1969). *Rollo May and Human Encounter.* Film. Santa Ann, CA: Psychological Films.

—— (1967). *Psychology and the Human Dilemma.* Princeton: Van Nostrand.

—— (1953). *Man's Search for Himself.* New York: Norton.

—— (1939). *The Art of Counseling.* New York: Abingdon-Cokesbury.

MAY, R., ANGEL, F., & ELLENBERGER, H. (1958). *Existence.* New York: Basic Books.

MAYNARD, P. K., & OLSON, D. H. (1987). Circumplex model of family systems: A treatment tool in family counseling. *Journal of Counseling and Development, 65,* 502–504.

MAZER, G. E., MANGRUM, O. L., HOVESTADT, A. J., & BRASHEAR, R. L. (1990). Further validation of the family of origin scale: A factor analysis. *Journal of Marital Family Therapy, 16,* 423–426.

MCCULLOUGH, L., & FARRELL, A. D. (1983). *Procedures Manual for CASPER: The Computerized Assessment System for Psychotherapy Evaluation and Research (Version 1).* Unpublished manuscript.

MCCULLOUGH, L., FARRELL, A. D., & LONGABAUGH, R. (1986). The development of a microcomputer-based mental health information system. *American Psychologist, 41,* 207–214.

MCCULLOUGH, L., STOUT, R. L., LONGABAUGH, R., & STEVENSON, J. (1982). *Major Problem Rating System (1), Manual No. 1.* Unpublished manuscript.

MCGOLDRICK, M., & GERSON, R. (1985). *Genograms in Family Assessment.* New York: Norton.

MCGRATH, E., KEITA, G., STRICKLAND, B., & RUSSO, N. (1990). *Women and Depression: Risk Factors and Treatment Issues.* Washington, DC: American Psychological Association.

MCGUIRE, F. J. (1980). Strong's Christian counseling: A Buddhist response. *Personnel and Guidance Journal, 53,* 592–595.

MCWHIRTER, E. H. (1991). Empowerment in counseling. *Journal of Counseling and Development, 69,* 222–227.

MEADOR, B. D., & ROGERS, C. R. (1984). Person-centered therapy. In R. J. Corsini (Ed.), *Current Psychotherapies* (3d ed.). Itasca, IL: F. E. Peacock.

MEEHL, P. E. (1973). *Psychodiagnosis: Selected Papers.* New York: Norton.

MEICHENBAUM, D. H. (1986). Cognitive behavior modification. In F. H. Kanfer & A. P. Goldstein (Eds.), *Helping People Change.* New York: Pergamon Press.

—— (1985). *Stress Inoculation Training.* New York: Pergamon Press.

—— (1977). *Cognitive-Behavior Modification: An Integrative Approach.* New York: Plenum.

MEICHENBAUM, D., TURK, D., & BURSTEIN, S. (1975). The nature of coping with stress. Paper presented at the NATO Conference on Stress and Anxiety, Korsor, Denmark.

MENDELSOHN, G. A. (1966). Effects of client personality and client-counselor similarity on the duration of counseling: a replication and extension. *J. Counsel. Psychol., 13,* 228–234.

MERIKANGAS, M. W., & FRETZ, B. R. (1986). Preretirement programming: Beyond lectures. In Z. B. Lei-bowitz & H. D. Lea (Eds.), *Adult Career Development: Concepts, Issues and Practices.* Alexandria, VA: American Association for Counseling and Development.

MICHIGAN STATE UNIVERSITY. (1956). *How to Make Referrals.* East Lansing, MI: Guidance and Counselor Training, College of Education, Michigan State University.

MILLER, D. (1970). The effects of immediate and delayed audio and videotaped feedback on group counseling. *Comparative Group Studies I.*

MILLER, S., NUNNALLY, E. W., & WACKMAN, D. B. (1977). *The Couple Communication Instructor Manual.* Minneapolis, MN: Interpersonal Communication Programs, Inc.

MILLER, W. R., & MARTIN, J. E. (1988). *Behavior Therapy and Religion.* Newbury Park, CA: Sage.

MILLON, T. (1981). *Disorders of Personality: DSM-III, Axis II.* New York: Wiley.

MILLON, T., MILLON, C., & ANTONI, M. (1987). Sources of emotional and mental disorder among psychologists: A career development perspective. In R. Kilburg, P. Nathan, & R. Thoreson (Eds.), *Professionals in Distress.* Washington, DC: American Psychological Association.

MINTZ, L. B. (1992). Assistant professor: Paranoid or self serving? *The Counseling Psychologist, 20,* 39–46.

MINTZ, L. B., & O'NEIL, J. M. (1990). Gender roles, sex, and the process of psychotherapy: Many questions and few answers. *Journal of Counseling and Development, 68,* 381–387.

MINUCHIN, S. (1974). *Families and Family Therapy.* Cambridge, MA: Harvard University Press.

MINUCHIN, S., & FISHMAN, H. C. (1981). *Family Therapy Techniques.* Cambridge, MA: Harvard University Press.

MINUCHIN, S., MONTALVO, B., GUERNEY, B., ROSMAN, B., & SCHUMER, F. (1967). *Families of the Slums.* New York: Basic Books.

MINUCHIN, S., ROSMAN, B., & BAKER, L. (1978). *Psychosomatic Families.* Cambridge: Harvard University Press.

MISCHEL, W. (1973). Toward a cognitive social learning reconceptualization of personality. *Psychol. Rev., 80,* 252–283.

MONTAGUE, A. (1950). *On Being Human.* New York: H. Schuman.

MOONEY, R. L. (1950). *Mooney Problem Checklist.* New York: Psychological Corp.

MORENO, Z. T. (1983). Psychodrama. In H. I. Kaplan & B. J. Sadock (Eds.), *Comprehensive Group* (2d ed.). Baltimore, MD: Williams and Wilkins.

——— (1959). A survey of psychodramatic techniques. *Group Psychotherapy, 12.*

MORGAN, C. (1984). A curricular approach to primary prevention. *The Personnel and Guidance Journal,* 467–469.

MORRIS, R. J. (1986). Fear reduction methods. In

F. H. Kanfer & A. P. Goldstein (Eds.), *Helping People Change.* New York: Pergamon Press.

MORTON, R. B. (1955). An experiment in social psychotherapy. *Psychol. Monogr., 69,* 1–17.

MOWRER, O. H. (1957). Some philosophical problems in psychological counseling. *J. Counsel Psychol., 4,* 103–111.

——— (1953). Tension changes during psychotherapy with special reference to resistance. In *Psychotherapy: Theory and Research,* ed. O. Mowrer. New York: Ronald Press.

——— (1951). Anxiety theory as a basis for distinguishing between counseling and psychotherapy. In R. Berdie (Ed.), *Concepts and Programs of Counseling.* Minneapolis: University of Minnesota Press.

——— (1950). *Learning Theory and Personality Dynamics.* New York: Ronald Press.

MUELLER, W. J. (1969). Patterns of behavior and their reciprocal impact in the family and in psychotherapy. *Journal of Counseling Psychology, 16,* (2, Pt. 2).

MURRAY, E. J. (1956). A content-analysis method for studying psychotherapy. *Psychological Monographs, 70,* (13, Whole No. 420).

MYERS, D. G. (1978). *The Human Puzzle: Psychological Research and Christian Belief.* New York: Harper & Row.

MYERS, J. E. (1985). Using links to help older disabled persons with transitions. *Rehabilitation Counseling Bulletin, 29,* 143–149.

MYERS, J. E., & SALMON, H. E. (1983). Counseling programs for older persons: Status, shortcomings and potentialities. *The Counseling Psychologist, 12,* 39–54.

MYERS, R. A., THOMPSON, A. S., LINDEMAN, R. N., SUPER, D. E., PATRICK, T. A., & FRIEL, T. W. (1972). *Educational and Career Exploration Systems: Report of a Two-Year Field Trial.* New York: Teachers College.

NEFF, P. (1984). *Tough Love: How Parents Can Deal with Drug Abuse.* Nashville: Abingdon Press.

NELSON, R. O., & BARLOW, D. H. (1981). Behavioral assessment: Basic strategies and initial procedures. In D. H. Barlow (Ed.), *Behavioral Assessment of Adult Disorders.* New York: Guilford Press.

NOBLE, K. (1987). Psychological health and the experience of transcendence. *The Counseling Psychologist, 15,* 601–614.

NORCROSS, J. C., & PROCHASKA, J. O. (1982). A national survey of clinical psychologists: Characteristics and activities. *The Clinical Psychologist, 35,* 4–8.

NYGREN, A. (1953). *Agape and Eros.* London: SPCK.

O'HANLON, W. H., & WEINER-DAVIS, M. (1989). *In Search of Evolutions: A New Direction in Psychotherapy.* New York: Norton.

O'NEIL, J. M. (1981). Male sex role conflicts, sexism, and masculinity: Psychological implications for men, women, and the counseling psychologist. *Counseling Psychologist, 9,* 61–81.

O'NEIL, J. M., & FISHMAN, D. M. (1986). Adult men's career transitions and gender-role themes. In Z. B. Leibowitz & H. D. Lea (Eds.), *Adult Career Development: Concepts, Issues and Practices.* Alexandria, VA: American Association for Counseling and Development.

O'NEIL, J. M., FISHMAN, D. M., & KINSELLA-SHAW, M. (1987). Dual-career couples' career transitions and normative dilemmas: A preliminary assessment model. *The Counseling Psychologist, 15,* 50–96.

OLSON, D. H., RUSSELL, C., & SPRENKLE, D. (1983). Circumplex model of marital and family systems: IV. Theoretical update. *Family Process, 22,* 69–83.

OLSON, D. H., SPRENKLE, D., & RUSSELL, C. (1979). Circumplex model of marital and family systems: I. Cohesion and adaptability dimensions, family types and clinical applications. *Family Process, 18,* 3–15.

ORLINSKY, D. E., & HOWARD, K. I. (1986). Process and outcome in psychotherapy. In S. L. Garfield & A. E. Bergin (Eds.), *Handbook of Psychotherapy and Behavior Change.* (3d ed.), pp. 311–384. New York: Wiley.

——— (1978). The relation of process to outcome in psychotherapy. In S. Garfield & A. Bergin (Eds.), *Handbook of Psychotherapy and Behavior Change.* New York: Wiley.

OSHERSON, S. (1980). *Holding On or Letting Go.* New York: Free Press.

OSIPOW, S. H. (1990). Convergence in theories of career choice and development: Review and prospect. *Journal of Vocational Behavior, 36,* 122–131.

——— (1983). Counseling psychology: Applications in the world of work. *The Counseling Psychologist, 10,* 19–26.

PACKER, J., & BAIN, J. (1978). Cognitive style. *J. Educ. Psychol., 70,* 864–871.

PAPP, P. (ED.). (1977). *Family Therapy: Full Length Case Studies.* New York: Gardner Press.

——— (1973). Family sculpting in preventive work with "well" families. *Family Process, 12,* 197–212.

PARNES, H. (1981). *Work and Retirement.* Cambridge, MA: MIT Press.

PATTERSON, C. H. (1984). Empathy, warmth, and genuineness in psychotherapy: A review of reviews. *Psychotherapy, 21,* 431–438.

PEABODY, S. A., & GELSO, C. J. (1982). Countertransference and empathy: The complex relationship between two divergent concepts in counseling. *Journal of Counseling Psychology, 29,* 240–245.

PEARLIN, L., & SCHOOLER, C. (1978). The structure of coping. *Journal of Health and Social Behavior, 19,* 2–21.

PEARSON, L. (ED.). (1965). *The Use of Written Communications in Psychotherapy.* Springfield, IL: Charles C. Thomas.

PECK, J. S., & MANOCHERIAN, J. (1988). Divorce in the changing family life cycle. In B. Carter & M. McGoldrick (Eds.), *The Changing Family Life Cycle:*

A Framework for Family Therapy (2d ed., pp. 545–578). New York: Gardner Press.

PECK, M. S. (1987). *The Different Drum: Community Making and Peace.* New York: Simon & Schuster.

——— (1978). *The Road Less Traveled.* New York: Simon & Schuster.

PEDERSEN, P. B. (1991). Introduction to the special issue on multiculturalism as a fourth force in counseling. *Journal of Counseling and Development, 70,* 5–6.

PENDAGAST, E. G., & SHERMAN, C. O. (1977). A guide to the genogram. *The Family, 5,* 3–14.

PENN, P. (1982). Circular questioning. *Family Process, 21,* 267–280.

PEPINSKY, H. B., & PEPINSKY, P. N. (1954). *Counseling Theory and Practice.* New York: Ronald Press.

PERLS, F. S. (1973). *The Gestalt Approach.* Palo Alto: Science and Behavior Books.

——— (1969a). *Gestalt Therapy Verbatim.* Moab, UT: Real People Press.

——— (1969b). *In and Out the Garbage Pail.* Moab, UT: Real People Press.

PERLS, F. S., HEFFERLINE, R. F., & GOODMAN, P. (1951). *Gestalt Therapy.* New York: Julian Press.

PERRY, M. A., & FURUKAWA, M. J. (1986). Modeling methods. In F. H. Kanfer & A. P. Goldstein (Eds.), *Helping People Change.* New York: Pergamon Press.

PERSONS, J. B. (1991). Psychotherapy outcome studies do not accurately represent current models of psychotherapy. *American Psychologist, 46,* 99–106.

PFEIFFER, J. W., & JONES, J. E. (EDS.). (1975). *The 1975 Annual Handbook for Group Facilitators.* San Diego, CA: University Associates.

PHILLIPS, E. L. (1956). *Psychotherapy; a Modern Theory and Practice.* Englewood Cliffs, NJ: Prentice-Hall.

——— (1951). Attitudes toward self and others; a brief questionnaire report. *J. Consult. Psychol., 15,* 79–81.

PHILLIPS, E. L., & AGNEW, J. W., JR. (1953). A study of Rogers' "reflection" hypothesis. *J. Clin. Psychol., 9,* 281–284.

PINSOF, W. M. (1981). Family therapy process research. In A. S. Gurman & D. P. Kniskern, *Handbook of Family Therapy.* New York: Brunner/Mazel.

POLKINGHORNE, D. E. (1991). Two conflicting calls for methodological reform. *The Counseling Psychologist, 19,* 103–114.

POLSTER, E., & POLSTER, M. (1973). *Gestalt Therapy Integrated.* New York: Brunner/Mazel.

PORTER, E. H., JR. (1950). *An Introduction to Therapeutic Counseling.* Boston: Houghton Mifflin.

——— (1949). Understanding diagnostically and understanding therapeutically. In F. C. Williamson (Ed.), *Trends in Student Personnel Work.* Minneapolis: University of Minnesota Press, 113–119.

POSTMAN, L., BRUNER, J. S., & MCGINNIES, E. (1948). Personal values as selective factors in perception. *J. Abnorm. Soc. Psychol., 43,* 142–154.

POWER, P. W., HERSHENSON, D. B., & SCHLOSSBERG, N. K. (1985). Midlife transition and disability. *Rehabilitation Counseling Bulletin, 29,* 100–112.

PRICE, R. H., COWEN, E. L., LORION, R. P., & RAMOS-MCKAY, J. (EDS.). (1988). *Fourteen Ounces of Prevention: A Casebook for Practitioners.* Washington, DC: American Psychological Association.

PROCHASKA, J. O. (1984). *Systems of Psychotherapy: A Transtheoretical Analysis* (2d ed.). Homewood, IL: Dorsey Press.

PROCHASKA, J. O., & DICLEMIENTE, C. C. (1982). Transtheoretical therapy: Toward a more integrative model of change. *Psychotherapy: Theory, Research, and Practice, 19,* 276–288.

PROGOFF, I. (1975). *At a Journal Workshop.* New York: Dialogue House Library.

QUATROCHI-TURBIN, S., & JASON, L. A. (1980). Enhancing social interaction and activity among the elderly through stimulus control. *Journal of Applied Behavior Analysis, 13,* 159–163.

RAIMY, V. (1975). *Misunderstanding of the Self.* San Francisco: Jossey-Bass.

RAMA, S., BALLENTINE, R., & AJAYA, S. (1976). *Yoga and Psychotherapy: The Evolution of Consciousness.* Honesdale, PA: Himalaya Institute.

RASKIN, A. (1961). Factors therapists associate with motivation to enter psychotherapy. *J. Clin. Psychol., 17,* 62–65.

RASKIN, N. (1974). Studies on psychotherapeutic orientation. AAP Psychotherapy Research monograph. Orlando, FL: American Academy of Psychotherapy, 1974.

RAYMAN, J. R. (1990). Computers and career counseling. In W. B. Walsh & S. H. Osipow (Eds.), *Career Counseling: Contemporary Topics in Vocational Psychology.* Hillsdale, NJ: Erlbaum.

REDDY, W. B. (1972). On affection, group composition, and self-actualization in sensitivity training. *J. Consult. and Clin. Psychol., 38,* 211–214.

REID, D. K., & SNYDER, W. U. (1947). Experiment on "recognition of feeling" in non-directive psychotherapy. *J. Clin. Psychol., 3,* 128–135.

REMER, P., O'NEILL, C. D., & GOAS, D. C. (1984). Multiple outcome evaluation of a life career development course. *Journal of Counseling Psychology, 31,* 532–540.

RENNIE, D. L. (1984, May). Client's tape-assisted recall of psychotherapy: A qualitative analysis. Paper presented at the annual meeting of the Canadian Psychological Association, Ottawa, Canada.

RENNIE, D. L., PHILLIPS, J. R., & QUARTARO, G. K. (1988). Grounded theory: A promising approach to conceptualization in psychology. *Canadian Psychology, 29(2),* 139–150.

REST, J. R. (1983). Research on moral development: Implications for training counseling psychologists. *The Counseling Psychologist, 12,* 19–29.

REUSCH, J., & PRESTWOOD, A. R. (1949). Anxiety. *Arch. Neurol. Psychiat., 62,* 1–24.

REYNOLDS, D. K. (1976). *Morita Psychotherapy.* Berkeley: University of California Press.

RICE, L. N., & GREENBERG, L. S. (1984). *Patterns of Change: Intensive Analysis of Psychotherapy Process.* New York: Guilford Press.

RICHARDSON, H. B. (1945). *Patients Have Families.* New York: Commonwealth Fund.

RICHARDSON, H., & BOROW, H. (1952). Evaluation of technique of group orientation for vocational counseling. *Educ. Psychol. Measmt., 12,* 587–597.

RIMM, D. C., & MASTERS, J. C. (1979). *Behavior Therapy: Techniques and Empirical Findings* (2d ed.). New York: Academic Press.

RIMM, R. C., & MARKLE, A. (1977). Parent effectiveness training: A review. *Psychological Reports, 41,* 59–109.

RING, K. (1984). *Heading Toward Omega: In Search of the Meaning of the Near Death Experience.* New York: William Morrow.

RIPPEE, B. D., HARVEY, W. E., & PARKER, C. A. (1965). The influence of counseling on the perception of counselor role. *Pers. and Guid. J., 43,* 600–606.

RIZZUTO, A. M. (1979). *The Birth of the Living God.* Chicago: University of Chicago Press.

ROBINSON, F. P. (1950). *Principles and Procedures in Student Counseling.* New York: Harper.

ROBINSON, M. (1979). A study of the effects of focused video-taped feedback in group counseling. *Comparative Group Studies, 1,* 47–77.

ROGERS, C. R. (1984). One alternative to nuclear planetary suicide. In R. Levant & J. Shlien (Eds.), *Client-Centered Therapy and the Person-Centered Approach: New Directions in Theory, Research, and Practice.* Westport, CN: Praeger.

———— (1980). *A Way of Being.* Boston: Houghton Mifflin.

———— (1977). *Carl Rogers on Personal Power.* New York: Delacorte.

———— (1973). Some new challenges. *American Psychologist, 28,* 379–387.

———— (1970). *Carl Rogers on Encounter Groups.* New York: Harper & Row.

———— (1968). The increasing involvement of the psychologist in social problems. *California State Psychologist, 9,* 29.

———— (1961). *On Becoming a Person.* Boston: Houghton Mifflin.

———— (1958). A process conception of psychotherapy. *American Psychologist, 13,* 142–149.

———— (1957a). A therapist's view of the good life. *The Humanist, 5,* 291–300, American Humanist Association, Yellow Springs, OH.

———— (1957b). The necessary and sufficient conditions of therapeutic personality change. *Journal of Consulting Psychology, 21,* 95–103.

———— (1955a). A personal view of some issues facing psychologists. *American Psychologist, 10,* 247–249.

_____ (1955b). Persons or science? A philosophical question. *American Psychologist, 10,* 267–278.

_____ (1954). *Becoming a Person.* Oberlin, OH: Board of Trustees, Oberlin College.

_____ (1953). Some directions and end points in therapy. In O. H. Mowrer (Ed.), *Psychotherapy: Theory and Research.* New York: Ronald Press.

_____ (1951). *Client-Centered Therapy.* Boston: Houghton Mifflin.

_____ (1946). *Counseling with Returned Service Men.* New York: McGraw-Hill.

_____ (1942). *Counseling and Psychotherapy.* Boston: Houghton Mifflin.

_____ The fully functioning personality. Unpublished paper.

ROGERS, C. R., & DYMOND, R. E. (1954). *Psychotherapy and Personality Change.* Chicago: University of Chicago Press.

ROSE, S. D. (1986). Group methods. In F. Kanfer & A. Goldstein (Eds.), *Helping People Change.* New York: Pergamon Press.

ROSEN, G. M. (1987). Self-help treatment books and the commercialization of psychotherapy. *American Psychologist, 2,* 46–51.

ROSENBAUM, J. E. (1979). Tournament mobility. Career patterns in a corporation. *Administrative Science Quarterly, 24,* 220–241.

ROSENFIELD, M., SHIMBERG, B., & THORNTON, T. R. (1983). *Job Analysis of Licensed Psychologists in the U.S. and Canada.* Princeton, NJ: COPA, Educational Testing Service.

ROSEWATER, L. B. (1985). Feminist interpretation of traditional testing. In L. B. Rosewater and L. A. Walker (Eds.), *Handbook of Feminist Therapy: Women's Issues in Psychotherapy.* New York: Springer.

ROTH, D., BIELSKI, R., JONES, M., PARKER, W., & OSBORNE, G. (1982). A comparison of self-control therapy and combined self-control and antidepressant medication in the treatment of depression. *Behavior Therapy, 13,* 133–144.

ROTTER, J. B. (1954). *Social Learning and Clinical Psychology.* Englewood Cliffs, NJ: Prentice-Hall.

RUDESTAM, K. E. (1982). *Experiential Groups in Theory and Practice.* Pacific Grove, CA: Brooks/Cole.

RUSH, A. J., BECK, A. T., KOVACS, M., & HOLLON, S. (1977). Comparative efficacy of cognitive therapy and pharmacotherapy in the treatment of depressed outpatients. *Cognitive Therapy and Research, 1,* 17–37.

RUSK, T. (1971). Opportunity and technique in crisis psychiatry. *Comprehensive Psychiatry, 12,* 249–263.

RUSSELL, D. M. (1988). Language and psychotherapy: The influence of nonstandard English in clinical practice. In L. Comas-Diaz & E. E. H. Griffith (Eds.), *Clinical Guidelines in Cross-Cultural Mental Health.* New York: Wiley.

SAGER, C. (1981). Couples therapy and marriage contracts. In A. S. Gurman & D. P. Kniskern, *Handbook of Family Therapy.* New York: Brunner/Mazel.

_____ (1976). *Marriage Contracts and Couple Therapy.* New York: Brunner/Mazel.

_____ (1966). The treatment of married couples. In S. Arieti (Ed.), *The American Handbook of Psychiatry,* New York: Basic Books.

SANFORD, N. (1966). *Self and Society.* New York: Atherton.

SATIR, V. (1964). *Conjoint Family Therapy.* Palo Alto, CA: Science & Behavior Books.

SCHACHT, T. E. (1991). Formulation-based psychotherapy research: Some further considerations. *American Psychologist, 46,* 1346–1347.

SCHER, M., STEVENS, M., GOOD, G., & EICHENFIELD, G. (EDS.). (1987). *Handbook of Counseling and Psychotherapy with Men.* Newbury Park, CA: Sage.

SCHLOSSBERG, N. (1984). *Counseling Adults in Transition.* New York: Springer.

_____ (1981). A model for analyzing human adaptation to transition. *The Counseling Psychologist, 9,* 2–18.

SCHLOSSBERG, N., TROLL, L., & LEIBOWITZ, Z. (1978). *Perspectives on Counseling Adults: Issues and Skills.* Pacific Grove, CA: Brooks/Cole.

SCHMIDT, L., & STRONG, S. (1971). Attractiveness and influence in counseling. *J. Counsel. Psychol., 18,* 348–351.

SCHRAM, R. W. (1979). Marital satisfaction over the family life cycle: A critique and a proposal. *Journal of Marriage and the Family, 41,* 1–7.

SCHUTZ, W. C. (1975). *Elements of Encounter.* New York: Bantam Books.

_____ (1971). *Here Comes Everybody.* New York: Harper & Row.

SCHWARTZ, R. C. (1985). Has family therapy reached the stage where it can appreciate the concept of stages? In D. C. Breunlin (Ed.), *Stages: Patterns of Change over Time.* Rockville, MA: Aspen.

SCHWEBEL, M. (1965). Learning and the socially deprived. *Pers. and Guid. J., 43,* 646–653.

_____ (1955). Why unethical practice? *J. Counsel. Psychol., 2,* 122–127.

SEEMAN, J. A., & OTHERS. (1949). A coordinated research in psychotherapy. *J. Consult. Psychol., 13,* 154–195.

SELVINI PALAZZOLI, M., BOSCOLO, L., CECCHIN, G., & PRATA, G. (1980). Hypothesizing—circularity—neutrality: Three guidelines for the conductor of the session. *Family Process, 19,* 3–12.

SELYE, H. (1974). *Stress Without Distress.* Philadelphia: Lippincott.

SHAFFER, W. F. (1986). An improved version of the counselor case-management advisor computer program. Paper presented at the annual meeting of the American Educational Research Association, San Francisco, CA.

_____ (1976). Heuristics for the initial diagnostic interview. Paper presented at the annual convention of the American Psychological Association, October, 1977, ED136152.

SHANNON, J. W., & WOODS, W. J. (1991). Affirmative psychotherapy for gay men. *The Counseling Psychologist, 19,* 197–215.

SHEIN, E. H. (1978). *Career Dynamics: Matching Individual and Organizational Needs.* Reading, MA: Addison-Wesley.

SHEINBERG, M., & PENN, P. (1991). Gender dilemmas, gender questions, and the gender mantra. *Journal of Marital and Family Therapy, 17,* 33–44.

SHERMAN, D. (1945). An analysis of the dynamic relationships between counselor techniques and outcomes in larger units of the interview situation. Unpublished doctoral dissertation, Ohio State University.

SHOBEN, E. J. (1955). Special review: Some recent books on counseling and adjustment. *Psychol. Bull., 52,* 251–262.

SHOEMAKER, M. E. (1977). Developing assertiveness: Training or therapy? In R. E. Alberti (Ed.), *Assertiveness Innovation, Applications, Issues.* San Luis Obispo, CA: Impact.

SHOSTROM, E. L. (1987). FACETS theory. Unpublished manuscript.

———— (1974a). *Three Approaches to Group Therapy.* 16-mm color films. Santa Ana, CA: Psychological Films.

———— (1974b). *Touching: Importance for Human Growth.* Film. Santa Ana, CA: Psychological Films.

———— (1968). *Man, the Manipulator.* New York: Bantam.

———— (1966a). *Caring Relationship Inventory.* San Diego: EDITS.

———— (1966b). *Three Approaches to Psychotherapy.* Films of Rogers, Perls, and Ellis. Santa Ana, CA: Psychological Films.

———— (1963). *Personal Orientation Inventory.* San Diego: EDITS.

SHOSTROM, E. L., & BRAMMER, L. M. (1952). *The Dynamics of the Counseling Process.* New York: McGraw-Hill.

SHOSTROM, E. L., KNAPP, L., & KNAPP, R. (1976). *Actualizing Therapy: Foundations for a Scientific Ethic.* San Diego: EDITS.

SHOSTROM, E. L., & LOCKWOOD, G. (1980). *Growth Process Inventory.* San Diego, CA: EDITS.

SHOSTROM, E. L., & MONTGOMERY, D. (1981). Actualizing Therapy. In R. Corsini (Ed.), *Innovative Psychotherapies.* New York: Wiley.

SHOSTROM, E. L., & RILEY, C. M. D. (1968). Parametric analysis of psychotherapy. *J. Consult. and Clin. Psychol., 32,* 628–632.

SILVERMAN, L. H. (1974). Some psychoanalytic considerations of non-psychoanalytic therapies: On the possibility of integrating treatment approaches and related issues. *Psychotherapy: Theory, Research, and Practice, 2,* 298–305.

SIMKIN, J. S., & YONTEF, G. M. (1984). Gestalt therapy. In R. J. Corsini (Ed.), *Current Psychotherapies,* (3d ed.). Itasca, IL: Peacock.

SIMONTON, O. C., MATTHEWS-SIMONTON, S., & CREIGHTON, J. L. (1980). *Getting Well Again.* New York: Bantam Books.

SINGER, B., & LUBORSKY, L. (1977). Counter-transference: A comparison of what is known from the clinical vs. quantitative research. In A. Gurman & A. Razin (Eds.), *Effective Psychotherapy: An Empirical Assessment.* New York: Pergamon Press.

SINGER, J. (1974). *Imagery and Daydream Methods in Psychotherapy.* New York: Academic Press.

SINICK, D. (1977). *Counseling Older Persons: Careers, Retirement, Dying.* New York: Human Sciences.

SKINNER, B. F. (1953). *Science and Human Behavior.* New York: Macmillan.

SLOANE, R. B., STAPLES, F. R., CRISTOL, A. H., YORKSTON, N. J., & WHIPPLE, K. (1975). *Psychotherapy versus Behavior Therapy.* Cambridge, MA: Harvard University Press.

SLUZKI, C. E. (1978). Marital therapy from a systems theory perspective. In T. J. Paolino, Jr. & B. S. McCrady (Eds.), *Marriage and Marital Therapy.* New York: Brunner/Mazel.

SMITH, A. J., & SIEGEL, R. F. (1985). Feminist therapy: Redefining power for the powerless. In L. B. Rosewater & L. A. Walker (Eds.), *Handbook of Feminist Therapy: Women's Issues in Psychotherapy.* New York: Springer.

SMITH, D. (1982). Trends in counseling and psychotherapy. *American Psychologist, 37,* 802–809.

SMITH, M. J., & VASQUEZ, M. J. (EDS.). (1985). Ethnic minorities: life stress, social support, and mental health issues. *The Counseling Psychologist, 13,* 531–581.

SMITH, M. L., GLASS, G. V., & MILLER, T. I. (1980). *The Benefits of Psychotherapy.* Baltimore, MD: Johns Hopkins University Press.

SMYER, M. A. (1983). Life transitions and aging: Implications for counseling older adults. *The Counseling Psychologist, 12,* 17–28.

SNYDER, D. K., WILLS, R. M., & GRADY-FLETCHER, A. (1991). Long-term effectiveness of behavioral versus insight-oriented marital therapy. *Journal of Consulting and Clinical Psychology, 57,* 39–46.

SOLOMON, M. A. (1973). A developmental, conceptual premise for family therapy. *Family Process, 12,* 179–188.

SOROKIN, P. A. (1950). *Explorations in Altruistic Love and Behavior.* Boston: Beacon Press.

SPERRY, R. W. (1988). Psychology's mentalist paradigm and religion/science tension. *American Psychologist, 43,* 607–613.

SPITZ, R. A. (1949). Role of ecological factors in emotional development of infants. *Child Development, 76,* 145–146.

SPOKANE, A. R. (1991). *Career Intervention.* Englewood Cliffs, NJ: Prentice-Hall.

SPOKANE, A. R., & OLIVER, L. W. (1983). The outcomes of vocational intervention. In W. B. Walsh & S. H. Osipow (Eds.), *Handbook of Vocational Psychology, Vol. 1: Foundations*. Hillsdale, NJ: Erlbaum.

SPRENKLE, D. H., & STORM, C. L. (1983). Divorce therapy outcome research: A substantive and methodological review. *Journal of Marital and Family Therapy, 9*, 239–258.

STANTON, M. D., & TODD, T. C. (1979). Structural family therapy with drug addicts. In E. Kaufman & P. Kaufman (Eds.), *The Family Therapy of Drug and Alcohol Abuse*. New York: Gardner Press.

STAPP, J., TUCKER, A. M., & VANDENBOS, G. R. (1985). Census of psychological personnel: 1983. *American Psychologist, 40*, 1317–1351.

STEIN, M., & STONE, G. (1978). Effects of conceptual level and structure on initial interview behavior. *J. Counsel. Psychol., 25*, 96–102.

STENSRUD, R., & STENSRUD, K. (1981). Counseling may be hazardous to your health: How we teach people to be powerless. *Pers. and Guid. J., 60*, 71–79.

STERNS, H. L., WEIS, D. M., & PERKINS, S. E. (1983). A conceptual approach to counseling older adults and their families. *The Counseling Psychologist, 12*, 55–62.

STILES, W. B., SHAPIRO, D. A., & ELLIOTT, R. (1986). "Are all psychotherapies equivalent?" *American Psychologist, 41*, 165–180.

STIVER, I. (1986). The meaning of care: Reframing treatment models for women. *Psychotherapy, 2*, 221–226.

STONE, C. H. (1948). Are vocational orientation courses worth their salt? *Educ. Psychol. Measmt., 8*, 161–181.

STRONG, S. R. (1980). Christian counseling: A synthesis of psychological and Christian concepts. *Pers. and Guid. J., 58*, 589–592.

—— (1968). Counseling: An interpersonal influence process. *Journal of Counseling Psychology, 15*, 215–224.

STRONG, S., & SCHMIDT, L. (1970). Expertness and influence in counseling. *J. Counsel. Psychol., 17*, 81–87.

STRUPP, H. H. (1986). Psychotherapy: Research, practice, and public policy (How to avoid dead ends). *American Psychologist, 41*, 120–130.

—— (1963). The outcome problem in psychotherapy revisited. *Psychotherapy: Theory, Research, and Practice, 1*, 1–13.

STRUPP, H. H., & BINDER, J. L. (1984). *Psychotherapy in a New Key*. New York: Basic Books.

STUART, R. B. (1980). *Helping Couples Change*. New York: Guilford Press.

SUE, D. W. (1992). The challenge of multiculturalism. *American Counselor, 1*, 6–15.

—— (1981, January). Cross-cultural counseling competencies. A position paper presented to Division of Counseling Psychology. Mimeographed.

SUE, D. W., ARREDONDO, P., & MCDAVIS, R. J. (1992). Multicultural counseling competencies and standards: A call to the profession. *Journal of Counseling and Development, 70*, 477–486.

SUE, D., & SUE, S. (1977). Barriers to effective cross-cultural counseling. *J. Counsel. Psychol., 24*, 420–429.

SUE, S. (1977). Counseling the culturally different. *Pers. and Guid. J., 55*, 422–425.

SUE, S., AKUTSU, P., & HIGASHI, C. (1985). Training issues in conducting therapy with ethnic minority group clients. In P. Pedersen, *Handbook of Cross-Cultural Counseling and Therapy*. Westport, CT: Greenwood Press.

SUE, S., & MORISHIMA, J. K. (1982). *The Mental Health of Asian Americans*. San Francisco: Jossey-Bass.

SULLIVAN, H. S. (1954). *The Psychiatric Interview*. New York: Norton.

—— (1953). *The Interpersonal Theory of Psychiatry*. New York: Norton.

SUPER, D. E. (1990). A life-span, life-space approach to career development. In D. Brown & L. Brooks. (Eds.), *Career Choice and Development* (2d. ed., pp. 197–261). San Francisco: Jossey-Bass.

—— (1957). *The Psychology of Careers*. New York: Harper & Row.

SURAN, B. G., & SHERIDAN, E. P. (1985). Management of burnout: Training psychologists in professional life span perspectives. *Professional Psychology: Research and Practice, 16*, 741–752.

SUSSKIND, D. J. (1970). The idealized self-image (ISI): A new technique in confidence training. *Behavior Therapy, 1*, 538–541.

SZASZ, T. S. (1978). *The Myth of Psychotherapy: Mental Healing as Religion, Rhetoric, and Repression*. Garden City, NY: Doubleday.

—— (1960). The myth of mental illness. *American Psychologist, 15*, 113–118.

SZYMANSKI, E. M., & DANEK, M. M. (1985). School-to-work transition for students with disabilities: Historical, current, and conceptual issues. *Rehabilitation Counseling Bulletin, 29*, 81–89.

TART, C. (1975). *Transpersonal Psychologies*. New York: Harper & Row.

TAYLOR, C. B. (1983). DSM-III and behavioral assessment. *Behavioral Assessment, 5*, 5–14.

TAYLOR, J. R., & STRASSBERG, D. S. (1987). The effects of sex composition on cohesiveness and interpersonal learning in short-term personal growth groups. *Psychotherapy, 2*, 267–273.

TENNYSON, W., & STROM, S. (1986). Beyond professional standards: Developing responsibleness. *Journal of Counseling and Development, 64*, 298–302.

TERRY, L. L. (1989). Systematic assessment of families through individual treatment: A teaching module. *Journal of Marital and Family Therapy, 15*, 379–386.

TEYBER, E. (1983a). Effects of the parental coalition on adolescent emancipation from the family. *Journal of Marital and Family Therapy, 9*, 305–310.

———— (1983b).   Structural family relations: Primary dyadic alliances and adolescent adjustment. *Journal of Marital and Family Therapy, 9,* 89–99.

THORESON, C. (1969).   The counselor as an applied behavioral scientist. *Pers. and Guid. J., 47,* 841–848.

THORESON, C. E., & EAGLESTON, J. R. (1985).   Counseling for Health. *The Counseling Psychologist, 13,* 15–88.

THORESON, C. E., & MAHONEY, M. J. (1974).   *Behavioral Self-Control.* New York: Holt, Rinehart & Winston.

THORNE, F. C. (1950).   Principles of personality counseling. Brandon, VT: Clinical Psychology Monograph.

TILLICH, P. (1957).   *Dynamics of Faith.* San Francisco: Harper & Row.

TINDALL, R. H., & ROBINSON, F. P. (1947).   The use of silence as a technique in counseling. *J. Clin. Psychol., 3,* 136–141.

TINSLEY, H., & HARRIS, D. (1976).   Client expectations for counseling. *J. Counsel. Psychol., 23,* 173–177.

TINSLEY, H., WORKMAN, K., & KASS, R. (1980).   Factor analysis of the domain of client expectancies about counseling. *J. Counsel. Psychol., 27,* 561–570.

TOMM, K. (1987a).   Interventive interviewing: Part I. Strategizing as a fourth guideline for the therapist. *Family Process, 26,* 3–13.

———— (1987b).   Interventive interviewing: Part II. Reflexive questioning as a means to enable self healing. *Family Process, 26,* 167–183.

———— (1985).   *Reflexive Questioning: A Generative Mode of Enquiry.* Unpublished manuscript, University of Calgary, Family Therapy Program.

———— (1984a).   One perspective on the Milan systemic approach: Part 1. Overview of development, theory and practice. *Journal of Marital and Family Therapy, 10,* 113–126.

———— (1984b).   One perspective on the Milan systemic approach: Part II. Description of session format, interviewing style and interventions. *Journal of Marital and Family Therapy, 10,* 253–274.

TOMM, K., & WRIGHT, L. (1979).   Training in family therapy: Perceptual, conceptual, and executive skills. *Family Process, 18,* 227–250.

TOOMER, J. (1983).   Counseling psychologists in business and industry. *The Counseling Psychologist, 10,* 9–18.

TRACEY, T. (1983).   Single case research: An added tool for counselors and supervisors. *Counselor Education and Supervision, 22,* 185–196.

TREBILCO, G. R. (1984).   Career education and career maturity. *Journal of Vocational Behavior, 25,* 191–202.

TRUAX, C. B. (1966).   Reinforcement and nonreinforcement in Rogerian psychotherapy. *Journal of Abnormal Psychology, 71,* 1–9.

———— (1963).   Effective ingredients in psychotherapy. *J. Counsel. Psychol., 10,* 256–263.

TRAUX, C. B., & CARKHUFF, R. R. (1964).   The old and the new: Theory and research in counseling and psychotherapy. *Pers. and Guid. J., 42,* 860–866.

———— (1962).   *Toward Effective Counseling and Psychotherapy.* Chicago: Aldine.

TRUAX, C. B., & MITCHELL, K. M. (1971).   Research on certain therapist interpersonal skills in relation to process and outcome. In A. E. Bergin & S. L. Garfield (Eds.), *Handbook of Psychotherapy and Behavior Change.* New York: Wiley.

TYLER, L. E. (1980).   The next twenty years. In J. M. Whiteley & B. R. Fretz (Eds.), *The Present and Future of Counseling Psychology.* Pacific Grove, CA: Brooks/Cole.

———— (1969).   *The Work of the Counselor* (3d ed.). Englewood Cliffs, NJ: Prentice-Hall.

ULRICH, D. N., & DUNNE, H. P. (1986).   *To Love and Work: A Systemic Interlocking of Family, Workplace, and Career.* New York: Brunner/Mazel.

U.S. DEPARTMENT OF LABOR, MANPOWER ADMINISTRATION. (1981).   *Career Thresholds.* (A training package of how people find jobs). Monograph 16. Washington, DC: Superintendent of Documents.

U.S. EMPLOYMENT SERVICE. (1977).   *Dictionary of Occupational Titles* (3d ed.). Washington, DC: U.S. Government Printing Office.

U.S. GOVERNMENT OCCUPATIONAL OUTLOOK SERVICE. (1986).   *Occupational Outlook Handbook.* Washington, DC: U.S. Government Printing Office.

VAILLANT, G. E. (1983).   *The Natural History of Alcoholism, Causes, Patterns and Paths to Recovery.* Boston: Harvard University Press.

VANDENBOS, G. R. (ED.). (1986).   Special issue: Psychotherapy research. *American Psychologist, 41,* 111–239.

VINES, N. (1979).   Adult unfolding and marital conflict. *Journal of Marital and Family Therapy, 5,* 5–14.

WACHTEL, E. F., & WACHTEL, P. L. (1986).   *Family Dynamics in Individual Psychotherapy.* New York: Guilford Press.

WACHTEL, P. L. (1977).   *Psychoanalysis and Behavior Therapy.* New York: Basic Books.

WACHTEL, P. S. (1980).   What should we say to our patients?: On the wording of therapists' comments. *Psychotherapy: Theory, Research, and Practice, 17,* 183–188.

WALLS, G. B. (1980).   Values and psychotherapy: A comment on "Psychotherapy and religious values." *Journal of Consulting and Clinical Psychology, 48,* 640–641.

WALSH, W. B. (1990).   A summary and integration of career counseling approaches. In W. B. Walsh & S. H. Osipow (Eds.), *Career Counseling: Contemporary Topics in Vocational Psychology.* Hillsdale, NJ: Erlbaum.

WALTZ, G. (1978).   *Searchlight: Relevant Resources in High Interest Areas. Mid Career Change: An Overview of Counseling Practices and Programs.* Ann Arbor, MI: ERIC Clearinghouse on Counseling and Personnel Services. (ERIC Document Reproduction Service No. ED 160 905).

WAMPLER, K. (1982). The effectiveness of the Minnesota Couple Communication Program: A review of research. *Journal of Marital and Family Therapy, 8,* 345–355.

WARNER, W. L., MEEKER, M., & ELLS, K. (1949). *Social Class in America.* Chicago: Science Research Associates.

WATERS, E., & GOODMAN, J. (1981). I get by with a little help from my friends: The importance of support systems. *Vocational Guidance Quarterly, 29,* 362–369.

WATKINS, C. E. (1992). Early professionals in counseling psychology: The academic setting. *The Counseling Psychologist, 20,* 47–53.

——— (1985). Psychoeducational training in counseling psychology programs: Some thoughts on a training curriculum. *The Counseling Psychologist, 13,* 295–302.

WATKINS, C. E., LOPEZ, F. G., CAMPBELL, V. L., & HIMMELL, C. D. (1986). Counseling psychology and clinical psychology: Some preliminary comparative data. *American Psychologist, 41,* 581–582.

WATTS, A. (1961). *Psychotherapy East and West.* New York: Random House.

WATZLAWICK, P., WEAKLAND, J., & FISCH, R. (1974). *Change: Principles of Problem Formation and Problem Resolution.* New York: Norton.

WEAKLAND, J., FISCH, R., WATZLAWICK, P., & BODIN, A. M. (1974). *Brief Therapy: Focused Problem Resolution.*

WEEKS, G. (1977). Toward a dialectical approach to intervention. *Human Development, 20,* 277–292.

WEEKS, G. R., & L'ABATE, L. (1982). *Paradoxical Psychotherapy: Theory and Practice with Individuals, Couples, and Families.* New York: Brunner/Mazel.

WELKOWITZ, J., COHEN, J., & ORTMEYER, D. (1967). Value systems similarity: Investigation of patient-therapist dyads. *Journal of Consulting Psychology, 31,* 48–55.

WELLNER, A. (ED.). (1978). *Education and Credentialing in Psychology: II.* Washington, DC: American Psychological Association.

——— (ED.). (1976). *Education and Credentialing in Psychology: I.* Washington, DC: American Psychological Association.

WHITE, M., & EPSTON, D. (1990). *Narrative Means to Therapeutic Ends.* New York: Norton.

WHITELEY, J. M. (1984). Counseling psychology: A historical perspective. *The Counseling Psychologist, 12,* 3–109.

——— (1980). *The History of Counseling Psychology.* Monterey, CA: Brooks/Cole.

WHITELEY, J. M., & FRETZ, B. R. (EDS.). (1980). *The Present and Future of Counseling Psychology.* Pacific Grove, CA: Brooks/Cole.

WHITELEY, J. M., KAGAN, N., HARMON, L. W., FRETZ, B. R., & TANNEY, F. (EDS.). (1984). *The Coming Decade in Counseling Psychology.* Schenectady, NY: Character Research Press.

WILBER, K. (1983). *Eye to Eye: The Quest for a New Paradigm.* Garden City, NJ: Avelon Books.

——— (1979). *No Boundary: Eastern and Western Approaches to Personal Growth.* Boston: Shambala.

WILSON, G. T., & DAVISON, G. C. (1971). Processes of fear reduction in systematic desensitization: Animal studies. *Psychological Bulletin, 76,* 1–14.

WILSON, G. T., & EVANS, I. M. (1977). The therapist-client relationship in behavior therapy. In A. Gurman & A. Razin (Eds.), *Effective Psychotherapy: A Handbook of Research.* New York: Pergamon Press.

WOLLERSHEIM, J., McFALL, M., HAMILTON, S., HICKEY, C., & BORDEWICK, M. (1958). Effects of treatment rationale and problem severity on perceptions of psychological problems and counseling approaches. *J. Counsel. Psychol., 27,* 225–231.

WOLPE, J. (1958). *Psychotherapy by Reciprocal Inhibition.* Stanford, CA: Stanford University Press.

WOOD, M. M., & LONG, N. J. (1991). *Life Space Intervention: Talking with Youth in Crisis.* New York: Pro-Ed.

WORLD FEDERATION FOR MENTAL HEALTH. (1989). *Declaration of Human Rights and Mental Health.* Baltimore, MD: Office of the WFMH General Secretary.

WORTHINGTON, E. L. (1989). Religious faith across the life span. *Journal of Counseling Psychology, 17,* 555–612.

——— (1986). Religious counseling: A review of published empirical research. *Journal of Counseling and Development, 64,* 421–431.

——— (1982). *When Someone Asks for Help: A Practical Guide for Counseling.* Downers Grove, IL: InterVarsity Press.

WORTHINGTON, E. L., & SCOTT, G. G. (1983). Goal selection for counseling with potentially secular settings. *Journal of Psychology and Theology, 11,* 318–329.

WRENN, C. G. (1985). Afterword: The culturally encapsulated counselor revisited. In P. Pederson (Ed.), *Handbook of Cross-Cultural Counseling and Therapy* (pp. 20–41). Westport, CT: Greenwood Press.

——— (1962). The culturally encapsulated counselor. *Harvard Educational Review, 32,* 444–449.

——— (1958). Psychology, religion, and values for the counselor, Part III, in the symposium, the counselor and his religion. *Pers. and Guid. J., 36,* 326–334.

YALOM, I. (1975). *The Theory and Practice of Group Psychotherapy* (2d ed.). New York: Basic Books.

YALOM, I. D., LIEBERMAN, M. A., & MILES, M. M. (1971). A study of encounter group casualties. *Archives of General Psychiatry, 25,* 16–30.

ZARLE, T., & BOYD, R. (1977). An evaluation of modeling and experiential procedures for self-disclosure training. *J. Counsel. Psychol., 24,* 118–124.

ZEIG, J. K. (ED.). (1982). *Ericksonian Approaches to Hypnosis and Psychotherapy*. New York: Brunner/Mazel.

ZELEN, S. L. (1954). Acceptance and acceptability. *J. Consult. Psychol., 18*, 316.

ZILBERGELD, B. (1978). *Male Sexuality*. New York: Bantam Books.

ZIMET, C. N. (1979). Developmental task and crisis groups: the application of group psychotherapy to maturational processes. *Psychotherapy: Theory, Research, and Practice, 14*, 2–8.

ZINKER, J. C. (1977). *Creative Process in Gestalt Therapy*. New York: Brunner/Mazel.

Index